TASMANIAN
Trout Waters

First published 1994

ISBN 0-646-19310-4

Typesetting: Ian Humble
Printing: Focal Printing

Maps supplied by TASMAP
For more detailed & comprehensive maps
contact your nearest Tasmap Sales Centre.

Lands Building   Henty House
134 Macquarie St   One Civic Square
HOBART   Launceston

Contents

PART 1: BACKGROUND / DECIDING WHERE TO GO

1. **ABOUT TASMANIA** 5

   Topography, weather, maps, abbreviations, regulations, the Salmon Ponds

2. **ABOUT OUR SPORTFISH** 9

   Spawning, growth and size, natural distribution, introduction to Tasmania, acclimatisation, current distribution in Tasmania, sea run populations, preferred environments, management

   2.1 **Brown Trout** *(including sea trout)* 10
   2.2 **Rainbow Trout** 17
   2.3 **Brook Trout** 23
   2.4 **Atlantic Salmon** 25
   2.5 **Pacific Salmon** *(did not establish)* 27
   2.6 **Triploids and Hybrids** 29

   Note: information on other species (introduced and native) is available in the book Tasmanian Freshwater Fishes *(Wayne Fulton, 1990).*

3. **WHERE THE LOCALS FISH** 31

   A short list of the State's most popular lakes and rivers. Notes on annual visitation, total fishing effort, annual harvest and average catch rates

4. **WHERE TO FISH – A REGIONAL BREAKDOWN** 33

   Introduction 34
   4.1 **Central Plateau** 34
   4.2 **North and Midlands** 36
   4.3 **West Coast** 38
   4.4 **Central South** 40
   4.5 **Far South** 42
   4.6 **Central North-West** 42
   4.7 **Far North-West** 43
   4.8 **South-West** 44
   4.9 **North-East** 45
   4.10 **East Coast** 46

5. FISHING IN NATIONAL PARKS 47

Introduction 48
    Includes notes on regulations and etiquette

5.1   **The Western Lakes (Walls of Jerusalem National Park /**
      Central Plateau Conservation Area) 49
5.2   **Southwest National Park** 64
5.3   **Franklin-Gordon Wild Rivers National Park** 65
5.4   **Cradle Mountain – Lake St Clair National Park** 66
5.5   **Mt Field National Park** 67
5.6   **Hartz Mountains National Park** 69
5.7   **Douglas-Apsley National Park** 70
5.8   **Rocky Cape National Park** 70

*Note: There are no recognised trout fisheries in the Ben Lomond, Asbestos Range, Maria Island,
Freycinet, Mount William or Strzelecki national parks.*

6. NOTES FOR THE SPECIALIST 71

6.1   **Fly Fishing** 72
6.2   **Lure Fishing** 74
6.3   **Bait Fishing** 74
6.4   **Trophy Trout** 77

PART 2:   TASMANIAN TROUT WATERS IN DETAIL

*Tasmania's lakes, rivers and estuaries listed in alphabetical order. Notes on
history, trout stocks, microhabitats, catchability, special features, facilities,
and access*

Introduction 81
    *How to look up waters in the alphabetical listing; what to do when a water
    is not listed; how to find current lake-levels; notes on the size of hatchery-
    reared trout; and how to keep informed*

Tasmanian Trout Waters in Detail 82

About Tasmania

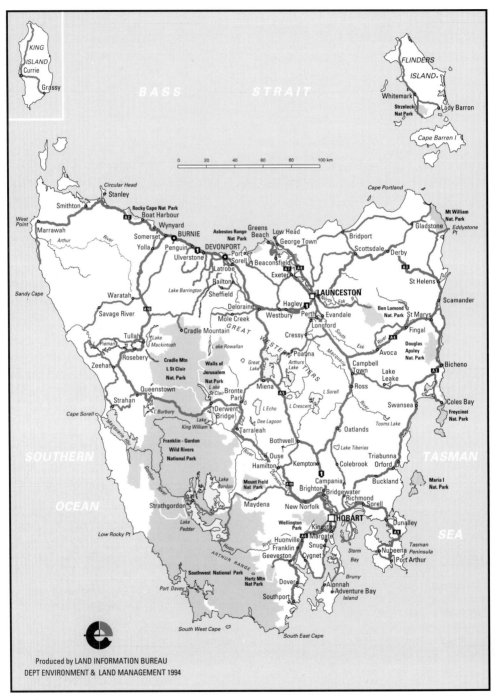

Produced by LAND INFORMATION BUREAU
DEPT ENVIRONMENT & LAND MANAGEMENT 1994

Geography

Tasmania is a group of islands comprising 68 331 sq km, of which the mainland occupies 64 409 sq km. It is the smallest of the Australian States.

The current resident population is about 460 000, the principal cities and towns being greater Hobart (population 200 000), Launceston (population 69 000), Devonport (population 22 000), and Burnie (population 20 000).

The Tasmanian mainland extends just 296 km from north to south and 315 km from east to west, with no point being more than 115 km from the sea. Although Tasmania is one of the most mountainous islands on the globe, few peaks exceed 1500 m and there are no permanent snowlines.

The climate is classified as temperate maritime. Tasmania is subject to prevailing westerly weather which comes in off vast oceanic expanses, so the west and south receive strong wind and heavy rain. The north-east is affected by less-frequent humid north-easterly winds and is also very wet. The driest areas are the Midlands, East Coast, south-east and Derwent Valley. Since there is no major spring thaw, floods are almost entirely associated with rainfall and are most common in winter and spring.

Typical daily maximum temperatures during summer are from 17-26°C. Normal winter minimums range from about 0-6°C.

The Tasmanian economy is driven by primary industry, mainly agriculture, forestry, mining and tourism. Extensive tracts of cleared land extend along the north-west coast and throughout the Midlands – but some 40% of the State is forested. Rainforest and dense wet-forest dominate in the west and south, while dry sclerophyll bushland is common on the Central Plateau and over the eastern half of the State.

Tasmania is recognised as one of the last bastions of environmental purity. The temperate wilderness is perhaps the major drawcard, catering for bushwalkers, trout fishers and other adventure-holiday enthusiasts. The State boasts 14 national parks, several of which are inscribed on the prestigious World Heritage list.

While some minor roads remain unsealed, the vast majority of routes are well surfaced. There is comfortable access to the major lakes, rivers and estuaries – as well as to the fringes of the wilderness.

Maps

While common road maps are adequate for those visiting only major trout fisheries, they are rarely as detailed or as accurate as those produced by the State's official map-maker, Tasmap. Tasmaps are available from most local tackle stores, outdoor shops and large newsagencies – or else you can buy direct from the Tasmap Sales Centres at the Lands Building, 134 Macquarie St, Hobart; and Henty House, 1 Civic Square, Launceston.

Tasmap produces a series of four general reference maps which cover *North West, North East, South West,* and *South East* Tasmania in a scale of 1:250 000. (In this book explicit details about access are only given if the information is not recorded on these maps.)

Recommended for bushwalkers and those visiting remote or obscure locations are the recently updated 1:100 000 Topographic Tasmaps. Avoid the Land Tenure series which can be difficult to read and do not indicate vegetation types. (So that readers may instantly recognise its rough location, each water listed in Part 2 – *Tasmanian Trout Waters in Detail* – is keyed to the 1:100 000 Tasmap index.)

The 1:25 000 maps are extremely detailed but are rarely advantageous. Each sheet covers only a relatively small area (you are continually 'walking off the map'), and in practical terms they are

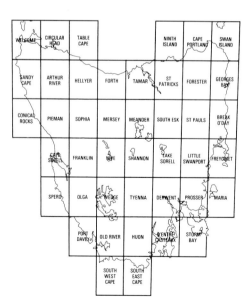

1:100 000 TASMAP INDEX

about 12 times more expensive than conventional 1:100000 sheets. The detail can be quite confusing too. For example, on the *Pillans* sheet it is difficult to distinguish small isolated ponds from major instream lakes. The few sheets which do show significant access routes, sub-aquatic features and other details of interest to anglers are recommended at relevant times throughout the text.

The 1:150000 *Central Plateau* map is an ideal general reference map for those visiting only the Central Plateau, but is not detailed enough for bushwalkers, nor is it especially useful if you already have the 1:250000 series. The 1:150000 *South East Tasmania* map indicates boat launching areas in the Derwent estuary and at several other waters.

The *Tasmanian Towns Street Atlas* (Tasmap, 1993) details access to boat launching ramps in residential areas.

Abbreviations used in this book

ANM   Australian Newsprint Mills Limited

APPM   Associated Pulp and Paper Mills

CSIRO Commonwealth Scientific and Industrial Research Organisation

HEC   Hydro-Electric Commission

IFC   Inland Fisheries Commission

NTAA   Northern Tasmanian Anglers' Association (an early name for the NTFA)

NTFA   Northern Tasmanian Fisheries Association

NWFA   North-Western Fisheries Association

PWS   Parks and Wildlife Service

SFFC   Salmon and Freshwater Fisheries Commission (the forerunner to the IFC)

STLAA Southern Tasmanian Licensed Anglers Association

RWSC   Rivers and Water Supply Commission

Fishing regulations

The Government authority responsible for fisheries management in inland waters is the Inland Fisheries Commission (IFC) which is located at 127 Davey St, Hobart 7000 (Ph 002 23 6622). The activities of the IFC are publicised in a regular newsletter which is available free from most tackle shops.

Laws governing activities at inland waters are tabled in the *Fisheries Act* (1959). The IFC is the principal law enforcement body for the Act, though officers from other departments (including the police force) also have authority.

Fishing regulations change from time to time and the information presented in this book is intended only as a summary at the time of publication. An up-to-date *Fishing Code* should be provided when you purchase your trout licence.

All people 14 years and older must obtain a current IFC angling licence before fishing in Tasmania's inland waters. This licence can be purchased from the IFC, tackle stores, police stations and some general stores.

Most inland waters are open to angling from the Saturday closest to 1 August to the Sunday closest to 30 April. The nominated rainbow trout fisheries – Dee Lagoon, Lake Rowallan, Lagoon of Islands and Lake Skinner – open in early October and close in late May. Special regulations apply at Great Lake and several other waters (check the *Fishing Code*).

The legal minimum (takeable) size for trout and salmon is 220 mm, and a bag limit of twelve fish per angler per day is imposed. These regulations apply at all public waters.

While bait fishing is allowed at most waters, some fisheries are reserved for the use of artificial lures and others are set aside for fly fishing only. Check the *Fishing Code*.

The Salmon Ponds

The Salmon Ponds, the IFC's hatchery museum, was established in 1862 as the first trout hatchery in the Southern Hemisphere (see notes on the introduction of brown trout in *About our Sportfish*, 2.1.) Of trout hatcheries which have maintained continuous operation, it is the oldest in the world today.

Shallow viewing ponds, set in a tranquil well-maintained park, offer visitors the chance to view at close range all of the salmonid species in Tasmania today. A kiosk and lunch rooms are conveniently located near the entrance.

Boating regulations

Boat operators must familiarise themselves with Tasmanian regulations and should contact one of the Port Authorities (Hobart, Launceston, Burnie, Devonport and Circular Head). Operators of speed boats (motor boats capable of exceeding 8 knots) must be licensed. Speed boat licences from other Australian States will be recognised for a maximum of 3 months.   ◆

About Our Sportfish

2.1 BROWN TROUT

The brown trout is the aristocrat of freshwater sportfish – and the success of the species in Tasmania has been nothing less than spectacular.

Natural distribution

The brown trout is native throughout mainland Europe. Significant natural populations also occur in the British Isles, Iceland, the Caspian Sea, the Black Sea, the Aral Sea, Turkey, Afghanistan, and in the Atlas Mountains in northern Africa.

Introduction to Tasmania

The early attempts to transport trout to Tasmania were linked with (and secondary to) the attempts to acclimatise Atlantic salmon. They are well documented in the early Parliamentary reports of the Salmon Commissioners and board members. Further information is available in Jean Walker's authoritative and highly readable *Origins of the Tasmanian Trout* (1988).

The Plenty River (some 50 km north-west of Hobart) was selected as the site for the first salmon and trout hatchery in the Southern Hemisphere – largely because of its cold clear water, because it was a tributary of the mighty Derwent, and because it offered young fish a clear passage to the sea. The Salmon Ponds were constructed in 1862.

The first successful shipment arrived in 1864. It included more than 100 000 Atlantic salmon ova as well as several thousand brown trout ova. The trout eggs, last minute gifts given shortly before the ship left Britain, were obtained from the Itchen near Winchester; the Wye at High Wycombe; the Wey at Alton; and perhaps the Test at Whitchurch.

Some 300 trout ova survived the voyage and on 4 May the first fry hatched. Of the original 300 or so trout, 40 were released into the Plenty in April 1865. The rest were retained for brood stock, ova being collected from them in the winter of 1866.

The trout from the original shipment probably were sufficient to populate the rivers and lakes of the colony – by 1866 it was considered that the acclimatisation of brown trout was guaranteed – but in order to cement the success, in the interest of supplying *'new blood'*, and in efforts to acclimatise 'different' species (such as sea trout and Loch Leven trout, both now recognised as strains of brown trout) there were many subsequent importations.

The Salmon Commissioners recorded the importation of 10 000-15 000 sea trout (sourced from the River Tweed) in 1866. This consignment resulted in about 1000 mature fish. In 1891-92 it was noted that Loch Leven trout *'produced from*

Highland gold

The Salmon Ponds today – history, tranquillity and live displays (see About Tasmania, section 1)

Ova purchased in New Zealand… have been placed in Lakes Sorell and Laycock, and a small lot in the River Esk'. In 1905 the NTAA reported that a *'shipment of ova was received from New Zealand consisting of Rainbow, Loch Leven and Fontinalis varieties'*, though it was conceded that the Loch Leven ova gave poor results because they were the *'product of pond fish'*. Each year from 1925 until at least 1928 the STLAA financed the importation of up to 50 000 sea trout ova from the Solway Fisheries at Dumfries in Scotland. And in 1933 the Commissioners for Fisheries claimed that they had *'regularly imported* [brown trout] *ova from New Zealand to improve the stock at Great Lake and Lake Sorell'.*

Acclimatisation

In winter 1866 (even though just 40 trout had been deliberately released by this time) the Commissioners were claiming that *'The English trout may now be regarded as established beyond all risk of failure'.* By this time the brood stock at the Salmon Ponds had been stripped and, while most of the subsequent ova were held at Plenty, some were laid down in hatching boxes

in the South Esk River at Strathmore. In August five pairs of trout were observed spawning in the Plenty River. By mid 1867 about 40 young fish had been reared at the Salmon Ponds, and the population in the Plenty River had increased markedly. Also, *'large'* fish had been seen (presumably in the Derwent) feeding on *'small fry'.*

During September and October 1867 most of the sea trout reared from the 1866 importation (about 900) were allowed to escape to the Plenty. But, as with the *'brown'* trout, brood stock was retained. By now trout were reputed to have been established in the South Esk, North Esk, St Patricks, North West Bay River, Ouse, Clyde, Lachlan Rivulet, Dry Creek, Dee River, Bagdad Rivulet, Sorell Rivulet, Jones River, Browns River and O'Briens Creek. It was noted that trout *'continued to prosper without interruption'* and that there had been a surprising increase in trout numbers.

One of the first releases of trout in the highland lakes occurred at Lake Sorell sometime between 1867 and 1870. The Commissioners recorded that in 1870 a further 1000 fry were released into *'Tasmanian Lakes'.* It is certain that about 100 of these fish were taken to Great Lake. The balance probably went to waters such as lakes Sorell and Crescent. Also in 1870 some 500 eyed ova were laid down in Lake Echo. The success of trout in lakes was no less spectacular than the success of the river liberations (see Part 2 – Tasmanian Trout Waters in Detail).

By 1871 trout ova and/or fry had been released at Swansea (on the East Coast) and Chudleigh (in the north of the State at the foot of the Great Western Tiers). By 1876 the distribution of trout had extended to rivers in the far north-east and the Forth system in the north-west. Other waters in the north-west were stocked in 1879. The West Coast probably was not stocked until 1881-82 when 2500 ova were transported to the mid reaches of the Gordon River.

The enthusiasm and efficiency of those involved with the early liberations was remarkable. William Senior (*Travel and Trout in the Antipodes*, 1880) wrote:

'… dwelling upon each [river]*, though it may not far exceed the dimensions of a rivulet, you shall ever find persons who tell you confidently that to them, and them alone, was entrusted the honour of depositing the first young fish. It is evidence at least to the importance they attach to the subject that, according to their own showing, three fourths of the male population of the country have with their own hands deposited salmon and trout in the rivers.'*

In 1888 the Fisheries Board recognised that brown trout had indeed established beyond all risk of failure. Matthew Seal wrote :

'Beyond the export of a large number of ova of brown trout to Victoria and New South Wales, the artificial culture of this species has for the present been abandoned. The fish is to be found in most of the rivers of Tasmania, and an increased stock is readily obtainable if required.'

Until the turn of the 19th century the overwhelming majority of ova and fry were produced at the Salmon Ponds. In 1897 anglers in the north of the State formed the NTAA/NTFA. This organisation fostered a renewed interest in the stocking of trout and by 1900-01 a hatchery had been erected at Waverley near Launceston. The operation of the hatchery is significant because it heralded a new era of trout stocking, facilitated the transportation of salmonids to the north-west and north-east, and enabled the distribution of trout to a number of previously unstocked waters. It remained in production at least until the 1930s.

From the early 1930s the Commissioners and the Associations began soliciting professional advice on stocking, trout growth, and the status of wild stocks. In 1947 the SFFC secured the services of Dr Aubrey Nicholls (of the Fisheries and Oceanographic Division of CSIRO) to study trout populations in the State. As a result of Nicholls' recommendations the SFFC, over several years

A typical small-stream fish

in the mid 1950s, wound down fish culture and trout liberation operations. While this action was met with anger from many anglers – and some minor politically-determined releases continued – the tradition of wholesale indiscriminate stocking was abandoned. The wisdom of Nicholls' arguments is now beyond question.

Of course it was never intended that stocking be scrapped altogether. There are significant fisheries which have little or no natural spawning facilities and at which stocking is essential. Moreover, fisheries managers were alert to measures which might improve the *quality* of fishing at popular waters. In 1959 the SFFC was replaced with the more professional IFC, and in 1960 a decision was made to test the feasibility of transferring adult brown trout from Great Lake to heavily-fished lowland waters. By 1961 the IFC was claiming that the experiment had *'paid off handsomely'*. In waters where trout populations were already large, and competition between fish was high, transferred trout failed to make significant growth – but in other waters (such as Lake Crescent and some of the Nineteen Lagoons) the fish fared extremely well. The programme was continued in earnest until the late 1970s but, as it was difficult to justify economically, it was finally wound back. Today adult trout transfers are largely confined to suitable lakes on the Central Plateau.

Although very young trout continue to be released statewide, liberations are largely confined to the relatively few waters which are unable to maintain significant self-supporting wild stocks. Virtually all hatchery fish are reared at the Salmon Ponds (which is owned and operated by the IFC) from ova collected from wild stock at Great Lake, Arthurs Lake and/or Lake Sorell. Most are released as swim-up fry, though others are on-grown to fingerling stage. Most fish to be on-grown are transferred to Association-operated rearing units in the north-west of the State.

While there are commercial trout and salmon farms in Tasmania, none produce brown trout.

Sea trout

The anglers' fascination with saltwater browns embodies both the visual perfection and physical strength of the fish, as well as our lust for variety and the unpredictable. Sea trout are invariably sleek, silvery and strong. They frequently provide exhilarating sight-fishing, and trophy specimens can be encountered at any time.

Sea trout look unique but are merely brown trout which 'choose' to spend time in the ocean. While it is true that there are distinct strains of sea trout, and that the progeny of sea trout are

Gordon River sea trout

more likely than river-resident stock to run to the ocean, sea runs readily establish from land-locked stock and vice-versa.

History

In 1867 the Salmon Commissioners reported several sightings of *'salmon'* feeding on *'small fry'*, presumably in the Derwent and/or Plenty rivers. By 1869 large fish had been sighted on many occasions but were still considered to be salmon because of their *'large size and bright glittering colour'*. We now believe that sea runs of salmon did not occur and, while it is probable that salmon smolts grew to reasonable size before going to the ocean, these early anecdotal accounts may be evidence of early sea trout populations. The dates of the sightings, as well as the reported size of the fish, suggest that sea runs may have resulted from the original importation of trout in 1864. But it is not possible to conclude that the first sea trout were the progeny of British river-residents. John Clements (*Salmon at the Antipodes*, 1988) noted that Francis Francis (who stripped the ova comprising one of the two gifts of brown trout in the original shipment) described his parent fish as being:

'... more like salmon than the common brown trout, and are brilliantly silver in colour, very short and thick in make, and weigh heavier than almost any fish I know ... They often run up to 7 or 8 lbs weight; the flesh is not alone pink as that of a salmon, but is of a much deeper red when at the height of condition.'

Recognised sea trout were imported in 1866, perhaps enhancing existing stocks, and significant sea runs soon established. In July 1877 a 20 lb (9 kg) trout (then assumed to be a salmon) was found spawning in the Plenty River. The attendant male weighed 14 lb (6.4 kg). By 1879 fish to 20 lb had been caught on rods, and in the same year a 28 lb 'brown trout' was found dead in the Huon River. Although fish continued to be mistaken for salmon, the success of sea trout had been widely recognised by the late 1870s. Regular runs of sea trout now occur throughout Tasmania.

Most (if not all) river systems containing trout were stocked at some time. Although it is known that sea trout will migrate between estuaries I have not found evidence of fish from stocked catchments 'seeding' unstocked systems. Major river systems in the south-west (such as the Davey River and the waters draining into Bathurst Harbour) do not appear to hold resident trout.

Life history

Studies completed by the IFC in 1988 shed light on the life history of sea trout in the River Derwent. Eggs are laid in fresh water and young fish migrate to saltwater during September/October when they are in either their second or third year of life. While there is no statistical preference, the growth advantage of early migration is significant. Among four year olds those which were two-year smolts are likely to be twice the weight of those which were three-year smolts.

Sea trout are tempted back from the ocean to the estuary when the runs of whitebait occur, usually from July to late November. The 'whitebait run' of sea trout consists mainly of maidens in their first or second year at sea. Such trout usually weigh from 0.5-1.5 kg. However, older maidens and mature trout also run, some of which attain 9 kg and more.

Whitebait

The whitebait in Tasmania belong to six or more species, including the Tasmanian whitebait (*Lovettia sealii*), four species of galaxias, and one species of smelt. The *Lovettia* are year-old adults returning upstream to spawn and die. Most of the galaxias are juveniles which were washed from freshwater to sea shortly after hatching and are returning to freshwater to live out their adult lives. Little is known of the life history of smelt but its contribution to the whitebait runs is relatively small. While all species are usually apparent in the runs at any time, *Lovettia* are normally dominant early in the season (July to September), while galaxias are more common in the late months (September to November). This is significant because the habits of the two major whitebait types are (in many respects) quite different.

As *Lovettia* are on a spawning run they do not actively feed. The run is 'direct' and, while many fish stray, the majority remain close to the deepwater channel (where it exists). As with the other whitebait species, *Lovettia* tend to avoid fast flows and move along the edge of main current. Unlike the case with other species, the runs are highly dependent upon the state of tide. *Lovettia* tend to move upstream on high incoming tides and fall back as tides recede. Also, there often are obvious congregations of spawning *Lovettia* away from the physical barriers on the river. While *Lovettia* prefer to spawn high in the upper estuary at the limit of tidal influence, they avoid freshwater and pollution – and the section of river where most spawning occurs varies from year to year according to changes in river conditions. Although eggs are deposited on almost any surface available, there appears to be a preference for submerged logs, rocks and rock shelves.

Most galaxias are feeding while migrating up the estuary and although they also roughly follow the edge of deepwater channels, they tend to stray further than *Lovettia*. Bottlenecks occur immediately below rapids. In most rivers the vast majority of migrating galaxias are jollytails (*G. maculatus*). These fish are less likely than any other whitebait to be intimidated by moderate freshes. The schools typically are smaller than those of *Lovettia* but the runs are usually more frequent and less dependent upon the state of the tide. While the main runs usually have been completed by November, small runs sometimes continue beyond December.

The importance of the whitebait runs to the angler should not be underestimated. Without whitebait some sea trout might stray into estuaries but mass springtime migrations would not occur. Following the decimation of whitebait during the 1940s, there was a dramatic and much publicised decline in the recreational sea trout fishery. Continued commercial harvesting until 1974 simply compounded the problem. Moreover, it is the spectacular visual display of trout charging through schools of baitfish – causing showers of frightened prey to leap clear of the water – that remains the major attraction of saltwater trout fishing. Still, while it is the whitebait runs which attract sea trout in from the ocean, the diet of sea trout when in estuaries

Sea trout – silver and sleek (photo by Rob Sloane)

is quite broad. Among significant dietary items are shrimps *(Paratya)* and crabs.

Sea trout re-enter the estuaries in March/April and migrate into freshwater to spawn. The exact timing of the major run is influenced by normal factors such as barometric pressure, water temperature and freshes. The spawning run is comprised mostly of fish in the fourth and fifth years of life but includes a significant number of much older specimens. As the spawning run does not include immature fish it is, on average, much smaller than the whitebait run. On the other hand, average spawners are much larger than average whitebait feeders.

Slob trout

Anglers fishing estuaries invariably catch a significant percentage of fish which lack classic silver hues – fish which are dull brown and have dark brown (and sometimes red) spots. Such trout are fish which have taken up residence in the estuary and do not migrate to sea. They are known as 'slob' trout. Residents typically range from 0.5-1.5 kg but can be 4 kg plus. They feed predominantly on shrimps, crabs and other invertebrates but also take advantage of the whitebait. Although slobs do not seem to migrate long distances after baitfish, they do contribute significantly to the spawning migrations.

Natural spawning

As with other trout, maturity in brown trout is primarily determined by age, not size. Males may mature in their second year but more commonly delay spawning until they are in their third year. Females usually mature as three year olds. Some fish (including a relatively high proportion of sea trout) do not spawn until the fourth or fifth years.

Brown trout are essentially winter spawners. In most Tasmanian waters peak spawning usually occurs in May and/or June – but in lakes on the West Coast the runs often do not get under way until July or even early August. Lake fish and sea trout (especially males) often begin congregating at stream mouths one or two months before the actual spawning run.

All brown trout (including sea trout and slobs) spawn in freshwater. Most lake fish migrate upstream but outflows may be used if tributaries are inadequate. Shore spawning is uncommon. Sea trout migrate into rivers and small tributaries. Most river residents spawn close to their home territory.

Although individuals have a strong tendency to migrate back to their birthplace to spawn, brown trout readily establish in new waters and

quickly invade entire systems. The ultimate upper limit of fish within a newly stocked catchment is usually determined by significant physical barriers such as waterfalls.

Growth and size

Although significant mortality occurs at first spawning, brown trout are very likely to survive for many years, especially if there is not a lot of competition for food and space. In heavily populated waters (such as Great Lake) most fish in the spawning runs are just three, four or (less commonly) five years old. But in less populated waters (such as Lake Crescent) fish commonly live for ten or more years. The maximum life span is probably in the order of 20 years.

Although there are genetic and other considerations, the average size of trout within a population primarily depends upon the amount of food available to each fish. The mechanisms by which the growth of an individual is controlled are not fully understood. Scientists have observed that the more food available to fish the greater their hunger. If rations are kept very low trout will go off their food and refuse to eat all that is offered.

In lakes and rivers where competition for food is high most fish do not put on much weight once they have matured. It seems that the younger fish are more efficient competitors and simply deny food to older fish – anyone who has fought a big maiden trout will realise just how much strength fish lose once they mature. There is no doubt that in environments where the trout population is large and the food limited, most fish will be small. There are exceptions though. For example, the biggest fish in a river pool will have taken up station in the most lucrative lie and, if it is very big, it has probably occupied that lie and dominated the pool for many years. Such a trout has reached a size at which it can no longer be intimidated by other fish, and will sustain growth until it becomes the victim of old age and/or disease. However, very large fish are most common in rich waters where there is limited recruitment.

Under ideal conditions brown trout can attain mammoth size. The book *Australian and New Zealand Fishing* (Summit Books, 1977) claimed that *'The world's record brown trout was one of 39½ pounds caught in Loch Awe, Scotland, in 1866 by W. Muir'*. In a newsletter in 1989 the IFC recorded a new world record brown, a fish of 39 lb 9 oz (18 kg) from the North Fork of the White River in Arkansas, USA. But sea run brown trout in the Caspian Sea often exceed 20 kg and can attain 50 kg (1.4 m in length). Unfortunately these trout apparently have no value as sportfish.

A slab

the surface in open water, or at great depth. In fact brown trout can usually be located wherever there is cool unpolluted water and some food. Still, it must be recognised that the habits of brown trout do differ from those of other salmonids, especially rainbow trout. Anglers wishing to target one or other species are well advised to assess local microhabitats and fish those areas *preferred* by the target species (see *Rainbow Trout*, 2.2).

Management

Brown trout are perhaps the most challenging of all freshwater sportfish. For example, the brown trout in Great Lake outnumber the rainbows by about 20:1 in their respective spawning runs, yet they account for just 50-70% of the annual harvest. And it is *because* they are challenging to catch that they are so respected by anglers. In Tasmania, with our vast variety of fishing waters, the opportunities for learning are infinite. Even the best of fishers never get to know it all.

Brown trout of at least 17 kg have been recorded in New Zealand. The largest fish in Australia have been taken in Tasmania. Sir Robert Hamilton (then Governor of Tasmania) caught a trout from the Huon River in 1887 which weighed 28¾ lb (about 13 kg) and was 35½ inches (about 900 mm) long. A fish taken by Ludwig Zotch from Lake Crescent in 1971 weighed 27 lb (about 12.3 kg) *cleaned* and was probably larger than the official record. And sea trout in excess of 9 kg (20 lb) are taken each season.

When brown trout become old and/or sick they begin to lose condition. If they do not succumb quickly they may, over one or several years, become increasingly slabby (thin).

Preferred environment

Brown trout are more robust than other trout and frequent an impressive array of habitats. They live in oceans, estuaries, rivers, small streams, coastal lagoons, and alpine lakes. They also utilize a broad range of microhabitats. In lakes and swollen rivers they take full advantage of the flood plains and marshes and, if there is significant forage food, they are prepared to move into water just centimetres deep. Brown trout are equally likely to be found feeding on

The IFC has an annual 'open day' at Liawenee (usually on the first Sunday in May) when the public is invited to examine displays on official projects, and watch staff 'stripping' eggs from wild brown trout spawners.

Tailing in the shallows – distinctive brown trout behaviour

Tasmanian brown trout waters are managed as wild fisheries. Most have ample natural recruitment and stocking is avoided where possible. In a very few cases, spawning facilities are inadequate and some stocking is necessary. In such cases the fish released are fry and/or fingerlings reared from ova collected from wild stock. Some liberations of triploid browns have been trialled at waters such as Lake Crescent and Lake Leake (see *Triploids and Hybrids*, 2.6) but these fish are still the progeny of wild stock. None of the commercial fish farms cultivate brown trout and, while display fish are held at the Salmon Ponds, there are no truly domestic fish in the State.

As brown trout are the most widely distributed salmonid in Tasmania, the fishing regulations are primarily geared for brown trout management. The only waters not closed to fishing during the peak brown trout spawning period (May, June and July) are those few given specific mention in the *Fisheries Act*.

2.2 RAINBOW TROUT

While most anglers agree that brown trout are the aristocracy of freshwater sportfish, there is significant and universal respect for the rainbow trout. In Australia rainbows are relatively scarce and therefore offer something of the exotic. They also fight extremely well, being noted for their long runs with the line and their tendency to leap high out of the water. But most of all, rainbow trout fishing simply is different from brown trout fishing – it is a chance to observe water in a new light and to develop new angling techniques.

Natural distribution

Rainbow trout are native to Pacific drainage waters between the Bristol Bay region of Alaska and the north-western Mexican State of Baja California. Other natural populations occur in some headwater tributaries of the mighty Mackenzie River (which flows north from central Canada to the Arctic Ocean). Outside of North America rainbows are native to the Kamchatka Peninsula in south-eastern Siberia.

Introduction to Tasmania

Rainbows were first introduced to Tasmania in 1898. In 1899 the NTAA recorded that :

'Amongst the fry liberated were the first lot of the newly introduced American Rainbow Trout, hatched from ova obtained from New Zealand by the Fisheries Commissioners, at the suggestion of northern anglers...'

Another shipment of rainbows to Tasmania was recorded the following year, and yet another in 1904-05.

According to Charles Harrison (*Fishing and Tourists*, 1934) the stripping of wild fish in Tasmania began in 1906 when the *'rainbow in lakes were sufficiently matured to give supply of ova'*.

During the early years, despite the development of healthy wild stocks, there were concerns about inbreeding, and anglers were likely to blame any unfavourable change in the size, condition or quantity of fish on poor bloodlines. In the absence of scientific research this fear was not entirely illogical. Harrison's book, Association records and Parliamentary reports indicate that from 1917 until at least the late 1930s there were almost annual shipments of rainbow ova from New Zealand, the main purpose of these importations being to provide *'fresh blood'* at Great Lake and Lake Leake. From the 1930s anglers sought professional advice on the status of trout stocks in Tasmania and it became apparent that most changes in fisheries could be attributed to environmental factors. The emphasis on fresh blood faded. Parliamentary records show that since the formation of the IFC in 1959 there have been only two importations of rainbow trout – 100 000 ova from New Zealand in 1964 (probably in con-nection with the first commercial trout farm) and an unspecified number of ova from the Ballarat Fish Acclimatisation Society in 1969-70 *'for farm dams'*.

Acclimatisation and current distribution

Rainbow trout were first liberated (as fry) in the 1898-99 season. The NTAA indicated that 550 fish were released into the South Esk River, 400 into the North Esk River, and 200 into *'Blue Peak'* (in the Chudleigh Lakes). It is likely that further releases were undertaken in the south of the State but few records survive.

Streams

NTAA/NTFA reports indicate that in the early years efforts were concentrated on stream stocking and that, in waters where brown trout were absent, acclimatisation was initially very successful. In 1914 (by which time rainbows had established in many small streams) the advice from the north-west was to *'put them in small streams above falls or other obstacles, as they readily make their way down from open water to the sea and disappear.'* Therefore it seems that rainbows were doing best in headwaters which had not yet been invaded by brown trout.

Many anglers developed a dislike for rainbows and in 1912 one prominent north-wester wrote:

Rainbow trout – classic lake-patterning

'The rivers here are well stocked with fish and some good catches were reported. One angler caught 85 Rainbow Trout in one day, but as a rule the fish caught were on the small side.

The last consignment of Brown Trout (yearlings) were much appreciated as they are not so plentiful here as the Rainbow, which were barred in the competitions, it being said that they were too easily caught. Some fishermen here caught good bags of them on the ordinary hook and worm, so it was passed that they should not count for the trophies.'

Within a few years contributors to the Annual Report had all but stopped mentioning stream rainbows. It is to be assumed that brown trout were rapidly introduced into rainbow streams to provide variety and 'better sport'. Once established the browns competed heavily for food and space and in most instances ultimately replaced the rainbows.

Rainbow trout populations are also threatened when formerly crystal streams become subject to siltation (see Part 2 – *Tasmanian Trout Waters in Detail* – *Florentine River* and *Leven, River*).

In streams which have remained free of brown trout, rainbows have survived to the present. Such waters include the Weld River (north-east),

A maiden. Note the olive back and silver flanks

the upper Mersey River, the Lawrence River and Halls Creek. Wild rainbows also survive in streams where migrants from stable upstream populations (such as lake populations) contribute to natural recruitment. Then there are a few streams, such as the Arve River, the upper St Patricks River and the Eldon River, where small numbers of rainbows maintain a fragile coexistence with brown trout.

The most significant rainbow streams in the State are the Weld River (Huon system) and the Vale River. In these systems rainbows have for many years vastly out-numbered browns in anglers' bags. Perhaps it is no coincidence that the best rainbow trout streams in Tasmania are located in limestone and dolomite country.

Lakes

In Tasmania, rainbow trout have been far more successful in lakes than streams. The first lake stocked probably was *'Blue Peak'* (1898-99) followed by Lake Sorell (1902-03), Lake Leake (1904), Arthurs Lake (1904-05), Great Lake (1910), and Lake St Clair (1928). Subsequently many more lakes, especially new hydro-electric storages, were stocked.

In most lakes repeated liberations were carried out until the 1950s, after which the SFFC ceased most stocking programmes. Rainbow trout have since demonstrated an ability to maintain self-supporting wild populations in most highland lakes. While brown trout are almost always dominant, rainbows have firmly established. In recent years rainbows have accounted for about 30% of the annual harvest at Great Lake; 15-20% at Bradys Lake, Bronte Lagoon, Lake Mackintosh, Lake St Clair and Pine Tier Lagoon; 10% at Lake Echo, Lake King William and Lake Sorell; and about 5-10% at Lake Gordon. In highland waters where brown trout are absent (such as the upper Mersey lakes, Lake Skinner and Lake Hayes) wild rainbow trout populations also appear to be stable.

The relative success of rainbow trout in lakes may be at least partially attributable to the fact that the preferred environment of the species differs from that of the brown trout – competition for food and space may not be as intense as it is in streams. However, in some waters (such as Arthurs Lake) fragile populations have eventually become extinct, and in other waters (such as the Chudleigh Lakes) the species has apparently failed to establish at all.

Saltwater

Despite the overwhelming urge of rainbows to migrate to the sea, sea run rainbow trout (steel-

The perfect adversary for the lure fisher

head) have not established anywhere outside of the fish's native range.

As early as 1914 anglers in northern Tasmania had noted that rainbows *'readily make their way down from open water to the sea and disappear'*. Despite the repeated stocking of many rivers (especially the Forth) and the occurrence of substantial wild riverine populations in apparently suitable river systems (such as the Leven), sea runs never established.

In the mid to late 1980s escapees from saltwater fish farms were caught by recreational anglers along the south-east coast – and sea cage escapees are still common in Macquarie Harbour and some West Coast rivers – but these fish are not wild *migratory* stock.

Natural spawning

A small percentage of male rainbows mature during the first year of life and some females mature in their second year. But, while early maturity is common among domestic fish, most wild fish do not spawn until they are three years old. Some fish delay first spawning for four or, more rarely, five years.

In Tasmania spawning takes place between late July and early November, and peak migrations at most if not all lakes usually occur in August/September. There does not appear to be any significant overlap between rainbow trout and brown trout spawning seasons.

The preferred spawning habitat is swift-flowing coldwater streams with shingle beds. Most lake rainbows spawn in lake tributaries, but they will utilise outflow streams, especially if the inflows are grossly inadequate or inaccessible. Rainbow trout also seem to be far more inclined than brown trout to lay eggs in loose lakeshore gravel.

Growth and size

Rainbow trout are relatively short-lived. While some specimens may survive for ten years or more, longevity is rare – certainly far less common than in brown trout. Even excluding infant mortality the great majority of fish die within the first five years of life.

Mortality at spawning appears to far exceed that of brown trout. The actual death rate depends upon the environment and seasonal factors, but it is common for 30% of fish to die after first spawning and few fish survive to third spawning.

Older brown trout may find it difficult to regain condition after spawning but they commonly survive as 'slabs' for one or more seasons. Rainbows generally succumb quickly. For this reason poor-conditioned browns are more common than slabby rainbows.

Although rainbow trout are short-lived they tend to grow faster than brown trout. In hatchery situations this can be partially attributed to the ability of the species to adapt quickly to domestication and artificial feed. However, even in the wild, rainbows tend to grow quickly. Studies undertaken by the IFC at Great Lake indicate that, despite early competitive disadvantages, during the first year of life rainbows grow significantly faster than browns.

While the diet of rainbows may not appear to differ much from the diet of brown trout, the two fish tend to occupy separate microhabitats, and in any water the relative quantity of dietary items taken by each species can be quite different. The mechanisms which govern trout growth are discussed under *Brown Trout, 2.1*.

Dr Robert McDowall (*New Zealand Freshwater Fishes*, 1990) noted that the largest recorded steelhead (sea run rainbow) of which he was aware weighed 16.3 kg and that a lake fish from Canada was reputed to have weighed 23.6 kg. John Clements (*Salmon at the Antipodes*, 1988) noted that a 42 lb (19 kg) steelhead was taken by rod and line off Alaska in 1970. As far as I am aware the largest rainbow trout taken in Tasmania was the 17 lb 2 oz (7.8 kg) specimen caught by C.V. Batchelor from the River Ouse in 1933.

Commercial fish farming

The potential for commercial trout farming was seriously examined in the early 1960s, prompting the IFC in 1965 to alter the Fisheries Act so as to provide an elaborate series of controls protecting the interests of recreational anglers. Farming was limited to licensed professionals and the sale of wild stock remained unlawful. The company 'Sevrup' established the first commercial hatchery and farm at Bridport in 1964. Rainbow trout were chosen because they are easy to rear and because they were marketable.

Sevrup found that runts and early-maturing fish were unsuitable for on-growing and offered some such fish to the IFC. These trout proved ideal for stocking enclosed waters where natural recruitment was low and high returns desirable. A demand soon developed. More recently domestic rainbows have created interest in underutilized storages such as Lake Barrington and Lake Crescent (even though these waters contain worthwhile numbers of brown trout).

Today there are commercial hatcheries at Bridport, Cressy, Springfield and National Park. Donations of fish to the IFC continue and occasionally further stocks are purchased. Domestic fish are only released into public waters where put-and-take fishing is appropriate; the IFC takes great care not to jeopardise any wild fishery.

Property owners may *purchase* domestic rainbow trout from commercial hatcheries. Applications for permits must be presented to the IFC so that the transport of fish within the State can be monitored – but the Commission does not require that privately owned fish be made available for public recreation.

Wholly private trout fisheries

The availability of privately-owned domestic rainbows led to the development of 'fish-out ponds' – storages where customers pay for the right to catch fish. While applications for this type of fishery were received as early as 1969, there was much opposition from anglers who believed that the legalising of private fisheries might eventually lead to the privatisation of public waters, and that contrived angling for tame fish might alter anglers' expectations of the wild fishery. Consequently the original proposals never proceeded.

In the face of increasing pressure from entrepreneurs to formally allow fish-out ponds, and in recognition of existing confusing provisions, the IFC in 1989 moved to provide for the registration of wholly private fisheries. Registration attracts an annual fee and clearly establishes the status of legitimate private trout fisheries. Patrons are permitted to fish without licences and without the need to adhere to normal provisions regarding bag limits and closed seasons. Regulations and fees are set at the discretion of the owner. However, while *bona fide* tourist trout-lakes on private land are normally registered on application, the IFC remains firmly opposed to the privatisation of public waters.

Private rainbow fisheries are not discussed in detail in this book.

Sea cages and how they affect recreational trout fisheries

Commercial trout farming has recently resulted in the advent of rainbow trout in coastal waters. Pilot studies on the feasibility of sea water culture (mariculture) of rainbow trout were undertaken in 1980. By the mid 1980s many leases had been issued and numerous sea cages had been established along the south-east coast from the Tasman Peninsula to Recherche Bay. In 1987 sea cages were also established in Macquarie Harbour. Inevitably some trout jumped out of the pens and some cages were damaged, so recreational anglers were soon catching escapees in coastal waters.

Lower than expected returns resulted in significant rationalisation of the industry and many of the less-adequate farm sites were abandoned. By the 1990s many of the remaining farms in the south-east had scaled down or phased out the mariculture of rainbows and embraced the cultivation of the more lucrative Atlantic salmon.

Surprisingly, the sea farming of rainbow trout in Macquarie Harbour has been very successful – a phenomenon probably due to the harbour's diluted salt content – and here the mariculture of rainbows is likely to continue for many years. Currently anglers catch large numbers of domestic rainbow trout in Macquarie Harbour, the Gordon River and the lower Henty River. Smaller numbers of fish are taken off the beaches along the central West Coast.

Preferred environment

Experienced anglers are well aware of the differences in preferred habitat between brown trout and rainbow trout. Rainbows are rarely seen foraging or tailing in shallows – they have a penchant

A wind lane – rainbow territory

for deep open water and are prominent in wind lanes.

In lakes rainbow trout are noted for 'schooling'. It is common for spin fishers and deep trollers to hook several rainbows in quick succession, even if the species is locally rare or has been difficult to locate. When polaroiding, immature fish are often spotted swimming in small groups and, although larger fish usually appear to be feeding alone, adults often concentrate into selected areas. 'Schooling' may be attributable to the tendency of the fish to gather in lucrative feeding areas, though in open water feeding in groups probably has strategic advantages.

A hot spot for rainbow trout is in rips. Wherever a stream pushes out into a lake or, within a stream, where running water pushes into a pool rainbows will be found *in* the current. If brown trout are present in the same water they usually will lie on the edge of the current. Many scientists and popular writers have speculated that, while rainbows in currents have first choice of inflowing food, they must expend considerable energy in obtaining it. The claim is that rainbows stay in the fast water only because the more competitive brown trout forcibly occupy the more

lucrative feeding stations nearby. However, even when brown trout are absent from a water many rainbows *choose* to station themselves in the current. Moreover, observant anglers will notice that the fish are not swimming hard against the flow – they are lying in pockets of 'dead' water. I suspect that rainbows simply prefer swift-flow habitats.

Rainbows are more likely than browns to strike at gaudy lures. Even on bright calm days, when browns can be very difficult for spin fishers to catch, rainbow trout are likely to provide fair to good sport.

Generally rainbows are much more catchable than browns. In Great Lake brown trout outnumber rainbows 10:1 in the respective spawning runs but account for only 50-70% of the annual harvest. A similar trend is evident at other waters, both in Tasmania and elsewhere throughout the world.

Management options

In the hatchery successive generations are often reared from parents chosen for their fast growth, so the brood stock are often among the least suspicious fish. Inevitably domestic trout lose much

Triploid rainbow from Dee Lagoon (photo by Rob Sloane)

of their fear of humans, especially if they are on-grown beyond fingerling stage. There are also problems in maintaining sufficiently broad gene pools – and after several generations hatchery stock develop dulled senses. They grow quickly but are easily caught in the wild. While these fish offer good returns for novice anglers, they are inferior sportfish.

Wild fish are the result of natural selection – only the strongest fish with the most keenly developed senses survive – and anglers must rely heavily on skill and experience. This is what most serious fishers value about trout fishing.

It may be appropriate to stock domestic fish in small enclosed waters close to centres of habitation, and in selected under-utilized major waters, but every effort is given to maintaining the status of wild fisheries.

The advantages and disadvantages of triploid rainbows are discussed under *Triploids and Hybrids*, 2.6.

2.3 BROOK TROUT

In Tasmania there are only one or two fragile wild populations of brook trout. In common with New Zealand and mainland Australia acclimatisation has been difficult and largely unsuccessful.

Brook trout are perhaps the most easily caught of our freshwater sportfish and are generally regarded as inferior fighters. But what the species lacks in sporting quality is compensated for by its rarity and beauty – brook trout have an enduring novelty value.

Native range

The brook trout's native habitat extends along the east coast of North America from the Arctic to New England in the United States. Native inland populations are also found in highland areas in the Appalachian Mountains as far south as Georgia.

Growth and behaviour

Brook trout prefer cold water and do best in headwater streams and alpine lakes. The most prolific native populations occur in alkaline waters. Spawners prefer shallow water with low flows and are especially attracted to springs and upwellings.

Males commonly mature in the first year of life and females when they are one year older. In environments where competition is high the early maturation of brook trout results in extreme stunting (see notes on growth and size under *Brown Trout*, 2.1). However, if food and space

Brook trout

are not limiting brook trout can grow faster than either browns or rainbows. In the book *Familiar Freshwater Fishes of America* (1964), Howard T. Walden claimed that the largest recorded brook trout was taken in 1916 from the Nipigon River (Ontario). It weighed 14½lb (about 6.6 kg), and was 31½ inches (80 cm) long. Brook trout to at least 4.5 kg have been taken in Tasmania.

While their diet is diverse, brook trout appear to be more predisposed than other trout to bottom food. When fish can be seen they are likely to take any lure or fly presented to them but in hot summer conditions they are likely to retreat to deep water and 'go off the bite'.

Early attempts at acclimatisation

Early Parliamentary reports indicate that brook trout were first introduced to Tasmania (from New Zealand) in May 1883. From the 100-200 healthy ova received upwards of 100 yearlings resulted. These fish were held as brood stock and spawned in 1885. More than 3000 fry from the first stripping were liberated in waters throughout the State (including St Patricks River, the Styx River, Sorell Creek, the River Dee, Lake Sorell and the Elizabeth River). By 1887 brook trout were in *'great demand'* – several more streams had been stocked and *'large numbers'* of ova were being fertilized at the Salmon Ponds.

By 1892 lakes Crescent and Dulverton had been stocked. In 1893 it was claimed that annual liberations were being undertaken at Lake Sorell and that releases had occurred at Woods Lake and Lake Echo.

Perhaps the most successful attempt at acclimatisation occurred at Lake Leake where, it seems, a wild population was maintained for many years.

The NTAA recorded widespread brook trout liberations throughout the early 1900s. Small numbers of (mostly) yearlings were taken to the South Esk system, the North Esk system, Lake Sorell, Pipers River, the Chudleigh Lakes, and the Blythe system.

Besides the original shipment of brook trout ova there was at least one other importation – in 1905 the NTAA noted that a *'shipment of ova was received from New Zealand consisting of Rainbow, Loch Leven and Fontinalis varieties'*. Propagation of the species continued until at least 1908-09 when 1800 fry were reared from hatchery stock. However, with the exception of the fishery at Lake Leake, no wild populations established.

Where can brook trout establish?

Within its natural range the brook trout has been

A male brook trout in full spawning regalia

unable to withstand the changes in environment which have resulted from the introduction of non-native trout. Rainbow trout are widely recognised as the most serious threat but this may simply be because the species has been so widely translocated – brown trout are known to have eliminated some native riverine populations.

In retrospect it is no surprise that, despite extensive stocking in Australia and New Zealand, brook trout have not established wild populations in waters already occupied by other salmonids.

There is no doubt that the greatest threat to Tasmania's brook trout fisheries is the introduction of other trout. This could happen accidentally through mix-ups of ova and/or young fish at the hatchery – so there is a strong argument for a greater reliance on catch-and-release to maintain stocks at wild fisheries. Widespread illegal stocking of both rainbows and browns in Tasmania is also a potential danger. The capture of a brown trout at Clarence Lagoon in 1991 is cause for concern.

Origins of existing brook trout stocks

In 1962 the IFC announced that :

'Through the generosity of the Canadian Department of Fisheries a consignment of 50 000 eyed ova was received by air on 6th

February. The eggs were from the Cobequid Fish Culture Station, Collingwood, Nova Scotia.'

Despite *'premature'* hatching and many deformities an *'adequate quantity'* of healthy fish survived. Brood stock has been maintained at the Salmon Ponds ever since.

Current distribution

Despite attempts to establish brook trout at Lake Lilla and Little Pine Lagoon, the only (proven) self-supporting population occurs at Clarence Lagoon.

Recognising the difficulty of acclimatising brook trout the IFC has (in the past) managed put-and-take fisheries at Harveys Lagoon, Little Waterhouse Lake, Briseis Hole, Blackmans Lagoon, Vaucluse Reservoir, Edgar Pond, Lake No Where Else and Lake Dulverton. No brook trout survive in these waters today.

Perhaps the most exciting development in recent times has been the liberation of brook trout into previously unstocked streams and lakes in the headwaters of the Anthony River on the West Coast. While the long-term future of the species in the Anthony system is uncertain, the IFC has already found evidence of natural

Tasmania's wild brook trout waters receive complementary stocking with hatchery-reared fish. These ova are almost ready to hatch. Note the eyes and backs of the embryos.

recruitment. The waters of most significance to anglers are lakes Plimsoll, Rolleston and Selina.

Genetic diversity

Brood fish have been maintained at the Salmon Ponds since 1962-63. Most of the current stock are descendants of hatchery fish and are now truly domestic. However, in the interest of maintaining strong blood lines, both ova and live fish have occasionally been transported to the hatchery from the wild population which eventually established at Clarence Lagoon.

Although the hatchery fish at the Salmon Ponds produce poor quality ova, this may not be entirely attributable to inbreeding. Jenny Ovenden completed a study of the genetic diversity of Tasmanian salmonids in 1991 and with reference to brook trout concluded that *'numerous maternal lineages have survived the 13 or more generations since their introduction'.*

Clarence Lagoon

2.4 ATLANTIC SALMON

The Atlantic salmon (Salmo salar) is capable of attaining at least 40 kg and is perhaps the world's most prized freshwater sportfish. It is native to coastal areas of western Europe (from

Iceland, Greenland, Scandinavia and the Baltic Sea to northern Spain) and along the east coast of North America (as far south as New England in the United States). The species is essentially sea-migratory, though landlocked populations occur in New England where they are known as sebago salmon.

Although wild stocks have not established in Tasmania, fish farm escapees are taken by anglers in southern waters, and domestic stock has been released into several lakes.

Early introductions to Tasmania

Early attempts to introduce salmon were driven by commercial interest. Of the original 100 000 ova which arrived in 1864 (see *Brown Trout*, 2.1), only about 3000 healthy fish resulted.

On 4 October 1864 a leak from one of the rearing ponds was discovered and it was estimated that some 1500 salmon had escaped to the Plenty River. Later that season some 500 fish were deliberately released into the river. Many fish were retained at the Salmon Ponds. From a second importation of about 100 000 ova in 1866, approximately 6000 smolts were eventually released into the Plenty.

From the beginning there were serious doubts about the success of the salmon experiment, but authorities were eager to assure the public that sea runs had established. On 18 April 1874 *The Mercury Supplement* told the colony:

'... the Salmon recently captured at Bridge-water, and for which a reward of £30 was paid by the Salmon Commissioners, has been exhibited at the Public Library here during the month, and has attracted great attention.'

In his book *Travel and Trout in the Antipodes* (1880) William Senior summed up the sentiment prevailing in the colony:

'... to many well-informed persons it is still an open question whether the few captured fish said to have been salmon were not, after all, salmon trout [sea trout]. It is heresy to suggest this doubt to a Tasmanian ...'

During the 1880s there were four further importations of Atlantic salmon – one in 1884 which resulted in about 1250 healthy fry, two in 1885 which resulted in about 36 000 healthy fry, and one in 1888 which resulted in several hundred thousand healthy fry.

Fry released between August 1885 and December 1886 included 10 950 in the Derwent system, 6000 to the South Esk, 250 to the North Esk, 4000 to the Huon, 4000 to the Mersey, 2000 to the Leven, and 200 to the Inglis and Forth. Also during this period nearly 1000 smolts were released into the Plenty.

In 1887 some 300 fry were transported to the Forth and Inglis. In 1888 about 50 fry were liberated at the Plenty while a further 250-300 were taken to the northern rivers. Another 130 000 smolts were allowed to escape to the Plenty late in 1889.

It is not known how many fish were actually reared at the Salmon Ponds but brood stock was still being maintained in 1892 and *'a quantity'* of fry was liberated in the Arthur River system during the 1892-93 season.

Why no sea runs?

There are many variables which influence the ability of sea run salmonids to find their way back to their birthplace (or place of release) and establish self-supporting populations. The fact that most salmon species and rainbow trout 'drift' with ocean currents is significant. Off Tasmania there are few currents, and those which do exist are incompatible with the breeding cycles of salmonids – the fish feel the spawning urge when they are far away from home and apparently become disoriented and lost. Other determinants, such as the role of pheromones, are poorly understood. The fact remains that Atlantic salmon have not established sea runs anywhere outside of the native range.

Landlocked populations

By the 1900s the failure of the salmon experiment was widely accepted and the NTAA sought the introduction of non sea-migratory stock with a view to establishing landlocked fisheries. On first application in 1906-07 sebagos were unavailable and sea-migratory stock was sent. These fish were eventually liberated in Great Lake, Lake Leake and the Chudleigh Lakes.

About 20 000 sebago ova were finally received in March 1910 and some 6200 yearlings had been reared by 1911. About 260 were retained for breeding and the balance distributed to Great Lake and the *'Upper Arthur Lakes'*. However, only a small number of salmon were caught by anglers.

The brood fish failed to give satisfactory results so in 1916 another 20 000 ova were imported. Some of the resulting fry were sent to Lake Dove. The rest were on-grown at Waverley and most were released as yearlings into Lake Leake.

Brood stock was held at Waverley until at least 1918. But, like the sea-migratory stock before them, sebagos failed to adapt to Tasmanian conditions.

Interest in Atlantic salmon rekindled in the 1930s and in 1934 the Commissioners reported an importation of 25 000 ova from New Zealand

Domestic Atlantic salmon from the Esperance River. Note the rounded and stunted fins – a state of condition common among fish which have been held in intensively-stocked hatcheries and/or sea pens. Note also how closely the fish resembles a sea run brown trout.

(in the book *New Zealand Freshwater Fishes* (1990) Dr Robert McDowall suggested that several lots of Atlantic salmon ova were sent to Tasmania, though exact dates were not given). About 8000 yearlings resulted, some of which were released into Great Lake, but the ultimate result was as it always had been – a few fish were caught by anglers but natural spawning (if it occurred at all) was insufficient for the establishment of wild stocks.

Atlantic salmon today

Atlantic salmon caught in Tasmania today are domestic stock from commercial seafood operations.

The pioneer work for commercial salmon farming in Tasmania began in 1984 when 100 000 domestic salmon ova were imported from the Gaden hatchery in New South Wales. Atlantic salmon were chosen in preference to Pacific salmon partly because of the Norwegian involvement in the programme and partly because of their superior farm-performance. The company 'Saltas' initiated and financed the operations.

The IFC and the Department of Sea Fisheries have issued several licences for the sea cage cultivation of Atlantic salmon and rainbow trout in southern waters and in Macquarie Harbour. The major freshwater salmon hatchery and rearing unit, which produces all of the State's smolts, has been in operation at Wayatinah (on the banks of the River Derwent near Wayatinah Lagoon) since 1985.

Many sea cage escapees have been caught by amateur fishers in recent seasons. Most have been taken in gill nets along the south-eastern coastline but others have been caught on lures, baits and flies in southern rivers (including the Huon, Esperance and Lune) and Macquarie

Harbour. To date the normal size range has been 0.5-4.5 kg but fish as large as 10 kg are cultivated. Anglers speculate that since salmon sometimes escape into estuaries at spawning time they might move upstream and spawn. While this is not impossible, it is extremely unlikely that the progeny of escapees will ever return to the rivers.

A few small salmon are caught at Wayatinah Lagoon, and the IFC has also released some salmon into Great Lake and Big Waterhouse Lake. However, it is unlikely that wild stocks will ever establish in waters where brown or rainbow trout are already present.

In the late 1980s there were one or two illegal liberations of Atlantics at Lake Ophion. The current status of this fishery has not been assessed.

2.6 PACIFIC SALMON

Excluding rainbow trout there are six species of Pacific salmon, all of which belong to the genus Oncorhynchus. *These fishes are essentially migratory, spending most of their lives in the ocean and returning upstream to their birth-places to spawn and die. Under certain conditions it is possible for some Pacific salmon to establish self-supporting landlocked populations, though such fish rarely attain the weights of their saltwater counterparts.*

Sockeye salmon

There has only been one small importation of sockeye salmon to Tasmania. The NTAA recorded that in October 1901 about 750 000 ova arrived at the Salmon Ponds from Canada. Of these only 60 000 hatched and many fry succumbed to heat stress. About 10 000 fry were taken to *'the north'*. Most of those which survived were released into the North Esk (1900), South Esk (5200), and

Mersey (900), but some were retained at Waverley. The following year (1902-03) 13 yearlings were liberated into the South Esk at First Basin. The fate of the stock held at the Salmon Ponds is unknown, though it is probable that most were eventually liberated into the Derwent system. There was no attempt to propagate the species at Waverley, nor does it seem that significant brood stock were held at Plenty. In 1908 the Commissioners conceded that there was no evidence that sockeyes had established in Tasmania.

Quinnat salmon

The importation of quinnat salmon to Tasmania was recommended by the NTAA as early as 1899. The first attempt occurred in 1902 and was recorded by the NTAA in 1903:

'... the United States Government had kindly presented the Tasmanian Fisheries Department with a quantity of ova of the Pacific Salmon known as "Quinnat"... the consignment arriving on the 29th December ... The ova, numbering 495,000, were splendidly packed and arrived in wonderful condition ... The eggs soon began to hatch, but the temperature of the water made itself felt and 177,500 died in the hatching troughs, the remainder being turned out into the Derwent and its tributaries in an immature state, while 50,000 were retained in the large pond at the hatchery. An attempt was made to rail 20,000 alevins to the North, but nearly all died in transit ...'

At the end of the 1903-04 season the NTFA claimed that:

'... when netted off, the pond only yielded 854 eight-months-old fish, 529 of which were railed to the North and placed in the South Esk and Mersey Rivers; 200 were put into the Plenty River, and 125 were sent to the Davey River ... A consignment of fry was sent to the Waverley Ponds.

The few that survived the Summer's heat, numbering 36, were liberated this Autumn when 17 months old ... Very little good can be expected from the immature fry liberated, and the results of the shipment may be said to rest with the 886 reared fish.'

The stocking list for that year detailed several releases of quinnat yearlings – 446 in the South Esk, 10 in the North Esk and 105 in the Mersey. But by 1906 it was conceded that there was no evidence of salmon having returned from the sea.

No further attempts were made to import quinnats until 1910 when, inspired by the success of the species in New Zealand, the Commissioners began an extended programme of importation, rearing and liberation. Each season from the winter of 1910 to the winter of 1917 small batches of quinnat ova (usually 25 000 per year) were brought in from New Zealand. The vast majority (if not all) resulting salmon were turned out into the Derwent system. Each of the annual liberations included 12 000-23 000 fry and (in some years) 600-2000 yearlings. There was no attempt to maintain brood stock.

Importations resumed in the winter of 1921 and continued almost without interruption until at least 1930. The number of ova in each ship-

A quinnat salmon taken from the Plenty River in March 1931. It is unlikely that this fish had ever been to sea

ment ranged from 25 000 to 200 000 according to the availability of parent fish in New Zealand. Significant stocking of the Derwent continued until at least 1923 and probably until the late 1920s. But this time the focus shifted to the River Forth, where major stocking occurred until the late 1920s (see *Forth, River* in Part 2 – *Tasmanian Trout Waters in Detail*).

In 1933 the Commissioners of Fisheries wrote: *'After 1930 – In view of the fact that no quinnat appear to have returned to the Forth, and none was reported as being caught in the Derwent, it was decided to discontinue the experiment.'*

In November 1931 some 5000 yearling quinnats were liberated at Great Lake. At least one other shipment (of 25 000 ova in 1934) was imported from New Zealand in the 1930s, and in 1935 the Commissioners noted that 10 000 yearlings reared at Plenty had been released into Lake St Clair, the Franklin River and the King River. These were probably among the last liberations of the species in Tasmania.

There appear to be many poorly understood factors which affect the ability of quinnat salmon to survive and propagate in the wild. Despite the success of the species in New Zealand, it is unlikely that any Tasmanian stock ever returned from the sea or that any natural recruitment occurred at our lakes.

2.7 TRIPLOIDS AND HYBRIDS

Upon reaching maturity trout undergo hormonal and metabolic changes which cause reductions in sturdiness of form and overall strength. Anyone who has caught a 2 kg maiden rainbow or sea trout will know just how powerful and muscular such a fish is – maidens completely outshine mature fish of the same size.

Growth at maturity is reduced because fish lose appetite during the spawning season and because energy is expended in egg/milt production, migration, and aggressive defence behaviour. Moreover, many fish (males especially) become subject to scarring and disease.

In the wild most browns and rainbows mature in the third year of life and maidens of greater than 1.2 kg are rare. Any fish which do delay spawning until the fourth or fifth year are able to dominate weaker fish of the same age and so usually feed well and enjoy rapid growth. The advantages of releasing sterile fish into the wild are self evident.

In lakes where there are already large populations of trout, sterile fish usually provide better-than-average sport. This has been proven at locations such as Dee Lagoon and Lagoon of Islands. However, the most logical places to release sterile trout are waters which have to be stocked in any case by virtue of the fact that

Tiger trout

they have poor natural recruitment. In Tasmania some of the most successful releases have occurred at Lake Crescent and in the Nineteen Lagoons.

There are several methods of producing sterility – and each has its own advantages and disadvantages.

Triploids

Normal fish are diploids – that is to say that their chromosomes are found in pairs. It is possible to treat freshly-fertilised normal eggs (which are single cells) in such a way that each pair of chromosomes becomes a triplet. As the cell multiplies the chromosomes continue to be replicated in triplicate. Resulting fish are sterile but visually indistinguishable from immature diploids.

Triploid salmonids are produced by applying short heat or pressure shocks to newly fertilised ova. Such treatment rarely results in 100% of the treated eggs being triploided. The greater the shock, the greater the percentage of triploids – but greater too is the mortality of ova.

Male triploids produce milt (though it is largely infertile) and are subject to normal stresses at spawning time. There is even some evidence to suggest that they can cause minor interference when among normal trout spawners. Females are totally sterile, are not prone to disease at spawning time, and display particularly fast growth.

It is possible to produce all-female triploids by shocking eggs fertilized with milt from sex-reversed females. Unfortunately the creation of sex-reversed brood stock involves feeding female fry hormone-treated food and then on-growing them in the hatchery for several years. And, as females have no sperm ducts, each fish must be killed when the time comes to extract the milt. The whole process is time-consuming and costly.

Currently in Tasmania rainbow triploids are favoured. This is because rainbows are easy to on-grow in hatcheries and, in terms of survivability, it is preferable to stock with advanced fingerlings rather than fry. Also triploid research has had a commercial component and historically rainbows have been of most interest to fish farmers.

Exceptional triploid rainbows more than 5 years old have been caught at Dee Lagoon and in the Nineteen Lagoons but, while triploid rainbows may not be any easier to catch than normal rainbows, they are still far more catchable than brown trout. The reality is that most triploid rainbows are killed within one or two years of release – before the benefits of sterility are realized.

Triploid rainbow trout could be of great value to recreational anglers if the catch-and-release philosophy was embraced at relevant waters. If anglers are not yet prepared to release most or all of their catch it may be more beneficial to stock with triploid browns and/or sterile hybrids.

Hybrids

Most trout and salmon can be successfully crossed. Hybrids are usually sterile and so possess favourable attributes in common with triploids – and there is no need to hold sex-reversed brood stock. In addition they often have distinctive patterning and high novelty value.

The IFC has produced several crosses at the Salmon Ponds and undertaken trial releases of two.

Most notable is the tiger trout, a fish produced by fertilizing brown trout eggs with brook trout milt. This cross invariably results in a very low survival of eggs and fry. However, if the eggs are triploided the success rate can be lifted significantly. Experimental work with Tasmanian fish has shown that triploid tigers grow well and have many of the highly desirable feeding habits of brown trout. While some tigers have escaped from the Salmon Ponds to the Plenty River, the hybrid has been deliberately turned out only at the Pet Reservoir. Unfortunately the Pet is deep and murky and far from ideal for experimental releases. The best lakes to stock would be small shallow clearwaters (such as many of the popular waters in the Nineteen Lagoons) where anglers would actually see most of the fish – and stand a reasonable chance of catching one. Also, small waters are ideal for monitoring growth, survivability and catchability. If over-harvesting became a problem, reduced bag limits could be encouraged.

More recently there have been releases of brown trout x Atlantic salmon hybrids. This fish is much easier to produce but is practically indistinguishable from triploid brown trout and does not have the high novelty value of the tiger. Stocked waters include the Beaconsfield Reservoir, The Big Lagoon, Blackmans Lagoon, the Brandy Pond, Bruins Pond, Curries River Dam, the Guide Reservoir and the Little Wonder Pond. ◆

Where the Locals Fish

Where the Locals Fish

The tables below list Tasmania's most-fished lakes and rivers in order of popularity. The statistics represent an average of postal questionnaire results collated by the IFC between 1985-86 and 1991-92. They have been verified by official creel surveys.

In recent seasons Brushy Lagoon, Lake Burbury and Lagoon of Islands have been annually visited by more than 1500 anglers. Each is highly recommended, though returns to trout fishers over the next few seasons will be difficult to predict (see

Part 2 – *Tasmanian Trout Waters in Detail*).

The Western Lakes also receive very high visitation (probably more than 1500 anglers per year) but, for a variety of reasons, the questionnaires results for these waters have been difficult to interpret.

Note that the river statistics make no distinction between 'traditional' stream sport and sea trout fishing. In some rivers most angling may be carried out in the lower reaches during spring (see Part 2 – *Tasmanian Trout Waters in Detail*).

Lakes visited by more than 1500 anglers each year

	Average number of licenced anglers visiting the water at least once in a season	Average effort expressed as the total number of angler-days spent at the water in a season	Average number of fish caught per angler per day	Average number of fish caught at the water over a season
Arthurs Lake	9 700	49 900	2.4	121 400
Great Lake	9 150	50 400	1.0	52 100
Lake Sorell	8 100	44 500	1.7	76 500
Bronte Lagoon	3 750	14 900	1.5	22 300
Lake Crescent	2 650	9 100	1.1	9 600
Lake Pedder	2 500	12 600	1.6	19 300
Bradys Lake	2 150	6 400	1.1	7 200
Lake Rowallan	2 000	7 200	1.9	13 400
Lake Echo	1 850	5 600	2.0	11 500
Dee Lagoon	1 800	5 400	0.7	3 700
Woods Lake	1 800	5 300	1.6	8 600
Little Pine Lagoon	1 750	6 900	1.3	8 700
Craigbourne Dam	1 600	5 200	0.9	4 600

Rivers visited by more than 800 anglers each year

	Average number of licenced anglers visiting the water at least once in a season	Average effort expressed as the total number of angler-days spent at the water in a season	Average number of fish caught per angler per day	Average number of trout caught at the water over a season
South Esk River	2 950	18 000	1.6	28 900
River Derwent	2 900	16 900	0.8	13 400
Mersey River	2 800	20 100	1.3	25 200
Brumbys Creek	2 650	15 000	1.2	17 300
Macquarie River	2 400	12 400	1.6	19 200
River Leven	2 150	12 900	1.4	17 700
Meander River	2 050	12 500	1.9	23 800
North Esk River	1 650	8 600	2.1	17 700
Tyenna River	1 600	6 900	2.9	19 700
St Patricks River	1 600	5 400	3.2	17 500
River Forth	1 200	5 500	0.7	3 700
Huon River	1 200	5 300	0.8	4 200
Lake River	1 150	6 100	2.1	11 300
Inglis River	950	7 700	1.2	9 000
River Clyde	950	3 700	1.8	6 500

Where to Fish –
A Regional Breakdown

Introduction

This section is designed to familiarise visitors with the nature of trout fishing in Tasmania and to pinpoint the best fisheries in each of the major trout fishing districts. Specific information on each water is given in Part 2 – *Tasmanian Trout Waters in Detail*.

For the purposes of this overview the State has been divided into ten regions, each of which is defined by its geography, accessibility and relevance to trout fishers.

In summary, the Central Plateau offers the cream of the State's lake fishing; the North and Midlands is the best stream fishing district; and the West Coast includes some of the most noteworthy sea trout rivers. The Central South, Far South, and Central North-West are not among Tasmania's very best fishing areas, though each offers good sport and is conveniently close to one or more of the main population centres. Overall the South-West is a poor fishing district, though it does incorporate lakes Pedder and Gordon. The least remarkable areas are the Far North-West, the North-East, and the East Coast.

4.1 CENTRAL PLATEAU

The Central Plateau is Tasmania's highland lakes district, location of the State's premier trout fisheries. It includes our three most popular waters (Great Lake, Arthurs Lake and Lake Sorell) as well as dozens of other renowned stillwaters. The major attractions for anglers include the variety of fishing conditions, the water clarity, the reliability of the sport, the scope for shore-based fishing, and the proximity to the major population areas. The weather is relatively mild, though wind, rain and snow can occur at any time.

The lakes district remains in a relatively natural state with open woodlands, moors and snowgrass plains providing superb scenery. Despite massive hydro-electric developments, there has been little wholesale clearfelling and there are no big towns. While there is significant roading in the east and south, the area between Great Lake and Lake St Clair (the Western Lakes) is a major wilderness recreation zone. Hotels and accommodation can be found at Miena, Tarraleah, Derwent Bridge and Bronte Park, and informal lakeshore camping is permitted at most waters.

Sight fishing – the glory of the Central Highlands

Although all waters are covered in this book, further information is given in the publication Trout Guide *(Rob Sloane and Greg French, 1991).*

The big three – Lake Sorell, Great Lake and Arthurs Lake

Despite the murky water, Sorell with its natural woodland setting is my favourite of the big three. Fish in the open water are mostly 0.8-1.5 kg and many taken from the marshes top 2 kg, yet the average catch is an impressive 1.7 trout per angler per day. Browns dominate but up to 10% of the annual harvest comprises rainbow trout.

Great Lake is a clearwater storage which suffers from severe drawdowns so the shore zone is usually barren and ugly. While much of the lake's modern popularity is rooted in tradition, it does give up good trout at the average rate of one per angler per day. Typical fish weigh 1 kg and some attain 2 kg. More than 30% are rainbows.

Arthurs Lake teems with 0.4-1 kg brown trout (no rainbows) and yields fish at the average rate of 2.4 fish per angler per day. It is an artificial impoundment and, though not as aesthetically bland as Great Lake, there are significant seasonal drawdowns.

Lure fishing

Intending lure fishers should read the section *Notes for the Specialist*, 6.2. The most popular trolling and drift-spinning waters are Arthurs Lake, Lake Sorell, Great Lake, Lake King William, and the Bradys chain of lakes. Spinning from the shore is possible at most waters, some of the best being Lake Sorell, the Western Lakes, Lake Echo, the Bradys chain of lakes, and Lake St Clair.

Fly fishing

The basics of fly fishing in the Central Highlands are discussed under *Notes for the Specialist* 6.1. While Little Pine Lagoon, Penstock Lagoon, some of the Western Lakes, and Bruisers Lagoon are reserved for fly fishing only, most other waters also offer superb sport.

Wet flies

Wet-fly fishing is very popular in waters where fish can be seen foraging. The best lakes are those with extensive shoreline marshes and/or weedy shallows – waters such as Little Pine Lagoon, Lake Sorell, Lake Crescent, Bronte Lagoon, some of the Western Lakes, and Lagoon of Islands.

Polaroiding

The best polaroiding waters include the Western Lakes, Great Lake, Dee Lagoon, Lake St Clair, St Clair Lagoon, and Lake Echo.

Natural environs and wild trout

Traditional dry-fly fishing

The best hatches of mayflies occur on Little Pine Lagoon, Arthurs Lake, some of the Western Lakes, Penstock Lagoon and Lake Sorell. Beetle falls are prominent on Dee Lagoon and Great Lake.

Bait fishing

Detailed notes on getting started are given under *Notes for the Specialist*, 6.3. The traditional bait fishing areas are at Great Lake, Arthurs Lake, Lake Crescent, the Bradys chain of lakes, and Pine Tier Lagoon.

Where am I most likely to catch fish?

By far the most impressive average catch-rates belong to Lake King William and Arthurs Lake. The yield at Lake Sorell is also notable, especially so because the fish are relatively large.

The rewards for going further afield include bigger fish, more challenging sport, and variety.

Trophy trout

See *Notes for the Specialist*, 6.4.

Stream fishing

Stream fishing is not exceptional and is completely overshadowed by the lake fishing. While enthusiasts may care to try Serpentine Rivulet, the River Ouse, the Nive River, the Clarence River or any of the other creeks, much better stream sport is to found in the North and Midlands.

4.2 NORTH AND MIDLANDS

The commercial and industrial heart of the region is Launceston (population 69 000), while the major rural centre is Deloraine (population 2100).

Vast expanses of flat pasture extend from the highways to the foothills. The region receives little direct rain so the rivers rely heavily on precipitation in the surrounding highlands. Summer/autumn irrigation demands often result in poor flows, a situation worsened by

Classic meadow stream (photo by Rob Sloane)

virtue of the fact that over-clearing has resulted in erosion and reduced water-retention. However, land degradation and the liberal use of fertilizers have not yet resulted in dangerous algal blooms – and the stream fishing remains exceptional.

The meadow streams

Fishing in the North and Midlands is centred on the meadow streams – sluggish waterways in the South Esk catchment which feature long weedy broadwaters. Among the most renowned locations are the Macquarie River, the Meander River, the Lake River, Brumbys Creek, the Elizabeth River and the Liffey River. Also, while not specifically in the North and Midlands region, the upper South Esk River, St Pauls River and the Break O'day River are major meadow streams commonly fished by Launceston-based anglers.

The normal size range of trout in anglers' bags is 0.3-1.2 kg and the best waters produce fish to 2 kg and more.

While there is plenty of scope for lure casting, the rivers are especially attractive to fly fishers. After heavy rains trout bow-wave and tail in flooded backwaters, and from early spring until the end of the season spectacular rises are to be expected. Terrestrials, caddis flies, damselflies, black spinners and many other insects stimulate worthwhile surface activity, though it is the handsome red spinner which provides the feature fishing.

Other streams

The North Esk catchment differs from the South Esk in that the streams are mostly steeper, faster, less weedy and (during moderate to low levels) clearer. Such waters are ideal for Celta fishing and bait casting but also provide plenty of entertainment for fly enthusiasts. The best streams include the North Esk River and St Patricks River where there are plenty of 0.2-0.6 kg trout. The smaller tributaries (such as Distillery Creek, Musselboro Creek, Patersonia Rivulet and Camden Rivulet) harbour large numbers of 0.1-0.3 kg fish.

The lower reaches of Pipers River support some reasonable trout but the upper reaches and tributaries contain mostly small fish.

The Rubicon River and other tributaries of Port Sorell are mini meadow-streams which produce some surprising trout in excess of 1 kg.

Choosing which streams to fish

Springtime

Fly fishing on the meadow streams peaks after spring rains when fish can be found foraging in

Catching tailers in the flooded margins of the Macquarie River (courtesy Rob Sloane)

the backwaters and/or taking mayflies and other insects from the surface along the edges. Breezes kill the hatches – but remember that prevailing winds can be neutralized by contrasting sea breezes. (For example on the Break O'Day, northerly to north-westerly weather often counters easterly sea breezes.) Among the best waters are the Macquarie, Meander, Break O'Day, and Lake rivers

Springtime on the fastwaters is not so remarkable. The water is usually flowing high and cold, and the flies are dormant. Even Celta fishing gives relatively poor results. The worm caster who works swollen (but not raging) creeks is often rewarded, though he too is better off in the meadows.

Summer and autumn

Post Christmas, when the water is low and warm, there is a lull in the meadows, though calm muggy days usually result in worthwhile surface activity. Often there is an autumn surge – a secondary hatch associated with a cooling of the water. Wet-fly enthusiasts and Celta fishers will also find that very bad autumn weather often causes the trout to be bold and savage. Try fishing upstream in pockets of clear water.

Weather conditions are not critical on the fastwaters when levels are low. However, I tend to explore the fastwaters only when it is either moderately cold, or warm and windy – it is a shame to neglect the meadows on potentially perfect days.

Camping

Most of the land flanking the meadow streams is privately owned and camping is not encouraged.

Essential reading

For those intent on fishing the rivers of the North and Midlands I strongly recommend the works of David Scholes. My favourite books are *Fly-fisher in Tasmania* (1961), *The Way of an Angler* (1963), *Trout Quest* (1969), and *Fly Fishing in Australia* (1974). Reprints of *Fly-fisher in Tasmania* and *Trout Quest* are available from Compleat Angler stores and selected book sellers, while the other two books can be found in the State Library. David's later titles are also a delight, if only because of his literary skill, but they lack optimism and freshness.

Read David at the *beginning* of the season. Enjoy his style and wit, and glean from him what practicalities you can. Re-read him at the end of the season... and next season... and in five years time. David does not bash you over the head with facts. He knows the power of subtlety, that some things can only be fully appreciated after certain levels of experience are gained. The beginner will find his notes useful, the intermediate angler will find them invaluable, and the experienced will be amazed at how much they failed to pick up in the first half dozen readings.

Another most capable meadow-stream enthusiast is Tony Ritchie. Tony is a regular contributor to the annual *Tasmanian Angling Report* and writes occasionally for national fishing magazines such as *Freshwater Fishing*.

Lakes

Brushy Lagoon (north of Westbury) produces 1-3 kg browns and rainbows, and has until recently been the local glory water. Curries River Dam (near Georgetown) is also very popular with locals. Tooms Lake, on the headwaters of the Macquarie River, contains plenty of 'average' trout and is well worth a visit.

Sea trout

Although under-utilised by local anglers, the Tamar estuary boasts very good runs of sea trout. Sea trout are also taken from the lower reaches of the North Esk River, the Rubicon River and Pipers River.

4.3 WEST COAST

The West Coast lies directly in the path of the Roaring Forties, icy winds which rip in from the Indian Ocean bringing with them clouds bursting with rain. The topography too is daunting, a mosaic of steep peaks, ranges and valleys. Rainforest features in the valleys and on the more sheltered hillsides, while exposed plains and coastal hills support thick heath and/or buttongrass.

West Coast society reflects a long tradition of mining. In the 1970s and 1980s the focus of the economy shifted to hydro-electric development, and now it is tourism driven. Some towns (such as the enchanting port of Strahan) have been able to take advantage of the changing industrial and social climate and are enjoying unprecedented growth. But the overall population of the region is in decline.

Traditionally the West Coast has been geographically isolated. In recent times modern highways have been constructed providing comfortable vehicular access between towns. However, minor roads are usually unsealed and access beyond the highways remains limited.

For the trout fisher the feature attraction is the sea trout fishing.

Sea trout

Angling for wild sea-run brown trout begins in August and continues in earnest throughout November (and sometimes well into December).

The best waters for the shore-based angler are the Henty and Little Henty rivers. Boat handlers prefer the Gordon River, the Pieman River and Macquarie Harbour.

Stream fishing

Invariably the water is tea-coloured, acidic, infertile and unfavourable for trout growth. Yet, as conditions for spawning are very good, natural recruitment is enough to cause severe overpopulation and stunted growth.

Most streams are too overgrown and/or deep to allow comfortable angling. Exceptions include locally-popular Celta waters such as the Little Henty River, the Huskisson River, the Wilson River and the upper Franklin River.

The only exceptional streams are the Fossey and Hatfield rivers. These waters differ from most others in that they flow through plains and marshes and carry trout in excess of 1 kg.

Lake fishing

How good is the lake fishing?

Lakes on the West Coast can hardly be recommended over those on the Central Plateau. The water is tea coloured, the weather is often uncomfortable and the sight fishing is unreliable. However, each water has its own attributes and local devotees.

Hydro-electric scheme lakes

The Pieman River Power Development lakes are established waters set in steep forested valleys. The best waters are Lake Mackintosh and Lake Rosebery. Both Lake Pieman and Lake Murchison are held in little regard by local trout fishers.

In 1993-94 the recently formed Lake Burbury offered even the novice angler a good chance of taking browns and rainbows.

Brook trout are found in the Henty/Anthony district, most notably at lakes Plimsoll, Rolleston and Selina.

The West Coast Range

As well as the brook trout waters in the Anthony drainage there are several lakes on the West Coast Range with established trout populations. The Lake Margaret drainage waters (including lakes Margaret, Mary, Paul, Peter and Polycarp) are accessible to backpackers and contain plenty of brown trout. Lake Beatrice, a wilderness destination in the King River drainage, contains both browns and rainbows.

Typical West Coast stream

In 1993-94 Lake Burbury was teeming with rainbows

Henty River

Other waters

Many anglers consider Talbots Lagoon to be one of the best small fisheries in the State. Parting Creek Lake, near Zeehan, is quite notable at mudeye time and the Waratah lakes are renowned for their traditional dry-fly fishing. Of interest to the bushwalker are lakes Dixon and Undine on the upper Franklin River.

4.4 CENTRAL SOUTH

The Central South is essentially a lowland region with large areas of relatively flat marginal pasture and pockets of degraded dry bushland. There is little rainfall during summer and autumn and over-clearing has resulted in reduced water retention. Wet mountainous terrain is confined to the far west, in the vicinity of the Wellington Range and Mt Field.

Hobart, the State capital, sprawls out along the Derwent estuary in the shadow of Mt Wellington. Although it has a population of some 200 000 it retains much of its colonial charm.

Most visiting anglers will spend time in Central South and many will, for one reason or

The rivers on the eastern side of the Derwent are weedy silt-bottomed 'meadow streams'. (courtesy Rob Sloane)

another, find themselves based in Hobart for at least some of their stay. So it is a comfort to learn that the region boasts an impressive array of worthwhile trout fisheries.

The Derwent estuary

Despite significant environmental degradation, the Derwent is a major sea trout fishery.

Lakes

Five major dams have been constructed in the mid reaches of the River Derwent. While none of these impoundments are especially popular, all carry brown trout. Meadowbank Lake and Wayatinah Lagoon are highly recommended to fly fishers and lure casters. Cluny Lagoon, Lake Repulse and Lake Catagunya are less appealing.

Craigbourne Dam, just ½ hr drive from Hobart, is quite worthwhile. Lake Dulverton (near Oatlands, 80 km north of Hobart) is normally a shallow weedy lagoon and has earned a reputation as a consistent producer of large trout.

At present Hobart's water supply dams are not open for public fishing.

The tributaries entering the Derwent from the west are mostly shingle-bottomed fastwaters.

Silencing the critics of the lower Derwent estuary (photo by Ashley Hallam)

Tributaries of the Derwent

Streams entering the River Derwent from the west are mostly fast clearwaters which provide ideal conditions for Celta fishing, bait casting and (where there is room) fly fishing. The very best is the Tyenna River, though the Styx and Plenty are also highly recommended.

The rivers entering the Derwent from the east flow through pasture and have reduced flows. The broadwaters are deep, silty and fertile and commonly harbour fish to 1.5 kg. Bait fishing is popular, and lure casting is worthwhile during periods of high to moderate flow. The fly fishing is fair but nowhere near as good as in the rivers of the North and Midlands.

Other rivers

Beyond the Derwent catchment the Coal River is the most significant stream. The fly fishing is superb.

Mt Field

Mt Field is one of the State's most spectacular national parks and it boasts many good clearwater trout lakes. The fishing is discussed in *Fishing in National Parks*, 5.5.

Mt Wellington

There are no fish on the plateau.

4.5 FAR SOUTH

Although much more sheltered than the South-West or West Coast, the Far South receives significant rain and remains lush year round. Pockets of productive lowland pasture feature along the coast and in the Huon Valley. The Huon Valley is also one of the State's primary fruit growing districts.

The hill country back from the seaboard is densely forested. Some is protected in national parks but much (including the Picton valley) is being logged. As much of the production forest is wilderness old-growth, there is continuous (and often bitter) debate over the options for future management.

The commercial centre, Huonville, has a population of some 1500.

For the visiting angler the Far South is conveniently close to Hobart. Features include superb runs of sea trout in the coastal rivers, as well as traditional stream-sport in the fastwater tributaries.

Sea trout

The major sea trout waters are the Huon, Esperance, Lune, D'Entrecasteaux and Catamaran rivers. All offer some scope for shore-based sport but are best fished from a dinghy.

Streams

Most streams in the Far South are shingle-bottomed fastwaters with little or no weed growth. The banks are often overgrown and wading is essential. While the water is tea coloured and mildly acidic, conditions for spawning are good and the survival of fish is high. On the whole, trout growth is much better than in West Coast streams, though most resident fish are under 0.5 kg and few exceed 1 kg. The fishing is best when levels are low, and at such times large bags are to be expected. Celtas, grasshoppers and flies are all effective.

The best streams are in the Huon drainage. Perhaps the very best is the Weld River, a curious water where rainbows greatly outnumber browns in anglers' bags. Other locally popular waters include the Little Denison River, the Arve River, Mountain River, Judds Creek and the Kermandie River. The Picton River contains brown trout but is deep, overgrown and difficult of access.

Beyond the Huon system the only easily accessible trout streams are the Esperance River and some tributaries of the Lune River.

Lake fishing

There are several mediocre brown trout fisheries in the Hartz Mountains National Park, including lakes Osborne, Perry and Esperance. Rainbows are found in Lake Skinner, a small natural lake on the Snowy Range. Most other alpine lakes in the region are located in rugged wilderness and have not been invaded by trout.

Bruny Island

The Big Lagoon on the neck has been stocked with browns, rainbows and hybrids – and delivers fish to 3 kg. There is no impressive river fishing, though several streams (including Cloudy Creek and Captain Cook Creek) contain small brown trout.

4.6 CENTRAL NORTH-WEST

The Central North-West is a wet, fertile farming district. The deep red volcanic loams near the coast have proven ideal for the cultivation of potatoes, root vegetables, legumes and pasture. Yet the lush green paddocks are divided by wind breaks and pockets of native bushland and, unlike the stark and often dry Midlands, the land retains scenic charm.

Beyond the coast only relatively flat land has been extensively cleared. The steep valleys and hillsides still support significant tracts of dense old-growth forest.

In the far south-west of the region, from the Middlesex Plains and the Vale of Belvoir to the Cradle Mountain district, there are extensive grasslands and sedgelands.

While agriculture and forestry are the traditional primary industries, tourism is increasingly important. Of all of the State's national parks the Cradle Mountain – Lake St Clair reserve is the one most visited by interstate and overseas visitors.

Burnie (population 20 000) is the commercial centre of the whole North-West. The local economy is dependent upon the town's heavy industries, including pulp-and-paper and pigment production. Unfortunately effluent from the factories has degraded much of the coastline.

Other major population centres include Devonport (population 22 000) and Ulverstone (population 10 000).

For the trout fisher there is broad scope. The Central North-West offers good stream and still-water fishing as well as reasonable runs of sea trout.

Stream fishing

The most respected trout river in the North-West is the Leven, an essentially-natural fastwater. The Vale River is a limestone stream noted for its fine rainbows and browns. The Mersey suffers

from low flows but also holds good fish.

The River Forth is not popular outside of the sea trout season, though it contains plenty of resident browns. Locals prefer to fish tributaries such as the Wilmot River, Forth Falls Creek and the Dove River.

Most of the very small coastal rivers, such as Cooee Creek, Chasm Creek, Sulphur Creek, Buttons Creek and Claytons Rivulet, contain large numbers of very small brown trout.

Sea trout

My pick of the sea trout waters is the River Leven, though the Forth and Mersey are quite noteworthy. Sea trout are also taken from the lower reaches of the Emu, Blythe and Don rivers.

Mersey Forth Power Development lakes

Most of the impoundments in the Mersey Forth Power Development are set in steep forested valleys. The best waters are lakes Rowallan and Parangana on the Mersey. Of the tea-coloured River Forth lakes, lakes Barrington and Cethana are most popular with local anglers. Lake Gairdner holds small fish but has the luxury of grassy banks.

Other stillwaters

Of the other lakes in the Central North-West, Lake Lea is the most notable. Most of the lakes at Cradle Mountain do not contain trout, the exception being Lake Dove. Burnie Anglers hold the Pet and Guide Reservoirs in high regard, though many prefer the West Coast region's Talbots Lagoon.

4.7 FAR NORTH-WEST

Northerly and westerly winds roar in from Bass Strait and the Indian Ocean bringing with them torrential rain. Lush pasture (intermingled with stands of native forest and wind breaks) has been cultivated on the deep red volcanic loams along the northern seaboard. Further south, in the Arthur River valley and beyond, there are dense old-growth forests – areas currently the subject of bitter debate between pro-loggers and conservationists.

The Far North-West is bypassed by the major tourist circuits and is not a major trout fishing district. However, it gives up fine sea trout and stream fish.

Sea trout

The Duck River (near Smithton) is accessible to shore-based anglers and is probably the best sea trout fishery in the region. The Arthur River, the

A typical small-stream fish from the North-West

Streams in the Arthur catchment are mostly shingle-bottomed fastwaters.

largest river in the Far North-West, flows through dense wet-forest, is accessible by boat, and gives up many good sea trout. Other respected sea trout fisheries include the Black, Detention and Inglis rivers.

River fishing

My favourite stream is the sluggish silt-bottomed Duck River, though the Flowerdale with its superb backwaters runs a close second. The Hellyer River is a classic fastwater, ideally suited to Celta fishing and wide enough to permit practical fly casting. The Montagu and Inglis rivers are also worthwhile.

Lakes

There is no remarkable stillwater fishing in the Far North-West. Lake Mikany offers scope for all angling tastes but produces only small browns. Lake Llewellyn is even less inspiring.

The Tarkine

The Tarkine is an area of high conservation value, most of which has no protection from logging, mining or other development. It is loosely defined as the land bounded by the Arthur River, the Murchison Highway, the Pieman River and the coast. The region is being promoted as a wilderness recreation area by conservation groups and is becoming popular with bushwalkers.

The trout fishing appears to be uninspiring. Stunted browns frequent most of the shingly fastwater tributaries in the Arthur and Pieman catchments, though the status of trout in most of the coastal streams remains unknown to me. In the late 1940s and early 1950s brown trout were liberated into Nelson Bay River, Big Eel Creek, the Dawson River, the Thornton River and the Pedder River. Trout may not have invaded some of the other coastal creeks.

King Island

Several coastal lagoons have been stocked with trout, though none appear by name on official stocking lists published after 1984 (see *King Island* in Part 2 – *Tasmanian Trout Waters in Detail*).

4.8 SOUTH-WEST

The South-West is a spectacular wilderness, a mosaic of vast plains divided by imposing ranges. The vegetation comprises mostly button-grass and heath, though dense scrub and some forest grows on the sheltered slopes. Although extremely harsh fronts whip in from the Antarctic, bringing with them bitter winds and torrential rain, conditions in summer and autumn can be quite mild.

Despite early European activity, which was mostly associated with pining in the Port Davey area and tin mining at Melaleuca, no significant towns were established and roading did not occur.

Today the Southwest National Park is an extremely high-profile wilderness.

Gordon River Power Development lakes

The South-West was made famous in the angling world as a result of the phenomenal trophy trout fishing which occurred in the new Lake Pedder in the mid to late 1970s. While the big fish are a thing of the past, Lake Pedder and its sister storage Lake Gordon remain the best trout waters in the region.

The wilderness lakes

Of the numerous wilderness lakes in the South-West only Lake Judd and Lake Curly are known to contain trout. Trout have not invaded any of the lakes on the Frankland, Arthur or Denison ranges.

Rivers

Most rivers in the South-West are tea-coloured fastwaters. The Huon system and the tributaries of Lake Gordon hold small brown trout but are remote, largely overgrown and not often fished. The Florentine River (in the Derwent catchment) contains many browns and a few rainbows and provides fair sport. The rivers draining into Bathurst Harbour and Port Davey (including the Davey, Crossing, Spring, North and Old rivers) do not appear to hold any resident trout at all. The status of trout in the Lewis, Giblin and New rivers (if they exist) has never been assessed.

4.9 NORTH-EAST

The North-East incorporates some of the wettest mountains and most pleasant scenery in Tasmania.

The coastal strip is a blend of native heath and flat pasture. The hinterland (near the Tasman Highway) is a patchwork of native production forest, pine plantations, and lush pasture. Dominating the views from the foothills are heavily-forested mountains such as Ben Lomond, Ben Nevis, Mt Saddleback, and Mt Victoria.

The history of the North-East is intricately linked with tin mining, though most minesites have been reclaimed by Nature. The economy is now driven by forestry and agriculture. The largest town (Scottsdale) has a population of just 2000.

For the trout fisher the North-East is generally unremarkable and it cannot be recommended above traditional trout fishing districts such as the Central Plateau, and the North and Midlands.

Waterhouse Protected Area

The principal fishery in the Waterhouse Protected Area is Blackmans Lagoon, a coastal basin which supports worthwhile numbers of large browns and rainbows. Little Waterhouse Lake is also quite productive.

Other lakes

The best lakes in the hinterland are the Cascade and Frome dams. Both are set in dense forest and produce plenty of small brown trout.

Stream fishing

Most streams in the North-East have steady year-round flows. They feature fast water, shingle beds, and little weed growth. Many are tea coloured, and any which flow through active logging operations and/or pasture are prone to become turbid during periods of high flow. Celta fishing and grasshopper casting are favoured, though tight fly casting is possible in many areas.

While the lower reaches of the Ringarooma River have been devastated by tin mining, the upper reaches remain good for trout fishing. The major tributaries (the Dorset, Maurice and New rivers) also produce good bags. A unique stream in the Ringarooma catchment is the Weld River above Harridge Falls which supports only rainbow trout.

The upper St Patricks River is a prized trout stream and is highly recommended.

The upper reaches of Great Forester River produce plenty of small fast-stream fish, while the sluggish mid-reaches harbour some fish in excess of 2 kg.

The lower Little Forester River is noted for its big resident browns.

Other good streams include the Brid River and the George River. The Great Musselroe, Ansons and Tomahawk rivers all contain trout but receive limited attention – even from local anglers.

Sea trout

The major sea trout fishery is the lower Great Forester River. The estuary of the Little Forester River supports both sea trout and large resident fish and is popular with locals. Other sea trout fisheries include the lower reaches of Ansons River and perhaps the Great Musselroe River, though neither is popular.

Flinders Island

Several coastal lagoons and farm dams on Flinders Island have been stocked from time to time but none appear to be capable of maintaining self-sustaining populations of trout (see *Flinders Island* in Part 2 – *Tasmanian Trout Waters in Detail*).

Frome Dam

Ben Lomond

The lakes and streams on the Ben Lomond plateau do not appear to support trout.

4.10 EAST COAST

The eastern seaboard is Tasmania's sunshine coast. Buffered from our prevailing westerly weather it receives relatively little rain, cloud and cold wind. It is a region noted for its charming seaside villages and white-sand beaches.

Agriculture has been a major influence on the economy and social structure since the earliest days of European settlement. Along the coastline, and on the river flats, there is a patchwork of cleared pasture and open woodland.

Inland, beyond the flats, there are significant tracts of dry sclerophyll forest, much of which is being logged. The largest remaining area of old-growth forest has recently been incorporated into a new reserve – the Douglas-Apsley National Park.

While the region is not recommended to the visiting angler, it is not exactly a trout fishing desert.

Rivers and creeks

By far the best streams are those in the South Esk catchment – notably the Break O'Day and St Pauls rivers. These waters feature long sluggish broadwaters, open banks – and superb rises! (see *North and Midlands*, 4.2).

Of the rivers traditionally thought of as East Coast rivers only a few can be recommended to anglers. The Scamander River holds plenty of fat browns and is one of my very favourite fastwater streams. The George River also provides reasonable fastwater fishing and is locally popular. The broadwaters of the Apsley River give up large silvery residents, and the Prosser River and its tributaries also carry good fish.

Creeks such as the Douglas River, the Swan River and its tributaries, the Meredith River, the Buxton River, Lisdillon Rivulet, the Little Swanport River, Maclaines Creek and Sandspit Rivulet are mostly shingle-bottomed waters with poor summer/autumn flows. While none can claim

Typical Swan-catchment stream

anything of special significance for the visitor, all contain catchable trout and many have a share of local devotees.

Lakes

The only significant stillwater is Lake Leake.

Sea trout

By standards set elsewhere in Tasmania the runs of sea trout are very poor. Perhaps the best fishery is the Scamander River, though small runs also occur in the lower reaches of the George, Swan, Little Swanport and Prosser rivers.

Tasman Peninsula

Very small browns survive in several of the tiny overgrown creeks, but there is nothing of special significance. ◆

Fishing in National Parks

About National Parks

Tasmania is renowned for its natural scenery and wild environs, and has reserved 14 National Parks. Of most interest to anglers is the Walls of Jerusalem National Park which, together with the Central Plateau Conservation Area, incorporates all of the Western Lakes. While most other parks also include significant fisheries, there are no recognised trout waters in the Ben Lomond, Asbestos Range, Maria Island, Freycinet, Strzelecki or Mount William national parks.

What is a National Park ?

National Parks are reserves of (generally) larger than 4000 ha which feature outstanding natural and/or cultural assets. The protection given to flora, fauna and the land can only be absolved with the approval of both houses of Parliament.

The controlling body

The Parks and Wildlife Service (PWS) manages land reserved under both the *National Parks and Wildlife Act* (1971) and the *Crown Lands Act* (1976). The IFC retains control over all freshwater aquatic life – including native species.

Regulations

Recreational pursuits, including fishing, are encouraged within National Parks. However, conservation is a primary objective and restrictions apply on activities likely to severely impact on flora and fauna, or which are not sustainable. Generally it is illegal to take pets and firearms into reserves, and to take vehicles off formed roads. Many areas have been zoned *'Fuel Stove Only'* (ie. no open fires are allowed).

Entrance fees were reintroduced in May 1993.

The World Heritage Area

Tasmania's Cradle Mountain – Lake St Clair, Franklin-Gordon Wild Rivers, and Southwest national parks were originally inscribed on the World Heritage List in 1982. In 1989 the listing was expanded to include extensions to the original parks, the Walls of Jerusalem National Park, the Hartz Mountains National Park, the Central Plateau Conservation Area, and several other adjoining reserves. The World Heritage Area (WHA) now covers about 1.37 million ha.

The WHA is subject to joint Commonwealth/State management agreements and has considerably more protection than any park without World Heritage status.

Other reserves

Conservation Areas and Wildlife Sanctuaries provide protection for fauna and flora, and nesting or breeding places, but unless tabled in specific management plans, do not offer protection to habitat in the broad sense. Moreover, the statutory powers of other agencies may be exercised to permit mining, forestry and hydro-electric developments. Usually it is illegal to take pets and firearms into Conservation Areas, but if in doubt check with the PWS.

Protected Areas are administered by the PWS but are protected under the *Crown Lands Act* (1976) and can be revoked by the State Government of the day without the approval of the Upper House. Pets are permitted in some reserves – check with the PWS.

Park etiquette

With ever increasing numbers of visitors utilizing our reserved areas, the need for users to minimise their impact on the environment has become paramount. Bushwalkers in Tasmania have embraced the Minimal Impact Bushwalking (MIB) philosophy, challenging themselves to leave no trace of their visits. The PWS has produced a respected brochure on the topic – a publication available free from outdoor shops and PWS offices.

Bait

Bait fishing causes genuine management problems in wild areas (see *Notes for the Specialist, 6.3*).

While not specifically mentioned in the *Fisheries Act,* the use of most natural baits is effectively prohibited under provisions of the *National Parks and Wildlife Act.* Bait fishing enthusiasts are encouraged to use scented soft plastics.

5.1 THE WESTERN LAKES

The Walls of Jerusalem National Park and the Central Plateau Conservation Area are the Western Lakes – Tasmania's showcase wilderness fishery and one of the most spectacular fly fishing regions in Australia.

It must be recognised that, on the whole, the fishing is difficult. In the Chudleigh Lakes the average catch rate is just 1.7 fish per angler per day, and in the Nineteen Lagoons the average is less than one trout for every 10 hrs of effort. Most devotees have transcended the desire for 'meat in the bag' and have come to savour the challenge and atmosphere.

'...no matter how you arrive, these highland moors are a sight to behold, their charm growing steadily upon you the more you wander their remote expanses investigating their many waters... But there is something other than the fishing which draws you back; perhaps the remoteness and feeling of treading unknown paths like that of the explorer, or maybe the weird landscape which, not withstanding its desolation, seems to whisper a soft message of beauty. Even though the wind be shrieking, tearing the breath from your chilled face, through your screwed-up eyes you can see it, inside you can feel it and would I be wrong if I said that sometimes you can hear it?'

David Scholes, Fly-fisher in Tasmania (1961)

Description

The Nineteen Lagoons, the Chudleigh Lakes and the Julian-Pillans area

The moors and rock outcrops east of the Great Pine Tier are stark but inspiring. Snowgrass is characteristic of the flood plains and wet areas, and heath dominates on elevated (dry) ground. While there are some stands of stunted eucalypts, especially in the south, much of the land north of Pillans Lake has been severely ravaged by wildfire.

The lakes were scoured out during the last glaciation by a vast ice sheet and are relatively shallow silt-bottomed affairs. Most banks are well defined, though some lakes recede markedly during during summer and break out into marshes and tussocks during floods. While the water is usually crystal clear, wave action can cause short-term discolouration on exposed shores.

The elevation varies from about 1100-1200 m and sudden blizzards can occur at any time. Snow settles and ice forms in winter, though mild days are common in summer.

Moorland at Blue Peaks

WESTERN LAKES

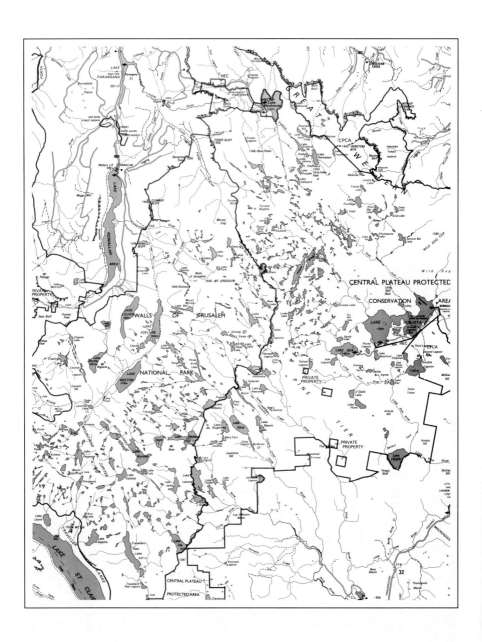

The east includes the two main fishing districts – the Chudleigh Lakes and the Nineteen Lagoons. The Chudleigh Lakes are the waters of the Fisher River drainage and are accessed from the north of the State via the Lake Mackenzie Road. The Nineteen Lagoons are the popular easy-access waters near Lake Augusta, and are reached via the Lake Augusta Road from Liawenee (Great Lake). The area between is simply known as the 'Julian-Pillans area'.

West of the Great Pine Tier

West of the Great Pine Tier the lakes tend to be sheltered by low hills and dry forest, though

Alpine woodland at Lake Malbena

there are distinct grassy valley-floors. Typically the waters lie behind (natural) moraine dams and are relatively deep. Most have well-defined rocky perimeters and are gin clear.

History

The Chudleigh Lakes

Natural pasture within the Chudleigh Lakes region was utilised for summer grazing as early as the 1830s or 1840s. In 1850 the area was formally surveyed and the first official grazing leases were let. Stock was herded onto the plateau via a number of formed tracks from lowland rural properties at Chudleigh, Mole Creek and Western Creek. Indeed the current Mole Creek, Parsons, and Higgs (walking) tracks are former stock routes. Grazing continued in the area for more than a century, but the practice wound down during the 1950s following the development and irrigation of lowland pastures.

Because of the severe gradient of the Fisher River, trout were unable to migrate from the Mersey River system into the Chudleigh Lakes. The region was first stocked in 1895 when Charles Harrison and three others ascended the Great Western tiers above Mole Creek and liberated brown trout into (the natural) Lake Mackenzie. The party was so impressed with the locality that they made a second trip two weeks

Reward for backpacking

later to liberate more fish into nearby waters.

According to the records of the NTAA / NTFA the first rainbow trout (200) were released at *'Blue Peak'* during the 1898-99 season; the first brook trout (500) were released at *'the Chudleigh Lakes'* in 1902-03; and the first Atlantic salmon (1500) were turned out in *'various'* of the Chudleigh Lakes in 1906-07. In addition to the fish first released by Harrison's party, by 1908 a further 32 250 fry had been turned out – 5000 *'brown'* trout, 23 000 *'migratory'* (brown) trout, 550 *'Loch Leven'* (brown) trout, 1700 rainbow trout, 500 brook trout, and 1500 Atlantic salmon. However, only the brown trout were able to establish viable wild populations.

A tourist hut was completed at Sandy Lake (now beneath the Mackenzie impoundment) in 1903 and, soon after, several hundred anglers and tourists were annually visiting the Chudleigh Lakes, enduring the arduous walk up the Great Western Tiers. During the 1912-13 season a hut was completed at Lady Lake on the edge of the tiers beside Higgs Track. From this time Higgs Track became the main access route for anglers. Another tourist hut, the Ironstone Hut, was built at Lake Nameless in 1916. By 1919 a *'fine boat with sailing and rowing gears'* had been transported to Lake Nameless and a substantial boat house had been built on the lakeshore.

The NTFA reported the details of the early years of angling in the Chudleigh Lakes. But after the construction of the northern access to Breona the *'Deloraine folk'* turned their attentions to the phenomenal fishing at Great Lake.

During the 1935-36 season 8000 rainbow trout were liberated in the Chudleigh Lakes, but this failed to rekindle interest in the region. By the time the Great Lake fishery began to decline the Nineteen Lagoons had become more accessible and were receiving the attentions of those who might otherwise have 'rediscovered' the Chudleigh Lakes.

In the 1960s the HEC began work on the Mersey Forth Power Development and during the latter part of the decade the Lake Mackenzie Road was completed – resulting in a resurgence of interest in the Chudleigh Lakes. Today the region includes some of the most popular wilderness fisheries in the State.

The Nineteen Lagoons

While it is probable that natural pastures within the Nineteen Lagoons were first utilized for summer grazing in the 1820s and 1830s, the first official survey of grazing leases was not completed until 1840. Pastoralism continued in earnest until the 1950s, by which time rabbit plagues and over-grazing had caused severe deterioration of the highland vegetation and farmers were coming to favour cleared irrigated lowland runs. The suitability of the Nineteen Lagoons for grazing continued to decline and the practice was finally phased out in 1991.

There are no early records of brown trout being liberated in the Nineteen Lagoons and it seems that the wild trout fishery resulted from natural upstream colonisation of the Derwent system. By 1893 the Fisheries Department had confirmed that trout were *'firmly established in all these lakes'*.

For many years the spectacular fishery at Great Lake overshadowed the potential of the Western Lakes. There were only brief accounts of the fishing in the Nineteen Lagoons at the turn of the century. Moderate interest in the area surfaced in the late 1930s as the Great Lake fishery began to decline.

According to NTFA records 3000 rainbow trout were transported to the upper Ouse and Little Pine rivers in the 1940-41 season. This was thought to be the first stocking of rainbow trout in the Nineteen Lagoons. Wild populations soon established in the James River, the River Ouse and Lake Augusta.

Interest in the Nineteen Lagoons boomed in the 1940s and early 1950s when the HEC began work on the Lake Augusta project. The Lake Augusta Road (between Liawenee and the Augusta Dam site) was almost completed by 1950. By the time the Augusta dam had been finished in 1953, the HEC had formed several spur tracks to recording stations at Double Lagoon and Lake Kay. The Lake Ada extension was also carried out by HEC workers at this time. For many years these tracks received little maintenance and little use.

In the winter of 1960 the IFC began its programme of transferring adult brown trout from Great Lake to other waters. The first liberations in the Carter Lakes occurred prior to 1965. Howes Lagoon had received adult browns by 1966 and Lake Botsford was first stocked in 1971. These activities did much to popularise the area.

Roads within the Nineteen Lagoons were upgraded in 1978 (following the proclamation of the Central Plateau Protected Area) providing a vast improvement in access to key waters beyond the Augusta Dam.

The Walls of Jerusalem

From the mid 1800s to the mid 1900s the Walls

A flooded gutter-connection

of Jerusalem area was used for summer grazing, and from the turn of the 19th century to the 1950s trapping was commonly practised throughout the (current) national park.

From the early 1920s several local identities, including Dick Reed and Reg Hall, began promoting the bushwalking and recreation potential of the region. In the early days access to the Walls was from the Chudleigh Lakes and the Nineteen Lagoons, and the Walls did not become very popular with recreational walkers until after the construction of the Mersey Valley Forest Road in the mid 1950s.

Lake Meston was stocked (with rainbows) in 1956-57 and significant numbers of trout fishers have been visiting the upper Mersey valley since the 1960s. Most other lakes in the national park have been virtually ignored by anglers – and the waters at the southern end (excluding the Pine River lakes) remain among the least-fished lakes in the State.

Land tenure

As a result of national interest in the protection of Australia's high country, the Lands Department in the early 1970s began a process of public consultation, the aim of which was to obtain a background for the creation of a comprehensive management plan for the Central Plateau. The Central Plateau Protected Area (including all of the Western Lakes) was finally proclaimed in 1978.

In 1981, 11 510 ha in the vicinity of the Walls was declared National Park, while the status of much of the rest of the land west of the Great Pine Tier was upgraded to Conservation Area.

In 1990 the Walls of Jerusalem National Park was expanded to about 51 000 ha to include the former Conservation Area and the parts of the western Central Plateau formally within Cradle Mountain – Lake St Clair National Park. At the same time all of the Western Lakes not included in the new national park were given Conservation Area status.

The current national park and Conservation Area were inscribed on the World Heritage List in 1989.

Vehicular access

2WD

The Nineteen Lagoons are reached via 13 km of unsurfaced road (the Lake Augusta Road) which leads from the Lake Highway at Liawenee. The road beyond the Augusta Dam is closed to vehicular traffic in the early months of the fishing season, but remains open from about the end of September. Within the Nineteen Lagoons conventional vehicles can be driven to within short distances of Lake Augusta (dam), Lake Augusta (natural), Double Lagoon, Howes Lagoon (Bay), the Carter Lakes, Lake Botsford, Rocky Lagoon, and Lake Ada. Other lakes in the region are accessible on foot. All vehicles must stay on formed roads and tracks.

The vehicular access to the Chudleigh Lakes is up the Great Western Tiers from the Mole Creek district via the steep corrugated Lake Mackenzie Road. The road terminates at Lake Mackenzie and all other lakes are accessible only on foot.

4WD

All 4WD access is strictly controlled. The tracks are subject to periodic closures during wet periods and PWS permits are required at other times.

The main 4WD track, which extends from the Nineteen Lagoons to the Julian-Pillans area, crosses the bed of Lake Augusta (dam) and is sometimes inundated and impassable.

According to the original log book in Kerrisons Hut, the track to the hut-site (which approximates an old stock route) was constructed by anglers in 1963. In 1967 another well known angling identity, Cliff Turner, used a bulldozer to extend Kerrison's track to his Lake Field hut-site. In 1970 Turner bulldozed yet another track to his Pillans Lake hut-site. These routes became increasingly popular in the late 1970s and throughout the 1980s.

Most of the growth in vehicular activity has occurred in the last (exceptionally dry) decade, yet erosion and visual scarring are major problems and the track degenerates from year to year. In recent seasons the track has been closed in the early (wet) season. The timing of the opening has been arbitrary but the District Ranger is (understandably) reluctant to enforce mid-season closures once the track has been opened.

While there is clear justification for closing the track on environmental grounds, there is strong user pressure to retain the track as a 'traditional' angling access. However, it must be recognised that the route is not sustainable and cannot be maintained as a 4WD route in the long term. Ultimately the PWS will need to limit vehicular use, upgrade the track to all-weather 2WD standard, or close the track to all vehicles.

Another route extends from Lake Ada to Talinah Lagoon. This track was originally a cart track (dating back to at least the 1840s) and passes over wet areas and soft flats. Erosion and loss of aesthetic appeal are major problems. Currently 60% or more of people using the route choose to walk and there is strong lobbying to have the route

Undercut banks in the Bar Lakes system

closed to vehicular traffic. The track beyond Talinah has been closed to vehicles since 1982.

From the Lyell Highway there is a rough vehicular access to Clarence Lagoon. This track passes over Forestry Commission land and a PWS permit is not required.

A small number of vehicles cross private land beyond Pine Tier Lagoon and use rugged logging tracks to gain access to the south-eastern extremities of the WHA boundary in the vicinity of Lake Ina and Olive Lagoon. But remember to get permission from the property owner and that vehicular access into the WHA is prohibited.

Walking tracks

The walking on the Central Plateau is relatively easy – certainly within the capabilities of people of average fitness. However, as is the case at all of Tasmania's wilderness areas, a knowledge of bushcraft is essential. Novices should ensure that they are well informed about bush safety, and that they have essential camping equipment.

The main walking tracks are shown on the Mersey, Meander and Nive 1:100 000 Tasmaps. Unfortunately, some of the 'tracks' on these sheets are merely ill-defined cross-country routes.

Tracks from Lake Augusta

A 4WD track extends along the western shore of the natural Lake Augusta, terminating at the lake's north-western corner. The old 4WD route which continued on to Little Blue Lagoon and Tin Hut Lake has been closed to vehicular traffic since the late 1980s and is now managed as a foot track. You can walk to Tin Hut Lake from the 2WD road at the western end of the Lake Augusta Spillway in ¾-1 hr. The 'tracks' to Tin Hut Lake from Rocky Lagoon, Lake Ada and Sandy Lake (shown on the *Mersey* map) are informal routes and, since they do not represent the best cross-country accesses, are best ignored. Similarly, there is no formal route beyond Tin Hut Lake to Stumps Lake.

Baillie, Flora and O'Dells

A good walking route follows a disused (and rehabilitated) 4WD track from the Lake Kay road (halfway between Lake Botsford to Lake Kay) past Lake Baillie and O'Dells Lake to a modest hut near Lake Flora. This trip takes about 1½-2 hrs (each way).

Ada to Talleh Lagoons and the Pine River valley

The walking track from Lake Ada to Talleh Lagoons follows a formal 4WD route as far as Talinah Lagoon and then continues over an old cart track (which has been formally closed to vehicular traffic since 1982), taking about 2-3½ hrs each way. The spur to the Lake Antimony hut is less well defined and occupies another 1-1½ hrs (each way). The 'track' from Talleh Lagoons to Lake Fanny is ill defined and is little more than an appropriate cross-country route.

The Chudleigh Lakes

The only formal walking tracks from Lake Mackenzie lead to Blue Peaks (1½-2½ hrs each way) and Lake Explorer (1-1½ hrs each way). The tracks which lead from the foot of the Great Western Tiers onto the Plateau (including Higgs Track and Parsons Track) are well-defined, but have been superseded by the Lake Mackenzie Road and are not often used by anglers.

Deep and Grub

From the end of the Meander Falls Road a walking track extends up the Tiers past Meander Falls emerging on the Plateau in the vicinity of Deep and Grub lakes. Although this walk is not used by many anglers, it is popular with a small but dedicated band from the Deloraine area.

Long Tarns and the Daisy Lakes

The Little Fisher River Track extends from the end of the Little Fisher Road up through the

The rise to the fly

Scree bank at Lake Lucy Long

rainforested Little Fisher valley and terminates on the Plateau in the vicinity of Long Tarns – a walk of 1½-2½ hrs. The path is well defined and provides convenient access to the trout lakes on the eastern fringes of the original Walls of Jerusalem National Park.

The upper Mersey

Well-used foot paths extend from the Mersey Valley onto the western side of the Plateau. The track of most interest to anglers is the Lake Myrtle Track which leads from the Mersey Forest Road at Juno Creek. The first part of the journey is ½-1 hr up a very steep forested tier and can be quite heartbreaking if you are not prepared for the climb. The rest of the track passes over flatter more open terrain and is quite easy. Unfortunately, most of the surrounding land was severely burned in 1982 and regeneration has been slow. The total trip from the road to the Lake Meston hut takes 3-5 hrs.

Lake Meston is also accessible via the Walls of Jerusalem and Junction Lake tracks. This route takes off from a well-signposted car park beside the Fish River and leads (for about 1-1½ hrs) up a not-so-steep slope, emerging on the Plateau in the vicinity of Lake Loane. From Lake Loane you follow a path down a classic U-shaped valley, passing Lake Adelaide and arriving at the idyllic

grassy campsites at the northern end of Lake Meston. The track then continues down the north-western shore to the Lake Meston hut. The total walking time from the carpark to the hut is quite long (5-7 hrs) but the route is very scenic.

Junction Lake is best reached via the Junction Lake Track from the Lake Meston Hut – a trip of 1-1½ hrs. The Moses Creek track, from the end of the Mersey Forest Road via Cloister Lagoon, encompasses some of the most spectacular scenery on the Plateau but is ill defined and not recommended for the inexperienced.

A reasonably well defined link route has evolved from the end of the Walls of Jerusalem Track (at Lake Salome) to the Junction Lake Track at the northern end of Lake Adelaide via the northern bank of Lake Ball. The walk to Lake Ball from the Fish River carpark (by either track) takes about 3½-5½ hrs.

Gowan Brae

A walking route follows a disused vehicular access from the end of a logging road north of Gowan Brae to Olive Lagoon and Lake Naomi. The walk to Lake Naomi from the WHA boundary takes about 1¼-2 hrs. But remember that the logging roads pass through private property and permission for access must be gained from the land owner.

Cross-country routes

Almost all of the Western Lakes are easily accessible without the aid of walking paths. The area east of the Great Pine Tier is so flat and open that it provides some of the easiest cross-country walking in the State. West of the Great Pine Tier the most convenient walking is along the river valleys, but overland excursions between river systems are relatively straight-forward.

A warning

Intending walkers please remember that it is essential that you are competent in map and compass reading and that you carry a full camping kit. If in doubt seek advice from experienced people *before* you plan your trip!

Huts

Several public huts exist in the Western Lakes. As they are all small, they are likely to be fully occupied and must be treated as emergency shelters only.

Boating

Only Lake Ada, Lake Augusta (dam), Lake Augusta (natural) and Lake Mackenzie are suitable for boat use. These waters are relatively shallow and small dinghies are most practical. Large runabouts are totally inappropriate.

Boating on small shallow headwater lakes is a major risk to the long-term stability of the trout fisheries. Problems include physical disturbance of the lake bed, and pollution from raw fuel and exhaust fumes. In large waters, or waters with big flow-throughs, pollutants are diluted and/or flushed away. In small isolated waters there is a significant cumulative effect. Consequently boating at most lakes is not recommended.

Trout stocks

The Nineteen Lagoons

The trout lakes on significant water courses receive adequate natural recruitment. These waters include Lake Ada, Ada Lagoon, Lake Augusta (dam), Lake Augusta (natural), Lake Kay and (to a lesser extent) Double Lagoon, Lake Agnes, Lake Baillie, Lake Flora, O'Dells Lake, and Sandy Lake. These lakes hold typical Western Lakes brown trout of 0.7-1.5 kg with a reasonable blend of bigger fish to 2.5 kg. They are managed as wild fisheries and should not require supplementary stocking in the foreseeable future – if realistic bag limits are adopted.

Significant populations of wild rainbow trout are also present in Lake Augusta (dam), Lake Augusta (natural), the River Ouse, the Julian Lakes and the lower reaches of the James River. These fish usually weigh 0.3-1.2 kg.

Other waters in the Nineteen Lagoons have very limited spawning grounds and rely on intermittent recruitment from nearby lakes during floods. Waters such as Lake Chipman, Lake Dudley, East Rocky Lagoon, First Lagoon and Tin Hut Lake have traditionally been recognised as trophy brown trout waters. In the past they yielded small numbers of brown trout in the 2-5 kg class. In recent years all have received some supplementary stocking. Catch-and-release fishing is advocated on these waters and a bag limit of two fish per angler per water per day is recommended.

Other waters such as Lake Botsford, the Carter Lakes and Rocky Lagoon have negligible recruitment. They are now intensively stocked with (mostly) adult wild browns from Great Lake. Here too catch-and-release is advocated.

While the emphasis is on brown trout, in recent years rainbows have also been liberated. Little Blue Lagoon, Tin Hut Lake, Lake Chipman, Lake Dudley, Lake Botsford and the Carter Lakes have all received experimental releases – including triploids.

Rocky banks at Wadleys Lake

The Chudleigh Lakes

The Chudleigh Lakes district is a wild brown trout fishery and all waters connected to significant tributaries support reasonable numbers of naturally spawned fish. Trout of 0.7-1.5 kg are the norm.

There are few exceptional trophy waters, though several of the small low-lying tarns remain isolated from the main lakes in all but the wettest months and hold fair numbers of 2-3 kg fish. Most such waters are in the vicinity of Blue Peaks and Lake Halkyard.

Several illegal liberations of domestic rainbows have occurred in certain isolated waters in recent years, but wild rainbows have not established.

Elsewhere

The Western Lakes is primarily a wild brown trout fishery and all lakes and tarns connected to significant tributaries can be expected to carry reasonable numbers of wild fish. Typical fish weigh 0.7-1.5 kg but in lakes where recruitment is low very large specimens may be caught (see notes on trophy trout on page 59).

While brown trout have invaded most lakes in the River Derwent system, they have not been able to move past the waterfalls in the Mersey system. Trout-free waters include the Lees Creek system (the Orion Lakes, Lake Pallas, Lake

The ability to cast a long line is rarely a great advantage – fish cruise in close!

Fisheries which must be stocked can be managed to produce trophy fish. Wild hybrids and triploids are viable options – but only if the catch-and-release philosophy is adopted.

Catch-and-release is essential if trophy fishing is to be maintained

Merope, Lake Eros and Lake Artemis); the Moses Creek system (Chalice Lake, Cloister Lagoon and Chapter Lake); Lake Bill and Lake Myrtle; the Juno Creek system (Lake Adelaide, Lake Charles, Lake Poa and Lake Louisa); the Fish River system (Lake Salome, Lake Tyre, Lake Sidon, Lake Thor, Lake Paterson, George Howes Lake and Solomons Jewels); Lake Norman and the Ling Roth Lakes; the lakes above Travellers Rest Lake; all of the lakes draining from the Plateau into Lake St Clair (including Lake Sappho, Rim Lake, Lake Payanna, Lake Riengeena and Lake Athena); and New Years Lake.

Lake Meston was stocked in 1956-57 and as a result the upper Mersey system (including Lake Youd and Junction Lake) is the only major rainbow-only fishery in the State.

Clarence Lagoon was first stocked in 1963 and now supports a fragile wild population of brook trout.

East vs West

It must be recognised that, on the whole, the waters west of the Great Pine Tier do not provide a better standard of fishing than exists in the Nineteen Lagoons and the Chudleigh Lakes.

The waters east of the Great Pine Tier are mostly uniformly shallow, biologically productive, and (because they often are not connected to major streams) they are usually just adequately populated. The fish grow to good size and are easily seen.

The trout in the deeper instream lakes west of the Tier are quite different from their eastern counterparts. It seems that, while one part of a shallow lagoon is much the same as any other, very deep waters suffer from the 'Great Lake syndrome'. Brown trout seem to feed best among the rich weedbeds deep down and are not often seen during 'good' polaroiding or tailing conditions. Only the very young fish without established territories, or older fish which have been forced off the weedbeds by their younger, more energetic brothers, are noticeable along the fringes of the lakes. And, as the spawning is often very good, many waters suffer from overpopulation.

Go west only if you enjoy bushwalking in very pleasant surrounds and like to get away from it all.

Trophy trout

Big fish are found in isolated waters where recruitment is low. As browns are able to take advantage of any marginally suitable spawning areas, ideal lakes must have negligible inflow streams. Usually the best waters are dead-end lakes fed from run-off. The outflow must be good enough to permit occasional recruitment from nearby lakes but must not be well suited to spawning.

After heavy rain many lakes break out into outlying shallow basins.

Tailing in the flooded margins

A typical trophy water will have gutter connections to significant lakes or streams only during floods. Alternatively the lake will be elevated and have a moderate but steep outflow creek. It is also worth remembering that, as competition for space is more acute in streams than lakes, isolated lakes connected to well-populated lakes are likely to contain fewer fish than lakes connected to well-populated streams.

Most of the big-fish waters in the Nineteen Lagoons are now well known and a summary is given on page 57. Beyond the near waters the best places to search for trophy waters include the network of catchments feeding Pillans Lake, the Christys Creek system and the Powena Creek system – but suitable lakes are to be found throughout the Western Lakes. The real thrill is the discovery.

Please remember that trophy fishing in small waters can only be maintained if the catch-and-release philosophy is embraced.

Catch-and-release

In Tasmania catch-and-release is most appropriate when the object is to maintain trophy fishing in waters which have limited natural recruitment. Nowhere is this more vital than in the Western Lakes.

In the Nineteen Lagoons waters such as East Rocky Lagoon, First Lagoon, Lake Dudley and Lake Chipman were once prized big-fish waters where dedicated locals commonly took ten-pounders. Today, as a result of increased user pressure, most of the best fish have been cropped, and the younger fish simply do not survive long enough to attain trophy size. If quality fishing is to be maintained catch-and-release is essential.

Fly fishing

Tailing trout are a feature of the Western Lakes, especially from October to Christmas. Spring floods produce the most activity, with brown trout urgently foraging in the shallows after frogs, tadpoles and drowned terrestrials. These fish will often take any well presented wet fly. The best areas are in the Nineteen Lagoons – places such as the backwaters and lagoons around Lake Kay, Lake Ada, Double Lagoon and Howes Lagoon. However, suitable flood basins are found throughout the Western Lakes.

When levels subside trout will tail while feeding on snails and amphipods and, while these fish are often difficult to catch, they offer excitement in the extreme. Snailing fish are common along the rocky shores of Carters, Augusta, Howes, Chipman, Baillie and Blue Peaks. Amphipod feeders are more typical of the shallow weedbeds of Lakes Kay, Double Lagoon, Lake Ada and Lake Antimony.

Wade polaroiding

Summertime dun hatches (and associated black spinner hatches) feature on many of the Western Lakes, and are prolific on a few. The hatches on Lake Kay, Christys Creek, Silver Lake and Lake Nameless are as good as any in the State (with the possible exception of those at Little Pine Lagoon).

In many lakes west of the Great Pine Tier where there are no obvious good dun hatches, there are still superb black spinner hatches. On these waters the nymph of the dominant mayfly crawls out onto emergent rocks before hatching. The dun of this species is quite large, but much more frail than the classic highland dun. When the spinners emerge from the dun they fly back over the water in the normal manner. The black spinner hatches at Olive Lagoon, Lake Naomi, Lake Rotuli and Three Arm Lake are second to none.

'Bread and butter' fishing for the Western Lakes angler is polaroiding. All waters are suitable for this style of fishing, though some are better than others. At lakes with well-defined 'deep' (1 m plus) shorelines, spotting from the banks is worthwhile. However, shallow water is best waded. Small waves help to 'open up' the water to give a better view of the trout, and by

And if it has been hard during the day, using a wet at dusk is a good fall-back.

wading the angler presents a low profile thereby reducing the chance of being seen. Chest waders are essential. Experienced polaroiders wade smoothly and constantly scan the water ahead. Trout usually first appear as a dark shadow on the pale silt-sand bed but, as you are usually wading down-wind and the fish usually feed up-wind, by the time you get to present your fly the fish is often very close and it is possible to see every spot. The best wade polaroiding waters are the beaches at Lake Augusta (natural) and Lake Ada; and the open silty shallows at Lake Botsford, Rocky Lagoon and Lake Antimony. When cruising fish are spotted (either from the bank or when wading) they may not be rising but they usually will take any well-presented nondescript dry-fly. Good light is essential, so the best fishing occurs from late spring to early autumn between the hours of 10.00 am and 4.00 pm. Still, enthusiastic anglers will spot fish at any time of year and at any time of day.

Lure casting

Lure casting is most productive in rough overcast conditions. The best months are September

Bank polaroiding. Another is spotted – and the first hasn't been played out!

WESTERN LAKES TRIP PLANNER

	SUGGESTED DESTINATIONS	IDEAL CONDITIONS	WHEN TO FISH
SHORT WALKS	Double Lagoon, Lagoon Lake, Chipman, First Lagoon, Lake Kay, O'Dells Lake, Lake Flora, Tin Hut Lake, Sandy Lake	Depends on angling method	Peak fishing times vary according to preferred angling method
2WD ACCESS	Lake Augusta, Lake, Botsford, Rocky Lagoon, Carter Lakes, Lake Mackenzie	Depends on angling method	Peak fishing times vary according to preferred angling method
BROOK TROUT	Clarence Lagoon	Cool water	(see graph)
STERILE TROUT	Lake, Botsford, Little Blue, Lagoon, Lake, Chipman, Carter Lakes, Tin Hut Lake, Lake Dudley	Depends on angling method	Peak fishing times vary according to preferred angling method
NATURALLY SPAWNED RAINBOWS	Lake Meston, Junction Lake, Lake Youd	Depends on angling method	Peak fishing times vary according to preferred angling method
BLACK SPINNER HATCHES	Christys Creek, Lake Naomi, Olive Lagoon, Lake Rotuli, Three Arm Lake	Hot and calm	(see graph)
DUN HATCHES	Lake Kay, Christys Creek, Silver Lake, Lake Nameless	Warm with high-level cloud	(see graph)
BANK POLAROID-ING	Lake Meston, Pillans Lake, Julian Lakes, Chudleigh Lakes, Most lakes west of the Great Pine Tier	Bright, sunny and calm	(see graph)
WADE POLAROID-ING	Lake, Augusta, Lake Ada, Lake, Botsford, Rocky Lagoon, Lake, Antimony	Bright and sunny with a stiff breeze	(see graph)
MARSH & BACKWATER FISHING	Lake Kay, Kay Lagoons, Double Lagoon, Lake Ada, Howes Lagoon, Blue Peaks, Westons Lake	Rising lake levels after heavy rain	(see graph)
SPINNING	Lake Augusta, Lake Ada, Double Lagoon, Pillans Lakes, Julian Lakes, Lake Mackenzie, Blue Peaks, Lake Meston	Stormy. Dull or overcast. Windy.	(see graph)
BOAT FISHING	Lake Augusta, Lake Ada, Lake Mackenzie	Depends on angling method	Peak fishing times vary according to preferred angling method

WHEN TO FISH (months): AUG, SEP, OCT, NOV, DEC, JAN, FEB, MAR, APR, MAY, JUN, JUL

SEASON CLOSED

KEY to fishing conditions: Peak — Good — Fair — Modest — Poor

63

Many waters in the Nineteen Lagoons are ideal for spinning. (photo by Jane Andrew)

Even when it snows the dedicated can get results. This fish was polaroided!

to December, and April. In summer, when the lakes are clear and low and the weather is pleasant, the fish tend to follow lures to the bank but refuse to strike. When lure fishing at this time of the year, the best results are usually achieved early in the morning and late in the evening.

As the lakes are mostly shallow, fish-spoons and small Devon spinners work best.

Climate

The Western Lakes region is subject to sudden blizzards at any time. While mild (even hot) days are common in summer and autumn, thermal underwear and rainproof, windproof garments must be carried at all times!

Maps

The latest 1:100 000 Tasmaps *(Mersey, Meander* and *Nive)* are perfectly adequate for bushwalkers and 4WD enthusiasts. The 1:25 000 series tends to be confusing (compare the *Pillans* 1:25 000 sheet to the *Mersey* 1:100 000 sheet).

5.2 SOUTHWEST NATIONAL PARK

The Southwest National Park includes some of the most rugged and most renowned bushwalking country in Australia. While there is little of interest to the backpacker angler, the reserve does include one of the country's most famous trout fisheries – Lake Pedder.

Description

The Southwest National Park incorporates 608 000 ha and is recognised as one of the world's prime temperate wilderness reserves. The bulk of the land consists of vast buttongrass plains divided by imposing ranges, but it is the spectacular southern coastline and the enchanting alpine lakes which most inspire the modern-day bushwalker.

Vehicular access

The park is essentially a wilderness and vehicular access is restricted to fringe areas. The family car can be taken to Cockle Creek (south of Catamaran at the far south-eastern corner of the reserve) and to Lake Pedder.

Backpacking

Only two lakes are of interest to backpacker anglers. Lake Judd (near Lake Pedder) supports plenty of slow-growing browns, while Lake Skinner (on the eastern fringes of the park) contains good-sized rainbow trout.

The only stream of note is the upper Weld River, a rainbow fishery.

Trout stocks at other waters

Although sea trout are reputedly taken from time to time at Port Davey and in the Bathurst Channel, resident trout have not been reliably recorded from any of the streams which drain to the south-west coast, Port Davey, Bathurst Harbour or the South Coast.

While brown trout are found throughout the upper Huon system and in Lake Pedder, waterfalls have prevented them from invading the alpine lakes on the Arthur and Frankland ranges. In fact most alpine waters are so isolated that they do not support any native fish, not even the highly-invasive climbing galaxias.

5.3 FRANKLIN-GORDON WILD RIVERS NATIONAL PARK

The angling feature of the Franklin-Gordon Wild Rivers National Park is the sea trout fishing in the lower reaches of the Gordon River. Most other waters are unremarkable, though fair sport is to be found in a few of the remote lakes.

Description

The reserve is 440 000 ha of rugged wilderness, characterised by mighty tea-coloured rivers, spectacular gorges, rocky peaks, and jagged ranges. The vegetation is typical of Tasmania's wet mountainous areas – ancient rainforests, buttongrass plains, and dense alpine heath.

The park comprises all of the Gordon River catchment except the Serpentine system and the Gordon River Power Development lakes. The fringes also include some of the coastal streams south of Macquarie Harbour, some of

Wild Rivers wilderness. Lake Dixon in the foreground

Gordon River sea trout

65

the headwater streams in the King River catchment, and the Derwent system lakes at the foot of the King William Range.

The trout fishing

The major trout fishery, the lower Gordon River, is accessible by boat from Strahan. Peak fishing occurs from August through until December – during the sea trout migrations.

Waters of interest to the bushwalker are lakes Dixon and Undine in the upper Franklin valley; lakes George, Rufus and Richmond at the foot of the King William Range near Lake King William; and Lake Curly near Lake Gordon. The trout are invariably small and slow growing.

Other lakes, including all of those in the vicinity of Frenchmans Cap, have not been invaded by trout. In most cases waterfalls have prevented access even to highly invasive native fish such as the climbing galaxias.

While trout have infiltrated most lowland streams, the water is always tea coloured, acidic and overgrown – and the trout are usually stunted. Enthusiastic Celta fishers take big bags from the Franklin and Collingwood rivers.

5.4 CRADLE MOUNTAIN – LAKE ST CLAIR NATIONAL PARK

The Cradle Mountain – Lake St Clair reserve is one of Australia's best known national parks. Although trout waters are not widespread, there are some remarkable fisheries – especially in the vicinity of Lake St Clair.

Description

The southern end of the reserve is of most interest to anglers. Rainforests dominate on the sheltered slopes, sclerophyll woodland is common elsewhere – and most lakes are crystal clear. The main physical feature is Lake St Clair.

While the north of the park is dominated by the dolerite peaks of Cradle Mountain and Barn Bluff, most of the underlying rocks are quartzites and schists which give rise to infertile acidic soils. Moorland is the major vegetation type and, as rainfall is very high, the waters are invariably tea-coloured.

Vehicular access

The family car can be taken to Lake Dove in the north and Lake St Clair in the south, but the reserve is essentially wilderness and there is no vehicular access beyond the major fringe developments.

Walking tracks

The major walking track is the internationally-famous Overland Track, which traverses the north-south axis of the reserve. Unfortunately this route encompasses few trout waters.

Anglers will be most interested in the circuit walk from Cynthia Bay (Lake St Clair) via Mt Rufus and the Hugel Lakes (6-7 hrs); the Cuvier Valley Track to Lake Petrarch (about 4 hrs from Cynthia Bay and 2½ hrs from the north end of Lake St Clair); and the track from the north end of Lake St Clair to Lake Marion (about 1½-2 hrs each way).

Trout stocks

The origin of trout stocks within the park is discussed in Part 2 – *Tasmanian Trout Waters in Detail (St Clair, Lake; Dove, Lake;* and *Labyrinth, The)*

Recommended fishing destinations

In the Cradle Valley the only recognised stillwater fishery is Lake Dove. Small brown trout, which are easily caught on Celtas, frequent the Dove River and Pencil Pine Creek.

Wilderness fishing near Lake St Clair

Lake St Clair and St Clair Lagoon are major (if underrated) clearwater fisheries containing good stocks of both brown and rainbow trout. Waters recommended for the backpacker angler include the Hugel Lakes which hold good-sized browns and fat rainbows; Lake Petrarch which is tea coloured but gives up large numbers of worthwhile brown trout; and Lake Marion which is reputed to hold smallish browns. Lake Ophion has been illegally stocked with Atlantic salmon.

Facilities and services

Southern end

See *St Clair, Lake* in Part 2 – *Tasmanian Trout Waters in Detail.*

Northern End

Accommodation huts are available in the Cradle Valley, the facilities being similar to those at Lake St Clair. No camping is permitted within a day walk of Lake Dove. A formal camping ground has been established beside the Cradle Mountain Road some 2 km north of the park boundary. Bookings are by arrangement with the PWS.

Luxury accommodation is available at the privately-owned Cradle Mountain Lodge, near the Cradle Mountain Road just north of the park boundary.

Maps

The best map is the 1:100 000 *Cradle Mtn Lake St Clair National Park* sheet. However, this publication is not essential if you already have the *Sophia, Mersey, Franklin* and *Nive* 1:100 000 Tasmaps.

Brown trout from Mt Field

5.5 MT FIELD NATIONAL PARK

Mt Field is located just 80 km north-west of Hobart. It is a small but spectacular reserve and, as a result of its popularity with skiers and picnickers, it has the distinction of being Tasmania's most visited national park. Although currently ignored by the majority of anglers, the reserve offers very good trout fishing.

Description

Mt Field National Park encompasses 16 257 ha. While the park entrance lies at an altitude of about 150 m, the vast majority of the reserve is higher than 900 m and all of the lakes of interest to anglers are located in alpine areas.

The heart of the reserve is not a single mountain but rather a labyrinth of peaks, valleys and moors. Forests are confined to sheltered areas such as small valleys and east-facing slopes. Elsewhere there are only scatterings of stunted gums and pencil pines. The moors feature a variety of grasses, mosses and heaths and are reminiscent of the more extensive plains in the Western Lakes.

As the park lies in the south-western quarter of the State, rainfall is high and winter conditions are harsh. In alpine areas heavy snowfalls are to be expected from June through until September, during which time the lakes may be frozen over. While the snow has usually completely melted by late spring, and pleasant sunny conditions are normal throughout the rest of the trout season, it must be recognised that blizzards can occur at any time.

Vehicular access

Within the park a single gravel route, the Lake Dobson Road, winds up through the closed-canopy forests to the exposed alpine heartland, terminating at Lake Dobson. This road is narrow and steep, and is subject to enforced closures during very heavy snowfalls. The small extension beyond the public carpark, leading up to the ski village at Mt Mawson, is strictly a supply route and is available to the public only as a foot access.

Facilities/Huts

Family picnics are encouraged near the park

entrance where there are PWS offices, picnic facilities, shelter sheds, a kiosk, toilets, a formal camping ground with caravan sites, and extensive lawns.

At Lake Dobson there are public toilets and a good day-shelter hut. The State owns and operates several rugged accommodation huts beside the Lake Dobson Road a kilometre before the road terminus. These shelters are in high demand only during the ski season. Bookings can be made through the PWS. Other buildings scattered about Lake Dobson and Eagle Tarn belong to various ski clubs and bushwalking groups.

Modest public (bushwalker) shelter huts exist at Lake Newdegate, Twilight Tarn, Lake Nicholls, Lake Belcher, and K-Col. As these huts are small and often fully occupied, they should be regarded as emergency shelters only. No fees are charged.

Walking tracks

Most walking tracks within the park are well maintained and easy to follow. In recent years many of the notorious wet areas have been corded and/or duckboarded. Visitors are encouraged to use the paths provided and (where possible) to avoid making cross-country expeditions.

The most spectacular and popular walking track is the circuit from Lake Dobson via the forested Broad River valley (incorporating lakes Seal and Webster) and the elevated, exposed Tarn Shelf (incorporating Twisted Tarn and Lake Newdegate). The entire circuit walk takes about 5-8 hrs.

Another pleasant circuit leads past Lake Nicholls and Mt Field East and rejoins the Lake Dobson Road at Lake Fenton, 2.6 km uphill from the start. The direct access to Lake Nicholls takes about ½-¾ hr (each way), while the full circuit via Mt Field East takes 2-3 hrs.

Lakes Belton and Belcher are also prime destinations for trout fishers. The access track to these waters is a no-through route of about 1½-2½ hrs duration (each way). The first half of the walk is over open plains. This is followed by a steep descent through low (but thick) forest undergrowth. The track forks about ½ hr from either lake. The main track to Lake Belcher is quite distinct. The spur to Lake Belton is not so well defined.

Trout stocks

Brown trout probably had invaded negotiable waterways within the park (including Lake Webster) via the Derwent system by the late 1860s. However, most lakes would have remained trout-free until they received their first direct liberations. An early Parliamentary report recorded the liberation of 1000 brown trout fry at 'Russell's Falls' in 1870. This most probably was a record of

Lake Hayes rainbow

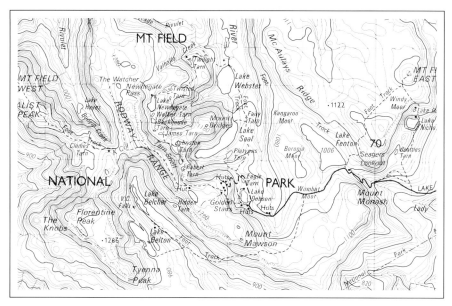

MOUNT FIELD NATIONAL PARK

an early stocking of the Tyenna River (which was formally known as 'Russell's Falls'). In 1893 The *Mercury* reported the stocking of Lake Webster. Later reports indicate that almost 100 000 rainbow trout fry were turned out in *'National Park'* and *'National Park Lakes'* between 1917 and 1922, and that a similar number of brown trout were released between 1920 and 1923. The NTFA recorded a further liberation of 120 000 rainbow fry in *'Lakes Mt. Field, Fenton, Dobson.'* in 1940-41. Subsequent releases of rainbows and browns, undertaken between 1957 and 1967, were carried out at various named waters (see Part 2 – *Tasmanian Trout Waters in Detail*). Today all trout stocks are maintained by natural recruitment. Brown trout dominate, though rainbows do well at Lake Hayes.

Recommended fishing destinations

While only lakes Fenton and Dobson are accessible by 2WD, there are several significant fisheries located within a day-walk of formed roads. Lake Webster is easily waded and holds large numbers of small brown trout. Lake Seal holds larger fish but much of the shoreline is of difficult access. Lake Nicholls holds relatively few trout and is not highly regarded.

Among the more distant brown-trout waters are Lake Belcher, Lake Belton, Twisted Tarn and Lake Newdegate. Lake Hayes is unique in that it contains only rainbows.

Maps

The most detailed map is the *Dobson* 1:25 000 Tasmap. The popular *Mount Field National Park* map provides topographic detail at a scale of 1:50 000 but does not include all features of interest to anglers.

5.6 HARTZ MOUNTAINS NATIONAL PARK

While the trout in the Hartz Mountains are small and slow growing, the scenery is superb.

Description

The current park encompasses 7250 ha and was inscribed on the World Heritage List in 1989. While it includes densely-forested valleys and mountain sides, the centre with its open moors, alpine lakes and rocky peaks is easily accessible.

Trout stocks

In 1908 the *Handbook of Tasmania* claimed that the Hartz Lakes were stocked with *'Loch Leven'* (brown) trout.

A new era of stocking began in the 1930s following the construction of the Geeveston hatchery. The STLAA reported that in 1931 about 30 000 fry *were "packed" to the Hartz Lakes by Members and friends'* and that during the 1933-34 season *'...Rainbow ova as well as brown trout ova were hatched and liberated in Hartz lakes, Lune River and other streams, the former being very successful'.* Other reports suggest that further stocking of both browns and rainbows may have occurred in 1935-36.

In 1953 it was noted that good conditioned browns existed in lakes Perry and Osborne, and that Lake Esperance was reputed to carry browns and rainbows. It was also suggested that a *'lake Laurie'* (1½ miles south of the hut, beside the track) had been stocked but no longer contained trout.

The last official stocking occurred in 1964 when the IFC allocated 30 000 brown trout fry to the *'Hartz Lakes'.* But at least two very small illegal consignments of brown trout fry were taken to Hartz Lake during the 1980s.

Today small slow-growing browns abound in lakes Esperance, Perry and Osborne. Hartz Lake appears to hold very few trout and it is possible that significant wild stocks never established.

Access

A 2WD gravel road extends some 2-3 km into the park, terminating on the alpine moorland near the lakes district. From the end of this road a small circuit walk (½-¾ hr) encompasses lakes Perry and Osborne.

A longer track extends 3.5 km south from the end of the road, passing Lake Esperance and terminating at Hartz Lake. This trip takes 1½-2 hrs (each way).

All tracks are well corded and signposted.

Facilities

There are basic roadside facilities for day visitors, including a picnic area, a wood barbecue, an open shelter and a pit toilet. The old Hartz hut, located a few minutes walk along the Hartz Lake track from the end of the road, is in a modest state of repair but serves as an adequate emergency shelter.

Weather

As with all of Tasmania's alpine areas sudden blizzards can occur at any time. Day-trippers must carry warm waterproof windproof clothing.

Maps

The best map for walkers is the 1:50 000 *Hartz Mountains Day Walk Map*, though this is hardly worthwhile if you already have the *Huon* 1:100 000 Tasmap.

5.7 DOUGLAS-APSLEY NATIONAL PARK

The Douglas-Apsley National Park was reserved in 1989 and gives protection to 16 080 ha of the last pristine dry-sclerophyll forest in Tasmania.

Relatively small numbers of tiny brown trout frequent the upper Apsley River. Trout are reputed to be absent from the Douglas River above Tevelein Falls.

5.8 ROCKY CAPE NATIONAL PARK

Rocky Cape National Park was first proclaimed in 1967 and now reserves 3064 ha. It features spectacular coastlines, with white-sand beaches backed by small hills covered with heath and bushland.

While trout are found in Lake Llewellyn and Sisters Creek, the quality of the fishing is unremarkable. ◆

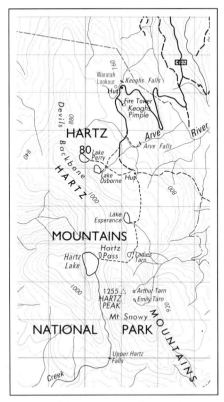

HARTZ MOUNTAINS NATIONAL PARK

Notes for the Specialist

6.1 FLY FISHING

The nature of the fishing

In Tasmania the emphasis is on sight fishing. As most waters are shallow and/or clear, polaroiding is our 'bread and butter', but in waters that are deep and discoloured there usually are risers and/or visible foraging fish. By world standards Tasmanians have a lot of leisure time and, because the State is so small, anglers are able to fish pretty much where and when they like. Locals tend to frequent specific waters only during periods of feature fishing, and at each fishery relatively unproductive water is more or less ignored. Angling pressure simply is not great enough to force people from prize fishing spots to less attractive areas. The advice given in this book reflects local attitudes.

Tasmania has such a reputation for its quality trout fishing that many visitors come here expecting to catch lots of fish. But quality does not necessarily equal quantity. Wild brown trout are rarely easy to catch, so accept the sport as a challenge.

Essential reading

This publication is primarily a 'where and when' guide so you are well advised to chase up some local 'how to' literature. Rob Sloane's book *Fly Fishing Fundamentals* (1993) is invaluable, especially for beginners and intermediates – I simply cannot recommend it too highly. Rob's earlier 'how to' guide *The Truth about Trout* (1983), which concentrates on 'observation, presentation and the functional fly', is out of print but is held at the State Library and provides compelling reading. Tony Sloane's *The Truth About Trout Flies* (1986) explains how to tie the fly patterns recommended in *The Truth About Trout*.

The works of David Scholes are also highly recommended (see *Where to Fish – A Regional Breakdown*, 4.2).

Equipment

A 6 or 7 wt fly rod is the best general purpose rod for use in Tasmania. As you are usually sight fishing, floating lines are ideal – and conventional double tapers or *Teeny* weight-forwards are recommended. While tippets of 2 kg are best for clearwater fishing, especially when using small dries or nymphs, larger diameter lines of 2.5-3 kg are more practical in snaggy and/or discoloured water.

As far as flies go it is rarely essential to have exact imitations and it is possible to get by with just a few patterns. My favourites are Red and Black Matukas, Green and Silver Matukas, Rabbit Fur Flies, Black Beetles, Green Nymphs, Red

Polaroiding – the Tasmanian fly fisher's 'bread and butter'

FLY FISHERS' TRIP PLANNER

	SEA TROUT	INLAND GALAXIID FEEDERS	FORAGING FISH IN FLOOD MARGINS	CLASSIC TAILERS (snail and shrimp feeders)	MAYFLY HATCHES ON LAKES	MAYFLY HATCHES ON RIVERS	POLAROIDING	MUDEYE FEEDERS
SUGGESTED DESTINATIONS	Henty River, Gordon River, Pieman River, River Derwent, Huon River, Great Forester River, D'Entrecasteaux Rvr, Inglis River, Duck River, River Forth, River Leven, Mersey River	Lake Crescent, Lake Sorell, Curries River Dam	Bronte Lagoon, Macquarie River, Lake River, Western Lakes, Lake Sorell, Lake Crescent	Little Pine Lagoon, Western Lakes	Little Pine Lagoon, Penstock Lagoon, Western Lakes	Macquarie River, Lake River, Break O'Day River	Great Lake, Dee Lagoon, Western Lakes, Lake Echo, Lake Rowallan	Lake Pedder, Lake Burbury, Lake Mackintosh, Brushy Lagoon
IDEAL CONDITIONS	Rivers not in flood	Dull weather and high water	Warm-weather floods	Overcast with a slight breeze	Warm to hot with some high-level cloud	High water, warm weather, and some high-level cloud	Lots of sun	Muggy calm evenings

WHEN TO FISH (AUG, SEP, OCT, NOV, DEC, JAN, FEB, MAR, APR, MAY, JUN, JUL)

MOST WATERS CLOSED TO ANGLING

ALL WATERS CLOSED TO ANGLING

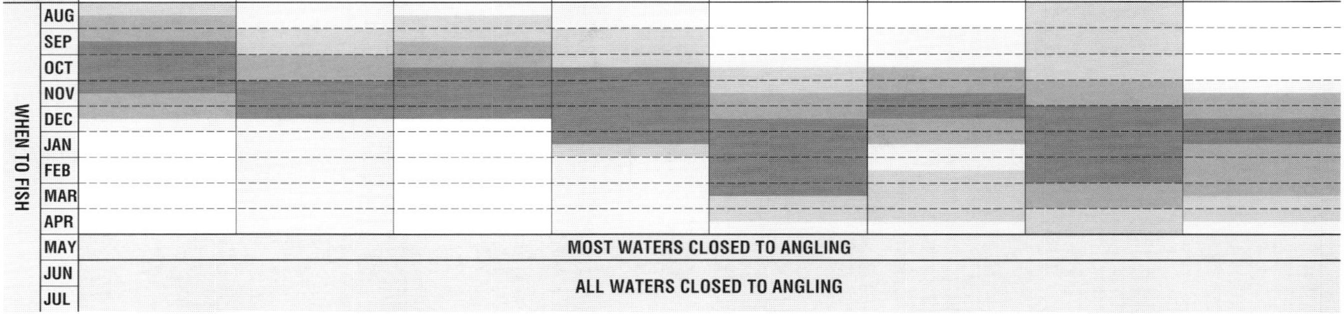

KEY to fishing conditions: Peak | Good | Fair | Modest | Poor

73

Tags, Black Spinners, Highland Duns, Deer Hair Gum Beetles, and Cork Flies.

Where wading is advocated (in marshes and shallow polaroiding water) chest waders are usually preferable to thigh boots. And tough plastic is normally more practical than heavy, hot neoprene.

Fishing schools

Among the services offered by the Department of Education are courses on fly casting and fly tying. Further information can be obtained from the Adult Education Centre.

6.2 LURE FISHING

Lure casting

Tasmanian lakes are mostly shallow so light lures in conjunction with 2-3 kg monofilaments are preferred. Locals favour the use of fish-spoon wobblers, Cobras and Devon spinners – in colour combinations of green and gold, green and black, and red and black.

Anglers fishing estuaries and the lower freshwater reaches of sea trout rivers use lake-style rigs – but the preferred lure colours are silver, green and white.

In small fastwater streams Size 1 Celtas and 1.5-2 kg lines are most effective – green and gold being the best colour combination. In larger rivers small Devon spinners and fish-spoons in the traditional lake-colours work best.

Trolling

Warm water is not a problem so trout are rarely forced from the surface down to cooler clines. And, unlike some New Zealand and mainland fisheries, no waters contain forage food such as smelt which encourage trout to feed at great depth. With the exception of Great Lake, where significant feeding take place on weedbeds beyond the extensive littoral zone, down-rigging and deep trolling are of little value.

The most popular trolling lures are large Cobras, Devon spinners, and spoons. Flatfish, Kwickfish, Rebels, Rapalas and Canadian Wigglers are used in some of the deeper waters but are no more effective than simpler (not to mention cheaper) lures. Lines of 3-4 kg are adequate.

Regulations limit the number of rods to one per person, and the maximum number of lures to two per rod. Local anglers often fix a Matuka-style fly on a 15-20 cm dropper from the anti-kink, about 60-80 cm in front of the lure.

Remember that it is an offence to fish from a

Spinning – exciting and easy

boat that is within 100 m of an angler fishing from the shore unless the boat is securely moored.

Locally made lures

Most lures sold and used in Tasmania are made locally. The popular Cobras are *Tassie Devils, Tillins, Lofty's, Bill Monks,* and *Johnson.* Devons are made by *Ashley, Tillins, Lofty's* and *Johnson.* Locally-manufactured conventional wobblers include those by *Tillins* and *Johnson,* though mainland produced wobblers (such as *Wonder Wobblers* and *Halco* lures) remain most popular.

6.3 BAIT FISHING

The popular baits

Wattle grubs (which can be bought from most tackle stores) are the traditional freshwater night-bait, being used on set-rods and for cast-and-retrieve fishing. Worms are one of the best daytime baits, especially for set-rod fishing in the rising flood margins of lakes and rivers, and for cast-and-retrieve fishing in small fastwater streams when levels are moderately high. Another good cast-and-retrieve bait for streams is the ever-popular grasshopper. Bush cockroaches (found under

LURE FISHERS' TRIP PLANNER

	SEA TROUT	SHORE-BASED LURE CASTING IN LAKES	TROLLING AND DRIFT SPINNING	SPINNING IN LARGE RIVERS	CELTA FISHING IN SMALL STREAMS
SUGGESTED DESTINATIONS	River Derwent, Huon River, Henty River, Gordon River, Pieman River, Great Forester River, D'Entrecasteaux River, Duck River, River Forth, River Leven, Mersey River	Lake Sorell, Great Lake, Bradys chain of lakes, Western Lakes, Lake Echo, Lake Pedder, Lake St Clair, St Clair Lagoon, Lake Burbury	Arthurs Lake, Great Lake, Lake Sorell, Lake King William, Lake Echo, Lake Rowallan, Lake Crescent, Bradys chain of lakes, Lake St Clair, Lake Pedder, Lake Mackintosh, Lake Barrington	River Derwent, Huon River, Mersey River, River Leven	Upper River Leven, Tributaries of the River Derwent, Tributaries of the Huon River, North Esk River and tributaries
IDEAL CONDITIONS	Rivers not in flood	Stormy, dull, overcast and/or windy	Overcast and/or breezy	Vary from water to water	Low water and some cloud
WHEN TO FISH				Peak fishing times vary from water to water	

WHEN TO FISH (months): AUG, SEP, OCT, NOV, DEC, JAN, FEB, MAR, APR, MAY, JUN, JUL

MOST WATERS CLOSED TO ANGLING

ALL WATERS CLOSED TO ANGLING

KEY to fishing conditions: ■ Peak ■ Good ☐ Fair ☐ Modest ☐ Poor

BAIT FISHERS' TRIP PLANNER

	TRADITIONAL SET-ROD FISHING	POLAROIDING IN LAKES	SEA TROUT	BAIT CASTING (worms)	BAIT CASTING (grasshoppers)	FLOOD-MARGIN FISHING	CAST-AND-RETRIEVE GRUB FISHING
SUGGESTED DESTINATIONS	Lake Crescent / Bradys chain of lakes / Pine Tier Lagoon / Craigbourne Dam / Meadowbank Lake / Curries River Dam / Lake Burbury	Great Lake / Lake Echo	Henty River / River Derwent / Huon River / Duck River / Inglis River / Mersey River / River Forth / River Leven	Upper River Leven / Tributaries of the River Derwent / Tributaries of the Huon River / Tributaries of the Mersey River / North Esk River and tributaries / South Esk River and tributaries	Upper River Leven / Tributaries of the River Derwent / Tributaries of the Huon River / Tributaries of the Mersey River / North Esk River and tributaries / South Esk River and tributaries	Flowerdale River / Inglis River / Meander River / Macquarie River	Most waters
IDEAL CONDITIONS	Vary from water to water	Bright and sunny	Rivers not in flood	Rivers swollen but not raging	Warm weather and moderate to low flows	Warm-weather floods	Warm, moderately-calm evenings
WHEN TO FISH	Peak fishing times vary from water to water						Peak fishing times vary from water to water

WHEN TO FISH (months): AUG, SEP, OCT, NOV, DEC, JAN, FEB, MAR, APR, MAY, JUN, JUL

MOST WATERS CLOSED TO ANGLING

ALL WATERS CLOSED TO ANGLING

KEY to fishing conditions: ■ Peak ■ Good ■ Fair □ Modest □ Poor

logs and rocks in dry bushland) are a very effective daytime bait when presented to cruising fish. Frogs are still commonly used as bait but, in light of local and international concern over recent dramatic declines in frog populations, their use is not advocated. Strangely, mudeyes are not popular among Tasmanian bait fishers.

Sea trout are taken on sandies (freshwater flathead), strips of flesh cut from large fish, galaxias and whitebait – or (when set-rod fishing) crabs and scallops. Sandies and galaxias are easily caught on small hooks baited with worms. In some estuaries and coastal lagoons (check the *Fishing Code*) you are allowed to take live bait with a seine net not exceeding certain dimensions or having a mesh greater than 12 mm. Anglers are permitted to take live bait in estuarine waters with a bush pole (a length of wood not less than 1 m in length) seven days before the Saturday nearest 1 August in any year until the Sunday nearest 30 April next. During the angling season live bait may be taken at inland waters on normal trout fishing equipment.

Please respect the regulations banning the importation of bait to Tasmania. Non-native species pose serious threats to our unique local animals. It is also illegal to use perch, tench, carp or goldfish for bait – whether dead or alive.

Ground bait or berley is prohibited, as are electronic or sonic devices capable of attracting or influencing the movement of fish.

Rigs

The use of handlines is not allowed at inland waters and rods must be attended (within 8 m) at all times. Each person is allowed just one rod and no rig may be fitted with more than two baits. Strike indicators such as bottles, jars and cans have been banned in an effort to reduce litter on lakeshores and river banks.

Most anglers use 3-4 kg line. Sliding-sinker rigs can be used for set-rod fishing but when cast-and-retrieve fishing additional weights are not favoured.

The status of bait fishing in Tasmania

Bait fishing is considered by many to be a second-class angling technique. This attitude is attributable, in part, to bigotry on the part of a minority of lure fishers and fly casters. However, a tradition of irresponsible behaviour by some bait fishers has led to legitimate concerns being voiced by managers and the wider angling community.

Littering has long been blamed on bait fishers – and bait fishers must take it upon themselves to discredit the association.

Another view voiced by many anglers is that set-rod fishers often occupy lucrative hot spots for unacceptably long periods. Two or three parties of bait fishers with lines stretched out over shallow margins can effectively deny access to a much larger number of mobile anglers. This is a real problem in places such as Lake Crescent. In New Zealand there is a universally respected voluntary code which prohibits anglers from taking prolonged control of river pools and sections of shore. The adoption of this philosophy in Tasmania is essential if bait fishers are to be widely accepted by other trout fishers.

Bait fishing is also a genuine problem in national parks. The inadvertent introduction of exotic bait species poses serious ecological dangers, while the collection of bait within reserves results in environmental damage.

Another valid reason for restricting the use of bait is to preserve fish stocks. Bait fishing is incompatible with the catch-and-release approach to trout management. Trout are usually hooked in the gills or gut, resulting in an unacceptably high mortality of up to 50-60% of fish released.

The sport in trout fishing is the ability to see the quarry and present an appropriate bait, lure or fly. Many of the die hard cast-and-retrieve bait fishers I have known are second-to-none sportsmen. Even set-rod fishing has social value, especially when practised by children and the handicapped. Many anglers would not fish at all if denied the opportunity to use bait, and any reduction in angler numbers simply lowers the voice of the angling lobby. But, while it is in the interests of all trout fishers that bait fishing be promoted as a worthwhile and legitimate sport, it is up to bait fishers to make themselves acceptable to other anglers.

6.4 TROPHY TROUT

The mechanisms which govern trout growth are fully described under *About Our Sportfish*, 2.1 – but basically ultimate size is determined by the amount of food available to each fish. It is possible therefore for some trout in small-fish waters to attain good size, especially if they can dominate a lucrative food source. In Tasmania very big fish are regularly taken from power station tailraces (where they feed on eels and other fish minced by the turbines), at popular boat ramps (where they feed on the remains of cleaned fish), and outfalls from slaughter yards and fish farms. But trophy fish are much more likely to be found in fisheries which contain few trout – in places where there is little competition for food. In

Tasmania the best freshwater trophy fisheries are shallow lakes which have few natural spawning facilities. The main waters are Lake Crescent and Lagoon of Islands, though several small waters in the Western Lakes also offer remarkable sport (see *Fishing in National Parks*, 5.1).

Sea trout, too, grow to impressive size, largely because they have access to the infinite larder of the ocean but also because they often delay spawning until they are 4-5 years old. Twenty pounders are taken every year. While the Gordon, Henty, Pieman, Huon and Derwent rivers are among the best fisheries, memorable fishing can be found in most coastal rivers. Anglers interested in catching sea trout should refer to *About Our Sportfish*, 2.1.

Trophy rainbows from Lake Crescent (photo by Rob Sloane)

Reward for searching remote water (photo by Rob Sloane)

PART 2

Tasmanian Trout Waters in Detail

Photo by Rob Sloane

About the waters index

How to look up waters in the alphabetical listing

There are several accepted ways of listing words alphabetically. The method used in this book is outlined below.

Essentially the main part of the place name appears first, so *Lake Sorell* appears as *Sorell, Lake*. Double-barrelled names are not broken down, so *Little Pine Lagoon* appears under 'L' and *Upper Jukes Lake* under 'U'. Also, the space between words is treated as a letter preceding 'A', so *New Years Lake* is listed before *Newdegate, Lake*.

Abbreviations formally accepted by the Nomenclature Board are acknowledged, thus *St Clair Lagoon* proceeds *Spring River*. Similarly *McCoy, Lake* appears after *Maurice River*.

What to do when a water is not listed

An effort has been made to include all significant waters under individual headings. However, it is senseless to individually list every minor tributary of a particular stream if they are all mediocre and alike. Similarly a single blanket statement such as 'there are no trout in the lakes on the Frankland and Arthur ranges' is often appropriate. If the water you want is not listed it will probably be mentioned in the discussion of its arterial stream. If not, look up the appropriate entry in *Where to Fish – A Regional Breakdown,* section 4; or *Fishing in National Parks,* section 5.

Lake levels

HEC impoundment levels are usually published weekly in the angling columns of the local daily newspapers *(The Mercury, The Examiner* and *The Advocate).* Alternatively you could contact the Public Services section of the HEC. While levels are usually given in metres below full supply, they are sometimes given as metres above sea level. Consequently, an attempt has been made in this book to give full supply levels accurate to within one centimetre.

Notes on the size of hatchery-reared trout

An explanation of the terms used in this book is given below.

Fry

Very small fish released within a couple of months after hatching.

Advanced Fry

Applied here mostly to brown trout of less than 1g released when 2-6 months old. Hatchery-reared rainbows grow faster and often reach fingerling stage during this time.

Small Fingerlings

Average fish in the batch weigh 1-10g.

Large Fingerlings

Average fish in the batch weigh 10-60g.

Extra Large Fingerlings

Average fish in the batch are greater than 60g.

Yearlings

Fish aged one year or slightly more. Rainbows of this age often weigh 60-120g, though runts can be less than 20g.

Adults

Most adults used for stocking are wild browns transferred from Great Lake or Arthurs Lake during the winter spawning runs. Typical fish weigh 0.7-1.5kg.

Keeping your finger on the pulse

The information in this book is complete and accurate as at May 1994. As management policies change and some fisheries are volatile, you are well advised to subscribe to the IFC's quarterly newsletter, a superb publication which details all of the Commissions activities (including stocking) and gives up-to-date information on happenings around the State. Further updates can be gleaned from the Angling Associations' annual *Tasmanian Angling Report* which is available from most tackle stores.

ADA LAGOON

Tasmap Mersey
Drainage Derwent system (via the Little Pine River)
Location Nineteen Lagoons

History

Ada Lagoon originally had extensive beds of bottom-hugging *Isoetes* weed and boasted prolific mayfly hatches. Consequently, in 1962 boating was prohibited; while the lagoon, the connecting channel to Lake Ada, and the Little Pine River for 400 yards downstream were declared 'fly-only' waters.

Since the early 1960s silt has built up and the weed has died. The source of the problem can be traced back to the 1950s when Lake Ada was severely affected by drought and anglers built a crude low-profile rock weir at the outlet of Ada Lagoon. This weir (which still exists) prolongs the time the two lakes remain at 0.5 m or so above natural minimum levels and prevents adequate flushing. Turbid water from Lake Ada is held back long enough for silt to settle in the lagoon.

The fishing today

Today the hatches are very mediocre and the bottom is too boggy to wade. The best fishing occurs early in the season when levels are high. Spinning and blind wet-fly fishing are both worthwhile.

Trout can be caught in the middle of the lake but the hot spot is along the undercut banks.

As levels subside and the weather warms, lure casting becomes increasingly unproductive. Fly fishers are usually able to polaroid some fish over the silty flats – but the sport is always better at Lake Ada.

Special regulations

Ada Lagoon, the channel to Lake Ada, and the Little Pine River for 100 m downstream of Ada Lagoon are reserved for artificial lures. In the lagoon proper it is illegal to fish from a boat propelled other than by oars worked by manual labour, while in the channel to Lake Ada it is illegal to fish from *any* boat.

See also *Fishing in National Parks*, 5.1.

ADA, LAKE

Tasmap Mersey
Drainage Derwent system (via the Little Pine River)
Location Nineteen Lagoons

Description

Lake Ada is relatively shallow with extensive sand/silt flats. Most of the perimeter is rocky and well defined. As levels drop the eastern shore recedes and a wide beach is exposed. In wet

Brown trout from Lake Ada

periods the lake breaks its north-eastern banks, filling deep channels, gutters and backwaters.

During rough weather wave action causes significant turbidity.

A crude rock weir at the outflow of Ada Lagoon helps keep Lake Ada from falling quickly to natural minimum levels (see *Ada Lagoon*).

Trout stocks

In 1982 some 830 fry and yearlings salvaged from Liawenee Canal were liberated into Lake Ada – but the brown trout population is quite capable of maintaining itself by natural recruitment and there is no regular stocking programme. Fish of 0.7-2 kg are typical and some grow much larger.

Rainbows are scarce. Those which do turn up are emigrants from nearby stocked waters (such as Tin Hut Lake and the Zig Zag Lakes).

Lure fishing

Trolling is productive but, because of the shallow nature of the lake, drift spinning is most efficient. Lure casting from the bank is also very worthwhile. Wading can be a distinct advantage, especially when levels are low.

Fly fishing

Fly fishing is superb – providing you avoid turbid windswept shores. If you seek out sheltered bays and beaches, good polaroiding can be enjoyed on all but the most windy days. The best area extends along the north-eastern shoreline. Fish can often be seen from the banks but it is best to wade.

When the weather is very rough it is worthwhile blind-fishing a nymph along the distinct line where the moderately clear water merges with very turbid water.

When levels are high concentrate on fishing wet flies along the undercuts and in the backwaters and channels adjacent to the north-eastern shore.

Special regulations

Bait fishing has been prohibited since 1962.

See also *Fishing in National Parks*, 5.1.

ADAMS CREEK

Tasmaps Hellyer and Forth
Drainage Direct to the Blythe River

A small slightly-turbid fastwater which contains plenty of small slow-growing brown trout. Wading is recommended, especially in the forested mid-reaches. At times of low flow Celta fishing and bait casting often result in big bags.

ADELAIDE, LAKE

No trout. See *Meston, Lake* and *Fishing in National Parks*, 5.1.

AGNES, LAKE

Tasmap Meander
Drainage Derwent system (via the Little Pine system)
Location Nineteen Lagoons

Despite its small size Lake Agnes is a popular fishery – especially when levels are high. When levels are low the shores recede markedly and, although there is permanent holding water along the southern snowgrass undercuts, the sport becomes quite mediocre. Typical trout weigh 0.7-1.5 kg.

See also *Fishing in National Parks*, 5.1.

AGNES RIVULET

Tasmap D'Entrecasteaux
Drainage Direct to the Huon River at Cygnet

A tiny creek with limited summer flow. It supports brown trout to 0.5 kg or so – but the population is relatively small.

AGNEW, LAKE

No trout. See *Fishing in National Parks*, 5.4.

AH CHEES LAKE

Tasmap Mersey
Drainage Derwent system (via the Pine system)
Location Western Lakes

Ah Chees Lake is surrounded by alpine eucalypt forest. The shores are mostly rocky and well defined, though there are some peat banks and marshy shallows. Several very large fish to 7 kg have been caught – but not in recent seasons. Most fish now weigh 1-1.5 kg and the catch rate is unimpressive. The deep banks are well suited to spin fishing and polaroiding. Rises are generally small and infrequent.

See also *Fishing in National Parks*, 5.1

AMBER CREEK

Tasmap Pieman
Drainage Direct to the Little Henty River

A typical tea-coloured West Coast fastwater holding plenty of tiny brown trout. There is better sport in the nearby Little Henty.

ANDREW RIVER

Tasmap Franklin
Drainage Gordon system (via the Franklin River)

A remote wilderness fastwater. The trout fishing is similar to that in the Franklin.

See also *Fishing in National Parks*, 5.3.

ANDREWS, LAKE

No trout. See *Fishing in National Parks*, 5.4.

ANSONS RIVER

Tasmap Georges Bay
Drainage Direct to Ansons Bay

This river is set in thick bushland and is accessible by road only at The Bottleneck (upstream from Ansons Bay) and in the headwaters.

While a few sea trout and good-sized residents are caught in the lower reaches, the mid reaches hold mainly small slow-growing fish. The overgrown headwaters are best suited to set-rod fishing.

The NTFA recorded the liberation of 25 000 rainbow fry in 1918 – but this species failed to establish.

The combination of poor access and unimpressive sport has discouraged anglers.

ANTHONY, LAKE

See *Plimsoll, Lake*.

ANTHONY RIVER

See *Plimsoll, Lake* and *West Coast Range*.

ANTIMONY, LAKE

Tasmap Mersey
Drainage Derwent system (via the Pine River)
Location Western Lakes

While Lake Antimony is surrounded by rocky woodland, there are sedge esplanades along the eastern shore and a large moor extends from the north. When the lake is very full water floods out into the moor, filling ditches and small basins. At low levels most of the lake, even the centre, is wadeable.

The wade polaroiding is superb, and there are reliable morning and evening tailers in the northern bays.

Lake Antimony

84

The trout average about 0.7 kg but many attain 1.5 kg.
A modest hut is located on the elevated land back from the north-eastern shore.

See also *Fishing in National Parks*, 5.1.

APOLLOS, LAKE

This lake undoubtedly holds slow-growing brown trout but is seldom fished. See *Lake Margaret*.

APSLEY RIVER

Tasmap Break O'Day
Drainage Direct to Moulting Lagoon

Although the Apsley Marshes have been cleared and laced with drains, they remain wet and extremely boggy throughout the year. The river here has been channelised but is overgrown with dense tea-tree scrub and is seldom fished.

Feature fishing occurs in the long deep rush-lined broadwaters, which extend through the dry woodland and paddocks from the top of the marshes to above the Lilla Villa Bridge (on the Tasman Highway). The water is always slightly murky and polaroiding is difficult – but on warm calm days there are fair rises. You have to cast out over narrow bands of dense emergent rushes, so fly fishing is most practical, yet there is scope for spinning and bait casting. Fat browns to 1 kg are common and some attain 2 kg or so. I once thought that there was a reasonable run of sea trout, though I now suspect that most silvery fish are residents.

While some of the mid reaches are narrow and overgrown, the river above the Rosedale Road is reminiscent of the Swan catchment. Much of the wide rock/shingle bed is exposed when levels are low, and most of the permanent pools are small and shallow. The water is usually very clear (though it can be very turbid after heavy rain) and looks promising for polaroiding. Unfortunately the fish are mostly very small – usually less than 15 cm long.

Fishing in the national park

In the national park the Apsley flows through pristine dry forest. When levels are low you can walk up the river bed from the park boundary to the Apsley Gorge and beyond. There is also a formal foot track which extends 2 km from the park entrance to the gorge.

I have taken small brown trout in the gorge and presume that they extend upstream at least as far as the first falls (about 9-10 km above the gorge).

There is an extreme fire risk in dry weather and there are restrictions on camp fires. Check details with the PWS.

ARBA HOLE

(sometimes misspelled 'Arbor Hole')

Tasmap Forester
Location Branxholm

Stocked with 2000 brook trout fry in 1981 and 1982. Does not contain trout today.

ARBOR HOLE

See *Arba Hole*.

ARGENT DAM

Tasmap Pieman
Drainage Pieman system
Location Beside the Murchison Highway south of Renison Bell

A small pond surrounded by thick scrub, and choked with weeds and dead trees.

The water is reserved for artificial lures but fly fishing is most practical. Fair rises occur on warm calm days and wet-fly fishing is a reliable fall-back. Wading is essential.

Liberations of 10 000 brown trout fry occurred in 1975 and 1976, and in 1978 the IFC claimed that fish to 2 kg had been caught. Today the water is severely overpopulated and many fish mature before they are of takeable size. Trout in excess of 0.5 kg are relatively uncommon.

ARM RIVER

Tasmap Mersey
Drainage Direct to the Mersey River above Lake Parangana

A fast clearwater stream which carries plenty of small brown trout. Most pools are shallow and, as the banks are overgrown with trees and scrub, wading is recommended. Celta fishing and bait casting commonly result in big bags.

ARTEMIS, LAKE

No trout. See *Fishing in National Parks*, 5.1.

ARTHUR RIVER

Tasmaps   Sandy Cape, Arthur River, and Hellyer
Drainage   Direct to the Southern Ocean

The Arthur system drains an extensive mountainous tract of dense wet-forest. While logging occurs in many areas, the conservation lobby is fighting to protect the remaining old-growth – and the battle for the 'Tarkine' wilderness is likely to become one of the big conservation issues of the 1990s. Brown trout are found throughout the system but, with the exception of the sea trout in the lower reaches, there is little to recommend for the angler.

Access

There is convenient 2WD access to the township of Arthur River at the river mouth. Much of the rest of the river is wilderness, though logging roads cross at several points.

Most of the Arthur is deep, fast and dark with tannin – and in most places the banks are overgrown with rainforest and dense scrub.

Trout stocks

The origin of the brown trout is unclear, though early Parliamentary reports show that the *'Way'* (the Wey feeds the Arthur via the Hellyer) was stocked with fry as early as 1881.

In 1892-93 it was noted that *'a quantity'* of Atlantic salmon had been conveyed to *'a tributary of the Arthur River'*, but this species failed to establish.

Sea trout fishing

Sea trout are caught from August until November (and sometimes later). The runs are sporadic but underrated.

While fishing from the rocky banks at the mouth is worthwhile, boating is recommended. Some 20 km of the lower reaches are accessible by dinghy and runabout (in fact cruise boats are taken up as far as the confluence of the Frankland River). Trolling with large spoons and Cobras is most productive yet there is some sight fishing. In the early months, sea trout are likely to be seen as they chase spawning *Lovettia* on shallow bankside rock shelves. Later, in October/November, they follow galaxias up to the bottlenecks below the rapids.

In 1958 the NWFA claimed that *'a few years ago a trout weighing 29 ¼ lbs (cleaned weight) was caught at the mouth'* and, even allowing for a measure of 'story telling', there is no doubt that very large fish are taken from time to time. The sea trout I have taken have been comparable with those in the Gordon and Pieman rivers – mostly 0.7-2 kg but with a sprinkling of 3-4 kg trophies.

River residents

While anglers largely ignore the Arthur once the sea trout have stopped running, there are appreciable numbers of residents in the lower reaches – especially from a couple of kilometres upstream of the Temma Road to the limit of boating. Most of these fish weigh 0.5-1 kg but others to 1.5 kg are reasonably common. Spinning is consistently productive and modest rises occur on hot calm evenings.

The mid reaches are not often fished, though fish to 1 kg are taken near the bridges on the logging roads by set-rod fishers and, when levels are low, lure casters.

The uppermost reaches, some distance above the Hellyer junction, were once severely polluted with sludge and tailings from tin mining operations. Tin was discovered at Mt Bischoff in 1871 and by the mid 1870s the mountain had become the world's biggest and most profitable tin mine. From about 1910 the quality of the ore went into decline, but mining continued in a fashion until after World War II. Since then there have been only small-scale operations – and environmental controls have been strengthened. Trout have re-established over much of the upper river in modern times, but the area remains of little interest to the serious angler.

The tributaries

Most of the small tributary streams contain trout and, when flows are low, any which are shallow enough to wade give up large numbers of half-pounders. Because of the dense overhanging scrub, Celta fishing and bait casting are most practical.

Only a few of the bigger tributaries are easily accessible. The Hellyer River is the most popular, though fish are also taken from the Rapid and Frankland rivers.

ARTHURS LAKE

Tasmaps   Shannon and Meander
Drainage   Natural – South Esk system (via the Lake River system)

Arthurs Lake is one of the most popular and productive of Tasmania's trout lakes. It offers even the inexperienced angler a realistic chance of catching a Central Highlands trout, though the best fishing is often boat dependent.

Arthurs is discussed in great detail in the book Trout Guide *(Rob Sloane and Greg French, 1991). A summary only is given here.*

Description

Arthurs Lake is a large hydro-electric impoundment. At full supply it is about 952 m above sea level but slow seasonal drawdowns of up to about 4 m are to be expected. For many years the HEC aimed to maintain very low levels of up to 9 m below full supply, mainly to safeguard against spillage during flash floods. Following representation from the IFC the flood risk was reassessed – and in 1993 the HEC agreed to less severe drawdowns.

Arthurs originally drained into Woods Lake via the Upper Lake River but the water is now pumped up into Great Lake. Small amounts of water are released via the natural drainage only when riparian requirements cannot be met from water stored in Woods Lake.

Many shores, especially those exposed to the predominantly westerly weather, are barren clay expanses. However, there are grassy verges and thick beds of Canadian pondweed in the sheltered bays (such as Pump House Bay, Cowpaddock Bay, Lawrence Bay and Jones Bay), and there are many dense stands of drowned timber.

The water is generally crystal, though some windswept shores get quite murky.

History

The modern Arthurs Lake inundated two natural lakes (Sand Lake and Blue Lake) and the Morass marsh.

The original lakes may have been stocked with brown trout in 1870 – at the same time as a number of other unspecified highland lakes – but this is difficult to substantiate. The NTFA recorded the release of 500 rainbow trout fry at *'Upper Arthur Lake'* in 1904-05 – and by 1915 more than 35 000 rainbow fry and 2500 rainbow yearlings had been turned out. The *'Upper'* lake also received 200 Atlantic salmon in 1907-08 and over 2000 sebago salmon in 1910-11.

During early stocking experiments the Upper Arthur Lake was closed to fishing and it was not *'thrown open to angling'* until 1 February 1913. At this time roading was poor but access could be made via Interlaken from the Midlands, and via Bothwell from the south. Between 1913 and 1915 *'fair sport'* was enjoyed. Rainbows dominated but a few salmon were also taken. Strangely there was no mention of brown trout. By 1922-23 a small dam had been completed on the Upper Lake River below the lower Arthur Lake. Its purpose was to store and regulate water (in conjunction

Boating at Arthurs (photo by Viv Spencer)

ARTHURS LAKE

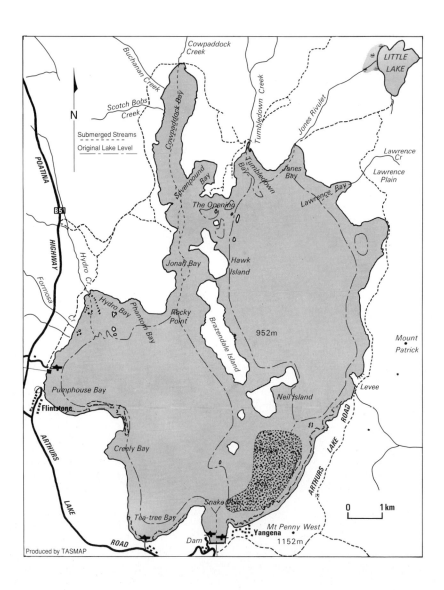

Cowpaddock
Creek

LITTLE
LAKE

Buchanan Creek

Scotch Bobs
Creek

Tumbledown Creek

Jones Rivulet

N

Submerged Streams

Original Lake Level

Cowpaddock Bay

POATINA

Sevenpound
Bay

Tumbledown
Bay

Jones
Bay

Lawrence
Cr

Lawrence
Plain

B51

The Opening

Lawrence Bay

HIGHWAY

Hydro Cr

Jonah Bay

Hawk
Island

Formosa

Hydro Bay

Phantom Bay

Rocky
Point

Brazendale Island

952m

Mount
Patrick

Pumphouse Bay

Neil Island

Levee

Flintstone

ARTHURS LAKE ROAD

ARTHURS

Creely Bay

LAKE

Tea-tree Bay

Snake Plain

0   1 km

ROAD

Dam

Mt Penny West

Yangena

1152m

Produced by TASMAP

with a pre-existing dam at Woods Lake), thus assisting the operation of the power station on the South Esk at Duck Reach near Launceston.

In 1934 the NTFA recorded that both rainbows and Loch Leven strain browns were present in Arthurs, and during the 1946-47 season 150 000 brown trout fry were released.

By the early 1950s the area had gained considerable popularity and the terms *'Blue Lake'* (for the western storage) and *'Sand Lake'* (for the Upper Arthur Lake) had been adopted. At about this time the trout in Blue Lake averaged 2-3 lb whereas those in Sand Lake were a little smaller. Both waters were relatively free of snags and trolling became popular. In fact one writer described Blue Lake in the summer of 1957 as resembling *'a miniature Regatta'*.

Reports of the 1950s offer the first good descriptions of the Morass – the marshland between the outflow of Sand Lake and the inflow to Blue Lake. The area was described as being laced with channels and lagoons and was said to provide exceptional fly fishing.

In 1954 Arthurs was described as *'perhaps the 3rd best lake fishing water in Tasmania'* and it was reported that *'many thousands of fish were taken last year'*. By 1956 the trout population consisted of *'mostly browns ... with a very occasional rainbow'*. Throughout the latter half of the decade thousands of brown trout fingerlings were released, mainly in the Morass. After this there were no significant records of rainbow trout captures.

In the early 1960s the HEC upgraded roads into the area, and by 1964 the small dam at Blue Lake had been superseded by the current 15 m high structure. By the winter of 1965 Arthurs had *'almost become one complete lake'*.

During the 1964-65 season most trout taken were about 1 kg, though a good number to 3 kg were taken from the Morass area. In the following year the average weight rose to about 2.7 kg and browns to 3.5 kg became common. But the boom was short lived, some reports suggesting that the average size dropped from about 2.3 kg in the pre-Christmas period of 1967 to about 1.4 kg post-Christmas. In June 1968 the average weight of spawners was only 0.7 kg.

Trout stocks today

Arthurs is a wild brown trout fishery supported entirely by natural recruitment. Fish of 0.4-1 kg can be expected but the quality and size vary from year to year depending on lake levels as well as climatic influences on spawning and recruitment.

Camping

A formal camping ground – with caravan sites (no power), camping areas, showers, toilets, water, and day-use picnic facilities – is located at Pump House Bay. Another camping ground is being developed at Jonah Bay. Informal camping is not encouraged but occurs in many places, especially around Cowpaddock Bay.

Boating

Arthurs owes much of its popularity to boat fishing. The most accessible launching area is near the Pump Station at Pump House Bay. A second (concrete) ramp, with deep water well-suited for big runabouts, is located at Arthurs Dam. A further ramp and parking area has been established at Jonah Bay.

Special regulations

All inflowing streams, and a radii of 50 m around where they meet the lake, are closed to fishing at all times.

Wet-fly fishing

Shore-based wet-fly fishing is at its best from September to November – when trout can be found tailing along the grassy edges.

Traditional British boat-fishing methods work very well. Try casting two flies out in front of a drifting boat and teasing them back right up to the sides. A large collapsible drogue is essential.

Dry-fly fishing

For the shore-based angler with the obligatory chest waders, the best fishing is from Jonah Bay to Cowpaddock Bay, and from Pump House Bay to Hydro Bay. The boat angler can add Phantom Bay, Sevenpound Bay, Camerons Opening, and the Lily Ponds.

The best dun hatches (they are exceptional) occur from early November to the end of summer. Peak fishing is usually from 11 am to 3 or 4 pm, ideal conditions being slightly overcast, or sunny with intermittent cloud. Wet nymphs, floating nymphs and mayfly patterns are needed.

On very bright days the rise can be quite disappointing and you may get better results by fishing in the shade among the trees.

The timbered shores offer good evening sport in mid summer when the mudeyes and beetles are about.

Lure fishing

It is generally conceded that the Morass area accounts for many of the best trout and so it is a popular trolling ground. Other popular circuits include the shores of Brazendale and Neil islands, the run between Pump House Bay and Hydro Bay, and the arm from Jonah Bay to the transmission lines at the mouth of Cowpaddock Bay.

Lure casting from a drifting boat is probably the best way to fish in rougher weather – and virtually all shores are suitable.

Spinning from the shore can be effective, though in many places weedbeds, surface strap weed, and drowned vegetation are a nuisance.

Bait fishing

The major boat ramps offer the best chance of catching good-sized fish. Literally hundreds of trout guts are discarded in these areas, providing easy pickings for big trout. The deep channel in front of the Pumping Station is especially good when the pump is in operation.

Generally the most popular bait fishing shores are in the traditional camping and shack areas – Pump House Bay, Tea Tree Bay, Arthurs Dam, Cowpaddock Bay and Jonah Bay.

Earthworms are the best bait, especially when the lake is flooding new ground after heavy rain.

ARVE RIVER

Tasmap Huon
Drainage Direct to the Huon River

The Arve contains both browns and rainbows.

The origin of the rainbows is unclear but it is probable that they are the progeny of fish released into the Hartz lakes in the 1930s (see *Fishing in National Parks*, 5.6). The population has been relatively stable since at least the late 1970s – and today you can expect rainbows to account for about 5-10% of your catch. The species appears to be confined to the stretch from the Huon River to the Arve Falls, and does well in the water near the Arve Road.

In 1953 the STLAA commented that the fish were small and in poor condition. The quality has not changed. Growth is extremely slow and most fish are less than 0.2 kg.

The lower reaches are deep and overgrown, and are not often patronised. The water near the Arve Road flows over a wide shingle bed and is easily fished with Celtas, baits and flies. You get the best results in summer and autumn when levels are low. On the Hartz plateau (above the Arve Falls) the creek is very small, overgrown and difficult to fish.

ASHFORD, LAKE

See *Ashwood, Lake*.

ASHWOOD, LAKE

(marked on some maps as Lake Ashford)

Tasmap Cape Sorell
Drainage Isolated coastal lagoon
Location North of Strahan

Lake Ashwood was first stocked in 1970 when 30 000 brown trout fry were released. It was managed as a brown trout fishery for more than a decade, receiving regular consignments of fry until the last release of 10 000 fish in 1983. There is no scope for natural recruitment and surveys undertaken by the IFC suggest that there were no fish left by 1987.

In its heyday Ashwood was the best of the Strahan Lakes. Fish of 0.7-1 kg were common and some attained 2 kg and more. Future liberations are possible, especially if the IFC receives formal requests from local clubs.

The lake is set amid pine-planted coastal dunes and, because of the shifting water table, it has an ability to fill during relatively dry weather and to remain fairly static during periods of moderate rainfall. The quality of the water varies too – from a distinct tea-colour to a reasonable clarity.

At low levels there are wide sandy beaches and extensive wadeable shallows. But at high levels the water backs up to the scrubline and movement along the banks can be quite arduous.

See also *Strahan Lakes*.

ATHENA, LAKE

No trout. See *Fishing in National Parks*, 5.1.

AUGUSTA DAM

See *Augusta, Lake*.

AUGUSTA, LAKE

Tasmaps Meander and Mersey
Drainage Natural – Derwent system (via Ouse system)
Location Nineteen Lagoons

The original Lake Augusta constitutes the western half of the artificial impoundment. But the new lake (as it is shown on most maps) exists for only brief periods – mostly during winter and/or spring. In the drier months the natural lake and outflow stream (the James River) remain much as they were before hydro-electric development, though there is always a body of water directly behind the Augusta Dam.

Augusta trout

Trout stocks

Lake Augusta and the associated section of the James River hold large numbers of naturally-spawned brown trout. Wild rainbows, the progeny of fish released in 1940-41, account for some 20-40% of the total annual harvest but are most likely to be caught by set-rod fishers in the Augusta Dam.

Augusta Dam

The 13m high rockfill/clay-core Augusta Dam was completed in 1953 and serves to retain water during very wet periods when Liawenee Canal (which diverts water from the River Ouse below the dam to Great Lake) is running at capacity. Low levels are maintained at other times, primarily to minimise losses from evaporation. Full supply is about 1141.6 m above sea level but the full drawdown of almost 9 m is to be expected after late spring. The foreshores are usually extensive, barren clay-flats.

Although the storage is unattractive it yields consistent bags of browns and rainbows in the 0.5-1 kg class (and sometimes larger). The theory is that the lower the water the more concentrated the trout.

Bait fishing is popular around the outlet structure, though the weather can get really bleak. A few anglers cast lures among the rocks (on both sides of the lake), and fly fishers sometimes polaroid the flats around the river mouths.

The James River

The deep James River between Augusta Dam and the natural Lake Augusta offers a better class of trout. After heavy rain, when the river has swollen to natural high levels, the water spills out into a number of small basins and lagoons and there is good sport for the wet-fly enthusiast (see *James River*).

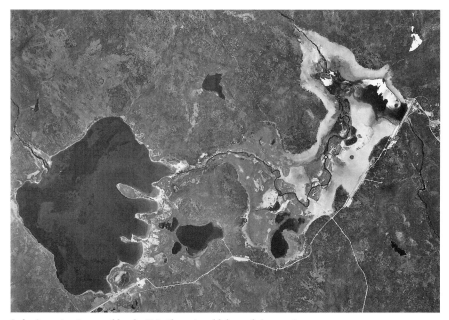

Lake Augusta at normal levels. Note the natural lake and river system.

The natural Lake Augusta

Although Lake Augusta rises to unnaturally high levels at times, it is normally retained within its original banks and the vegetation has been able to survive the brief periods of inundation. It remains an essentially-natural lake and is the second most popular water in the Western Lakes. It is moderately shallow, though most of the body is too deep to wade. While weed mounds grow like coral gardens over much of the lake bed, there are open sand/silt flats along the eastern shore.

The natural lake supports a very large population of wild brown trout and a significant number of wild rainbows. Most fish taken are 0.5-1 kg but there are plenty of others to 1.5 kg or so.

Lake Augusta is one of the very best lure casting waters in the Nineteen Lagoons. All the banks, except the south-eastern beaches, are suitable.

Trolling and spinning from a boat are very productive. Small boats can be launched in front of the levee, though you really need a 4WD.

Good hatches of duns occur throughout the summer. Polaroiding is good along all shorelines, but is best around the inflow of the James River and across the shallow finger-like eastern bays.

See also *Fishing in National Parks*, 5.1

AUSTRALIA TARN

Probably no trout. See *Fishing in National Parks*, 5.3.

AVENUE RIVER

Tasmap   Georges Bay
Drainage Direct to the Scamander River

The Avenue catchment is mostly hilly wet-forest and there are constant summer/autumn flows. The bed is wide and shingly and good pace can be made when wading upstream. Brown trout do well and fish to 0.7 kg are common. Celta fishing and bait casting often result in big bags, especially post-Christmas when levels are low.

There is no convenient 2WD access, and 4WD access is limited to the headwaters.

AYR, LAKE

Tasmap   Mersey
Drainage Forth system (via Douglas Creek)
Location Pelion Plains, Cradle Mountain – Lake St
            Clair National Park

The NTAA noted that 5000 eyed ova were planted in Lake Ayr in 1900 – but trout failed to establish. Today the Douglas Creek system appears to remain trout free, though there have been unsubstantiated claims that the system was recently illegally stocked.

BACK CREEK

Tasmap   South Esk
Drainage Direct to the South Esk River
Location Longford

A small creek typical of those in the South Esk drainage. It cuts through flat open farmland and, while there is often little post-Christmas flow, many pools are deep enough to hold trout throughout the year. Typical fish weigh 0.5-1.2 kg.

BACK RIVER

Tasmap   Derwent
Drainage Direct to the River Derwent
Location Near New Norfolk

A small silty creek which carries plenty of small brown trout.

BACK RIVER

Tasmap   Prosser
Drainage Direct to the Prosser River at Brockley

A tiny overgrown creek with minimal summer/autumn flows. Most locals prefer to fish other streams in the Prosser catchment. There are several semi-permanent backwater lagoons in the farmland near the mouth which give up the odd good trout after springtime floods.

BACKWASH, THE

See *Henty River*.

BADGER RIVER

Tasmaps   Cape Sorell and Pieman
Drainage Direct to the Henty River

A typical West Coast stream – fast, tea-coloured, acidic, overgrown, and full of tiny slow-growing brown trout.

BAGDAD RIVULET

Tasmap   Derwent
Drainage Derwent system (via the Jordan River)

Early Parliamentary reports indicated that brown trout were established in Bagdad Rivulet by 1869. The NTFA recorded the liberation of 2000 rainbow fry in 1917, but this species failed to establish. Today over-clearing of the surrounding land has resulted in the creek becoming a marginal habitat – even for brown trout.

During floods trout invade from the Jordan River – and surprising fish to 1.3 kg can be taken until the first prolonged dry-spell. Bait casting is most practical, though there is room for tight fly casting.

In summer there is no visible flow and the creek becomes a series of isolated shallow pools. In many places pasture extends to the banks and, as there is little cover to protect fish from heat and predators, the trout population dwindles.

BAILLIE, LAKE

Tasmaps Meander and Mersey
Drainage Derwent system (via the Little Pine system)
Location Nineteen Lagoons

A small but popular water ideally suited to fly fishing. Polaroiding from the banks is worthwhile but there are many areas where wading is advantageous. Brown trout of 0.7-1.5 kg are typical.

See also *Fishing in National Parks*, 5.1.

BAKER, LAKE

Probably no trout. See *Youl, Lake*.

BALL, LAKE

Tasmap Mersey
Drainage Derwent system (via the Pine River)
Location Western Lakes

Although contained between steep wooded hills, Lake Ball is surprisingly shallow and much of the shoreline is wadeable. Flat moorland stretches from the eastern end, and open elevated land exists along the western banks.

The lake supports an enormous population of 0.2-0.8 kg brown trout, though fish to 1 kg or so are quite common. When levels are high small lures cast along the edge of the marshy margins and rocky banks commonly induce savage strikes. In the height of summer it is normally best to cast well out – along the edges of the submerged shelves.

In wet periods wet-fly fishing along the flooded undercuts (along the eastern moors) is well worthwhile. On hot post-Christmas days the rises can be phenomenal. Black spinners cause most activity, though duns and beetles are also taken. The small fish are difficult to polaroid but,

Catch-and-release at Lake Baillie

Lake Ball

after a rise, the larger ones can usually be spotted and followed. While it is most comfortable to fish from the open banks, the forested shores should not be ignored.

A quaint slab-and-shingle hut (with a dirt floor and bunks for four) lies sheltered among the pencil pines midway along the northern shore.

See also *Fishing in National Parks*, 5.1.

BALMORAL, LAKE

Tasmap Mersey
Drainage Mersey system (via the Fisher system)
Location Chudleigh Lakes

Brown trout would have invaded Lake Balmoral soon after Lake Mackenzie was stocked in 1895, but there were direct liberations as well (300 Loch Leven strain brown trout in 1898-99, a part-share of 250 Loch Levens and 500 sea trout in 1900-01, and probably other consignments). Today the fishery is maintained entirely by natural recruitment and most trout taken weigh 0.5-1.3 kg.

Lake Balmoral is unique in that the surrounding land displays little obvious fire damage. It is one of the most picturesque of the Chudleigh Lakes.

Most shorelines are rocky and well defined but there are several shallow bays. Spinning and

Don't ignore the overgrown banks – if that's where they are rising you'll find a way to reach them.

polaroiding are the most reliable angling methods. Good rises, though not uncommon, are quite irregular.

See also *Fishing in National Parks*, 5.1.

BANANA LAKE

Tasmap Nive
Drainage Gordon system (via Lake Richmond)
Location 1 km north of Lake Richmond

I once helped electrofish the stream between Lake Richmond and Banana Lake and took brown trout to 1 kg in a section of water above all major physical obstacles. Moreover, there was freshly disturbed gravel at the mouth of the lake – probably redds. My guess is that Banana Lake holds a relatively small population of larger-than-average trout.

Extensive wadeable weedy shallows extend along the southern banks. The rest of the shoreline is steep and densely vegetated. There is only a hint of tannin and conditions for polaroiding look good.

See also *Richmond, Lake* and *Fishing in National Parks*, 5.3.

BANTIC, LAKE

Tasmap Cape Sorell
Drainage Isolated coastal lagoon
Location North of Strahan

The lake was managed as a put-and-take brown trout fishery from 1970 to 1983 (when it was regularly stocked with fry). There were also several minor illegal liberations of brown trout in the mid to late 1980s. I caught a few rainbow trout in 1984-85 and, while the origin of these fish cannot be confirmed, it is likely that they were stock allocated to Lake Bellinger. During the heyday, fish to 2 kg were reasonably common. There are probably no fish left now but future liberations are possible, especially if the IFC receives formal requests from local clubs.

Unlike the other Strahan Lakes the shores were not ravaged during the devastating Zeehan fires of the early 1980s, and the banks remain overgrown with plantation pines and coastal scrub. Dense emergent rushes choke the shores and the crystal water is too deep to wade. A dinghy is essential! Remember though that it is illegal to fish from a boat propelled other than by manal labour.

Access is via the Ashford 2 Road.

See also *Strahan Lakes*.

BAR LAKES SYSTEM

Tasmaps Meander and Mersey
Drainage Natural – Derwent system (via Ouse system)
Location Western Lakes

Generally the lakes on the upper Ouse east of the Julian Lakes hold many more fish than similar looking waters in the rest of the Western Lakes. The stream provides ideal spawning grounds and holding water – and carries large numbers of resident trout. In fact this is one of the few systems on the western Central Plateau where stream fishing is worthwhile. High competition forces young fish to move-on quickly and overpopulate the major instream lakes (including Second Bar Lake, Thompsons Lake, First Bar Lake and Lake Furmage). Trout from these waters are mostly 0.2-0.7 kg.

In side waters where you might expect to find very good fish (such as Deep Lake and Grub Lake) most trout weigh just 0.5-1.5 kg. Usually you will only find worthwhile numbers of 2-4 kg trout in waters which are very isolated – as isolated as Lake Botsford and Little Blue Lagoon in the Nineteen Lagoons.

See also *Fishing in National Parks*, 5.1.

BARRINGTON, LAKE

Tasmap Forth
Drainage River Forth (a major instream impoundment)

Lake Barrington, a picturesque hydro-electric scheme impoundment, was formed in 1969 following the completion of an 84 m high concrete-arch dam at Devils Gate. It has international recognition as a rowing venue but is much underrated as a trout fishery.

Description

The lake floods a steep densely-forested valley. It is long and narrow, and areas of shallow water are confined to the heads of bays with inflowing creeks. In most places forest and thick scrub extend to the waterline – but there are few drowned trees. The water is slightly tea-coloured and faintly turbid. Full supply is almost 122 m above sea level and normal drawdowns do not exceed 5.33 m.

Trout stocks

While brown trout stocks are essentially maintained by natural recruitment, most tributary streams are largely inaccessible to lake spawners. Undoubtedly some successful spawning occurs at the creek mouths but it is likely that most recruits are migrants from Lake Cethana. Largely because of the constraints on natural recruitment, the lake has not overpopulated and most fish taken by anglers weigh 0.6-1.5 kg.

At the instigation of the NWFA, the rearing units and the Salmon Ponds have (since 1984) supplied regular consignments of brown trout fry. The impact of these fish on the overall trout population (if any) has not been formally assessed.

Domestic rainbows were first liberated in 1975 – and there were further releases in the late 1980s. While many of these fish emigrated downstream, significant numbers have been caught by

95

anglers. There appears to be little (if any) natural recruitment and the quantity of fish caught is directly linked to the regularity and success of the stocking programmes. In recent years rainbows (mostly yearlings and two-year-old maidens to about 0.7 kg) have accounted for about 2-15% of the total trout harvest.

Trout liberations

Wild brown trout

YEAR	SIZE	NUMBER
1972	adults	200
1984	fry	4 000
1985	fry / advanced fry	22 000
1986	fry / advanced fry	106 000
1987	fry / advanced fry	82 000
1988	fry / advanced fry	220 000
1989	fry / advanced fry	5 000

Domestic Rainbow Trout

YEAR	SIZE	NUMBER
1975	?	10 000
1986	small fingerlings	25 000
1987	large fingerlings	1 000
1988	extra large fingerlings	2 000
1989	large fingerlings	2 000

Facilities

At Kentish Park there are toilets, barbeques, a kiosk, launching ramps, and cosy campsites.

About 180 ha in the vicinity of Billet Creek (on the eastern shore of Weeks Reach) has been reserved as a State Recreation Area. The feature of the reserve is the international-standard rowing course, complete with comprehensive spectator and visitor facilities. The course is used for rowing, water skiing and canoeing competitions. Facilities include toilets, barbeques, picnic areas, a kiosk, and launching ramps.

Boat access

On the eastern side of the lake, boats can be launched from good ramps at Kentish Park and Weeks Reach. A small launching area with a tight turning circle is located on the western shore at the end of the Lake Barrington Road (which extends from Wilmot).

Shore access

Most of the banks are steep, densely vegetated, and of difficult access – but there are extensive cleared areas at Kentish Park and the south-eastern corner of Weeks Reach. Access to small sections of the western shoreline can be made from

the Lake Barrington Road, and there is limited scope for fishing below the bridge on the Cethana Road.

Lure fishing

Trolling can be very productive. In the 1970s, as the newly flooded vegetation rotted, the cold stratified water on the bottom of the lake became low in oxygen and high in sulphide and was avoided by trout. Today the deep water is suitable for trout, but the fish still tend to concentrate near the top and deep trolling is not usually advantageous. All of the lake surface is productive – but a large area of Weeks Reach is utilized as a rowing venue.

Drift spinning is more practical than spinning from the shores, though shore-based anglers do take fish at Kentish Park and Weeks Reach.

Bait fishing

Set-rod fishing is popular, though blackfish often take baits intended for trout. Cast-and-retrieve fishing with grubs can be extremely rewarding, especially on warm calm evenings when the trout are taking beetles from the surface.

Fly fishing

Feature fishing occurs on warm days in summer and autumn when the trout rise to take gum beetles and other terrestrials. The best results are gained from a boat in the wind lanes. Polaroiding is difficult because of the tea-coloured water.

While limited bank access – and the tendency for wind lanes to remain off shore – result in frustration for the shore-based angler, fair bags are sometimes taken in the evening and at night.

BASIN LAKE

Probably no trout. See *West Coast Range*.

BATHURST HARBOUR

Tasmap   Old River
Drainage   Direct to Port Davey

Sea trout have been reported (but not confirmed) from Port Davey and the Bathurst Narrows. However, the IFC has failed to find resident fish in the tributary streams, and marine scientists have failed to catch slob trout during summer/autumn net surveys.

See also *Fishing in National Parks*, 5.2.

BATTERY DAM

Tasmap Tamar
Drainage Tamar system
Location Beaconsfield

According to NTFA reports the storage was stocked as early as 1959-60 when 4000 brown trout fingerlings were turned out, and each winter from 1970 to 1977 some 25-200 adult browns were released.

The most recent stocking occurred in mid 1992 when 200 rainbow yearlings were trialled.

BEACONSFIELD RESERVOIR

Tasmap Tamar
Drainage Tamar system (via Brandy Creek)

Stocking began as early as 1957 when small hatchery-reared brown trout were released, and peaked from 1964 to 1978 when there were almost annual liberations of 160-1450 adult browns. Several stockings of brown trout fry have occurred in modern times, and 1000 brown trout x Atlantic salmon hybrids were released in 1993. In 1993 the IFC promised annual releases of about 1000 rainbow yearlings.

The banks are mostly gentle but, as they are overgrown with thick scrub, wading is recommended. While there are patches of emergent rushes and thick weed, there is ample open water. Spinning, bait fishing, and fly casting are all worthwhile. The tea-coloured water makes polaroiding impossible but there are fair rises on warm days.

BEATRICE, LAKE

Tasmap Franklin
Drainage King system
Location West Coast Range (east of Mt Sedgwick)

Lake Beatrice holds plenty of naturally-spawned browns and rainbows. The origins of both species can probably be traced to stockings of the King River. Growth is slow and most fish weigh 0.2-0.7 kg.

The tea-coloured water is encircled by steep, densely-forested hills. Access along the banks is difficult but there are plenty of wadeable shoreline shallows.

Spinning is usually very productive and good rises occur on warm days in the post-Christmas period.

Access to the bottom of the outflow stream can be made by boat via Lake Burbury. From

Lake Beatrice

there you face a 1½-2½ hr upstream rock-hop – and this is only possible when levels are low. Small informal tent-sites can be found along the lakeshore – but they are few and far between.

See also *West Coast Range*.

BEATTIES TARN

Tasmap Tyenna
Drainage Derwent system (via the Tyenna system)
Location Mt Field

In 1961 the STLAA recorded that *'this tiny farm* [sic] *has some small trout in it and can be taken on spinners'*. It is unlikely that trout survive today.

BELCHER, LAKE

Tasmap Tyenna
Drainage Derwent system (via the Tyenna system)
Location Mt Field

Lake Belcher is impounded by dramatic towering ranges. Tall heath and ancient pencil pines grow along many banks (especially on the western shore) but there are also some long grassy/mossy esplanades.

As the lake is relatively shallow and crystal clear, most of the bottom is visible from the banks. The sand/gravel shallows close to the shores are hard and open – but loose silt beneath the 'coral gardens' of *Isoetes* prevents you from wading far out.

Spin fishing is productive when the lake is full. Wading is essential as many banks are overgrown and the open foreshores are likely to be wet and boggy. When levels are low, lures tend to snag in the weeds.

Polaroiding is productive whenever the shores are not frozen or snowed-over, but is especially good during low levels in summer and autumn.

Lakes Belcher (foreground) and Belton

Although fish can be spotted from the banks, wading is often advantageous. Tailing fish and rises are not features.

The trout population is surprisingly large yet fish from 1-1.5 kg are common and others attain 2 kg and more.

A hut is located beside the walking track about ¼ hr walk before the lake. It is a modest two-bunk shelter with a coal-fired pot-belly stove. Comfortable informal campsites can be found at the lakeside.

See also *Fishing in National Parks* 5.5.

BELLINGER, LAKE

Tasmap Cape Sorell
Drainage Isolated coastal lagoon
Location North of Strahan

Lake Bellinger was first stocked in 1966 when 10 000 rainbow fry were released. In early 1972 a further 230 rainbows were electrofished from Halls Creek and transported to the lake. Subsequent releases of hatchery-reared fry occurred from 1973-1975. The lake was not well patronised but the NWFA reported that fish of 5-6 lb were taken.

In 1975 a landslip occurred on the high ground rising between Lake Bellinger and Lake Ashwood. Lake Bellinger drained to a puddle,

and there was a corresponding rise in the level of Lake Ashwood. Only a few fish were salvaged and the IFC theorised that most had been washed via an underground 'tunnel' to Lake Ashwood

Although Lake Bellinger failed to recover, it was listed on official stocking summaries for 1981 and 1982. The ultimate fate of these fish is unknown, though some may have been released at Lake Bantic.

See also *Strahan Lakes*.

BELLS LAGOON

Tasmap Lake Sorell
Drainage Isolated
Location North-west of Tunbridge

This water is reputed to have produced good fish, but since the early 1980s it has been intermittent and has not been a prospect for further trout liberations.

BELTON, LAKE

Tasmap Tyenna
Drainage Derwent system (via the Tyenna system)
Location Mt Field

Belton lies in the shadow of Tyenna Peak, in a hollow on the hillside some 300 m above Lake

Belton browns

Belcher. While most approaches are steep and overgrown with forest undergrowth, flat open moorland extends from the southern, south-western and north-western shores – and in these areas there is ample scope for fishing from the banks. There are also stretches along the deeper banks where it is possible to sneak out, knee to thigh deep, beyond the fringes of the overhanging bushes.

The trout (all browns) are mostly from 0.5-0.7 kg, though there are others in excess of 1 kg.

Many good bags are taken on lures. The rises are irregular but fish can be easily polaroided along the edges.

See also *Fishing in National Parks*, 5.5.

BEN LOMOND RIVULET

Tasmaps South Esk and St Pauls
Drainage Direct to the South Esk River

According to Parliamentary reports this stream was stocked as early as 1878-79, though by this time trout probably had already invaded from the South Esk. Today wild brown to 1 kg are common.

In 1955-56 some 1700 rainbow yearlings were liberated and, although David Scholes wrote in *The Way of an Angler* (1963) that rainbows were 'still' being caught, the species failed to establish.

BIG CREEK

Tasmaps Table Cape and Hellyer
Drainage Direct to the Inglis River

Like other waters in the Inglis system, Big Creek has no noticeable tannin but remains turbid even during periods of low to moderate flow.

The surrounding land is a blend of farmland and plantations, and the banks are overgrown and of difficult access. However, the water is very shallow and at normal levels it is possible to wade through the middle of most pools and runs.

The bed is essentially firm but there are significant deposits of silt and most pools are littered with logs and debris.

The creek becomes impossibly overgrown in the vicinity of Upper Mt Hicks.

There are countless brown trout, most of which weigh less than 0.2 kg.

In 1912 the NTFA recorded liberations of rainbow trout – but this species failed to establish.

Although Celta fishing and bait casting are most efficient, there is room for tight fly casting. When levels are low limit bags are to be expected.

Tributaries (such as Dowlings Creek) hold lots of trout but are very small and difficult to fish.

BIG EEL CREEK

See *Nelson Bay River*.

BIG JIM, LAKE

See *London Lakes*.

BIG LAGOON, THE

Tasmap D'Entrecasteaux
Drainage Isolated coastal lagoon
Location Bruny Island (north-east of the isthmus)

Description

The dunes impounding the lagoon are covered with dense heath, but at normal levels an open sand/silt esplanade extends around the shoreline.

The water is shallow and the south-western end (about one third of the total area) often dries up. While much of the northern end is choked with emergent rushes and strapweed, an open wave-worn channel runs along the shore. South-east of the weedbed there are extensive open wadeable flats. The only deep channel runs down the middle of the lake along the outer edge of the weedbed. The water is tea coloured and slightly brackish.

Trout stocks

There are no spawning grounds and trout stocks can only be maintained through artificial stocking. According to NTFA reports stocking may have occurred as early as 1956 (when 50 000 brown trout fry were turned out at 'Bruny Island Lagoon'). Stocking recommenced in 1983, but there is no clear policy regarding future liberations.

The fish grow well and, although sometimes infested with worms (see *Curries River Dam*), they can attain 3 kg and more.

Trout liberations (since 1983)

Wild brown trout

YEAR	SIZE	NUMBER
1983	fry	10 000
1984	fry	20 000
1986	small fingerlings	3 500

Domestic rainbow trout

YEAR	SIZE	NUMBER
1986	large fingerlings	3 500

Brown trout x Atlantic salmon hybrids

YEAR	SIZE	NUMBER
1993	advanced fry	3 000

Access

The access track leaves the Bruny Island Main Road about 3 km north of the isthmus, where it is signposted as the route to Moorina Bay and Cape Queen Elizabeth. It was formerly a 4WD track but is now reserved for foot traffic. The walk takes about 20-30 minutes each way.

The fishing

There is plenty of scope for both spinning and fly casting. The best times to fish are early morning and late evening. Brown trout can often be seen moving in the channel between the weeds and the shore – but they avoid shallow water during hot summer weather. Modest hatches of mudeyes occur from early summer to early autumn.

BIG WATERHOUSE LAKE

Tasmap   Cape Portland
Drainage   Coastal lagoon

A large coastal lagoon situated between two fine trout fisheries, Big Waterhouse appears to be full of promise. Yet in over 60 years of trout fishery management it has failed to give even remotely adequate returns.

Description

The storage is encircled by exposed dunes, coastal scrub, and grassy flats. Much of the lake is choked with weed but there is ample open water beyond the shoreline shallows. Fishing from a dinghy is most practical.

As the lake is sometimes open to the sea (via Lake Creek) and is quite saline, it supports a variety of estuarine species (including mullet and long-finned eels).

History of trout stocks and angling

Big Waterhouse Lake was first stocked in 1931 (when 20 000 brown trout fry were liberated). Originally it was intended that it be maintained as a brown trout water but by the mid 1930s there had been releases of rainbow trout.

The lake has been stocked regularly throughout its history as a trout water. In fact, in terms of fish per unit of surface area, the amount of stocking has been quite extraordinary. Yet the early reports of the NTFA chronicle disappointment after disappointment – there were very few years when branch members were able to catch any trout at all. The modern history is no better. Between 1970 and 1974 about 1 000 000 brown trout fry and nearly 1000 adults were liberated yet very few were ever taken by anglers. From the late 1970s to the mid 1980s there were several more significant (but poorly documented) releases, and there was continued optimism from the local angling club. In the *Tasmanian Angling Report* for 1981 is was predicted that 'in a few years time Big Waterhouse will fish as well or better than Blackmans'. But the IFC test netted the lagoon in 1985 and could not locate any trout at all.

In 1990 the NTFA lobbied the IFC to trial Atlantic salmon. Despite the previous history of the lake, and the fact that salmon would be even more inclined than brown trout to run to the sea, the experiment went ahead. Between August and October 1990 more than 51 000 Atlantic salmon fingerlings (most of which weighed 25-70 g) were released. These fish were runts and late-smolters and were donated by Saltas. In July 1991 there was a major test-netting exercise and just five salmon were caught. The growth rate had been good (the fish weighed 1-1.5 kg) but the surviving population was extremely small. By

1993 the Scottsdale club conceded that few salmon had been seen or caught by anglers.

The release of 20 000 rainbow trout yearlings in 1993 can be written-off as a waste of time.

BILL, LAKE

No Trout. See *Fishing in National Parks*, 5.1.

BINNEY, LAKE

Tasmaps Nive and Shannon
Drainage Derwent system
Location Central Highlands (north-east of Tarraleah)

Binney is a worthwhile water, though it is not as popular as Bronte Lagoon and Bradys Lake. It is given comprehensive coverage in the book Trout Guide *(Rob Sloane and Greg French, 1991).*

Description

Lake Binney, Bradys Lake and Tungatinah Lagoon are the 'Bradys Chain' of hydro-electric impoundments. Binney receives water from Bradys via a short canal and, in turn, is linked via another short canal to Tungatinah. All three waters have a full supply level of 651.2 m above sea level and a normal operating range of about 4.6 m. The water is normally clear but wave action sometimes causes turbidity along exposed margins.

The lake is impounded by rolling forested hills and the shorelines are mostly steep.

Trout stocks

Trout stocks are maintained by natural recruitment, the main spawning ground being located beyond Bradys Lake. Fish of 0.5-1 kg are typical and rainbows account for up to 10% of the annual harvest. Slightly bigger fish are taken at Tungatinah.

History

See *Bradys Lake*.

Facilities

The recommended boat launching area is on the western shore just south of the dam. Small boats can pass freely through the canals to Bradys and Tungatinah.

Informal camping is permitted; the most popular areas being the north-western corner from the dam wall to the boat ramp, and the flat near the Binney-Tungatinah canal.

Fishing

Early season wet-fly fishing is best along the shallow Island Shore (just south of the canal outlet). This area is also the best for summer polaroiding. Any sheltered shore can provide excellent dry fly fishing when beetles fall on hot days.

Drift spinning is often more effective than trolling. Take your boat along the shores and cast towards the banks.

The dam offers very worthwhile sport for shore-based spin fishers, especially in rough weather.

The inflows and outflows of the canals are the most reliable bait fishing spots.

BISCHOFF RESERVOIR

Tasmap Hellyer
Drainage Arthur system
Location Near Waratah

Description

Bischoff Reservoir is a large dam, apparently constructed in the early 1900s. It is encircled by dense wet-forest and is full of emergent tree trunks. The banks are deepish clay affairs but you can usually wade out beyond most overhanging scrub. Though not obviously tea-coloured, the water is always moderately turbid.

Trout stocks

The origin of the trout is difficult to trace, a situation compounded by a history of confusing nomenclature. To locals the *'Magnet Dam'* is the Waratah Reservoir, but officially it is a small water some 6 km east of Waratah. In IFC records it seems that *'McKays Dam'* is a synonym for the Bischoff Reservoir. Also, the Bischoff and Waratah reservoirs are often referred to as the *'Waratah Dams'* or the *'Magnet Dams'*.

According to NTFA records, in 1910 the *'Magnet Mine Dam'* was stocked with almost 800 Loch Leven strain brown trout fry and 1500 rainbow trout fry. Another report noted the release of 1000 rainbow fry at *'Magnet'* in 1918 – and there were releases of brown trout fry at *'Waratah'* in the 1920s. In modern times the record is no less obscure.

Trout liberations (since 1960)

Wild brown trout

PLACE	YEAR	SIZE	NUMBER
Waratah dam	1970	fry	10 000
Magnet dam	1970	fry	10 000
Waratah Dams	1972	fry	15 000
Magnet Dams	1977	adults	250

Rainbow trout

PLACE	YEAR	SIZE	NUMBER
Waratah Dams	1962	fry	22 500
McKays dam	1975	fry	10 000
McKays Dam	1980	fry	10 000
McKays Dam	1981	fry	10 000
McKays Dam	1982	fry	10 000
Waratah Dams	1991	yearlings	1 000

Note: the IFC has promised annual liberations of 500-1000 rainbow fingerlings at the 'Waratah Dams'.

Natural overpopulation is a problem. But while the water teems with 0.2-0.7 kg fish, some attain 1 kg and more.

Anecdotal evidence suggests that rainbows have been spawning successfully since at least the 1960s – and natural recruitment was confirmed by the IFC in 1991.

Prior to the 1991 liberations rainbows accounted for about 10-15% of the annual harvest.

The fishing

Feature fly fishing occurs on warm summer/autumn days when there are spectacular rises to mayflies, damselflies and terrestrials. There is also year-round sport for lure casters and bait enthusiasts.

BLACK RIVER

Tasmaps Circular Head and Arthur River
Drainage Direct to Bass Strait

According to early Parliamentary reports the Black River was stocked with brown trout as early as 1881. Wild populations soon established.

Sea trout

While there can be worthwhile runs of sea trout in August, the best sport usually occurs from late September to November.

At high tide the estuary backs up to the forested banks but at low tide it is simply a small stream cutting through a wide sand flat.

The stream

Above the tidal influence the Black River is small, fast and dark with tannin. The lower section flows through dense bushland, though there is some pasture above the Mawbanna Road.

There are plenty of small slow-growing brown trout to about 0.3 kg. The water is best suited to Celta fishing and bait casting, and fishes well when levels are low. Wading is essential.

BLACK BOBS RIVULET

Tasmap Shannon
Drainage Derwent system (via Lake Catagunya)

A small, very shallow, shingle-bottomed fastwater. It holds plenty of very small brown trout and, when levels are low, Celta fishing and bait casting usually result in big bags.

BLACK SUGARLOAF CREEK

Tasmap Tamar
Drainage Direct to the Meander River

A small creek which flows through pasture and has some deep sluggish pools. The lowest reaches support worthwhile numbers of 0.3-0.6 kg brown trout. Bigger fish, some in excess of 1 kg, are taken in the small flood plains near the confluence with Four Springs Creek.

BLACKBURN CREEK

Tasmap Shannon
Drainage Derwent system (via the Shannon River)

A small stone-bottomed creek which generally flows only when water is being drained from Lagoon of Islands. It is not recognised as a worthwhile fishery.

BLACKFISH CREEK

Tasmap Huon
Drainage Direct to the Huon estuary

A tiny stream which supports a lot of fat brown trout to 0.5 kg.

BLACKHOUSE TARN

Tasmap Tyenna
Drainage Derwent system (via the Broad system)
Location Mt Field

A clearwater lake which contains a few better-than-average trout. The fishing is always very tough.

See also *Fishing in National Parks*, 5.5.

BLACKMAN RIVER

Tasmap Lake Sorell
Drainage South Esk system (via the Macquarie River)

The Blackman River flows through cleared paddocks and most banks are open and grassy.

During prolonged dry weather some stretches dry up but there are many large permanent weedy pools.

According to early Parliamentary reports the river was stocked as early as 1876, though by this time brown trout would already have invaded from the Macquarie. Today stocks are maintained by natural recruitment. Most fish weigh 0.3-0.6 kg and some attain 1.5 kg.

The fishing is not as remarkable as that in the Macquarie – there are no significant backwaters or flood basins, and the rises are relatively mediocre. However, dedicated locals often take worthwhile bags.

The best fishing is found between the confluence with the Macquarie and the foot of the Great Western Tiers. In Mike Howes Marsh (adjacent to the Interlaken Road) the stream has been channelised and offers poor sport.

The Oatlands water supply dams

At the head of the Blackman River, about ½-¾ hr walk south of the Table Mountain Road, are two water supply dams.

The lower dam

The lower dam is a 13 m high concrete structure which was completed in 1938 to impound water for domestic use in Oatlands. Most of the lakeshore is fairly steep and forested but, as there is no understorey, there is ample casting space.

At the inflow there are significant shallow weedy margins.

The water is usually slightly murky.

Fly fishing is best after September. If levels are reasonably high in October/November fish may be found foraging in the shallows. There are fair mudeye hatches in summer and good beetle falls in autumn.

Spinning from the steep banks can be productive at any time of the season.

The upper dam

The upper dam, a long 7 m high earthfill structure, was completed in 1968. It floods a small alpine moor and serves to bolster the Oatlands water supply.

The banks are open and grassy (though there are stands of trees nearby) and much of the water is shallow and weedy.

Most trout weigh 1-2 kg and others to 3 kg are reported from time to time.

Fish move freely in the marshes in October and November, and good evening rises occur on balmy evenings in summer and autumn. The water is often slightly turbid but polaroiding

Tailing trout at the upper Blackman dam

along the edges is always a good fall-back.

There is scope for spinning from the dam wall.

BLACKMANS LAGOON

Tasmap Cape Portland
Drainage Coastal lagoon

Like other lakes in the Waterhouse dunes area, Blackmans is surrounded by coastal heath, marram grass, and some pasture. The fringes of the lagoon are shallow and, for those without a boat, wading is essential. While the fishing is slow, anyone prepared to work hard can expect to catch trophy trout.

Trout stocks

There is no scope for natural recruitment and the average size of the fish, the ratio of species caught, and the quality of the fish mirrors the nature of the stocking regimes.

Trout of 1.5-2 kg are common but fish which survive 4 years or more are likely to reach the optimum size of 3-5 kg.

History

In 1955 the NTFA recorded the first-ever liberations of trout (brown trout fry) at Blackmans Lagoon – and by 1960 anglers were taking fish to 8 lb. By 1960 anglers were able to drive to the shore, resulting in more fishing pressure.

Early liberations seem to have comprised brown trout only. However, the commercial fish farm which opened at Bridport in 1964 provided a convenient supply of domestic rainbow trout, and these fish dominated in the stocking programs from 1965 to the 1970s.

In 1970-71 some 8000 brook trout yearlings were released, but from 1970 to the mid 1980s the fishery was maintained primarily through releases of brown trout fry (5000 - 220 000 per year).

Since 1986 wild brown trout, domestic rainbows, and brown trout x Atlantic salmon hybrids have been turned out.

Throughout the history of the fishery the quality of the sport has remained fairly stable – Blackmans has always been renowned as a producer of large well-conditioned trout.

Trout liberations (since 1985)

Wild brown trout

YEAR	SIZE	NUMBER
1985	small fingerlings	50 000
"	fry and advanced fry	140 000
1986	fry and advanced fry	135 000
1987	fry and advanced fry	80 000
1988	fry	70 000
1989	fry	50 000
1990	fry and advanced fry	24 000
1991	yearlings	2 000
"	yearlings (T)	2 000

(T) = Triploid stock

Domestic rainbow trout

YEAR	SIZE	NUMBER
1986	small fingerlings	5 000
1989	large fingerlings	2 000
1990	small fingerlings	18 000
1992	yearlings	1 000
"	advanced fry	1 500

Note: in 1993 the IFC promised annual releases of 1000 yearling rainbows.

Brown trout x Atlantic salmon hybrids

YEAR	SIZE	NUMBER
1993	advanced fry	2 000

The rearing unit

The Scottsdale branch of the NTFA has operated a trout rearing unit at Kamona since the mid

Blackmans trophy (courtesy Ashley Hallam)

1970s and continues to ongrow significant numbers of fry for release into the Waterhouse Lakes.

Water levels

Concerns about the long-term survival of the lake have been voiced since the earliest days of the fishery. In 1962 the NTFA noted that the lagoon was just *'one third of five years ago because of encroaching sands'*, and as early as 1963 there was a proposal to divert Sheepwash Creek (which feeds Big Waterhouse Lake) into Blackmans.

The drought of the early 1980s renewed previous concerns and by 1985, during *'the lowest ever levels'*, the Scottsdale branch of the NTFA had completed the *'excavation of ditches for the collection and channelling of water into Blackmans Lagoon'*.

The lake filled in the mid to late 1980s and has remained high ever since. As the drains channel run-off from nearby fertilized pasture, the water has accumulated dangerously-high quantities of nutrients and in recent years there have been unprecedented algal blooms. The water also swamped once-grassy banks and there is now no convenient access for shore-based spin fishers.

Fly fishing

Blackmans fishes well from late September to December. Peak sport occurs from about 1 hr before first light until dawn, and (to a slightly lesser degree) late in the evening – when brown trout swirl and tail in weedy shallows. Small wets, such as fur flies, are ideal.

During hot weather the fish tend to avoid the warm algae-rich shallows and fishing becomes difficult. Rises are not a feature, though fair hatches of mudeyes occur in the deeper water in mid to late summer.

Late in the season, when the water cools, fish re-enter the shallows, albeit in fewer numbers.

Lure fishing

There is little scope for spinning from the banks. Drift spinning and row-trolling with shallow-running lures are recommended. As with fly fishing, peak sport occurs from late September to December.

Bait fishing

Cast-and-retrieve fishing is effective for tailers – try using a small wattle grub or large cockroach.

Set-rod fishing is inappropriate in the marshes but can be quite effective when practised from a dinghy.

BLUE LAKE

Tasmap   Forester
Drainage   Boobyalla system

Blue Lake is a drowned tin-quarry set in quartzite country at the foot of Mount Cameron. The surrounding land was once a stark moonscape, though significant regeneration has occurred in modern times.

The water is a striking milky turquoise, reminiscent of glacier melt, and does not appear to be well suited to trout. The STLAA recorded that *'Blue Lagoon (Mt Cameron)'* was stocked with 7000 brown trout fry in 1957, and the IFC documented the distribution of 130 000 brown trout fry to the *'BMI Dams at South Mt Cameron'* in 1974.

No formal assessment of the fishery at Blue Lake was ever undertaken. I doubt that trout exist there today.

BLUE PEAKS LAKES

Tasmap   Mersey
Drainage   Mersey system (via the Fisher system)
Location   Chudleigh Lakes

The Blue Peaks Lakes are among the most popular of Tasmania's wilderness trout fisheries.

Cruising fish at Blue Peaks

They lie between Blue Peaks and Turrana Heights and are accessed via a recognised walking track. Although vegetation on the surrounding hills has been devastated by wildfire, the moors encircling the lake shores remain healthy. The water is typically gin clear.

Naturally-spawned brown trout of 0.5-1.5 kg dominate in most lakes, though specimens to 2 kg are quite common. Several of the small lakes which remain isolated in all but the wettest months contain better-than-average trout of 2-3 kg. Domestic rainbows were illegally released in the mid 1980s (and perhaps recently as well) but they did not provide significant sport.

All of the main waters are suited to most traditional angling methods. Duns, spinners and terrestrials can cause good rises along any shore, and most banks are suited to polaroiding. Each lake has special features but none should be fished to the exclusion of any other.

Blue Peak Lake

This, the northernmost water (grid ref. 475 802), is one of the best early season destinations. When levels are high trout can be found foraging over the flats along the western shore. Fish in the tussocks, along the flooded banks, and in the mouths of the inflowing gutters. In summer, fish can be polaroided from the banks and in the wadeable shallows.

Middle Lake

As the name suggests, Middle Lake (grid ref. 481 800) lies between Blue Peak Lake and the main lake (Little Throne Lake). It is the most consistently-deep of the big lakes and is an exceptional spinning water. There are shallow sandy bays along the western shore in which evening tailers can be found throughout the year. These bays also offer very good wade polaroiding.

Little Throne Lake

This, the biggest lake, offers some of the best mayfly hatches in the Blue Peaks area. Search along the deep channels and necks.

The western shoreline recedes markedly in summer and autumn – but after heavy rain it floods out into significant gutters and basins, providing good wet-fly fishing.

Harry Lees Lakes

Harry Lees Lakes (grid refs. 460 789 and 455 802) are the two narrow waters west of Blue Peak Lake. They are well suited to spinning and bank polaroiding.

Shark Hole

The Shark Hole (grid ref. 495 784) lies at the foot of the eastern slope of Little Throne. It is deep and is well suited to spinning and bank polaroiding. Recruitment is modest and fish in excess of 2 kg are relatively common.

Grassy Lake

Grassy Lake (grid ref. 496 791) is the water which accepts the outflow from all the other Blue Peaks Lakes.

Excellent hatches occur near the inflow and outflow. The northern shore is very shallow and offers good wade polaroiding. Tailing fish can sometimes be found early in the morning and late in the evening.

See also *Fishing in National Parks*, 5.1.

BLUFF RIVER

Tasmap   Prosser
Drainage   Direct to the Prosser River

The fishable (lower to mid) reaches wind through poorly-developed farmland. Negligible flows can be expected during prolonged dry weather, but there are many deep silt-bottomed pools. As most banks are overgrown with scrub, set-rod fishing and bait casting are most practical. Typical trout weigh 0.5-1 kg.

BLYTHE RIVER

Tasmap   Hellyer
Drainage   Direct to Bass Strait

The best runs of sea trout occur from early September to November – during the galaxia migrations. The whole of the estuary is worthwhile but the hot spot is where baitfish bottleneck below the weir (some 3 km from the mouth).

The 10 km stretch of river from the weir to Camena flows through a steep densely-forested valley. It is of difficult access, and is rarely fished.

Near Camena the river is flanked by pasture and, although most banks are overgrown with native scrub and trees, there is some scope for productive angling. The long relatively-shallow broadwaters have considerable flow, even in the driest months. The water is tinged with tannin and becomes murky after heavy rain. The bottom is boggy in places and littered with submerged logs – and in many areas there is significant weed growth. Usually it is most practical to fish from the small stretches of cleared bank, but at times (awkward) wading is essential. Celta fishing and bait casting are most popular. Fly fishing is best from early summer to late autumn when levels are low and fish can be seen rising. Trout to 0.8 kg are reasonably common.

In the forested gorge which extends for some 6 km above the Camena district, the water usually flows underground and is of no interest to anglers.

Above the South Riana Road the river becomes a series of short steep rapids and boulder-strewn pools. There is some scope for wading but there is limited access along the steep forested banks. The water is slightly tea-coloured, slightly turbid, and full of very small brown trout. When levels are low Celta fishers commonly take big bags.

The headwaters are shallow and overgrown but also contain numerous tiny fish.

According to early NTFA reports rainbows were released in the *'Upper Blythe'* in 1913 – but this species failed to establish.

BOOBYALLA RIVER

Tasmaps Cape Portland and Forester
Drainage Direct to the Ringarooma estuary

A tea-coloured fastwater.

The lower to mid reaches are poorly serviced by roads and are rarely fished.

According to NTFA reports 4000 brown trout fry were placed above the falls in 1932. The over-grown headwaters now contain many small brown trout but are rarely fished.

BOTSFORD, LAKE

Tasmap Meander
Drainage Derwent system (via the Little Pine system)
Location Nineteen Lagoons

Lake Botsford has a very poor connection to Lake Baillie and originally contained few (if any) trout. It was first stocked in 1971 when the IFC released 300 yearling-plus brown trout and 200 yearling-plus rainbow trout (all of which were salvaged from Liawenee Canal). By 1974 anglers were taking browns up to 2.5 kg and rainbows up to 3.5 kg. Natural spawning is not possible and, because of the good returns, the IFC was able to justify continued stocking. From 1974 until present Lake Botsford has received almost annual liberations of (usually 200) 0.7-1.5 kg wild brown trout. There have also been occasional releases of rainbow trout.

Lake Botsford has a well-defined rocky perimeter but is very shallow. At normal levels almost all of the open sand/silt bed is wadeable. Despite the apparently barren nature of the lake, the trout do well. Isopods, small silt-dwelling crustaceans,

constitute the bulk of the trout's diet and, no doubt, are responsible for the good growth and condition of the fish.

During the early months of the season wet-fly fishing and spinning can be worthwhile. At this time of the year many of the fish taken are 'new transfers' – brown trout of unexceptional size and condition.

In summer and autumn the lure fishing becomes increasingly difficult. But the feature fishing, the wade polaroiding, is at its best. Mayfly hatches are poor and there is no significant marsh fishing. Bait fishing has been prohibited since 1979.

Catch-and-release

The IFC has found that adult trout released at Lake Botsford (in winter) do not gain significant weight until Christmas. But from Christmas to the end of the season growth is dramatic. Fish which survive a full year are likely to be 2 kg or so. Those which survive 2 years may grow to 3 kg. And any which last longer may attain the optimum size of 3.5-5 kg!

In the 1970s only 40-50% of the new transfers were taken in the first year. Today some 80% are harvested before the first Christmas – before they have been able to gain any weight.

Lake Botsford is of little special value if it is managed to produce scrappy Great Lake browns for just 5 months of the season – there are many waters nearby with ample stocks of naturally-spawned small fish. However, as a producer of large strong trout it is one of the best wade polaroiding waters in the State. The bottom line is that in order to maintain Lake Botsford (and similar waters) as a high-profile special fishery anglers must exercise restraint. Catch as many as you can – but never kill more than two. Better still, release *all* of your catch!

Trout liberations (since 1985)
Wild brown trout

YEAR	SIZE	NUMBER
1985	adults	300
1986	adults	150
1987	adults	400
1988	fingerlings-adults	125
"	adults	200
1989	adults	200
1990	adults	200
1991	adults	200
"	yearlings	600
1992	adults (T)	300
1993	adults	200

(T) = triploids

Rainbow trout

YEAR	SIZE	NUMBER
1985	yearlings (T)	350
1986	fingerlings (T)	500
"	advanced fry (T)	10 000
1988	fingerlings-adults	5

(T) = triploids

See also *Fishing in National Parks*, 5.1.

BOUNDARY LAGOON

Intermittent. Not recognised as a trout fishery.

BOWLERS LAGOON

Reputed not to contain trout.

BRADYS LAKE

Tasmaps Nive and Shannon
Drainage Derwent system
Location Central Highlands (north-east of Tarraleah)

Bradys Lake is one of the most worthwhile trout fisheries in the Tarraleah district, though it is overshadowed by its widely acclaimed neighbour Bronte Lagoon. It is discussed in detail in the book Trout Guide *(Rob Sloane and Greg French, 1991). A summary only is given here.*

Bradys Lake (photo by Rob Sloane)

Description

Bradys Lake is a hydro-electric storage impounded by a 20.42 m high rockfill dam. It lies at the head of a three-lake chain (Bradys-Binney Tungatinah). Inflows are received from Bronte Lagoon (via Woodwards Canal) and from Dee Lagoon (via the Dee Tunnel). Water discharges into Lake Binney. Full supply is 651.2 m above sea level and the normal operating range is 4.6 m. The lake is surrounded by wooded hills and the shoreline is relatively steep and rocky.

Trout stocks

Bradys is a wild trout fishery maintained by natural spawning. The main source of recruitment is from the gravel beds in the Whitewater. Brown trout dominate, though rainbows account for about 20% of the annual harvest.

Typical trout weigh 0.5-1 kg and others to 2 kg are taken every now and then. There are also some exceptional brown trout in excess of 3 kg – usually fish which feed heavily on redfin perch.

History

The original Bradys Marsh was an extensive swampland which supported a small wild population of brown trout. In 1950, after the start of work on Bradys Dam and the partial flooding of the marsh, the wild stock was supplemented by the addition of some 9000 hatchery-reared yearling browns. In order to assess the ability of new lakes to self-recruit, no further stocking of the Bradys chain was undertaken.

In 1953, upon completion of the dams, canals and diversions, the Bradys chain of lakes was opened to fishing. Well conditioned brown trout were caught in the first angling season. Indeed, angling records indicate that all of the lakes contained big fish (some in excess of 8 lb). During the next few seasons the average size of trout taken rose to about 6 lb.

By 1956 rainbow trout were evident in the system. It seems that these fish were downstream migrants from Bronte and Dee lagoons. Like the brown trout before them they soon established self-supporting stocks.

Redfin perch passed from Dee Lagoon and rapidly proliferated.

The Whitewater between Woodwards canal

and Bradys Lake developed as a natural spawning ground and there was an explosion of trout stocks. By 1956 there had been a noticeable decline in the average weight of trout taken. In 1958 the STLAA recorded that the trout in Bradys were generally small and in poor condition and by 1962 *'the average size was little more than one pound'*.

The IFC acknowledged that the trout had *'become too numerous and small'* and so at the beginning of the 1962-63 season, *'In the hope of improving the stocks by encouraging heavier exploitation'*, Lake Binney and Tungatinah Lagoon were opened to bait fishing. Similarly, at the beginning of the 1964-65 season the 'artificial lures only' was lifted from Bradys.

Fly fishing

The grassy shore in front of the shacks can produce great sport when the lake first rises after prolonged low levels – the trout gorge on drowned corby grubs.

In warm easterly weather the Bradys Sugarloaf Shore is well worth a look – the fish rise to take gum beetles and aquatics.

The snowflake caddis hatch in the Whitewater is worth investigating in early December if there are good flows.

For those with a boat there is notable wind lane fishing, especially for early-morning midging rainbows.

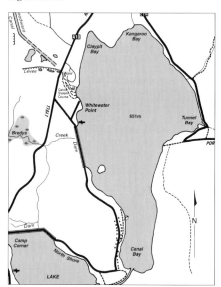

BRADYS LAKE

While the water is crystal, the small size of most fish and the deep water make polaroiding relatively difficult.

Lure fishing

Virtually any shore is suitable for lure casting – but there are several hot spots.

Tunnel Bay and the mouth of the Whitewater are particularly good when trout are congregating before spawning. The best months are August to October for rainbows and April for browns.

The inflows are also good in November and December when the trout feed heavily on redfin perch, and in the height of summer when fish are attracted to cool oxygenated water.

Trolling and drift spinning in the inflowing currents are effective too, though it can be worthwhile deep-trolling in the body of the lake when the traditional areas fail.

Bait fishing

The hot spots are around the two inflows, though Claypit Bay and Kangaroo Bay are also popular. Worms and grubs are favoured – and please remember that redfin perch are a prohibited bait. Set-rod fishing at night is most popular but cast-and-retrieve methods tend to be more productive

Special regulations

The Whitewater (between the radial gates and Bradys Lake) and the mouth of the Dee Tunnel (as defined by two white posts) do not open to fishing until the Saturday nearest 1 November, and close a month early on the Sunday nearest 31 March.

Facilities

There are no formal camping areas. The popular informal sites are found on the north side of the Whitewater, at Tunnel Bay, at Kangaroo Bay, and at Claypit Bay.

The recommended boat launching ramp is at Whitewater Point.

BRANDY POND

(also known as Brandy Creek Dam)

Tasmap   Tamar
Drainage Tamar system (via Brandy Creek)
Location West of Beaconsfield

A very small dark-water surrounded by bushland and thick scrub. Most banks are overgrown and dense weed extends along much of the shoreline, so convenient shore-based angling is limited to the dam wall.

The trout are mostly the result of artificial stocking and the optimum size is about 1 kg.

From 1979 to 1984 the pond received almost annual consignments of 10 000-25 000 brown trout fry. In 1992 about 150 yearling rainbows were turned out, and in 1993 there was a release of 150 brown trout x Atlantic salmon hybrids (advanced fry).

Set-rod fishing is most popular. Better sport can be found nearby at the Beaconsfield Reservoir.

BREAK O'DAY RIVER

Tasmaps St Patricks and Break O'Day
Drainage Direct to the South Esk River

The Break O'Day River is an integral part of Tasmanian fly fishing lore – a fact due in no small part to having featured strongly in the works of David Scholes. The fishing can be frustrating but if you strike it on a red-letter day it will live in your memory.

Description

The cream of the fishing is found in the lower two thirds of the river (from the confluence with the South Esk to Cullenswood) where there is a series of long sluggish broadwaters. These pools are lined with emergent rushes and support lush weedbeds. They are too deep to wade but, with the exception of a few short stretches of willows, there is open access along the banks. During floods the water spills out into the paddocks filling depressions and ditches.

Above Cullenswood there is a system of narrow deep creeks. Fish live here too but this area does not provide feature sport.

While the water can become quite murky after heavy rain, it clears appreciably in settled conditions.

Trout stocks

The quality and quantity of the trout has remained fairly static for decades. In 1936 the NTFA reported that :

'Although a much smaller stream than the South Esk, the average size would be higher, and an average of 1½ lbs for a day's catch would not be out of the way'.

Today trout taken by anglers still average 0.5-0.7 kg and others to 2 kg are reported from time to time.

Catch rates vary enormously according to conditions. Casual anglers are lucky to catch one or two fish per day. But devoted locals who fish only during ideal conditions often fare exceptionally well.

The fishing

Spinning and bait casting are worthwhile – but the water is most valued as a fly venue.

Break O'Day River (photo by Rob Sloane)

After heavy rains in August and September it can be worthwhile wet-fly fishing along the flooded edges and in the adjacent ditches and backwaters. At this time of the year the trout tend to feed on worms, grubs, frogs and other forage items.

Feature fishing occurs when the fish are taking mayflies off the top. While duns and black spinners are eaten, it is the handsome red spinner which causes most activity. The hatches usually peak from October through until early December. The best time is the hottest part of the day – from 10.00 am to 3.00 pm. Good rises occur when the river is at moderate levels but the most prolific feeding happens when the water is running a banker and spilling into the tussocks. Warm oily-calm conditions are ideal. The easterly sea breezes normally signal an immediate end to the mayflies and are quite exasperating. Consequently northerly to north-westerly weather, which tends to negate the sea breeze, is often essential for a full day's sport. If the hatches do fail the best approach is to work a nymph over the weedbeds, or to wait until the evening session when a small wet or buoyant-dry cast into likely spots will often prompt savage strikes.

In the post-Christmas period the water is usually low, temperatures are often higher than optimum for mayflies, and the fishing slows. There are still some daytime rises, and evening fishing can be quite good, but you really have to work for your fish.

Good spinner hatches usually recur as the temperatures moderate in autumn. The fly life is rarely as prolific as it is in spring but the fish are often slightly less cautious.

Further information

The *St Marys* 1:25 000 Tasmap shows all the broadwaters and backwaters and is invaluable for newcomers. See also *Where to Fish – A Regional Breakdown*, 4.2.

BRID RIVER

Tasmap   St Patricks
Drainage   Direct to Trent Water

Although escapees from the commercial rainbow trout farm at the mouth of the Brid are sometimes caught by anglers in the lower reaches, there is no major sea trout fishery.

The stream proper is a typical shingle-bottomed fastwater. The lower to mid reaches are fairly small and overgrown but, by wading and

scrub-bashing, you can make good progress upstream. Brown trout of 0.2-0.7 kg are common and in the post-Christmas period, when levels are low, Celta fishers and bait casters often take big bags.

The uppermost reaches, in the vicinity of the Tasman Highway, flow through open pasture and support many very small fish. Lures and baits work best here as well.

BRISEIS HOLE

Tasmap   Forester
Drainage   Drowned open-cut mine
Location   Derby

General history

Tin was discovered at Derby in 1875 and small scale mining had begun by 1876. In 1883 a syndicate, the Briseis Tin Mining Company, was formed to finance the opening of the deep lead, and by the turn of the century the open-cut was substantial. Disaster struck in 1929 when the Cascade Dam burst, swamping the mine. Mining resumed in 1934 but the heyday was well and truly over.

Trout stocks

Trout fishing can only be maintained through artificial stocking. Records of the NTFA indicate that the hole was stocked with trout as early as 1936-37, and in 1938 it was claimed that the fish were doing exceptionally well.

Stocking recommenced in 1966 when the IFC trialled brook trout. Follow-up releases occurred in 1968-69 and 1974-75. In 1976 the IFC noted that the average weight of brook trout caught by anglers was 1.8 kg and that some fish had attained 3.2 kg.

The last liberation occurred in 1982 when 5000 domestic rainbows were turned out.

Future stocking is likely only if there is a resurgence of interest from local fishers.

BROAD RIVER

Tasmap   Tyenna
Drainage   Derwent system (via Cluny Lagoon)

The lower to mid section is a small clear fastwater. It runs over a shingle bed through a forested valley and offers fast sport for 0.1-0.3 kg brown trout. While scope exists for fly fishing, Celtas and baits work best.

The upper reaches, in the Mt Field National Park, flow through a wide buttongrass valley-floor. After heavy rains and/or major snowmelt, the water rises and fish can be found foraging along the flooded banks. However, the trout never move far from the main channel so when the whole plain is flooded the angling is poor.

In times of low flow trout can be found in the permanent and semi-permanent backwater lagoons immediately downstream of Lake Webster. But, despite the marshes, most fish never exceed 0.4 kg and the angling at Lake Webster is usually more impressive.

BRONTE LAGOON

Tasmaps Nive and Shannon
Drainage Derwent system
Location Central Plateau (north of Tarraleah)

Bronte Lagoon is the feature water of the Tarraleah district. The main attraction is the springtime wet-fly fishing, but there is consistent sport throughout the angling season. Detailed information is contained in the book Trout Guide *(Rob Sloane and Greg French, 1991) A summary only is given here.*

Description

Bronte is a hydro electric scheme impoundment. It lies behind a 10.67 m high rockfill/clay-core

BRONTE LAGOON

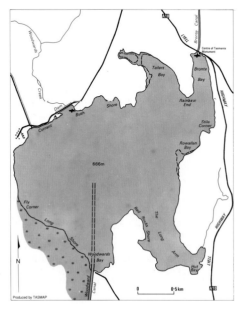

dam and has a full supply level of 666 m above sea level, though drawdowns of up to 3.65 m are to be expected.

Water is received from Pine Tier Lagoon (via Bronte Canal) and from Laughing Jack Lagoon (via the Clarence Weir and Pipeline). It is discharged into Bradys Lake via Woodwards Canal.

The lake is surrounded by sub-alpine woodland but the shores are characteristically open and grassy. The water is reasonably clear.

History

Bronte Lagoon was established in 1953, flooding a natural wet plain known as Woodwards Marsh. Despite thorough examinations at the time, there were no records of trout in the natural system.

In an effort to assess the ability of new waters to self-recruit, Bronte was initially left unstocked and consequently few fish were caught in the 1953-54 season. However, as was expected, fish migrated downstream from the upper Nive system, entering the lake via Bronte Canal, and a large brown trout population soon established.

During December 1955 some 17000 rainbow trout yearlings were liberated. Many of these fish were caught in 1956 – but so too were browns to 6 lb and rainbows to 5 lb. Presumably these bigger rainbows were migrants from the upper Nive.

A further 12000 rainbow fingerlings were stocked during the 1958-59 season, and in latter years there were some small-scale experimental releases of adult browns, but since its formation Bronte Lagoon has demonstrated an ability to maintain self-supporting stocks of both trout species.

In the 1960s trout of 2 kg were typical. In the last 15 years the average size has fallen from about 1.5 kg to below 1 kg.

Trout stocks today

While brown trout dominate, rainbows comprise about 15% of the annual harvest. Though not often taken, the odd brook trout strays into Bronte from Clarence Lagoon (via the Clarence Weir and Pipeline). There are no redfin perch.

Typical trout weigh 0.5-1 kg but others to 1.5 kg are taken regularly. The average size and condition is somewhat dependent upon lake levels and rainfall, and is prone to seasonal variation.

Bags of one to three fish per angler per day are normal.

Special regulations

Bronte Lagoon is reserved for the use of artificial lures and flies, as are the inflowing Bronte Canal and outflowing Woodwards Canal.

The tussocks at Bronte Lagoon – first class wet-fly fishing (photo by Rob Sloane)

Bronte Canal does not open for fishing until the Saturday nearest the 1 November and closes on the Sunday nearest 31 March. The mouth of the canal is designated by two white posts which are visible from the Surveyors Monument.

Fly fishing

From late August to October frogs spawn among the tussocks in the flooded shallows. The best time to fish is just after heavy rain when the lake is rising, or when the lake is at a sustained high level. The flooded tussocks in Tailers Bay (northerly to north-westerly winds), along the Long Shore and Woodwards Bay (westerly to southerly winds), and Woodwards Broadwater are the hot spots.

Tailing trout are most active in the early months of the season. However, summer floods flush out all manner of worms, grubs and caterpillars, causing fish to forage along the grassy edges. And there is a chance of finding a tailing fish or two at any time of the season regardless of water levels. Dawn is always best.

The best dun hatches occur across the southern shores from Fly Corner to Red Rocks Shore during January, and the heaviest gum beetle falls occur along the Eastern Shore on hot summer days.

Bronte Canal and Woodwards Canal are good fall-backs if trout are hard to find in the lake. In summer the fish rise freely and can be taken on nondescript patterns. On sunny days you can polaroid the larger fish but stealth is paramount as there is little cover along the banks.

Lure fishing

Bronte is essentially very shallow, so drift spinning and trolling are effective all over the lake.

Early in the season the best areas for lure casting are the currents around the mouths of the inflowing Bronte Canal and Clarence Pipeline. The mouth of the outflowing Woodwards Canal can be productive at any time of the year. The Rainbow End, the Currant Bush Shore and the dam are other favourite areas. Rough weather is best.

Bronte Lagoon is undeniably good for lure fishing, but it is a mistake to fish it to the exclusion of the Bradys chain of lakes.

Water level manipulations

Historically Bronte Lagoon has fished well when levels have been high. In recent seasons low rainfalls have resulted in the water often falling to near the minimum operating level. In the early 1990s the IFC lobbied the HEC to maintain higher levels. An agreement was finally reached whereby the HEC promised to attempt to maintain a stable level of 665.0 m for the first five months of the 1992-93 angling season.

The previous agreement was simply that water would not be drawn below 664.5 m during the angling season.

Despite the fact that fairly constant levels were maintained during the trial period, fishing did not improve dramatically. Still the IFC has advocated a continuation of the programme and an extension of the period of the trial beyond Christmas.

It must be recognised that it is not the high levels as such which stimulate shore feeding but rather the process of water rising and reflooding long-exposed flats. Long-term constant high levels may eventually result in the death of tussocks and trees, the siltation of the shoreline shallows, and irreparable damage to the fishery.

Facilities

The favoured sites for informal camping are near the Bronte Dam, in the eastern corner of Bronte Bay, near Woodwards Bay carpark, and west of Hut Bay.

The recommended launching area is near the Bronte Dam, but when levels are high small dinghies can also be launched at Bronte Bay.

BROWNS RIVER

Tasmap   Derwent
Drainage   Direct to the outer Derwent estuary

Although an improved sewerage treatment plant has operated at Kingston since the mid 1980s, a significant sea trout fishery has not yet re-established.

The stream proper is tiny and overgrown but supports numerous brown trout up to about 0.2 kg. Fish are taken as far upstream as Fern Tree. Bait casting and set-rod fishing are most practical.

BRUINS POND

Tasmap   Tamar
Drainage   Tamar system (via Brandy Creek)
Location   West of Beaconsfield

Like most of the Beaconsfield impoundments, Bruins Pond is set amid dense bushland and the water is dark with tannin. Rushes and thick weed mats extend over much of the water, limiting the scope for practical wading. Fishing is largely limited to spinning and bait casting from the dam wall.

Trout stocks are essentially maintained through artificial stocking. According to NTFA reports 'Brewins' dam was stocked with brown trout (fry) as early as 1933. The fishing peaked from 1970 to 1976 when there were annual releases of 100-200

adult browns. There were annual releases of 10 000 brown trout fry from 1982 to 1984 but fishing fell short of expectations. The most recent liberations occurred in 1992 and 1993 when 100 yearling rainbows and 100 brown trout x Atlantic salmon hybrids (advanced fry) were turned out.

Better sport is to be found nearby at the Beaconsfield Reservoir.

BRUISERS LAGOON

Tasmap   Meander
Drainage   Derwent system (via Shannon Lagoon)

Bruisers Lagoon is a 'fly-only' water located east of the Lake Highway near the turn-off to Tods Corner (Great Lake). It lies in flat scrubby moorland and is very shallow and weedy. When levels are low the shorelines recede markedly and the surface is reduced to as little as 10% of what it is at capacity. Much of the water is hidden beneath emergent rushes.

While fish of 1-2 kg are commonly caught, the optimum size is an impressive 3-4 kg. The best sport occurs at moderate to high levels when fish can be found foraging in the shallows. Fishing in summer is often frustrating, though there are evenings when the trout can be seen sipping mudeyes and terrestrials.

There are no spawning streams and the trout population is maintained by artificial stocking. According to IFC reports the liberations in the 1980s were *'the first for many years'*. At this time it was intended that the water be managed as a rainbow-only fishery, but it was soon recognised that conditions are best suited to the growth and survival of brown trout.

The 'fly-only' regulation dates back to the beginning of the modern era of management and reflects the fact that the water is not suited to lure casting.

Trout liberations

Rainbow trout

YEAR	SIZE	NUMBER
1980	fry	2 000
1981	fry	2 000
1982	fry	2 000

Wild brown trout

YEAR	SIZE	NUMBER
1984	adults	50
1985	adults	30
1986	adult	50
1987	adults	50

1989	adults	50
1990	adults	50
1991	adults	122
1992	adults	20
1993	adults	50

BRUMBYS CREEK

Tasmaps South Esk and Meander
Drainage South Esk system (via the Macquarie River)

The Brumbys system – the three low-profile weirs and what remains of the natural stream – is a lowland fishery in the heart of the renowned South Esk system. It provides exceptional sport, especially for fly fishers.

History

The early years

Brumbys Creek has long received the attentions of serious trout fishers. Interest can be traced back at least as far as 1900 (when 2000 sea trout were liberated). By the 1930s the water had gained quite a reputation. A typical report (by the NTFA in 1936) stated that:

'Brumby's Creek ... is a delightful stream for the dry fly. Although only a small creek and in places difficult to fish, good brown trout of excellent condition up to 3½ lbs. can be taken ...

Probably the best months ... are November and December, and even earlier. The streams are then usually full and the lagoons in excellent condition. It is usually during this period that the big fish are caught.'

An indication of the interest in the stream is reflected in the fact that the water featured strongly in stocking programmes throughout the 1930s and 1940s. Other reports describe phenomenal springtime fishing when trout could be found foraging in flooded backwaters, and suggest that fish rising to mayflies and terrestrials provided good sport in early summer and in autumn.

Hydro-electric development

Brumbys Creek as it exists today is the result of works associated with the Poatina Power Development.

Since 1964-65 the waters of Great Lake (which formerly flowed south via the Derwent system) have been diverted north (via the Poatina Power Station, the Tailrace Cut and Brumbys Creek) into the South Esk. The three major weirs, which flood the best of the original stream, were formed to provide buffers against the erosive force of additional water.

The snowflake caddis question

A major trout fishery in the natural outflow of Great Lake was lost when the waters were diverted

Brumbys Creek (courtesy Tasmap)

115

– and anglers have long hoped that the fishery could be recreated in the new outflow at Brumbys Creek. However, essential to the proliferation of the snowflake caddis hatch is a continuous flow of cool water throughout November, December and January – and this is incompatible with the HEC's primary objective of maintaining efficient power-generation.

Commercial trout farming

A licence for a commercial trout farm at Brumbys Creek was approved by the IFC in 1979, and the facility was operational by 1980. The farm is located near the southern bank of the creek, downstream of the lowest weir (Brumbys Weir 3), and it produces domestic rainbows (see *About Our Sportfish*, 2.2).

Description and regulations

Brumbys Creek is flanked by vast tracts of flat pasture and many banks are overgrown with willows.

The Weirs (especially Brumbys Weir 1) flood what were once the best stretches of stream – a network of deepwater channels. At exceptionally low levels mud flats are exposed and much of the original system is discernible. At moderate to high levels the pondages remain laced with currents.

In the early years the pondages had firm standing but they are now quite silty and in places wading is treacherous.

Unlike the natural stream, Brumbys below the Tailrace Cut is continually fed by cold water from the highlands and temperatures remain relatively constant throughout the year. Still, the periods of power generation are unpredictable and the water levels are prone to dramatic (sometimes daily) fluctuations.

The water is reasonably clear but becomes discoloured during periods of heavy rain.

Brumbys Weir 1

The pondage behind Brumbys Weir 1 (the uppermost storage) is perhaps the best all-round fly fishery in the system. While there is some scope for spinning, especially near the dam, conditions are hardly remarkable. Bait fishing is not permitted.

You are only allowed to fish from a stationary boat, and small dinghies are most appropriate.

Car access can be gained from the Cressy Road, and there is additional foot access from Brumbys Weir 2.

Brumbys Weir 2

The pondage impounded by Brumbys Weir 2 is very small and is choked with weeds. While fly fishing and bait casting are popular, there is little to excite the lure enthusiast.

Access is via a short road which leads west from the southern end of Lees Bridge on the Cressy Road.

Brumbys Weir 3

This pondage harbours large patches of weeds and reeds but, while fly fishing and bait fishing are most practical, there is limited room for accurate lure casting.

Access is via a short road which leads east from the southern end of Lees Bridge on the Cressy Road. Fishing from a stationary boat is permitted.

The rest of the system

Good fishing occurs in the short stretch of river between the Macquarie River and Brumbys Weir 3, and in the river between the uppermost pondage (Brumbys Weir 1) and the Tailrace Cut.

In the Tailrace Cut there is a series of small buffer dams – and a respectable population of trout.

Brumbys above the outfall of the Cut is fished infrequently but contains plenty of good-sized fish. Worthwhile tributaries include Palmers Rivulet, Poatina Creek, Westons Creek and Garcias Creek, all of which carry browns to 1 kg or so. In April you can expect to catch pre-spawners which migrate upstream from the Brumbys weirs.

Remember that fishing from a boat is prohibited in all of Brumbys Creek and its tributaries except in the pondages above Brumbys Weir 1 and Brumbys Weir 3, and that bait fishing is prohibited in the water between Brumbys Weir 1 (including the pondage) and Saundridge Road and all tributaries thereof.

Trout stocks

Since the 1950s brown trout stocks have been maintained essentially by natural recruitment, though there were occasional releases of adults in the 1960s and 1970s. During the early years of operation most fish taken from the weirs weighed 0.3-1.5 kg. In articles contributed to the *Tasmanian Angling Report*, Tony Ritchie noted that the average size has declined steadily, being 2½-3 lb in 1977-78 and 1¼-1½ lb in the late 1980s. It must be remembered though that the normal size and condition of the trout is prone to modest seasonal variation.

Rainbow trout were released in the natural creek as early as 1932 when 10 000 fry were turned out, but the species failed to establish. Further releases, comprising thousands of fry and yearlings, occurred in the pondages in 1965, 1968, 1977 and 1978. These fish provided some immediate sport but there was little if any natural recruitment. The very few rainbows taken from the weirs today are probably emigrants from Great Lake.

Domestic rainbows, escapees from the fish farm, are quite common in the stream below Brumbys Weir 3.

Redfin perch abound throughout the system.

Fly fishing

Brumbys is a lowland fishery and, as the weather is relatively mild, it tends to fire-up early. However, high water levels are essential for lucrative sport.

Tailers can be found from the beginning of August and are reliable from early September through until the end of January. Most fish are seen early in the morning and late in the evening, though activity does occur at other times of the day – especially during dull weather. The hot spot is the eastern side of the pondage above Brumbys Weir 1.

For dry-fly fishing I prefer Brumbys Weir 1, though reasonable activity occurs throughout the system.

On lowland rivers with natural flow, hatches tend to explode in mid spring when the water reaches optimum temperatures, and diminish in summer as heat becomes excessive. At Brumbys the hatches are tempered by the cool tailrace water – they are rarely prolific but they occur throughout the angling season. Significant surface activity is usually evident by September.

Red-spinner duns provide action during the day and red spinners stimulate frenzy feeding on warm calm evenings. The best hatches happen in late spring and early summer. Modest (but worthwhile) hatches continue in January and February – and there is often a late-season surge.

Smutting fish are a feature of calm mornings from early summer, but you must be on the water at first light. While trout rise all over, they are easiest to catch in the currents and against the willows.

Damselflies and dragonflies are another attraction. In spring, dry flies, or small sheeny wets skimmed along the surface, can be quite effective. In summer the fish, sometimes dozens at a time, put on a memorable performance leaping high out of the water and setting the heart apace – but you are usually doomed to frustration.

Superb rises occur on any warm evening. A variety of insects are taken, including cockchafer beetles and mayflies. Small dries work well before sunset but at last light, when activity peaks, small wets and large buoyants are best.

Fair hatches of snowflake caddis occur in early summer in the stream from the top of Brumbys Weir 1 to the top end of the Tailrace Cut.

Lure casting

While Brumbys is not a feature water for lure casters, it is quite popular with locals. Pockets of fishable water can be found in the pondages above Brumbys weirs 1 and 3. Hot spots exist in the fast water immediately below all three weirs.

Bait fishing

Bait fishing is not permitted in Brumbys Creek and all tributaries thereof between Brumbys Weir 1 and Saundridge Road.

There is room for cast-and-retrieve fishing in the stream between the Macquarie River and Brumbys Weir 3, and in the pondages above Brumbys weirs 3 and 2.

Maps

Anglers will find the *Cressy* and *Delmont* 1:25 000 Tasmaps to be useful. These sheets detail roads, footpaths, full-supply levels, and the network of original river channels.

See also *Where to Fish – A Regional Breakdown*, 4.2.

BRUSHY LAGOON

Tasmap   Tamar
Drainage   South Esk system (via the Meander system)
Location   On the upper reaches of Brushy Rivulet some 15 km north-west of Westbury (grid ref. 771 181)

Over the past few seasons Brushy Lagoon has been the glory water of the north coast. The fishing dropped away in 1993-94, and the long-term future of the lake is difficult to predict.

History

The 5 m high, 400 m long rockfill/clay-core dam on Brushy Rivulet was constructed in 1986-87 by the local branch of the Forestry Commission, primarily to impound water for fire fighting.

The land flooded was essentially an open grassy flat, and financial assistance from the IFC and NTFA enabled most pockets of trees and scrub to be removed before the lake was formed.

The lagoon filled in early 1987 and was stocked that winter. The water is shallow and in the summer of 1988 a combination of decomposing vegetation and high water temperatures resulted in fatally-low oxygen levels. Many of the larger fish died or were severely stressed. The bulk of the drowned vegetation has now rotted away and a repeat fish-kill is unlikely.

Description

Brushy Lagoon is surrounded by dry woodland but a narrow esplanade of grass and heath extends around most of the shoreline and there is comfortable access along most banks.

Emergent drowned scrub is found in the north-west corner, and in 1993-94 weeds proliferated over much of the rest of the lake. In recent seasons *Cumbungi* rushes (bullrushes) have exploded along the shoreline threatening to further restrict shore-based angling. The IFC began chemical spraying early in 1993 and the success to date raises hope that total eradication will eventually be achieved.

The lake has an average depth of about 3 m and levels remain fairly static throughout the year. The water has a faint tinge of tannin and is often slightly turbid.

Trout stocks

Brown trout have long been present in the upper reaches of Brushy Rivulet, but most fish taken from the lagoon have been hatchery-reared stock.

Trout growth boomed soon after the storage was formed, a scenario typical of new impoundments. Rotting vegetation provided food and shelter for a burgeoning population of aquatic insects which, in turn, provided easy food for trout. The average size of fish taken by anglers soon reached 1 kg and by the late 1980s browns and rainbows of 2-3 kg were common.

The normal trend in new impoundments is for the average size and condition of fish to go into decline a few years after the initial boom. This is usually associated with a reduction of the primary food source (rotting vegetation) and an increase in trout numbers. At Brushy there was a chance that good fishing could be maintained indefinitely. The lake is shallow and biologically productive and is capable of supplying more than sufficient food for a relatively large population of fish. For years there was negligible natural recruitment of trout and trout numbers could be manipulated to foster optimum growth. Early in 1992 (at the instigation of the NTFA and IFC) the Forestry Commission 'rebuilt' the inflow stream (Brushy Rivulet) and created a spawning channel. If this facility is successful it is likely that the lake will overpopulate with brown trout and that the average size of both brown and rainbow trout will drop markedly.

At present the lake is essentially a put-and-take fishery and most of the harvest is killed for food. The fish are usually in fine condition but are prone to have a 'muddy' flavour.

Trout liberations

Wild brown trout

YEAR	SIZE	NUMBER
1987	fry	45 000
1988	fry	20 000
"	adults	550
1989	fry	75 000
1990	fry	20 000
1992	advanced fry	6 400

Domestic rainbow trout

YEAR	SIZE	NUMBER
1990	fingerlings	16 000
1991	fingerlings	8 400
1992	yearlings	10 000
"	advanced fry	9 000
1993	yearlings	11 000

Note: in 1993 the IFC promised annual liberations of 10 000 rainbow fingerlings.

Redfin perch

Redfin perch were probably present in the original stream long before it was flooded – but they were not immediately obvious in Brushy Lagoon. In recent years the population has exploded.

Glory days at Brushy Lagoon

Large numbers of small fish school in all areas of the lake and commonly frustrate anglers by snatching baits, lures and flies intended for trout. They also impact upon the mudeyes.

Fly fishing

Brushy Lagoon is a lowland storage in the famous Meander catchment, so it is hardly surprising that prolific hatches of aquatic insects have been a major feature.

Both black and red spinner mayflies have established, with hatches occurring from about late October, peaking in November and December, and continuing throughout the rest of the season. But it is the dragonfly larvae that have caused most activity. In the late 1980s and early 1990s, warm evenings from October through until March saw the trout go wild. Peak activity began at dusk, and on the best nights it continued through until dawn.

Hot spots existed wherever there were emergent dead trees or scrub. In 1993-94 the fishing was very disappointing, some anglers believing that the redfin were out-competing the trout for mudeyes. Only time will tell if this was a hiccup or the beginning of an ongoing problem.

Polaroiding is difficult because of the poor water clarity, but on days when fish are not rising traditional wet flies are a reasonable fallback. If you are lucky you will find fish foraging in the shallows, especially early in the morning and late in the evening, but often blind casting is the only hope. Unfortunately, proliferating weeds are strangling the once snag-free shores.

Spinning

Lure casting has been worthwhile, especially in the early and late months of the season. However, each year the weeds encroach upon fishable water and in 1993-94 the only good spot was along the dam wall. Shallow-running lures are most practical.

Bait fishing

While set-rod fishing is extremely popular, bait casting is recommended when the fish can be seen taking mudeyes. Wattle grubs work as well as any bait.

Facilities

Roads extend along both the western and eastern sides of the lake – and there are several spur tracks leading to the lake shore. A comfortable picnic area with a modest day-shelter is located midway along the eastern bank. There are many splendid informal campsites on the flat grassy verges along both sides of the lagoon.

While large boats are inappropriate, dinghies can be launched from gravel ramps at the picnic area and at the western end of the dam.

Special regulations

Since 1992 Brushy Rivulet above Brushy Lagoon, and a radius of 50 m around the mouth, have been closed to angling at all times.

BRUSHY PLAINS RIVULET

Tasmap Prosser
Drainage Direct to the Prosser River at Buckland

The best angling is found in the farmland at Buckland and Whitemarsh, though good trout also exist in the forested mid-reaches. While many banks are overgrown and most pools are too deep to wade, there is plenty of scope for all fishing techniques. The water becomes murky after heavy rain but clears during prolonged dry weather.

Average trout weigh about 0.5 kg but others to 1.2 kg are quite common. While stocks are healthy (as far as sluggish rivers go) bags of more than two or three fish per angler per day are exceptional.

Lure casting is worthwhile when levels are high but becomes frustrating in summer and autumn.

Wet-fly fishing is good after heavy rain. Usually blind casting is necessary, though fish can sometimes be found foraging in the flood margins at Whitemarsh.

The most productive fishing occurs in warm weather when levels are low. During the day trout can be polaroided and (occasionally) seen sipping terrestrials. Evening fishing is a reliable fall-back, especially during beetle falls in summer and autumn.

BRUSHY RIVULET

Tasmap Tamar
Drainage South Esk system (via the Meander River)

Although Brushy Rivulet often stops flowing in late summer, the small shallow pools always contain large numbers of tiny brown trout. There is room in the lower reaches for productive Celta fishing and bait casting. The stream above Brushy Lagoon is closed to angling at all times.

BULL LAGOONS

No trout. See *Fishing in National Parks*, 5.1.

BURBURY, LAKE

Tasmap Franklin
Drainage King River (a major instream impoundment)

Lake Burbury is a huge hydro-electric scheme impoundment on the West Coast near Queenstown. Given the nature of the land flooded, and the water itself, it is understandable that hopeful anglers feel it has the potential to be 'another Lake Pedder'. However, militating against the establishment of a high-profile trophy fishery are pollution, planned fluctuations in water level, and apparent early overpopulation.

In 1993-94 the lake offered even the novice a good chance of catching wild rainbows and browns.

History

The King River was first investigated as a potential source of power in 1917 amid proposals for a zinc refinery on the West Coast. The scheme was abandoned when the company involved decided to establish the refinery at Risdon near Hobart.

Construction of the (current) King River Power Development was authorized in 1983 following the cessation of work on the Gordon River Power Development Stage 2 (see *Franklin River*). Lake Burbury began filling in the winter of 1991 and reached full supply in 1992.

Description

The water is impounded by an 80 m high rockfill dam (the Crotty Dam) set in the gorge between Mt Jukes and Mt Huxley. The smaller 15 m high rockfill dam across the Andrew Divide (the Darwin Dam) prevents the lake from spilling into the Franklin catchment.

The lake inundated a huge buttongrass (sedge) plain and most of the trees and scrub (which grew only along the rivers and on the elevated outcrops) were removed prior to flooding.

The surrounding land is reminiscent of that at lakes Pedder and Gordon. Sedgeland extends around much of the northern basin. South of Lyell Highway the water has backed up into forested valleys and against densely vegetated hillsides, though there are sedge flats at the foot of Mt Jukes at the Darwin end.

The lake is used to store water for power generation. It is likely to reach its full supply of 235 m above sea level during wet winters, but will be drawn down by a maximum of 9 m during dry months. By contrast Lake Pedder, which exists primarily to divert water (into Lake Gordon), has a normal maximum drawdown of just 1.53 m.

The water is tea-coloured and acidic.

The pollution problem

Linda Creek and Lyell Comstock Creek, which discharge along the north-western shore of Lake Burbury, are contaminated with copper from old Mt Lyell mine workings and tailing dumps. The pollution is so severe that both creeks are virtually lifeless.

Experiments undertaken by the IFC in 1986-88 indicated that, to guarantee the health of trout in the new lake, the input of copper would need to be reduced by about 85%. However, it was acknowledged that poisonous 'pure' copper can bind with dissolved organic matter such as tannins and that in such a form it poses no threat to trout.

Before the lake began to fill, a reduction of about 30% of the total copper was achieved. This was done through non-mechanical means – by simply diverting some of the polluted water back through Mt Lyell and via a new drain into the East Queen River (which was already heavily polluted, and discharges into the King River below Lake Burbury). It is also hoped that additional reductions will be achieved through the rehabilitation of mine tailing dumps. Further decreases in pollution, which were recommended by the IFC and other consultants to the HEC, could be met only by installing dams and pumps on the polluted streams and, as this work was estimated to cost millions of dollars, it was shelved. The State Government and the HEC opted for the soft option of 'wait and see'.

By 1993 the IFC had found that most copper *was* being locked into non-poisonous compounds and that, in most of the lake, the amount of pure copper, though higher than desired, was safe for trout. Very high copper levels are found only at the mouths of Linda Creek and Lyell Comstock Creek. These levels are accentuated at times of heavy flow.

Continued monitoring is being undertaken by the IFC (at the request and expense of the HEC) and will continue at least until 1995. If there is a major deterioration in water quality appropriate action will be taken – hopefully in time to preserve the fishery.

Trout stocks

Prior to the formation of the lake, the King River below Lyell Comstock Creek was mostly too polluted to carry trout. However, the upper King system (including the Eldon River, the South Eldon River, and Dante Rivulet) contained plenty of small browns and rainbows (see *King River*). Tributaries which drained into the polluted

Lake Burbury – Darwin end

lower stretch of the King (such as the Princess, Nelson and Governor rivers) contained only small brown trout.

Existing trout stocks would have been enough to populate the lake, but they were enhanced through liberations of 200 000 hatchery-reared wild brown trout fry in 1992, and 50 000 domestic rainbow fry in 1993.

Stocks of both brown and rainbow trout are maintained by natural recruitment. Rainbow trout accounted for about 50% of the annual harvest in the upper King River – and represented a similar percentage of the lake catch in 1993-94. Most good-sized rainbows caught to date would have hatched in the Eldon and South Eldon rivers. If spawning lake-rainbows come to make good use of former brown-trout-only streams (such as the Nelson and Governor rivers) it is conceivable that the species may eventually account for the majority of fish caught.

By the end of the 1993-94 trout season most fish caught by anglers weighed 0.3-1.2 kg, and others in excess of 2 kg were being reported from time to time. However, overpopulation is already a problem – many of the one-kilo fish have already reached maturity and can be expected to gain little more weight during the rest of their lives. In fact the trout population is so large that locals already expect to take big bags on most outings. As the primary food source (rotting drowned vegetation) depletes, the average size and condition of the trout is bound to decline. The ultimate average size will probably be similar to that in Lake King William.

Vehicular access

There is convenient 2WD access to both sides of the northern basin (see map overleaf).

Vehicles can also be taken via South Queenstown and the Mount Newall Road to the Darwin Dam, where there is scope for boating and shore-based sport. Note that the spur road to the Crotty Dam is not a public access.

Boat launching areas – northern access

The boat launching ramp at the picnic ground (on the eastern shore) is steep, unsurfaced, and only suited to 4WD vehicles. Moreover, the site is very exposed and is not appropriate for small boats.

The best launching site is at the (drowned) end of the Kelly Basin Road. This road extends from the Lyell Highway 1.5 km west of Bradshaws Bridge. Unfortunately, turning and parking are tight.

Small boats can also be launched from the drowned sections of the old Lyell Highway (near Linda Creek on the western shore, and a couple of kilometres north of the picnic area on the eastern shore).

Boat launching areas – southern access

There are two 2WD-standard boat launching areas at the Darwin end. However, the water is relatively shallow and care is needed when handling large runabouts.

Access for shore-based anglers

Much of the northern basin is encircled by flat sedgeland and is easily accessible to shore-based anglers. The real hot spot is the western bank for some 4 km either side of Bradshaws Bridge. The eastern bank near the drowned section of the Lyell Highway is also very productive, though it is exposed to the prevailing westerly weather.

At the southern (Darwin) end of the lake, some 4 km of narrow flat sedge-esplanade extends along

121

LAKE BURBURY

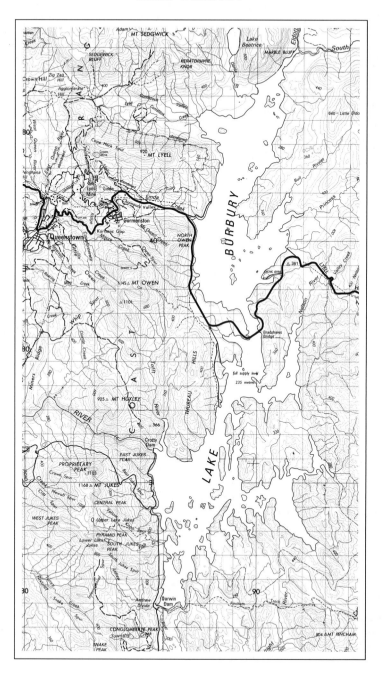

the foot of Mt Jukes (along the western bank, from near the Crotty Dam spur road to the Darwin Dam). Much of the rest of the southern basin backs up against densely-vegetated hills and into steep valleys and is of difficult access.

Fly fishing

Opportunities for fly fishing are similar to those which already exist on the West Coast (at lakes Rosebery and Mackintosh) and in the South West (lakes Pedder and Gordon). However, the sheer number of fish (not to mention the predominance of rainbows) ensures that even newcomers stand a good chance of success.

During crisp calm mornings from mid spring to the end of the season, large numbers of trout can be found rising to take midges. These fish always include a disproportionately high number of rainbows. Boating is almost essential, though good wind lanes form in the lake narrows and sometimes drift to within casting distance from the shore.

Good mudeye hatches occur on warm evenings from December through until mid autumn. Already there has been exceptional fishing when good rises have lasted from late evening to early morning. In the daytime trout can be found among the sticks charging and leaping at dragonfly adults. Usually these fish respond well to any semi-buoyant fly which faintly resembles a mudeye (such as a Mrs Simpson or fur fly).

Don't be disturbed if there are no rises. At any time of the year, under any conditions, you can rely on taking fish simply by blind casting among the sticks with small wets, or by persistent loch-style wet-fly fishing from a boat.

Hot spots for the shore-based fly fisher include all sites mentioned above in the discussion on shore access. I prefer the Darwin end – but only because it is relatively sheltered from the prevailing westerly weather. The best water is littered with drowned sticks and you must accept a few break-offs as being inevitable.

Boat operators should target any sheltered patch of drowned scrub adjacent to deep water – mudeyes like to crawl out onto emergent sticks – but avoid the polluted sections of the north-western shore near the mouths of the Linda and Lyell Comstock creeks.

Lure fishing

Traditional shallow-running daytime lures (such as Cobras and fish spoon wobblers) work well. At night the Fishcake is reliable – especially during the summertime mudeye migrations – though it is rarely as productive as a surface-fished wattle grub.

The shore-based angler can catch fish from any accessible shore except the areas near the Linda and Lyell Comstock creeks. Don't ignore the sticks.

Drift spinning and shallow trolling are also productive. Hot spots include the fringes of drowned scrub, though fish are caught all over. The stratified deep water is low in oxygen, high in sulphide, and avoided by trout.

Peak spawning time usually happens late on the West Coast. In the early years at lakes Rosebery and Mackintosh the brown trout did not really begin to run until late July, though this has moderated as the waters have matured. At Burbury the first major spawning run of brown trout was exceptionally late (July/August) and, while some moderation is expected over the next few years, spawning will never be as early as it is on the Central Plateau. Fishing close to the mouths of the main streams (the Eldon, Princess, Nelson and Governor rivers) is more productive early in the season (when fish are returning from spawning) rather than late in the season.

Bait fishing

Set-rod fishing is popular with locals – but bait casting with wattle grubs is usually more productive, especially at mudeye time (see above notes on fly fishing). Remember to avoid the polluted sections of the north-western shore in the vicinity of the Linda and Lyell Comstock creeks.

Special regulations

As yet there are no special regulations – the season is the same as the standard for brown trout fisheries, and angling is permitted in all inflow streams. However, in light of the late spawning and the predominance of rainbows, I would be surprised if local anglers do not push for a late opening of the angling season – and perhaps a late closing. Check your current *Fishing Code*.

Facilities

There are no formal camping facilities. While caravans are often parked at the ends of the access tracks, attractive tent-sites are almost non-existent (the sedge plains are wet and uneven). At present (1994) the State Government and its agencies have refused to commit themselves to recreational developments.

BURNS CREEK

Tasmap   St Patricks
Drainage   North Esk River

A tiny fastwater containing plenty of small brown trout. Celta fishing and bait casting are most practical.

BURNS DAM

Tasmap   Nive
Drainage   Natural – Gordon system (via Franklin system)

The HEC built a small earthfill weir on Burns Creek in 1967 so that water could be diverted into the Lake King William catchment. The pond so formed is surrounded by moorland. It is tea coloured and, in most places, very weedy. Slow-growing brown trout to 1 kg can be taken on lures and flies.

BUTTERS, LAKE

Tasmap   Mersey
Drainage   Natural – Derwent system (via James system)
Location   Western Lakes

A productive water containing brown trout of 0.7-2 kg. The banks are rocky and steep and polaroiding is most effective. Fair rises occur on warm days post-Christmas when the gum beetles are about. Lure casting can be productive on dull days.

See also *Fishing in National Parks*, 5.1.

BUTTONS CREEK

Tasmap   Forth
Drainage   Direct to Bass Strait

A tiny fastwater which supports numerous brown trout to 0.3 kg and a few others to 0.5 kg. There are many open grassy banks. Bait casting is most effective.

BUXTON RIVER

Tasmaps   Freycinet and Little Swanport
Drainage   Direct to Great Oyster Bay.

The lower reaches flow through flat farmland, though a ribbon of native bush extends along the banks, in many places forming a loose canopy over the water. The stream becomes turbid after heavy rain but clears during periods of moderate to low flow. At very low levels much of the shingle bed is exposed. Most permanent holes extend from bank to bank and, except for the heads and tails, are too deep to wade.

Undersized fish can often be seen in the riffles and shallows but, perhaps due to the abundance of forage food (galaxias), quite a few trout of 1-1.5 kg lurk in the deep holes.

At times of moderate flow Celta fishing can be quite worthwhile. As levels drop fly fishing and bait casting become more effective. Polaroiding and night fishing are the best ways to undo big trout.

Success at Lake Butters

While there is some scope for lure casting from the banks, fly fishing is best done from the river bed.

The stream is as good as any on the East Coast but never expect big bags.

The runs of sea trout are poor.

CALDER RIVER

Tasmap   Hellyer
Drainage   Direct to the Inglis River

A small fastwater flowing through a steep forested valley. Although the NTFA reported that rainbow trout were *'doing well'* in the upper reaches in 1912, and that more rainbows were released in 1912 and 1929, this species failed to establish. Today the stream supports plenty of small brown trout, and Celta fishing and bait casting often result in large bags.

CALVERTS LAGOON

Tasmap   D'Entrecasteaux
Drainage   Isolated coastal lagoon
Location   South Arm district

Association reports indicate that Calverts Lagoon was stocked as early as 1956 (when 200 brown trout yearlings were turned out), and that regular liberations continued until the early 1960s. The sport at this time was exceptional, dun hatches being a major attraction. In 1963 low levels and high alkalinity resulted in major fish kills.

Rainbow trout fry were liberated in 1966 but all died during the summer. During an experiment in 1970-71 it was found that yearling rainbows could not survive in the lagoon for more than a few hours.

Each year from 1975 to 1979 some 10 000-85 000 brown trout fry were released. By 1977 there were numerous fish above the legal minimum size, and by late 1978 specimens to 2.5 kg were being taken. However, as early as 1978 there were minor fish kills, and by 1980 the alkalinity was again too high for the survival of trout fry.

For the last few years the lagoon has been a dry basin. It is still an official 'fly-only' water, and will probably be restocked when it refills.

Land surrounding the lagoon was acquired by the Crown in 1976-77 and eventually gazetted as a State Recreation Area.

CAM RIVER

Tasmap   Hellyer
Drainage   Direct to Bass Strait

A small fastwater flowing through a steep forested valley.

According to early Parliamentary reports trout were liberated as early as 1881. Today the stream teems with resident browns to 0.5 kg – and they respond well to Celtas and baits.

Sea trout are taken from the estuary (at Somerset) and the lower freshwater reaches. Peak fishing (such as it is) occurs from late September to early November, coinciding with the galaxia migrations.

Rainbows were released in 1911-12 but failed to establish.

CAMDEN RIVULET

Tasmap   St Patricks
Drainage   North Esk system (via St Patricks River)

A small fastwater with many open grassy banks. Brown trout to 0.4 kg are plentiful. Rainbows were released in 1910 and a remnant population survives today. While Celta fishing and bait casting are most efficient, room exists for pleasant fly casting.

CAMERONS LAGOON

(known to some locals as Murderers Hill Lagoon)

Tasmap   Meander
Drainage   Spills towards Great Lake (only during floods).
Location   Beside the Lake Highway about 3 km north of the Marlborough Highway junction.

A very shallow silt-bottomed lagoon reminiscent of many of the Western Lakes. It usually fishes well early in the season, but levels often become critically low in summer. Wet-fly fishing and polaroiding are most practical, though small lures are effective when levels are high.

The fishery is maintained entirely by artificial stocking, mostly with adult brown trout. Fish taken by anglers usually weigh 1-1.5 kg but any which survive two or more seasons are likely to attain 2 kg or more.

Trout liberations

Wild brown trout

YEAR	SIZE	NUMBER
1984	adults	40
1985	adults	40
1986	adults	50
"	fingerlings – adults	55
1987	adults	50
1989	adults	50
1991	adults	22
1992	adults	20
1993	adults	30

Rainbow trout

YEAR	SIZE	NUMBER
1972	fry	1 000
1986	fingerlings	2

Note: a large but poorly recorded liberation of small rainbows occurred in 1987 or 1988.

CAMP CREEK

Tasmaps   Table Cape and Hellyer
Drainage   Direct to the Inglis estuary

A small fastwater which flows through a mosaic of native bush, plantations and farmland. As with most tributaries of the Inglis, there is no noticeable tannin but the water remains slightly turbid even during periods of low flow. The clay bed is safe to wade.

There are plenty of well-conditioned browns to 0.2 kg, as well as a few to 0.4 kg. Big bags are to be expected.

Records of the NTFA indicate that yearling rainbows were released in 1911-12, but this species failed to establish.

CARDIGAN RIVER

See *Collingwood River*.

CARLTON RIVER

Tasmap Prosser
Drainage Direct to Frederick Henry Bay

Sea trout fishing is mediocre, though some fish are taken at the head of the estuary.

The creek proper is best fished in the rural areas immediately above the estuary, and in the vicinity of the Arthur Highway. There is very little summertime flow but there are many deep permanent holes. Despite the often scrubby banks there is scope for spinning and fly fishing. The water becomes murky after rain and clears during long dry spells. Most trout weigh 0.2-1 kg and some attain 1.5 kg.

The uppermost reaches, in the vicinity of the Kellevie Road, are surrounded by dry forest. Most pools are small, overgrown and cool – and hold trout throughout the year. Typical fish are less than 0.5 kg. Set-rod fishing is most appropriate.

CAROLINE CREEK

Tasmap Forth
Drainage Direct to the Mersey River

A tiny creek which supports small slow-growing brown trout. Fishing is not permitted in the crayfish sanctuary between the Latrobe-Railton road and Dawson Siding.

CARTER LAKES

Tasmap Meander
Drainage Natural – Derwent system (via James system)
Location Nineteen Lagoons

The Carter Lakes lie in flat moorland and comprise a large deep storage (locally known as Carters Lagoon) and two shallow lagoons. These waters are connected by narrow inconspicuous channels which permit limited movement of trout from one water to another.

Trout stocks

Natural stocks were limited, though some fish invaded from the James River. In 1951 the NTFA mentioned a '30 lb' trout found dead in 'Crater Lake'.

Early IFC records are sketchy but it seems that the first trout liberations occurred in 1962. Almost every winter since then consignments of

adult brown trout have been transferred to the main lagoon. In modern times there have also been releases of rainbow trout.

As the fishery depends on stocking, the average size and quality of the trout taken is variable. Browns of 1-2 kg are typical but fish of 3-4 kg are not unknown.

Trout liberations

Wild brown trout (since 1985)

YEAR	SIZE	NUMBER
1985	adults	100
1987	adults	200
1988	adults	200
1989	adults	150
1990	adults	200
1991	adults	150
1992	adults	200
1993	adults	150

Wild rainbow trout

YEAR	SIZE	NUMBER
1980	fingerling-adults	62
1985	yearlings	100
"	yearlings (T)	884

(T) = triploids

Regulations

Although the Carter Lakes have been managed as 'fly-only' waters since 1962, there is little of special interest for the fly fisher. At the time that the law was introduced the primary intention was to *'balance the concessions to Lake Binney and Tungatinah Lagoon'*.

Fishing from a boat was also banned in 1962.

The fishing

Traditionally Carters has been noted for its Christmas-time tadpole feeders which make smash-and-grab raids into the gutters and shoreline recesses.

Tailing fish are often found feeding on snails along the rocky southern shore. The deep northern bank is good for dry fly fishing on hot summer days when there are fair rises to duns and spinners.

See also *Fishing in National Parks*, 5.1.

CASCADE DAM

Tasmap Forester
Drainage Ringarooma system (via the Cascade River)

This slightly tea-coloured water is impounded by densely forested hills and is reminiscent of the

Cascade Dam

Frome Dam. Big drawdowns in summer and autumn result in much of the clay bed becoming exposed.

History

The first major dam on the Cascade River was a 12 m high structure built in 1924-25 to provide water for sluicing in the Briseis mine at Derby. This dam was raised about 10.5 m in 1927-28. In 1929, following an extended period of unprecedented heavy rain, the dam spilled and burst – swamping Derby and Briseis, killing 14 people, and devastating property and equipment. The mine reopened in 1934 and the current 27 m high rockfill dam was built in 1936. The mine ceased operation in 1948.

Trout stocks

Despite an abundance of trout in the Cascade River, the new dam was stocked soon after its completion. In 1940 the NTFA mentioned that good brown trout were being caught and that a prize had been claimed for the *'first rainbow'* – a fish of *'2 lb 5 oz'*. Further stocking occurred in 1955 (brown trout fry) and 1966 (190 adult browns), but brown trout stocks have essentially been maintained through natural spawning.

Rainbow trout did not establish.
Today fish of 0.3 - 0.7 kg are typical and a few exceed 1 kg.

The fishing

The 'how to' notes given for the Frome Dam can be applied equally to the Cascade.

Access and facilities

Access is via a very rugged 2WD track. The worst section (the last 2 km) can be walked in ½ -1 hr. Informal camping is permitted.

CASTLE FORBES RIVULET

Tasmap   Huon
Drainage Direct to the Huon estuary

A small creek containing many very small brown trout. Room exists for Celta fishing and bait casting. Low flows are best.

CATAGUNYA, LAKE

Tasmap   Shannon
Drainage River Derwent (a major instream impoundment)

Description

The 49 m high pre-stressed concrete Catagunya Dam was completed in 1962, flooding a steep forested section of the Derwent valley. The lake is deep and narrow with few shallow margins. Although dense undergrowth occurs along most banks, grassland and/or open paddocks exist at the head of the lake and in the vicinity of Black Bobs Rivulet. There is also an area of open woodland extending from the southern shore.

The water has the faintest tinge of tannin and is often very slightly turbid.

At full supply the lake is 169.16 m above sea level, and the normal maximum drawdown is just 1.52 m.

Trout stocks

Fish stocks are maintained by natural recruitment. Brown trout of 0.3 - 1 kg are common but rainbows are rare. Small redfin perch often annoy anglers by snatching lures, flies and baits intended for trout.

The fishing

Lake Catagunya is not very popular with anglers, largely because there are several more noteworthy waters nearby (including Meadowbank Lake, Wayatinah Lagoon, Bronte Lagoon and the Bradys chain of lakes).

127

While trolling, drift spinning, and set-rod fishing are favoured, there is good warm-weather dry-fly fishing during the summer/autumn beetle falls.

Facilities

A mediocre launching site exists near the Catugunya Power Station at the head of the lake.

CATAMARAN RIVER

Tasmap South East Cape
Drainage Direct to Recherche Bay

The runs of sea trout are superb. Good fishing can occur in August but is more likely in September, October and early November. The estuary is just 20-100 m wide and is flanked by thick scrub and forest. Although there is some room for shore-based sport (especially if you are prepared to wade) fishing from a boat is recommended. Drift spinning and fly fishing are most effective.

The freshwater reaches are tea coloured and support large numbers of slow-growing brown trout. However, the banks are overgrown with impenetrable scrub and convenient access is restricted to small areas at the head of the estuary and near the South Cape Road.

CECILY, LAKE

No trout. See *Fishing in National Parks*, 5.3.

CETHANA, LAKE

Tasmaps Forth and Mersey
Drainage River Forth (a major instream impoundment)

Description

Lake Cethana was formed in 1971 and lies in a steep densely-forested valley behind a 110 m high rockfill dam. There are extensive drowned forests along most shores, especially in the mid to upper reaches. Full supply is 220.98 m above sea level and seasonal fluctuations of up to 6.1 m are to be expected. The water is slightly tea-coloured and fairly turbid.

Trout stocks

As a trout fishery Lake Cethana is much less popular than Lake Barrington – but this appears to be so only because it is further from the main population centres. Natural recruitment of brown trout is high and the overall trout population exceeds that of Lake Barrington. Brown trout

usually weigh 0.5-1 kg, though others of 1.5-2 kg are taken every now and then. The IFC has determined that the average daily catch is about two trout per angler per day, which compares to one fish per angler per day at Barrington.

Domestic rainbow trout were released in 1979 (20 000 fingerlings) and 1990 (16 000 fingerlings). While many of these fish migrated downstream, significant numbers stayed behind and provided novelty fishing for a few years. There appears to be little or no natural recruitment of rainbows, so the average size and quantity of the fish is highly variable. In the-first one or two years after release small maidens account for up to 20% of the total trout harvest. Mature fish are less common but specimens in excess of 2 kg are not unknown. Rainbows appear to grow faster than the browns, probably because they make better use of surface food in the wind lanes.

Access

The daunting topography greatly restricts shore-based fishing. The best places are at Lorinna (a small farming community midway down the eastern shore) where there are small grassy approaches to the water. Other (small) angling sites, best suited to set-rod fishing, can be found near the damsite. There is no convenient access from the Wilmot Power Station.

A seaworthy dinghy or small runabout is essential for serious fishing. The recommended launching ramp is near the eastern end of the dam.

The nature of the fishing

The fishing is very similar to that at Lake Barrington. Drift spinning among the emergent trees and trolling are most popular. Fly fishers will find plenty of fish rising to take beetles from the wind lanes on warm summer/autumn days. Night fishing with big wets is also effective – especially on warm summer evenings during the mudeye migrations when any patch of emergent trees is likely to provide good sport.

A hot spot for rainbows is where water enters the lake from the Wilmot Power Station.

The major spawning areas are in the Dove River and the River Forth, so the top end of the impoundment is usually very productive towards the end of the season. The minor tributaries are steep and largely inaccessible to lake spawners.

CHALICE LAKE

No trout. See *Fishing in National Parks*, 5.1.

CHAMBERS, LAKE

See *Johnny, Lake*.

CHAPTER LAKE

No trout. See *Fishing in National Parks*, 5.1.

CHARLES, LAKE

No trout. See *Fishing in National Parks*, 5.1.

CHASM CREEK

Tasmap Hellyer
Drainage Direct to Bass Strait

Early NTFA reports show that Chasm Creek was stocked with 1750 rainbow fry in 1903. At this time no other trout were present and the fishery was to be closed to angling for three years to allow stocks to develop. Today Chasm Creek contains only very small brown trout.

The lower reaches flow through a small steep forested valley and are easily fished with Celtas and baits.

In the vicinity of Stowport the creek is flanked by open paddocks, and many verges are boggy.

Fly fishing is appropriate here, especially when levels are high.

CHIPMAN, LAKE

Tasmap Meander
Drainage Derwent system (via the Little Pine system)
Location Nineteen Lagoons

Access

Lake Chipman is a significant but little-known water located between Double Lagoon and Lake Augusta (just out of sight from the main road). It can be reached by walking along the long-disused vehicular route which follows the fenceline from the eastern end of the levee at (the natural) Lake Augusta – or else you can walk cross-country from Double Lagoon. Either way the trip is little more than 1 km.

Trout stocks

Spawning facilities at the lake are negligible and most fish are upstream migrants from the outflow creek and Double Lagoon. Because natural recruitment is poor, Chipman was a traditional big-fish water renowned for its 2-6 kg browns.

Domestic rainbows were released in 1979 (2000 large fingerlings) and 1986 (5000 small triploid fingerlings). Net surveys undertaken in

Lake Chipman

129

1991 showed that rainbow trout then accounted for about 30-50% of the total trout population, and that the normal size range for both browns and rainbows was 1-2.5 kg. It is likely that the lake was overstocked, and that this was compounded by less-than-expected harvesting. As the older fish die off the condition of the young fish is bound to improve. Managed carefully Chipman has the potential to be a productive trophy water.

The nature of the fishing

Lake Chipman has well-defined banks and is ideal for lure casting.

Fly fishing is reasonable in springtime when trout are to be found snailing along the rocks. Later in the year polaroiding can be effective – providing that the lake is not too discoloured by wave action.

The water is quite shallow but the bottom is silty and only parts can be waded.

See also *Fishing in National Parks*, 5.1.

CHISHOLM, LAKE

Reputed to have been stocked some years ago, but does not contain trout today.

Typical mayfly feeder from Christys Creek

CHRISTYS CREEK

Tasmap Mersey
Drainage Derwent system (via the Little Pine system)
Location Western Lakes

In many places the creek itself is deep and undercut and holds trout throughout the year. But the real attraction is the extensive labyrinth of lakes and ponds. Perhaps the best known water is Christys Lagoon (grid ref. 510 644), though fish have invaded the main system as far upstream as the two big lakes above Lunka Lake. Trout are also found in the lakes of the tributary system south of the Talinah-Talleh track.

Quite a few of the permanent lakes are deep rocky-shored affairs with stable weedbeds. These are suitable for lure casting, and in summer they boast impressive hatches of duns and black spinners.

Many other waters are shallow and sometimes only semi-permanent. Such lagoons are noted for their tailing fish, especially when the system is swollen after heavy rain.

In most waters the normal size range is 0.5-2 kg.

See also *Fishing in National Parks*, 5.1.

CHUDLEIGH LAKES

See *Fishing in National Parks*, 5.1.

CLARENCE LAGOON

Tasmap Nive
Drainage Derwent system (via the Clarence River and the Nive system)
Location Western Lakes

While recent attempts to establish brook trout in the Anthony system look promising, Clarence Lagoon remains the only proven wild brook trout water in Australia.

Description

The southern shore is a lightly wooded moraine, and the rest of the lake is fringed by flat moorland. There is an extensive reedy marsh at the northern end, and bottom-hugging *Isoetes* weed grows like coral over the rest of the lake bed. The lake is quite shallow but only the edges are wadeable. A crude low-profile rock weir, which was illegally constructed across the outflow in the late 1980s, serves to hold the lake about 0.5 m above natural minimum levels. The water is very slightly tea-coloured.

Trout stocks

When brook trout were re-introduced to Tasmania in 1962 it was widely recognised that the species did not compete well with other salmonids and that, to have any chance of establishing a viable wild population, fish would have to be released into previously unstocked waters. Clarence Lagoon was chosen because a small waterfall about 1 km below the outlet prevents the invasion of brown trout.

The first brookies (604 fingerlings) were released in November 1963. IFC records from the 1970s detail many good catches of 0.3-3.6 kg fish, and clearly indicate that a small self-supporting population had established.

In 1979 the IFC carried out a survey of the lagoon and, while some fish were netted in the lake, an absence of recruits in the spawning streams raised concern that the fishery was in delicate balance.

The modern era of regular stocking began in October 1979. Since then hatchery-reared stock has formed the basis of the recreational fishery. Ova is collected both from brood stock at the Salmon Ponds and from Clarence residents.

In 1991 IFC staff netted a brown trout of unknown origin in Clarence Lagoon. If brown trout establish, the brook trout fishery will certainly collapse.

Brook trout liberations

YEAR	SIZE	NUMBER
1963	fingerlings	604
1979	fry	20 000
"	small fingerlings	950
1980	fry	77 000
"	extra large fingerlings	1 030
1981	fry	18 000
1982	fingerlings	230
1986	small fingerlings	4 000
1988	large fingerlings	1 500
"	yearlings	400
"	small fingerlings	5 000
1989	fry/fingerlings	11 000
1990	advanced fry	6 870
1992	small fingerlings	3 000
1993	small fingerlings	4 500

Fly fishing

As brook trout dislike warm water the early and late months of the season are most productive.

Wet-fly fishing with large matuka-style lures usually works best. All open shores can be productive but fish are rarely found in the marshes. Late in the season it pays to concentrate on the

Clarence Lagoon

open shallows in the north-eastern corner, and on the area near the outflow. The inflowing creek, where it cuts through the marsh, is also worthy of inspection.

Polaroiding is extremely difficult, primarily because the fish are camouflaged in the weeds. The secret is to be alert to the white slashes on the edges of the fish's pectoral and pelvic fins. Cruising fish often ignore dry flies but will usually take nymphs and large wets.

Modest rises can occur whenever the weather is mild – but such activity is irregular and unpredictable.

Lure casting

Spinning can be very productive, especially in the early and late months of the season. Rough overcast weather is undoubtedly the best, though you can get surprising results on calm bright days.

Small shallow-running lures are most appropriate. The best areas are along the southern and eastern shores. Alternatively, wade out along the north-western fringe of the marsh.

Access

The access track leaves the Lyell Highway 3 km west of the Clarence River bridge (8 km east of

Derwent Bridge). Vehicles with good clearance can be taken to within 300 m of the water. There are plenty of comfortable informal campsites among the trees near the outflow.

Clarence galaxias

The Clarence galaxias (*Galaxias johnstoni*) occurs only in the Clarence system above the waterfall and in a small lake on the Wentworth Range. Biologists note that the fish's current distribution is confined to waters without brown trout and suggest that brown trout have overtaken much of its former range. However, it is more likely that the natural range has always been limited to areas above major physical barriers where the species has been isolated from its close relative the climbing galaxias (*Galaxias brevipinnis*).

It *is* highly likely that brown trout would make a severe impact on the Clarence galaxias, especially in riverine environments. The effect of brook trout has not been assessed, and there has been no attempt to determine safe stocking densities.

Ethics

Boating is inappropriate because motors cause physical damage to the lake bottom, and because like most small headwater lakes it is especially vulnerable to pollution from raw fuel and exhaust fumes.

Stocking with hatchery-reared fish is undesirable because hatchery fish may eventually swamp the wild gene pool, and because there is always the risk of accidental releases of brown and/or rainbow trout. Anglers can help preserve the fishery by adopting a voluntary two-fish bag limit.

See also *About our Sportfish*, 2.3 and *Fishing in National Parks*, 5.1

CLARENCE RIVER

Tasmap   Nive
Drainage   River Derwent (via the Nive system)

Because water is diverted at the Clarence Weir, the lowest reaches are often nearly dry.

Between the Clarence Weir and the Clarence waterfall (about 1 km below Clarence Lagoon) the creek is a typical stony-bottomed fastwater. It contains plenty of very small brown trout and the odd emigrant brook trout (from Clarence Lagoon). Most banks are overgrown with native scrub so Celta fishing and bait casting are most practical. Low flows are best.

Above the waterfall the river contains only brook trout. Most of these fish are undersized,

though lake emigrants are taken from time to time.

CLARENCE WEIR

Tasmap   Nive
Drainage   Derwent system (via the Clarence Pipeline and Bronte Lagoon)

The 7 m high concrete gravity dam impounding Clarence Weir was completed in 1953. Full supply is 694.94 m above sea level and drawdowns of more than 2.1 m are to be expected.

While the pondage is surrounded by open woodland, there are several wide grassy verges. The silty bottom supports some weed, there are plenty of emergent drowned trees and scrub, and the water is slightly tea-coloured.

Slow-growing brown trout of 0.2-0.6 kg abound, and emigrant brook trout from Clarence Lagoon are taken from time to time.

High levels (which are common in spring and summer) provide for pleasant Celta fishing, especially on dull days. Bait casting and fly fishing are also productive.

CLARRIES CREEK

Intermittent. Few if any trout.

CLAYTONS RIVULET

Tasmap   Forth
Drainage   Direct to Bass Strait

A small overgrown creek with year-round flow. Rainbow trout were liberated in 1916 but failed to establish. Small brown trout thrive today. Bait casting and Celta fishing are most practical.

CLEVELAND LAGOON

Tasmap   South Esk
Drainage   Isolated flood basin
Location   Eastern side of the Midland Highway at Cleveland

Cleveland Lagoon is a small weedy basin. When full it has a maximum depth of around 6 m – but it tends to dry up after successive dry seasons.

According to NTFA reports stocking occurred as early as 1918-19 when 100 rainbow fingerlings were liberated. The IFC recorded that between 1970 and 1981 there were regular stockings of 10 000 - 50 000 brown trout fry. Good fishing occurred throughout most of this period and fish to 3 kg are reputed to have been taken. The fishery collapsed during the drought of the early 1980s. The lake partially refilled in 1987 and was restocked with brown trout fry, only to dry up again during the summer.

Restocking will probably occur when the lake refills – providing it seems likely that levels will remain reasonably high for at least several seasons.

CLOISTER LAGOON

No trout. See *Fishing in National Parks*, 5.1.

CLUNY LAGOON

Tasmap   Tyenna
Drainage   River Derwent (a major instream impoundment)

The quality of the trout and the average catch rate are comparable to those at Meadowbank Lake. However, Cluny is not especially appealing to shore-based anglers and, while there are local devotees, it remains relatively unpopular.

Description

The 30 m high Cluny Dam was completed in 1968 as part of the Lower Derwent Power Development. Full supply is 97.84 m above sea level and drawdowns of up to almost 4.9 m are to be expected.

The lake has a rural setting and is flanked by a patchwork of pasture, bushland and scrub. The shoreline incorporates cliffs and gentle slopes.

The water is very faintly tea-coloured and is sometimes slightly turbid. The major input is from Lake Repulse via the Repulse Power Station. A smaller but more constant contribution is maintained by the Broad River.

Trout stocks

Trout stocks are maintained almost entirely by natural recruitment, though 7000 advanced brown-trout fry were released in 1993. The main spawning area is the Broad River but spawning fish also congregate near the outfall of the Repulse Power Station.

Most trout taken by anglers are browns of 0.5-1.3 kg. Rainbows are extremely uncommon.

Schools of diminutive redfin perch abound, especially in the shallows.

Fly fishing

There is room for fly fishing from the shore but a dinghy or small runabout is recommended.

The best daytime sport occurs on warm days in the post-Christmas period when the fish rise to take gum beetles and other terrestrials. The hot spots are where the wind funnels food along the shores of Punchbowl Bay, and in the wind lanes further out.

Late in the season wet-fly fishers target pre-spawners at the mouth of the Broad River and near the Lake Repulse Road bridge.

Lure fishing

Trolling and drift spinning are favoured but, while weed is a problem in some areas, there is ample room for shore-based sport.

The shores

The best areas for shore-based fly fishing and spinning are along the grassy southern banks from Punchbowl Bay (the biggest bay) to the mouth of the Broad River.

The north-eastern shore, from the launching ramp to the western side of Doctors Point, is also worthwhile.

The uppermost reaches, in the vicinity of the Lake Repulse Road bridge, are best fished late in the season.

Facilities

The recommended launching ramp is located on the northern side of the lake near the dam.

Picnic tables exist near the boat ramp and at the mouth of the Broad River.

Camping is discouraged.

CLYDE, RIVER

Tasmaps   Tyenna, Shannon, and Lake Sorell
Drainage   Derwent system (via Meadowbank Lake)

Description

The river from Meadowbank Lake through Hamilton and Bothwell to the hills beyond Dennistoun Plain is flanked by dry pasture – but many banks are overgrown with willows and/or scrub. Hilly woodland predominates from Dennistoun to Lake Crescent.

Much of the river is a series of long sluggish pools, most of which are too deep to wade.

Water is stored in Lake Crescent during wet periods and released into the Clyde during dry spells (usually sometime after October) to supply irrigation and domestic requirements at Bothwell and Hamilton.

Floods commonly occur in the lower to mid reaches in the early months of the angling season (August to October). The lowest flows usually happen between the last major early-season rain and the beginning of the irrigation period.

133

When water is being drawn from Lake Crescent the river swells but does not flood.

The water is quite muddy during floods but clears appreciably during periods of low flow.

Fish stocks

According to early Parliamentary reports brown trout had established by 1869.

When water is being drawn from Lake Crescent some large emigrant trout (including the odd rainbow) are caught in the uppermost 2 km or so. Resident browns of 0.3-1 kg dominate throughout the rest of the system.

Stunted redfin perch abound in the lower to mid reaches – but they do not extend above the large waterfall in the hills beyond Dennistoun.

The golden galaxias, which is endemic to the Clyde system, is found above the waterfall where it has evolved in isolation from its close relative the climbing galaxias (see *Crescent, Lake*).

Where to fish

The lowest reaches, near Hamilton, are extremely overgrown with willows and are best suited to

The Coal River (photo by Rob Sloane)

set-rod fishing and bait casting.

The most fishable water exists in the Meadsfield region. Bait casting is favoured but there is ample room for fly fishing and spinning.

There are also some good open-banked pools at Bothwell.

The uppermost reaches are really only worthwhile when water is being drawn from Lake Crescent.

How to fish

There are no major flood basins or backwaters so early-season fly fishing is unremarkable.

Polaroiding is reliable only when the water is low and clear. There are few good weedbeds and hatches are small and irregular. However, terrestrials such as beetles and grasshoppers cause fair rises on warm days and muggy evenings.

Spinning is best when levels are high and the water discoloured. Small lures (such as Celtas and light fish-spoon wobblers) are most appropriate.

When the pools are still and clear, bait casting is much more productive than spinning. Try grasshoppers in the mid to late months of the season, and grubs on warm evenings when the fish are mopping up beetles. Surface-fished golden galaxias are dynamite in the river immediately below Lake Crescent when water is being drawn.

COAL RIVER

Tasmaps Derwent, Lake Sorell, and Little Swanport
Drainage Direct to Pitt Water

Description

The Coal catchment is a low-rainfall area and most of the land flanking the river is flat marginal pasture. While overhanging willows, blackberries and scrub are prevalent along many banks, there is ample room for all trout fishing techniques.

Below the Craigbourne Dam the river is a series of deep silt-bottomed weed-lined pools. The water is regulated to meet local irrigation requirements (see *Craigbourne Dam*), so flows are relatively cool and constant. The river only breaks its banks during major floods when the dam spills. The water is often very clear but becomes turbid after heavy rain, and when the dam has been stirred up by big winds. Minor algal blooms occur in some pools following prolonged warm weather.

Above the Craigbourne Dam the river relies on natural inputs. In summer/autumn flows are often minimal or non-existent and the water recedes into isolated pools. The deepest holes are located between the reservoir and the gorge. Much of the uppermost stretch, in the vicinity of Stonor and Tunnack, is prone to dry up – but even here there are a few permanent pools.

Trout stocks

According to early Parliamentary reports brown trout had been taken to the Coal River by 1870. Self supporting stocks soon established.

Today, the lower reaches from the estuary to the Craigbourne Dam carry an adequate supply of trout but, with the improved habitat resulting from the constant flows, natural recruitment probably results in something short of the optimum carrying capacity. While there have been several liberations of fry in modern times, stocking with very small fish is of dubious value because the water is infested with predatory redfin perch.

Currently most trout caught weigh 0.3-0.9 kg but others to 1.5 kg are relatively common. Rainbows, emigrants from the Craigbourne Dam, are also taken, though they account for only a very small percentage of the total trout harvest.

Above the dam, in the vicinity of Brandy Bottom, the river pools harbour normal-sized river residents and an impressive number of 1.5-2 kg specimens – presumably one-time lake fish. Spawning rainbows are caught from September to November.

Further up, near Stonor and Tunnack, stocks are prone to depletion during droughts. However, fish of surprising size manage to survive the cruellest conditions.

Trout liberations (since 1980)

Wild brown trout

YEAR	SIZE	NUMBER
1981	fry	10 000
1982	fry	10 000
1983	fry	30 000
1988	fry	20 000

Fly fishing

Fly fishing is best on warm or hot days after mid spring. Fish cruise the banks and weedbeds and can be easily polaroided when the water is clear. Although there are irregular daytime rises to mayflies and grasshoppers, surface activity is most pronounced on warm calm evenings when the caddis flies and cockchafer beetles are about.

Lure casting

Spinning is most productive when the river is high and discoloured. As the pools are relatively narrow and shallow, small lures such as Celtas and fish-spoon wobblers are most appropriate. When levels drop and the water clears, lure casting can be quite frustrating and bait fishing becomes more attractive.

Bait fishing

Grasshopper casting is dynamite when the water is low and clear, especially since the fish can be easily polaroided.

Surface-fished grubs work exceptionally well in the evening and at night, particularly during balmy weather when the fish are mopping up beetles.

Hot spots

From August to November small bottlenecks of whitebait occur below the gauging weir just downstream from the Richmond Bridge. Resident fish, as well as the odd sea trout, can sometimes be seen bulging and charging, though the activity is quite irregular.

The best fishing occurs between Richmond and the Craigbourne Dam. While there are good stretches immediately north of Richmond and adjacent to the Fingerpost and Brown Mountain roads, the more distant pools should not be ignored.

The river at Brandy Bottom is very good but the current land owner does not encourage angling.

Although persistent locals take a few good fish from the uppermost reaches, the fishing here is quite unremarkable.

The best tributary stream is White Kangaroo Rivulet.

COATES CREEK

Tasmap Nive
Drainage Derwent system (via Lake King William)

A small fastwater flowing through buttongrass plains. It contains plenty of small brown trout.

COCKATOO DAM

Tasmap Mersey
Drainage Forth system (via Machinery Creek and Lake Barrington)

A small impoundment on the upper reaches of Machinery Creek. It features shallow margins and static levels, and produces trout to 3 kg. The water is drained from time to time but the fishing usually recovers quickly. It was reputedly restocked in 1988.

COCKLE CREEK

Tasmap South East Cape
Drainage Direct to Rocky Bay

Small numbers of good sea trout are taken from the estuary.

COILERS CREEK

Tasmap Tamar
Drainage Direct to the Mersey River

A small but locally popular shingle-bottomed creek. Low flows are common in summer/autumn.

While recruitment is relatively poor, the fish are small. Artificial stocking has occurred as recently as 1979 when 5000 brown trout fry were released – but with little effect on the fishing.

COLLINGWOOD RIVER

Tasmap Franklin
Drainage Gordon system (via the Franklin River)

Like most rivers in the Franklin catchment, the Collingwood is flanked with rainforest and dense scrub. The water is tea coloured and maintains good flows throughout the driest of seasons.

While the river below the Lyell Highway is commonly used by rafters and canoeists to gain access to the Franklin, deep water and steep overgrown banks prevent convenient foot access.

The mid reaches, which run adjacent to the Lyell Highway, are overgrown but largely wadeable. Big bags of 0.1-0.3 kg fish are taken on Celtas when levels are low.

Most of the tiny overgrown tributaries (including the Cardigan River, Raglan Creek and Snake Creek) support lots of very small fish.

See also *Fishing in National Parks*, 5.3.

COMPANION RESERVOIR

Tasmap Hellyer
Drainage Emu River (an instream impoundment)

The 13 m high rockfill dam was built in 1964 by APPM to impound water for industrial use. The lake is surrounded by scrubby hills and the banks are littered with fallen trees. The tea coloured water abounds with slow-growing 0.2-0.6 kg brown trout. Much better fishing exists nearby at Talbots Lagoon and the Waratah lakes.

COOEE CREEK

Tasmap Hellyer
Drainage Direct to Bass Strait

According to early NTFA reports Cooee Creek did not contain any trout until it was stocked with 1750 rainbow fry in 1903. Following this liberation the water was closed to fishing for 3 years to allow the trout to grow to maturity.

Today Cooee Creek contains brown trout only, and most fish are very small. The water is narrow and overgrown and is best suited to bait casting.

COQUET CREEK

Tasmap St Patricks
Drainage North Esk system (via the St Patricks River)

A small overgrown fastwater containing plenty of very small brown trout.

CRACROFT, LAKE

No trout. See *Fishing in National Parks*, 5.2.

CRAIGBOURNE DAM

Tasmap Derwent
Drainage Coal River (a major instream impoundment)

The 24 m high concrete Craigbourne Dam was constructed in 1986 to provide irrigation water for the rural districts of Campania and Richmond. It is not recorded on some current maps but is clearly visible from the Colebrook Road between Campania and Colebrook.

Description

The lake usually fills in winter but is drawn upon as soon as 'natural flows' in the lower Coal River begin to ebb – often in the early months of the trout season. Marked drawdowns are to be expected in summer and autumn.

The water is surrounded by farmland and most banks are grassy and open.

The land extending from the south-west is very flat and the shore recedes markedly as lake-levels drop. The clay/silt bottom is continually disturbed by wave action, and weed growth is relatively sparse. In most years there is some terrestrial regrowth.

Smaller grassy flats flank the original courses of the Coal River and Craigbourne Creek (at the Brandy Bottom end of the lake). These flood at high levels and remain sheltered under most weather conditions.

Many of the northern and south-eastern banks are fairly steep.

The water becomes quite murky after heavy rain and/or strong wind and, while it clears appreciably during prolonged spells of settled weather, there is little scope for polaroiding.

Access and facilities

A sealed road leads from the Colebrook Road along the south-western shore towards the dam-site. At the terminus of this access there is a boat launching ramp (which provides good service unless the lake is exceptionally low) and a toilet block.

There is also vehicular access to the eastern end of the storage from Colebrook via Brandy Bottom, and from the Colebrook Road north of Campania via the Brown Mountain Road and Hardings Road. Small boats can usually be launched from the drowned Craigbourne Road – but there is limited room for turning and parking.

Please remember that the maximum boat speed is 5 knots.

Camping is not encouraged.

Fish stocks

Prior to flooding, the Coal River contained estab-lished populations of brown trout and redfin perch, and both species are self-supporting in the new lake. However, as the Coal River provides relatively modest natural recruitment, brown trout stocks are supplemented with hatchery-reared fish and wild adults.

The rainbow trout fishing is wholly dependent upon artificial stocking.

The average size of the trout and the relative numbers of each species are heavily influenced by stocking regimes. In recent seasons rainbows have accounted for as little as 20% and as much as 60% of the annual harvest. Brown trout to 1.5 kg are to be expected and quite a few attain 2 kg and more. Maiden rainbows of 0.3-1 kg are most common, though mature rainbows often weigh 2 kg or so.

Trout liberations

Wild brown trout

YEAR	SIZE	NUMBER
1986	fry	100 000
1987	fry	50 000
1988	fry	20 000
1989	fry	30 000
1992	adults	150

Craigbourne Dam (courtesy The Mercury*)*

137

Domestic rainbow trout

YEAR	SIZE	NUMBER
1986	large fingerlings	10 000
1989	large fingerlings	6 000
"	adults	700
1990	large fingerlings	2 200
1991	fingerlings	10 000
"	yearlings	3 100
1992	yearlings and older	4 000

Note: in 1993 the IFC promised annual releases of 5000-10 000 rainbow fingerlings.

Bait fishing

Set-rod fishing is extremely popular but the merits of cast-and-retrieve should not be overlooked, especially not on warm muggy evenings when the trout can be seen sipping beetles and/or mudeyes. Worms are ideal bottom baits when rising waters are re-flooding grassy verges, and grubs are best for surface fishing.

Lure fishing

Bright lures work best in the murky water.

The deep banks are ideal for spinning, but those prepared to wade pick up plenty of browns in the shallows.

When trolling, it pays to fish along the deep shores and in the middle of the lake.

Lure fishing is most productive early and late in the season. In the heat of summer it is best to target rainbows by fishing over deep water (not necessarily deep down). Dull days are best.

Fly fishing

If levels are high, good early-season wet-fly fishing occurs over the flooded grassy flats at the eastern end of the storage.

You can expect fair mayfly hatches from mid spring to early autumn, especially on warm calm days. The best action happens along sheltered shores and in the middle of the lake.

Daytime wind lane fishing occurs on warm days in summer and autumn.

The best action is encountered on muggy calm evenings from late spring to early autumn when the trout mop up cockchafer beetles. Modest migrations of mudeyes also occur during this period.

CRATER LAKE

No trout. See *Fishing in National Parks*, 5.4.

CRESCENT, LAKE

Tasmap   Lake Sorell
Drainage   Derwent system (via the River Clyde)

Lake Crescent is a noted trophy-trout water. The fishing is described in detail in the book Trout Guide *(Rob Sloane and Greg French, 1991). A summary only is given here.*

Description

Lake Crescent is a large essentially-natural storage surrounded by open woodland and pockets of pasture. There are extensive weedy marshes along the northern and western shores, and the water in the main basin is usually quite discoloured. The average depth is 1.5 m and the maximum depth is just 2.3 m.

Water enters the lake from Lake Sorell via Interlaken Canal (which is regulated at Lake Sorell by a small gate). A shallow unregulated channel and natural floodway (Kermodes Drain) connects the two lakes when Sorell is at capacity.

The outlet (at the head of the River Clyde) is regulated to provide irrigation and domestic water for the rural districts of Bothwell and Hamilton.

History of water manipulation

The waters of both Lake Sorell and Lake Crescent have been manipulated since the first gates and sluices were erected in order to guarantee summer water flow to a major property at Hamilton on the River Clyde. After 1838 the original structures fell into disrepair.

As a result of prolonged drought, the Clyde Water Trust was established by Act of Parliament in 1857. Works on Sorell and Crescent were vested with five trustees who were charged '*to protect the sources of the River Clyde and to secure a supply of water to the inhabitants of the townships of Bothwell and Hamilton'*.

In 1921 the Clyde Water Trust deepened the outlet channel from Crescent to the River Clyde and built a sluice gate to control the water. In 1926 a hand operated lift-gate was installed on Sorell to allow the control of water into Lake Crescent. The canal between the two lakes was deepened in the late 1960s, as was the channel between Lake Crescent and the Clyde.

In 1983, in reaction to continued drought, the Trust constructed a new outlet on Lake Crescent, enabling the lake to be lowered an additional 0.6 m.

Water is now primarily used for flood irrigation of pasture, though there are significant draw-offs to supply Bothwell and Hamilton. The demand for water has increased in recent years and Lake

High-level at Crescent (photo by Rob Sloane)

Sorell is drawn upon early in the irrigation period (about November). However, largely in an effort to reduce losses by evaporation, the policy of the Trust is to keep Sorell as high as possible and Crescent as low as possible while still supplying sufficient flow to the Clyde.

History of trout stocks

The early stocking history of Crescent is linked to that of Sorell (see *Sorell, Lake*). It is likely that the lake was first directly stocked with trout between 1867 and 1870. Subsequent stocking occurred before the turn of the century and in the early 1900s. Liberations carried out between 1920 and 1960 are generally recorded as having taken place at Lake Sorell, though it is likely that on some occasions trout were placed directly into Crescent. Moreover, there has always been limited migration of trout between the two lakes, particularly in wet years.

Lake Crescent was never recognised in early literature as a noteworthy angling venue. Even in the 1930s, when Lake Sorell finally became popular, scant reference was made to Crescent. This is perhaps not surprising when the lack of natural recruitment and the difficulty of crossing the marshes to fish open water are considered. In short, the trout in Sorell have always been numerous and more catchable, and this has overshadowed the fishing at Crescent.

In the early years anglers showed little appreciation for (or knowledge of) the trophy brown trout fishing at Crescent. Even by the 1950s there were only a few devotees. However, in 1958 the NTFA reported that *'Anglers who fish this lake usually consider themselves unlucky if they grass a fish under 5 lb ... The type of angling is just about confined to spinning with a little natural bait fishing'*.

Moderate popularity of the fishery developed only after the newly formed IFC began transferring adult brown trout from Great Lake in 1960. These relocated trout exhibited unprecedented growth and the NTFA recorded a noticeable increase in the popularity of bait fishing. Anglers came to recognise that native golden galaxias were the staple diet of the trout and it soon became common practice to row a bait out into open water. This unique long-lining method was formally legalised on Lake Crescent in 1972.

In the late 1970s stocking with adult trout was discontinued, and the peak years for trophy trout at Lake Pedder diverted the attention of anglers away from Lake Crescent. Crescent became a forgotten fishery until revived by an intensive stocking programme in the late 1980s.

Golden galaxias

The golden galaxias *(Galaxias auratus)* is endemic to the upper Clyde system – and probably evolved from a population of climbing galaxias *(Galaxias brevipinnis)* long-isolated above the big fall on the River Clyde in the hills above Bothwell.

The species is very common within its range, especially in lakes Sorell and Crescent, and is a major food item for trout.

If other species closely related to the climbing galaxias (such as the Pedder galaxias and the Swan galaxias) are any indication, it is probable that the golden galaxias would not compete well with either climbing galaxias or redfin perch. Anglers are reminded that it is illegal to have in any bait can or elsewhere in your possession any live fish not already present in that water, and that it is illegal to use live or dead redfin for bait.

Trout stocks today

The large size and rapid growth of the trout is essentially a function of limited natural recruitment in combination with an abundant food supply. Only small intermittent creeks flow directly into the lake and the Interlaken Canal is of no real value as a spawning ground (though it does allow small numbers of trout to migrate from Lake Sorell). Yet the extensive shoreline marshes support prolific trout food, especially native golden galaxias.

Since 1985 increased attention has been given to supplementary stocking with both brown trout and rainbow trout. This stocking has boosted trout numbers and the annual harvest but there has also been a reduction in the average size of fish caught. Even so, rainbows of 1-3 kg and browns of 2-3 kg can be expected. Moreover, there is always a reasonable chance of taking browns of 4-6 kg – and fish in excess of 12 kg are reported every now and then.

One of the largest trout ever taken in Tasmania. It was caught by Ludwig Zotch from Lake Crescent in 1971. (courtesy The Mercury)

Trout liberations (since 1980)

Wild brown trout

YEAR	SIZE	NUMBER
1983	fry	100 000
1984	fry	100 000
"	small fingerlings	4 580
1985	small fingerlings	2 000
"	fry	30 000
1986	advanced fry	71 500
"	fry	100 000
1987	large fingerlings (T)	6 000
1989	fry	25 000
1993	yearlings	2 500
"	adults	2 500

(T) = triploid stock

Rainbow trout

YEAR	SIZE	NUMBER
1986	large fingerlings (D)	13 370
1988	large fingerlings (D)	4 000
"	advanced fry (W) (T)	2 000
1989	large fingerlings/yearlings (D)	5 600
1990	small fingerlings (D)	16 000
1991	fingerlings (W)	4 000
1992	fingerlings (W)	3 000

(T) = triploid stock
(D) = domestic stock
(W) = wild stock
Note: in 1993 the IFC promised annual releases of 2000-3000 rainbow fingerlings.

Bait fishing

The best fishing areas are Tea-tree Point, The Island, Triffitt Point and Jacks Point. The native galaxia (which can be taken with light line, a tiny hook and worm bait) are the best bait. The traditional method is to row the bait out 50 m or more – but fish can be caught equally well close in, especially in the band of clear water between the marshes and the shore. A bubble float is an obvious advantage only if extra casting distance is required. The best times to fish are evenings, nights and early mornings from August to early December.

Lure fishing

As the water is very shallow and discoloured, shallow-running Cobra lures with high contrast colours (such as yellow and black) fished as slowly as depth will permit are most effective.

The northern circuit between Tea-tree Point, The Island and Interlaken Marsh is popular with trollers, though the southern end of the lake is favoured in southerly weather.

Drift spinning is probably the most effective way to fish Crescent as it allows you to properly cover the edges of the marshes and the rocky shores.

Spinning from the bank is best done from the rocky points.

Fly fishing

Crescent is mainly a wet-fly water, the recommended flies being galaxia imitations such as large Matukas and fur flies.

The best brown trout fishing is in the marshes from September to early December – before receding water and summer weed growth make the shallows unfishable. Trout can often be *seen* charging after baitfish but blind casting is worthwhile when things are quiet.

Rainbow trout tend to frequent the deep water on the outer edge of the marshes and are best caught from a boat

CUMBERLAND LAKE

Tasmap Pieman
Drainage Little Henty system (via Cumberland Creek)

The current 10 m high dam on Cumberland Creek was constructed by the Cumberland mining company in 1936. The lake lies on a buttongrass shelf and, while there are steep rainforested banks at the foot of Cumberland Hill, most banks are fishable. The water is dark with tannin.

IFC records suggest that the lake was stocked with some 30 000 brown trout fry between 1970 and 1976, though there is no recognised trout fishery today. Blackfish are common.

Access is via a 2 km stretch of steep washed-out vehicular track which extends through dense wet-forest from the Trial Harbour Road.

CURLY, LAKE

Tasmap Wedge
Drainage Gordon system (via the Gell River)

A small wilderness brown-trout fishery surrounded by dense scrub. The easiest access is a cross-country expedition from Pokana Bay, Lake Gordon, though this is possible only if you have a seaworthy dinghy or runabout. Alternative (much longer) cross-country expeditions can be taken from the Rasselas (walking) Track.

See also *Fishing in National Parks*, 5.2.

CURRAJONG RIVULET

Tasmap Lake Sorell
Drainage South Esk system (via the Blackman system)

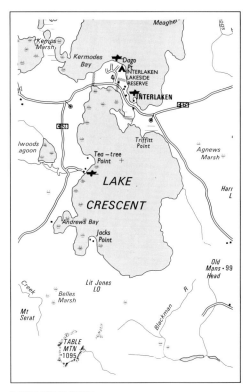

LAKE CRESCENT

An intermittent creek. While some fish are taken near the confluence with Tin Dish Creek, fishing in the mid to upper reaches is not recommended.

CURRIES RIVER DAM

Tasmap Tamar
Drainage Curries River (an instream impoundment)

Description

This domestic water supply storage lies behind a 26 m high earthfill dam and backs up against rolling forested hills. There are some steep banks but most shores are relatively flat. In places, high water floods pockets of dense tea-tree. An esplanade of cleared land extends along much of the southern shoreline, and another clearing (about 1 ha) extends north-east from the northern end of the causeway. Much of the southern shore is choked with dense weeds and rushes. The water is quite tea coloured and some shores become slightly murky after strong wind.

141

History

In 1963 the NTFA recorded that *'Through the I.F.C., title of the land to be flooded and the outskirts of the proposed lake have been registered in the name of the Fishermen of Tasmania'* but this proposal never went ahead.

The current dam was built in 1979 by the RWSC to supply domestic water to the George Town district. Following negotiations with the IFC and anglers, the laws which restricted public fishing were relaxed before the beginning of the 1990-91 trout season.

Boating was allowed from the beginning of the 1993-94 season, but only on the understanding that the IFC would legislate against fishing from motorised boats.

Access and facilities

The main access leads from the Bridport Road across a causeway (about three quarters of the way down the lake) to the western corner of the north shore. Here there is a clearing with parking areas, swings, fireplaces and a couple of modest picnic shelters. The road is gated about 1 km beyond the causeway and there is no public vehicular-access to the damsite.

Several short tracks lead from the Bridport Road to the southern shore – but these are usually closed to vehicular traffic.

Camping is not encouraged.

Small boats can be launched near the causeway.

Trout stocks

Brown trout existed in Curries River prior to the flooding, and there is still some scope for natural recruitment. However, since 1989 natural stocks have been complemented with hatchery-reared fish.

Illegal releases of rainbow trout occurred before the dam was opened to public fishing and the IFC made further releases in 1990. Unfortunately rainbows proved to be susceptible to tapeworms – a phenomenon not uncommon in coastal lagoons since the life cycle of tapeworms (and redworms) involves sea-bird hosts. Just why rainbows are more susceptible than browns is unclear, though it may be linked to the species' relatively high consumption of galaxias. While the worm poses no known threat to human health, its presence in trout flesh is unappealing and, because of complaints from anglers, the suitability of future stocking with rainbow trout is being questioned.

The average size, quality and quantity of fish taken alters with changes in stocking regimes.

Most fish in anglers' bags weigh from 0.5-1.5 kg – but specimens in excess of 3 kg are not especially uncommon and some of the galaxia feeders exceed 5 kg.

The spawning stream is very small and the lake is unlikely to suffer from natural overpopulation. My guess is that, in view of the abundance of forage fish (galaxias), there will always be respectable numbers of large trout.

To date rainbows have accounted for as much as 90% of the annual harvest – and bags of one fish per angler for every two days of effort have been average. However, these figures are heavily influenced by the high incidence of set-rod fishing, and both the catch rate and the incidence of brown trout captures are appreciably higher for fly fishers and lure casters.

Trout liberations

Wild brown trout

YEAR	SIZE	NUMBER
1989	advanced fry	15 000
1990	fry	50 000
1991	yearlings	5 090
1992	advanced fry	6 400
"	yearlings	3 000

Domestic rainbow trout

YEAR	SIZE	NUMBER
1990	fingerlings	21 000
"	yearlings	1 150

Note: illegal liberations of domestic rainbows have occurred since the mid to late 1980s.

Brown trout x Atlantic salmon hybrids

YEAR	SIZE	NUMBER
1993	advanced fry	10 000

Bait fishing

Set-rod fishing with worms and grubs is very popular with locals, the most patronised area being the causeway and nearby banks. However, the merits of cast-and-retrieve fishing should not be ignored.

Lure fishing

There is ample room for spinning from the shore, though wading is essential if you want to cover a lot of water. The most-open areas are along the northern banks.

Drift spinning and trolling (from boats worked by manual labour) are highly recommended. Try casting along the fringes of the weeds where the big trout hammer the galaxias.

Fly fishing

Shore-based fly fishing is generally unremarkable, though working a wet along the northern shores sometimes results in fair catches.

Feature sport occurs when the trout are charging about after galaxias – and to take full advantage of this activity you need a boat. The best action occurs along the outer fringes of the southern weedbeds. Rainbows have provided the most reliable sport, though browns also feed on baitfish.

While rises are irregular and fairly unpredictable, spectacular activity occurs from time to time. Good ant falls are possible in early spring, and mudeyes and beetles are taken on warm calm evenings in summer and autumn.

Because there is little scope for polaroiding, fly fishers (even those with boats) often end up blind fishing with wets. This can be tough play – but remember that there is always the chance of something big for your efforts.

CURRUTHERS, LAKE

No trout. See *Fishing in National Parks*, 5.4.

CUVIER RIVER

Tasmap Nive
Drainage Derwent system (via Lake St Clair)

A shallow shingle-bottomed fastwater. Small browns and rainbows are common in the lower reaches from Lake St Clair to the Hugel junction, whereas only brown trout are found in the upper reaches. Celta fishing when levels are low offers the best chance of success. Wading is essential.

See also *Fishing in National Parks*, 5.4.

CYGNET RIVER

Tasmaps Freycinet, Break O'Day, and St Pauls
Drainage Direct to the Swan River

Brown trout exist from the Swan junction to Meetus Falls. (There were no fish at all above the falls until the IFC released the endangered Swan galaxias in 1993.)

The quality and nature of the trout fishing is very similar to that of other Swan system streams (see *Swan River*). In times of low flow the water is quite clear, though the deep holes always have a slightly milky appearance. While there is relatively little weed growth or insect life, galaxias (especially jollytails) abound.

In the lower reaches, during typical summer/autumn flow regimes, much of the shingle bed is exposed. However, several of the permanent holes are long and deep and extend from bank to bank.

In the mid reaches there are numerous pools connected by distinct trickles of flowing water. Many holes cover the entire width of the stream and back up against undercut banks. Others are small 'puddles' encircled by exposed shingle.

The best fishing is found where there are pockets of deep water and reasonable amounts of cover. Most trout are small but some exceed 1 kg.

DAISY LAKES

Tasmap Mersey
Drainage Derwent system (via the Powena and Pine systems)
Location Western Lakes

The Daisy Lakes are three clearwaters located in one of the few places in the north-east of the Western Lakes not ravaged by wildfire. They are surrounded by verdant heath and pencil pines.

In Lake Nutting there are several large shallow silt-bottomed bays in which trout can be

Daisy Lakes

polaroided well out from the shore. Most other banks are deep and rocky.

Fair rises occur – but they are irregular.

Most trout weigh 0.3-1.2 kg and others exceed 1.5 kg.

See also *Fishing in National Parks*, 5.1.

DALE BROOK

Tasmaps Mersey and Meander
Drainage Meander system
Location Great Western Tiers

The water is crystal, fast, and (when levels are low) ideal for Celta fishing.

While early NTFA reports suggest that Dale Brook was stocked with rainbows between 1906 and 1918, this species failed to establish. In 1919 it was claimed that fish to 5 lb could be taken, but today brown trout of 0.2-0.5 kg are typical.

DAPHNE, LAKE

No trout. See *Fishing in National Parks*, 5.3.

DASHER RIVER

Tasmap Forth
Drainage Mersey River

A wide rocky shallow creek flanked by bushland and pasture. The water flows year-round and wading is a distinct advantage. The trout grow slowly but, while many are undersized, some exceed 0.5 kg. The best ways to fish are by bait casting with worms when the water is swollen, and by Celta fishing and grasshopper casting when levels are low. There is also scope for accurate fly casting.

DAVEY RIVER

Tasmaps Port Davey and Olga
Drainage Direct to the Southern Ocean

In 1904 the NTFA recorded that '... *125* [quinnat yearlings] *were sent to the Davey River, in the south, which contains no other salmonidae'*. This species failed to establish.

While there have been unconfirmed reports of sea trout taken in gill nets in Port Davey, it seems that brown trout have not taken up residence in the freshwater reaches.

See also *Fishing in National Parks*, 5.2.

DAWSON RIVER

See *Nelson Bay River*.

DEE LAGOON

Tasmap Shannon
Drainage Derwent system
Location Central Highlands

Dee Lagoon has a reputation for being a difficult trout water – but it contains superb fish and, if approached in the right manner, can be expected to provide outstanding sport. It is covered in detail in the book Trout Guide *(Rob Sloane and Greg French, 1991). A summary only is given here.*

Description

Dee Lagoon is a clearwater hydro-electric impoundment surrounded by tall eucalypt forests. It lies behind a 15.2 m high rockfill/clay-core dam and is primarily used to divert the upper Dee catchment via the Dee Tunnel into Bradys Lake. At full supply the water is 655.32 m above sea level, and the normal maximum drawdown is just 0.3 m. The lake is said to be 'full' or 'down' depending upon the input from Lake Echo via the Lake Echo Power Station.

History

Dee Lagoon was created in 1955 as part of the Tungatinah power development. Prior to flooding, the upper River Dee provided quality trout fishing. It was ideal for fly fishing, being sluggish and weedy with clear banks, and brown trout of 2-4 lb were common. The stream also held redfin perch, the progeny of early liberations into Lake Echo.

In June 1955 the IFC released the first rainbow trout into Dee Lagoon and by the end of that year more than 21 000 yearlings had been turned out. During the 1955-56 season many browns (former river-residents) and rainbows were caught. By the following season browns to 9 lb and rainbows to 5 lb were being landed.

Despite continued stocking with rainbow trout, naturally-spawned brown trout soon were dominant. In an effort to improve the rainbow fishing the Dee was closed during the 1964-65 season to enable yearling rainbow stock to *'grow to a bigger size before capture'*, but subsequent angling reports condemned the experiment as *'a waste of time'*.

Annual stocking with rainbow trout has continued to the present and Dee Lagoon is still managed as a rainbow trout fishery.

Trout stocks

Although the Dee is managed as a rainbow trout water, wild brown trout account for at least 50% of the annual harvest. The browns are mostly 0.8-1.5 kg, though specimens to 3 kg are not uncommon in the weedy Mentmore end.

Rainbow trout are more common in the deep open southern basin than in the weedy shallows. Hatchery-reared fish account for at least 80% of the rainbows caught – and among these fish are a significant number of triploids. The rainbows are typically 0.8-1.5 kg, though quite a few attain 2.5 kg or so.

The Dee also harbours a prolific population of redfin perch.

Trout liberations (since 1985)

Rainbow trout

YEAR	SIZE	NUMBER
1985	small fingerlings	8 000
"	yearlings	1 500
1986	large fingerlings (T)	4 000
1987	small fingerlings (T)	900
1988	small fingerlings (T)	2 000
1990	small fingerlings (T)	1 000
"	large fingerlings	3 000
1991	fingerlings (D)	2 000
1992	advanced fry	4 000

(T) = triploid stock
(D) = domestic stock
Note: in 1993 the IFC promised annual liberations of 4000 rainbow fingerlings.

Fly fishing

There is only limited scope for fishing from the shore and if you don't have a boat you are bound to get frustrated.

Warm days from December to March bring the gum beetles out of the surrounding forests, while red-and-black leaf hoppers feature on calm days from March to early May. Close imitation and precise presentation are essential because the water is very clear and the trout can be quite spooky. Don't forget your polaroids!

The heaviest beetle falls occur around the southern basin and the rainbows are the real challenge. The Neck, Station Bay Point, Hill 24, and Brownie Bay are normally the best areas. The beetles take to the air when the day warms up and the best fishing can be expected between 11 am and 3 pm. Very hot and bright conditions often produce an oversupply of gum beetles and the trout may go quiet during the middle of the day. In these conditions the browns often start mopping up on dusk.

*Triploid rainbow from Dee Lagoon
(photo by Rob Sloane)*

If fish are hard to find, wet-fly fishing in Station Bay and Paton Bay is a good fall-back, especially when the Lake Echo Power Station is running.

Dee Lagoon also offers excellent early-morning wind lane fishing. The best midge hatches occur after calm frosty mornings.

Lure fishing

The southern basin is ideal spinning water, though you can expect to lose lures on submerged tree stumps and logs. Rainbows take well in rough weather – and wind-exposed shores are best.

The Eastern Shore, Station Bay, and Brownie Bay are good lure-casting areas when the wind is on shore. Popular trolling circuits in the southern basin include Duckhole Bay, the island, the stump shore, and Station Bay.

Special regulations

The season opens on the Saturday nearest to 1 October and closes on the Sunday nearest to 31 May. The River Dee and Mentmore Creek above Dee Lagoon are closed to fishing at all times.

Boating

The recommended launching ramp is located 1 km west of the Dee Dam on the Victoria Valley Road. Small dinghies can also be launched near

145

the dam and further along the Victoria Valley Road at Brownie Bay and Paton Bay.

Camping

Informal camping is possible around all accessible shores. Favourite areas include the grassy point adjacent to the outlet canal in Paton Bay, near the launching sites in Brownie Bay, around the main boat ramp south of Spillway Bay, and on the eastern shore near the dam.

DEE, RIVER

Tasmaps Tyenna and Shannon
Drainage Direct to the River Derwent

Early Parliamentary records indicate that brown trout were established in the River Dee by 1869. In 1880 William Senior *(Travel and Trout in the Antipodes)* wrote:

'The Dee is a charming little tributary, reached by means of a spring cart over seven miles of

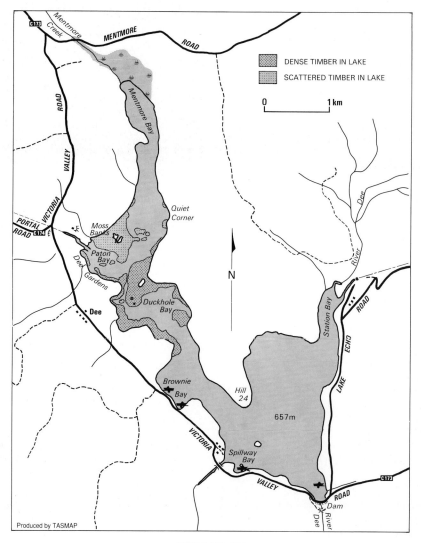

Produced by TASMAP

extremely rough bushroad. It is a mountain stream, and gives fair sport even with an artificial fly; it has, moreover, the additional recommendation of occasional clearings on the banks.'

The best section of river was drowned beneath Dee Lagoon in 1955. Today the best fishing occurs from the confluence with the River Derwent to just above the Lyell Highway. This stretch is flanked by pasture and, while most banks are overgrown with willows, there is room for tight Celta fishing and bait casting. There is a steady flow through the shallow riffles and stony pools – and trout of 0.3 - 0.5 kg are common.

From the head of the pasture to the Father of Marshes Road, the river winds through a steep densely-forested valley. Normal flows are disappointing and the pools are rarely fished.

The stretch between the Father of Marshes Road and the Dee Dam has negligible flow, the water being diverted via Dee Lagoon and the Dee Tunnel into Brady Lake.

Fishing is not permitted at any time in the River Dee between Dee Lagoon and Lake Echo.

DEEP CREEK

Tasmap Circular Head
Drainage Direct to Duck Bay

A small overgrown creek which supports plenty of small resident browns.

Fair catches of sea trout are taken at the estuary from August to November.

Some 6000 rainbow fry were released in 1929, but this species failed to establish.

DEEP LAKE

See *Bar Lakes System*.

DENISON RIVER

Tasmaps Olga, Wedge, and Nive
Drainage Direct to the Gordon River

A large tea-coloured fastwater in the heart of the south-west wilderness. It is known to harbour lots of slow-growing brown trout but is rarely visited by anglers.

See also *Fishing in National Parks, 5.3*.

D'ENTRECASTEAUX RIVER

(known to some locals as the Pigsty River)

Tasmaps South East Cape and Huon
Drainage Direct to Recherche Bay

The D'Entrecasteaux River flows through dense wet-forest and is dark with tannin.

The estuary and lower freshwater reaches are accessible by vehicular track from the Cockle Creek Road. There is only limited scope for shore-based fishing and a small dinghy is recommended. The sea trout fishing is superb, especially from early September through until mid December.

The mid section of the river, near the South Cape Road is narrow, deep and fast. Dense forest overhangs most banks and access is extremely difficult. Some trout, including a few in excess of 1.4 kg, have been taken on bait near the bridge – but the fishing can hardly be recommended.

The largely inaccessible uppermost reaches are small fastwaters which support plenty of very small brown trout.

DERBY HOLE

See *Briseis Hole*.

DERWENT, RIVER

Tasmaps Derwent, Tyenna, Shannon, and Nive
Drainage Direct to the Southern Ocean

Hobart, Tasmania's first European settlement, was established on the outer Derwent estuary in 1804, and farms were soon in production in the fertile New Norfolk and Ouse districts. The Derwent grew to be the commercial hub of the island so it was chosen from other suitable catchments to be the site of the first salmon/trout hatchery. It became the cradle of brown trout in Australasia.

At 182 km the Derwent is Tasmania's third largest river. Today it is a remarkable brown trout fishery, offering fine sea trout angling and, in the tributaries, traditional stream-sport.

History of salmonids in the Derwent

Brown trout

The story of the introduction and acclimatisation of brown trout in Tasmania is intricately linked with the Derwent system and is described in *About Our Sportfish*, 2.1.

The Salmon Ponds (the first trout hatchery in the Southern Hemisphere) was established on the banks of a tributary of the Derwent (the Plenty River) in the early 1860s. The first brown trout were turned out into the Plenty in April 1865 – and by 1867 further consignments had been taken to the Ouse, Clyde, Lachlan, Dee, Bagdad, Sorell and Jones rivers. Brown trout soon established throughout the system. Indeed, in 1869 the Commissioners noted:

> 'During the months of June and July last, at every suitable spot for a distance of several miles along the course of the [Plenty River], several, often many pairs of fish of all sizes, were to be seen at all hours of the day, busily engaged in forming their nests and depositing their spawn.'

Stocking of the Derwent system continued in earnest until the 1950s, though releases after the 1860s probably had little impact on existing populations or the overall quality of the fishing.

Rainbow trout

Rainbows were first introduced to Tasmania in the 1898-99 season and there is little doubt that the Derwent system received stocks almost immediately. Brood fish would have been held at the Salmon Ponds and stocking of southern waters would have been no less enthusiastic than that done in the north of the island (see *About Our Sportfish*, 2.2). However, wild populations established only in the highland lakes – and today rainbows are rare in the river and instream impoundments below Lake King William. The species has even failed to establish in most of the fastwater tributary streams, though wild fish are taken from the Florentine River and domestic fish are found in the Tyenna River.

Brook trout

Brook trout were reared at the Salmon Ponds from the early 1880s to the early 1900s, and new brood stock has been maintained since 1963. While small liberations (both deliberate and accidental) have occurred in the Derwent system, the species has fared poorly. A wild population exists in Clarence Lagoon, an isolated headwater lake.

Atlantic salmon

The Atlantic salmon was the inspiration behind the first attempts to introduce salmonids to the Antipodes. But, despite the release of significant numbers of fry and smolts, it seems that no fish ever returned from the sea.

A small number of Atlantic salmon are taken from the estuary today – but all are domestics which have escaped from nearby fish farms.

The attempts to establish Atlantic salmon are discussed more fully in *About Our Sportfish*, 2.4.

Pacific salmon

The failed attempts to establish Pacific salmon in the Derwent are discussed under *About Our Sportfish*, 2.5.

The Derwent Power Development

While a small weir with control gates had been built at the southern end of Lake St Clair by 1937, the first major instream hydro-electric impoundment (Lake King William) was not completed until 1949. Further dams were installed on the lower Derwent in subsequent years – Wayatinah (1957), Catagunya (1962), Meadowbank (1967), Repulse (1968) and Cluny (1968). In addition to drowning the entire mid section of the river, the dams have altered the very nature of the lower reaches and estuary. Flows are regulated and there is no longer any major flooding and flushing. Also, the dams are major physical barriers to migratory fish and mammals. Meadowbank Dam marks the upper limit of sea trout, whitebait, grayling, eels (though some are manually transported further upstream), and seals.

Of the instream impoundments only Meadowbank Lake, Wayatinah Lagoon and Lake King William are popular trout fisheries.

Trout fishing in the Derwent Estuary

Hobart, together with its suburbs and its satellite communities, dominates both banks of the lower Derwent estuary. There is no doubt that far more anglers reside in the Derwent valley than live near any other of Tasmania's other trout fisheries. Yet most of Hobart's anglers ignore the estuary, or pay only cursory attention to it. This lack of interest cannot entirely be attributed to Tasmanian anglers' traditional preference for lake fishing. Perhaps anglers are afraid of the unknown – the unpredictability of sea trout and the dynamics of tidal waters. Perhaps they are suspicious of pollution levels. Or maybe the Derwent is under-utilized simply because it seems so unlikely that good trout fishing can be found minutes from one's backyard in saltwater amid the urban sprawl and heavy industry.

General description

Urban development is concentrated on the banks of the outer estuary, south of the Tasman Bridge. From the wharves in the port of Hobart to the southern suburb of Taroona there are some 15 km of virtually unbroken suburbia. Similarly, the 10 km or so of eastern shore from the bridge to Tranmere is intensely residential. The outer estuary itself is up to 6 km wide and relatively featureless. Several well-known local anglers successfully target trout at Kangaroo Bluff, Howrah Point, and other places on the eastern shore as far south as Tranmere Point, but it is widely accepted that by far the best fishing is to be found upstream of the Tasman Bridge.

TASMAN BRIDGE TO BRIDGEWATER

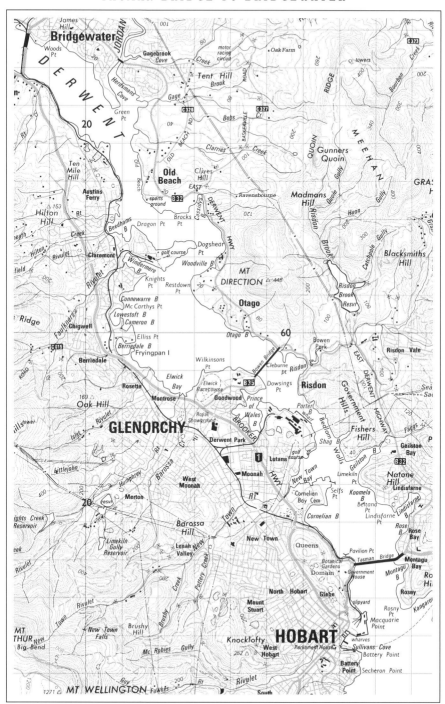

The upper 40 km or so of estuary between the Tasman Bridge and New Norfolk has a distinct, very salty, bottom layer, and a relatively shallow layer of less salty water (which becomes further diluted during periods of heavy flow). The only major inflow is at the head of the estuary – and this is regulated by upstream hydro-electric dams.

Between the Tasman Bridge and the Bowen Bridge the estuary varies in width from about 0.5 to 2 km. The water remains consistently deep and, while there are some relatively shallow bays, there is no significant deepwater channel. The shores are predominantly gentle slopes of gravel and/or rock but there are no extensive wadeable shallows. The major industrial areas are on the western shore – Selfs Point and the zinc works. Land along the eastern shore is residential. At Rose Bay, Lindisfarne and Geilston Bay many houses are located within 50 m of the water.

From the Bowen Bridge to the Bridgewater Bridge the river bed becomes complex. The most significant feature is the deepwater channel which serpents the bottom, in places running along the shoreline. While the bays and flats adjacent to the deepwater are not especially shallow, relative to the channel they are little influenced by tidal and freshwater currents. The shores mostly are rocky slopes similar to those south of the Bowen Bridge. Suburbia continues

along the western banks but most development is back from the water. Cadbury's chocolate factory, a major industry, is located near Dogshear Point (Cadbury Point). Land fronting the eastern shore is mostly rural-residential, though there are significant housing developments at Old Beach, Gagebrook and Bridgewater.

Above Bridgewater the most significant features are the extensive saline flats. While many of these shallow expanses are congested with semi-terrestrial rushes there also are vast open mud-flats. The marshes are inundated only during very high tides, and the mud is exposed only when tides are exceptionally low. Winding through the tidal shallows is the continuation of the deepwater channel, narrow and well defined but difficult to detect from the shore during normal tides. The surrounding land is mostly rural and rural-residential.

At Boyer there is a major pulp and paper industry. Above this complex the river is narrow (about 100 m average) and uniformly deep. The edges are too sharp to wade and overhanging willows and scrub impede access along the banks.

New Norfolk, one of the State's most significant rural centres, marks the head of the estuary. There are open grassy esplanades in the township (from which practical shore-based angling can be enjoyed) but most banks are

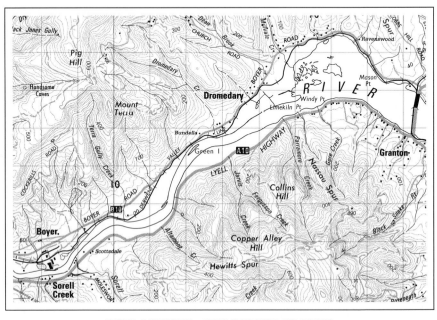

RIVER DERWENT – BRIDGEWATER TO BOYER

Near the zinc works

overgrown and the river remains deep and largely unwadeable.

The first significant rapid exists at Lawitta, about 3 km from New Norfolk, above which there is no tidal influence. A further 5 km upstream there is a much larger drop/rapid.

Pollution

The estuary has been highly degraded as a result of heavy industry and urban development. The major sources of pollution are sub-standard sewerage systems (from Hobart to New Norfolk), the zinc works at Lutana, and the pulp and paper factory at Boyer.

High levels of bacteria exist throughout the estuary as a result of poor sewerage systems. This has resulted in the closure of several beaches and calls for the upgrading of sewerage treatment plants. Some councils (eg. Hobart) have already taken steps to guarantee future tertiary treatment.

The zinc works at Lutana was established during World War 1 and has since diversified to produce a range of products. Currently it is operated by Pasminco Metals – EZ. Throughout the history of the plant toxic waste has been emptied into the Derwent. This waste has been high in heavy metals such as zinc, cadmium, lead, copper and mercury. In the 1970s there was considerable academic and public concern over very

high metal levels in fish. As a result of this concern the company, in the mid 1970s and early 1980s, undertook several measures to reduce toxic output. However, until recently the company still operated under three ministerial exemptions, the so called 'licences to pollute'. In 1991 an advanced effluent treatment system was commissioned, which removes virtually all metals from factory waste. The discharge now complies with requirements of the Environment Protection Act. In 1993 a new acid plant was commissioned removing the need for the final ministerial exemption. The big problem now is the existing heavy metal in the river sediments near the factory.

The pulp and paper factory at Boyer is owned by ANM and has operated since the mid 1940s. Discharge from the factory includes wood fibre, dissolved organic substances, toxic resin acids (from softwood), and some heavy metals (including mercury). Until recently all waste passed through only crude settlement ponds. Enormous quantities of wood fibre were flushed downstream – and have settled over the river bed in significant quantities as far downstream as the Bowen Bridge. Decaying organic matter consumes oxygen and releases foul-smelling sulphides. Consequently, water quality deteriorates significantly under conditions of moderate temperatures and reduced river flow (such as commonly exist for about

Looking for bow-waves on the rocky shores by the Tasman Bridge

eight months of the year). So severe is this pollution that bottom fauna has been severely depleted from some 20 km of the upper estuary (between Bridgewater and New Norfolk). In fact, in this section of the river, the water suitable for fish extends no more than about 2 m below the surface – and even this surface water deteriorates such that fish migrations are artificially curtailed for up to 6 months of the year.

In 1988 ANM commissioned a new effluent treatment plant and effectively reduced emissions by some 50%. In 1990 the second stage of the new plant was completed ensuring that wood fibre emissions were reduced to about 20% of the pre-1988 levels and that significant reductions in other pollutants were achieved. While the company no longer operates under a ministerial exemption, many academics believe that the maximum pollution levels set by law are inadequate. Moreover, there remain major long-term problems with the organic waste already in the river.

Despite past and current problems, trout still frequent the Derwent in very appreciable numbers. While heavy metals continue to be of concern, both sea run and resident trout remain edible.

Sea trout

Early-season sea trout fishing is dependent upon migrations of baitfish – mainly *Lovettia* and

galaxias (see notes on sea trout under *About Our Sportfish*, 2.1).

In the Derwent *Lovettia* are often present in all sections of the estuary by August. While *Lovettia* prefer to spawn high in the upper estuary at the limit of tidal influence, they avoid fresh water and pollution. The river section where most spawning occurs varies from year to year according to changes in river conditions. Usually it is between Bridgewater and the rapids at Lawitta.

Most galaxias are feeding while migrating up the estuary and, although they too roughly follow the edge of deepwater channel, they tend to stray further than *Lovettia*. Bottlenecks occur immediately below the rapids above New Norfolk. In the Derwent the vast majority of migrating galaxias are jollytails *(G. maculatus)*. These fish are less likely than other whitebait to be intimidated by moderate freshes. The schools are typically smaller than those of *Lovettia* but usually are more frequent and less dependent upon the state of the tide. While the main runs usually have been completed by November, small runs sometimes continue beyond December.

While it is the whitebait runs which attract sea trout in from the ocean, the diet of sea trout when in the estuary is quite broad. Among significant dietary items are shrimps *(Paratya)* and crabs. Shrimps frequently appear in impressive

Most Derwent sea trout are taken in the evening and after dark.

numbers on rocky shallows in the lower estuary and at such times sea trout can be found chasing, charging and tailing. Crab feeders are usually not so active but can sometimes be seen foraging along the shallow rocky fringes.

During late summer and early autumn there are negligible numbers of sea trout in the estuary. Sea trout re-enter the estuary in March/April and migrate into freshwater to spawn. Surprisingly, this run is barely exploited, not even by those who are devotees of the estuary during the early season. The spawning run probably is quite direct and the fish confine themselves to the deepwater channel. As they are not feeding (not enthusiastically anyway) they simply are not often seen. Also, it is probable that potentially-good early runs in the estuary above Bridgewater are often curtailed by low oxygen and high sulphide levels. The best runs occur after (or during) the first good post-summer fresh. Obviously the best places to fish are along the edges of the river channel and at the bottlenecks below the rapids above New Norfolk. Other hot spots exist upstream – at the mouths of major tributaries and below Meadowbank Dam.

Slob trout

While I have taken a few slobs as far downstream as Bellerive, residents are most prevalent in the upper estuary. The IFC has determined that during the whitebait runs approximately 30% of the trout taken at Dogshear Point are slobs. At Boyer about 70% of the annual harvest comprises slob trout. Residents typically range from 0.5-1.5 kg but can be 4 kg plus. They feed predominantly on shrimps, crabs and other invertebrates but also take advantage of the whitebait. Although slobs do not seem to migrate long distances after baitfish they do contribute significantly to the spawning migrations. They probably vacate severely polluted sections of the upper estuary during summer.

Other fish

The mid estuary is a marine/estuarine habitat and supports many fully estuarine species. Bottom fishers find that cod, flathead, dogfish, gummy sharks, eels and bream take baits intended for trout. Fly fishers and lure casters take many mullet as well as some blackback salmon, whiptail (juvenile blue grenadier) and couta. The tailing fish on the gravel/rock beaches include a large number of mullet and bream.

Above Bridgewater anglers are much less likely to encounter species other than trout. Part of the reason for this simply is that the freshwater/estuarine habitat supports fewer fully marine fish. Bait fishers take eels, bream and sometimes cod. Anglers fishing the surface layer catch a relatively small number of mullet and, above Boyer, some redfin perch.

When to fish

Anglers may fish the estuary downstream of Dogshear Point from May to July when the rest of the river is closed to angling – and there are rewards for the dedicated. However, the best fishing is from August through until the end of October. Good bags can be maintained throughout November and sometimes into December. Many local anglers insist that the fishing winds down from about mid September but I suspect that this attitude is more associated with improved fishing conditions further afield than with any dramatic decline in estuary fishing. Although slobs can be taken in the mid reaches throughout summer, the fishing is relatively unremarkable and cannot really be recommended to anyone other than those without the means or desire to look further afield. Between Bridgewater and New Norfolk the trout simply cannot tolerate summer pollution levels. If there has been a fair autumn flush the spawning run may start as early as late March. More commonly it does not get underway until mid April.

Trout can be taken throughout the day but evening fishing is usually most productive. It is best to be on the water at least an hour before sunset and to continue until at least one hour after dark. On very good evenings the fishing may continue throughout the night. Another period of peak activity can occur at dawn.

For the fly fisher interested in sight fishing, ideal evenings are warm and calm. The dedicated also find rewards in flogging a wet during cold rough weather. Lure casting and bottom fishing are productive under most conditions.

The tide influences the psyche of the angler at least as much as it influences trout. I first fished the estuary when I was a teenager and came to favour low incoming tides. Such was my preference for just the right tide that I frequently began fishing post midnight. And I took many big bags! Interestingly, most fish taken at low tide were crab feeders. Perhaps the re-inundation of the littoral zone stimulated benthic activity. Despite my personal preferences, several friends continued to insist that incoming high-tides were best. They claimed that whitebait (especially *Lovettia*) were much more obvious at such times – and this proved to be good advice. However, the more I fished the more I came to disregard the state of tide and rely upon the time of day. Evening undoubtedly is the best time to fish. State of tide most certainly affects the feeding pattern of trout but, providing the angler fishes according to prevailing conditions, it is not such an influence on overall productivity.

Significant freshes reduce surface activity and are bad news for fly fishers and lure casters. However, providing the river is not in flood, anglers who fish bait on the bottom often fare quite well. They probably catch fish which have moved deep to avoid the surface layer of freshwater. If the fresh is very big, fish drop downstream and probably vacate some sections of the estuary altogether. This is especially true above Bridgewater where fish otherwise could only avoid freshwater by moving into the stagnant deepwater. However, it should be recognised that sea trout are quite happy to chase whitebait into the lower freshwater reaches during periods of moderate to low flow.

Hot spots for the shore-based angler

In the lower estuary my favourite fishing spots include Rose Bay, the shoreline between Lindisfarne Bay and Geilston Bay, Church Point,

Dowsings Point, Otago Bay, the shoreline from Dogshear Point to Dragon Point, and Old Beach. At all of these sites the shores are gently sloping gravel/rock surfaces and there is little weed growth. These sites also are reasonably close to the deepwater channel. The water is deep enough for practical lure casting but shallow enough to permit sight fishing. Trout can often be seen ambushing whitebait from around miniature rock-projections. I have seen big fish feeding with such enthusiasm that they have temporarily run aground. Watching a 2 kg plus sea trout floundering around in a few inches of water, back and fins clearly visible between splashes, is quite an experience! These shores also are good for shrimp and crab feeders – and tails and/or bow waves can often be seen.

The upper Jordan estuary is accessible from the Cove Hill sub-division (on the eastern bank) and the Cove Hill Road (along the western bank). Here the banks are relatively deep and well suited to lure casting and bottom fishing. Fly fishers target the whitebait feeders at the head of the estuary.

At Bridgewater by far the best fishing is away from the extensive shallow flats! The channel under the bridge is extremely popular and can be fished from the north-eastern shore. There also is limited scope for fishing the southern side of the channel from the causeway. While the shore from the bridge to Woods Point is a typical gravel slope, at high tide the water backs up into a narrow band of rushes and weeds and sea trout can often be found chasing whitebait amongst the emergent vegetation.

Mason Point lies on the edge of the main channel and is further influenced by tidal currents which move (via a network of gutters) through the big bay to the north-west. It is a prime spot for all types of trout fishing. Whitebait feeders work along the edges of the rushes when tides are high.

While rush-choked flats and dense scrub extend along most banks between Bridgewater and New Norfolk, there are several very good fishing spots. Limekiln Point, on the southern bank, projects into the main channel and is extremely well respected among anglers even though it offers just 70 m or so of fishable shoreline. The banks are deep and the water usually is lapping grassy/weedy verges. Trout can often be seen chasing whitebait. As the name implies, the point formally was an industrial area. Ruins remain of the kiln and jetty. Another good shore exists below the aquatic club on the southern bank, about halfway between Bridgewater and

New Norfolk. A little further upstream, the Lyell Highway embraces the river. At the mouth of Sorell Creek a small section of shore is accessible. This is a good spot at spawning time as well as during the whitebait runs.

In New Norfolk there are several open grassy esplanades from which all fishing methods can be successfully employed.

There are congregations of whitebait (including *Lovettia* in dry seasons) below the rapids at Lawitta, though access to the water is severely impeded by willows and scrub.

The second rapid is easily accessed from the southern bank. *Lovettia* do not progress this far up river but bottlenecks of galaxias occur from time to time. Spawners also tend to 'rest up' below the fast water.

The mouths of major tributaries (such as the Plenty, Styx and Tyenna) are good at spawning time, as is the Derwent below Meadowbank Dam.

Tips for boat handlers

Boat handlers using the lower estuary should concentrate on areas near the main channel. Favourite trolling places include the Bedlam Walls, Dogshear Point, and the lower Jordan. Dogshear Point is subject to favourable tidal currents and is especially recommended.

Wind lanes are influenced by tidal currents, river channels, freshes, changes in salinity, and other factors – and they can be useful in locating freshwater currents and deepwater. Also, the wind lanes funnel food. Concentrations of plankton may be targeted by galaxias which in turn may be targeted by trout.

Above Bridgewater avoid the mud flats and 'coastal saline flats'. Concentrate on the deepwater channel but avoid fishing deep. Remember that water suitable for trout extends for just 2 m or so below the surface.

Whitebait invade the big channels leading into the 'marshes' and trout congregate accordingly. The mouths of the major gutters (such as Byers Creek, Jarvis Creek, and the very big gutter draining the marsh below Mt Dromedary) are superb for all types of fishing. They fish best when tides are high, and when baitfish drop back as tides recede. Whitebait feeders may also be found along the fringes of the rushes away from the creek mouths.

Remember that the effluent from the pulp and paper factory is avoided by trout (but not all whitebait). The point of discharge is about 1 km downstream of Boyer. The plume (which is discoloured with tannin and usually clearly visible) extends east for about 1.5 km. It hugs the northern

At the mouth of Sorell Creek

bank but extends out over a third to half of the river width.

In most years the piers of the jetties and over-water buildings at the pulp and paper factory are significant spawning areas for *Lovettia*. Congregations of whitebait (including *Lovettia* in dry seasons) and trout also occur below the rapids at Lawitta.

Regulations

The seaward limit is drawn east from Dogshear Point. The river north of this line is inland water subject to normal trout fishing regulations.

The estuary above Dogshear Point is a Conservation Area and all waterfowl are wholly protected.

Since 1992, the inland *Fishing Code* has stipulated that the normal closed season for inland waters (basically May, June and July) applies to '*...the taking of salmon and trout in the section of the River Derwent below its seaward limit to an imaginary line drawn between the extremities of Dowsing's Point and Store Point*'. However, while anglers may not *kill* trout in this section of river during the closed season, there is no restriction on catch-and-release fishing for salmonids, nor is there any restriction on the taking of other species.

Further information

Recommended for boat handlers is the *New Norfolk* 1:25 000 Tasmap. This publication details the channels, marshes, mud flats, and boat launching sites from Bridgewater to New Norfolk. The other 1:25 000 sheets covering the Derwent give little detail of sub marine features. The *Derwent* 1:100 000 Tasmap is excellent in its depiction of roads and topographic features but again gives limited sub marine detail. The *South East Tasmania* 1:150 000 Tasmap shows most boat launching areas on the River Derwent.

D'Entrecasteaux Waterways, a publication compiled by the Cruising Yacht Club of Tasmania, accurately records the topography of the river bed between the outer estuary and New Norfolk and is invaluable to the serious angler. It is available from most booksellers within the State, as well as the Tasmap sales centre in Hobart.

The estuary to Meadowbank Dam

The river between New Norfolk and Meadowbank Dam is deep, fast and mostly unwadeable. It is flanked with hop fields, cash crops, and pasture – and most banks are heavily overgrown with willows and scrub. The water has only the faintest tinge of tannin but is often slightly turbid and is not good for polaroiding.

There are good stocks of resident brown trout. Most fish caught weigh 0.2-0.5 kg, but others to 1 kg are quite common and some real monsters are taken from time to time. Stunted redfin perch are also common. Rainbow trout are extremely rare.

While there are many small clear spots where you can set-rod fish, access along the banks is mostly quite arduous. The most accessible stretches are on the southern side of the river – the most popular being the railway bridge south of Plenty, and the area near the mouth of the Plenty River. There are also significant stretches of open bank away from public roads, and these are well defined on the *Uxbridge* and *Bushy Park* 1:25 000 Tasmaps. Another hot spot is below the Meadowbank Dam, especially during the galaxia and elver migrations (October to January) and trout spawning runs (late April).

Despite the fact that trout are taken from the river proper, it is important to recognise that the fishing is usually much better in the tributary streams. If you want to catch good numbers of small fish you are best advised to fish the fastwaters which enter from the west – the Tyenna, Styx and Plenty rivers. If you are interested in broadwater fishing you can try the Jordan, Ouse and Clyde, though these do not compare favourably with the broadwaters in the North and Midlands.

Blackfish

Blackfish are not native to the Derwent system but Saville Kent of the Salmon Commission introduced 70-80 fish (some 10 inches long) from the Mersey River in 1887. The species now thrives in the mid reaches. Most fish are very small and are a bother to set-rod trout fishers, though impressive specimens in excess of 1 kg are taken every now and then.

Wayatinah to Lake King William

The Derwent between Wayatinah Lagoon and Lake King William is set in a steep forested valley, and flows over a largely-exposed boulder/shingle bed. Water stored behind Lake King William, which would naturally flow down the valley, passes through a power station at the foot of the Clark Dam and is diverted overland (via two canal/pipeline systems). Some 5 km down from the Clarke Dam there is a small weir from which the Derwent Pump pushes more water up into the canal system. Water in the canals passes through several power stations before re-entering the Derwent at Wayatinah Lagoon.

The bottom line is that, unless Lake King William is spilling (which is a rare event), very little water passes down the Derwent valley below the Derwent Pump. Still, there are always braided trickles and small clear pools.

Celta fishing and bait casting often result in big bags of 0.2-0.4 kg brown trout. Some better fish are taken from the pondage behind the weir at the Derwent Pump, and in the canals (see *Tarraleah Canals*).

Lake King William to Lake St Clair

The river between the Lyell Highway road bridge at Derwent Bridge and St Clair Lagoon is open to fishing from the beginning of November to the end of April. This stretch is deep, scrub-lined and mostly unwadeable.

There is always a steady flow of crystal water, flood-force if the radial gates at St Clair Lagoon are open and there is heavy rain in the St Clair catchment.

The water contains good numbers of 0.2-0.7 kg brown trout and the odd rainbow. Fishing can be worthwhile on hot evenings when there are rises to caddis flies, though it is rarely a more attractive proposition than fishing at Lake King William or St Clair Lagoon. The one place which *is* always worth a look is the water immediately below the radial gates at St Clair Lagoon, where you can often polaroid impressive fish to 2 kg. For decades there was a law prohibiting fishing for 50 m downstream of the gates, but this was lifted in 1992 when the shortened fishing season for the entire King William – St Clair stretch was adopted.

DETENTION RIVER

Tasmaps Circular Head and Table Cape
Drainage Direct to Bass Strait

As late as 1926 the NTFA was arguing that the Detention River *'be reserved for indigenous fish of which it has a wonderful supply and not be stocked with any species of trout'*. Today the system teems with brown trout.

The sea trout fishing can be very good, especially from September to late November. When the tide is high the estuary extends from forested bank to forested bank, but at low tide it is a distinct stream cutting through an exposed sandy flat. Good fishing can be found near the Bass Highway as well as at the head of the estuary. Rising tides are best.

The stream proper carries plenty of small browns. It is fast, shallow, overgrown and tea-coloured. Scope exists for productive Celta fishing and bait casting but, by standards set at nearby streams, the sport is unremarkable.

DIANAS BASIN

Tasmap Georges Bay
Drainage Coastal lagoon

A large coastal lagoon which occasionally breaks through to the sea. At the request of the NTFA a liberation of brown trout fry took place in 1965, but it seems that worthwhile fishing did not eventuate.

DIP RIVER

Tasmaps Circular Head and Arthur River
Drainage Direct to the Black River

A shallow fastwater stream which flows through dense forest and supports plenty of tiny brown trout. Fish are found both below and above the falls. Celta fishing and bait casting often result in big bags, especially when levels are low.

DIPROSE LAGOON

Tasmap South Esk
Drainage Isolated marsh
Location Near Cleveland, west of the Midland Highway.

This marsh was stocked with 40 000 brown trout fry in 1959 and fish survived for at least one or two seasons. In modern times the basin has not contained enough water to be a viable proposition for restocking.

DISTILLERY CREEK

Tasmap St Patricks
Drainage Direct to the North Esk River at Waverley

William Senior (*Travel and Trout in the Antipodes*, 1880) wrote:

'At Distillery Creek ... the stranger may see ... the rivulet in which the first trout was put ten years ago. The fish have thriven apace; so much so that, during the last season a big brown trout, roaming from his pool, was suddenly surprised in the stream in the garden – a stream so tiny that a child might step across it ... Though but thirty-two inches long this noble specimen ... turned the scales at fifteen pounds.'

In 1900-01 the NTAA set up the Waverley Hatchery (see *North Esk River*). While rainbow trout escaped from time to time and small liberations of yearling brook trout occurred between 1904 and 1906, neither species established.

Today the creek supports good stocks of brown trout, some of which exceed 0.5 kg. The water is clear and fast, and is best fished with Celtas and bait when levels are moderate to low.

DIXON, LAKE

Tasmap Nive
Drainage Gordon system (via the Franklin River)

According to early Parliamentary reports, in 1892 there was a failed attempt to place Atlantic salmon in Lake Dixon. Today the lake is a brown trout fishery. It carries plenty of slow-growing fish to about 0.6 kg, as well as a few others in excess of 1.5 kg.

Lake Dixon is surrounded by eucalypts and sedgeland, but most banks are overgrown with tea-tree and scrub. Wading is essential.

The easiest fishing is along the firm open bottom adjacent to the eastern shore. Although there is room for spinning and wet-fly fishing, the best sport occurs during stable low levels in the post-Christmas period when the fish rise freely. The water is tea coloured but polaroiding is worthwhile, especially in calm conditions.

While the boggy pin-rush marsh which extends over the western half of the lake is inaccessible when the Franklin is high, it is suitable for fly fishing and harbours the best trout.

Lake Dixon

Access is by a little-used foot track which leads from the end of the Rufus Canal Road. The route extends about 100 m through a fringe of dense wet-forest before descending through open woodland. The total walking time is about ¾ hr each way. Several small (but comfortable) informal campsites exist near the lakeshore.

See also *Fishing in National Parks,* 5.3.

DOBSON, LAKE

Tasmap   Tyenna
Drainage   Derwent system (via the Broad system)
Location   Mt Field

A shallow silt-bottomed clearwater surrounded by dense alpine woodland. While access along the banks is difficult, at normal levels much of the water is wadeable.

Rainbow trout were released in Mt Field between 1917 and 1922, and it is probable that some of these fish ended up in Lake Dobson. Another release of 120 000 rainbow fry at '*Lakes Mt Field, Fenton, Dobson*' was noted by the NTFA in 1940-41. However, the species failed to establish.

Brown trout probably had been released by 1920. Other releases took place in 1959 (600 yearlings) and 1966 (100 adults). Today the brown trout population is maintained by natural recruitment and fish of 1-1.5 kg are typical.

It seems that the standard of fishing has remained static since at least the 1950s when anglers were complaining of slabby fish and poor returns. At this time the SFFC carried out 'fertilization' experiments, placing bags of fertilizer over the lake bottom in the hope that nutrient levels could be bolstered. However, it seems that no practical advantage was gained. The bags are now overgrown with weed but remain clearly visible.

Despite criticisms of the lake, the fishing is quite worthwhile. Wade polaroiding is most exciting, though there is ample scope for spinning.

A formal 'artificial lures only' restriction was introduced in 1958.

See also *Fishing in National Parks,* 5.5

DON RIVER

Tasmap   Forth
Drainage   Direct to Bass Strait

From August to November there is good sea trout fishing in the estuary.

The stream proper is very small and many banks are overgrown with willows, blackberries and scrub. However, the pools are shallow and wadeable and there is scope for tight spinning and bait casting. When levels are low you can expect big bags of 0.1-0.3 kg brown trout.

Rainbow trout were released as early as 1907-08 – but they failed to establish.

DONALDSON RIVER

Tasmaps   Pieman and Arthur River
Drainage   Direct to the lower Pieman River

Sea trout are taken at the mouth. The upper reaches are remote, overgrown and not often fished, but are reputed to carry plenty of small brown trout.

DORA, LAKE

No Trout. See *West Coast Range.*

DORSET RIVER

Tasmap   Forester
Drainage   Direct to the Ringarooma River below
Ringarooma

While patches of forest grow along the lower reaches, most of the stream is flanked by open pasture. When levels are low the pools are relatively clear, the riffles are shallow, and much of the bed is wadeable.

Most trout weigh 0.2-0.4 kg and others in excess of 2 kg are taken every now and then. The best stretch is from Ringarooma to Alberton. Celta fishing, bait casting and fly fishing are all worthwhile.

DOUBLE BAR LAGOON

See *Double Lagoon*.

DOUBLE LAGOON
(known to some locals as Double Bar Lagoon)

Tasmap Meander
Drainage Derwent system (via the Little Pine system)
Location Nineteen Lagoons

The main feature of Double Lagoon is the extensive marsh system along the northern and north-western shores. When levels are high (usually in October and November) the lake spills out, filling gutters ditches and backwaters. As is the case at Lake Kay and the Little Pine River, the trout move in to the flooded shallows to feed on tadpoles, frogs and other forage food. Tailing fish are a feature, though blind casting in the gutters and along the submerged banks is a good fallback.

As the water recedes, polaroiding becomes bread-and-butter sport. Wade over the sand/silt flats and along the edges of the weedbeds.

Mayflies and terrestrials cause fair to good rises in the main body of the lake from about late spring.

Spinning is productive throughout the year. When levels are high it pays to search along the outer fringes of the marshes. As levels drop back, it is best to concentrate on the deep water in the body of the lake.

The trout usually weigh 0.5-2 kg, though specimens to 3 kg are not uncommon. While naturally-spawned browns dominate, a few emigrant rainbows from Lake Chipman have been taken in recent years.

The family car can be taken as far as the modest carpark several hundred metres from the lakeshore. The traditional vehicular access to the shore passes over delicate marshland and severe damage has been caused by indiscriminate 4WD use.

In 1967 the NTFA constructed a crude low-profile rock weir across the outlet stream. This structure still exists and serves to keep the lake from falling quickly to natural minimum levels.

See also *Fishing in National Parks*, 5.1.

DOUGLAS CREEK

No trout. See *Ayr, Lake*.

DOUGLAS, LAKE

See *Johnny, Lake*.

DOUGLAS RIVER

Tasmap Break O'Day
Drainage Direct to the Tasman Sea

Trout are reputed to exist only in the lowest 5-6 km – below Tevelein Falls (wrongly marked on some maps as Leeaberra Falls).

The fishing is similar to that in the Swan system (see *Swan River*). Sea trout are not a major feature and the resident fish are mostly small.

The lower reaches (where the trout are) are an important refuge for the rare native grayling. Please remember that this species is wholly protected.

DOVE, LAKE

Tasmap Sophia
Drainage Forth system (via the Dove River)
Location Near Cradle Mountain

Lake Dove is one of Tasmania's most photographed lakes, the stark towering rock-faces of Cradle Mountain providing a magnificent backdrop. The tea-coloured water is flanked by sedgeland, dense heath and pencil pines but, while many banks are inaccessible, there are wadeable shallows along the quartzite beaches near the outflow.

Slow-growing brown trout abound. Most weigh 0.3-0.5 kg but some exceed 1 kg.

Spinning can be very worthwhile when the weather is rough. Fly fishing is best on bright sunny days when you can spot fish cruising in the shallows; and on warm calm post-Christmas evenings when the shallow bays come alive with risers.

History of trout stocks
The NTFA recorded that 1000 sebago salmon fry were taken to Lake Dove in 1916, and that in 1916-17 some 1800 rainbow fry and 1500 brown trout fry were released. A further 3000 brown trout were liberated in 1951. While the salmon and rainbows

failed to establish, the brown trout are now maintained entirely by natural recruitment.

See also *Fishing in National Parks, 5.4.*

DOVE RIVER

Tasmaps Mersey and Sophia
Drainage Forth system (via Lake Cethana)

A small shallow stony-bottomed fastwater.

The lower half (from Lake Cethana to the boundary of the Cradle Mountain – Lake St Clair National Park) flows through a remote densely-forested valley and, while it supports plenty of small brown trout, it is rarely fished. The upper reaches (near Lake Dove) flow through open moorland, and are lined with pencil pines and heath. When levels are low Celta fishing is likely to result in limit bags of half-pounders.

DUCK RIVER

Tasmaps Circular Head and Arthur River
Drainage Direct to Duck Bay

The Duck is one of the very best trout rivers in north-west Tasmania.

Sea trout.

Sea trout are a major attraction from August to November.

All of the estuary is productive. At high tide you can fish from the grassy foreshores and rocky banks in Smithton, but at other times you must be prepared to wade out over mud flats and along the fringes of rush marshes. While blind fishing is sometimes essential, fish can often be seen smashing through schools of whitebait.

From mid September to November, when galaxias are dominant in the whitebait runs, trout can be found both in the estuary and in the freshwater reaches. Set-rod fishing is good along the heavily overgrown banks adjacent to the Bass Highway. A hot spot for all angling methods is below the gauging weir (just above the Trowutta Road bridge, the first bridge across the Duck, about 3-4 km upstream from the tidal reaches). The IFC built a permanent fish ladder here in 1981-82 but the whitebait still bottleneck.

Stream fishing

Most of the freshwater reaches flow through farmland but the banks are so overgrown with willows that canopies cover many pools. The banks and bed are soft and, while there is no obvious tannin, the water remains slightly murky

even during times of low flow. There are many sluggish holes and few riffles.

Under ideal conditions you can expect to take impressive bags of 0.1-0.7 kg brown trout as well as the odd fish in excess of 1.5 kg. Rainbow trout were released as early as 1908 but did not establish.

Unlike the Flowerdale, there are no significant flood plains and the fishing is best when levels are moderate to low. Celta fishing and bait casting are most practical, though there is scope for clever fly casting. Fair rises occur on hot summer/autumn days when grasshoppers and beetles are about. Some of the best fishing occurs in the stretch from the Scotchtown district to Edith Creek.

The uppermost reaches (above Roger River township) are small and overgrown with scrub. While the size of the trout is not impressive, you can take good bags on Celtas and baits.

DUDLEY, LAKE

Tasmap Meander
Drainage Natural – Derwent system (via Lake Augusta)
Location Nineteen Lagoons

Lake Dudley is a traditional big-fish water. It lies in flat moorland and is contained by rocky shores and undercut banks. Most of the crystal water is too deep to wade.

While there are no inflowing spawning streams, there is a gutter connection to Lake Augusta (or the James River).

Brown trout in excess of 5 kg were taken from the 1950s to the 1970s, but in recent seasons angling pressure has increased and most fish now weigh 1-2.5 kg. Trophy fishing can only be maintained if anglers adopt the catch-and-release philosophy.

In 1986 some 5000 triploid rainbows fingerlings were released, and some of these fish were still being caught in the early 1990s. The best specimens weighed 3-3.5 kg.

In rough weather spinning and wet-fly fishing along the undercut banks can be productive. On hot sunny days polaroiding is most effective. Rises are not a feature.

The easiest access is via the ½ km of vehicular track which leads west from the Julian Lakes track just north of Lake Augusta. Remember that when Augusta is high the Julian track floods and becomes impassable.

DULVERTON, LAKE

Tasmap Lake Sorell
Drainage Isolated lagoon
Location Oatlands

For some 40 years Lake Dulverton was a prime trophy water – then in early 1993 it dried up. Undoubtedly it will be restocked as soon as it refills, and the fishery should rehabilitate quickly.

Description

Lake Dulverton is a weedy natural lagoon encircled by dry pasture on the edge of the Oatlands township. The bed is uniformly flat and the average depth is normally just 2-3 m. Usually you need to scout around for sections of shoreline not choked by dense mats of emergent strapweed, and many anglers prefer to fish from a dinghy. The water can become quite clear in settled weather but is usually slightly turbid.

Water levels

In most years more water is lost through evaporation and seepage than is replaced by rain, and the lagoon occasionally dries up. Because of this the local council in about 1930 constructed a small retaining wall across the outflow. But the lake dried up again in 1945.

Members of the Oatlands branch of the NTFA improved the Red Rocks race which diverted water into the lagoon from adjacent farmland, and by 1951-52 (when the lake was restocked) levels were again appreciable. Work on the race continued throughout the 1950s and in 1960-61, at the instigation of the STLAA, the dam was raised 12 inches.

In November 1975, during a major flood, the dam spilled and was severely damaged. Later that season the structure was repaired and buttressed.

Throughout the 1980s low levels were a constant concern. Fish kills commonly occurred in summer, and the problem was exacerbated whenever the strapweed was cut (to cater for various watersports) and left to rot in the water.

The recent proliferation of farm dams on the intermittent inflows has probably compounded the water problem.

Fish stocks

There is no scope for natural recruitment and the trout fishery is maintained entirely by artificial stocking.

Trout liberations began as early as 1892 when brook trout were released. By the 1920s the lake was being managed as a trophy-brown water. The fishery collapsed during the drought of the 1940s.

The lagoon was restocked with small brown trout in 1951 and had fully recovered by 1953-54. By 1960 a hatchery had been established on the lakeshore, a unit which operated until at least 1966-67. The first releases of adult brown trout occurred in the early 1960s, and from 1971 to 1980 there were annual liberations of 400-2500 fish. From 1981 stocks were maintained primarily through liberations of fry and fingerlings. Brown trout took full advantage of the shoreline marshes and proved to be ideal sportfish. Most fish taken by anglers were 2-3 kg and a respectable number exceeded 4 kg.

Rainbow trout were released in 1966 and in the late 1980s. These fish grew well but were most common in the few pockets of open water beyond the reach of the shore-based angler.

While novelty releases of brook trout (surplus display-fish from the Salmon Ponds) occurred in 1987 and 1988, these fish provided only very short-term sport.

When the lake refills liberations of both browns and rainbows are likely. Instant fishing will occur if adult fish are translocated from highland lakes.

Redfin perch were abundant during the last two fishing eras. It is likely that fish still survive in marshes, puddles and dams in the catchment area, and that eggs, fry and/or adults will be washed into the lake as it refills.

The fishing

Surface fishing with grubs and frogs has been the traditional angling method. Spinning from the shore was difficult because of the dense weed.

Fly fishing was always very productive. Early in the morning and late in the evening browns could be seen bow-waving after frogs and other forage prey, and in daylight you could sometimes polaroid fish along the edges. Blind casting with large wets was a reliable fall-back.

The best fishing occurred from opening day to about November. Fishing was usually difficult in the hot summer months, when warm water and prolific weed growth caused all manner of frustrations, but there was often a late-season resurgence. Evenings, nights and early mornings always provided peak sport, though the persistent fisher was able to make worthwhile daytime catches.

After the lake refills, released fry should attain 2-3 kg within 3-4 years. Translocated adults will provide instant action. It will probably take 2-3 years for the weedbeds to fully re-establish and during this time there will be unusually broad scope for shore-based fishing. Take advantage of this situation while it lasts.

DUNCAN, LAKE

Tasmap Shannon
Drainage Isolated

This 'lake' is one of the two small flooded quarries adjacent to the Poatina Road between the Lake Highway and Arthurs Lake. For many years it has been regularly stocked by IFC staff, though most releases have been poorly documented. While small numbers of Atlantic salmon and rainbow trout were released in the late 1980s, you only *expect* to catch brown trout. Few fish exceed 1.5 kg.

Spinning, bank polaroiding and traditional dry-fly fishing can all be effective.

Trout liberations (since 1990)

Wild brown trout

YEAR	SIZE	NUMBER
1991	adults	20
1992	adults	20
1993	adults	20

DUNDAS RIVER

Tasmap Pieman
Drainage Direct to the Little Henty River

A small overgrown fastwater which carries plenty of small slow-growing brown trout. It fishes best when levels are low. Use Celtas or natural bait.

DUNNYS DAM

Tasmap Nive
Drainage Derwent system (via the Tarraleah Canal system)

A tiny turbid weedy water flanked by pasture and tea-tree. It teems with tiny brown trout, but can hardly be recommended to the serious angler.

See also *Hornes Dam*.

EAGLE LAKE

Tasmap Mersey
Drainage Derwent system (via the Nive system)
Location Western Lakes

Eagle Lake lies in a moorland basin which, in turn, is surrounded by rocky forested hills. There is comfortable access along most banks and many shores are wadeable. The fish are mostly 0.6 - 1.2 kg and they respond well to lures. While the polaroiding is far superior to that at Lake Malbena, the rises are irregular and unreliable.

See also *Fishing in National Parks,* 5.1.

EAGLE TARN

No trout. See *Fishing in National Parks,* 5.5.

EARLHAM LAGOON

Tasmap Prosser
Drainage An estuary connected to the Tasman Sea

Although sea trout are sometimes seen by the spear-and-light brigade, rod fishing can hardly be recommended.

EAST ROCKY LAGOON

(also known as Shark Lagoon)

Tasmap Meander
Drainage Derwent System (via the Little Pine System)
Location Nineteen Lagoons

A good fly fishing water which offers reasonable dun hatches and summer polaroiding. Fish of 3.5 - 5 kg are reported from time to time but the catch rate is poor. Catch-and-release is advocated.

See also *Fishing in National Parks,* 5.1.

EAST LAGOON

Location Toiberry

Intermittent. Not recognised as a trout fishery.

EAST QUEEN RIVER

Heavily polluted with heavy metals and sludge. No trout.

ECHO, LAKE

Tasmap Shannon
Drainage Derwent system
Location Central Highlands

Echo is a very productive lake which holds impressive trout. It is discussed in detail in the book Trout Guide *(Rob Sloane and Greg French, 1991). A summary only is given here.*

Description

Lake Echo is an extensive hydro-electric impoundment which draws water from Little Pine Lagoon and the River Ouse via Monpeelyata Canal. Water is discharged through a canal flume and pipeline to the Lake Echo Power Station at Dee Lagoon.

The water is clear and the shorelines feature extensive areas of drowned trees. The elevation is 846 m above sea level and, being a principal storage, seasonal drawdowns of up to 13.5 m can be expected.

Trout stocks

Trout stocks are maintained entirely by natural recruitment from the River Ouse, Monpeelyata Canal and a number of small lake-tributaries. Brown trout predominate, though rainbows account for up to 10% of the annual harvest. Fish to 1 kg or so are typical and some exceed 2 kg. Redfin perch are also common.

History

The first recorded stockings of the natural lake were the laying down of 550 brown trout ova in 1870 and the liberation of 500 fry in 1871, though the Salmon Commissioners reported that trout were already established in the River Dee by 1869. In 1893 it was reported that brook trout had been released into the lake, but this species failed to establish. The only significant recorded stocking after this time was that of 15 000 brown trout fry during the 1920-21 season, by which time a wild population had firmly established.

It was reported that by 1907 it was sometimes possible (depending on river flow) to collect ova for the hatcheries from the River Dee at the outlet of Echo. While there are few references to early angling in the lake, the NTFA report for 1919 displayed a fine photograph of *'the record brown trout of 24 lbs'* taken during the previous season.

An article by Major A N Woods in the NTFA report for 1933 mentioned that: *'It may be said that Lake Echo, which is known to hold a great quantity of trout, and very large ones, too, is somewhat of an enigma to anglers, as it is said that none have ever been taken by ordinary methods'*. It was also reported that trout would not rise, that the fish were *'confirmed bottom feeders'*, and that *'large quantities of crustacea and mollusca may possibly exist in these waters'*. A further suggestion was made that the young perch abounding in the lake might *'largely assist the trout in denying himself of the necessity of surface feeding'*. Such observations were consistent with other reports of the period – and the lake continued to be ignored by anglers until the HEC began activities in the area in the early 1950s.

An article by the STLAA in 1954 noted that the road from the Lyell Highway to the southern end

of Lake Echo had been constructed and that the popularity of the water was increasing. Consistent with other reports, the average weight was said to be about 5 lb and that fish over 10 lb were common. By this time the presence of rainbow trout had been recorded and they were said to account for one in every ten trout caught. The origin of these fish remains unclear.

By 1954 the HEC had constructed a cofferdam and raised the lake by about 4 m. However, the main structure, the 18 m high Echo Dam, was not completed until 1956. Also in 1956, the upper reaches of the Ouse and Little Pine rivers were diverted via the new Monpeelyata Canal into the northern end of the lake.

The new canal provided vastly increased spawning facilities, while the high dam and fluctuating water-level destroyed many of the lake's rich feeding grounds.

Fly fishing

The shallow weedy north-western bays (from Teal Bay to Broken Bay) are productive wet-fly waters early in the season, especially when the lake is approaching full supply. Brocks Bay is a good alternative in southerly weather.

Evening along Echo's barren rock shores (Photo by Rob Sloane)

The timbered western shore offers reliable dry-fly fishing when the gum beetles are flying on warm summer days. The water is clear and polaroids are essential.

Notable mudeye migrations along the timbered shores stimulate good rises on fine summer evenings.

There are outstanding wind lanes across the open reaches which provide superb opportunities for boat fishers. Most activity is caused by midges after calm frosty mornings, and gum beetles on warm days in summer and autumn. Remember, too, that rainbows are especially common in wind lanes.

Lure fishing

The best areas for drift spinning and trolling are the mouths of the north-western bays and the timbered shore in between. The best bags are taken by trolling just outside the tree-line, or by drifting along the edge and casting among the trees.

The mouth of the Monpeelyata Canal is a reliable area for spinning.

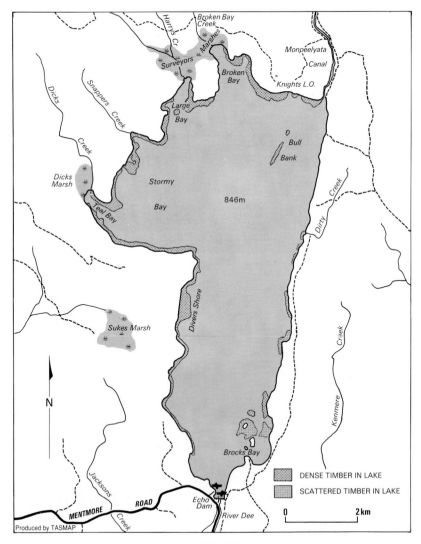

*Teal Bay – note the lush weed
(photo by Rob Sloane)*

Bait fishing

Cockroaches are dynamite when cast in front of rising, tailing or cruising trout. The timbered shores are best and polaroids are essential.

Access

The only reliable 2WD access is to the dam area at the southern end of the lake. However, 2WD standard forestry tracks now extend from the Mentmore Road to within easy walking distance of the north-western bays.

The traditional northern access via Monpeelyata Canal crosses private land and in recent years public access has been denied.

Boating

The recommended launching ramp is located on the western side of the Echo Dam. The water is large and exposed and extreme caution should be exercised in small dinghies.

Camping

Informal lakeshore sites can be found adjacent to the Echo Dam and at Brocks Bay. Other less-used sites exist at Teal Bay and Broken Bay.

EDGAR POND

Tasmap   Old River
Drainage Huon system
Location   The foot of the Edgar Dam, Lake Pedder

A tea-coloured water in a wet buttongrass flat. It was formed at the time of the construction of the Edgar Dam – simply because, while the face of the wall fulfils the primary purpose of stopping Lake Pedder from spilling through a narrow section of low-lying plain, the other side blocks the natural passage of the Edgar system of creeks. The Edgar system now spills through a small canal adjacent to the air strip before entering the Huon River below the Scotts Peak Dam. Full supply is about 302 m above sea level and the water remains fairly static throughout the year.

Some margins are choked with weed and drowned scrub, and some banks are overgrown with dense heath, but there is plenty of scope for shore-based sport.

Brown trout existed in the system prior to the formation of the lake and stocks continue to be maintained by natural recruitment. Most fish taken weigh 0.6 -1.2 kg.

Some 200 brook trout yearlings and 56 000 fry were turned out between 1979 and 1981 but, while these fish provided immediate sport, the species did not establish.

The pond is adjacent to a formal camping ground (see *Pedder, Lake*) and is well worth a look when Pedder is rough and uninviting. Remember that artificial lures only are allowed.

ELDON RIVER

Tasmaps   Franklin and Sophia
Drainage Direct to Lake Burbury

A large tea-coloured fastwater with overgrown banks. It holds plenty of small resident browns and rainbows, and is a major spawning ground for Burbury fish. It is an ideal Celta water, especially when levels are low.

See also *King River* and *Burbury, Lake*.

ELIZABETH RIVER

Tasmaps   South Esk, St Pauls, and Little Swanport
Drainage South Esk system (via the Macquarie River)

Although the Elizabeth is a typical meadow stream and can be quite productive, it is over-shadowed by the Macquarie River, the Lake River and Brumbys Creek.

Description

The lower section, from the confluence with the Macquarie to the hills 5 km east of Campbell Town, is a series of broadwaters surrounded by flat marginal pasture. Many banks are overgrown with willows and/or scrub, but there is ample room for spinning and fly casting. Although the river sometimes breaks its banks, the flood plains are much less impressive than those on the Macquarie. The water is often murky and rarely clears enough to permit memorable polaroiding.

From the fringes of the pasture to Lake Leake the river flows between rolling hills clothed with scrub. The upper 10 km or so of this stretch are flanked by narrow wet flats.

Lake Leake, at the head of the system, is a water storage for the Campbell Town district – and you can rely on releases of lake-water down the Elizabeth before natural flows reach critical lows.

Trout stocks

Brown trout probably invaded the Elizabeth shortly after the South Esk was first stocked (in 1866-67). The population soon grew and by the 1900s the fish were so numerous that the average size had become 'unimpressive'. As early as 1914 the NTFA conceded that 2 lb fish were uncommon. Today most trout caught are 0.2-0.5 kg and anything in excess of 1 kg is a surprise. The average catch rate is an impressive two to three trout per angler per day.

For a brief period in the late 1800s and early 1900s brook trout were established in Lake Leake and the Snowy River – but they were eventually displaced by rainbow trout. Small numbers of hatchery-reared brook trout were also released near Campbell Town in the early 1900s, but without success.

Rainbow trout were released in Lake Leake in 1904 and for decades emigrants from the resulting wild population kept the mid to upper reaches of the Elizabeth well stocked. Also there was enthusiastic stocking of hatchery-reared rainbows in the Elizabeth near Campbell Town throughout the 1920s and 1930s (and probably into the 1950s). But the wild rainbows in both the lake and stream were eventually displaced by brown trout. Rainbow trout are still released at Lake Leake but, while emigrants are commonly taken in the river below the dam, only a few are caught at Campbell Town.

The inaugural report of the NTAA indicated that redfin perch were released into the Elizabeth (probably at Campbell Town) prior to 1893. For many decades the species was confined to the lower to mid reaches of the system, but it appeared at Lake Leake in 1974 and is now well established there.

The fishing

Although the river is well patronised by locals, visitors who wish to experience the best of the meadow streams are probably best advised to try the Macquarie River and Brumbys Creek.

While spinning in the lower reaches peaks from August to October/November, there is often a resurgence in Autumn. Celta fishing below Lake Leake is worthwhile whenever there is reasonable flow.

For fly fishers the best sport is in the lower reaches near Campbell Town. When the river is running a banker you will take trout by fishing a wet along the flooded edges. Hatches occur too, essentially being miniatures of those in the Macquarie. When the fishing is tough at Lake Leake, nymphing in the outflow is a handy fall-back.

Set-rod fishing with worms and wattle grubs accounts for many fish, especially in the evenings, though cast-and-retrieve methods are usually more productive. Daytime grasshopper casting is recommended in summer and autumn.

See also *Where to Fish – A Regional Breakdown*, 4.2.

ELYSIA, LAKE

See *Labyrinth, The.*

EMMA TARNS

Tasmap Mersey
Drainage Derwent system (via the Little Pine system)
Location Nineteen Lagoons

Wet-fly fishing and polaroiding are good when levels are moderate to high. Typical trout weigh 0.7-1.5 kg.

See also *Fishing in National Parks*, 5.1.

EMMETT, LAKE

Possibly no trout. See *Fishing in National Parks*, 5.5.

EMU RIVER

Tasmap Hellyer
Drainage Direct to Bass Strait

According to early Parliamentary reports the Emu was stocked with brown trout as early as

1881. Stocks are now maintained entirely by natural recruitment.

Sea trout

From August to November (and especially in September and October) sea trout may be found throughout the short estuary. Bottlenecks of galaxias occur below the weir at Fern Glade (a little more than 1 km from the mouth).

Resident trout

The river proper flows through a steep densely-forested valley. In the mid to lower reaches the tannin is barely noticeable, but the water is often slightly turbid. In the upper reaches the water is distinctly tea-coloured.

The pondage above the weir is very small and soon narrows into a long, deep unwadeable broadwater. However, there is a small grassy esplanade which is sometimes patronised by set-rod fishers.

Above the broadwater the river is a series of small pools and long riffles. It holds plenty of slow-growing brown trout to 0.3 kg as well as a few fish in excess of 0.5 kg. Wading is essential so angling is best when levels are low. Celta fishing and bait casting are recommended, though there is plenty of scope for fly casting.

Access above Fern Glade is limited, though several forestry roads (some of which are suitable only for 4WD vehicles) lead to the valley floor. Most tracks are clearly marked on the *Hellyer* 1:100 000 Tasmap.

Although the uppermost reaches (beyond Hampshire) are very small and overgrown, they too are quite fishable.

EOS, LAKE

See *Labyrinth, The.*

EROS, LAKE

No trout. See *Fishing in National Parks, 5.1.*

ESPERANCE, LAKE

Tasmap Huon
Drainage Esperance system
Location Hartz Mountains

Although Lake Esperance lies at the foot of a steep scrubby peak, most of the eastern shore is fishable. Wading is advantageous at times.

Brown trout to 0.6 kg abound.

Spinning is productive throughout the fishing season. Fly fishing is best on warm calm days in summer and autumn when the fish rise to take mayflies and terrestrials.

See also *Fishing in National Parks, 5.6.*

ESPERANCE RIVER

Tasmap Huon
Drainage Direct to the D'Entrecasteaux Channel

Sea trout fishing peaks from late August to October, though good sport often continues until late November. The best stretch extends from the Esperance Narrows (1-2 km down the estuary from the Huon Highway) to the gauging weir (about 1 km upstream from the highway). A small dinghy enables easy access along the edge of the mud flats and overgrown banks. Anglers confined to the shore can fish from the open tussocks and mud flats immediately below the Huon Highway; from the bridge itself; or scrub-bash to small stretches of fishable bank upstream of the highway.

The freshwater reaches are slightly tea-coloured and flow fast over a shallow rock/shingle bed. Much of the surrounding old-growth production forest is being clearfelled. The stream abounds with 0.2-0.5 kg browns and, when levels are low, big bags can be expected. Celta fishing and bait casting are most popular but traditional upstream-nymphing is also worthwhile.

EVA, LAKE

Possibly no trout. See *Fishing in National Parks, 5.3.*

EXPLORER CREEK

Tasmap Mersey
Drainage Mersey system (via the Fisher system)
Location Chudleigh Lakes

Between Lake Mackenzie and Lake Explorer there are several deep, slow turbid pools in which there are fair to good summer/autumn rises.

When in flood, sections of the stream near Lake Explorer spill into large backwaters providing good wet-fly fishing.

Most fish are small but some exceed 1 kg.

EXPLORER, LAKE

Tasmap Mersey
Drainage Mersey system (via the Fisher system)
Location Chudleigh Lakes

The first stocking of trout probably occurred in

1895 (see *Mackenzie, Lake*). A part-share of 2000 brown trout fry was liberated in 1889, and small numbers of Loch Leven and sea-migratory strains (of the same species) were turned out in 1901-02. While it is probable that releases of other salmonids occurred in subsequent years, the lake now holds only naturally-spawned browns.

Lake Explorer is characterised by its extreme murkiness. Water discolouration began in the 1970s and has steadily worsened. The problem may be caused by swans uprooting *Isoetes* weed over the extensive shallows, exposing the silt bottom to wave turbulence. However, the turbidity of the water does not seem to affect fish growth and most trout range from 0.5-1.3 kg.

As most shorelines are rocky and well-defined the lake is well suited to spinning from the banks. The real hot spots are near the inflows from Lake Johnny and Snake Lake.

Polaroiding is practical only in the clear waters near the inflowing streams. Rises are modest and irregular.

See also *Fishing in National Parks, 5.1.*

FALLS CREEK

See *Forth Falls Creek.*

FALLS RIVER

See *Russell Falls Creek.*

FANNY, LAKE

Tasmap Mersey
Drainage Derwent system (via Powena Creek and the Pine system)
Location Western Lakes

Lake Fanny is a clearwater surrounded by grassland and open woodland. The shores are well-defined (there are no marshes), moderately deep, and well-suited to spinning. There are reasonable dun hatches and superb rises to black spinners.

The water teems with 0.2-0.5 kg brown trout and fish in excess of 1 kg are relatively uncommon.

The easiest access is via the old cart route from Lake Ada. The last leg, from Talleh Lagoons to the southern end of Lake Fanny, is ill-defined and is best treated as an 'easy' cross-country route.

See also *Fishing in National Parks, 5.1.*

FENTON, LAKE

Tasmap Tyenna
Drainage Derwent system (via the Tyenna system)
Location Mt Field

Chomping down the Red Tag – Lake Fanny

Lake Fenton (photo by Frances Latham)

Essentially Lake Fenton is a very deep natural lake. In the 1930s the Hobart City Council undertook the ambitious project of incorporating the crystal waters in its town supply. The idea had been mooted in the 1920s but became practical only after the State organized unemployed workers to construct an access road to the lake. The water scheme, which involved the construction of a low-profile weir (about 3 m high) at the outflow and some 80 km of pipeline, was formally opened in April 1939. The dam was raised (by less than 1 m) in the 1950s. In addition to the artificial capacity, water can be pumped below the natural full-supply level, and today the scheme still contributes about 15% of Hobart's domestic water.

Lake Fenton is contained between rolling hills. The banks are rocky, and overgrown with heath and stunted eucalypts. When the lake is at or below normal levels there is an obvious barren perimeter scar. However, the shores do not recede markedly and the surface area and shape of the lake remain quite static throughout the year. As there are very few drowned trees on the littoral fringe, access along the banks is usually quite easy. While there is vehicular access to the lake, there are no boat launching facilities.

The first stockings of brown and rainbow trout probably occurred in the decade preceding 1920 (see *Fishing in National Parks*, 5.5). The NTFA recorded the liberation of 120 000 rainbow fry in *'Lakes Mt Field, Fenton, Dobson'* in 1940-41, while the STLAA documented the release of 2000 brown trout yearlings in 1956-57. Further releases of 170 and 165 adult browns were undertaken by the IFC in 1965 and 1966 respectively. Lake Fenton now supports a very large population of naturally-spawned browns, but I have not heard of any rainbow trout being taken in modern times.

Most fish weigh less than 0.5 kg and very few exceed 1 kg.

The deep shores are ideal for spinning. Polaroiding is best over the silt flats at the northwestern end. Promising evening rises are often curtailed by sudden cool breezes.

See also *Fishing in National Parks*, 5.5.

FERGUS, LAKE

Tasmap Meander
Drainage Derwent system (via the Little Pine system)
Location Western Lakes

In 1949 the NTFA claimed that Lake Fergus was *'one of the heaviest fished lakes in Tasmania this season'*. Today it remains among the most popular of the Western Lakes.

Lake Fergus lies in a moorland basin but is bounded by steep wooded tiers. The water is clear and shallow, and much of the bed is wadeable. There are extensive beds of *Isoetes* weed as well as significant sand/silt flats. Emergent pinrushes feature along the western shore.

The water was reserved for artificial lures in 1962 but is most prized for its superb fly fishing. After spring floods fish can be found foraging in the margins. Later in the season, when levels are low, they tail over the sand flats, especially early in the morning and late in the evening. Wade polaroiding is a delight, and on good days you are bound to see dozens of trout! There are also extraordinary rises to duns, black spinners, beetles and damselflies.

Typical brown trout weigh 0.5-1.5 kg. Although very rare, emigrant rainbow from the Nineteen Lagoons may also be encountered.

The most convenient access is via the rugged vehicular track which extends north-west from the Marlborough Highway just east of Little Pine Lagoon. This 12 km track traverses private land and has been extensively damaged through unrestricted wet-season use. Private land owners have voiced support for seasonal closures to 4WD traffic. The route can be walked in 3-4½ hrs. Please remember that, at any time of the year, it is illegal to take vehicles along the lakeshore.

A modest hut is located on the edge of the tree line, some 200 m back from the south-eastern shore. It is a single-roomed vertical-board structure with room on the floor to sleep five or six. As with all huts in the Western Lakes, it is frequently fully occupied.

See also *Fishing in National Parks*, 5.1.

169

FIELD, LAKE

Tasmap Mersey
Drainage Natural – Derwent system (via the Ouse system)
Location Western Lakes

Lake Field is a rocky-banked water encircled by moorland. The shoreline remains fairly static, though the water breaks its banks in several places when levels are very high. There are extensive beds of bottom-hugging *Isoetes* weed out from the shore.

Most fish taken range from 0.7-1.5 kg. Spinning and bank polaroiding are most effective, though fair mayfly hatches occur on suitable days, and the odd fish may be found foraging in the small flood basins when levels are high.

Most 4WD operators leave their vehicles at the Julian Lakes crossing and walk the remaining 2 km or so of track. The hut is a private lease and is always locked.

See also *Fishing in National Parks*, 5.1.

FIRST BAR LAKE

Tasmap Meander
Drainage Natural – Derwent system (via the Ouse system)
Location Western Lakes

Most trout are taken in summer and autumn by polaroiding and traditional dry-fly fishing.

When levels are high early in the season, trout can be found along the flooded edges. However, few anglers venture this far when the weather is wet and cold – much better marsh fishing exists in the Nineteen Lagoons.

Typical fish weigh 0.2-0.7 kg.

See also *Bar Lakes System* and *Fishing in National Parks*, 5.1.

FIRST LAGOON

Tasmap Meander
Drainage Natural – Derwent system (via the Ouse system)
Location Nineteen Lagoons

Although First Lagoon is surrounded by flat moorland, the shoreline is quite well-defined and there are few marshes. The bottom is shallow and rocky and the water is clear.

There are few spawning facilities and recruitment from the outflow stream (Block Creek) is very limited. Largely because of the small trout population, the lake has received relatively little attention from anglers, even though it has long been recognised as a trophy water. A well-known local identity claimed that until recently he had

First Lagoon

never shot or speared a fish of less than 11 lb. In the late 1980s, in what was a poorly documented liberation, the IFC turned out a significant number of brown trout fingerlings. These fish grew well and by 1993-94 had attained 1.5-3.5 kg. Many of the old hands claim that the water is now overstocked and lament the end of the huge-fish era. However, in light of the increase in attention from anglers, continued (if less zealous) stocking is justified.

Feature fishing occurs throughout the angling season when the trout are charging about in the shallows after galaxias and tailing for snails. But, if there is little obvious activity, wade polaroiding is a good fall-back. There is also some scope for spinning. Access is gained by walking down the snowgrass plain from the Double Lagoon track near Second Lagoon.

See also *Fishing in National Parks*, 5.1.

FLANNIGAN, LAKE

Tasmap King Island Special
Drainage Coastal lagoon

Received almost annual stockings of 10 000-30 000 rainbow fry from 1966 to 1982. Has not been mentioned by name in recent IFC reports.

See also *King Island.*

FLINDERS ISLAND

Trout liberations on Flinders Island were poorly documented but probably quite widespread. The NTFA recorded the release of 2000 brown trout fry in the 1933-34 season. A further 3000 fry were released in Scotts Lagoon (near Lady Barron) in 1951, and in 1954 the fishing in the *'lagoons on Flinders'* was reported to be very good. Unfortunately, none of the coastal lagoons appear to be capable of maintaining trout stocks by natural recruitment, and none appear by name on recent stocking lists.

FLORA, LAKE

Tasmap Mersey
Drainage Derwent system (via the Little Pine system)
Location Nineteen Lagoons

When levels are very high the south-eastern end of the lake spills out into substantial flood basins. There are also significant backwaters along the south-western shore. However, these areas are rarely fished – it is usually impossible for keen anglers to walk past the bow-waves and tails in the Kay Lagoons.

Lake Flora is usually fished after the spring-time floods when the weather has stabilized. Polaroiding is the fly fishers bread-and-butter sport, the hot spot being the extensive wadeable sand-flats at the south-eastern end.

The weedbeds are significant, but not superb, and the hatches are rarely as good as those at nearby O'Dells Lake.

There is plenty of deep water, especially along the north-eastern shore, and when levels are low Flora is a much better proposition than O'Dells for lure fishers.

A small rock and mortar dam (about 0.6 m high) was constructed by anglers in the 1960s. This structure keeps the lake from falling quickly to natural-minimum levels, but it also prevents efficient flushing. Anecdotal evidence suggests that, during the last few decades, deposits of silt have degraded the weedbeds and impacted upon the mayfly hatches.

An obvious two-bunk hut exists against the rocky outcrop back from the north-eastern shore. It is clad with sheet metal and has no internal lining. Though unattractive in fine weather, it is a good emergency shelter.

See also *Fishing in National Parks,* 5.1.

FLORENTINE RIVER

Tasmaps Nive and Wedge
Drainage Direct to the River Derwent above Lake Catagunya

A large fastwater almost entirely located within production forest. Substantial clearfelling is carried out adjacent to the river but, in contrast to prior practice, the bankside vegetation (old-growth and regeneration) is now reserved.

The lower few kilometres, from the Derwent to above the first road bridge, flow through dry rocky woodland over a boulder-strewn bed.

The mid to upper reaches are located in lime-stone country and are flanked by dense wet-forest. Here the substrate is firm but there are substantial deposits of silt. The bed is shallow and the current is obvious, but there are few classic riffles. Weeds grow in dense beds, reaching the water surface and trailing in the current. Most stretches are cluttered with huge semi-submerged logs.

The water is tea-coloured and slightly turbid, especially so after heavy rain.

Trout stocks

While brown trout of 0.1-0.2 kg abound, quite a few fish attain 0.4 kg and some exceed 1 kg.

Anecdotal evidence suggests that in the 1960s and early 1970s rainbows accounted for up to 50% of the annual harvest – but rainbows appear to be much less common today.

The rainbows in Lawrence Rivulet appear to be isolated from the Florentine by virtue of the fact that the lower 2 km flow underground.

Access

Forestry roads (comfortable 2WD standard) extend from both the Wayatinah and Maydena ends of the river to the lower and mid reaches. However, all entry points are gated and access can be gained only by prior arrangement with ANM.

The Timbs Track (a public footway) extends 4 km from the Gordon River (Lake Pedder) Road near The Needles to a flying fox over the Florentine. It is a rehabilitated 4WD route and is well-defined. There are several comfortable camp-sites on a grassy clearing beyond the riverbank forest. The two huts are very run-down and provide emergency shelter only.

Where to fish

The lower section of river, from the River Derwent to above the first road bridge, is little different from most of Tasmania's dolerite-bottomed streams and, while it carries many small trout, it offers nothing of special interest.

The most attractive fishing sites are in the weedy limestone runs. In the active production forest I favour the stretches crossed by the Tiger Road – near the junctions of Coles Creek and Eden Creek. The Station Marsh is located beyond the riverbank forest and does not offer noteworthy fishing. Moreover, the river adjacent to the marsh is scoured during floods and does not support the lush weedbeds typical of the rest of the limestone country.

The river at the end of the Timbs Track is as good for fishing as any stretch accessible by car.

The headwater streams crossed by the Gordon River Road are tiny trickles and cannot be recommended to serious anglers.

Ilow to fish

Fishing is practical only when the water is low, and is best in summer and autumn.

Wading is essential and, while the banks are soft and deep, there are firm shallows centre-river. You must be prepared to crawl over submerged logs and scrub-bash around the deeper runs.

Celta fishing is highly recommended.

Polaroiding is difficult because of the small fish and discoloured water, though fish can sometimes be seen stationed close to the surface on the edge of the weed. Traditional daytime dry-fly fishing is possible on warm days when the trout take beetles and a variety of aquatics, and the evening rise is often spectacular. When all else fails, persistent upstream nymphing is bound to get results.

FLOWERDALE RIVER

Tasmaps Table Cape and Hellyer
Drainage Direct to the Inglis River

Flowerdale Flats

Feature fishing occurs in the lowest 3-4 km of river. This turbid stretch is completely overgrown with willows, and during normal levels has little to recommend visitors (though it is well patronised by local set-rod fishers). On the other hand, when the river floods and the water spills out past the willows into the paddocks, it briefly becomes a fishery worthy of praise.

Most locals fare well by using worms in conjunction with set-rods, but there is a lot to be said for wading along the banks. Bow-waves can be seen on the outer edge of the willow trunks, in relatively open patches between the willows, and sometimes in small open flood-basins tens of metres from the nearest trees.

Most fish taken during the floods weigh 0.4-1.3 kg and big bags are quite normal.

The rest of the river

Most of the Flowerdale beyond the Moorleah farming district is set in a steep densely-forested valley. Here the river is a typical fastwater with holding pools and lots of shingly riffles. The bottom is firm and the water is relatively clear. Celta fishing and bait casting are recommended when levels are low. Traditional upstream nymphing works quite well, but the hatches are irregular and relatively small.

Most fish weigh 0.2-0.5 kg – but there are surprises.

Rainbow trout

While the NTFA reported that rainbows were doing well in the upper reaches in 1912, and that 5000 fry were released in 1929-30, the species failed to establish.

FOLLY LAGOON

Tasmap Lake Sorell
Drainage Isolated
Location West of Ross

A small intermittent marsh. According to NTFA and IFC reports it was stocked with rainbow trout by airdrop in 1958-59. Apparently the fish could not tolerate the alkaline water and soon died.

FORD RIVER

Tasmaps Forester and St Pauls
Drainage Direct to the North Esk River

A shallow overgrown fastwater which carries plenty of small brown trout. Angling is best when levels are low, and Celta fishing and bait casting are most practical.

See also *North Esk River*.

FORESTER RIVER

See *Great Forester River*.

FORGOTTEN LAKE

Tasmap Nive
Drainage Derwent system (via Lake St Clair)

Forgotten Lake is a deep rocky-shored clearwater surrounded by sub-alpine woodland. Most shores are wadeable, and those which are not can be fished from the banks.

Lure fishers who cast well-out into deep water catch some impressive rainbows. Fly fishers usu-

ally find that polaroiding is most productive –
but they work hard for the odd 2-3 kg brown
trout. While rises occur on hot days in the post-
Christmas period, such activity is always more
pronounced at nearby Shadow Lake.

Access is via a well-formed walking path from
Cynthia Bay (Lake St Clair).

See also *Fishing in National Parks*, 5.4.

FORTH FALLS CREEK

Tasmap Forth
Drainage Forth system (via Lake Barrington)

A small fastwater which contains plenty of 0.1-
0.4 kg brown trout.

The steep lower reaches, in the vicinity of
Forth Falls and Lake Barrington, are set in dense
forest. Most of the rest of the river flows through
flat pasture. When levels are low the fish respond
well to Celtas and baits.

See also *Forth, River*.

FORTH, RIVER

Tasmaps Forth and Mersey
Drainage Direct to Bass Strait

Description

The river proper between the estuary and the
Paloona Dam is deep and overgrown with scrub.
Flows are almost wholly regulated by upstream
hydro-electric developments and are usually
quite fast.

The 50 km or so of densely-forested valley
between Paloona and the Lemonthyme has been
completely inundated by the Paloona, Barrington
and Cethana impoundments.

Above Lake Cethana the river is a pristine, tea-
coloured, shallow water flowing through a
forested valley flat.

The Mersey Forth Power Development

Work on the Mersey Forth Power Development
began in 1963 and was completed in 1973.

Since the late 1960s water from the Mersey
catchment has been diverted at Lake Parangana
through tunnels and penstocks to the River Forth
at Lemonthyme (above Lake Cethana).

Three major instream dams and associated
power stations were constructed on the Forth
itself, utilizing the combined flows of the Forth
and upper Mersey catchments. Lake Barrington
was completed in 1969, Lake Cethana in 1971,
and Lake Paloona in 1972.

While the scheme denies water to the lower

Forgotten Lake

Mersey, it increases overall flows through the
lower Forth. Flows are now more or less constant
and there is little major flooding of the estuary.

History of trout stocks

Brown trout

In 1869 the Salmon Commissioners said that
they were delaying the stocking of trout into *'the
best rivers in the colony'*, including the Forth,
until salmon were established. The first recorded
liberation of brown trout occurred in 1876 when
500 fry were taken to the *'River Forth and tributary'*. Wild stocks soon established – and subsequent releases (which continued in earnest from
the early 1900s to the 1950s) probably had little
influence on the existing fishery.

Sea trout

Sea trout were first mentioned by the NTFA in the
early 1900s but there is no indication that at this
time the runs were exceptional. In the early
1920s it was suggested that there were *'no whitebait'* and that the fishing was *'bad'*. However,
anecdotal evidence suggests that by the 1930s
the runs were large, and that by the early 1940s
the sea trout fishing was at its peak.

Following the advent of commercial whitebait fishing (see *About Our Sportfish*, 2.1) the sea trout fishery went into serious decline, from which it has never fully recovered. The reasons for the collapse are likely to be complex. Remember that the runs of the 1930s and 1940s were not typical of previous decades, and the impact (since the late 1960s) of massive water manipulation by the HEC is difficult to assess.

Quinnat salmon

In the 1920s the NTFA acted upon its desire to establish quinnats in northern Tasmania and announced to its members:

'*Intense stocking in the headwaters of one stream only is recommended, and the River Forth has been selected. This is a fine salmon stream, rising in the mountains, with numerous tributaries, and the estuary is subject to little or no netting.*'

The first consignment of fry was delivered in August 1922. About 15 000 were taken to the Iris River about 3 km beyond Moina – a site chosen because it gave clear passage to the sea and because it fed one of the major tributaries of the Forth (the Wilmot). A further 4000 fry were deposited in Forth Falls Creek and some were taken to the Lea River.

In mid 1923 some 11 000 yearlings were distributed in the Forth, and a few months later a further 44 000 fry were released in the Iris (most at Moina but some on the Middlesex Plains). By 1924 a hatchery for the expressed purpose of rearing quinnats had been erected at Moina – but ova was not available until 1925.

Each winter from 1925 to 1929 up to 150 000 ova were laid down at Moina. Annual liberations to the Iris ranged from 64 000 to 98 000 fry – and in some years yearlings were released as well (some of which were taken as far away as Forth Falls Creek).

Much to the disappointment of those involved, no sea run salmon were ever caught, and in 1930 the experiment was discontinued. The Moina hatchery was subsequently used to hatch brown trout, but in 1933 it was dismantled and transported to the northern end of Great Lake.

See also *About Our Sportfish*, 2.5.

Atlantic salmon

In 1887 some 300 Atlantic salmon fry were taken to the Forth and Inglis Rivers. As proved to be the case in other Tasmanian rivers, none returned from the sea.

Rainbow trout

The Forth system was probably first stocked with rainbow trout in 1907 when 2600 fry were turned out at the township of Forth. There was continuous and often significant stocking of both fry and yearlings until the 1950s, but wild populations did not establish.

Perhaps the most thorough stocking occurred in the years from 1948 to 1951-52, when the NTFA made a concerted effort to establish steelhead. Of the 5400-120 000 yearlings released annually, none returned from the sea.

The few rainbows taken in the river today are emigrants from artificially-maintained populations in the instream lakes.

Sea trout fishing today

The sea trout fishery is a shadow of what it was in the 1930s and 1940s – but is significant nonetheless.

The runs of *Lovettia* peak in September/October and at this time fishing is best in the estuary. One of the favourite spots is on the eastern side of the river beneath the Bass Highway bridge. There are other vantage points at Turners Beach (inside the estuary) and Leith. If you have a boat you can gain access along the overgrown banks and to the deep water beyond. The best fishing usually occurs adjacent to the main river channel, which runs close to the eastern shore upstream of the Bass Highway and is well marked on the *Ulverstone* 1:25 000 Tasmap.

From early October to late November there are likely to be reasonable runs of galaxias. These baitfish move further upstream than the *Lovettia* and bottleneck at the Forth Weir. This hot spot is clearly visible (and easily accessible) from the Wilmot Road above Sayers Ripple, about 1.5 km south of the Forth Road bridge. Spinning and bait casting are locally popular and there is room for fly fishing.

Resident trout

Much of the river between the estuary and the Paloona Dam is of difficult access and, while there are good stocks of 0.2-0.7 kg browns, the fishing can hardly be recommended. The best sport is found in the Wilmot River, a major tributary which enters the Forth below the Paloona Dam. Other tributaries feeding the lower reaches of the Forth are very small. Those which do not dry up in summer contain plenty of tiny trout, but the sport is poor.

Most of the creeks feeding the hydro-electric impoundments are small permanent streams which fall down steep densely-forested slopes. While they contain lots of small brown trout, most are rarely fished. The only waters of note are Forth Falls Creek, the Dove River and the remote Hansons River.

Above Lake Cethana the Forth is accessible from the Lemonthyme Road and Patons Road. The stream here is shallow and fast and contains plenty of 0.2-0.3 kg brown trout. Generally you get the best results with Celtas when levels are low. However, a little rain late in the season will often trigger an early run of spawners from Lake Cethana. And, at any time of the year, better-than-average can be taken at the outfall of the Lemonthyme Power Station.

FOSSEY RIVER

Tasmap Sophia
Drainage Arthur system (via the Hellyer River)

Among small streams on the West Coast the Fossey is exceptional, the high quality of the trout fishing being recognised by the NTAA/NTFA as early as 1904.

Feature fishing occurs in the open plains adjacent to the Murchison Highway (White Marsh and Micklethwaite Marsh). After springtime floods, when the weedy silt-bottomed stream begins to break its banks, trout can be found along the undercuts and foraging in the gutters among the tussocks. In summer and autumn the current remains quite strong but there are few obvious riffles. While the water is slightly tea-coloured, it is clear enough to polaroid and good results can be expected when dry-fly fishing and bait casting. Fish to 0.7 kg are common and a few exceed 1.2 kg.

The stream beyond the marshes is steep, overgrown and full of small fish.

FOUR SPRINGS CREEK

Tasmap Tamar
Drainage South Esk system (via the Meander system)

An enthusiastic lobby – the Four Springs Lake Development Committee – was set up in the mid 1970s to press for the construction of a trout lake at Four Springs Plain (in the Four Springs Recreation area). Government agencies have given in-principal support but have not provided funding. It is unlikely that the project will get off the ground in the foreseeable future.

FOX, LAKE

Tasmap Mersey
Drainage Mersey system (via the Fisher system)
Location Chudleigh Lakes

Lake Fox lies on a small piece of high ground overlooking lakes Johnny, Chambers and Douglas. Most of the lake bottom is rocky, and the fringes are shallow enough to wade. There are no spawning grounds and the outflow creek is too small and steep to permit the invasion of trout from the lakes below. While there are unconfirmed reports of past brown trout liberations, this species has not established.

In 1986 there was an illegal release of 400-500 rainbow trout fingerlings. Most of these fish were caught within a few years, though a few fish of 2-4 kg were reported in 1990-91.

See also *Fishing in National Parks*, 5.1.

FRANKLAND RIVER

Tasmap Sandy Cape
Drainage Direct to the Arthur River.

The tea coloured Frankland and its fastwater tributaries (such as the Lindsay and Horton) are set in dense old-growth production forest. They abound with slow-growing brown trout but, as they are remote and difficult of access, they are rarely fished. There is a 2WD route to the mid reaches via the Blackwater Road (which leads from the Sumac Road south of Kanunna Bridge over the Arthur River). The lower reaches are accessible by boat and give up good sea trout (see *Arthur River*).

FRANKLIN RIVER

Tasmaps Olga, Nive, and Franklin
Drainage Direct to the Gordon River

The Franklin is one of Australia's most-renowned wild rivers. It flows through spectacular gorges and ancient rainforests – and features a blend of tranquil basins and tumultuous whitewater. The catchment is a true wilderness, the only major development being the Lyell Highway.

A dam abandoned

In 1982 the State Government sanctioned the construction of a hydro-electric dam on the Gordon river below the confluence of the Franklin – a proposal that would have flooded much of the Franklin and destroyed wilderness values – and sparked one of the most divisive conservation struggles in Australia's history. In 1983 a new Federal Government passed the World Heritage Properties Conservation Act and used the legislation to override the will of the State. The State took the case to the High Court, but the appeal failed and work on the power scheme was abandoned.

Trout stocks

The history of the trout stocks in the Franklin is discussed under *Gordon River*. Today the water teems with slow-growing brown trout. Most fish weigh 0.1-0.5 kg, though a few exceed 1 kg.

The fishing

Celta fishing is very productive, especially when levels are low. The water between the Gordon and the Lyell Highway is largely inaccessible on foot but is very popular with rafters and canoeists. If you are camped near a still pool it is usually a simple matter to secure enough fish for the evening meal.

The river at the Lyell Highway is flanked by dense wet-forest but is shallow, shingly and easily waded.

Lakes Dixon and Undine (which are accessible by foot from the Rufus Canal Road) are full of small brown trout – and there is worthwhile Celta fishing in the stream between.

Trout exist in the streams at the foothills of the Cheyne Range but have not invaded the elevated lakes (such as Lake Hermione and, perhaps, Australia Tarn).

See also *Gordon River* and *Fishing in National Parks*, 5.3.

FRANKLIN RIVULET

Tasmap Tamar
Drainage Direct to Port Sorell

A small sluggish stream.

Sea trout are taken from the South East Arm (of Port Sorell) to the weir (about 2 km upstream of the estuary, just downstream of the bridge on the logging road).

Resident brown trout to about 0.8 kg are fairly common throughout the rest of the stream. Some 5000 fry were liberated in 1988, though this had no obvious effect on the quality of fishing.

The lowest 6 km or so of river flows through forest and the banks are quite overgrown. Fishing is best in the vicinity of Wisedale, where the river is flanked by paddocks and there are plenty of open banks. During floods trout can be found in the small backwaters and along the drowned edges. When levels subside bait casting and dry-fly fishing are recommended.

Better fishing exists nearby in the Rubicon.

FRANKS LAKE

Tasmap Meander
Drainage Natural – Derwent system (via the Ouse system)
Location Western Lakes

The lake is sheltered in an amphitheatre of low tiers, and the surrounding vegetation has largely escaped the ravages of wildfire. The most striking features are the scree shores (on the eastern side) and the stands of pencil pines. Flat moorland extends from the western bank, and the outflow passes through a maze of undercuts. The water is relatively deep but, when conditions are bright, most of the weedy bottom can be seen.

The fish are a class better than those in Lake Furmage. Polaroiding and spinning from the bank are usually most appropriate.

FREESTONE CREEK

Tasmaps Freycinet and Break O'Day
Drainage Direct to the Swan River

The small weedy rush-lined broadwater near the Tasman Highway usually holds a few brown trout to 0.5 kg or so. The rest of the stream is intermittent. Much better fishing is to be found in the other Swan tributaries (see *Swan River*).

FROME DAM

Tasmap Forester
Drainage Ringarooma system

The 18 m high concreted-faced rockfill dam on the Frome River was completed in 1909, its primary purposes being to store water for the generation of electricity and (once it had passed through the turbines) sluicing operations at Pioneer. Today the power station is connected to the State grid and electricity is sold to the HEC. Full supply is about 325 m above sea level but big drawdowns can be expected by late summer or autumn.

The lake is contained by densely-forested hills. At full supply the water backs up to the tree line but there are wadeable pin-rush flats along the southern shore where fish can sometimes be found foraging.

At normal levels a barren clay littoral-scar is exposed and you can walk right around the lake. There is a scattering of logs and emergent tree stumps.

Trout would have existed in the Frome River prior to the formation of the lake, and existing stocks would have been sufficient to ensure the establishment of a significant lake population. However, the NTFA noted enthusiastic stocking of brown trout, especially in the 1920s. The last liberation occurred in 1973 when 100 000 brown trout fry were turned out. Today stocks are maintained entirely by natural recruitment and over-population is a problem. While the condition of

Frome Dam

much of the shoreline is wadeable. The banks vary from grassy undercuts on the west to rocky slopes on the east.

As with other instream lakes in the Bar Lakes system, Furmage carries plenty of small brown trout. Most fish weigh less than 1 kg and many are just 0.5-0.7 kg.

There are fair mayfly hatches but polaroiding and spinning are the most reliable angling methods. Remember to wade when polaroiding!

See also *Bar Lakes System* and *Fishing in National Parks*, 5.1.

GAIRDNER, LAKE

Tasmap Forth
Drainage Natural – Forth system (via the Wilmot system)

Lake Gairdner lies behind a 34 m high dam which was completed by the HEC in 1970. It serves to divert the upper Wilmot catchment via pipe to the Wilmot Power Station on the banks of Lake Cethana. Full supply is about 475 m above sea level.

While there are steep forested hills near the damsite, gentle grassy slopes extend from most other shores, and small marshes exist at the heads of the tiny bays. The water is slightly tea-coloured.

Existing stocks of brown trout in the Iris and Lea rivers resulted in almost immediate overpopulation. Today most trout caught range from takeable size to about 0.5 kg and fish in excess of 1 kg are rarities.

Fly fishing is best on warm summer/autumn days when the water comes alive with risers. Fishing from the banks is quite productive but you need a boat to take advantage of the wind lanes. Wet-fly fishing in the evening is a reliable fall-back.

Lure casting from the shore and drift spinning are likely to result in good bags at any time of the fishing season, especially in rough weather.

A good launching ramp exists near the dam. While there is ample room for camping on the grassy flats, there is no public vehicular access beyond the launching area.

most fish caught is pleasing, typical weights are 0.3-0.7 kg and few fish exceed 1.2 kg.

Spinning is superb, big bags being taken throughout the year.

The trout rise freely on warm days, especially in the post-Christmas period when there are good beetle falls. And despite the slightly tea-coloured water, fish can be polaroided in the shallows.

Access is via a rugged 2WD track and there are many comfortable informal campsites on the grassy glades halfway along the southern shore.

FROZEN LAGOON

Tasmap Mersey
Drainage Mersey system (via the Fisher system)
Location Chudleigh Lakes

A shallow weedy lagoon. Although illegally stocked with rainbows in the mid 1980s, it seems that no trout survive today.

See also *Fishing in National Parks*, 5.1.

FURMAGE, LAKE

Tasmap Mersey
Drainage Natural – Derwent system (via the Ouse system)
Location Western Lakes

The lake bottom mostly comprises silt flats and

GALAXIAS, LAKE

Tasmap Mersey
Drainage Derwent system (via the Pine system)
Location Western Lakes

A rocky-shored clearwater surrounded by open woodland and best suited to spinning and

Lake Galaxias – success after two days of effort

polaroiding from the bank. Fish are sometimes seen on the fringes of the pin-rush marshes, though the open-water bays are usually most productive. While the trout are often bigger than those in the instream Pine River lakes, the angling is tough.

See also *Fishing in National Parks*, 5.1.

GANYMEDE, LAKE

No trout. See *Fishing in National Parks*, 5.2.

GARCIA, LAKE

Tasmap   Cape Sorell
Drainage   Isolated coastal lagoon
Location   North of Strahan

Thick scrub grows along most banks, and dense rushes extend into the lake from the western and southern shores. The water is dark with tannin and is mostly too deep to wade. Although some sandy beaches are exposed at times of low water, shore-based sport is largely confined to set-rod fishing. Small dinghies can be man-handled into the lake, but it is illegal to fish from boats propelled other than by manual labour.

There is no scope for natural recruitment of trout. Although regular stocking with brown trout fry occurred from 1970 to 1983, there have been no liberations in recent times.

See also *Strahan Lakes.*

GARDEN ISLAND CREEK

Tasmap   D'Entrecasteaux
Drainage   Direct to the Huon estuary.

A small shingle-bottomed creek with poor summer/autumn flows. According to early Parliamentary reports it was stocked with 400 brown trout ova in 1884. Today the trout population is relatively small, though fish of 0.3 kg and more are easily caught on Celtas when levels are moderate to low. Galaxias (which abound in the lower reaches) annoy bait fishers by snatching worms and grasshoppers intended for trout.

GAWLER DAM

See *Isandula, Lake*.

GAWLER RIVER

Tasmap   Forth
Drainage   Direct to the Leven estuary

Fair to good numbers of 0.5-1.5 kg sea trout are taken at the estuary from late August to early November. If flows are not too low during September and October, sea trout will chase galaxias 3 km or more up into freshwater.

The stream proper mostly flows through farmland and many banks are overgrown with blackberries, willows and scrub. While there is room for Celta fishing, locals favour bait casting with grasshoppers – especially in the post-Christmas period. Resident brown trout of 0.3-0.5 kg, as well as the odd emigrant lake-rainbow, can be taken below Lake Isandula.

Both major tributaries (the West Gawler and East Gawler) are very small fastwaters which hold plenty of tiny brown trout. They are best fished in the radiata pine forest north of Preston/Castra.

GAYE, LAKE

No trout.

GEEVES, LAKE

No trout. See *Fishing in National Parks*, 5.2.

GEORGE, LAKE

Tasmap Nive
Drainage Derwent system (via Lake King William)

A clearwater lake surrounded by thick bushland. The eastern end is surprisingly shallow and much of the shoreline is wadeable. The water teems with 0.2-0.5 kg brown trout and few fish exceed 1 kg. Spinning is productive throughout the year. Fly fishing is best post-Christmas when the fish rise to take beetles. Polaroiding is worthwhile, though small fish tend to slip by unnoticed.

The easiest access route is cross-country from where the transmission lines almost touch Harbacks Road (the Guelph logging road). Buttongrass plains extend to within 50 m or so of the outflow so the walking time is just 1-1½ hrs (each way).

The ground is wet, and comfortable campsites are few and far between.

See also *Fishing in National Parks, 5.3.*

GEORGE RIVER

Tasmaps Georges Bay and Forester
Drainage Direct to Georges Bay

The water has a strong year-round flow and in summer and autumn it is quite clear.

Most of the lower 5-6 km of the freshwater reaches flow through dry forest. Here the river is wide and shallow and, at times of low flow, much of the shingle bed is exposed.

In the mid to upper reaches the water usually extends from bank to bank. While there are significant areas of cleared farmland where willows have taken-over the banks – notably near Priority, and adjacent to the Tasman Highway at Goshen – many stretches are flanked by native woodland.

The fish

According to early Parliamentary reports Goulds Country had been stocked with brown trout by 1878-79. The species soon established and today the population is very large. Most fish taken weigh 0.2-0.3 kg, though some exceed 0.5 kg.

Rainbow trout were once established above St Columba Falls on the South George River but were eventually displaced by brown trout (see *South George River*).

Stream fishing

All of the river is worth fishing, though casting is most comfortable in bushland areas away from the willows. Wading is always advantageous.

When levels are low (usually after spring) big bags are to be expected. Bait casting and Celta fishing are most popular. Fly fishers spend a lot

Typical stream fish

of time blind casting with nymphs, though modest rises occur in the forested areas.

Sea trout

From August to November sea trout are taken in the estuary but, while the runs are better than those in most East Coast streams, they are not as well respected as those in the Scamander River.

Tributaries

The tributaries are shallow fastwaters which give up big bags of small brown trout. Most notable are the Ransom, Groom, North George, and South George.

GERTRUDE, LAKE

No trout. See *Fishing in National Parks*, 5.3.

GLEN DHU RIVULET

Tasmap Derwent
Drainage Derwent system (via Sorell Creek)

A typical small fastwater containing lots of brown trout to about 0.2 kg. It fishes best post-Christmas when levels are low. As the lower 5 km or so is rural-residential and drawn upon for riparian and domestic water, trout habitat is best in the mid to upper reaches. Celta fishing and bait casting are most practical.

GLEN MORRISTON RIVULET

Tasmap Little Swanport
Drainage South Esk system (via the Macquarie River)

When levels are high the lower 3 km or so (near the confluence with the Macquarie) provide worthwhile backwater fishing.

Sluggish weedy silt-bottomed pools extend some distance upstream and provide fair dry-fly fishing even when levels subside.

The size and condition of the fish are comparable to those of Macquarie River trout.

See also *Macquarie River*.

GORDON LAGOON

No trout. See *Fishing in National Parks*, 5.3.

GORDON, LAKE

Tasmaps Olga and Wedge
Drainage Gordon River (a major instream impoundment)

Lake Gordon remains very much the poor brother of Lake Pedder. It harbours some good trout, and has its share of devotees, but for most anglers it is simply ugly and uninspiring.

Description

Lake Gordon is a massive tea-coloured hydro-electric storage. The 140 m high concrete-arch Gordon Dam was completed in 1974, impounding water from the Gordon catchment (notably the Gordon, Holley, Pokana, Boyes and Adams rivers) and from Lake Pedder (which enters via McPartlan Canal). It took several years for the lake to reach full supply (307.85 m above sea level). Since 1978, when the first two generators were installed, the scheme has been the major power source for the State and the drawdowns have been dramatic. Fluctuations are more seasonal than rapid, and levels of 20-25 m below full supply have been typical. A third generator was commissioned in 1988, resulting in more rapid (and potentially more extreme) drawdowns. The projected minimum operating level is some 52 m below full supply. Unless there is a succession of major floods it is unlikely that the lake will spill in the foreseeable future.

The lake floods vast buttongrass plains but backs up against steep densely-forested hills. Very little timber was removed prior to flooding and,

Lake Gordon – note the littoral scar

while some salvage operations are undertaken today, there are extensive stands of drowned trees.

Because of the drawdown a large barren littoral-scar is visible. Some of the steep slopes have eroded back to rock – and the flats are little more than black bogs.

Trout stocks

Brown trout were well established in the rivers and streams long before the lake formed (see *Gordon River*).

Rainbow trout fry were released in 1976 (500 000), 1977 (200 000), and 1982 (100 000).

In the early years the trout did well and, while the average size was always much less than that in Pedder, growth was impressive. In 1978 brown trout of 2-4 kg were quite common and two-year-old rainbows weighed 1-1.5 kg. By 1979 rainbows accounted for almost 30% of the annual harvest and some had attained 4 kg.

By the early 1980s the average weight of the brown trout had stabilised at about 1.1 kg and only a few fish exceeded 2 kg. Things remain pretty much the same today. Brown trout dominate but naturally-spawned rainbows are reasonably common – especially in the wind lanes and at the mouths of the inflows.

Redfin perch

The IFC noted that a redfin perch was caught at Lake Gordon in December 1978. By the end of that season there had been several other captures, and by 1980 schools of small fish could be found all over the impoundment.

The origin of the perch is uncertain, though they may have escaped from illegally-stocked dams at Adamsfield. As yet they have not invaded Lake Pedder.

Vehicular access and boating

The *Olga* and *Wedge* Tasmaps show most roads and tracks and are strongly recommended to all anglers.

Convenient 2WD access is limited. A clearly-marked road leads from the Gordon River Road to a good gravel launching site at Ragged Basin, and another good ramp exists at Knob Basin near the Gordon Dam. However, the forestry roads extending along the banks of Ragged Basin, from Adams Bay to Boyes Basin, and from the Gordon River Road to Holley Basin are closed to the public.

Boat handlers are reminded that the lake is very large and can become very rough at little notice. It also has many bays and necks which sometimes confuse and disorientate the inexperienced – a problem compounded by the fact that

at low levels the shape of many inlets bear only scant resemblance to the full-supply level shown on most maps. Moreover, many bays (including Ragged Basin) are so choked with dead trees that it is often difficult to get a clear view of the banks and/or other reference points.

Access for the shore-based angler

There is only limited fishing space near the Gordon Dam – the best sites are at the south-eastern end of the storage.

A good stretch of fishable shore is to be found near the 2WD access to the drowned forest at Ragged Basin. The enthusiastic angler may also walk along some of the gated roads to Holley Basin, Adams Bay, and the Island Road bay, though the effort is hardly worthwhile.

The real hot spot is Wedge Inlet, which can be reached by walking along the track which follows the northern bank of McPartlan Canal.

Lure fishing

As explained above (under the notes on access) there is limited scope for spinning unless you use a boat. There is always a good chance of hooking fish in the head of Wedge Inlet, and there is room at Ragged Basin to cast among the drowned sticks, but really the shore fisher is best advised to try Lake Pedder.

Undoubtedly the best way to fish is by drift spinning from a large dinghy or small runabout. The hot spots are in (or along the edge of) the drowned trees and scrub in Ragged Basin, Wedge Inlet, Adams Bay, Boyes Basin, Pokana Bay and Holley Basin. Ragged Basin is as good as anywhere else – so don't be tempted further afield unless you have a seaworthy boat or special permission to use the gated forestry roads.

Brown trout congregate at the rips of inflowing streams in April and August. The rips are also good for spawning rainbows from August to November, and for resident rainbows throughout the rest of the season.

On warm evenings after October, when the trout are taking mudeyes among the emergent trees and sticks, try a wet-fly dropper used in conjunction with a surface lure.

Fly fishing

Blind fishing with matukas and streamers in the rips at the mouths of McPartlan Canal and the Gordon River will often produce savage strikes, especially from rainbow trout. Otherwise it is worthwhile blind casting with rough mudeye imitations (Mrs Simpsons, fur flies, etc) among emergent sticks.

181

The best sport occurs on warm days after October when the trout feed on migrating-mudeyes, dragonflies and damselflies. If you are restricted to the shore, Wedge Inlet and Ragged Basin will provide all the action you can handle. However, fishing from a boat offers greater mobility, more opportunity to manoeuvre fish away from snags, and appreciably more comfort. On the best days fish can be seen leaping and charging among the sticks from late morning until after dark. When things are tough a wet fly flicked among the trees at dusk is a reliable fall-back.

Wind lane fishing is exceptional, though you really need a good boat. Midging trout can be found after calm frosty mornings from September on, and gum beetles provide daytime and evening sport throughout summer and autumn.

The action can be very good – but you must remember that for sight fishing you rely heavily on rises. Since the weather is notoriously unpredictable, the angler with limited time is likely to be disappointed.

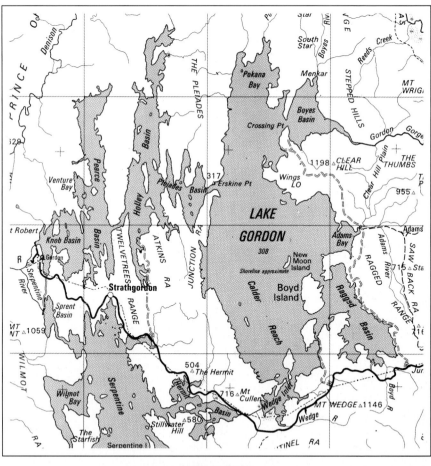

LAKE GORDON

Facilities

All toilets, camping grounds and picnic areas are located at Strathgordon and Lake Pedder (see *Pedder, Lake*).

Special regulations

Lake Gordon is reserved for the use of artificial lures. It is illegal to fish any inflowing water (and within a radius of 50 m around where that water enters the lake) except for the Holley, Pokana, Boyes, Gordon and Adams rivers.

GORDON RIVER

Tasmaps Franklin, Olga, Wedge, and Nive
Drainage Direct to Macquarie Harbour

At 185 km the Gordon is the second-longest river in the State. The catchment is mostly wilderness and, except for the Lake Gordon/Adamsfield district, it is entirely within the Gordon-Franklin Wild Rivers National Park.

Feature fishing occurs in the lower reaches at sea-trout time.

Origin of trout stocks

According to early Parliamentary reports, the Gordon River was stocked with brown trout in 1881 when 2500 ova were taken to the *'Great Bend'* (presumably Gordon Bend, above what is now Lake Gordon). In 1892 there was a failed attempt to place Atlantic salmon fry into Lake Dixon *'with a view to stocking the Gordon'*.

Some 7000 quinnat yearlings were released into the Franklin in 1934, but none returned from the sea.

Rainbow trout were placed in Lake Gordon in 1976 and a self-supporting lake-population soon established. Emigrants are taken from time to time in the middle Gordon River near the Franklin junction.

Commercial fish farms were established in Macquarie Harbour in 1987 and domestic rainbows have been common in the lower Gordon ever since. While domestic Atlantic salmon also escape from the sea pens, they do not feature strongly in anglers' bags.

The lower Gordon – sea trout country

Description

The lower Gordon, from Macquarie Harbour to the Gordon Dam, flows through gorges and dense rainforest. The bottom 40 km or so (from Macquarie Harbour to near the Franklin junction) is navigable, but none of the river is easily fished from the banks.

Though not always obvious, there is tidal influence at the mouth. However, the surface water is always fairly fresh.

While water is regulated at the Gordon Dam, there are natural inputs from major downstream tributaries – and the flow below the confluence of the Franklin *seems* natural.

The Gordon and Franklin rivers (courtesy The Wilderness Society)

Gordon River sea trout

Access

The most convenient access is via runabout (or seaworthy dinghy) from Strahan. This involves a 40 m journey across the open tidal waters of Macquarie Harbour – so you have to choose your weather. Additional party members can be dropped off by local cruise boat operators. Remember, though, that because of erosion caused by the wakes of big craft, cruise boats are now only permitted to travel upstream a short distance beyond Pine Landing.

Camping, huts and facilities

There is only very limited room for camping on the river bank and, as you can spend ages looking for tent-sites, you are best advised to use the Boom Camp at Pine Landing (some 10 km from the river mouth). This large sheet-metal shed lies 50 m or so back from the river bank and is quite inconspicuous from the water. It is served by a crude jetty and can sleep 8-12 people with comfort.

While other huts exist at the Lower Gordon Camp (some 40 km from the mouth), they are too far from the prime fishing areas to be of interest to sea-trout enthusiasts.

A public walkway, serviced by a cruise-boat standard jetty, has been built through the rainforest at Kathleen Sound just upstream of the Boom Camp. Other walkways and a jetty exist at Sir John Falls (upstream from the Lower Gordon Camp).

When to fish

Although sea trout (and domestic rainbows) run from early August to December, peak fishing occurs from September to mid November. The action is reliable providing that the river is not in flood. The state of the tide does not appear to have a major effect on catch rates.

River residents, and a smaller number of domestic rainbows, can be taken throughout the fishing season but are not a major attraction.

Where to fish

The best fishing occurs from the mouth to Pine Landing (some 10 km upstream). There are also some good spots adjacent to the spit in Macquarie Harbour (see *Macquarie Harbour*).

What can I expect to catch ?

The feature attraction is the wild sea-run brown trout, and in the peak months these fish account for about 40-50% of the harvest. Most weigh 0.7-2 kg and quite a few exceed 3 kg. River-resident browns (mostly from takeable-size to 1.5 kg) are also common, though the larger ones are inclined to be dark and in 'average' condition.

In recent years domestic rainbow trout have accounted for up to 40% of the early-season harvest. These fish are typically 0.7-1.5 kg.

Domestic Atlantic salmon are also taken, though they are relatively uncommon. Many (most?) of the reported salmon are actually sea trout and (believe it or not) rainbows.

During the peak fishing months, bags of two to four fish per angler per day are typical. After November the catch rate drops markedly, though you can still take fair numbers of river-resident brown trout and rainbows. As you go upstream past Pine Landing you can expect the numbers of resident browns to increase slightly, and the numbers of rainbows to drop significantly.

Lure fishing

Trolling with cobras and spoons is very worthwhile. Try working the spit (in Macquarie Harbour) and along the narrow fringes of strapweed near the banks. It matters not whether you troll upstream or downstream.

Drift spinning enables you to get lures into small pockets of likely water – among the weeds, under the overhanging forest, and in recesses in the banks. The current can be a little annoying at times – but the effort is well worthwhile.

Try Fishcakes at night.

Fly fishing

You rarely find sight fishing as good as that in the Henty River. However, on the best days the mouth can be quite memorable. Much of the water adjacent to the spit is wadeable (see *Macquarie Harbour*) and is productive both day and night when fished with large wets. Blind casting is often essential, though you are likely to see the odd slash and/or bow wave.

On the river proper you must fish from a boat. If you are lucky you may find trout charging after bait on the bank side of the strapweed – and then the sport is second to none. In September/October there are other hot spots along the rocky banks in the First Gorge (about 7-8 km above the mouth) where the *Lovettia* spawn.

Power developments

The Gordon River Power Development was approved by the State Government in 1967. As the works were to be carried out in wilderness, and involved the inundation of a National Park, there was an unprecedented public outcry (see *Pedder, Lake*). Nonetheless, by 1974 the major dams had been completed.

In the late 1970s the HEC proposed additional dams on the lower Gordon. The option eventually approved by the State Government involved the construction of a huge dam below the Franklin junction. This project would have drowned part of a new World Heritage Area and destroyed one of Australia's last remaining 'wild rivers'. The conservation lobby had gained strength since the Pedder days and the issue became one of national prominence.

Acting on an election promise, a new Federal Government in 1983 sought to protect the wilderness by enacting the World Heritage Properties Conservation Act. The State Government lost a High Court challenge to the Act – and work on the power scheme was abandoned (see *Burbury, Lake*).

The Gordon-Franklin Wild Rivers National Park is now a high-profile wilderness recreation area.

The upper Gordon

The Gordon River between Lake Gordon and Lake Richmond is large, fast and overgrown with forest undergrowth. Access can only be made on foot (most conveniently via the Rasselas Track) and the river is only wadeable at times of low flow.

While slow-growing resident browns are found throughout the upper reaches, and Lake Gordon spawners (both browns and rainbows) use the water in the Gordon Gorge, there is little to recommend to the serious angler.

See also *Fishing in National Parks*, 5.3.

GOULDS LAGOON

Location   Beside Main Road, 2 km south-east of Granton

Intermittent. No trout.

GRANTS LAGOON

Tasmap   Georges Bay
Drainage   Direct to the Tasman Sea
Location   Near Binalong Bay

The NTFA proposed the stocking of this water as early as 1963. Some 300 adult browns were liberated in winter 1974, but their fate was not recorded. No trout survive today.

GRASSY LAKE

See *Blue Peaks Lakes*.

GREAT FORESTER RIVER

Tasmaps   St Patricks, Cape Portland, and Forester
Drainage   Direct to Bass Strait

Sea trout

The lower Forester is a tea coloured deepwater. It supports 0.3-1.5 kg resident browns throughout the year but is very popular with anglers only at sea-trout time. Peak fishing occurs from late September to late November.

The lowest stretch passes through open beach and offers spectacular fishing reminiscent of that in the lower Henty River. It can be accessed by walking downstream from the bridge on the Waterhouse Road.

The channelized section of river adjacent to the Waterhouse Road is flanked by flat pasture – and the banks are open and grassy. Though the surface layer is always quite fresh, the water is heavily influenced by tide – and incoming high water is best for angling. Trout ambush whitebait from recesses in the deep weedy clay-banks and are usually very noticeable. In fact this is one of my very favourite sea-trout fly-waters. It is also well suited to spinning and bait casting. The weedy backwaters (which are connected year-round to the main river) hold plenty of good-sized resident browns.

The stream proper

While most of the mid reaches flow through dense tea-tree swamps and are quite inaccessible, there are open flats in the Wonder Valley and at Footrot Flats where the water meanders through deep undercuts. When the water is running a banker trout can be caught along the edges and in the gutter recesses. In summer there are fair rises as well as some scope for polaroiding. Fish of 0.4-0.6 kg are common and some exceed 2 kg. The access roads and open stretches of bank are clearly defined on the current (1992) *Forester* Tasmap.

The uppermost reaches (in the vicinity of Forester Flats, the Tasman Highway and South Springfield) flow fast over a wadeable sandy bed. Some stretches are overgrown with willows but there is plenty of scope for Celta fishing, bait casting and fly fishing. When levels are low, and the water clear, big bags of 0.2-0.3 kg fish are to be expected. Browns dominate but since 1974, when the (commercial) Springfield trout hatchery began operating, domestic rainbows have been reasonably common.

Pollution

In April 1994 a major spill of pyrethrum occurred at Hogarth Rivulet, devastating the trout population from Tonganah down past the Wonder Valley. While fishing for resident brown trout is bound to be affected in 1994-95, there will be no lasting damage.

GREAT LAKE

Tasmap Meander
Drainage Natural – Derwent system (via the Shannon River)

Though aesthetically bland, Great Lake is one of the most-fished waters in Tasmania. It is covered in detail in the book Trout Guide *(Rob Sloane and Greg French, 1991). A summary only is given here.*

The natural lake

At the time of European colonisation, Great Lake was the largest lake on the island. While the overall shape and size of the water was not too different from what you see today, the maximum depth was about 6 m, the average depth was about 2 m, and there was dense weed throughout.

Arthur Flemming (*Highland Memories*, 1990) remembered the natural Great Lake thus:

'Todds Corner was a reedy lagoon separated from the Lake by about half a mile of land with a creek connecting the two. Lake Elizabeth was also a separate lake, very dirty and muddy, while just north of here the lake was practically cut into two sections. Howells Neck jutting out from the eastern shore to within half a mile of the western shore just north of what is now Canal Bay – and Split Rock jutting out south of Canal Bay and overlapping Howells Neck on the southern side about 500 yards distant to within half a mile of the eastern shore – with the water separating the two in several places only about three feet deep.

Boggy Marsh (now Cramps Bay) was more like Todds Corner, a reedy lagoon separated by a high ridge of sand about 200 yards wide with a connecting creek. Sandbanks at that time was true to name and from a point about a mile south of where the Poatina tunnel intake now is

to the timbered point on the northern end of the lake about two miles distant from the tunnel entrance was all sandbanks.

Little Lake at Breona was also a separate lake standing approximately one mile from Great Lake and joined by one of the best streams entering the lake (Half Moon Creek).

Other accounts claim that many of the shoreline shallows were choked with large-leaved thick-stemmed weeds – but that in many places it was possible to wade out up to 50 m from the banks.

Walch's Tasmania Guide Book (1871) recorded that:

'A sort of trout about six inches long, and nearly transparent, abounds in Great Lake and, after high winds they may be picked up on the beach in bucketsful, and make very fine eating indeed.'

Changes to the lake

In 1910 a proposal went before Parliament to dam Great Lake for the purposes of generating electricity. This proposal involved diverting the Shannon River below Great Lake so that the water could be taken by canal to a point high above the River Ouse (near Waddamana) and dropped some 80 m to a power station on the valley floor. By 1912-13 an 8 ft coffer weir had been erected across the Shannon river at the mouth of Great Lake, and in 1915 a larger permanent masonry dam had been completed.

In 1922, in response to increased demands for power, a new 10 m high concrete multiple-arch dam superseded the original masonry dam. Also in that year the River Ouse was diverted into Great Lake via the newly completed Ouse Diversion Canal (Liawenee Canal).

Since 1964-65 the waters of Great Lake have been diverted north through the Poatina Power Station, eliminating traditional flows in the Shannon River. Also at this time the Upper Lake River catchment was diverted into the lake at Tods Corner. In 1967 yet another new dam was completed, superseding the old Multiple Arch Dam and raising the lake by a further 3.4 m.

Great Lake reached its highest recorded level (approximately 1033 m above sea level) in 1975. The existing rockfill dam was raised 6 m in 1982 but, to date, the lake has never reached its previous full-supply level. In fact it is expected to do so only once in every 30 years or so.

Great Lake now has the capacity to be filled some 19 m above its natural level.

A description of Great Lake today

Great Lake is surrounded by moorland (along

extensive tracts of the southern and western shores) and forests of stunted alpine eucalypts. Full supply is 1039 m above sea level but, to date, the water has never exceeded 1033 m. The normal operating range is some 21 m, though fluctuations are slow.

The main inflow is from Liawenee Canal which discharges into Canal Bay about halfway up the western shore. Water from Arthurs Lake is pumped up to Great Lake and discharged at Tods Corner. There are also several natural streams entering the lake, most notably Sandbanks Creek, Breton Rivulet, Halfmoon Creek, Brandum Creek and Stony Creek.

The natural outflow, the Shannon River at the southern end of the lake, is now blocked off and water is diverted north over the Great Western Tiers to the Poatina Power Station and the South Esk system.

The water is generally cold and clear, though heavy wave action can cause temporary discolouration along exposed shores.

At low (normal) levels the shores are barren expanses of rock, gravel and mud. Semi-submerged trees litter the shoreline in several places, particularly on the eastern side.

Great Lake is the main centre for holiday-home development in the Central Highlands,

and the traditional fishing shacks that burgeoned in the late 1960s have gradually given way to more sophisticated dwellings. The main shack areas are at Miena and Breona, with smaller clusters at Brandum and Tods.

The weedbeds

Because the lake fluctuates markedly, and many areas are subject to erosive wave-action, much of the shore zone is quite barren, and most of the rest of lake is now too deep to support lush weed growth. Today weedbeds cover only some 5% of the lake bottom. They have developed in sheltered bays below the extent of normal drawdowns and are significant to anglers because they harbour the greatest concentrations of brown trout. At low levels the productive feeding grounds are more easily reached from the shore – and this explains the better catches and improved quality of the fish.

Trout stocks

Brown trout and rainbow trout

The first stocking of Great Lake is attributed to James Wilson, the local police superintendent, who conveyed 120 juvenile brown trout to the lake in December 1870, and it is generally accepted that these were the only trout stocked

A typical bag of Great Lake brown trout from the pre-dam glory days. The weights left to right are 9½lb, 7½lb, 10lb, 14lb, 16lb, 10lb and 7½lb. (photo from the Handbook of Tasmania, *1908)*

GREAT LAKE

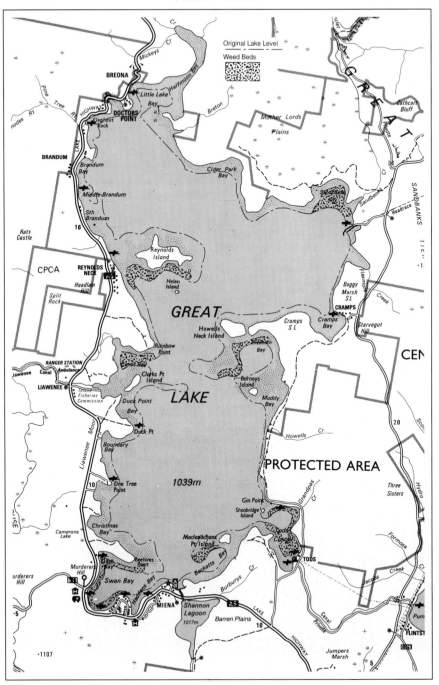

into the main lake until 1910.

The success of the species was remarkable. In a Parliamentary report of 1887-88 it was suggested that:

'In places like the Great Lake, where large trout have accumulated to a great extent, it would improve the fishing to thin them out by means of well adapted nets, of a proper mesh, to allow small fish to escape; and those large fish might be brought to the market, or the right of taking such, under proper regulations and restrictions, might be let.'

Large fish indeed! From 1890 to 1905 anglers took exceptional bags of trout – and the *average* weight was 8-10 lb. Matthew Seal is credited with the largest-ever Great Lake fish – a 25 lb monster taken in March 1897.

In 1910, following a drought-driven lull in the fishing, Great Lake received 4900 yearling rainbows and 500 Loch Leven strain brown trout. In fact concern over trout stocks prompted the Salmon Commissioners to approve the construction of a hatchery at the Shannon outlet to provide for annual restocking.

The Miena Hatchery commenced operation in the 1910-11 season. In the first year some 130 000 brown trout fry and 21 000 rainbow trout fry were released – heralding an era of regular and heavy annual stocking.

After 1910 the average size of brown trout caught went into decline and by 1916 it had fallen to less than 5 lb. In the winter of 1915 the lake was raised and by 1917-18 the fishery was making a comeback.

A substantial increase in the rainbow trout population was formally recognised in 1920, and in appreciation of the species' springtime spawning the opening of the angling season was moved forward to 1 November each year. This was the first season that rainbows exceeded browns in anglers' bags, and official catch records documented fish to 13 lb.

During the 1922-23 season new Government tourist houses opened at both ends of the lake to cater for the rapidly increasing interest in fishing.

The diversion of the Ouse into the lake (in 1922-23) gave the rainbow trout access to some 10 km of uniform gravel substrate and huge spawning runs soon developed. Also, with waters rising over new ground following the completion of the Multiple Arch Dam, the weight of the brown trout was restored to pre-1910 levels.

Browns and rainbows from Great Lake in the 1930s (courtesy Inland Fisheries Commission)

In the 6 years or so after 1922 the Great Lake fishery was at its peak. During this period power demand was such that lake levels were relatively static. The rainbow population was probably enhanced by successful shore-spawning, and both trout species had access to bountiful food.

Throughout the 1930s rainbow trout dominated in anglers' catches by a ratio of more than 50 to 1. They averaged 5-6 lb and many weighed 10-12 lb. Tremendous fishing continued until about 1940, when the rainbows went into decline. This crash has since been related to the progressive concreting of Liawenee Canal (from 1933-1941) which removed the area ideally suited to rainbow trout spawning. Also, increases in power consumption resulted in marked lake-level fluctuations, possibly denying rainbows areas for effective shore-spawning. An extensive stocking programme failed to reverse the trend.

By 1950 the size and condition of the trout had further declined and brown trout had become the dominant species (even though more than 5 000 000 rainbow trout were stocked between 1930 and 1950). Since then the fishery has remained fairly stable – despite management efforts to boost both the numbers of rainbow trout and the condition of the brown trout.

The adult transfer programme was a unique strategy adopted in an attempt to improve the quality of brown trout. From 1960 to 1980 some 110 000 browns trout spawners were trapped in Liawenee Canal and transferred to other waters. The programme failed to enhance the Great Lake fishery and, while it was of benefit to many lowland impoundments, high costs forced the operation to be radically scaled-down.

Today wild rainbow spawners are taken as they run up Liawenee Canal and placed in gated-off sections of an elaborate Zig Zag Canal. This canal was built expressly to optimise the success of the natural rainbow spawning run by giving each pair of fish a guaranteed minimum redd area, and minimising the chances of subsequent disturbance by other fish. It lies adjacent to, and utilises water from, Liawenee canal. The eggs hatch naturally, and swim-up fry quickly drop back into Great Lake.

Usually more than enough fish run to fill the Zig Zag and eggs from some of the surplus are hatched artificially at Salmon Ponds. Most of the resulting fish are returned to Great Lake as fry and fingerlings. The outcome of this activity has not been adequately tested, though the results (in terms of percentage of hatchery-reared fish vs naturally spawned fish in anglers' bags) are likely to be poor – especially when fish are released at fry stage.

Liberations of wild rainbow trout (since 1985)

YEAR	SIZE	NUMBER
1985	small fingerlings	10 000
"	yearlings	2 000
1986	large fingerlings	6 870
1987	small fingerlings	40 000
"	large fingerlings	4 000
1988	advanced fry	32 000
1992	advanced fry	10 000

Atlantic salmon

In 1907 about 1000 sea-migratory Atlantic salmon were released in Lake Elizabeth, but few were taken by anglers and the species soon disappeared.

A further 2000 eight-inch Atlantic salmon were released in Great Lake in 1936, again with disappointing results.

Experimental releases of domestic Atlantic salmon were undertaken in the late 1980s. These fish grew up to 1 kg or so and, for several years, made a significant contribution to the annual harvest. While most were long and lean, they were appreciated by the majority of anglers. There was little if any natural spawning and the species was not caught in 1993-94.

Modern liberations of domestic Atlantic salmon

YEAR	SIZE	NUMBER
1988	adults	88
"	small & large fingerlings	2 400
1989	yearlings	11 000
"	small & large fingerlings	140 000
1990	yearlings	400

Quinnat salmon

In November 1931 some 5000 yearling quinnat salmon were released. A 5 lb fish was landed in April 1932, and in 1932-33 numerous 5-7 lb fish were caught. However, the species did not establish.

Where and when to fish

Deep trolling

In general terms the major weedbeds (see map) lie between the 1020 and 1024 m contours. An echo sounder is a great aid to locating the best trolling course. If you can identify the gently sloping shelf just above the distinct edge of the original lake bed, then you are well on the way. At normal lake levels trolling depths of 5-10 m are needed – and this is best achieved by using down-riggers, lead-core lines, paravanes or specialised deep-trolling lures. A wobbler run behind an appropriate length of lead-core seems to work as well as any other method.

Lure casting

The deeper points are especially suited to spinning from the bank because the weedbeds, though less extensive than in other areas, are likely to be within reach of the shore at most lake levels. Reynolds Island, Rainbow Point, Beehives Point, Maclanachans Point and Howells Point are hot spots.

Other shores are good for spinning when heavy wave action has stirred up food in the shallows. Rainbow trout in particular will come close to the shore and feed in the waves when conditions are rough.

The mouths of the spawning creeks are hot spots in April/May (for brown trout) and August/September/October (for rainbow trout). Remember, though, that recent changes in fisheries regulations prohibit fishing within 50 m of stream mouths.

Bait fishing

With the exception of areas where bait fishing is prohibited by law, the areas recommended for lure casting are just as productive for bait fishers. Wattle grubs and earthworms are the standard baits.

Fly fishing

The best general areas for wet-fly fishing include Little Lake Bay, parts of Brandum Bay, Reynolds Neck, Canal Bay, Swan Bay and Tods Corner. As described for lure casting, the places where spawning streams discharge are hot spots early and late in the angling season.

The most accessible polaroiding shores are Little Lake Bay, Reynolds Neck, Canal Bay, Duck Point Bay, Boundary Bay and Tods Corner. A strong northerly wind is ideal as it tends to stir up food along the shore zone. Trout will be found cruising just outside the band of discoloured water, and in the extreme shallows.

On warm summer days good falls of beetles are to be expected. The best rises occur along sheltered shores in the evening.

Stable and persistent wind lanes form regularly in many areas, including Reynolds Neck, Canal Bay, Swan Bay, Tods Corner and Cramps Bay. Prolific midge hatches occur from October to March. A steady early-morning breeze following a clear frosty night is ideal.

Accommodation / Services

Petrol is available at Miena. A larger general store and petrol station is located at the Great Lake Hotel (at the intersection of the Lake and Marlborough highways).

The Great Lake Hotel provides meals and accommodation year-round – and includes a public bar. The Compleat Angler Lodge at Haddens Bay operates as a lodge and restaurant during the peak months of the fishing season.

Camping

There is no formal camping ground, though powered caravan sites are available at the Great Lake Hotel.

Informal lakeshore camping is common but not appealing. The western shore from Canal Bay to Swan Bay, and Tods Corner are most popular.

Boating

Boats can be launched at the many sites around the lake where old roads and tracks have been flooded. However, the only regularly maintained sites are at Cramps Bay, Brandum Bay, Swan Bay and Haddens Bay.

Special regulations

The season opens on the Saturday nearest 1 August and closes on the Sunday nearest 31 May. Canal Bay is an exception in that it opens on the Saturday nearest 1 November and closes on the Sunday nearest 31 March.

Little Lake Bay, Canal Bay and Tods Corner are reserved for the use of artificial lures. And all waters flowing into Great lake (and a radii of 50 m around their mouths) are closed to fishing at all times.

GREAT MUSSELROE RIVER

Tasmaps Swan Island and Georges Bay
Drainage Direct to the Tasman Sea

The Great Musselroe is rarely fished. It is isolated from the major population centres and fishing districts, there is limited vehicular access, the banks are overgrown with dense scrub, and the tea-coloured water is mostly too deep to wade.

The origin of the brown trout is unclear, though the NTFA reported liberations in the '*Musselroe*' in 1917-18.

Small resident fish are sometimes taken by set-rod enthusiasts near the road bridges, and I presume that there are runs of sea trout in the lower reaches.

GREENS CREEK

Tasmap Tamar
Drainage Direct to Port Sorell

A small sluggish silt-bottomed stream cutting

through pasture. Many of the deep pools are overgrown with willows and scrub, so bait fishing is most practical. Brown trout to 0.7 kg are reasonably common and some exceed 1 kg.

GRUB LAKE

See *Bar Lakes System*.

GUIDE RESERVOIR

Tasmap Hellyer
Drainage Cam system (via the Guide River)

The 15 m high earthfill dam on the Guide River was completed in 1982 as an extension to the Burnie water supply.

Description

The reservoir flooded a grassy plain in the middle of a radiata pine plantation. Trees grow close to the western banks and extensive flat grassy esplanades extend along the eastern shore. The water is usually clear.

Trout stocks

At the time of flooding the Guide River carried enough small naturally-spawned brown trout to guarantee immediate sport. However, local anglers quickly carried out one or more illegal liberations of rainbow trout. Fish to 1.5 kg were reasonably common in 1983-84 but by 1985 natural overpopulation was evident. Despite the poor average weight, locals successfully lobbied for artificial stocking.

Today the storage abounds with brown trout from 0.2-0.5 kg, and fish in excess of 1.2 kg are relatively uncommon. While maidens are often in good condition, older fish are mostly disappointing. Rainbow trout have not made a major contribution to anglers' bags in recent times and, while the IFC has promised annual liberations of 500-1000 fingerlings from 1993-94, these fish will do little to improve the overall status of the fishery.

Trout liberations

Wild brown trout

YEAR	SIZE	NUMBER
1984	fry	10 000
1985	fry	10 000
1986	fry	16 700
1987	advanced fry	6 700
1990	fry/advanced fry	10 000

Domestic rainbow trout

YEAR	SIZE	NUMBER
1991	large fingerlings	500

Brown trout x Atlantic salmon hybrids

YEAR	SIZE	NUMBER
1993	advanced fry	2 000

The fishing

There is plenty of scope for spinning and fly fishing from the banks. Spinning is best during the early and late months of the angling season, but there are so many fish that reasonable bags can be expected whenever conditions are not too calm.

Fly fishing (with wets) is worthwhile as early as August/September, though things really pick up in mid to late spring. Prolific evening rises occur on warm evenings from about November.

Small dinghies can be launched near the dam. Drift spinning in the deeper water is recommended when the shoreline shallows warm in the heat of summer. Boats are also good for reaching the bigger trout – which have a tendency to rise just beyond the reach of the shore-based angler.

GUIDE RIVER

Tasmap Hellyer
Drainage Direct to the Cam River

A usually-turbid fastwater containing plenty of brown trout to 0.3 kg. Rainbows from the Guide Reservoir are taken from time to time.

When levels are low Celta fishing and bait casting often result in big bags. The most attractive areas are in the vicinity of the falls.

GUN LAGOON

Tasmap Mersey
Drainage Mersey system (via the Fisher system)
Location Chudleigh Lakes

A small rocky-banked lake. It was probably invaded by brown trout soon after the Chudleigh Lakes were first stocked (in 1895) but was one of the *'Two lakes northwest of Lake Mackenzie'* restocked with 1900 brown trout fry in 1972. Recruitment is relatively poor and the fish grow to good size.

See also *Fishing in National Parks*, 5.1.

GUNNS LAKE

Tasmap Meander
Drainage Natural – South Esk system (via Arthurs Lake)

Gunns is the smallest of the two natural lakes north-east of Arthurs Lake and is often erroneously called 'Little Lake'.

While it lies in moorland, there are forests of stunted eucalypts on nearby elevated outcrops. Emergent rushes extend along the north-eastern and south-western shores. When levels are high trout forage in the clearwater channel which forms between the rushes and the banks. The rest of the lake is shallow and open and ideally suited to spinning and polaroiding. Exceptional mayfly hatches occur from November to March. The shores recede markedly during extended dry spells.

The history of the trout stock is discussed under Arthurs Lake. Today the water teems with naturally-spawned browns to about 0.8 kg, though some exceed 1 kg. Generally the average weight is slightly better than that at nearby Little Lake.

The road from Cowpaddock Bay (Arthurs Lake) includes built-up sections across the marshes and a good bridge over Tumbledown Creek. When the land is very dry there is rugged 2WD access to Tumbledown, though high clearance 4WD vehicles are recommended.

There are plenty of comfortable informal campsites, the most popular being at the south-western corner of Little Lake.

GWENDOLYN, LAKE

No trout. See *Fishing in National Parks*, 5.3.

GWENDY, LAKE

Tasmap Mersey
Drainage Natural – Derwent system (via James system)
Location Western Lakes

A small water surrounded by open heathland but sheltered from the prevailing westerly weather by a substantial rock outcrop. The shores vary from deep and rocky to shallow and silty. Extensive weedbeds grow in the deeper areas, promoting good mayfly hatches. Brown trout of 0.5-1.5 kg are typical.

See also *Fishing in National Parks*, 5.1.

HALKYARD, LAKE

Tasmap Mersey
Drainage Mersey system (via the Fisher system)
Location Chudleigh Lakes

Lake Halkyard supports a large population of brown trout and is one of the most consistently productive of the Chudleigh Lakes. Trout average about 0.6-0.7 kg and some fish attain 1.3 kg.

The water is surrounded by moorland and the open banks are good for spin fishing and polaroiding. Hatches of duns and black spinners occur throughout summer and autumn.

See also *Fishing in National Parks*, 5.1.

HALLS CREEK

Tasmaps Franklin and Cape Sorell
Drainage King system (via the Queen River)

A tiny tea-coloured fastwater which carries plenty of tiny rainbow trout.

Most fish are well under the legal minimum size (220 mm), though a few attain 0.2 kg or so. Undoubtedly the rainbows breed well because the heavily polluted Queen River has isolated the fish from headwater brown trout populations. The stock probably originated from the Lake Margaret Hatchery sometime in the 1930s.

The stream is very narrow, and in most places it is covered by a low ceiling of dense scrub. While

A typical rainbow from Halls Creek

193

access along the banks is almost impossible, the pools and riffles are very shallow and, when levels are low, you are able to wade quickly. Room exists for tight Celta fishing and bait casting.

Access is from South Queenstown via the Mount Jukes Road and the Old Mount Lyell Railway (now a disused 4WD track). 2WD vehicles can be taken as far as the first road bridge over Halls Creek. There is no room for comfortable camping.

HANSON, LAKE

No trout. See *Fishing in National Parks*, 5.4.

HARRY LEES LAKES

See *Blue Peaks Lakes*.

HARTZ LAKE

Tasmap Huon
Drainage Huon system (via the Picton system)
Location Hartz Mountains

Hartz Lake is the largest of the stillwaters in the Hartz Mountains. Dense wet-scrub overhangs most banks but much of the bed is hard and wadeable. The water is crystal clear.

Stockings have been poorly documented, though it is certain that (at least two) illegal liberations of brown trout fry occurred in the mid 1970s and 1980s.

The current status of trout stocks is unknown. I have noticed an abundance of *Anaspides* shrimps free-crawling all over the lake bed, and this is normally an indication of poor fish stocks. But I find it difficult to reconcile the apparent lack of trout with the fact that in the early 1980s I caught two small browns near the outflow.

The fishing is much more reliable in lakes Esperance, Perry and Osborne.

See also *Fishing in National Parks*, 5.6.

HARVEYS LAGOON

Tasmap Little Swanport
Drainage South Esk system (via the Kittys system)
Location Some 20 km east of Oatlands

A small intermittent pond. Each season from 1966-67 to 1969-70 it was stocked with brook trout fry and/or yearlings. The fish grew well and provided good short-term sport, but there was no natural recruitment.

HATFIELD RIVER

Tasmap Sophia
Drainage Pieman system (via the Huskisson River)

Feature fishing occurs in the Romney Marsh, an open tussock flat adjacent to the Murchison Highway. Here the stream has generous flow but is deep and weedy. During floods, when the water starts to break the banks, trout can be found along the undercuts and in the gutters. Later in the year there are fair rises and the fish can be polaroided. Most trout weigh 0.5-0.7 kg but some exceed 1.2 kg. Fly fishing and bait casting work best, though there is scope for spinning with light lures. Although you usually fish from the banks, waders are a good insurance against the snakes which abound in damp areas among the tussocks.

The lower reaches are typical of West Coast streams – steep, overgrown and shingle-bottomed. They are difficult of access and provide quite ordinary sport.

HAYES, LAKE

Tasmap Tyenna
Drainage Derwent system (via the Florentine system)
Location Mt Field

Being a rainbow fishery, Lake Hayes is unique in Mt Field. The origin of the fish is unclear, though the STLAA recorded two releases of 5100 rainbow yearlings at the Lawrence Rivulet in 1957-58 and 1958-59.

I have taken many big bags. Most fish have weighed 0.3-1.2 kg and some have exceeded 2 kg.

While the centre of the lake is very deep, a wide gravel shelf extends along most shores. Lure fishers and wet-fly enthusiasts should concentrate on fishing the edge of the drop-off. Fish are rarely polaroided but there are good rises on warm days.

Access involves a walk along one of the formal foot tracks to K Col followed by a steep 2 km cross-country descent through waist-high heath.

See also *Fishing in National Parks*, 5.5.

HAZELWOODS LAGOON

Tasmap Lake Sorell
Drainage Derwent system (via the Clyde system)

A semi-intermittent marsh which is quickly invaded by brown trout from the River Clyde each time it fills. When levels are very high in the early months of the season, wet-fly fishing can be quite successful. Later, when the weeds

the Murchison Highway). Here there is a grassy glade laid out with barbeques, picnic facilities, toilets and a small riverside foot path.

There is also good water beside the new Guilford Road (which supersedes the old Murchison Highway).

HENDERSON LAGOON

Tasmaps Break O'Day and Georges Bay
Drainage Coastal lagoon

Stocked with 60 adult brown trout in 1966 but did not become a viable fishery.

HENTY, LAKE

Tasmap Sophia
Drainage Natural – Henty River (an instream impoundment)

A small impoundment with steep densely-vegetated banks. The 23 m high concrete-faced rockfill dam was completed in 1988 and serves to divert the tea-coloured upper Henty River into the Henty Canal (also completed in 1988), from where it flows into Lake Plimsoll. Full supply is 523 m above sea level and drawdowns are marked.

The impoundment offers little prospect as a fishery and has not been stocked, though it may eventually be invaded by brook trout from the Anthony system.

See also *West Coast Range*.

HENTY RIVER

Tasmaps Cape Sorell, Pieman, and Sophia
Drainage Direct to the Southern Ocean

I rank the Henty as Tasmania's best sea trout fishery. Its attributes include the unique setting; the reliability of the runs; the action in the shallows; the polaroiding; and the scope for shore-based sport.

General description

There is no true estuary and there is no marked daily tidal influence. However, the ocean backs into the lowest reaches during spring tides and storms.

The lowest 2-4 km cuts through the vast white sands of Ocean Beach. Immediately behind this beach there is a further kilometre or so of stable vegetated dunes. The rest of the river flows through dense wet-forest. In the vicinity of the Henty Bridge (on the Henty Road between Strahan and Zeehan)

Lake Hayes

proliferate, the fishing drops away. Most fish taken weigh 1-3 kg.

HELLYER RIVER

Tasmap Hellyer
Drainage Direct to the Arthur River

A large shallow fastwater with plenty of wide shingly riffles. The water is quite clear, though it becomes slightly tea-coloured after heavy rain, and forestry operations can cause moderate turbidity at any time of the year. The lower reaches, from the Arthur River to Guilford, flow through densely-forested hills and gorges. In the vicinity of Guilford there is some pasture but the banks are still overgrown with forest. Wading is essential and fishing is best when levels are low.

Brown trout of 0.2-0.5 kg are typical and the best fish weigh 0.7-1 kg. Bags of 4-12 fish per angler per day are normal when levels are moderate to low. While Celta fishing and bait casting are most productive, traditional upstream nymphing works well and there are modest rises on warm afternoons.

The most popular stretch of water lies in the 569 ha Hellyer Gorge State Reserve (adjacent to

Henty River

the water is deep and access along the banks is difficult. Near the Zeehan Highway (the Queenstown to Zeehan road) there are deep pools and steep rapids set in a forested gorge. The headwaters, near the Anthony Road, are small and overgrown.

The recent Anthony Power Development resulted in the uppermost section of the river being diverted into the Anthony catchment (see *West Coast Range*) and this makes a visible difference to low-level flows at the Zeehan Highway.

The whole system is dark with tannin.

More about the mouth

As the lower portion of the river flows through shifting sands, the mouth is somewhat variable. For many years the water flowed more-or-less directly west, crossing just 1 km or so of true beach. In the late 1970s the river turned at the back of the beach, taking a course south along the fringes of the semi-stable dunes before meandering over 2-3 km of open sand. During this era there was no clear channel to the sea – the mouth had become a wide sandbar – and the runs of whitebait were subdued. By 1987, after some spectacular storms and floods, the river altered course yet again, breaking through to the sea about 2 km north of the previous spit, and since then the fishing has been exceptional.

Fish stocks

By standards set at other waters, the sea trout runs peak late, usually from early October to early December. This is probably due to the lack of a classic estuary and a subsequent dominance of galaxias over *Lovettia* in the whitebait runs (see *About Our Sportfish*, 2.1). The sea trout move well upstream and can be taken at the upper limit of practical boating (1 km or so above the Henty Bridge).

From time to time domestic rainbow trout (escapees from commercial fish farms in Macquarie Harbour) also enter the lower reaches.

Large numbers of impressive river-resident brown trout frequent the broad water (from the ocean to the first rapid above the Henty Bridge) throughout the year. These fish are typically 0.5-1.5 kg, though quite a few are much bigger.

While plenty of slow-growing browns live in the fast stretches of water adjacent to the Zeehan Highway, they have not invaded the headwaters.

The Langdon River, a headwater tributary, contains naturally-spawned brook trout, and other headwater streams and lakes may eventually be invaded by brook trout from the Anthony system (see *West Coast Range*).

Access, boat ramps, camping

Because of the daunting gorges and dense vegetation, practical fishing is largely confined to the lower reaches.

Shore-based anglers should head straight to the dunes and beach. There is a 3 km stretch of sandy vehicular track between the Henty Road about 2 km south of the Henty Bridge and the southern bank of the river. There are idyllic informal camp-sites where the track meets The Backwash – lawn-like clearings sheltered by dense walls of high heath. The river is often slightly brackish so it pays to bring your own drinking water.

The recommended boat launching area is at the south-western corner of the Henty Bridge. Small dinghies can also be launched near The Backwash.

When to fish

Respectable numbers of brown trout and resi-dent baitfish live in the lowest reaches through-out the year. However, feature fishing occurs during the sea trout runs – usually from late September to late December. The sport is quite reliable so long as the river is not in flood.

When there is a lot of whitebait about it is visible along the edges of the deep water as a fragmented black ribbon. It can be a metre or more wide and of indiscernible depth. However, even modest runs of bait trigger frenzy-feeding by sea trout and river-residents.

Shore-based fishing

For fly fishers and bait casters the best approach is to walk from The Backwash to the mouth, blind casting the edge of the deep water as you polaroid the shallows. While water greater than thigh-deep is almost black with tannin, trout cruising over sandy flats stand out remarkably well.

Often there is a good deal of swirling and splashing in the middle of the river, and many fish race into the shoreline shallows spraying ribbon-like sheets of water high into the air.

Although the Henty is tea-coloured, trout stand out against the white sand. Note the dark edge of the deep water.

I favour the use of whitebait-imitation flies, though nondescript lures featuring green and silver work extremely well.

Spin fishers usually do best when fishing along the edges of the drop-offs – but don't ignore the middle of the river.

The Backwash

The Backwash is a shallow, weedy, sometimes brackish lagoon located on the southern bank of the river near the main camping area. It is con-nected to the Henty only during major floods and there is no well-defined outlet channel. The shores recede markedly during prolonged dry spells, yet there are always pockets of deep open water.

The lagoon contains eels, blackback, mullet – and a surprising number of brown trout to 2 kg. While it is hardly a feature attraction, trout can often be seen charging at baitfish and rising to aquatic insects. It can be a welcome fall-back after a long tough day on the Henty. Fly fishing and bait casting are most practical.

The old river course

Scattered over the beach along the old river course are several significant lagoons. They are usually isolated but possibly become connected to the ocean and river during major storms and floods. They hold appreciable numbers of resi-dent brown trout in the 1-4 kg range.

Boat fishing

When fishing from a boat, the whole of the navi-gable water is worthwhile. There is ample room for trolling and drift spinning with shallow-run-ning lures. Fly fishers and bait casters will find trout ambushing whitebait along the edges of the overhanging scrub.

HERBERT, LAKE

Tasmap Sophia
Drainage Pieman system (via Lake Mackintosh)
Location Mt Farrell

A small tea-coloured rocky-shored lake flanked by eucalypts and open sedgeland. According to NTFA reports it was stocked in 1910 with 780 Loch Leven strain brown trout fry and 1500 rainbow fry, but there were no reports of subsequent captures. The lake was restocked in 1983 with 2000 brown trout fry, and again no fish were taken by anglers.

HERMIONE, LAKE

No trout. See *Fishing in National Parks*, 5.3.

HIGHLAND WATERS

See *London Lakes*.

HOBART RIVULET

Tasmap Derwent
Drainage Direct to the Derwent estuary

In Hobart city the water flows underground through concrete canals. Between Molle St and the Cascade Brewery the river follows its natural course and is open to the air – but it remains little more than an urban drain, polluted with domestic waste, stormwater, and effluent from the brewery. While small trout can be found throughout this stretch, fish kills are common.

The most healthy section of the river is above Cascade. Here Hobart Rivulet and Guy Fawkes Rivulet are shallow rocky-bottomed fastwaters which support plenty of very small brown trout. Fishing is best when levels are low. Celtas and baits are most effective.

HOOD LAGOON

See *Kay Lagoons*.

HORNES DAM

Tasmap Nive
Drainage Derwent system (via the Tarraleah Canal system)

The Wentworth Canal development was undertaken by the HEC during the drought of 1967 to enable the diversion of a series of small creeks into the Tarraleah Canals. In addition to the new canal, the system comprises three small dams: Dunnys, Wentworth and Hornes. All hold small trout, though only Hornes is of significant size.

Hornes Dam is located in dense forest behind a rockfill dam. While the southern end is choked with emergent trees and drowned sticks, the dam end is deep and open. The water is slightly murky.

Brown trout of 0.1-0.3 kg abound and big bags can be taken on lures, baits and flies. There are good rises on balmy afternoons.

HOT SPRINGS CREEK

Tasmap Huon
Drainage Direct to the Lune River

A small tannin-tinged shingle-bottomed fastwater

surrounded by dense wet-forest. As in other tributaries of the Lune, tiny brown trout abound. Wading is essential, and you must be prepared to clamber over fallen logs. The best results are obtained when casting Celtas or baits during periods of low flow.

HOW, LAKE

Tasmap Mersey
Drainage Mersey system (via February Creek)
Location February Plains

Probably no trout, though the lake and creek were rumoured to have been illegally stocked with brown trout fry in the late 1980s.

HOWE, LAKE

Probably no trout. See *Fishing in National Parks*, 5.1.

HOWES LAGOON (BAY)

Tasmap Meander
Drainage Natural – Derwent system (via James system)
Location Nineteen Lagoons

When water is being held behind the Augusta Dam, Howes becomes a bay of Lake Augusta – but for most of the year it exists as a separate 'natural' lagoon, much as it was before hydro-electric development.

Howes is a fly-only water and fishing from a boat has been banned since 1974. There is good wet-fly fishing along the flood-banks early in the season, and wade polaroiding is worthwhile on sunny days. Tailers feature across the rocky shallows in the south-eastern corner.

Trout stocks

There is natural recruitment from the James River via well-defined gutter connections, and from Lake Augusta during periods of inundation. However, stocks are augmented with occasional releases of adult brown trout. This stocking programme began as early as the winter of 1966 (when 100 fish were turned out), and from 1970 to 1976 there were annual liberations of 200 fish. In modern times liberations have been more conservative, occurring only after emergency salvage operations at Liawenee Canal.

You can expect to take brown trout from 0.7-1.5 kg, though rainbows are caught from time to time.

Trout liberations

Brown trout liberations (since 1980)

YEAR	SIZE	NUMBER
1986	fingerlings-adults	50
1988	fingerlings-adults	250

Rainbow trout liberations

YEAR	SIZE	NUMBER
1986	fingerlings	3
1988	fingerlings-adults	28

See also *Fishing in National Parks*, 5.1.

HUGEL LAKES

See *Shadow Lake* and *Forgotten Lake*.

HUGEL RIVER

Tasmap Nive
Drainage Derwent system (via Lake St Clair)

A shallow fast clearwater set in dense forest. While it carries small browns and rainbows and is good for Celta fishing when levels are low, the serious angler will be more interested in Lake St Clair and the Hugel Lakes.

See also *Fishing in National Parks*, 5.4.

HUNTLEY, LAKE

No trout. See *West Coast Range*.

HUON RIVER

Tasmaps D'Entrecasteaux, Huon, Tyenna, and Old River
Drainage Direct to the D'Entrecasteaux Channel

At 170 km the Huon is the fourth largest river in Tasmania. It is a deep tea-coloured water which flows fast between densely-forested banks. While the mid to upper reaches hold little of special interest to the angler, the estuary, lower fresh-water reaches, and tributary streams are all highly recommended.

Description

The lower estuary is flanked by a mosaic of pasture, orchards, woodland, scrub, small towns, and large rural residential areas. The tidal area of most interest to trout fishers (from Port Huon/ Lower Wattle Grove to the first rapid, some 4-5 km above Huonville) features banks overgrown with ribbons of forest and undergrowth.

From upper reaches of tidal influence (above Huonville) to the junction of the Little Denison River, the water flows quickly through big rapids and deep broadwaters. The surrounding land is rural but trees and scrub overhang the mostly-deep banks.

Between the Little Denison and the Picton River, the Huon is surrounded by dense production forest. The bankside vegetation is almost impenetrable, and most of the water is too deep and fast to wade.

From the Picton to The Razorback range, the water rushes between steep hills and virgin forest. This area is mostly unroaded and convenient access is limited to the Huon (walking) Track. Manuka Creek marks the edge of the Southwest National Park.

Between The Razorback and Lake Pedder the river is a large stream overgrown with heath and scrub. Flows weaken as you move upstream, dwindling to a trickle at the Scotts Peak Dam. The Scotts Peak Dam floods and diverts the upper Huon (see *Pedder, Lake*).

History of trout stocks

In 1869 the Salmon Commissioners claimed that there had been a delay in stocking brown trout into the best rivers, including the Huon, so that Atlantic salmon might first be established.

The first trout were released in 1870, when 300 'brown trout' fry were conveyed to Mountain River and 500 'sea trout' fry were released into the Huon proper. There were subsequent small liberations throughout the 1870s, and a viable population soon established.

According to early Parliamentary reports a 28 lb brown trout was found dead in the Huon in 1880. And in November 1887 Governor (Sir Robert) Hamilton landed a fish of 28¾ lb – which remains the official State record for a trout caught on a rod and line.

Rainbow trout are firmly established in the Arve and Weld rivers, though they are rare in the Huon itself. While the origin of these fish is unknown, it probably could be traced back to the days of the Geeveston hatchery (1930-?) and the Glen Huon hatchery (1939?-1949?).

Trout stocks today

Resident brown trout survive in the estuary throughout the year but are most common above the Egg Islands. Fish of 0.3-1.3 kg are typical, but many attain 1.5 kg and a surprising number exceed 5 kg. The average size decreases markedly as you move upstream beyond Tahune.

Sea trout are usually 0.6-2 kg, and each year local anglers take a number of 5-7 kg monsters.

Rainbow trout are mostly confined to the tributary streams (see notes above on the history of trout stocks).

In recent years domestic Atlantic salmon (escapees from the sea cages scattered along the south-east coast) have featured in rod-and-line creels, most of which have been 0.3-1.5 kg. However, it is unlikely that wild populations will establish (see *About Our Sportfish*, 2.4).

The Tasmanian blackfish was introduced from northern waters (probably by Saville-Kent, Superintendent of Fisheries) sometime in the late 1880s and is now abundant in the lower to mid freshwater reaches. Most of those caught by anglers are taken by set-rod fishers and weigh 0.1-0.3 kg. A few exceed 1 kg.

Sea trout

The Huon is one of the most productive sea trout fisheries in the State, and it is renowned for giving up trophies.

When to fish

While sea trout are sometimes found in appreciable numbers at the very beginning of the angling season, early runs are unreliable. Generally whitebait begin to congregate from about mid August and the best fishing is from early September to late November.

The action is fairly consistent provided the river is not in flood. There are no releases of water from Lake Pedder so flows can be reliably judged from rainfall alone.

Pre-spawners re-enter the river in April and provide worthwhile sport at the mouths of some tributary streams.

What to use

Local bait anglers favour the use of sandies (freshwater flathead). These can be left on the bottom but are more effective when retrieved like a lure. Other good baits include wattle grubs, galaxias and commercial saltwater baitfish.

Traditional shallow-running lures such as Cobras and fish-spoon wobblers are recommended for spinning and trolling.

The fly fishing is superb, though you really need a boat. Whitebait imitations and large matuka-style wets are essential.

Which part of the river is best?

Sea trout and slobs can be taken throughout the outer estuary (I have caught fish at Garden Island, Beaupre and Surges points) but the best and most reliable sport seems to be upstream of Port Huon / Lower Wattle Grove.

Night-time sea trout – Huon River

Hot spots for the shore-based angler

As most banks are overgrown, boating is highly recommended. However, there are several places popular with shore-based lure casters and bait fishers.

In the estuary proper it is worth trying Shipwrights Point (at Port Huon) and the accessible sections of bank at Lower Wattle Grove.

In Huonville the locals prefer to fish from the Bridge – the relatively shallow rock-shelf below is a major spawning site for *Lovettia*. The favoured method is to drift a bait down the current beneath a bubble float, letting out 20-30 m of line at a time. Trout strike the baits both on the drift and during the retrieve, and catches are simply walked like a dog on a lead to the nearest bank. This method is particularly effective at night in September/October.

There is also room for casting from the grassy esplanade on the north-eastern bank.

Galaxia feeders are taken in the *Lovettia* areas *and* above the first rapids, so from October to early December you can add the Judbury bridge and the mouth of the Little Denison River to the list of hot spots.

In late April good catches of pre-spawners are taken at the mouths of the Russell and Little Denison rivers.

Fishing from a boat

Trolling and drift spinning are very effective, and a boat is essential for serious fly fishing.

The real hot spots, especially for sight fishing, are where the whitebait spawn and/or bottleneck – the shallow rock-shelf under the Huonville bridge, and the first and second rapids (several kilometres above Huonville).

Trout also ambush baitfish from the recesses and roots in the overgrown banks. Explore the main channels both sides of the Egg Islands, and the Huonville area. Trolling along the edges is effective, but when the fish can be seen slashing and charging you will do best if you cast *to* them.

Dinghies can be taken above the rapids to Judbury and beyond, though there usually is little advantage in moving far above Huonville. Also, the further upstream you go, the greater the percentage of river residents among your catch.

The recommended launching ramps are at Huonville and Franklin. Other launching areas are shown on the 1:150 000 *South East Tasmania* Tasmap.

Fishing in summer and autumn

While the best post-Christmas sport is found in the freshwater tributary streams (see *Where to*

Fish – A Regional Breakdown, 4.5), resident brown trout can be taken throughout the Huon itself. Fish of 0.3-1.3 kg are quite common from the Egg Islands to Judbury, and there is always a small chance of taking a monster of 4-7 kg.

The water above Judbury teems with fish to 0.6 kg or so.

There is no worthwhile fishery at the foot of Scotts Peak Dam.

Domestic Atlantic salmon

Atlantic salmon escape from sea pens along the south-eastern coastline and are commonly taken by trout fishers. Most are caught during the springtime whitebait runs but others are taken in summer and autumn. The species is difficult to target and is really nothing more than a novelty. For further information see *About our Sportfish*, 2.4.

Special regulations

The Huon River above Lake Pedder is closed to angling at all times.

HUSKISSON RIVER

Tasmaps Pieman and Sophia
Drainage Pieman system (via Lake Pieman)

A relatively wide tea-coloured fastwater set in dense wet-forest. When levels are low many pools and riffles can be waded. Celta fishing and bait casting usually result in big bags of 0.1-0.3 kg brown trout.

ILA, LAKE

Tasmaps Meander and Mersey
Drainage Natural – Derwent system (via the Ouse system)
Location Western Lakes

A silt-bottomed lake with low rocky banks. There are no inflowing spawning streams and, while there is a significant gutter connection to Thompsons Lake, the trout population is relatively small. Browns of 1.5-3 kg are typical and some exceed 4 kg. Spinning and bank polaroiding are most effective. Catch-and-release is advocated.

See also *Fishing in National Parks*, 5.1.

INA, LAKE

Tasmap Nive
Drainage Derwent system (via the Nive system)
Location Western Lakes

Alpine bushland extends from the rocky western shoreline, while the southern and eastern approaches are a patchwork of moors and forested moraines.

The western banks are steep and moderately deep; the southern shore is a gentle gravel beach; the eastern shore features a variety of bouldery bays, gravel beaches, and rocky banks; and at the northern end there are patches of emergent pin-rushes.

Lake Ina holds plenty of 0.5-1.2 kg brown trout. When levels are high and the weather rough, the fly fisher should use wets and search the bays and the gutters behind the pin rushes. When there is adequate sunshine wade polaroiding over the beaches is exceptional. Tailing fish can be found early in the morning and late in the evening along the eastern beaches. Daytime rises are usually small and irregular. Spinning is worthwhile on rough and/or overcast days.

The lakes downstream of the outflow produce 'average' fish but are well suited to spinning and fly fishing. The lakes feeding Lake Ina from the north hold trout in the 1-2.5 kg class.

Lake Ina is accessible from Gowan Brae (Pine Tier Lagoon), but the roads are privately owned and sometimes gated. Remember that vehicles

Some of the lagoons north of Lake Ina hold good-sized trout.

cannot be taken into the World Heritage Area – the last boggy leg of the traditional access route must be walked. Alternative cross-country walks can be taken from Clarence Lagoon and all other Western Lakes access points.

See also *Fishing in National Parks*, 5.1.

INGLIS RIVER

Tasmaps Table Cape and Hellyer
Drainage Direct to Bass Strait

Sea trout

Although irregular, the runs of sea trout in the Inglis are as good as any in the North-West. From August to mid September the sea trout are largely confined to the estuary, but from September to late November they chase galaxias into the freshwater reaches, sometimes moving up beyond the Flowerdale junction.

The shore-based angler can enjoy good sport in the estuary, the best areas being along the southern bank from the mouth to Gutteridge Gardens, on the northern bank at the end of the Golf Course Road, and near the Table Cape Bridge (about 2 km from the mouth). Another hot spot, when the galaxias are running, is in the freshwater below the weir about 0.6 km above the Bass Highway (accessible from Godwins Road and the Pump Station Road).

Dinghies and runabouts can be launched at Gutteridge Gardens in Wynyard. Boat anglers have access to all of the estuary below the Table Cape Bridge, and the long stretches of overgrown bank further upstream. The best sport occurs when the trout are slashing at baitfish along the edges of the overhanging vegetation.

The Inglis Flats

The lower freshwater reaches, from the Bass Highway to the Flowerdale junction, flow through flat pasture and are very overgrown with willows. The pools are mostly long, deep, silty, and impossible to wade.

For most of the year this stretch receives scant attention from anglers (though good fish can always be taken on set-rods). However, during rising floods (usually in spring) the fishing is superb! As the water starts to spill out beyond the willows into the paddocks, trout of 0.4-1.5 kg move into the shallows to forage. While set-rod fishing with worms is most popular, there is plenty of scope for sight fishing with wet flies.

Locals seem to greatly favour fishing the nearby Flowerdale Flats, but this is probably only because the Flowerdale is close to the main roads.

The rest of the river

Most of the Inglis upstream of the flats flows between steep forested hills. The water riffles over shingly shallows and through wadeable pools – and is usually reasonably clear. Low levels are best for angling. Celta fishing and bait casting are most productive, though there is room for upstream nymphing. Modest rises occur on warm evenings during caddis hatches.

The best stretches include the Calder junction and Thunders Flat (about 5 km above the Calder junction). The majority of fish are 0.2-0.4 kg, though some exceed 1 kg.

The uppermost reaches, in the vicinity of Takone, are small but give up plenty of 0.1-0.2 kg fish.

History of trout stocks

According to early Parliamentary reports, brown trout were released into the Inglis as early as 1881.

A part-share of 300 Atlantic salmon fry were turned out in 1887, though none were ever caught.

Reports of the NTFA indicate that rainbows were probably first stocked in 1912 and that a further 9000 fry were released into the *'Inglis and Calder'* in 1929. There were probably many unrecorded liberations as well, but no rainbows survive today.

INGRID, LAKE

Tasmap   Mersey
Drainage   Derwent system (via the Nive River)
Location   Western Lakes

Although Lake Ingrid is surrounded by rocky alpine bushland, it is not especially deep and there are many pin-rush bays along the western shore.

Celta fishing along the channels between the rushes is recommended when levels are high, otherwise it is best to use small wobblers in the open water at the inflow and along the eastern bank.

During the early months of the season, fly fishers target tailing fish in the western bays. In summer and autumn, polaroiding is most effective.

Brown trout of 0.5-1.2 kg are typical.

See also *Fishing in National Parks*, 5.1.

IRIS RIVER

Tasmaps   Forth, Mersey, and Sophia
Drainage   Forth system (via Lake Gairdner)

A shallow tea-coloured fastwater containing plenty of tiny brown trout.

The lower reaches flow through a densely-forested valley and, with the exception of the stretch immediately above Lake Gairdner, are rarely fished. The uppermost reaches (accessible from the Cradle Mountain Road) flow through open sedgeland and are easily fished with lures, baits and flies. Big bags can be expected when levels are low.

History of trout stocks

According to early NTFA reports brown trout were taken to the upper reaches, on the Middlesex Plains, as early as 1906-07.

In an attempt to establish sea-runs of quinnat salmon in the River Forth, fry were released in the Iris during 1922 – and by 1924 a salmon hatchery had been erected at Moina. Stocking continued until 1929-30 but no fish ever returned from the sea (see *Forth, River*).

IRON CREEK

Tasmap   Prosser
Drainage   Direct to Pitt Water

A small creek with a rural setting. Summer/autumn flows are often very poor but brown trout hold-over in the deep shady pools. Fish of 0.2-0.4 kg are typical and some exceed 0.7 kg. Fishing peaks as flows moderate after floods. Bait casting is most effective.

The odd sea trout is taken from the estuary.

IRONSTONE, LAKE

Tasmap   Mersey
Drainage   Mersey system (via the Fisher system)
Location   Chudleigh Lakes

A very sheltered water lying between small steep hills. While most of the water is too deep to wade, all of the bed is clearly visible from the banks. Dense bottom-hugging *Isoetes* weed grows in most areas, promoting good mayfly hatches. All banks are suited to both polaroiding and spinning. Brown trout of 1-2 kg are typical.

See also *Fishing in National Parks*, 5.1.

ISANDULA, LAKE

(known to locals as the Gawler Dam)

Tasmap   Forth
Drainage   Leven system (via the West Gawler River)

A small water-supply lake impounded between steep (mostly forested) hills. The 15 m high rock-fill dam was built in 1966 and the normal operating range is quite marked. The water is slightly turbid and is best suited to lure casting and bait fishing. However, there is scope for fly fishing near the dam, and in the few small wadeable bays at the south-western access. Fair rises occur on warm summer/autumn evenings.

While there is ample natural recruitment of brown trout, the local angling clubs regularly liberate fry and fingerlings. Most fish caught weigh 0.3-0.5 kg but some approach 1 kg. Depending upon stocking regimes, domestic rainbows account for 0-50% of the annual harvest.

Trout liberations (since 1985)

Wild brown trout

YEAR	SIZE	NUMBER
1985	advanced fry	3 000
1987	fry	850
1988	fry	5 000
1989	small fingerlings	1 000
"	advanced fry	5 000
1991	fry	626

Domestic rainbow trout

YEAR	SIZE	NUMBER
1990	advanced fry	1 460

Note: legitimate (but poorly documented) releases of rainbows occurred throughout the 1980s.

ISIS RIVER

Tasmaps South Esk and Lake Sorell
Drainage South Esk system (via the Macquarie River)

Though small and easy to overlook, the Isis is an impressive trout water.

The best sport occurs where the river flows through flat (marginal) pasture. While many stretches are overgrown with willows and scrub, there are open banks at the confluence with the Macquarie; adjacent to the Macquarie Road; and further upstream.

The wet-season backwater fishing is very good, and when levels moderate good rises persist in the narrow weedy pools.

Most fish weigh 0.2-0.5 kg and some attain 0.7-1 kg.

See also *Macquarie River* and *Where to Fish – A Regional Breakdown*, 4.2

JACKS LAGOON

Tasmap Mersey
Drainage Mersey system (via the Fisher system)
Location Chudleigh Lakes

The Jacks Lagoon / Last Lagoon system has not been invaded by brown trout – in fact the lakes are so physically isolated that they do not even contain native fish.

The system was reputedly illegally stocked in the mid 1980s with rainbow trout but, while there is plenty of opportunity for natural recruitment, the current status of the species has not been formally assessed.

See also *Fishing in National Parks*, 5.1.

JAMES RIVER

Tasmaps Meander and Mersey
Drainage Natural – Derwent system (via the River Ouse)
Location Nineteen Lagoons

Augusta Dam to Lake Augusta

Although not obvious from most maps, the Lake Augusta impoundment is usually kept at such low levels that it is two lakes separated by the 'natural' James River (see *Augusta, Lake*). This section of the James carries brown trout (and a few wild rainbows) throughout the year and is of special interest to anglers after heavy rain when natural flows cause it to spill out into adjacent gutters, ditches, backwaters and lagoons. Browns tail in the shallows, and can also be tempted out of the flooded undercuts. The best fishing is in the snowgrass plains west of the Julian Lakes track. Avoid places where the bed of the Augusta impoundment has eroded back to bedrock and clay.

Since 1962 it has been illegal to fish from a boat in the lower James River and the associated lagoons. Also in 1962, the waters were reserved for fly fishing only, though this law was later repealed.

The upper reaches

Between the natural Lake Augusta and Pillans Lake the James is a large turbulent clearwater flowing through rocky heathland. It holds brown trout from 0.5-1.5 kg throughout the year, and can provide worthwhile sport during December/ January when there are goods hatches of snowflake caddis.

See also *Fishing in National Parks*, 5.1.

JAMES TARN

Probably no trout. See *Fishing in National Parks*, 5.5.

JANE RIVER

Tasmap Franklin
Drainage Gordon system (via the Franklin River)

A large tea-coloured fastwater flowing through wet-forest wilderness. It holds plenty of slow-growing brown trout and is best fished when levels are low. Celtas are very effective.

See also *Fishing in National Parks*, 5.3.

JEAN BROOK

Tasmap Forth
Drainage Direct to the River Leven at the Leven Canyon

A small overgrown shingle-bottomed fastwater containing lots of tiny brown trout. It is quite popular among local bait casters when levels are low.

JETTY LAKE

No trout. See *Fishing in National Parks*, 5.3.

JOCKS LAGOON

Tasmap Georges Bay
Drainage Isolated coastal lagoon
Location 2 km south of Stieglitz

A deep tea-coloured water with rush-choked shores. There is little space for shore-based fishing, so it pays to bring a dinghy.

The trout population is maintained entirely by artificial stocking and, while fish can attain 1.5-2 kg, the average size is highly variable. The last recorded stocking occurred in may 1992 when some 500 brown trout fingerlings were turned out.

JOHNNY, LAKE

Tasmap Mersey
Drainage Mersey system (via the Fisher system)
Location Chudleigh Lakes

While lakes Johnny, Chambers and Douglas appear to support relatively few trout, the normal size of fish caught (0.8-2.5 kg) suggests that recruitment from the gutter connection to Lake Explorer may be quite significant. In 1989-90 the IFC undertook experimental releases of 1000 brown trout fry into each lake.

During wet periods Lake Johnny breaks out into the flats flanking its western shore, but most banks in the system are rocky and well-defined.

Spinning is worthwhile in rough weather. During summer the water can become slightly turbid – but not so much that you can't polaroid. The hatches are disappointing.

See also *Fishing in National Parks*, 5.1.

JOHNSONS LAGOON

No trout. See *Fishing in National Parks*, 5.1.

JOHNSTON TARN

Probably no trout. See *Fishing in National Parks*, 5.5.

JONES RIVER

Tasmap Tyenna
Drainage Derwent system (via Meadowbank Lake)

A small creek with moderate summer/autumn flows. It meanders through farmland and, while some stretches are overgrown with trees and scrub, there is ample room to cast from the banks.

According to early Parliamentary reports, brown trout were established by 1869. Today the system teems with fish to 0.3 kg.

Celtas and natural baits are recommended, and you get the best results when levels are low. The best areas are near Meadowbank Lake and adjacent to the Jones River Road. The headwaters (including Ironstone Creek and Montos Creek) are very small and overgrown but contain plenty of tiny fish.

JORDAN RIVER

Tasmaps Derwent and Lake Sorell
Drainage Direct to the Derwent estuary at Gagebrook

The Jordan is flanked by flat marginal pasture and many banks are overgrown with willows and scrub. After heavy rain (usually in spring) some sections break the banks, but by late summer the system has usually receded into a series of flowless weedy pools. While the water is often very murky, it can clear appreciably during dry spells.

The best fishing is in the deep pools from the head of the estuary to Lower Marshes. Good stretches exist near the Tea Tree road, adjacent to the Elderslie Road, adjacent to the Lake Highway, and at Lower Marshes.

Trout also manage to survive throughout the year in the puddles above the Midland Highway – and no doubt move into Lake Tiberias during floods.

Trout stocks

According to early Parliamentary reports brown trout were established in the Jordan by 1869. The NTFA recorded the release of rainbow fry at Pontville as early as 1917, but this species failed to establish. While most trout taken today weigh 0.4-0.5 kg, many attain 0.7 kg and some exceed 1.2 kg.

Fly fishing

The Jordan is essentially a 'meadow stream'. When levels are high trout can be taken on wet flies along the flooded edges, and when levels subside there can be fair rises as well as limited scope for polaroiding. However, while locals appreciate the fishing on their doorstep, visitors are better advised to fish the South Esk system (see *Where to Fish – A Regional Breakdown*, 4.2).

Lures and bait

Fishing with small lures works well when the river is flowing fast but becomes increasingly futile as flows subside.

On hot days in summer and autumn grasshopper casting is worthwhile, and on warm evenings surface fishing with wattle grubs is recommended.

Sea trout

Good sea trout are taken throughout the estuary – don't be put off by the adjacent housing developments. The best spots for the shore-based angler are the open deepwater banks between the East Derwent Highway and the Cove Hill Road. There is also scope for trolling and drift spinning.

See also *Derwent, River*.

JUDD, LAKE

Tasmap   Wedge
Drainage   Huon system (via the Anne River)

This deep rocky-shored clearwater lies at the foot of the dramatic cliff-faces of Mt Eliza and is surrounded by dense wet-forest.

Brown trout probably invaded the lake shortly after the Huon was first stocked (in 1870) and are now well established. Some fish exceed 1.5 kg but most weigh 0.4-0.7 kg.

While access along the banks is mostly difficult, you can wade close to the shore and pick up good numbers of fish while spinning or polaroiding. Hatches are not a feature, though fair rises occur on warm evenings.

Access is via the well-formed foot track which extends east from the Scotts Peak Road at Red Tape Creek. The trip takes about 2½-3½ hrs each way. There is a well-established informal camping area in the forest near the outflow.

See also *Fishing in National Parks*, 5.2.

JUDDS CREEK

Tasmap   Tyenna
Drainage   Direct to the Huon River at Judbury

A slightly tea-coloured fastwater. The lower reaches flow through cleared farmland and feature deep clay-banked pools. Further up, the valley is steep and well-forested.

There are plenty of 0.2-0.5 kg brown trout and, when levels are low, bait casters commonly take big bags.

JULIA, LAKE

No trout. See *West Coast Range*.

JULIAN LAKES

Tasmap   Mersey
Drainage   Natural – Derwent system (via the River Ouse)
Location   Western Lakes

The Julian Lakes are clearwaters surrounded by rocky heathland and, in contrast to nearby Pillans Lake, there is little sign of fire damage. The system comprises two main waters (the Lower and Upper lakes), which are separated by 30 m or so of steep wide creek, and a myriad of much smaller waters.

The Lower Julian Lake

The lower lake has some deep banks (notably at the upper end near the track crossing) but features extensive wadeable shallows. Brown trout in excess of 2 kg are not unknown, though smaller fish of 0.5-1 kg predominate. A few naturally-spawned rainbows are also taken.

While spinning and wade polaroiding are usually most effective, good rises occur off the deep banks on warm calm afternoons.

The Upper Julian Lake

The upper lake is a labyrinth of deep well-defined necks, arms and bays. Brown trout of 0.7-1.5 kg are typical but many exceed 2 kg. Naturally-spawned rainbows are reputed to account for up to 5% of the annual catch, though I have found them to be rare. While bank polaroiding and spinning are the main fishing methods, good rises can occur on muggy afternoons.

Bridge Lake (Grid Ref. 558 730)

Brown trout of 1.5-2 kg are reasonably common but there are some much larger fish as well. Spinning, polaroiding and night fishing with wet flies give the best results.

Cliffs Lake (Grid Ref. 560 728)

A silt-bottomed water with rocky banks at the southern end and grassy marshes at the northern end. It supports good stocks of 1-2 kg brown trout. Wet-fly fishing is recommended when the marshes are full, and polaroiding is good at other times.

Grassy Lagoon (Grid Ref. 565 722)

A shallow silt-bottomed lake with many grassy undercuts and a poor gutter connection to the Lower Julian Lake. It holds some exceptional fish but the angling is always very tough.

Other waters

Scattered around the main lakes there is a multi-tude of small tarns. Many receive limited natural recruitment from the main waters and sport fish of 2-3 kg and more. Polaroids are essential.

See also *Fishing in National Parks*, 5.1.

JULIUS RIVER

Tasmaps Arthur River and Sandy Cape
Drainage Direct to the Arthur River

A shallow slightly tea-coloured fastwater set in dense rainforest. When levels are low Celta fishing and bait casting result in big bags of tiny brown trout.

JUNCTION LAKE

Tasmap Mersey
Drainage Mersey River (an instream lake)
Location Western Lakes

Junction Lake is a rainbow-only water (see *Meston, Lake*) which carries plenty of fat fish. Most weigh 0.2-0.7 kg and a few exceed 1.5 kg.

The southern shore is steep, thickly forested and largely inaccessible. The best areas for fishing are at the inflow of the Mersey and the grassy flats (Frog Flats) midway along the northern shore. The bed is weedy and soft and unsuitable for wading.

In fine weather the rises are phenomenal, and even blind fishing with nondescript dry flies will get results.

While the charming rustic hut is frequently fully occupied, there are plenty of good informal campsites.

See also *Fishing in National Parks*, 5.1.

Junction Lake

JUPITER, LAKE

No trout. See *Fishing in National Parks*, 5.2.

KARA, LAKE

Tasmap Hellyer
Drainage Emu system (via Tittie Gee Creek)

Lake Kara was built by the NWFA for the expressed purpose of providing public fishing. For many years it was a major disappointment but, since a recent rehabilitation programme, it has shown some promise.

Description

Kara is a small tea-coloured water surrounded by dense wet-bushland. While there are a few open banks and wadeable shallows, a small dinghy is a definite asset.

History

Construction of the earthfill dam across Tittie Gee Creek was a NWFA project carried out in March 1968. Brown trout were removed from the creek prior to flooding, and in May 1968 the new impoundment received some 10 000 rainbow fin-gerlings. A follow-up liberation of 10 000 rain-bow fry occurred in the following year, and a formal opening ceremony was held in November 1969. While there were isolated catches of large well-conditioned trout, the fishing was generally poor and by 1979 it was apparent that the rain-bows had failed to establish.

In an effort to improve the fishing some 10 000 brown trout fry were turned out each year from 1979 to 1983, and a further 20 000 rainbow fry were liberated in 1982. But still the lake was a disappointment.

The IFC surveyed the lake in 1984-85 and concluded that the main problems were the acidity of the water, and the effect of rotting vegetation on oxygen levels. It was also pointed out that, since rainbow trout tended to migrate downstream or frequent deep water well out from shore, the lake was best suited to brown trout.

In 1987 the lake was completely drained. The NWFA cleared and burned most of the dead scrub and trees on the bed, and applied lime and limestone to the lake and its inflow. It is intended that liming will be an ongoing management strategy.

The lake was restocked in 1988 and now provides fair sport.

Trout liberations (since 1988)

Wild brown trout

YEAR	SIZE	NUMBER
1988	adults	400
1989	adults	300
"	fry	30 000
1990	adults	200
1991	adults	200
1992	adults	200
1993	adults	200

Note: the adult fish are typically 0.9-1.2 kg.

Domestic rainbow trout

YEAR	SIZE	NUMBER
1991	fingerlings	1 000
1992	yearlings	500

The fishing today

The adult trout released since 1988 have maintained condition, and there has been significant natural spawning. But, while the fishing has definitely improved and is much appreciated by locals, there is nothing special to attract visitors.

Set-rod fishing is worthwhile, though small blackfish often snatch baits intended for trout.

While there is limited scope for lure casting from the shore, drift spinning is often more productive.

Blind fishing with wet flies can induce savage strikes, especially from brown trout in the small weedy bays. Also, there are fair beetle falls on warm summer/autumn days.

KAY LAGOONS

Tasmap   Meander
Drainage   Derwent system (via the Little Pine system)
Location   Nineteen Lagoons

The Kay Lagoons are the backwaters upstream of Lake Kay. They include several permanent pools

(such as Hood Lagoon) and a number of intermittent flood basins. The fishing is discussed under *Kay, Lake*.

KAY, LAKE

Tasmap   Meander
Drainage   Derwent system (via the Little Pine River)
Location   Nineteen Lagoons

Lake Kay is a shallow silt-bottomed clearwater surrounded by vast snowgrass flats. After periods of heavy rain the lake and the inflowing river back up into the tussocks, spilling into backwaters and semi-permanent lagoons. Fish work their way up gutters and ditches and forage furiously in the shallows, providing phenomenal wet-fly fishing.

Once the floodwaters subside, Lake Kay quickly recedes and becomes a small inconspicuous lagoon. However, the combination of shallow water, weed growth, and river flushing creates ideal conditions for mayflies. Hatches of duns begin in spring, peak in summer, and continue into autumn. While the best activity occurs when there is a wisp of high-level cloud, any warm day can be worthwhile. The dun hatches normally peak between midday and mid afternoon, and black spinners fly back over the water in the afternoons and evenings. When there is no surface activity polaroiding is a good fall-back.

In times of drought Kay can become very shallow and turbid. Such conditions subdue the mayflies and the trout tend to lie lazily on the lake bed or retreat to the river. However, the fishing picks up quickly during the next good rain. A bad summer should not be seen as an indication of a long-term decline in the fishery.

Wading is advantageous at any time of the year. Spinning is not recommended. In the early season your often-vain attempts to reach pockets of fishable water are likely to spook the prized foraging fish and ruin the action for fly fishers. In summer and autumn the trout simply do not respond well to lures.

Many of the foraging fish taken early in the year are river residents of 0.7-3 kg. Mayfly feeders tend to range from 0.5-1.5 kg. While rainbows sometimes migrate down from some of the nearby artificially-stocked lakes, they are rarities in Lake Kay.

The family car can be driven to within 1 km of the lake. From here a convenient foot track leads to the lakeshore.

See also *Fishing in National Parks*, 5.1.

KELLAWAYS CREEK

Tasmap D'Entrecasteaux
Drainage Direct to the Huon estuary at Woodstock

A small shallow shingle-bottomed creek with sluggish summer/autumn flows. It holds a fair number of brown trout to about 0.5 kg and fishes well when not in flood. While Celta fishing and bait casting are most practical, there is scope for fly fishing.

KENNETH LAGOON

Tasmap Nive
Drainage Derwent system (via the Nive system)
Location Western Lakes

A shallow clearwater with permanent marshes along the western shores and rocky-bottomed open water near the outflow. Typical trout weigh 0.4-1.5 kg.

See also *Fishing in National Parks*, 5.1.

KERMANDIE RIVER

Tasmap Huon
Drainage Direct to the Huon estuary at Kermandie

From August to December sea trout can be taken throughout the kilometre or so of estuary. The hot spot is directly below the weir.

Most of the browns in the pondage above the weir are less than 0.5 kg, though there some surprises.

The stream proper is a clear fastwater running over a rocky bed. While most banks are overgrown with willows and blackberries, at normal levels there is plenty of room for wading. Celta fishers and bait casters are assured of big bags of 0.2-0.5 kg browns. Some of the best stretches are in the township (Geeveston).

KERRISONS LAKES

Tasmap Mersey
Drainage Natural – Derwent system (via James system)
Location Western Lakes (grid refs. 550 721 and 547 727)

Kerrisons Lakes are the two larger stillwaters north of Kerrisons Hut. They are contained by low boulder-encrusted hills and share a permanent gutter connection to Pillans Lake.

While there is anecdotal evidence of very large fish being taken from time to time, brown trout of 1-2 kg are typical.

Spinning and polaroiding are usually most practical.

KING ISLAND

Trout were taken to King Island as early as 1900 when the NTAA recorded a consignment of 5500 brown trout ova.

John Clements (*Salmon and Trout in the Antipodes*, 1988) noted that in the 1930s a small hatchery and rearing pond was established on the island. Brown trout ova were supplied from Tasmania and Victoria, while brown and rainbow fry were imported from Tasmania. Some 6000 quinnat salmon ova from New Zealand were also received. However, Clements assumed that the hatchery was relatively short-lived.

Brown trout fry were taken to the island in the late 1950s and early 1960s, and rainbows were released in 1960. The NTFA also noted that redfin perch had been illegally introduced by 1964. Unfortunately, early records do not detail release sites, though it is likely that the coastal lagoons, including Martha Lavinia, were targeted.

A new era of trout stocking began in the mid 1960s. Between 1966 and 1982 Lake Flannigan received almost annual shipments of rainbow fry, and from 1970 to 1976 Penny Lagoon was stocked with brown trout fry.

None of the coastal lagoons are capable of maintaining trout stocks through natural recruitment and, while there may have been some poorly documented releases in recent years, the fishery has never been well respected by mainland Tasmanians.

KING RIVER

Tasmaps Cape Sorell and Franklin
Drainage Direct to Macquarie Harbour

The King River below its confluence with the Queen River is heavily polluted with heavy metals and sludge and is effectively dead. However, the upper tributaries teem with browns and rainbows and provide more than adequate recruitment for Lake Burbury.

General history

From Macquarie Harbour to the Crotty Dam the King flows through a densely-forested gorge, and at one time the river's beauty was said to rival that of the famed Gordon.

Small-scale gold mining in the King system began in 1883 leading to the discovery in 1891 of payable copper at the Iron Blow (near Mt Lyell). The Mt Lyell Mining and Railway Company was formed in 1892 and the first of the Mt Lyell smelters began operating in 1896. Trees on the hills around Queenstown were cut down to feed the furnaces – and sulphur smog combined with repeated wild fires killed the regrowth. Torrential West Coast rains then washed away millions of tonnes of topsoil. By 1905 the hills were partially denuded and severely eroded.

Ultimately the soil washed down the tributary streams into the lower King River, and within a few years the port of Teepookana had silted up so much that it had to be abandoned.

Mine tailings too were pumped into the system, killing all life in the Queen River, Linda Creek, the Lyell Comstock Creek, and the King River below the outfall of the Lyell Comstock. The pollution has hardly abated – the Queen is still little more than an open gutter for toxic sludge.

The Mt Lyell mine is no longer viable and, after many reprieves, it is now due to close at the end of 1994. Still, much of the King catchment will remain lifeless for years to come.

In 1991-92 the HEC completed the King River Power Development, flooding the huge buttongrass basin flanking the upper King. The dam is upstream of the Queen River, but downstream of the Linda and Lyell Comstock creeks – raising doubts about the long-term health of the new impoundment (see *Burbury, Lake*).

History of trout stocks

Trout fared well only in the King River above Lyell Comstock Creek and in the unpolluted tributaries. These fish were typically 0.1-0.3 kg, though some exceeded 0.5 kg.

Brown trout

Parliamentary records indicate that from 1931 to 1933 the King, Nelson and Princess rivers were stocked with brown trout fry, though it is unlikely that these were the first or only liberations.

The Governor River (which fed a moderately polluted stretch of the King) and the West Queen River have also long supported small brown trout.

Rainbow trout

The King was stocked with 40 000 rainbows (fry) in 1934 and major wild populations soon established in brown trout waters such as the upper King River, the Eldon River, the South Eldon River, Dante Rivulet and Lake Beatrice.

In Halls Creek (a tributary of the polluted Queen River) rainbows have thrived in the absence of brown trout.

Quinnat salmon

Some 3000 quinnat yearlings were released in 1934, but this species failed to establish.

The King today

The water below the mouth of the polluted Queen is unlikely to support trout in the foreseeable future.

The river between the Queen junction and the Crotty Dam was probably never severely polluted, as contaminated water from the Linda and Lyell Comstock creeks would have been greatly diluted by contributions from clean downstream tributaries. In 1993-94 the stretch from the Queen to the outfall of the King Power Station was awash with vile sulphide-contaminated water typical of that found in the bottom stratum of newly formed lakes. While this condition will probably persist for a few years, the highly-active rotting vegetation on the lake bottom will eventually be consumed and the water will become more habitable to fish. There will come a time when the King between the Queen and the power station will hold large numbers of brown and rainbow trout, though the steep forested gorge will always be a deterrent to anglers.

The King between the power station and the Crotty Dam is deprived of water and, while small fish can be taken from the puddles scattered along the river bed, the angling will never be attractive.

The upper King River has been completely inundated by Lake Burbury. The tributary streams at the north end of the lake (most notably the Eldon and South Eldon) support worthwhile stocks of resident rainbows and browns. The other major clean tributaries (such as the Princess, Nelson and Governor rivers) hold plenty of resident browns and, as they are bound to be used by lake spawners, they may eventually become home to significant numbers of resident rainbows.

KING WILLIAM CREEK

Tasmap Nive
Drainage Derwent system (via Lake King William)

A small shallow fastwater flowing through buttongrass plains. When levels are low Celta fishing and bait casting result in big bags.

KING WILLIAM, LAKE

Tasmap Nive
Drainage Derwent system (a major instream impoundment)

Although King William trout are small, the high catch-rate is very appealing to beginners. Further information is available in the book Trout Guide *(Rob Sloane and Greg French, 1991). A summary only is given here.*

Description

Lake King William is a clearwater hydro-electric storage, established to store and regulate the upper Derwent catchment. The Clark Dam is 67 m high and full supply is 719.94 m above sea level. Drawdowns of up to 29 m are to be expected, so the size and shape of the lake are quite variable.

The high banks along the eastern and southern shores, and between the Guelph Basin and the main lake, support substantial eucalypt forests, and significant stands of drowned trees still exist in many areas. The littoral zone in these areas has eroded back to bedrock and clay.

Vast buttongrass plains extend from the northwestern shores and around the Guelph Basin. At low levels silt and mud flats are exposed and, after extended exposure during successive drought years, terrestrial vegetation re-establishes.

Trout stocks

The fishery is maintained entirely by natural recruitment, the main spawning areas being the upper Derwent, the Navarre River, the Little Navarre River, the Guelph River, the Middle River and Rufus Rivulet. Brown trout dominate, though rainbows account for about 10% of the annual harvest. Most fish are very small (0.2-0.6 kg) but when the lake rises over long-exposed flood plains foraging browns quickly gain weight and condition. At almost four trout per angler per day, the average catch rate is the highest recorded in the Central Highlands.

Lake King William – what the fish lack in size is compensated by quantity

History

The Tarraleah Power Development was approved by Parliament in 1934 and by 1937 dams, pumps and control gates had been constructed at Lake St Clair. At the same time a small weir was erected on the River Derwent at Butlers Gorge to enable water to be diverted via a series of flumes canals and pipelines to the Tarraleah Power Station in the Nive valley. The power station was commissioned in 1938.

Further expansion of the Tarraleah project began at the end of the War, and by 1949 the small weir at Butlers Gorge had been superseded by the 61m high Clark Dam.

There were sufficient trout already in the natural river system to guarantee both instant sport and continued natural recruitment. However, during the last few months of 1949 some 22 000 brown trout yearlings and 76 000 rainbow trout yearlings were liberated into the rising waters of the new impoundment. Extensive stocking of the lake continued for several years.

During 1951 the lake almost filled and the fish reached an average of about 3 lb. In the following few years many fish to 7 lb were taken. From the outset limit bags were common and the fishery remained very popular for about a decade. But by the 1960s the relative abundance of rainbows had declined and the average weight of the brown trout had fallen below 2 lb.

By the standards set at other new impoundments, average trout were never large. This can be attributed to the tremendous number of fish and the fluctuating water levels. A less-zealous stocking programme may have been beneficial in the early years – but by the mid 1950s enormous stocks of trout were being maintained solely through natural recruitment.

In 1966 the Clark Dam was raised by 6 m to a new height of 67 m, though the new full supply level was not reached for some time.

Fly fishing

When the lake fills, foraging trout provide exciting sport. Bedlam Bay, Navarre Bay and the bays around the Guelph basin are hot spots. Fishing is best when rising water is flooding long-exposed flood plains where vegetation has started to re-establish. Brown trout gorge on worms, frogs, drowned insects and a variety of other forage items, quickly gaining weight and condition.

When levels recede fishing is more enjoyable from a boat. Consistent dry-fly fishing is available, with good rises to beetles, caddis and mayflies on warm settled days. The shallow bays

211

in the Guelph Basin, the south-western shore of the main lake, and the western fringes of the northern end of the lake are very good, though rises can occur anywhere.

Mudeyes feature among the drowned trees and sticks during summer and early autumn.

If trout are not moving, good results can be achieved by blind casting with nymphs and small wets. Concentrate on the fringes of drowned bushes and trees.

Lure fishing

Lure casting from a drifting boat is extremely effective, especially when fishing among the flooded bushes.

Shore-based spinning is largely confined to the banks near the dam.

By far the majority of fish taken in King William are caught by trolling with Cobras and Devons. Undoubtedly the best areas are the Guelph Basin and the northern end of the lake. Most anglers prefer to troll close to the shores but, when the fish are biting, good catches can be made anywhere. Limit bags are common – even on bright days.

Bait fishing

Cast-and-retrieve surface fishing with grubs in the evening is a deadly method. Otherwise it is worthwhile set-rod fishing with worms or grubs.

Access

Normally the most convenient access is via the unsealed Butlers Gorge Road to the Clark Dam at the southern end of the lake.

When levels are high, the northern end of the lake can be reached from the Lyell Highway near Derwent Bridge. However, the storage is often well below full supply and can recede kilometres down the old river course.

A rough 2WD track extends south from the Lyell Highway (10 km west of Derwent Bridge) to the Guelph Basin.

Rugged 4WD tracks extend from the Lyell Highway to Navarre Bay, and along the eastern banks (north from Butlers Gorge).

Camping

Informal lakeshore camping is permitted. At the southern end there are a few unattractive sites near the boat launching ramp and along the 4WD track. At the northern end there are suitable campsites at Navarre Bay. But the most attractive camping is at the Guelph basin.

The Derwent Bridge Hotel offers accommodation and is recommended when the lake is high enough to fish from the northern access.

Boating

A substantial launching ramp exists at the southern end near the Clark Dam. When the lake is full boats can also be launched near the Derwent inflow. At low levels boat access from the north is almost impossible.

LAKE KING WILLIAM

KITA LAKE

Tasmap Mersey
Drainage Derwent system (via the Nive system)
Location Western Lakes.

A deep rocky-shored clearwater which contains some larger-than-average brown trout. The fishing is always exceptionally tough.

See also *Fishing in National Parks*, 5.1.

KITTYS RIVULET

Tasmap Little Swanport
Drainage South Esk system (via the Macquarie River)

A narrow gutter-like creek flowing through open farmland. It holds some surprising brown trout to 1 kg or so. After heavy rain fish can be taken with wet flies along the flooded edges. In summer and autumn dry-fly fishing and bait casting with grasshoppers are recommended. The best sport is in the lowest reaches.

KNIGHTS CREEK RESERVOIR

Public fishing is not allowed.

KNIGHTS LAGOON

Mentioned in the Fishing Code as being reserved for artificial lures. Not listed with the Nomenclature Board and unknown to current IFC staff.

KOONYA, LAKE

Tasmap   Cape Sorell
Drainage   Manuka Creek system

A deep dark tea-coloured water encircled by dense tea-tree scrub. While it contains blackfish and (probably) brown trout, it is difficult to fish.

LABYRINTH, THE

Tasmap   Mersey
Drainage   Pieman system (via the Murchison system)
Location   Some 10 km north-west of Lake St Clair

The Labyrinth is a small wilderness plateau encircled by spectacular peaks, and studded with a dozen or so crystal lakes. While none of the waters have been invaded by brown trout, Atlantic salmon were illegally released into Lake Ophion in the 1980s and specimens to 2.5 kg were taken in the early 1990s. If the salmon do not migrate to sea and are able to spawn successfully they may eventually establish in Lake Ophion, Cyane Lake, Lake Erytheia and (further downstream) Long Lake. However, the success of the species is by no means assured.

The easiest access is from Lake St Clair via a well-formed walking track.

See also *Fishing in National Parks*, 5.4.

LACHLAN RIVER

Tasmap   Derwent
Drainage   Direct to the River Derwent at New Norfolk

A clear fastwater flowing over a shingle bed.

According to early Parliamentary reports brown trout were established by 1869, William Senior (who visited Tasmania around 1877) wrote that the stream *'was not opened for angling till last season'*.

Today the water teems with fish to about 0.5 kg and, when levels are low, Celta fishing and bait casting commonly result in big bags. The lower reaches, from New Norfolk to the Lachlan district, flow through farmland but, as the banks are overgrown with willows and scrub, wading is essential. The pools in the forested upper reaches are mostly very small.

LADY LAKE

No fish. See *Fishing in National Parks*, 5.1.

LADY BARRON CREEK

Tasmap   Tyenna
Drainage   Derwent system (via the Tyenna River)

Brown trout exist throughout the stream but the upper reaches are very small and overgrown and practical fishing is confined to the lowest 3 km or so where the stream flows clear and fast through dense wet-forest. Brown trout to about 0.3 kg are quite common and when levels are low big bags are taken on Celtas.

Access is via a well-formed walking track from the Mt Field National Park picnic area to Lady Barron Falls; or via the Weir Road from National Park (township).

See also *Fishing in National Parks*, 5.5.

LAFFER DAM

See *Maa Mon Chin Dam*.

LAGOON OF ISLANDS

Tasmap   Shannon
Drainage   Derwent system (via the Shannon system)

A well-respected trophy water, showing renewed promise after a disastrous crash.

Description

Lagoon of Islands is a shallow swampy storage, heavily overgrown with strapweed and featuring numerous islands of dead tea-tree. It receives water from its limited natural catchment and from the Ripple Diversion. Water is discharged via Blackburn Creek.

213

The main purpose of the storage is to allow the HEC to meet its riparian requirements without having to take more-valuable water from Shannon Lagoon and/or Great Lake.

History

In its natural state the Lagoon of Islands was a large swampland. A unique feature of the area was the extensive weed mat which floated on a bed of liquid organic slime. Numerous floating tea-tree islands were anchored to the lake sediments through their extensive root systems.

The damming of the lagoon was a joint venture between the IFC and the HEC. The perceived advantage to anglers was the creation of a new rainbow fishery, while the HEC was interested in being able to supply riparian water to properties along the lower Shannon and Ouse rivers. The IFC contributed 25% of the construction costs and received the guarantee of a minimum drawdown level.

Dam construction commenced in January 1964 and all works were completed by early May. The first stocking occurred in April 1964 when 2200 rainbow fingerlings were turned out. By May 1965 nearly 29 000 rainbows had been released.

Prior to the liberation of rainbow trout it was believed that eels and tench were the only fish in the natural lagoon. IFC staff were therefore surprised to find that 25% of the trout caught during early netting surveys were brown trout.

The new lagoon was opened to fishing at the beginning of the 1965-66 rainbow trout season. The fish averaged 4 lb and were reported to be 'deep almost as they are long'.

Owing to a succession of dry seasons it was not possible to draw riparian water from the storage until February 1970 – and the lake did not spill until 1971. By 1973 many of the tea-trees had died and there were signs that the weed mat was fragmenting.

Contrary to expectations, the brown trout population blossomed and by 1972 this species was dominant. Consequently the IFC altered the angling season to make it consistent with other brown trout waters. In October of the same year the Commission released 56 000 brown trout fry. Rains were never as heavy or consistent as had been expected. Indeed dry winters frequently denied brown trout access to the mediocre spawning beds in Mary Creek. However, there were often sufficient spring rains to enable significant natural recruitment of rainbow trout. In 1974 the open season was again managed for the conservation of rainbow trout. At this time the fishing began to improve. Many rainbows and browns to 3 kg were taken and angling effort intensified.

Also in 1974 was the first recorded capture of a redfin perch. The origin of this species in the lake is unknown but a thriving population soon established.

Throughout the 1970s and early 1980s the Lagoon of Islands continued to be artificially stocked with rainbow trout. The lake developed a reputation as a trophy water, with fish averaging close to 2.5 kg and ranging up to 7 kg.

Because of the inability of the storage to hold sufficient water for riparian use during drought years, the scheme had largely been a white elephant for the HEC. In 1983 it was proposed to divert water from Ripple Creek (a tributary of the upper Shannon) into Jacks Creek (a tributary of Woods Lake) and to establish weirs on Jacks Creek to enable the manipulation of extra water into Lagoon of Islands and (if required) to Woods Lake. Rather than discharge directly from an underground pipeline into the Lagoon of Islands and risk damage to spawning fish, a 500 m long spawning channel was constructed. The works were carried out the following year.

By the winter of 1984 there was a strong flow through the Ripple Diversion and some 650 adult brown trout spawners from Great Lake were placed directly into the new spawning grounds. The channel soon became the primary spawning area for both trout species. In addition there was continued artificial stocking and, despite the substantial increase in trout numbers, trophy fishing was maintained for several years.

A decline in the fishery was first noticed by anglers in 1987 and by the summer of 1988 there was dramatic discolouration of the water, and an especially dramatic crash in both the size and condition of the trout.

From this time until the end of the 1990-91 season the lake was a major concern for fisheries management. Trout which were able to survive grew slowly and were usually less than 1 kg at maturity. After first spawning the fish became slabby and few survived to spawn a second time. The triploid rainbows fared best but, while they maintained condition, few were able to exceed 1 kg. Anglers considered the slimy green water to be virtually worthless.

With funding from the HEC, IFC research staff eventually found that the problem (a severe algal bloom) was caused by increased nutrient levels. Most nutrients were being flushed into the lake from artificially-fertilized farmland in the Ripple catchment. But the problem was compounded by the fact that the strapweed, which could not

IFC staff catching rainbow spawners from the Ripple Diversion in order to collect ova and milt (photo by Viv Spencer)

tolerate high levels and poor water, was rotting and releasing further nutrients.

Water-quality safeguards were introduced. These included lowering the maximum permitted lake level to 1 m below full supply, maintaining the minimum level at a little more than 2 m below full supply, minimising the use of the Ripple Diversion, and negotiating with land owners to reduce the use of superphosphates.

There has since been a dramatic upturn in both the water quality and the trout fishing. By the end of the 1991-92 season trout spawners (both rainbows and browns) averaged 2.2-2.5 kg and by the end of the 1993-94 season the fishing had returned to its former glory.

It must be stressed though that the lagoon remains in an extremely delicate state of balance and its long-term future is by no means assured.

Trout liberations (since 1985)

Wild brown trout

YEAR	SIZE	NUMBER
1985	adults	600
1986	small fingerlings	9 500

Rainbow trout

YEAR	SIZE	NUMBER
1985	fingerlings	3 800
"	small adults	600
"	yearlings	1 500
1986	large fingerlings (T)	9 100
1987	large fingerlings (T)	3 900
1992	fingerlings (D)	4 000

(T) = triploid stock
(D) = domestic stock
Note: in 1993 the IFC promised that, subject to assessments on optimum stocking densities, there would be annual liberations of 4000 rainbow fingerlings.

The fishing today

The fishing is usually best when levels are high early in the season. At such times the trout feed in patches of open water around the shoreline behind the strapweed. The sheltered western and south-western margins are favourite areas, especially at dawn and dusk. Fly fishers delight in finding big fish swirling, bow-waving and rising.

The sandy flats across the far north-eastern corner are productive areas for wet-fly fishing, and the wave-cut weed-free trough along the exposed eastern shore is good for fly fishing and lure casting.

There are fair to good mudeye migrations in January/February.

Anglers with boats usually concentrate on the deeper weed-free depressions in the middle of the lake. Drift spinning and fly fishing are most appropriate.

Camping

Informal lakeshore camping is permitted in the area just west of the dam.

Boating

Because of the dense weedbeds and shallow water, small dinghies are most appropriate. A ramp exists on the western side of the dam.

Special regulations

The angling season opens on the Saturday nearest to 1 October and closes on the Sunday nearest to 31 May. All inflowing waters are closed to angling at all times, as are radii of 50 m around their mouths. Bait fishing is prohibited.

LAKE RIVER

Tasmaps South Esk and Lake Sorell
Drainage South Esk system (via the Macquarie River)

The Lake River encompasses all that is good and special about the meadow streams and ranks behind only the Macquarie and the Meander in its status as a trout fishery.

The best fishing occurs in the flat pasture from the confluence with the Macquarie to the foothills at Parknook and, to a lesser degree, at Bluff Bottom. When these areas flood, the water backs out into grassy basins, backwater lagoons and a lacework of former river channels. In summer the river recedes back into long weed-lined silt-bottomed broadwaters. The size of the fish and the nature of the fishing are almost identical to those in the fabled Macquarie (see *Macquarie River*) and need no further discussion here. All the important physical features (including the flood basins, backwaters, and bankside vegetation) are marked on the *Delmont* and *O'Connors* 1:25 000 Tasmaps.

Above Bluff Bottom there is an unimpressive forested stretch followed, on Regents Plain, by a series of small broadwaters and flood margins. Above Regents there is another forested valley. When water is being drawn from Woods Lake there is good fishing in the Devils Throat (below the Woods dam).

See also *Where to Fish – A Regional Breakdown*, 4.2.

LANGDON LAGOON

See *West Coast Range*.

LANGDON, LAKE

See *Langdon River*.

LANGDON RIVER

Tasmaps Franklin and Sophia
Drainage Henty system (via the Yolande River)
Location West Coast Range

A small overgrown tea-coloured fastwater which has never been invaded by brown trout.

In the mid 1980s work began on a hydro-electric scheme dam. A re-evaluation of costs and benefits resulted in the project being shelved. As the proposed lake would have had great potential as a fishery, the river was seeded with brook trout. I have taken fat fish to 0.5 kg on Celtas, but it is likely that as the fish prosper the average size will drop markedly. In New Zealand most brook trout in headwater creeks mature before they are 220 mm long and make little growth thereafter. The most convenient access is via the vehicular track from the Anthony Road to the damsite.

Liberations of brook trout

YEAR	SIZE	NUMBER
1986	fingerlings	*
1987	advanced fry	1 000
1989	advanced fry	1 000
"	small fingerlings	1 300

* = part-share of 5060

See also *West Coast Range* and *About our Sportfish*, 2.3.

LAST LAGOON

See *Jacks Lagoon*.

LAUGHING JACK LAGOON

Tasmap Nive
Drainage Derwent system
Location Central Highlands

While Laughing Jack produces good-sized trout and has its devotees, it is difficult to recommend above other waters.

Description

Laughing Jack is a hydro-electric storage lying behind a 17 m high concrete dam. Full supply (762 m above sea level) is often met during wet winters, but there are massive drawdowns of up to 11 m during summer and autumn (when the water is directed to the Bronte/Bradys system).

The water is normally slightly tea-coloured and can become very dirty after windy weather, especially when the water is low.

The surrounding hills feature significant stands of eucalypts but have been heavily logged.

Trout stocks

The lake supports a modest population of strong silvery brown trout. Fish of 1-1.5 kg are typical and quite a few attain 2.5 kg.

Spawning is confined to small creeks, and each year stocks are depleted when the water is drawn down. Stranded trout are salvaged from below the dam and returned to the lake – but losses are significant.

History

The lagoon was formed in 1957 to augment the Tungatinah power scheme. The dam flooded a natural marsh system and fish of 6-8 lb were taken in the early years.

How to fish

Generally the lake fishes best when levels are reasonably high before Christmas.

Trollers concentrate on fishing the deeper water from the dam to the lake centre – and when the lake is full it pays to get down deep.

Spinning is good along the deep banks near the dam and along D'Arcys Bluff. The shallower waters at the top end are best fished from a drifting boat.

Fly fishers are advised to fish from a drifting boat. The marshy edges around the creeks at the top end can provide worthwhile shore-based sport in spring, but as levels recede they become boggy and difficult to wade.

LAURA, LAKE

Tasmap Nive
Drainage Derwent system (via Lake St Clair)

A deep clearwater lake where heavy timber and thick undergrowth extend to the waterline. According to the tourism publication *The Haunt of the Giant Trout* (1941) the lake was *'well stocked with trout'* by the 1940s. Today naturally-spawned brown trout of 0.7-1.4 kg are common.

Spinning and polaroiding are most practical, though wading is essential.

The easiest access is by boat across Lake St Clair and then by foot (cross-country) through the dense closed-canopy forest.

See also *Fishing in National Parks*, 5.4.

LAWRENCE RIVULET

Tasmaps Wedge and Tyenna
Drainage Derwent system (via the Florentine River)

A rainbow-only stream, apparently isolated from the Florentine by virtue of the fact that the lower 2 km flow underground. The origin of the trout can be traced back to 1957-58 and 1958-59 when the STLAA recorded releases totalling 10 200 yearlings. Rainbows now abound throughout the system, from the Eden Creek Road to Lake Hayes.

Rainbow trout – Lawrence Rivulet

The clear water tumbles over boulders and shingles through production forest. It is an ideal Celta stream, especially when levels are low, delivering big bags of 0.1-0.4 kg fish. Vehicular access can be made only by prior arrangement with ANM.

LEA, LAKE

Tasmap Sophia
Drainage Forth system (via the Wilmot system)

Lake Lea is a moderately tea-coloured natural storage. The bottom is mostly firm and fairly shallow, though there are two deep basins in the middle.

The south-western end is flanked by snow-grass plains and incorporates pin-rush marshes and large wadeable flats. Most of the rest of the lake is impounded by elevated woodland. Some banks are overgrown with tea-tree but others are quite open.

Trout stocks

Early reports of the NTFA show that Lake Lea was stocked as early as 1902 when 1000 brown trout fry were released. By 1908 a further 500 sea trout fry had been turned out. In 1909 some 2000 rainbow fry were stocked, followed by a further 1000 rainbow fry in 1910. And a part-share of 10 000 brown trout fry was taken to the lake in 1919.

Anecdotal evidence suggests that brown trout were doing well in the 1930s and that by this time the rainbows had failed to establish. Yet the NWFA was convinced that the early liberations of brown trout had been unsuccessful and, in 1957, members organised the release of a further 3700 brown trout fingerlings. Even in 1960 the NWFA claimed that there were *'no fish to be seen in Lake Lea'*.

By the 1970s Lake Lea had shaken off its bad reputation and had become popular with 4WD enthusiasts and bushwalkers, and by the 1980s the water was recognised as an important fishery.

Today the lake teems with naturally-spawned brown trout. Fish of 0.3-1 kg are typical, though some exceed 1.5 kg.

Private development

For many years Lake Lea was accessible only by a rugged 4WD route or on foot. In the late 1980s permission was sought from local government to build a 140-bed resort on a small parcel of private land at 'The Knoll' (midway along the north-western shore). As the lake is otherwise surrounded by pristine crown land, anglers and conservationists opposed the development. Despite continued lobbying, a 2WD road was pushed to The Knoll in 1989-90. In autumn 1994, after gaining approval for a septic system (the treated effluent was to be taken via 3 km of pipe to the Vale River), the developer put the land on the market.

The fishing

Spinning is best in the early and late months of the angling season. Shallow-running lures retrieved along the edges of the overhanging tea-tree work very well, especially when levels are high. In the height of summer it pays to concentrate on the deep water further out.

Early-season wet-fly fishing peaks in October and November. The marshes at the south-western corner (including the 'backwater' west of the ford) are recommended.

Despite the tea-coloured water and dark bottom, proficient anglers are able to polaroid fish in the shallows.

In summer and autumn fish rise to take damselflies, mudeyes, mayflies and beetles.

There is also impressive fishing in the nearby Vale River.

A better than normal fish from the 'backwater' at Lake Lea

Facilities/regulations

Although there are no public toilets, there is ample scope for pleasant informal camping. Please remember that you are not permitted to take vehicles off the formed road. It is also illegal to fish from a boat propelled other than by oars worked by manual labour.

LEA, RIVER

Tasmaps Forth, Mersey, Sophia, and Hellyer
Drainage Forth system (via Lake Gairdner and the Wilmot River)

A small tea-coloured fastwater flowing through a forested valley. Brown trout of 0.1-0.3 kg are typical, though some to 1 kg are taken at the outflow from Lake Lea. The biggest bags are taken on Celtas and baits when levels are low.

See also *Forth, River.*

LEAKE, LAKE

Tasmaps Little Swanport and St Pauls
Drainage South Esk system (via the Elizabeth River)

Lake Leake is the only major stillwater on the East Coast. It provides good trout fishing, though it is difficult to recommend above the lakes on the Central Plateau.

The 6 m high rockfill dam on the upper Elizabeth River was built to impound water for domestic use and irrigation at Campbell Town. Work began in 1882 and was completed in 1883. At the time of its formation, Lake Leake was the largest artificial lake in Australia.

Description

Lake Leake is surrounded by dry woodland and features stands of drowned trees. The bottom is soft and the water is always slightly murky, especially on wind-swept shores. There are extensive weedy marshes in Kalangadoo Bay and Chock 'n Log Bay, and further weedbeds exist deep down over much of the lake body. Much of the northern shore is rocky and relatively deep, while much of the exposed eastern shore is shallow and sandy.

Early season levels commonly approach full supply (571 m above sea level) but substantial drawdowns occur during summer and autumn.

History of fish stocks

It seems that at the time of its formation Lake Leake did not contain trout – and since brown trout were already well established in the lower

to mid Elizabeth, I assume that there is a significant fall somewhere below the damsite.

For a time Lake Leake and the Snowy River
supported a viable brook trout population. Don
Gilmour (*The Tasmanian Trout*, 1973) made the
unsubstantiated claim that the species was originally released in 1889. In 1904 the NTFA reported
that the '*Snow River*' was the only stream in the
State carrying '*fontinalis*' and that on New Years
Day A F Sharland caught 24 fish, the largest
being 2 lb.

In May 1904 A F Sharland and noted angler
Charles Harrison assisted in releasing 210 rainbow

yearlings. This was followed with releases of 184
yearlings in 1905 and 600 yearlings in 1906. In
1907 the NTFA reported:

'*Most satisfactory progress has taken place
with the stocking of Lake Leake with Rainbows
... last spring the fish spawned, and some 20 000
eggs, of a deep red and very fine quality, were
obtained and conveyed to the Waverley Hatchery,
being the first instance of stripping "wild"
Rainbows in the state. The fish, although hardly
three years' old, had grown to a fine size, and 12
carefully weighed averaged almost 7 lb., the
largest scaling 8 1/4 lb ... The locality affords an*

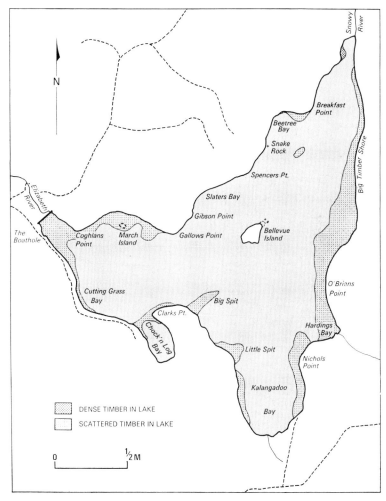

LAKE LEAKE

excellent source of obtaining an annual supply of ova, and recognising that the spawning grounds are limited, the Midland folks have subscribed, through the agency of Mr. A. F. Sharland ... enough funds to put up a small hatchery at the lake dam ...'

Lake Leake was opened to angling on 1 December 1907. At this time there was limited accommodation available from 'Mrs Spencer' (near the dam) and at the 'halfway house' (near the eastern end of the lake). Both houses kept accurate records of trout captures. In the first year 115 fish averaging almost 6 lb were recorded. Two of these were brown trout 'present in the lake owing to a small lot of fry being mixed'.

During the 1907-08 season the hatchery came into full production and more than 30 000 rainbow fry were turned into the lake.

The success of the rainbows signalled the end of the brook trout. The Snowy River produced good fish to 4 lb in 1905-06, at least 27 fish averaging ¾-1 lb in 1906-07, and a few more fish in 1907-08. But thereafter there were no records of 'fontinalis' captures.

The period from 1908 to 1920 was the boom era for Lake Leake. The average weight fluctuated from about 3.5-5 lb and each season specimens of 8-10 lb were taken. Lake Leake became 'the finest

Rainbow Trout Fishery in the Commonwealth'. The popularity of the water was such that in 1912 the Government had a Tourist House erected at the dam end. It was placed under the control of the Northern Tourist Association and leased.

In the boom time the NTFA recorded only rainbow trout captures and a few incidental salmon captures (see below) – so it is somewhat of a surprise to read in the 1920 report that:

'A feature of the season was the large increase in English fish, all in good condition and scaling up to 6 lb'.

A further significant increase in brown trout was reported in 1921. By 1922 the species accounted for more than one third of the annual harvest – and by 1923 one in every two fish caught was a brown. From about this time the rainbow population was probably maintained mainly by artificial stocking, and the brown trout by natural recruitment.

Until the mid 1940s the ratio of browns to rainbows fluctuated from 4:1 to 1:1, reflecting changes in the intensity of rainbow stocking. The browns averaged 3-3 ½ lb, while most rainbows weighed 2 ½-3 lb. Throughout this period the lake continued to be very popular and in 1954 the NTFA described it as 'the best fishery in the State'. However, by 1965 the average weight was

Lake Leake

reputed to be 'only a little over 1 lb' and there was general disappointment about the quality of the fishing. At about this time the IFC made a controversial decision to attempt to rehabilitate the water as a rainbow fishery. Over 3 years from 1964 brown trout fry were trapped and removed from the Snowy River spawning beds. In winter 1967 the entire spawning run of brown trout (6576 fish) was culled, and in 1968 all ova was stripped from the spawners. Some 25 000 rainbow trout were liberated in August 1967, followed by a further 2000 fish in 1968.

In the 1967-68 season the IFC recorded the average weight of the fish as 2 lb 2 oz before Christmas and 1 lb 8 oz post-Christmas. However, the new management strategy had resulted in only a slight increase in the proportion of rainbow trout in anglers' bags – and the poor results bolstered the public outcry over the culling of trout spawners.

By 1970 the average weight of fish taken by anglers was 1½ lb and the proportion of rainbows had fallen to the lowest on record. In 1972 the angling season was readjusted to bring it back in line with other brown trout fisheries.

In an effort to bolster angler interest, stocking with rainbows resumed in 1983. However, this action is intended to complement rather than replace the existing brown trout fishery.

Atlantic salmon

About 1000 Atlantic salmon fry were released in 1906-07, followed by 52 yearlings in 1909-10. A few were subsequently caught by anglers but there was no natural recruitment.

Some 600 yearling sebago salmon (a landlocked form of Atlantic salmon) were released in 1916-17, followed by a further 20 in 1917-18. Again a small number were caught but no natural spawning was observed.

Redfin perch

According to Parliamentary reports, the first recorded redfin perch at Lake Leake was taken in January 1974. The origin of this species remains unknown, though eggs may have been inadvertently transferred from other waters on commercial eel-fishers' nets. Large schools of stunted fish are now found all over the lake.

Trout stocks today

Stocks of brown trout are essentially maintained by natural recruitment. Recent artificial stocking of the species has been driven more by politics than by any real concern about the health of the fishery. Typical fish weigh 0.7-1 kg, though quite a few attain 1.5 kg.

The rainbow trout are now maintained almost entirely by artificial stocking, and changes in the relative abundance of the species in anglers' bags simply reflect changes in the annual stocking rate. In the last few seasons rainbows have accounted for 7-20% of the annual harvest, and most fish caught have been maidens of 0.3-0.8 kg.

Trout liberations (since 1985)

Wild brown trout

YEAR	SIZE	NUMBER
1985	fry	30 000
1986	small fingerlings	25 000
"	fry	100 000
1987	small fingerlings	30 000
1988	fry	50 000
1989	fry	65 000
1992	small fingerlings	7 400
"	advanced fry	12 000
1993	small fingerlings (T)	5 600
"	advanced fry	10 000

(T) = triploid stock

Rainbow trout

YEAR	SIZE	NUMBER
1987	large fingerlings (W)	2 500
1989	large fingerlings (D)	7 000
1990	small fingerlings (D)	14 000
1991	fingerlings (D)	3 000
1992	fingerlings (D)	2 500
"	advanced fry (D)	3 000
1993	yearlings (D)	3 000

(W) = wild stock
(D) domestic stock
Note: in 1993 the IFC promised annual liberations of 2000-3000 rainbow fingerlings.

Special regulations

Lake Leake is reserved for the use of artificial lures, and it is illegal to fish from a boat propelled other than by manual labour. All inflowing streams are closed to angling at all times.

Fly fishing

Tailing fish have not been a feature in modern times. Early in the angling season you have to rely on blind casting with wets. This can be very productive, especially in Kalangadoo Bay and Chock 'n Log Bay.

Warmer water in mid to late spring brings on the hatches, with the most reliable sport occurring in November and December. Among the best areas are the marshes in Kalangadoo Bay and Chock 'n Log Bay, though good rises occur all over the lake. Smutting fish feature early in the morning followed by rises to red spinners throughout the rest of the day. And if the daytime sport has been difficult, evening fishing with wet or dry mudeye imitations is a reliable fall-back.

Polaroiding is mostly difficult, though fish can sometimes be seen between rises as they cruise in shallow water over the weeds. Keen-sighted fishers may also be able to spot fish as they move through the slightly-turbid silt/sand shallows in Hardings Bay and along the Big Timber Shore.

In the height of summer the daytime hatches become subdued, though there are fair evening rises to mudeyes and terrestrials.

Beetle falls and spinner hatches provide renewed excitement in autumn.

Lure fishing

The fishing usually peaks between late September and mid December. Often there is a hot-weather lull during summer before the fishing picks up again in autumn.

I prefer spinning along the outer fringes of the weedbeds in Kalangadoo Bay and Chock 'n Log Bay – but most other shores also produce worthwhile numbers of trout.

Drift spinning and row-trolling among the stands of drowned trees is highly recommended.

The Duckhole (bay) at the mouth of the Snowy River is a hot spot late in the season.

Facilities

The best boat ramp is at the Boathole (bay) near the dam. There are public toilets and attractive informal camping areas nearby. Another popular launching area is located at Kalangadoo Bay.

LEGERWOOD RIVULET

Tasmap   Forester
Drainage   Direct to the Ringarooma River below Branxholm

A small overgrown creek with a permanent, though sometimes sluggish, flow. Brown trout to 0.3 kg are common and some grow much bigger. Fishing is best when levels are low. Celtas and baits are recommended.

LENONE, LAKE

Tasmap   Mersey
Drainage   Derwent system (via the Nive system)
Location   Western Lakes

A deep clearwater with well-defined rocky shores. It is surrounded by open forest, and patches of tea-tree impede progress along the western shore.

Cruising trout – northern end of Lake Lenone

There is plenty of scope for spinning and bank polaroiding. When levels are high you also find some fish tailing in the shallows along the northern shore.

Typical fish weigh 1-1.5 kg and some exceed 2 kg.

See also *Fishing in National Parks*, 5.1.

LEONIS, LAKE

Tasmap   Mersey
Drainage   Mersey system
Location   West of Lake Rowallan

Illegally stocked with rainbows in the late 1980s – with the outflow offering some chance of natural recruitment.

The easiest access is cross-country from the forestry spurs on Maggs Road.

LEPERA, LAKE

Tasmap   Mersey
Drainage   Natural – Derwent system (via James system)
Location   Western Lakes

Lake Lepera (photo by Steve McArdle)

A clearwater feeding Wadleys Lake. It supports a good stock of 0.7-1.5 kg brown trout and a few larger fish.

See also *Fishing in National Parks*, 5.1.

LESLIE CREEK

Tasmap Pieman
Drainage Direct to the Little Henty River

A small overgrown tea-coloured fastwater containing large numbers of tiny brown trout.

LEVEN, RIVER

Tasmaps Forth, Hellyer, and Sophia
Drainage Direct to Bass Strait

The Leven is one of the State's few essentially-natural large rivers – there are no major dams and little streamside development. It ranks as one of the very best trout streams in the Central North-West.

Description
The Leven is always tea-coloured, heavily so after big rains. Rain associated run-off from headwater forestry operations and lowland farms can result in significant turbidity, though the water clears as levels subside.

Ulverstone, at the heads, is a major town of some 10 000 people. Elsewhere the estuary is flanked by native trees and scrub. The upper tidal limit is 2 km or so above the Allison Bridge.

Beyond the estuary the river is a large shingle-bottomed fastwater.

The lower stretch to Gunns Plains is mostly steep and heavily wooded. Some 15 km at Gunns Plains is flanked by pockets of flat pasture, though the banks are still overgrown and the bed remains predominantly shingly. While much of the body of the stream is deep, there are plenty of wadeable shallows along the banks and at the heads and tails of pools. During major floods the water breaks out into the paddocks.

Above Gunns Plains there is 10 km or so of dramatic densely-forested valley. At the spectacular boulder-strewn Leven Canyon there are two significant falls, so severe that they halt the upstream migration of eels, crayfish and blackfish.

Above the Canyon, in the Loongana district, the streamside is mostly forested. There are small pockets of lush pasture but no flood plains. At low levels there is plenty of wadeable shingle.

In the headwaters, in the vicinity of Cattley Creek and the Medway River, the Leven is small, shallow and overgrown.

Undoubtedly the best areas to fish are the estuary (for sea trout), Gunns Plains and Loongana.

Sea trout
The estuary gives up sea trout from August to November. Hot spots for the shore-based angler are the pockets of stillwater formed behind rocky points which jut out into the main current. My favourite areas include the south-eastern bank between the Leven Bridge (in Ulverstone) and the bridge on the Bass Highway, and the mouth of the Gawler River.

With a boat you can get access to trout which ambush baitfish along the steep banks in the narrows at the head of the estuary. There are several good launching ramps in Ulverstone.

From early October to November sea trout chase galaxias up into the freshwater reaches. I have taken numerous fish near the pumphouse (some 3 km above the Allison Bridge), and many locals insist that incidental sea trout can be taken as far upstream as Gunns Plains.

Stocking with brown trout
Since the mid 1980s the NWFA has attempted to bolster the sea trout runs by releasing brown trout fry immediately above the estuary. However, the Leven is already overpopulated with brown trout and it is unlikely that the stocking programme will improve the current quality of fishing.

Brown trout liberations (since 1980)

YEAR	SIZE	NUMBER
1985	advanced fry	8 000
1986	advanced fry	8 000
1987	advanced fry	5 120
1988	advanced fry	9 800
1989	advanced fry	10 000
1991	fry	8 000

Fishing at Gunns Plains
From August to October the water is usually fast and cold and you are only likely to find very good sport if the river is so high that it has spilled out into the paddocks. Ideally the river will be running at slightly more than a banker – just enough for the water to creep out beyond the scrubby fringes of the banks into small basins and gutters. At these times worms and wet flies work well. When levels are exceptionally high there is simply too much water between the fish.

The best fishing usually starts in summer when the water is low, warm and wadeable.

River Leven at Loongana

Celtas and grasshoppers are dynamite. Fly fishers find that the numerous rising fish will take well-presented nymphs and dries. Notorious cool breezes often curtail the fishing late in the afternoon – but when you do get an evening rise the action is fast and furious. When all else fails try traditional upstream nymphing.

Most fish weigh 0.2-0.3 kg and a few exceed 1.5 kg.

Loongana and the rainbow story

In 1909 the NTFA reported:

'This Association also put a number of Rainbow in the Leven above the big Falls at Hell's Gates, some 40 miles up, where no other fish except mountain trout are found, and in the course of a few years will be worth fishing.'

The rainbows soon established and throughout the 1920s and 1930s the Loongana district was noted as a prime fishing destination. The fishery was maintained mostly by natural recruitment, though 5000 rainbow fry were released in 1920 and there may have been a few other stockings.

In 1948 it was noted:

'For dry fly fishing the best water is at Loongana, in the Leven River ... Many visitors have described it as the most beautiful fly stream in Australia. The Tasmanian Fisheries'

Commissioners some years ago decided that it is the only stream in the island for which Rainbow would be supplied. Unfortunately it has not received fry or yearlings for many years past ...'

Records of the NTFA and STLAA show that from 1948-49 until at least the early 1950s many thousands of rainbow fry and yearlings were turned out at Loongana. More significantly, it is recorded that 5000 brown trout yearlings were released in 1948-49 followed by a further 2500 in 1951-52.

By 1960 a member of the NWFA had conceded:

'The river used to be renowned for its fighting rainbow but in showing now have a greater percentage of about 60% brown and 40% rainbows. "Goodbye Rainbow".'

A contributor to the *Tasmanian Angling Report* of 1985 suggested that the final nail in the coffin was the *'heavy earthworks in the headwaters* [which] *left at least 6 mm of silt over the entire stretch of rainbow water for 18 months'.*

By the 1970s the natural rainbow population was close to extinction. Experimental liberations of rainbows have done little to rehabilitate the fishery, and it is most unlikely that a viable wild population will ever re-establish.

Rainbow trout liberations (since 1970)

YEAR	SIZE	NUMBER
1972	fry	16 000
1985-86	fingerlings (W)	1 000
1986-87	fingerlings (W)	1 000
1989	fingerlings (D)	400
1990	fingerlings (W)	850
1991	fingerlings (D)	4 100

(W) = wild stock
(D) = domestic stock

Loongana today

The shallow riffly water at Loongana is best fished during warm weather when levels are low, usually in summer and autumn.

On calm days there is a good deal of rising and bulging, and upstream nymphing is a good fall-back when things are quiet.

Celta fishing and bait casting are reliably productive.

Most trout taken are browns of 0.1-0.3 kg, though quite a few fish attain 0.5-1 kg. Appreciable numbers of rainbows are likely to be caught only in the first few months after significant stocking.

LEXIE, LAKE

Tasmap Mersey
Drainage Natural – Derwent system (via James system)
Location Western Lakes

The lake bed is mostly silty and the hatches are much less impressive than those at Lake Gwendy. Polaroiding and lure casting are usually the best techniques. Few fish exceed 1.5 kg.

See also *Fishing in National Parks*, 5.1.

LIAPOOTAH, LAKE

Tasmap Nive
Drainage Derwent system (via the Nive system)

Lake Liapootah was created by the HEC in 1958. Water backs up behind the 40 m high Liapootah Dam, flooding the steep forested Nive valley, and is diverted via tunnel to the Liapootah Power Station near Wayatinah Lagoon. The normal operating range is about 3.5 m.

The Liapootah Dam Road leads only to the foot of the dam, and the road from the Lyell Highway near the Tungatinah Power Station is managed as a public foot access. While the few open banks are patronised by local set-rod fishers, movement along the shores is difficult.

Brown trout of 0.5-0.9 kg are quite common. Rainbows are scarce.

LIFFEY RIVER

Tasmaps South Esk and Meander
Drainage South Esk system (via the Meander River)

The Liffey was stocked with brown trout as early as 1878, though by this time fish had probably already invaded from the South Esk and Meander. It soon became a well respected fishery and today it remains a favourite among local fly fishers.

The lower reaches

From the confluence with the Meander to the township of Liffey, the Liffey River flows through flat pasture. Willows, blackberries and scrub feature along many banks but, while some stretches are overgrown, there is plenty of fishable water.

The creek comprises shallow riffles and deep silt-bottomed pools, and becomes quite murky after heavy rain.

Most fish caught weigh 0.2-0.6 kg and some attain 1.5 kg. Under normal conditions big bags are common.

Bait casting is very popular among locals. A worm cast into likely lies and allowed to drift with the current is likely to undo many fish, especially when the water is moderately high and discoloured. Grasshoppers work well post-Christmas when the weather is hot and the water low and clear.

Celta fishing is productive throughout the season.

Fly fishing is very rewarding. When levels are very high and the water breaks out into the paddocks, fish can be found in the shallows foraging after worms and grubs, or taking both aquatic and terrestrial insects from the surface. Such activity is most reliable after mid spring but can occur early in August. In fact the first good flood of the season is usually a highlight. As levels moderate, upstream nymphing becomes increasingly productive, and you may even encounter fair daytime rises.

The upper reaches

Beside the Gulf Road (upstream of Liffey) the stream is flanked by both forest and farmland. The water flows over shingles and is wadeable in its entirety.

About 5 km along the Gulf Road is the edge of the Liffey Forest Reserve/Liffey Falls State Reserve – part of the World Heritage Area. Within the protected area the Liffey is a crystal fastwater which bounces over shingles through rainforest. The water teems with brown trout to 0.4 kg and provides fast sport – especially when Celta fishing and upstream nymphing.

Facilities in the reserved area

The Liffey Forest Reserve is accessible by 2WD from Liffey (via the Gulf Road) and from the Lake Highway (via the Riversdale Road). A well formed foot path (suitable for families and casual visitors) extends through the reserve between the two major access points. Another more arduous walking track leads up the valley to the alpine moors adjacent to the Lake Highway near Pine Lake.

A wet-forest day-use recreation area complete with barbeques, toilets, and day-shelters has been developed at the terminus of the Riversdale Road.

Hydro-electric development

In the 1960s the uppermost section of the Liffey (in the moorland above the Lake Highway) was diverted via Pine Lake into Great Lake. This diversion contains some very small brown trout but can hardly be recommended to serious anglers.

See also *Where to Fish – A Regional Breakdown*, 4.2.

LILLA, LAKE

Tasmap Sophia
Drainage Forth system (via the Dove system)
Location Near Cradle Mountain

While some 1275 brook trout fingerlings were released in October 1964, none were ever caught by anglers. No trout of any species survive today.

See *Fishing in National Parks*, 5.4.

LIMEKILN GULLY RESERVOIR

Public fishing is not allowed.

LINDA CREEK

No trout. See *Burbury, Lake*.

LING ROTH LAKES

No trout. See *Fishing in National Parks*, 5.1.

LISDILLON RIVULET

Tasmaps Freycinet and Little Swanport
Drainage Direct to the Tasman Sea

According to early Parliamentary reports brown trout fry had been transported to Lisdillon by 1878. The species was soon firmly established.

The rivulet flows through a small scrubby valley

but, while the banks are in places very overgrown, you can easily bypass unattractive stretches by skirting through adjacent pasture and woodland.

Much of the river flows knee-deep over a shingle bed and is less than a rod's length wide. However, there are also some deep long sluggish pools. While the water becomes quite murky after heavy rain, it clears appreciably in summer and autumn.

Spinning and bait-casting are most practical. When wading up the riffles you tend to catch lots of fish under 0.2 kg. In the big pools fish to 0.5 kg are common and some exceed 1 kg.

LITTLE BELLINGER

Tasmap Cape Sorell
Drainage Isolated coastal lagoon
Location North of Strahan

Though there are no formal records, Little Bellinger is known to have been irregularly stocked between 1970 and 1983, and again in the late 1980s. No trout survive today.

See also *Strahan Lakes*.

LITTLE BLUE LAGOON

Tasmap Mersey
Drainage Natural – Derwent system (via James system)
Location Nineteen Lagoons

Little Blue Lagoon has no inflowing spawning streams and only a tiny intermittent gutter connection to Lake Augusta. Prior to artificial stocking it supported a negligible population of brown trout.

The first liberation of rainbow trout occurred in 1974 and by 1979 fish to 6 kg had been caught. As a result of this initial success irregular stocking with rainbow trout has continued. Today the average size of the trout caught is related to the time since the last liberation. Fish which survive 3-5 years usually weigh 2.5-4 kg and, since it is these big fish which are the main attraction, catch-and-release is advocated.

Rainbow trout liberations

YEAR	SIZE	NUMBER
1974	fry	10 000
1979	fingerlings (D)	2 000
1982	fry (D)	5 000
"	fingerlings (T)	500
1985	fingerlings (T)	350
1986	fingerlings (T)	5 500

(D) = domestic stock
(T) = triploid stock

Although the lake is too deep to wade, the maximum depth does not exceed 2-3 m. The shores are mostly rocky and well defined.

It is usually difficult to polaroid fish (they tend to stay off shore) and the rises are irregular, so fly enthusiasts prefer to fish late in the evening with big wets.

The most convenient access is by foot via the disused vehicular route which extends from the western shore of Lake Augusta.

See also *Fishing in National Parks*, 5.1.

LITTLE DENISON RIVER

Tasmaps Huon and Tyenna
Drainage Direct to the Huon River

A shallow rocky-bottomed fastwater with forested/ scrubby banks.

Sea trout are taken from the mouth and lower reaches during the late-spring galaxia runs and the April spawning migration (see *Huon River*).

While resident brown trout to 0.5 kg have long been a feature, smaller rainbow trout have been quite common since Lake Skinner was first stocked in 1978. Try Celta fishing and traditional upstream nymphing.

LITTLE FORESTER RIVER

Tasmaps Ninth Island and St Patricks
Drainage Direct to Bass Strait

Sea trout are taken all over the estuary from August to December, while impressive 0.3-3kg slobs are caught throughout the season. The residents appear to move up with the tide and are best targeted near the bridge on Sandy Point Road. They often rise and can be taken on dry flies and surface baits.

Above the estuary the stream is very overgrown and, while there are numerous fish to 0.4 kg or so, the sport can hardly be recommended.

LITTLE HENTY RIVER

Tasmap Pieman
Drainage Direct to the Southern Ocean

The lowest reaches flow across the open sands of Ocean Beach and the position of the mouth is variable. Good sea trout are taken, especially in October and November, and river residents are caught throughout the season. The style of fishing is similar to that practised at the Henty River (see *Henty River*). Access is via vehicular track from Remine, Trial Harbour.

Success at the mouth of the Little Henty

Beyond the dunes the river flows through a steep densely-vegetated valley and many stretches are inaccessible. The best fishing occurs in the water adjacent to the Henty (Strahan to Zeehan) Road. When levels are low there are many wadeable riffles and Celta fishing usually results in big bags of 0.2-0.3 kg brown trout. Near the Zeehan (Queenstown to Zeehan) Highway the pools are mostly deep and overgrown.

LITTLE LAKE

Tasmap Meander
Drainage Natural – South Esk system (via Arthurs Lake)

A shallow clearwater lined on the western and southern shores with emergent reeds. It is heavily populated with brown trout and few individuals exceed 0.7 kg. Early season wet-fly fishing in the flooded marshes is superb, and from November to January there are steady dun hatches. The open rocky eastern banks are well suited to spinning. Access and camping are discussed under *Gunns Lake*.

LITTLE NAVARRE RIVER

Tasmap Nive
Drainage Derwent system (via Lake King William)

A small clear fastwater flowing through buttongrass plains. Celta fishing and bait casting are preferred, and the best results are gained when levels are low. Expect big bags of very small brown trout.

LITTLE PINE LAGOON

Tasmaps Shannon and Meander
Drainage Natural – Derwent system (via the Little Pine River)
Location Central Highlands

Little Pine Lagoon is the State's premier fly water. It is noted for two annual highlights – springtime tailers and summertime dun hatches. Detailed information is available in the book Trout Guide *(Rob Sloane and Greg French, 1991). A summary only is given here.*

Description

The present lagoon was formed by the damming of the Little Pine River behind a dam almost 4 m high and is used to divert water via Monpeelyata Canal to Lake Echo. As storage is not the principal function, the normal operating range is little more than 1.2 m. Full supply is 1007.07 m above sea level.

Little Pine is very shallow and at times all but the original river/lake bed is wadeable. The shores are flat, grassy and exposed. The water is generally clear but can become discoloured during strong winds, especially if the level is down.

By special agreement a minimum level of 0.74 m below full supply is maintained throughout the summer – but the IFC has to compensate the HEC for water lost through extra evaporation.

Trout stocks

Little Pine is noted for its hard-fighting naturally-spawned brown trout. Well-conditioned fish in the 0.8-1.5 kg class are typical, though average size and condition can vary from year to year. Rainbow trout are very rare, the few caught being emigrants from artificially-stocked waters in the Nineteen Lagoons.

History

Originally the area now flooded by Little Pine Lagoon included a sizeable natural lake (Bluff Lagoon) on the western side of the Little Pine River, and two smaller lagoons on the eastern side. In 1930 the NTFA recorded that:

'... during the first few months of the fishing season many [brown trout] *frequent the* [lagoons] *... They are without doubt the finest conditioned and fighting ... brown trout to be found in our lakes today ... The size runs from 2½-6 lb ... As summer approaches and the water becomes lower they move from the lagoons back into the waters of the river. They may be readily seen here and sometimes taken, but owing to the high banks and very clear water become very shy.'*

The exceptional fishing which followed the formation of the new lagoon in 1954 came as no surprise. In recognition of the possible conflict of interest between fly fishers stalking fish in the margins and lure casters disturbing the shallows in search of pockets of open water, the impoundment was immediately reserved for fly fishing only.

Although existing stocks were adequate to ensure both immediate sport and continued natural recruitment, a once-only seeding of 25 000 brown trout fry was undertaken in 1955. Apart from several small-scale experimental liberations of trout from Great Lake in later years, the only other stocking occurred in the winter of 1966 when more than 9000 yearling brook trout were turned out. This species failed to establish.

The prolific growth of exotic Canadian pond weed became a cause for concern in the mid 1970s. Coincident with low water levels, rich summer growth made fishing quite difficult.

Since 1976-77 efforts have been made to control the weed by maintaining high water levels during the peak summer fishing period and lowering the lake during late autumn and early winter.

In 1982, following a dispute in relation to private ownership of the fishery, the Crown acquired 358 ha of land around the foreshore. This land is now a designated Fishing Reserve and public access is guaranteed.

Tailers

Little Pine tailers are usually preoccupied with tiny amphipods in the weeds. There is no consistently reliable method of catching them – hence the ongoing fascination and challenge. It pays to keep moving along the shore and cover as many fish as possible in the hope that one will take. Some anglers prefer to drift a dry fly in front of the fish, but most opt for a small beetle or nymph.

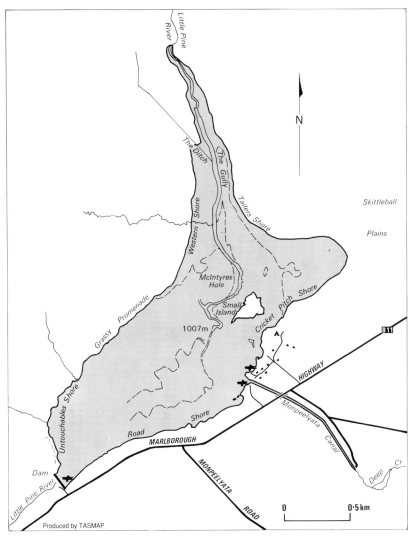

LITTLE PINE LAGOON

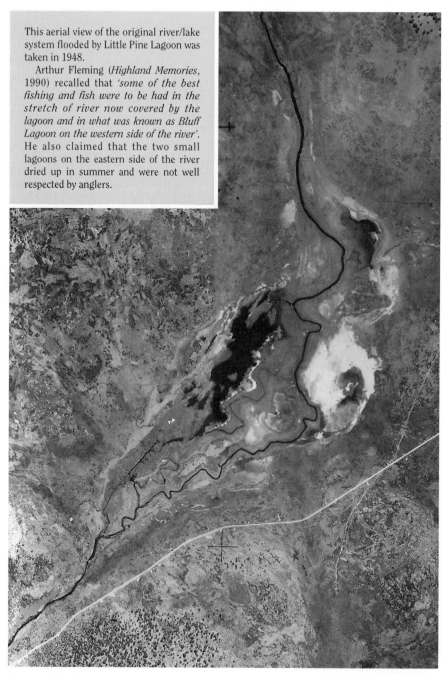

This aerial view of the original river/lake system flooded by Little Pine Lagoon was taken in 1948.

Arthur Fleming (*Highland Memories*, 1990) recalled that *'some of the best fishing and fish were to be had in the stretch of river now covered by the lagoon and in what was known as Bluff Lagoon on the western side of the river'*. He also claimed that the two small lagoons on the eastern side of the river dried up in summer and were not well respected by anglers.

(courtesy Tasmap)

Looking for tails – Little Pine Lagoon (photo by Rob Sloane)

October and November are the best months to find tailing trout, though the odd fish may be found in the shallows at any time. An overcast day with a slight breeze is ideal, peak activity occurring at dawn and dusk. The fish become very unobliging when conditions are calm and bright.

All shores are suitable, though the Tailers Shore, the Cricket Pitch and the Western Shore are hard to beat.

Dun hatches

Little Pine is regarded as the best dry fly water in the Central Plateau – the dun hatches are legendary.

The best hatches usually start in early December and may extend until the end of March. And such is the reputation of the rise that at Christmas you are likely to be one of hundreds of fishers scattered over what is really quite a small lagoon.

The hatch usually peaks from noon to 3 pm, but times vary according to the weather. While warm slightly-overcast days generally produce the best rises, surprising activity can occur in bleak conditions.

Camping

Informal lakeshore camping occurs along the eastern side of the lake adjacent to the Marlborough Highway.

Boating

Some anglers like to use dinghies, though most of the lake can usually be covered by wading. The recommended boat ramp is on the eastern side of the lake at the outlet of Monpeelyata Canal.

LITTLE PINE RIVER

Tasmaps Nive, Shannon, Meander, and Mersey
Drainage Derwent system (via the Nive system)

The rocky-bottomed stream between the Pine River and Little Pine Lagoon suffers from greatly reduced flows (water is diverted at the lagoon) and, while it supports small brown trout, the fishing can hardly be recommended.

Between Little Pine Lagoon and Ada Lagoon, the river flows through snowgrass plains. The banks are deep and undercut, and there are long stretches of sluggish water. While there are some shingly runs below Lake Kay, most of the bottom is silty and weedy. Food is abundant and there is an absence of prime spawning grounds. Wild brown trout of 0.7-2 kg are typical and some exceed 3 kg. Rainbows are scarce, the few caught being emigrants from artificially stocked waters in the Nineteen Lagoons. During summer and autumn the fishing is usually very difficult. Most good fish lurk out of sight in the undercuts, and the banks are so honeycombed that as you walk they move and disturb the water. Fair hatches occur on some days – but mostly attract the attention of the smaller trout. Serious anglers prefer to fish nearby lakes such as Little Pine Lagoon, Lake Fergus and Lake Kay.

Feature fishing in the Little Pine River occurs in mid to late spring after heavy rain. Water soon backs out into the snowgrass, filling gutters, backwaters and lagoons. Fish can be found tailing, or lured out of the deeper water by careful blind fishing with wet flies. The prime spots are between Double Lagoon/Lake Kay and Ada Lagoon (see *Kay, Lake* and *Kay Lagoons*). As soon as levels begin to drop the trout start to retreat back to the main river.

See also *Fishing in National Parks*, 5.1.

LITTLE PIPERS RIVER

Tasmap St Patricks
Drainage Direct to Bass Strait

The odd sea trout is taken from the mouth. The stream proper is extremely small and overgrown and, while it supports small brown trout, the fishing is unimpressive.

LITTLE SWANPORT RIVER

Tasmap Little Swanport
Drainage Direct to the Tasman Sea

The estuary is a disappointing sea trout water, though the odd fish is taken near the Tasman Highway.

The lower 25 km or so of the river proper flows through a steep dry-woodland valley and is typical of East Coast waterways. Much of the shingle bed becomes exposed as flows diminish in summer and autumn. While trout of 0.1-0.5 kg can be taken from the shallow clearwater pools, the fishing is quite unimpressive.

The best sport occurs in the flat farmland in the vicinity of Stonehenge where trout to 1 kg or so can be expected. After heavy rain murky water breaks out into the paddocks and trout can be caught along the flooded edges. In summer the river recedes back into scrubby-banked silt-bottomed pools and the water clears. There are also a few worthwhile permanent and semi-permanent backwater lagoons.

LITTLE THRONE LAKE

See *Blue Peaks Lakes*.

LITTLE WATERHOUSE LAKE

Tasmap Cape Portland
Drainage Coastal lagoon

Little Waterhouse is contained between sand dunes, some exposed but most overgrown with banksia and coastal scrub. The water surface is choked with weeds and rushes. Although there is some scope for shore-based fishing, a small dinghy is recommended. Wet-fly fishing and set-rod bait fishing are most practical. The average catch rate is much less than one fish per angler per day, but the trout are always in good condition and grow to impressive size.

History

In 1932 the NTFA recorded:

'Last year our Scottsdale Branch expressed a wish to stock with fry two Lakes at Waterhouse. Permission for this was granted, at the same time it being suggested that Brown trout should be liberated in one Lake and Rainbow in the other.'

Despite the inconsistent nomenclature in subsequent reports, it is evident that Little Waterhouse Lake was the water originally managed as a rainbow fishery, while Big Waterhouse Lake (which failed as a trout fishery) was the water originally stocked with browns.

The original 20 000 rainbow fry did well. In 1934 it was noted that *'In November 1933, or exactly two years later, many fine Rainbow were taken varying in weight from 3½-5 lbs'*. Stocking continued in earnest but it was not until the 1935-36 season that brown trout were liberated. By 1938 the rainbows were averaging 5-6 lb and brown trout to 8½ lb were being taken.

Little Waterhouse remained the feature stillwater of the North-East until the 1950s when it was overshadowed by Blackmans Lagoon.

The dam

During spring floods in 1952 Little Waterhouse broke its banks and local anglers, concerned about the erosion of the retaining dunes and the loss of fish to the ocean, attempted to dam the outflow. The original sand, soil and brush structure was inadequate and in 1954 the NTFA was calling for donations towards an enlarged wall and spillway. In 1955 it was reported that the SFFC had granted funds sufficient to complete a dam such as had been recommended in a recently compiled engineers report. Work was finished in July.

Trout stocks

As there is no opportunity for natural recruitment, the quantity of fish, the average size, and the relative abundance of trout species is directly linked to stocking regimes.

Young fish are caught but the optimum size is an impressive 3-4 kg.

Although originally managed as a rainbow-only fishery, since 1935-36 there have been regular liberations of both browns and rainbows. Brook trout were released in 1966 (1820 fingerlings) and 1968-69 (5500 fish) but stocking with this species was short-lived.

Trout liberations (since 1985)

Wild brown trout

YEAR	SIZE	NUMBER
1985	advanced fry	15 000
1987	advanced fry	20 000

Domestic rainbow trout

YEAR	SIZE	NUMBER
1986	small fingerlings	5 000
1991	fingerlings	2 000
1992	yearlings	1 000
"	advanced fry	1 500

Note: in 1993 the IFC promised annual liberations of 1000 rainbow fingerlings.

Camping

The family car can be taken to the lakeshore where there is ample room for informal camping. The lagoon can be brackish so remember to bring your own drinking water.

LITTLE WONDER POND

Tasmap Tamar
Drainage Tamar system
Location Beaconsfield (grid ref. 834 392)

A dark tea-coloured water surrounded by bushland and thick scrub. According to NTFA reports stocking occurred as early as 1933 when 3000 brown trout were turned out. It has received ad hoc stocking ever since, the last being a consignment of 50 rainbow yearlings in 1992, and 50 brown trout x Atlantic salmon hybrids (advanced fry) in 1993.

Better fishing exists nearby at the Beaconsfield Reservoir.

LLEWELLYN, LAKE

Tasmap Table Cape
Drainage Sisters Creek (an instream impoundment)

Lake Llewellyn is a tea-coloured slightly-turbid impoundment formed in 1968 behind an 8 m high earthfill dam. The banks are mostly steep and overgrown with dense wet-bushland and, as bullrushes choke the few shallow bays, convenient shore-based sport is limited to the shack frontages (no public access) and the dam wall (no vehicular access). Most fish are taken by drift spinning and bait casting from a boat, the recommended launching area being near the shacks.

The lake was stocked with 4000 brown trout fry in 1973 but the fishery is now maintained by natural recruitment from Sisters Creek. Slow-growing browns to 0.6 kg are typical in anglers' bags.

LOANE, LAKE

No trout. See *Fishing in National Parks*, 5.1.

LOBSTER CREEK

Tasmap Forth
Drainage Direct to the River Leven

A small fastwater which gives up large bags of small brown trout.

Fishing is best when levels are low.

A hatchery was constructed on the banks in 1930, and it probably operated for two decades or more.

LOBSTER RIVULET

Tasmaps Forth, Tamar, Meander, and Mersey
Drainage Direct to the Mersey River

A small fastwater. Brown trout of 0.2-0.4 kg are typical, though some attain 1 kg. Rainbows were liberated as early as 1907 but failed to establish.

LONDON LAKES

Tasmap Shannon
Drainage Derwent system (via Dee Lagoon)
Location Central Highlands

London Lakes is a private wild-trout fishery developed purely for fly fishers. The purpose-built lakes were originally seeded with some 50 000 brown trout fry purchased from the IFC in 1978 – but stocks are now maintained through natural recruitment. Lake Big Jim carries plenty of 1-1.5 kg fish while Lake Samuel holds a smaller head of fish to 2 kg or so. The angling is exceptional. There are reliable tailers from September, prolific caddis hatches from late October, and the revered caenid mayflies from the beginning of summer. Midges, large mayflies and mudeyes also cause surface activity, and there is scope for polaroiding.

233

A Professional guiding service is offered (and recommended), though there are special no-guide rates. Anglers who wish to fish for more than one day have the luxury of an on-site lodge, superb meals and wine.

Highland Waters, a private lake set within a large bushland estate, was formed in 1990. One hectare waterfront lodge-sites are now being sold, with owners receiving a share in ownership of the lake and fishing rights. The fishery has been producing large brown trout and was recently stocked with rainbows.

For further information contact:

London Lakes Fly Fishing Lodge
P.O. Box Bronte Park Tasmania 7140 Australia
Phone: (002) 89 1159

LONELY LAKE

No trout. See *Fishing in National Parks*, 5.1.

LONG TARNS

Tasmap Mersey
Drainage Natural – Derwent system (via James system)
Location Western Lakes

A group of clearwater lakes characterised by relatively-deep rocky banks. Brown trout of 0.5-1.5 kg are taken, mostly by bank polaroiding and spinning.

See also *Fishing in National Parks*, 5.1.

LORETTA, LAKE

Tasmap Mersey
Drainage Derwent system (via the Nive system)
Location Western Lakes

A clearwater in a woodland setting with open sedge esplanades. It holds plenty of 0.5-1.3 kg brown trout. Spinning and bank polaroiding are most productive.

See also *Fishing in National Parks*, 5.1.

LOUISA, LAKE

No trout. See *Fishing in National Parks*, 5.1.

LOWER GLENORCHY RESERVOIR

Tasmap Derwent
Drainage Derwent system (via Humphrey Creek)

Good trout are taken from the smaller lakes near Long Tarns

A clearwater surrounded by well-maintained public parkland. Tame rainbow trout can be viewed through the security fence. Fishing is not allowed.

LOWER LAKE JUKES

No trout.

LUCY LONG, LAKE

Tasmap Mersey
Drainage Mersey system (via the Fisher system)
Location Chudleigh Lakes

A rocky-banked clearwater. While most of the water is too deep to wade, there are several extensive sand/silt flats and much of the lake-bottom can be seen from the banks.

The southern shore is defined by a steep relatively-high tier. While, myrtles and pencil pines grow near the water and access along the banks is awkward, there are some elevated vantage points from where you can gain good views of cruising fish.

Flat moorland extends from the northern shore.

Most fish weigh 0.5-1.5 kg though some exceed 2 kg. They are best caught by spinning and bank polaroiding.

Superb sheltered campsites exist against the tier at the eastern and western ends of the lake.

See also *Fishing in National Parks*, 5.1.

LUNE RIVER

Tasmap Huon
Drainage Direct to Southport

Very good runs of sea trout occur in the estuary from August to early December. A dinghy is recommended as thick scrub impedes access along the banks.

The lower freshwater reaches are deep, tea-coloured, impossibly overgrown, and rarely fished.

The mid reaches flow over a wide shingle bed, much of which is exposed at low levels, and can be accessed from the South Lune Road. Celta fishing and bait casting often result in big bags of 0.1-0.3 kg brown trout.

Accessible tributaries such as Hot Springs Creek and Mesa Creek also give up plenty of tiny browns.

LUNKA LAKE

Tasmap Mersey
Drainage Derwent system (via Christys Creek)
Location Western Lakes

A clearwater lake with well-defined rocky banks. Trout of 0.7-1.5 kg are typical and some exceed 2 kg. Spinning and bank polaroiding are the most reliable fishing methods, though there are irregular mayfly hatches.

See also *Christys Creek* and *Fishing in National Parks*, 5.1.

LYELL COMSTOCK CREEK

No trout. See *Burbury, Lake*.

LYNCH, LAKE

Tasmap Shannon
Drainage Isolated

One of two drowned quarry pits adjacent to the Poatina Road between the Lake Highway and Arthurs Lake. It has long been stocked with brown trout (and a few rainbows), though formal records are scant. Usually you can catch fish to 1 kg or

so. Spinning, polaroiding and traditional dry-fly fishing all work well.

Trout liberations (since 1990)

Wild brown trout

YEAR	SIZE	NUMBER
1991	adults	20
1992	adults	20
1993	adults	20

MAA MON CHIN DAM

(known to locals as the Laffer Dam)

Tasmap Forester
Drainage Ringarooma system
Location About 2 km south-west of Weldborough

According to NTFA reports, the Laffer Dam was stocked with both browns and rainbows in the 1930s, and by 1937 fish in excess of 8 lb were being caught. From the mid 1960s to the mid 1970s the 'Laffa' was included in the adult-brown-trout stocking programme. Today the trout are all browns, the product of natural spawning, and most weigh less than 1 kg.

Most banks are steep and overgrown with dense scrub. Set-rod fishing is practised from the grassy esplanade along the mid-western shore.

MACHINERY CREEK

See *Cockatoo Dam*.

MACKENZIE TARN

Probably no trout. See *Fishing in National Parks*, 5.5.

MACKENZIE, LAKE

Tasmap Mersey
Drainage Mersey system (via the Fisher system)
Location Chudleigh Lakes

The current Lake Mackenzie was formed following the completion of the 14 m high concrete-faced rockfill hydro-electric dam across the Fisher River in 1972. The rising waters inundated two large natural lakes (Lake Mackenzie and Sandy Lake) and a significant wetland (the Pine Marsh). At full supply the impoundment is 1120.75 m above sea level, but drawdowns of up to almost 10 m are normal. At low levels the original lakes are discernible.

Releasing the first trout into Lake Mackenzie, 1895 (photo courtesy Inland Fisheries Commission)

The littoral zone consists mostly of bare rock and silt, and there is little weed growth. The water is normally clear but wave action can cause turbidity along some shores.

Brown trout, the only salmonid to establish, were first released in 1895 (see *Fishing in National Parks*, 5.1). Fish of 0.5-1 kg are quite common and some exceed 1.2 kg. Rainbow trout are scarce, though in recent years a few emigrants from illegally-stocked upstream lakes have been recorded.

Trolling is popular and productive. When levels are high Pine Marsh Bay and Sandy Lake Bay are well patronised, but as levels fall boats are confined to the 'natural' Lake Mackenzie.

All shores are suited to spinning.

Trout can often be seen cruising along the face of Mackenzie Dam and along the rocky banks on the south-western shore. Polaroiding in the shallows in Pine Marsh and Sandy Lake bays and near Explorer Creek is also worthwhile.

Reasonable rises to duns, spinners and gum beetles occur during summer and autumn.

See also *Fishing in National Parks*, 5.1.

MACKINTOSH, LAKE

Tasmap Sophia
Drainage Pieman system

Lake Mackintosh supports good-sized browns and rainbows and is the best of the Pieman River Power Development lakes for boat fishing.

Description

Mackintosh is a huge tea-coloured impoundment. The major dam (the Mackintosh Dam) is a 75 m high concrete-faced rockfill structure on the Mackintosh River. A smaller dam (the Tullabardine Dam) prevents the lake from spilling down a nearby valley.

The lake started to fill in August 1980 and the full supply of 229.5 m above sea level was reached in August 1981. The power station at the foot of the Mackintosh Dam was commissioned in March 1982. Fluctuations can be quite rapid, the full drawdown of 10.65 m being achievable in as little as three weeks.

While much of the land flooded was buttongrass plain, the lake backs up against steep densely-forested hills. Big stands of drowned trees feature in the Mackintosh valley, in Brougham Inlet, along the eastern shore, and at the Tunnel End.

Trout stocks

A one-off seeding of brown trout occurred at the time of initial flooding – but the system was already well populated with river residents and the species is now maintained entirely by natural recruitment.

Rainbows have long been present in the Mackintosh system (see *Vale River*) but in the lower reaches they comprised only a small proportion of the total trout population. In Lake Mackintosh naturally-spawned rainbows account for only 5% or so of the total trout harvest. However, in the first couple of years after a significant release of hatchery-reared rainbows, the species can comprise as much as 50% of the catch.

In the early to mid 1980s most trout caught weighed 1-2 kg. Today the average weight of the browns is about 0.9 kg, The average weight of the rainbows varies with stocking regimes, but specimens in excess of 1.3 kg are by no means rare.

Trout liberations

Wild brown trout

YEAR	SIZE	NUMBER
1980	fry	100 000

Rainbow trout

YEAR	SIZE	NUMBER
1980	advanced fry (W)	10 000
1986	large fingerlings (D)	13 000
1989	large fingerlings (D)	3 000

(W) = wild stock
(D) = domestic stock

Shore-based fishing

Fish can be taken (by all methods) from any of the relatively open areas between the Mackintosh and Tullabardine dams. Another fair access is at the Tunnel End – the southernmost bay where water enters via the tunnel from Lake Murchison. However, if you don't have a boat you are really better off fishing at Lake Rosebery.

Trolling and drift spinning

The best spots are on the fringes of the drowned timber and sticks. The Mackintosh valley arm and Brougham Inlet are reliable and well-sheltered.

The rip from the tunnel discharge at the Tunnel End is a hot spot for rainbows.

Bait fishing

While local set-rod fishers frequent the dams area and the Tunnel End, you are likely to get better results by cast-and-retrieve fishing from a boat among the trees. The best sport occurs on warm summer/autumn evenings.

Fly fishing

Early season sport is quite unreliable so it is best to plan a trip for summer and/or autumn.

On warm days trout can be found leaping after dragonflies and damselflies among the stands of drowned timber. And if the daytime sport has been tough, fishing at dusk with a wet or dry mudeye imitation is a reliable fall-back. The best results are gained from a boat in areas well sheltered from cool breezes.

Daytime wind lane fishing is also a feature. On warm breezy summer/autumn days you can often see rainbows mopping up beetles near the dams, but the serious angler will want to work the lanes from a boat. Some of the best action occurs over the open water in the main body of the lake.

Access, facilities, launching areas

The best access is via the sealed road from Tullah to the dams. Near the Tullabardine Dam there are unimpressive informal campsites, a picnic area and a sheltered launching ramp.

The southern end of the lake can be reached via 1 km of unsealed 2WD road from the Murchison Dam Road – but there are no facilities.

MACLAINES CREEK

Tasmaps Prosser and Little Swanport
Drainage Direct to Spring Bay

The lower reaches are flanked by dry bushland and open pasture. Most banks are overgrown with scrub and it is usually best to fish from the shingly creek bed. In dry times there is little visible flow and the water recedes into isolated pools. Some of these pools are short and shallow, whereas others are deep, long and extend from bank to bank. Unless there has been recent heavy rain the water is usually clear enough to polaroid. Brown trout to 0.7 kg are fairly common in the shady permanent holes, though they are often difficult to locate. Modest bags are taken on Celtas and grasshoppers.

The upper reaches are within the Buckland Military Training Area where public access is strictly prohibited.

MACQUARIE HARBOUR

Tasmaps Cape Sorell and Franklin
Drainage Direct to the Southern Ocean

Description

Macquarie Harbour is a large tea-coloured tidal water surrounded by wet-forests, dense heathland and buttongrass. While the surface water is often surprisingly fresh, the tidal influence is marked and estuarine/marine species (such as whiptails, cod, flounder and dogfish) are found as far south as Birchs Inlet and the mouth of the Gordon River.

Although the only major development is at the small village of Strahan, the harbour is steeped in history. There are the ruins of an infamous penal settlement at Sarah Island, and the ghost of a short-lived mine-associated port at Pillinger.

The environmental toll of the Mt Lyell mine is hard to ignore, the mouth of the King River being a wasteland of mine tailings, and eroded soil (see *King River*).

Access

2WD access is limited to the northern end and, while rough roads extend from Strahan to Macquarie Heads, you really need a seaworthy boat to reach the best trout fishing areas.

Boating

A good boat launching ramp (with jetty) exists at Strahan. Seaworthy runabouts are recommended. Do not attempt to explore the harbour in a dinghy unless you have lots of open-water experience and are prepared to make emergency camps on exposed shorelines.

Trout stocks/When to fish

The harbour contains wild resident brown trout (slobs) throughout the year. These fish are typically 0.5-2.5 kg, though exceptionally large specimens are taken from time to time. Those taken are mostly incidental captures made by sea trout enthusiasts and recreational net fishers – they are not a major attraction in their own right.

Sea run brown trout are common in the harbour from August to December. These fish are usually 0.5-3 kg and are the feature of the recreational fishery.

Commercial trout farming in Macquarie Harbour began in 1987 and is now a reliable industry. Rainbow trout are taken to the sea pens as smolts and are on-grown for 1-2 years. Most fish are harvested when they are 1-2 kg, though brood stock can be much bigger. Many fish jump out of the cages, or escape when the cages are damaged by storms. Such fish are now common in the harbour and lower Gordon River and can be caught at any time of the year.

Domestic Atlantic salmon are also on-grown by the fish farmers, though they are not especially common in anglers' bags. In fact most of the fish reputed to be salmon turn out to be sea trout or (believe it or not) rainbow trout.

What to use

Trolling and spinning are by far the most productive angling methods. However, sight fishing with

wet flies is possible at the mouth of the Gordon and around Sarah Island, and blind fishing with gaudy wets works well near the sea cages.

Where to fish

While trout can be taken throughout the harbour, there are only a few spots worth recommending.

Macquarie Heads can be fished from the white-sand beaches. The tidal rip is extremely strong and spinning with heavy lures works best. Locals do not often target trout here but I have taken many good sea-run fish and domestic rainbows while fishing for native estuarine species.

The hot spots for domestic rainbows are near the commercial leases – but make sure you stay a polite distance (50 m or more) from the pens. There are sites at King Point, and from the heads to Liberty Point.

At sea trout time (August to December) the best place to fish is the Gordon River spit (from Gordon Point to the river mouth) and the lower Gordon River (see *Gordon River*). The southern shore adjacent to the spit is shallow, sandy and easily waded – and is a hot spot for fly fishing. Before the time of the fish farms, sea trout accounted for 50% or more of the annual harvest of trout. Now the catch is complimented with plenty of domestic rainbows. However, the rainbows are mainly after whitebait and/or on spawning migrations, and numbers in and near the river drop appreciably during summer.

The only other place I have enjoyed good sport is from the shores of Sarah Island. While the action is irregular, on good days you can find surprising numbers of trout slashing after baitfish in the shallows.

MACQUARIE RIVER

Tasmaps South Esk, Lake Sorell, and Little Swanport
Drainage Direct to the South Esk River at Longford

The Macquarie is probably Tasmania's most respected fly stream. Rising and foraging trout provide ample opportunity for sight fishing, though the water is often murky.

Description

From its confluence with the South Esk to the hills beyond Trefusis, the Macquarie is a series of long deep weed-lined broadwaters flanked by flat marginal pasture. There are stretches of overhanging willows and scrub, but there is also plenty of open bank. Below the junction of Brumbys Creek there are regular injections of cold tailrace water from the Poatina Power Station (see *Brumbys Creek*). Above Brumbys

Macquarie River (photo by Rob Sloane)

the flows are more-or-less natural and largely rain-dependent.

In the forested hills beyond Trefusis there are many shingly runs and stony pools.

Brown trout stocks

Brown trout may have invaded the Macquarie shortly after the South Esk was first stocked (in the mid 1860s), but there were direct liberations of hatchery-reared fry in the 1870s. By the turn of the century the river was teeming with naturally-spawned fish and the average size had probably stabilized at something near what it is today. The NTFA claimed that the largest fish taken from the Macquarie and Elizabeth rivers in 1913-14 was no more than 2 lb.

Heavy artificial stocking continued until the 1950s, since when the fishery has been maintained entirely by natural recruitment.

Today most fish taken weigh 0.3-0.7 kg, though specimens in excess of 1.5 kg are to be expected from time to time. In editions of the *Tasmanian Angling Report*, noted angler Tony Ritchie claimed that the average weight was 0.9 kg in the 1970s and just 0.6 kg in the early 1980s. However, the average rose considerably in 1986-87 before falling again in the late 1980s. Such observations parallel reports of previous decades, indicating that seasonal variations in size are influenced by rainfall and the subsequent availability of forage food.

Rainbow trout stocks

Rainbow trout were probably first liberated in the early 1900s. By 1933 the Campbell Town branch of the NTFA was claiming that all streams in the Midlands were well stocked with browns and rainbows. Stocking with rainbows continued in earnest until at least the 1940s (and probably until the 1950s) but the species failed to establish.

Today rainbow escapees from the commercial fish farm at Brumbys Creek are taken from the lower reaches, and emigrants from Tooms Lake are caught in the upper reaches. However, the species accounts for only a very small percentage of the total trout harvest.

Other species

At least 160 brook trout yearlings and 1000 brook trout fry were liberated between 1904 and 1906, but this species soon disappeared.

Redfin perch are common in the lower to mid reaches but are absent from Tooms Lake and most headwater streams. Following the construction of Lake Yalleena in the mid 1980s (which effectively joined portions of the upper Elizabeth and Macquarie catchments) redfin perch have invaded Brodribb Creek. The threatened Swan galaxias (see *Swan River*), which exists in isolation of other fish species in several

Macquarie headwaters, is now facing extinction in Brodribb Creek.

The nature of the fishing/When to fish

The Macquarie fishes best when levels are high, but not during major floods when the water extends well out into the paddocks and there is no access to the main river channel. Ideally the river will be level with the bank, or lapping out into small backwaters and basins.

Early in the season you are likely to find trout foraging along the flooded edges after worms, corby grubs and frogs. At such times the best results are gained by working a wet fly in the backwaters and drains, or by casting upstream so as to cover likely cavities in the banks. Avoid traditional cross-stream techniques – the majority of the fish will have vacated the deep open water. Peak fishing usually occurs early in the morning and at dusk, but bad weather or heavily overcast skies can tempt the fish to stay in the shallows throughout the day. The fishing is reliable during rising water, and usually worthwhile when levels are high and stable. Falling water is likely to make the trout spooky and/or cause them to retreat back to the river depths.

Insects, including the famous red spinner mayfly, appear as early as mid September. High levels are still best – the trout rise along the edges and charge after surface food in the flooded shallows. Falling levels and stable low-levels are less than perfect, but they are not hopeless! Scholes and Ritchie will tell you that peak fishing occurs as the air temperature approaches 20°C. Insects do not hatch in the cold early weeks of the season, and high summer temperatures are also unfavourable. Rises are likely to occur throughout the day but often peak in the evening. The best days are warm and still with a wisp of high-level cloud. If the fishing proves difficult, it pays to hang on until evening and then search likely lies with a small wet.

The mayflies peak from October to December. Fishing in the post-Christmas period can be relatively slow, though notable rises occur at times. A good secondary hatch happens as temperatures moderate in autumn. Late-season risers are less spectacular to watch but are often fairly easy to catch. The river is likely to be low at this time, so search the clear strips of water between the weedline and the bank.

Also in autumn there is a resurgence of wet-fly fishing – but only when the weather is very bad. Fish upstream along the edges.

Where to fish

The lowest stretch, from the confluence with the South Esk to the Brumbys junction, receives cool tailrace water. While the hatches here are never as prolific or as reliable as those further upstream, they are likely to continue in dribs and drabs throughout the summer.

The best backwaters are near the junction of the Lake River, at Wyldes Plain (near the junction of the Isis River), and along the stretch between Fosterville and Glen Morriston Rivulet

The tributaries

Among the most notable tributaries are the Elizabeth River, Glen Morriston Rivulet, Kittys Rivulet and Tin Dish Rivulet.

The future

In 1991 the IFC began a three-year assessment of the water requirements for trout in the South Esk, Macquarie, Meander and Mersey rivers. Minimum-flow regulations are necessary in light of increasing demands for irrigation and riparian needs.

See also *Where to Fish – A Regional Breakdown*, 4.2.

MAGDALA, LAKE

I do not know whether the connecting stream between Lake Martha and Lake Magdala is negotiable to trout. See *Margaret, Lake* and *West Coast Range*.

MAGDALEN, LAKE

No trout. See *Fishing in National Parks*, 5.3.

MAGNET DAM

See *Bischoff Reservoir* and *Waratah Reservoir*.

MALBENA, LAKE

Tasmap Mersey
Drainage Derwent system (via the Nive River)
Location Western Lakes

A clearwater contained between rocky wooded hills. Most of the lake is very deep, though there are several silty shallows, notably in the southern arm and near the inflow from Eagle Lake. The trout prefer to feed deep down on the weedbeds and most fish seen along the edges are either young fish without established territories or older less well-conditioned specimens.

Fishing is most comfortable along the southern and western shores. Lure casters should concentrate on fishing deep down in the main body of the lake where they are likely to hook superb silvery browns to 1.5 kg. Fly fishers spot a few fish cruising along the edges but, by standards set at many nearby waters (including Eagle Lake), the fishing is poor.

See also *Fishing in National Parks*, 5.1.

MANUKA CREEK

Tasmap   Cape Sorell
Drainage   Direct to Macquarie Harbour at Strahan

A small overgrown tea-coloured creek which contains plenty of good-sized blackfish and (reputedly) small brown trout.

MARGARET, LAKE

Tasmap   Sophia
Drainage   Henty system (via the Yolande system)
Location   West Coast Range

History / Description

The 17 m high concrete dam impounding Lake Margaret was commissioned as part of the Mt Lyell Mining and Railway Company's private power scheme and was completed in 1914. In 1985 the scheme was bought by the HEC and leased back to the mining company. When the Lyell mine finally dies (projected to be the end of 1994) the electricity will be fully integrated into the State grid.

The lake is impounded by steep densely-vegetated hills. At full supply (some 660 m above sea level) there is no convenient access along the banks. However, big drawdowns are normal (especially in summer and autumn) and it is usually possible to walk along the barren white-quartzite littoral scar. While most banks are very steep, there are beaches at the north-eastern end. The water is distinctly tea coloured.

Trout stocks

According to early NTFA reports, trout were taken to Mt Lyell as early as 1917-18. From 1922 to at least 1943 the Mt Lyell Mining and Railway Company operated a hatchery at Leslie Creek, about a kilometre below the village of Lake Margaret. Browns and rainbows were reared and both species were liberated into the Lake Margaret system. Parliamentary reports and hatchery records show that in the early 1930s yearling trout were taken to lakes Margaret, Mary and Polycarp. Some 300 quinnat fry were liberated at Lake Margaret in winter 1935, but none were taken by anglers.

In the hope of providing forage food for trout, the SFFC in 1957 granted permission to the Mt Lyell Fisheries Association to liberate redfin perch into Lake Margaret. However, it seems that this never occurred.

In 1976 the IFC supplied some 10 000 brown trout fry for release in Lake Margaret – but in modern times there has never been any serious doubt about the lake's ability to maintain brown trout by natural recruitment. While the fish grow slowly, and are usually in modest condition, many exceed 1 kg.

I am not aware of any rainbow trout captures.

The fishing

Fly fishing is best in summer and autumn. Despite the tea-coloured water, fish can be spotted along the banks – they stand out remarkably well against the white substrate. In late summer and autumn there are fair rises to beetles. Surface food tends to funnel in towards the dam wall, but all shores provide worthwhile sport.

The deep banks and open bays are ideal for spinning. While overcast days are best, the trout population is so large that you can get surprising results even in bright calm conditions.

Lake Margaret – note the littoral scar

241

Access

Access is by foot from Lake Margaret village. The first leg follows the haulage and steel pipeline up a steep hill, a walk of ½-1 hr. From the top of the haulage, a wooden tramway follows a section of wooden pipeline along a single contour to the dam, a delightful stroll of ½-¾ hr.

Camping

A few small damp informal tent-sites can be scouted out at the foot of the dam. Alternatively you can camp on the damp white-sand beaches at the north-eastern end of the lake.

See also *West Coast Range*.

MARGATE RIVER

Tasmap D'Entrecasteaux
Drainage Direct to North West Bay

A small creek with poor summer/autumn flows. No doubt it contains small brown trout.

MARILYN, LAKE

No trout. See *Fishing in National Parks*, 5.3.

MARION, LAKE

Tasmap Mersey
Drainage Derwent system (via Lake St Clair)

A tea-coloured lake with significant shoreline shallows, set in an amphitheatre of densely-vegetated mountains. It is reputed to carry plenty of brown trout.

See also *Fishing in National Parks*, 5.4.

MARS, LAKE

No trout. See *Fishing in National Parks*, 5.2.

MARTHA, LAKE

Tasmap Sophia
Drainage Henty system (via the Yolande system)
Location West Coast Range

In light of the trout fishery at Lake Mary, and the relatively large connecting stream, it seems likely that Lake Martha contains a viable population of brown trout.

See also *West Coast Range*.

The peat tarn beside Mary Tarn holds lots of small browns.

MARTHA LAVINIA, LAKE

See *King Island*.

MARY, LAKE

Tasmap Sophia
Drainage Henty system (via the Yolande system)
Location West Coast Range

Records from the Lake Margaret Hatchery show that in the early 1930s Lake Mary was stocked with thousands of yearling browns and rainbows. Only brown trout survive today.

The most convenient access is via a little-used (and ill-formed) foot track which leads from a buttongrass recess about 80 m west of where the outflow stream enters Lake Margaret.

A small rock weir at the lake mouth enables water to be held about 2 m above natural maximum levels. When the gates are closed the lake spills out into the surrounding heath and sedge and there is little chance of lure fishers finding snag-free water. When levels are low, fish can sometimes be seen cruising in shallow water over the white sand beaches. More reliable sport is found at Lake Margaret.

See also *West Coast Range*.

MARY TARN

Tasmap Mersey
Drainage Derwent system (via the Nive system)
Location Western Lakes

Similar in most respects to Lake Loretta. Never expect big bags – you can often circumnavigate the lake without spotting a single fish.

Lots of slow-growing 0.5-0.8 kg trout exist in the small peat tarn adjacent to the south-eastern shore.

See also *Fishing in National Parks*, 5.1.

MAURICE RIVER

Tasmap Forester
Drainage Direct to the Ringarooma River above Ringarooma

A tea-coloured shingle-bottomed stream flowing through bushland and pasture. The fishing is similar to that at the Dorset River.

McCOY, LAKE

Tasmap Mersey
Drainage Mersey system
Location West of Lake Rowallan

Reputed to have been illegally stocked with rainbows in the late 1980s.

See also *Fishing in National Parks*, 5.4.

McFARLANE, LAKE

No trout. See *Fishing in National Parks*, 5.4.

McKAYS DAM

See *Bischoff Reservoir*.

McRAE, LAKE

No trout. See *Fishing in National Parks*, 5.4.

MEADOWBANK LAKE

Tasmap Tyenna
Drainage River Derwent (a major instream impoundment)

Meadowbank Lake is located just an hour from Hobart and is a much underrated trout fishery.

History / Description

The 43 m high concrete-buttress Meadowbank Dam was built as part of the Lower Derwent Power Development. The lake started to fill in December 1966 and soon reached its full supply of 73.15 m above sea level. It is principally a storage for the power station at the foot of the dam, and fairly rapid drawdowns to more than 6 m below full supply are to be expected.

The lake floods a well-defined valley. Most of the surrounding land comprises marginal pasture and the water is very slightly turbid.

The Dunrobin Bridge divides the impoundment into two distinct fishing areas.

The North End

At the North End the lake floods out over a flat grassy basin. The western and north-western shores are a mosaic of thickly-matted semi-aquatic weeds, dense pin-rushes and pasture. Beyond the well-defined fringe of emergent vegetation there are wadeable shallows.

The eastern shore is well-defined (no marshes), wave-washed and relatively barren.

While much of the lake bed is covered with weeds, there are patches of open silt.

South of the Dunrobin Bridge

South of the Dunrobin Bridge the valley is steep and narrow. The banks are grassy and open but the water is mostly too deep to wade.

Fish stocks

Meadowbank Lake was stocked with 350 tagged adult browns in 1967 – but this was done only to gain information on growth and migration. Today all brown trout are the result of natural spawning. Most weigh 0.5-1.2 kg, and in the North End a surprising number exceed 2 kg.

Wild rainbows are extremely scarce, the few taken in recent times being emigrants from upstream impoundments. Some 10 000 domestic rainbow fingerlings were released in 1986, but the benefit to Meadowbank anglers proved to be little and short-lived. A further 25 000 fingerlings were released in 1993.

Schools of small redfin perch are an ever-present nuisance.

Fly fishing

Fly fishing is best along the western and north-western shores of the North End.

When the lake is high fish forage in the pockets of shallow open water among the weeds and rushes.

Wade polaroiding can be quite effective too, but only when there is plenty of light.

Meadowbank Lake

Traditional dry-fly fishing is best from mid spring to Christmas, though good sport continues to the season's end. Smutting fish are a feature on calm mornings and evenings, while gum beetles and mayflies cause fair to good daytime rises. When all else fails, a wet or dry mudeye imitation used at dusk is a reliable fall-back.

Trolling

The best place to troll is in the North End. The basin is shallow and weedy but, once you get to know the area, you can easily avoid the snags. The hot spots are in the middle and along the outer edge of the marshes.

Fishing south of the bridge can also be productive, though the fish are usually smaller. While some anglers fare well using deep-running lures, I prefer to work traditional lures close to the banks. The mouths of the River Clyde and the Jones River are hot spots in autumn.

Spinning

I have taken my best bags when wading out along the western shore of the North End. The deep open banks south of the bridge are popular among locals.

Access

The only convenient public access is to the Dunrobin Bridge from the Lyell Highway or Westerway. The Meadowbank Road (which extends from the Gordon River Road near Glenora, past the western side of the Meadowbank Dam, to the Meadowbank Ski Club) is not freely available for public use. And since early 1994 the road from the Lyell Highway to the foot of the Meadowbank Dam has also been gated and locked.

Facilities

On the western side of the lake, north of the Dunrobin Bridge, a small paddock has been reserved for camping. Facilities include a toilet block and a picnic shelter.

At the eastern end of the bridge there is a serviced picnic area and (on the southern side of the bridge) a good launching ramp.

MEANDER, LAKE

No trout. See *Fishing in National Parks*, 5.1.

MEANDER RIVER

Tasmaps South Esk, Meander, Tamar, and Mersey
Drainage Direct to the South Esk River at Hadspen

The Meander is one of the best flood-time trout streams in Tasmania.

Trout stocks

According to early Parliamentary reports hatchery-reared brown trout were liberated as early as 1877, though by this time fish would already have invaded from the South Esk. Although regular artificial stocking continued until the 1950s, it is now known that natural spawning results in ample recruitment. There were experimental releases of 20 000 fry in 1981 and 1982 and these had little or no effect on the fishing in subsequent years. Association records suggest that the average size of the fish has altered little in the past six decades.

According to NTAA reports rainbow trout were first released in 1899 when 500 fry were taken to Deloraine. Over the next five decades countless thousands of fry and yearlings were turned out, both in the Meander itself and in the coldwater tributaries at the foot of the Great Western Tiers, but returns were poor and the species failed to establish.

The release of 100 brook trout yearlings in 1905-06 proved to be of no benefit at all .

Redfin perch exist throughout the broadwaters and sluggish tributaries but are not found in the cold fastwaters at the foot of the Great Western Tiers.

The meadows

The stretch of river from Hadspen to the Deloraine district flows through pasture. At normal levels it is a series of long broadwaters, deep pools, and short riffles. Many banks are lined with willows and/or native scrub but there is ample room for casting. The water is usually turbid, especially so after heavy rain, though it can clear appreciably during long periods of settled weather.

Feature fishing occurs when the river floods and spills into adjacent ditches, depressions and semi-permanent backwaters. The river rises and falls quickly, and you may only have one or two weeks a year when the conditions are just right.

Floods are most common in spring, though high water at any time of the year should be fished hard. Rising and static high levels are best – the trout retreat back to the main river channels as the water starts to recede.

The best area to fish is between Westwood and Exton. The *Westbury* and *Deloraine* 1:25 000 Tasmaps show all the important features – backwaters, ditches, flood plains, and access roads. Hot spots are the flooded mouths of tributaries, the distinct backwaters, and (when they can be

seen) the submerged banks of the river and inflows. Usually you will find tails, bow waves, and/or rising fish. If not, try blind fishing with small wets.

Unlike the Macquarie, the hatches are rarely spectacular, though very good rises do occur on warm evenings when the spinners and caddis are about. Peak fishing occurs in October and November but there is often an autumn resurgence. During floods fish rise in the drowned paddocks – and good results can be expected at normal levels as well.

Lure casters do best when the river is high but still within its banks. When levels are very low you are best advised to fish the fast water between the town of Meander and the Great Western Tiers.

Most fish weigh 0.4-1 kg but others to 1.5 kg can be expected from time to time.

Fastwater fishing

Beyond Deloraine the broadwaters become increasingly broken by shallow riffles until, at a point several kilometres outside of the township, the river becomes a wide clear shingle-bottomed fastwater. Ribbons of native scrub extend along most banks but there is ample room for wading. Most fish weigh 0.2-0.5 kg and, when levels are low, big bags are to be expected. Celta fishing, bait casting, and traditional upstream nymphing work best.

The headwaters

In the production forest at the foot of the Great Western Tiers the Meander is fed by small stony-bottomed fastwaters. All contain plenty of small brown trout and can be effectively fished with Celtas and baits. Among the most productive are Jackeys Creek, Warners Creek, Sales Rivulet and Smoko Creek. Trout have not invaded beyond Meander Falls.

On the edge of the Meander Forest Reserve there are toilets, day shelters, picnic areas and a large public shelter hut (the Huntsmans Hideaway Hut). A network of well-formed foot tracks transect the reserve, and several lead up to the Central Plateau.

The future

In response to increasing demands for irrigation the IFC in 1991 began assessing the flow requirements of fish and invertebrates in the Meander River. Minimum flow regimes will be recommended.

While it has long been proposed that the Meander be dammed so that water can be stored for irrigation, it is unlikely that such a scheme will be approved in the short to medium term.

See also *Where to Fish – A Regional Breakdown*, 4.2.

MEDWAY RIVER

Tasmaps Hellyer and Sophia
Drainage Direct to the River Leven

A small fastwater which passes through forest and plains. It supports plenty of 0.1-0.3 kg brown trout.

MEREDITH RIVER

Tasmaps Freycinet and Little Swanport
Drainage Direct to Great Oyster Bay

The quality and nature of the fishing are similar to those of the Swan system (see *Swan River*).

A few sea trout are taken from the estuary.

The lower freshwater reaches flow through marginal pasture and the banks are overgrown with trees and dense scrub. Much of the shingle bed becomes exposed during extended dry spells. Only the largest of the permanent pools cover the full width of the river, though many of the smaller holes back up against one undercut bank.

There is ample room for fly fishing, Celta fishing and bait casting. In some areas you can spot trout from the elevated banks, but you must always return to the river bed to cast.

While most trout caught weigh 0.1-0.4 kg, some exceed 1 kg. Many of the biggest fish feed heavily on galaxias.

MEROPE, LAKE

No trout. See *Fishing in National Parks*, 5.1.

MERSEY RIVER

Tasmaps Forth and Mersey
Drainage Direct to Bass Strait

The Mersey is essentially a major fastwater stream, though the lowland reaches are severely affected by hydro-electric operations. While the state of the river today is much maligned by those who remember the pre-hydro glory days, there is still plenty to recommend for the angler. Feature attractions include the rainbow trout in the headwaters and the sea trout in the estuary.

The Mersey Forth Power Development

Power development in the Mersey and Forth catchments began in 1963 and was completed in 1973.

Water is impounded by the Rowallan Dam and released through a power station before entering another impoundment, Lake Parangana. From Parangana the entire upper Mersey catchment is diverted, via tunnel, to the Lemonthyme Power Station in the Forth valley. Cold alpine water reaches the lower Mersey only during exceptional floods when Parangana spills.

Brown trout stocks

In 1869 the Salmon Commissioners reported that the stocking of brown trout into the Mersey had been delayed in the hope that Atlantic salmon could be established first. However, brown trout fry had been released by 1877 and the species adapted well.

Many old-hands claim that trout stocks have suffered in recent decades, though few have publicly emphasised the link between the former nature of the river and adverse effects of water manipulation by the HEC.

With the support of the IFC, the NWFA has sought to bolster brown trout numbers by releasing hatchery-reared fry into the lower reaches (some 120 000 from 1986 to 1993), and by building a spawning channel at Latrobe into which ripe highland spawners are transferred (400 since 1991). While the intentions of those involved are honourable, this style of management has been discredited time and time again, both in Tasmania and overseas.

Natural spawning is not a problem in the Mersey – trout numbers are limited by low flows and poor water quality (though it seems to me that natural overpopulation occurs nonetheless).

In 1991 the IFC began a three-year assessment of the flow requirements of fish and invertebrates in the Mersey, and it is likely that minimum flow regimes will be recommended. These measures may protect the river from further deterioration (proposed new projects such as the Wesley Vale pulp mill threaten to extract even more water) but it is unlikely that flows can be improved.

Rainbow trout stocks

Rainbow trout were introduced to the Mersey as early as 1904 when the NTFA recorded the liberation of 1000 fry. Stocking of the lower to mid reaches (with fry, fingerlings and yearlings) continued in earnest until at least the 1930s but, with the exception of tributary streams such as York Creek, wild populations did not establish.

Rainbows were not liberated above Hartnett Falls until 1956-57 when fish were air-dropped into Lake Meston (see *Meston, Lake*). As the upper reaches are isolated from brown trout, rainbows have thrived.

Other species

There were unsuccessful attempts in the early 1900s to establish sockeye and quinnat salmon (see *About Our Sportfish*, 2.5).

Fishing for sea trout

Early records of the NTFA reveal that good numbers of sea trout were taken from the Mersey in the early 1900s, but that from the War to the early 1920s poor whitebait runs resulted in very poor trout fishing. The whitebait began to build up again in the mid 1920s and by 1927 the Mersey was *'fast becoming one of the principal trout waters'*. The sea trout fishery peaked in the 1930s and 1940s, and the decline appears to have been related to the severe depletion of baitfish by commercial interests (see *About Our Sportfish*, 2.1). By the 1960s the heyday was well and truly over.

Despite reports to the contrary, todays angler still has a reasonable chance of success. The best spots for the shore-based fisher include the stretch from the heads to Ambleside (don't be put off by the industrial and urban development), the Latrobe area (especially the channel adjacent to Bells Parade and Pig Island), and all accessible banks between Latrobe and The Great Bend. Boat handlers often find trout ambushing bait against the emergent rushes at the head of the estuary, especially on the edge of the main river channel.

The best time to fish is from September to November. The impact of heavy rain is greatly reduced because of the upstream dams, but minor flooding is quite common and it invariably subdues the fishing.

The estuary to the Parangana Dam

Rural flats are found at Latrobe, Merseylea, Mole Creek and Liena. Elsewhere the river flows between steep forested hills. While there is a Forest Reserve at The Great Bend and a State Reserve at the Alum Cliffs gorge (at the base of the Gog Range), most undeveloped areas are in designated production forests.

As explained under the notes on power development, the river below Parangana was once a powerful shingle-bottomed fastwater, but since the commissioning of the Mersey Forth scheme it has relied almost entirely on contributions from relatively-warm lowland streams. While marked rises in water level occur after heavy rain, flushes

are stemmed and inadequate. In many areas, especially in the lower reaches, there have been substantial build-ups of silt and weed.

Fishing at Latrobe, The Great Bend and Merseylea is well worthwhile. When levels are high locals like to cast-and-retrieve worms among the willow roots. When levels subside it is usually best to work wet flies and baits over the weed beds, though fair rises can occur on warm afternoons. Most river residents weigh 0.2-0.7 kg and a few exceed 1.2 kg.

From the Mole Creek district to the Parangana Dam the river is often reduced to a series of big pools scattered along a largely-exposed shingle bed. Trout of 0.2-0.6 kg are quite common – but the fishing is usually better further downstream.

Parangana to beyond Rowallan

The water between Lake Parangana and the Rowallan Dam is almost totally regulated. When the Rowallan Power Station is operating there is considerable whitewater, but at other times there are only isolated pools scattered along an exposed shingle bed. While trout exist in some of the larger pools throughout the year, the fishing is quite unremarkable.

The 4 km or so of river between Lake Rowallan and Lewis Falls enjoys natural flow and is a major spawning area for browns and rainbows from Lake Rowallan. It is closed to angling from the Sunday closest to 1 May to the Saturday closest to 31 October, but gives up trout of 0.2-1 kg at other times.

Lees Paddocks

Lees Paddocks, a large freehold encircled by national parks, can be accessed via the well-formed foot track which leads from the end of the Mersey Forest Road. The land is an expanse of flat snowgrass amid dense forest and, in addition to some quaint huts, there are plenty of idyllic campsites.

The river here is a large fastwater slightly discoloured with tannin. It features deep weedy pools and shingly riffles and carries browns and rainbows. Most fish are small but some exceed 1 kg. Celta fishing and fly fishing are very effective. While the most reliable sport occurs in summer and early autumn, spring floods can tempt fish to forage along the grassy edges.

Trout (mostly browns) to 2 kg are sometimes taken from the oxbow and the semi-permanent backwaters.

The headwaters – rainbow country

As explained under the notes on trout stocks, the Mersey above Hartnett Falls contains only rainbow trout. It is essentially a wilderness, being within the Cradle Mountain – Lake St Clair and Walls of Jerusalem national parks.

The river between the Overland (walking) Track at Hartnett Falls and Junction Lake is accessible by an informal (but well used) cross-country walking route. Most of the stream is shallow and shingly, but there are some deep weedy holes. Many fish weigh less than 0.2 kg, though quite a few are 0.5-1 kg. While Celta fishing is usually most practical, in places there is scope for nymphing and traditional dry-fly fishing.

See also *Junction Lake*; *Meston, Lake*; and *Fishing in National Parks*, 5.1, 5.4.

MESA CREEK

Tasmap Huon
Drainage Direct to the Lune River

A shallow fastwater which supports plenty of very small brown trout.

MESTON, LAKE

Tasmap Mersey
Drainage Mersey River (an instream lake)

Meston, a rainbow-only trout water, is a deep clear lake contained between relatively-steep scrubby tiers. The best campsites are found on the wide grassy valley-floor at the northern end, and near the hut halfway down the north-western shore.

While the shallows teem with small immature fish, trout of 0.7-2.5 kg (and even bigger) are common in the deep water. Lure casters should fish from the steep banks along the eastern and southern shores, or wade out along the edge of the shelf which runs parallel to the north-western shore. Fly fishers should concentrate on polaroiding the northern end of the rocky south-eastern bank, where wind lanes regularly blow on-shore. Even deep-cruising fish will rise eagerly to take a dry fly.

The origin of the rainbows

Rainbow trout were first liberated by air drop in 1956-57. These fish had been intended for Lake Adelaide but Ned Terry (the inflight supervisor of the fish) recalled that the weather was so bad that they simply dropped the fish into the first big body of water that was seen.

NTFA reports indicate that until the early 1960s most (if not all) local anglers still believed that it *was* Lake Adelaide which had been stocked. In light of poor returns a *'second'* liberation (of 3000 rainbow yearlings) was planned for Adelaide in 1959-60 – though it seems this was never carried out.

Lake Meston

Access is by well-formed foot tracks. The most direct route is via the Lake Myrtle Track (from the Mersey Forest Road at Juno Creek to the hut midway along the north-western shore) – a walk of 3-5 hrs (each way).

See also *Fishing in National Parks*, 5.1.

MIDDLE ARM CREEK

Tasmap   Tamar
Drainage   Tamar system

A very small silty creek. Some sections adjacent to the Tamar Highway are overgrown with dense scrub, but there are open banks in the vicinity of the Holwell Road. While most fish are 0.2-0.3 kg, a few attain 1 kg or so.

MIDDLE LAKE

See *Blue Peaks Lakes*.

MIKANY, LAKE

Tasmap   Circular Head
Drainage   Deep Creek (a small instream impoundment)

Lake Mikany lies behind a long 9 m high rockfill dam and was formed in 1972. It is the principal domestic supply for Smithton and marked drawdowns can be expected in summer and autumn.

The surrounding land is forested and many banks are overgrown. There are open stretches from the dam wall to 'The Island', and along the south-western shore.

The water is slightly turbid and has a hint of tannin.

Access

There is vehicular access from the Bass Highway to the dam wall via the Reservoir Road. Alternatively you can reach the southern end via Faheys Lane and Hilders Road.

Trout stocks

Naturally-spawned brown trout abound. Most weigh 0.2-0.6 kg, though there are a few to 1 kg. There are no rainbows.

Fly fishing

The best fly fishing areas are the weedy shallows around 'The Island', and along the south-western bank. Blind fishing with a wet is worthwhile, and fair evening rises occur in summer and autumn. Some of the bigger trout can be seen slashing at galaxias along the dam wall.

Lure fishing

The best stretch for spinning is the deep open water along the dam wall and down the western shore to 'The Island'.

Special regulations

In the interest of maintaining clean water the council prohibits boating and camping.

MIKANY, LAKE

Tasmap   Mersey
Drainage   Derwent system (via the Little River system)
Location   Western Lakes

A clearwater contained between rocky wooded hills. The deep shores are ideally suited to spinning and polaroiding. Typical brown trout weigh 0.5-0.9 kg.

See also *Fishing in National Parks*, 5.1.

MILLICENT, LAKE

No trout. See *Fishing in National Parks*, 5.3.

MINNOW RIVER

Tasmap   Forth
Drainage   Mersey system (via the Dasher River)

A small clear fastwater which carries plenty of very small brown trout. Big bags are taken by Celta fishers and bait casters.

MOLE CREEK

Tasmap   Mersey
Drainage   Direct to the Mersey River

A small water with plenty of open banks and a few deep pools. After prolonged dry weather the flow dwindles to a mere trickle. Big bags of small brown trout are taken on Celtas and baits.

MONTAGU RIVER

Tasmaps   Welcome and Sandy Cape
Drainage   Direct to Robbins Passage

The lower reaches

The lower reaches are narrow, deep and sluggish. The bed consists largely of soft clay, and the water is usually turbid. Since the banks are overgrown with native trees, set-rod fishing is most practical. Sea trout are taken from August to December, while resident browns to 1.5 kg are caught throughout the fishing season.

249

The mid reaches

In the vicinity of the Bass Highway, the river flows through lush flat pasture. The main channel has been straightened, widened and de-snagged. At low flow the resulting canal floor is mostly a mosaic of grassy rushes, semi-aquatic weeds, pools, and narrow riffles, though there are some significant broadwaters. The water is always slightly turbid but is often clear enough to polaroid. Despite the often-poor summer/autumn flows and the lack of bankside shelter, there are enough 0.5-1.5 kg brown trout to provide exciting sport.

Wet flies work well when the river is flooding out over the canal floor and the trout are working along the weedy edges. As levels subside, traditional upstream nymphing and dry fly techniques become more appropriate, though you may find trout slashing at galaxias at any time of the year. In the height of summer, when the water is very warm, it pays to fish early in the morning or (second best) late in the evening.

Spinning is worthwhile when levels are up, providing you use small shallow-running lures. At other times weed and warm water become quite exasperating.

Bait casting is highly recommended.

Further up

Upstream of the pasture the river drains an extensive scrubby wetland known as the Montagu Swamp. Here, too, the river has been channelised, but access along the banks remains difficult and the area is rarely fished.

The uppermost reaches, in the vicinity of the Rodger River Road, contain plenty of very small trout.

MONTOS CREEK

See *Jones River*.

MOSSY MARSH POND

Tasmap Nive
Drainage Derwent system (via the Tarraleah Canal system)

Mossy Marsh pond is a part of the second overland channel between Lake King William and Tarraleah, a project completed in 1955. It lies in wet-forest behind a 4 m high earthfill dam and, as it is primarily used to divert water, levels remain fairly static. There are stands of emergent trees and plenty of weed so wading is essential.

The pond was originally stocked with rain-

bows, and apparently produced large fish for a few years. However, it eventually became over-populated with migrant trout from Lake King William and nearby creeks – and by the early 1980s small browns of 0.2-0.8 kg were dominant.

The adult browns released in 1978 and 1981 resulted in a short-term improvement in the quality of trout taken, but failed to bolster angler interest.

MOUNTAIN RIVER

Tasmap D'Entrecasteaux
Drainage Direct to the Huon River at Huonville

A shallow rocky-bottomed fastwater flanked with scrub. According to early Parliamentary reports brown trout were first released in 1870 (see *Huon River*). Today there are plenty of naturally-spawned 0.2-0.5 kg resident browns, and a few sea trout are taken in the lower reaches. Celta fishing and bait casting are most popular. Wading is essential.

MT PARIS DAM

Tasmap Forester
Drainage Ringarooma system (via the Cascade River)

The large concrete dam was built in 1936, and the resulting lake was stocked with brown trout fry in the 1940s and 1950s. The wall fell into disrepair, and in the 1960s the precautionary measure of draining the lake was undertaken. The lake partially refilled in the early 1980s when the outlet blocked, and years passed before the obstruction was removed.

MURCHISON, LAKE

Tasmap Sophia
Drainage Pieman system (via the Murchison River)

The 94 m high concrete-faced rockfill Murchison Dam was completed in 1982. It serves the dual purpose of diverting the Murchison River into Lake Mackintosh (so that the water can be used in the Mackintosh Power Station) and water storage (especially when Lake Mackintosh is full). Full supply is 241 m above sea level but rapid drawdowns of up to 22 m are normal. Most trees were removed from the impoundment prior to first flooding and the littoral zone is steep and stark. No doubt the lake supports plenty of small brown trout – and the odd brook trout from Lake Plimsoll – but the fishing can hardly be recommended.

Boating and camping are prohibited.

MURDERERS HILL LAGOON

See *Camerons Lagoon*.

MUSSELBORO CREEK

Tasmap   St Patricks
Drainage   Direct to the North Esk River

A small shallow stony-bottomed fastwater. As there is limited spawning shingle, the trout population is not as large as you might expect and the lower reaches carry a few fish in excess of 0.5 kg.

While native trees form a canopy over most of the stream, there is room for tight Celta fishing and bait casting.

MUSSELROE RIVER

See *Great Musselroe River*.

MYRTLE CREEK

Tasmap   Forth
Drainage   Direct to the Leven estuary

A small fastwater which carries plenty of small brown trout. Celta fishing and bait casting are most popular.

MYRTLE, LAKE

No trout. See *Fishing in National Parks*, 5.1.

NAMELESS, LAKE

Tasmap   Mersey
Drainage   Mersey system (via the Fisher system)
Location   Chudleigh Lakes

A clearwater contained between low hills. Most shorelines are rocky and well-defined and, while there are some shallow beaches at the southern end, there are no marshes or flood plains. *Isoetes* weed extends over much of the lake bed.

By late spring good dun hatches are likely to occur whenever the water is moderately calm. And in midsummer the rises are comparable to those at Little Pine Lagoon, Lake Kay and Silver Lake. Polaroids are essential, both to follow the fish between rises and to locate cruising fish when surface activity subsides.

All shores are well-suited to spinning from the banks.

The trout (all browns) average about 0.8 kg but commonly range up to 1.5 kg.

The ruin of the Ironstone Hut was dismantled in 1993 by local hut 'preservers', who have PWS permission to 'restore' it.

See also *Fishing in National Parks*, 5.1.

A good-sized brown sucks down a floating nymph – Lake Nameless

NANCY, LAKE

No trout. See *Fishing in National Parks*, 5.3.

NAOMI, LAKE

Tasmap Mersey
Drainage Derwent system (via the Little River system)
Location Western Lakes

Naomi is surrounded by open woodland, though expanses of open sedgeland extend from the eastern, northern and south-western shores. There are extensive sand/silt shallows and wading is always advantageous.

The lake supports a phenomenal number of 0.5-1 kg brown trout and when the black spinners are about (in summer and early autumn) the fishing is fast and furious. Trout rise all over the lake but the hot spots are among the emergent pin rushes and in the open channels between the rushes and the banks. Polaroids are essential.

Spinning can be very productive at any time but is best in bad or overcast weather.

See also *Fishing in National Parks*, 5.1.

NARCISSUS RIVER

Tasmaps Nive and Mersey
Drainage Derwent system (via Lake St Clair)

The deep sluggish lower-reaches flow through a relatively barren sand/clay flood plain. Evening and night fishing with large wets and buoyant dries often results in exceptional bags of typical St Clair fish.

The upper reaches, which are flanked by buttongrass and woodland, are shallow and fast. When levels are low, daytime Celta fishing is recommended. Most fish taken are browns of 0.2-0.4 kg.

See also *Fishing in National Parks*, 5.1.

NAVARRE RIVER

Tasmap Nive
Drainage Derwent system (via Lake King William)

A clear shallow fastwater flowing through sedge plains. It gives up good bags of very small brown trout.

A typical Naomi fish

A better than normal fish from Lake Nearana

NEARANA, LAKE

Tasmap Mersey
Drainage Derwent system (via the Pine system)
Location Western Lakes

Lake Nearana is surrounded by alpine woodland. Most shorelines are rocky and well defined, and most banks are too deep to wade. The clear water is best suited to lure casting and polaroiding. The trout are bigger than those in the instream lakes along the Pine River, but the fishing is always very tough.

See also *Fishing in National Parks*, 5.1.

NELSON CREEK

Tasmap Franklin
Drainage King system (via the Nelson River)

A tiny, overgrown, clear fastwater which supports lots of very small brown trout.

NELSON RIVER

Tasmap Franklin
Drainage King system (via Lake Burbury)

A clear shallow fastwater flowing through wet-forest and dense scrub.

The Nelson and Princess rivers were stocked with 35 000 rainbow fry in 1934 but the species did not establish. Today the water teems with very small brown trout.

A short well-formed foot path leads from the Lyell Highway to the picturesque Nelson Falls.

See also *Burbury, Lake* and *Fishing in National Parks*, 5.3.

NELSON BAY RIVER

Tasmap Sandy Cape
Drainage Direct to the Southern Ocean

According to a SFFC report printed by the NTFA in 1954, Nelson Bay River was first stocked in 1947 when brown trout fry were turned out.

Some yearling browns were released during the next few years, and in August 1953 a further 2000 marked yearlings were distributed among the Nelson Bay River, Big Eel Creek, Possum Creek, the Dawson River, the Thornton River, the Pedder River and Rebecca Lagoon. It was noted that:

'It is doubtful if these rivers have ever been populated with trout and it is probable that the sand bars forming obstacles at their mouths have prevented the entry from the sea of such fish which may have come from adjacent rivers.'

All of the rivers are tea-coloured permanent

streams which rise from scrubby hills and pass through coastal dunes and beaches.

NEPTUNE, LAKE

No trout. See *Fishing in National Parks*, 5.2.

NEW RIVER

Tasmap Forester
Drainage Ringarooma system (via the Dorset River)

In summer and autumn the water usually recedes into a series of isolated pools scattered along an exposed shingle bed. While most of these pools contain small brown trout, there is much better fishing in the nearby Dorset, Maurice and Ringarooma rivers.

NEW RIVER

Location Southwest National Park

Possibly no trout. See *Fishing in National Parks*, 5.2.

NEW RIVER LAGOON

Possibly no trout. See *Fishing in National Parks*, 5.2.

NEW TOWN RIVULET

Tasmap Derwent
Drainage Direct to the Derwent estuary

A shallow shingle-bottomed clearwater creek.

Brown trout were liberated as early as 1869 and the species soon established.

The lowest reaches flow through suburbia. Small trout still frequent these developed stretches, but pollution combined with high water temperatures often results in fish kills.

The mid reaches, above Main Road (Moonah), contain plenty of 0.1-0.2 kg trout and can be effectively fished with Celtas and baits.

NEW YEARS LAKE

No trout. See *Fishing in National Parks*, 5.1.

NEWDEGATE, LAKE

Tasmap Tyenna
Drainage Derwent system (via the Broad system)
Location Mt Field

Perched on the Tarn Shelf, in the shadow of the

stark rock-faces of the Rodway Range, Lake Newdegate is one of the most picturesque waters on Mt Field. The western shore backs on to steep fagus slopes and convenient access is limited to the overgrown eastern banks.

The deep water is suited to spinning and polaroiding. Brown trout of 1-2 kg are typical, though they are often difficult to locate.

Access is by well-formed walking track from Lake Dobson, a trip of 1¾-2½ hrs (each way). A good hut with a coal-fired pot-belly stove and eight bunks exists near the ouflow. Informal tent-sites can be found near the hut and along the eastern shore.

See also *Fishing in National Parks*, 5.1.

NEWTON, LAKE

Tasmap Sophia
Drainage Natural – Henty system
Location West Coast Range

A small impoundment with steep densely-vegetated banks. The 37 m high concrete-faced rockfill dam was completed in 1990, impounding the tea-coloured Newton Creek. Water is pumped from the lake up into the Henty Canal from where it flows into Lake Plimsoll. Full supply is 480 m above sea level and the normal operating range is 5 m.

The impoundment offers little prospect as a trout fishery and has not been stocked. While it is unlikely to be invaded by brook trout from the Anthony system, it may eventually receive hatchery-reared fish.

See also *West Coast Range*.

NICHOLLS, LAKE

Tasmap Tyenna
Drainage Derwent system (via the Tyenna system)
Location Mt Field

Lake Nicholls is a clearwater contained by rocky forested hills. Most banks are steep and, with the exception of a few small bays, the edges are deep.

The STLAA recorded releases of 3000 rainbow fingerlings in 1958, 500 rainbow yearlings in 1959, and 900 brown trout yearlings in 1959. In 1961 it was claimed that:

'The lake has had trout in it for many years, but ... numbers had recently fallen off. However, during the past three years Maydena anglers have re-stocked the water ... and during the past season good bags of [rainbows] *up to 15 inches were taken ... several large Brownies up to 4½ lb. were taken early in the season.'*

The IFC recorded a liberation of 40 000 rainbow fry in 1967.

As spawning is restricted to the mediocre substrate in the outflow, natural recruitment is modest. I have taken brown trout to 2 kg in recent years – but the fishing is very tough.

There are places where you can fish from the shore, but you often find it convenient to wade along some of the more overgrown banks.

A modest two-bunk shelter exists near the outflow. Informal camping is permitted, but there are few attractive tent-sites.

See also *Fishing in National Parks*, 5.5.

NICHOLLS RIVULET

Tasmap D'Entrecasteaux
Drainage Direct to the Huon estuary at Port Cygnet

A small clearwater creek in a rural valley. The flow dies to a trickle in summer, but the deep permanent pools always hold fish. Brown trout to 0.5 kg are typical. Bait casting and accurate fly fishing are most productive.

NINETEEN LAGOONS

See *Fishing in National Parks*, 5.1.

NILE RIVER

Tasmaps South Esk and St Patricks
Drainage Direct to the South Esk River

A shallow stony-bottomed clearwater with good year-round flows. While most of the surrounding land is rural, many banks are overgrown and wading is advantageous. The water teems with brown trout to 0.5 kg – and there are a few larger fish as well. Celta fishing and bait casting often result in big bags, especially when levels are low. The most popular stretches are located in the Deddington district.

NIVE, LAKE

Tasmaps Nive and Mersey
Drainage Derwent system (via the Nive system)
Location Western Lakes

A clearwater contained between low wooded hills where the fish average about 0.9 kg. The rocky shores are relatively deep and are well-suited to lure-casting and polaroiding.

See also *Fishing in National Parks*, 5.1.

NIVE RIVER

Tasmaps Shannon, Nive, and Mersey
Drainage Derwent system (via Wayatinah Lagoon)

As water is diverted at Lake Liapootah, the natural water course between Wayatinah Lagoon and the Liapootah Dam is usually almost dry. There are always some shallow pools scattered along the wide stony bed, and most of these contain small redfin perch and brown trout, but the fishing is poor.

The river immediately above Lake Liapootah is also often near dry, though it becomes a torrent when water is being released through the Tungatinah Power Station. At such times the set-rod fishing is good and the spinning is fair. While brown trout of 0.5-1 kg are typical, those which feed on fish minced in the turbines can attain extraordinary size.

From the Tungatinah Power Station to the Clarence Pipeline the river passes through a steep forested gorge, and from the pipeline to the Pine Tier Dam it is flanked by marginal highland pasture. Both sections were once shingly fastwaters but, since water is now diverted at the Pine Tier Dam, todays flows are usually poor. Plenty of very small brown trout frequent the trickles which run over the largely-exposed bed, and the deep pools hold the odd fish in excess of 0.7 kg, but there is little to recommend for the serious angler.

The river between Pine Tier Lagoon and the Western Lakes is a wide fastwater. It contains numerous resident brown trout to 0.7 kg, and is used by brown and rainbow spawners from the lagoon. Celta fishing and bait casting are most productive. The best times to fish are after moderate rain in April and September/October (when pre-spawners move upstream from Pine Tier Lagoon), and in summer and early autumn (when the water is shallow enough to wade).

Brown trout have invaded most of the headwater lakes (see *Fishing in National Parks*, 5.1).

NO WHERE ELSE, LAKE

Tasmap Forth
Drainage Don system (via the Whitehawk system)
Location on the eastern side of the No Where Else Road between West Kentish and the Devils Gate Dam road

A small steep-sided water supply with a rural setting. It was formed in 1960 and was stocked as early as 1963 when 10 000 brown trout fry were released. From 1964 to 1979 it received regular consignments of adult brown trout (usually 100-

200 each year), and some 10 000 brook trout fry were turned out in 1982. In recent years it has been stocked only with small browns.

Trout liberations (since 1985)

Wild brown trout

YEAR	SIZE	NUMBER
1985	advanced fry	500
1986	fry	10 000
1987	advanced fry	5 400
1988	advanced fry	3 600
1991	fry	4 000

NORMAN, LAKE

No trout. See *Fishing in National Parks*, 5.1.

NORTH ESK RIVER

Tasmaps St Patricks, South Esk, and Forester
Drainage Direct to the Tamar estuary at Launceston

The North Esk is a large fast clearwater. It flows through a variety of land types and the nature of the fishing varies considerably from one area to another.

History of trout stocks

Early Parliamentary reports indicated that brown trout were well established by 1869, and early NTAA/NTFA reports offer convincing evidence that the quality of fishing has remained fairly static since the turn of the century.

In the mid 1950s, Dr Aubrey Nicholls conducted a detailed census of trout stocks in the North Esk system, and in 1985 the IFC conclusively demonstrated that, after 30 years, the quantity and average size had essentially remained unchanged.

Rainbow trout were first liberated in 1898-99, and extensive stocking of the system with both fry and yearlings continued until the late 1950s. While stocking has not occurred for more than 30 years, remnant populations still exist in Camden Rivulet and the mid reaches of St Patricks River.

Early this century, small numbers of sockeye and quinnat salmon were released, but none returned from the sea (see *About Our Sportfish*, 2.5).

Some 300 brook trout yearlings were turned out between 1904 and 1906, again without success.

Hatcheries

In 1900-01 northern anglers built a hatchery and rearing unit at Waverley near Distillery Creek (see notes on acclimatisation in *About Our Sportfish*, 2.1). At various times browns, rainbow,

brooks, sockeyes, quinnats and Atlantics were handled – and doubtless many fry and fingerlings escaped into the lower North Esk.

The Waverley hatchery was never intended to be a major hatchery. As early as 1900 the NTFA was arguing for the construction of a state-of-the-art hatchery and rearing facility on *'the clear space on the left side of the North Esk at Corra Lynn'*. After years of lobbying, the SFFC in 1946 finally began construction of the Corra Linn project. The unit was intended to be more than just a replacement for the out-dated (and by now little used) Waverley facility – it was expected that it would supply the (then) enormous demand for all of the north of the State. By 1947 four concrete rearing ponds had been completed, and in subsequent years a hatchery and further ponds were added. However, the site was soon found to be inadequate, water from the North Esk being too warm and too little. The problem was exaggerated in the early 1960s as a result of the North Esk regional irrigation scheme.

The Corra Linn site was offered for sale in 1965, but removed from the market when it was realised that money from asset sales would be taken by the State Government and not benefit the IFC. Since then the hatchery has operated on an ad hoc basis. From time to time in recent years aquaculture students have used the facilities for small-scale rearing and triploiding experiments – and some fish (mainly rainbows) have escaped into the river.

The grounds and picnic facilities remain open to the public during daylight hours.

The lower reaches

The lower reaches, from Launceston to Corra Linn, flow through flat lush pasture. The water is deep, sluggish and slightly turbid, and the banks are overgrown with willows.

Sea trout are caught from August to December. Near the mouth, in the heart of Launceston, you can cast flies, baits and lures from the wharves and embankments. Elsewhere the willows impede access and in most places set-rod fishing is most appropriate. In any case, the fishing is never as good as it is in the River Tamar at the Trevallyn tailrace.

The broadwaters also harbour plenty of resident browns. Most weigh 0.3-1 kg, though some in excess of 4 kg are reported from time to time. The hot spot is near Hobblers Bridge below the outfall of the Killafaddy abattoirs. Willows are a curse but, while set-rod fishing is easiest, there are stretches (especially near St Leonards) where you can cast a lure or fly.

At the beginning of major floods, just as the water is creeping out beyond the willows into the pasture, you can find big trout foraging in pockets of open water. At such times cast-and-retrieve worm fishers and wet-fly enthusiasts can fish most of the broadwaters. The fishing deteriorates as levels rise to the point where you lose access to the main channel.

Traditional stream fishing

From Corra Linn to beyond Watery Plains, the river flows through rocky boulder-strewn gorges and steep valleys. When levels are moderate to low, there is good Celta fishing and bait casting for 0.3-0.7 kg brown trout, and every now and then you hook something much bigger.

From the bridge on the Musselboro Road to the bridge on the Burns Creek Road, there is a flat expanse of snowgrass tussocks. Here the river is fairly sluggish and clear. The bed is sand/silt and the sides are wadeable. In the 1960s and 1970s David Scholes wrote of superb fly fishing from the banks. Today willows impede access, though many banks have recently been rehabilitated. The trout are mostly 0.2-0.5 kg yet some exceed 1 kg. When the river floods you can take fish along the submerged edges, and when levels moderate there are fair to good rises. By mid summer the flow is usually poor and the trout become spooky. Under such conditions it is best to fish the fastwater further up.

Above Burns creek most stretches are fast, shallow and shingly. On mild summer and autumn days, traditional upstream fly fishing with dries and nymphs is recommended. Celtas and grasshoppers also work well. The fish are usually small (up to about 0.4 kg) but there is always a chance of hooking a trout to 1 kg or so.

Tributaries

The main tributary, St Patricks River, is a well-respected trout water. Most other tributaries (including Distillery Creek, Pig Run Creek and the Ford River) are small fastwaters which support large numbers of very small trout. Slightly larger fish are taken from Musselboro Creek.

See also *Where to Fish – A Regional Breakdown*, 2.4.

NORTH GEORGE RIVER

Tasmap Forester
Drainage Direct to the George River

The lower reaches, from Pyengana to above the Tasman Highway, are similar to the upper George River.

The small fast headwaters have a rainforest setting and give up plenty of tiny brown trout.

NORTH LAGOON

Location Toiberry

Intermittent. Not recognised as a trout fishery.

NORTH WEST BAY RIVER

Tasmaps D'Entrecasteaux and Derwent
Drainage Direct to North West Bay

The odd sea trout is reported from the lower reaches but few if any move beyond the weir (4 km from the mouth).

In summer and autumn the lower reaches have poor flow and much of the wide shingle bed is exposed. While the clearwater pools contain small brown trout, the fishing can be relatively disappointing.

The uppermost reaches, on the slopes of Mt Wellington, also contain small brown trout.

NUGARA, LAKE

Tasmap Mersey
Drainage Derwent system (via the Little River system)
Location Western Lakes

Lake Nugara is impounded by rocky lightly-wooded hills. The slightly turbid water is clear enough for practical polaroiding, and the deep banks are ideal for spinning. Brown trout of 1-1.8 kg are quite common.

See also *Fishing in National Parks*, 5.1.

NUGETEENA, LAKE

Tasmap Mersey
Drainage Derwent system (via the Nive system)
Location Western Lakes

A deep clearwater impounded by rocky lightly-wooded banks. While the fishing can be very difficult, patient polaroiders and spin fishers have their share of success. Most trout weigh 1-2 kg and a few exceed 3 kg.

See also *Fishing in National Parks*, 5.1.

NUTTING, LAKE

See *Daisy Lakes*.

Just when you think it's played out – Lake Nugeteena (photo by Frances Latham)

OBERON, LAKE

No trout. See *Fishing in National Parks*, 5.2.

O'DELLS LAKE

Tasmap Mersey
Drainage Derwent system (via the Little Pine system)
Location Nineteen Lagoons

A shallow clearwater set in moorland. When levels moderate, much of the lake is wadeable. While there are sandy flats at the southern end and extensive rock shallows elsewhere, bottom-hugging weeds grow over much of the lake centre.

There is some scope for fishing from the banks but wading is a distinct advantage, especially when levels are low.

At times the water backs up into the tussocks and fish can be found foraging along the submerged banks, but there are no substantial flood basins. The best high-water fishing is in the Kay Lagoons and at Lake Flora.

When the lake is at normal levels the wade polaroiding is superb. There are also good rises to duns and black spinners on warm days in summer and early autumn.

Spinning is worthwhile, though the weed becomes a problem when levels are very low.

Bait fishing is prohibited

While brown trout of 0.9-1.5 kg are typical, the average size varies considerably according to seasonal conditions.

Access is by foot via a long-disused vehicular route from Lake Botsford, or via a selection of cross-country options. Allow 1½-2 hrs each way. A modest emergency shelter exists nearby at Lake Flora.

See also *Fishing in National Parks*, 5.1.

OLD RIVER

Probably no trout. See *Fishing in National Parks*, 5.2.

OLIVE LAGOON

Tasmap Mersey
Drainage Derwent system (via the Little River system)
Location Western Lakes

A shallow clearwater surrounded by woodland. Most shores are fringed with tea-tree and emergent pin-rushes. There are several shallow flood basins along the western bank.

When levels are low, all of the shores and much of the middle can be waded. In summer and early autumn, hatches of black spinners

A black spinner feeder taken from amongst the pin rushes at Olive Lagoon

cause intense surface activity. Fish can be polaroided in the narrow bands of open water between the pin rushes and the shore, and as they cruise over the sandy shallows further out.

After heavy rain, the water spills out into the mossy flats on the western shore and trout soon move in to forage for worms and frogs.

Most fish taken weigh 0.5-0.9 kg.

See also *Fishing in National Parks*, 5.1.

OLIVE, LAKE

Tasmap Mersey
Drainage Derwent system (via the Little River system)
Location Western Lakes

A deep clearwater contained between steep forested hills. The shores are rocky and there are no marshes or flood plains.

Although best suited to spinning, fish can be sometimes spotted along the banks.

Brown trout of 0.4-1.2 kg are typical.

See also *Fishing in National Parks*, 5.1.

OPHION, LAKE

See *The Labyrinth*.

ORB LAKE

No trout. See *Fishing in National Parks*, 5.2.

ORIELTON LAGOON

Tasmap Prosser
Drainage Direct to Pitt Water

Orielton Lagoon is a bay of Pitt Water, partially impounded when the causeway on the Tasman Highway was completed in the late 1950s.

In 1962 the IFC placed weirs and baffles on the outlets in order to minimise tidal influence and reduce salinity, and from 1963-64 to 1971 there were annual liberations of 200-2000 adult brown trout.

A minor fish kill occurred in February 1970 and by 1974 such disasters had become commonplace. The fishery soon collapsed.

The deterioration of the lagoon was found to be due to severe pollution. The causeway had so reduced tidal flushing that nutrients washing in from adjacent fertilized pasture had built up to unacceptably high levels. More importantly, the Sorell and Midway Point sewage schemes (completed in 1969) were discharging effluent directly into the lagoon. Algal blooms and obnoxious smells became the order of the day.

The lagoon deteriorated even further in the early 1990s, and in January 1993 the first bloom of toxic blue-green algae was recorded. After intense lobbying, Local and State Governments finally began addressing the problem. By early 1994 the openings in the causeway had been deepened and widened so as to permit major tidal flushing. It has also been decided that sewage effluent will be chlorinated, though this is of questionable benefit.

While the water is still technically an inland water reserved for the use of artificial lures, it is questionable whether the trout fishery will ever be restored.

ORIELTON RIVER

Tasmap Prosser
Drainage Direct to Orielton Lagoon

In the days of the Orielton Lagoon fishery, resident browns and lake spawners could be taken in the lower reaches. Today the estuary is polluted and the creek is often dry. Undoubtedly the odd trout could still be found in the few permanent holes – but there is little to recommend for the angler.

ORION LAKES

No trout. See *Fishing in National Parks*, 5.1.

OSBORNE, LAKE

Tasmap Huon
Drainage Huon system (via the Arve system)
Location Hartz Mountains

A deep clearwater impounded by steep densely-vegetated slopes. While fishing from the banks is awkward, there are wadeable shallows near the outflow and at the northern end.

Brown trout to 0.5 kg or so are plentiful. Spinning is the most reliable method, though there are fair rises to duns on warm days in summer and early autumn.

Access is via 1 km of well-formed foot path. Day-use is advocated.

See also *Fishing in National Parks*, 5.6.

OUSE, RIVER

Tasmaps Tyenna, Shannon, Meander, and Mersey
Drainage Direct to the River Derwent at Ouse

Hydro-electric development

When the Great Lake power scheme began operation (1916), water from the head of the Shannon catchment was diverted, by canal, to the newly-created Penstock Lagoon, from where it was dropped 80 m to the Waddamana Power Station on the banks of the Ouse. This served to considerably bolster the Ouse catchment and, because the Great Lake scheme was at that time the only major power development in the State, steady flows were maintained throughout summer and autumn.

In 1918-19 work began on the Liawenee Canal – the diversion of the Ouse (8 km below what is now the Augusta damsite) into Great Lake. When this project was complete (1922-23), the Ouse between the entrance of the canal and Waddamana was denied flow, changing from a shingly fastwater to a warm-water trickle. The situation below Waddamana altered in that, while all of the headwater was eventually returned through the power station, it was delivered at a steady rate. Winter floods and summer lows were significantly subdued.

In 1955 the Augusta Dam was completed, permitting even greater control of the headwaters (see *Augusta, Lake*). Since 1964-65 Great Lake has been diverted north out of the Shannon and Ouse catchments into the South Esk catchment. Small amounts of water are released through Waddamana only when the HEC is compelled to supply riparian requirements.

Trout stocks

Early Parliamentary reports indicated that brown trout were established in the River Ouse by 1869, and that the species had infiltrated the Nineteen Lagoons well before 1893. Today brown trout continue to be maintained by natural recruitment, though the average size and relative abundance varies from stretch to stretch.

Rainbow trout were probably first liberated in the early 1900s. After the commissioning of the Waddamana Power Station (1916), the tailrace became a small-scale trophy water. In 1933 a rainbow of some 7.8 kg was landed (see *About Our Sportfish*, 2.2), a State record fish. The tailrace fishery ended when Great Lake was diverted in 1964-65.

Today rainbows are largely confined to the headwaters above Liawenee Canal. Wild populations exist in Lake Augusta and the Julian Lakes (see *Fishing in National Parks*, 5.1).

The River Derwent to Ousedale

The lowest portion of the Ouse flows through relatively flat marginal pasture. It is a string of long, deep, weedy silt-bottomed pools. Most banks are overgrown with willows, and there are no major flood plains or backwaters.

Trout to 0.7 kg are quite common and some exceed 1 kg. Set-rod fishing and bait casting work well. Lure fishers have to search the banks for pockets of open water.

Ousedale to Waddamana

Above Ousedale the river flows between wooded hills and gorges and there is no public road-access. I enjoy polaroiding good-sized trout in the long deep pools, though the banks are overgrown and the water is often slightly murky.

Waddamana to the Marlborough Highway

The surrounding terrain is much like that in the Ousedale-Waddamana stretch – but the summer/autumn flows are abysmal and usually much of the creek bed is exposed. There are plenty of brown trout to 0.3 kg in the shallow shingle-bottomed pools, and a few 1 kg fish are taken from the deeper shady lies.

The Marlborough Highway to Liawenee Canal

This is the most accessible and most fished section of river. It flows through moorland, over a wide largely-exposed shingle bed. While the water becomes very warm in the height of summer, there are plenty of 0.2-0.3 kg brown trout. The fish respond well to Celtas and baits.

Liawenee Canal to the Augusta Dam

There is usually a constant flow of water, though summer/autumn flows are rarely more than what is permitted by natural run-off. Water is shut off at the Augusta Dam only when it is necessary to carry out maintenance to Liawenee Canal.

Moorland extends from the banks and there is ample room for casting. Trout of 0.2-0.5 kg are typical, though larger emigrants from Lake Augusta are not uncommon. Rainbows account for about 10-20% of the fish caught.

Although this section of river fishes well, it is completely overshadowed by the nearby lake fishing (see *Fishing in National Parks*, 5.1).

The headwaters

Unlike most other streams in the Western Lakes district, the Ouse carries a year-round supply of takeable trout. Celta fishing is always worthwhile, and fair rises occur on suitable days (see *Bar Lakes System*). Trout have invaded most of the headwater lakes (see *Fishing in National Parks*, 5.1).

OVAL LAKE

No trout. See *Fishing in National Parks*, 5.2.

PADDYS LAKE

Tasmap   Hellyer
Drainage Leven system
Location Black Bluff

A small tea-coloured alpine lake impounded by steep heath-covered slopes. Though stocked with 10000 rainbow fry in 1968, no fish (trout or natives) are present today.

PALLAS, LAKE

No trout. See *Fishing in National Parks*, 5.1.

PALOONA, LAKE

Tasmap   Forth
Drainage River Forth (a major instream impoundment)

Lake Paloona is the most isolated of the Mersey Forth Power Development lakes. It harbours some good trout, but can hardly be recommended over Lake Barrington.

Description

The Paloona Dam, a 40 m high concrete-faced rockfill structure, was completed in 1972. It floods a steep densely-forested section of the River Forth yet there is little emergent timber. While full supply is 53.35 m above sea level, there is a normal operating range of almost 4.6 m. The water is slightly tea-coloured and faintly turbid.

Access and facilities

Convenient 2WD access is limited to the banks near the eastern side of the dam, and the power station below Lake Barrington. However, there are several little-used vehicular tracks leading to the mid reaches, all of which are marked on the *Castra* 1 : 25 000 Tasmap.

There are no formal boat launching areas or campsites.

Trout stocks

Some 10000 brown trout fry were released in 1977, though by this time the species was already well established. Naturally-spawned brown trout to 1 kg are quite common today.

Rainbow trout are incapable of natural recruitment, though emigrants from lakes Barrington and Cethana are sometimes quite common.

The nature of the fishing

While the nature of the fishery is similar to lakes Barrington and Cethana, the absence of access roads, launching areas, and open banks makes the angling largely unappealing.

There is some scope for set-rod fishing near the dam, but the best fishing areas are in the mid reaches at the ends of the vehicular tracks.

Local set-rod fishers report taking a few better-than-average fish at the outfall of the Devils Gate Power Station (below Lake Barrington).

PARANGANA, LAKE

Tasmap   Mersey
Drainage Natural – Mersey system (a major instream impoundment)

Although much less popular than Lake Rowallan, Parangana is a rewarding fishery.

Description

Lake Parangana floods steep forested sections of the Mersey and Fisher valleys. It lies behind a 53 m high earth and rockfill dam (completed in 1968) and serves to divert the upper Mersey catchment into the nearby Forth valley. The water is faintly tea-coloured. Full supply is 381 m above sea level, and the normal operating range is little more than 2.1 m. While there are few emergent trees, there are many submerged logs and snags at southern end of the Mersey arm.

There is always some input from the Mersey (mainly because the Arm River enters a little upstream of the lake) but whenever the Rowallan Power Station is operating (irregularly) the flow becomes a torrent. The input from the Fisher end is also regulated and irregular.

Access, boating and facilities

There is an extensive grassy area – complete with picnic facilities, informal campsites and launching ramps – adjacent to the Mersey Forest Road 1.5 km south of the dam.

The inflow from the Mersey is accessible via a vehicular track from the Mersey Forest Road.

Trout stocks

Natural spawning occurs in both the Mersey and Fisher inflows, and a significant number of lake fish emigrate downstream from Lake Rowallan.

In 1969 the IFC reported that most of the fish taken were rainbows (possibly hatchery-reared stock). A couple of seasons later brown trout had become dominant. In recent years rainbows have accounted for about 3% of the annual harvest, though this figure temporarily increases whenever Lake Rowallan is stocked.

Most fish caught weigh 0.3-0.7 kg and a few exceed 1 kg.

Shore-based fishing

As the banks are mostly very steep and overgrown, shore-based sport is limited.

The best area (for all fishing methods) is at the southern end of the Mersey arm. Warm summer/ autumn evenings are perfect – anyone prepared to wade over the submerged logs chasing risers is bound to take good bags.

There is also limited scope for casting at the picnic/camping area.

Boat fishing

Trolling and drift spinning are dynamite. All of the lake is worthwhile, though the recognised hot spot is the southern end of the Mersey arm.

There are good summer/autumn beetle falls and, while the wind lanes are never as good as those in Lake Rowallan, you can usually polaroid fish along the edges.

PARK CREEK

Tasmap Tyenna
Drainage Direct to the River Derwent at Bushy Park

A small fastwater, ideally suited to bait casting and Celta fishing. It supports plenty of very small brown trout.

PARTING CREEK LAKE

Tasmap Pieman
Drainage Little Henty system
Location North of Zeehan

Description

A dark tea-coloured water supply formed in 1969. It lies behind a 5 m high earth dam and is surrounded by sedge-clothed hills. Drowned trees extend over the northern end.

Access along the wet, sometimes steep banks is fairly tiresome, and care is needed when wading.

Trout stocks

The trout (all browns) are essentially maintained by natural recruitment. While there is pressure on the IFC to stock with hatchery-reared fry, I doubt that such fish make significant contributions to anglers' bags.

Most trout grow slowly and many of the older fish are just 0.4-0.6 kg. However, a significant number attain 1-2 kg, and each season the odd 3-4 kg fish is reported.

Trout liberations

Wild brown trout

YEAR	SIZE	NUMBER
1972	fry	21 000
1975	fry	10 000
1976	fry	10 000
1984	fry	4 000

Most trout in Parting Creek Lake grow slowly.

Facilities

Dinghies and small runabouts can be launched at the southern end. There are no comfortable campsites.

The fishing

Drift spinning and trolling are popular with locals. There is also scope for spinning from the banks, especially if you are prepared to wade.

Feature fishing occurs on muggy summer/ autumn evenings during the mudeye migrations. Flies and grubs cast to rising fish are usually eagerly accepted. The hot spot is among the drowned trees, though anglers without boats fare reasonably well at the dam end.

PATERSONIA RIVULET

Tasmap   St Patricks
Drainage   North Esk system (via St Patricks River)

A small fastwater with a rural setting. The water becomes murky after heavy rain but clears appreciably as levels moderate. While some banks are open, many are overgrown and wading is always a distinct advantage.

There are plenty of 0.1-0.5 kg brown trout. Celta fishing and fly casting are best when levels are low. Bait casting with worms is advocated when the water is swollen.

PATON CREEK

Tasmap   Hellyer
Drainage   Direct to the Blythe River

A small moderately tea-coloured fastwater.

In 1966 the IFC found plenty of naturally-spawned 0.5-1 kg rainbow trout. Today only browns are present.

The lower reaches flow over granite boulders and fine gravel. The banks are overgrown with dense scrub and wading is essential. There are numerous undersized fish and a few to 0.3 kg or so. Celta fishing and bait casting work well, especially when levels are low.

Near Upper Natone the creek is flanked by pasture and is so small that in many places you can step across it. There are still plenty of small fish but some, especially those in the deep pools and small dams, attain 0.5 kg and more.

The uppermost reaches, near the crossing of the Upper Natone Road, flow through open paddocks and are very small and shallow. There are fewer fish here, and most never exceed 0.2 kg.

PATRICK, LAKE

Probably contains plenty of slow-growing brown trout. See *Margaret, Lake.*

PATS TARN

Tasmap   Mersey
Drainage   Derwent system (via the Little River system)
Location   Western Lakes

While most of the lake is flanked by woodland, open flats extend from the southern and eastern shores. After heavy rain fish can be found foraging over the flooded edges. When levels are low, lure casting and polaroiding are usually most appropriate. Typical fish weigh 0.5-1.3 kg.

See also *Fishing in National Parks,* 5.1.

PAUL, LAKE

Probably contains plenty of slow-growing brown trout, See *Margaret, Lake.*

PAWLEENA RESERVOIR

Tasmap   Prosser
Drainage   Sorell Rivulet (a small instream impoundment)

The dam, a 9 m high concrete structure, was built in 1919 to satisfy domestic and minor irrigation requirements in the Sorell district. The lake has a rural setting and the water is usually turbid. When levels are high the northern end spills into the paddocks. But by mid autumn the lake is often reduced to less than half of its full-supply surface area and fish kills are common.

Trout liberations (since 1985)

Wild brown trout

YEAR	SIZE	NUMBER
1985	fry	20 000
1986	fry	10 000
1988	fry	5 000
1989	fry	5 000

Domestic rainbow trout

YEAR	SIZE	NUMBER
1986	small fingerlings	5 000

The peak fishing years were between 1965 and 1979 when there were almost annual liberations of 200-300 adult brown trout. Since 1980 the fishery has been maintained mostly by stocking with fry. There are still adequate numbers of 1 kg fish, but specimens in excess of 2 kg are much less common than they once were.

Feature fishing occurs early in the season (August to November) when the trout are charging at the schools of land-locked smelt.

Fishing in the post-Christmas period is often disappointing – especially if the water is low and warm.

PAYANNA, LAKE

No trout. See *Fishing in National Parks*, 5.1.

PEDDER, LAKE

(known to environmentalists as the Serpentine Impoundment)

Tasmaps Olga, Wedge, and Old River
Drainage Gordon system (via Lake Gordon)

For many years Lake Pedder was synonymous with huge trout – it was Australia's glory fishery. Today it produces much smaller fish, though they are still fat, silvery and strong.

Description

Lake Pedder is surrounded by wilderness and is incorporated in the Southwest National Park. It is a huge hydro-electric scheme impoundment, formed by the damming of two once-separate catchments. The Scotts Peak Dam (on the Huon River) is a 43 m high bitumen-faced rockfill structure, while the Serpentine Dam (on the Serpentine River) is a 30 m high concrete construction. The Edgar Dam (at the Scotts Peak end) serves to prevent the impoundment from spilling out through a gap in the encircling hills and ranges.

The impoundment is primarily used to divert the Serpentine and upper Huon catchments via McPartlan Canal into Lake Gordon, enabling the water to be utilized in the Gordon Power Station. Full supply is 308.46 m above sea level and the normal maximum drawdown is little more than 1.5 m.

The area flooded was mostly vast buttongrass plains but included several picturesque natural lakes. The tea-coloured water backs up against verdant slopes of thick sedge and heath. There are no major forests, though trees line some of the inflowing streams. While small pockets of drowned heath are found along many shores and there are drowned trees in Starfish Inlet, the lake is largely free of emergent vegetation.

The only town, Strathgordon, was the original HEC construction village. Beyond the town,

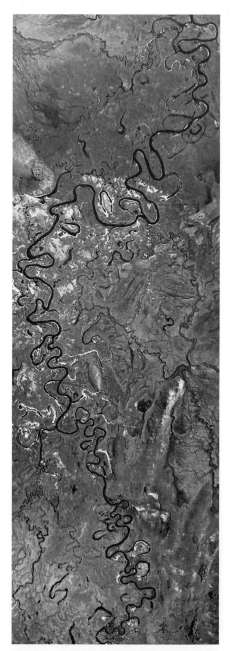

The Serpentine River between the natural Lake Pedder and the Bell – now beneath Serpentine Reach, Lake Pedder (courtesy Tasmap)

developments are limited to picnic grounds, camping areas and boating facilities.

The flooding

The wilderness value of the South-West had been recognised by 1955 when 23 880 ha surrounding the original Lake Pedder was proclaimed National Park. The intention of the HEC to flood Lake Pedder was made public in 1967 and, following unprecedented public outcry, the reserve was renamed the Southwest National Park and expanded to 191 625 ha. (There have been several hard-won extensions to the Southwest National Park and it now comprises 608 000 ha.) Most of the original Lake Pedder National Park was drowned in 1971-72. Public outrage continued and UNESCO described the event as the *'greatest environmental tragedy since European settlement of Tasmania'*. The incident gave birth to today's powerful environmental movement, a movement which has had considerable impact (see *Gordon River*) and which is actively lobbying for the eventual restoration of the natural Lake Pedder.

The origin of the trout

A large fall on the Serpentine River (not far upstream from its junction with the Gordon) was an effective barrier to all fish attempting to move up from the Gordon system. However, anecdotal evidence from well-known bushwalkers and anglers suggests that the natural Lake Pedder may have long held brown trout. In *The Tasmanian Tramp* (1955) it was said that *'Loch Leven trout were reportedly liberated there in 1905'*. And in 1967 the IFC noted that there were small brown trout in *'some parts of the Serpentine River'* (though it is not clear if these fish were found above the falls).

But regardless of the state of the Serpentine catchment, the flooded sections of the upper Huon system teemed with wild browns, and these fish would have been sufficient to populate the new impoundment.

In order to bolster existing stocks and to guarantee immediate sport, a once-only liberation of 350 000 brown trout fry was undertaken in September 1972.

Lake Gordon was first stocked with rainbows in 1976 and occasional migrants were being caught in Lake Pedder soon after.

Boom and bust fishing

The new Lake Pedder began filling in September 1971. By 1973 the quality of the fish was the talk of the town, and in winter 1974 IFC staff were handling spawners up to 4.6 kg.

The real glory years were from 1975 to 1978 when the average weight of fish taken remained at

The natural Lake Pedder, now beneath Pedder Reach (courtesy Tasmap)

about 4.5 kg and plenty of much larger specimens (some in excess of 10 kg) were being reported.

It is expected that trout in newly-created impoundments will grow quickly (see notes on trout growth in *About Our Sportfish*, 2.1). But Pedder was unique – the growth of the trout was simply phenomenal. In 1976 the IFC found one three-year-old brown trout to be 7.2 kg!

Part of the reason for the rapid growth was the abundance of large forage food. By 1974 there were huge schools of galaxias all over the lake – and the trout could be found charging through them much as sea trout chase whitebait. Mudeyes too were important dietary items, even in the early years, and the health of the fishery was enhanced by virtue of relatively static lake levels.

By 1980 the average weight had dropped to less than 3.5 kg, by 1982 it was little more than 2 kg, and by 1985 it was about 1.5 kg. The decline in size was to be expected. The rotting buttongrass could not last forever, and the abundance of spawning streams meant that the trout population would increase year by year. However, at about the time of the collapse of the trophy fishing there was a dramatic change in the nature of the lake – over a single season the galaxias practically disappeared. A contributor to the *Tasmanian Angling Report* (1983) wrote:

'When I first moved to Strathgordon in 1979 the lake was alive with the native galaxia and the trout would feed on these in the gravel shallows at night early in the season, and in bays like Wilmot Bay around December, the galaxia and hence the trout would be everywhere. By 1981 these galaxia had began to disappear and the fish changed their feeding habits quite dramatically. Whereas in previous years fish caught early in the season would be gorged on galaxia, very few fish caught had galaxia in them. Instead the trout were feeding on immature dragonfly larvae (mudeye). Areas where galaxia used to abound became almost uninhabited by trout and the fish moved to shorelines where tea-tree and other bushes hung over the water.'

The galaxias

Because of the fall on the Serpentine, the two galaxiid species in the natural Lake Pedder had evolved in isolation from the rest of the Gordon system and were found nowhere else on Earth. The swamp galaxias *(Galaxias parvus)* is quite distinct from other galaxiids, whereas the Pedder galaxias *(G. pedderensis)* is closely related to (and probably evolved from) the climbing galaxias *(G. brevipinnis)*. When the new Lake Pedder was formed, climbing galaxias from the Huon catchment were able to invade the Serpentine system.

Soon after the flooding, large schools of galaxias were observed in all areas of the lake. Most of the fish along the shores and in the shallows were Pedder galaxias and swamp galaxias, though by 1976 climbing galaxias were fairly common in the body of the lake.

A dramatic decline in galaxias was noted in 1980-81. While subsequent surveys have shown that swamp galaxias are still relatively common along the swampy edges and in the streams, the Pedder galaxias is now reduced to a handful of individuals in just a few streams and is facing extinction. The rapid decline of the Pedder galaxias over just one or two seasons suggests interference in spawning, and/or low survival of young, not direct predation of older fish. It is likely that the species is simply unable to compete with climbing galaxias.

The IFC has placed a handful of Pedder galaxias in a nearby fish-free tarn, though it is too early to determine if they will establish.

Glory days (photo courtesy The Mercury*)*

Trout stocks today

The decline in average weight has slowed considerably in recent years. In 1990 the average weight was about 1.2 kg and in 1993 it was about 1.1 kg. Trout of 1.5 kg are still common, though fish in excess of 2.5 kg are rarities. Most trout are fat and silvery and the catch rate compares favourably with the best of the big-name highland waters.

Rainbows account for only 1% or so of the annual harvest.

While redfin perch abound in Lake Gordon, they have not yet moved through McPartlan Canal to Lake Pedder.

Vehicular access and facilities

Access is via a single no-through-road (the Gordon River Road) from Maydena. There are no shops, and petrol (no outboard mix) can only be purchased on weekdays from the HEC at Strathgordon.

The sealed Gordon River Road extends some 45 km before reaching Lake Pedder at McPartlan Canal, where there is a good launching ramp. Some 14 km further along the lakeside, at Teds Beach, there is a shelter hut, elaborate picnic facilities, campsites, and another good launching area. At Strathgordon there is chalet accommodation

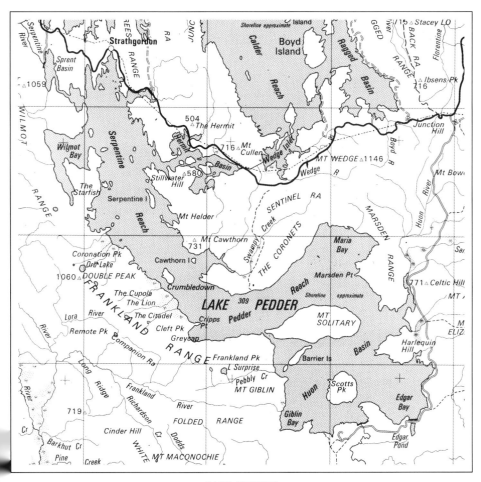

LAKE PEDDER

267

and a formal camping ground. Boat and tackle hire can be arranged at the Lake Pedder Motor Inn. Beyond Strathgordon, a 3 km gravel spur leads to a boat launching area and picnic facilities at the Serpentine Dam (Sprent Basin).

Some 29 km along the Gordon River Road from Maydena (long before McPartlan Canal) there is a 34 km gravel spur to the southern end of the lake. The first of the main southern camping developments is about 30 km along the Scotts Peak Road, beneath the Edgar Dam on the north-eastern shore of Edgar Pond. This is an exposed site, subject to cold wet winds. Toilets, tank water, and a large day shelter are provided. A good boat launching area (complete with jetty) is located nearby at the eastern end of the Edgar Dam – but this too is very exposed. In rough westerly weather you are best advised to tow your boat a couple of kilometres west to the less well-developed ramp at Tea Tree Cove. At the Scotts Peak Dam there is a small boat harbour, complete with a substantial launching surface and large jetty. If you turn right past the Scotts Peak Dam, you will come to a forested area on the banks of the Huon River where there is a cluster of formal very-sheltered camping recesses. Facilities include a pit toilet, a day shelter, tank water, individual fire places (wood supplied), and individual picnic tables.

Access along the shore

The thick heath and sedge, combined with wet boggy slopes, can make progress along the banks quite difficult and, if you don't have a boat, you are really confined to relatively small (though often productive) stretches of shoreline near the access roads. The choice of where to fish is often largely determined by the weather. Sheltered shores are best, so you often find yourself fishing the western aspects of bays and inlets.

The Strathgordon end

You can scrub-bash along some banks from the boat ramp at McPartlan Canal, or walk along the edge of the canal to the Wedge Inlet at Lake Gordon (see *Gordon, Lake*).

The north-western shore of the Hermit Basin can be reached from the Gabion Shore (where the Gordon River Road crosses over a small inlet).

The northern shore of Trappes Inlet and the eastern shore of Teds Beach are accessible by road, and a rough walking route extends along the banks between the two.

There is also scope for fishing from the jetties at Strathgordon, and from the banks near the Serpentine Dam.

The Scotts Peak end

About 1.7 km of rugged vehicular track leads from the Scotts Peak Road (at a point some 19 km south of the Gordon River Road, and 0.1 km north of Condominium Creek) to the Huon Inlet at the mouth of Condominium Creek. Vehicles can be taken 0.7 km or so before you meet a formal road-barrier. From here you have an easy walk to the lake, where there are several kilometres of open bank. This area is really only appealing in calm conditions or during (infrequent) easterly weather, though there are a couple of inlets sheltered from westerly winds.

Productive fishing can be enjoyed at all of the boat launching sites (see notes on vehicular access and facilities). Crude walking tracks lead north-west from Tea Tree Cove, giving access to some of the best of the conveniently accessible shoreline.

Boat-accessible shores

Boat operators are able to gain access to other popular shores, including Coronation, Crumbledown and Mt Solitary, though if you have a boat you tend to fish from it.

Trolling

In the glory days of the 1970s, trolling with large and/or deep-running lures, such as Rebels, Rapalas, Canadian Wigglers and Flatfish, was favoured. However, traditional Tasmanian lures (such as large Cobras and spoons) have always worked well and are increasingly popular.

The fishing is good throughout the year, though it should be remembered that the weather in the early months of the season is likely to be uninviting. While daytime fishing has always been most popular, row-trolling at dusk with a Fishcake is dynamite.

All areas of the lake produce fish so your choice of destination is usually determined by the weather. Some of the favourite circuits incorporate Bell Basin, Wilmot Bay, Hermit Basin and Stillwater Passage, the Crumbledown Shore, Maria Bay, the Huon Inlet, Giblin Bay, and Edgar Bay. The Huon Inlet is especially popular in April when spawners begin to congregate.

Spinning

All accessible shores are suitable for lure casting. Drift spinning among the trees in Wilmot Bay and the Starfish Inlet is also highly recommended.

In the daytime, especially when fishing among snags, I prefer light shallow-running lures such as small fish-spoon wobblers and Devon spinners.

Lake Pedder today (photo by Rob Sloane)

The most popular method has always been Fishcaking at night. While this style of spinning is not as reliable as it was in the lake's heyday, it is still very worthwhile. In the 1970s, when the trout fed on galaxias in the shallows, Fishcaking was at its best in the early months of the season. Trout can still be taken early, but peak activity is now in summer and autumn when the mudeyes are on the move. Ideal conditions are calm and dark, though you should never ignore the water just because of chop and/or moonlight.

Fly fishing

Sight fishing is possible at any time of the year, though the weather is most reliable in summer and autumn.

Midging fish can be found on frosty mornings from about mid spring, though they are never as active as those in rainbow waters such as Lake Burbury. While trout will sometimes keep sipping down midges until early afternoon, it pays to be out boating in the wind lanes at first light.

Dragonflies and damselflies provide the feature fishing. From mid spring to late summer, warm afternoons will see fish leaping and bow-waving to take adults and nymphs among the drowned sticks. Frequently the fish are accessible from the shore, but they also work further out, often finning in deep water. At such times I have had most success with wet mudeye-imitations, though many locals prefer dry adult-imitations.

On warm evenings in summer and autumn, mudeyes crawl out of the water to hatch, and any patch of sticks is likely to come alive with rising trout. The fishing usually peaks at dusk but can continue throughout the night. Big wet flies (such as fur flies) and buoyant dries (such as corks) are reliable favourites.

The mayfly hatches are no match for those in the Central Highlands, though they can prompt worthwhile surface activity. Smutting fish are especially common. Ideal conditions are warm, overcast and calm. Boating is a distinct advantage.

Because of the dark tea-coloured water, Pedder can hardly be recommended to the polaroid enthusiast, and herein lies the lakes biggest fault. If the weather is bad (and it often is) all you can really hope to do is blind-flog the banks. This usually results in one or two hard-earned trout, especially when fishing at dusk, but it is not as much fun as it is in Lake Burbury.

Special regulations

Lake Pedder is reserved for the use of artificial lures and flies. All inflowing waters, and radii of 50 m around each stream mouth, are closed to fishing at all times.

The impoundment is included in the Southwest National Park and special park regulations apply (see *Fishing in National Parks*, Introduction and section 5.2).

PEDDER RIVER

See *Nelson River*.

PENAH LAKE

Tasmap Mersey
Drainage Derwent system (via the Little River system)
Location Western Lakes

Penah is a labyrinth of bays and necks surrounded by relatively flat heathland and some woodland. There are a few deep shorelines but much of the periphery is quite shallow.

The trout (all browns) are generally in good condition and quite a few exceed 1.3 kg.

Spinning and polaroiding are most reliable.

See also *Fishing in National Parks*, 5.1.

PENCIL PINE TARN

Tasmap Mersey
Drainage Natural – Derwent system (via James system)
Location Western Lakes

Although not especially deep, Pencil Pine Tarn has no extensive wadeable shallows. Spinning and polaroiding are most reliable, though wet-fly

fishing in the small backwaters is worthwhile when levels are high. Typical brown trout weigh 0.7-1.2 kg.

Scattered along the main tributary stream are several undercut pools and marshy lagoons which harbour a few larger-than-average fish.

See also *Fishing in National Parks*, 5.1.

PENGUIN CREEK

Tasmap Forth
Drainage Direct to Bass Strait

A tiny overgrown water containing plenty of small brown trout. Bait fishing is most practical.

PENNY LAGOON

Tasmap King Island Special
Drainage Isolated coastal lagoon

Each year from 1970 to 1976 there were liberations of 5000-25000 brown trout fry, and the NWFA reported captures in excess of 3 kg. The water does not appear by name on official stocking records published after 1977.

See also *King Island*.

Some of the small lagoons near Pencil Pine Tarn provide exceptional sport.

PENSTOCK LAGOON

Tasmap   Shannon
Drainage   Derwent system (via the Waddamana Power
Station and the Ouse system)

This prized fly water is discussed in detail in the
book Trout Guide *(Rob Sloane and Greg French,*
1991). A summary only is given here.

Description

Penstock is surrounded by alpine woodland but
has many grassy esplanades. It lies behind a
6.1 m high rockfill dam and has a normal operating range of just 8 cm. Full supply is 919.58 m
above sea level.

The lagoon played a pivotal role in the original
Great Lake power scheme. Water from Great
Lake was conveyed via Shannon Lagoon and a
canal system to Penstock Lagoon, where it was
directed into penstocks and dropped nearly 80 m
to the Waddamana Power Station on the banks of
the River Ouse.

Since 1964-65 Great Lake has been diverted
north into the South Esk catchment, and only
water sufficient to meet downstream riparian
requirements is passed through the lagoon and
power station (see *Great Lake* and *Shannon*
Lagoon).

The water is often turbid, and the stable levels
have fostered heavy shoreline weed growth.

History

Penstock Lagoon was formed in 1915 in conjunction with the Great Lake power scheme and
it soon became a prized fly fishing venue, though
in the early years it was overshadowed by the
tremendous fishery at Great Lake.

While the early fishing at Penstock was not
well documented, NTFA reports indicate that by
the 1930s the average weight of the trout was
about 2½ lb and that browns were dominant.

A second canal between the Shannon and
Penstock was built between 1939 and 1949,
increasing considerably the flow through the
lagoon. Associated with this was the construction of a second power station at Waddamana
(Waddamana B).

In 1949 a portion of canal above the Shannon
Power Station burst, resulting in the severe siltation of Penstock. It is claimed that the revered mayfly hatches suffered as a result and, while dry fly
fishing later regained prominence, many old hands
maintain that the mayflies never fully recovered.

With the commissioning of the Poatina Power
Station in 1964-65, most of the water from Great
Lake was diverted away from Penstock. Small

amounts of electricity are generated from the
compulsory riparian requirement, but so little
water is used that the main power station at
Waddamana has already been closed and
Waddamana B will soon be shut down as well.
The No. 1 Canal from Shannon is no longer used,
and the No. 2 Canal carries greatly reduced flows.

The changed flow-regimes led to a reduction
in natural recruitment of brown trout. The
lagoon was stocked with 1000 yearling rainbows
in 1968-69, complimenting existing wild stocks,
and the subsequent canal changes began to
favour the recruitment of rainbows. While rainbows never dominated in Penstock, numbers
increased markedly in the 1960s and 1970s.

The diversion of Ripple Creek into the Lagoon
of Islands in 1984 promised to relieve the HEC
of the need to supply so much of its riparian
obligation from Great Lake via No. 2 Canal and
Penstock. Options for future management of the
fishery were considered and it was concluded that
regular releases of brown trout and occasional
supplements of rainbows would be desirable. At
the same time a small weir was constructed on
No. 2 Canal to ensure that naturally spawned ova
and newly hatched fry would not become exposed
during periods of low flow.

In 1987 there was a dramatic decline in the
water quality at the Lagoon of Islands (see *Lagoon*
of Islands) and since that time the HEC has again
been forced to utilise water from Great Lake,
though the HEC plans to allow the water to
bypass Penstock Lagoon and Waddamana.

In recent times anglers have voiced concern
about increased discolouration of Penstock. This
has largely been attributed to suspended sediment
entering from Shannon Lagoon, though the possibility of algal enrichment is being monitored.

Trout stocks today

Brown trout dominate, though rainbows usually
account for about 10% of the annual harvest.
Some natural recruitment (of both species)
occurs in No. 2 Canal but there is complimentary
artificial stocking.

Trout of 1-2 kg are typical and a few attain 3 kg.

Trout liberations (since 1985)

Wild brown trout

YEAR	SIZE	NUMBER
1985	small fingerlings	2 000
"	fry	15 000
1986	small fingerlings	7 000
1987	small fingerlings	10 000
1988	fry	40 000

271

The fishing

Penstock is a respected early-season wet-fly water. Fishing slowly from a dinghy, or wading around the prominent weedbeds can be very effective. Frog feeders feature in September and October, and tadpoles are prominent in November. By early December damsel nymphs are a major dietary item.

Calm frosty mornings result in good midge hatches, while balmy mornings favour prolific hatches of smut.

Summer dun hatches, the main attraction for anglers, peak between Christmas and early February. It pays to be on the water before 10am and to fish through until 3pm, though the hatch usually peaks around midday. The trout respond best when the water is clear.

Jassids cause good rises during late March and early April.

Fishing early in the morning is highly recommended at any time of the year – the fish tail freely and rise well.

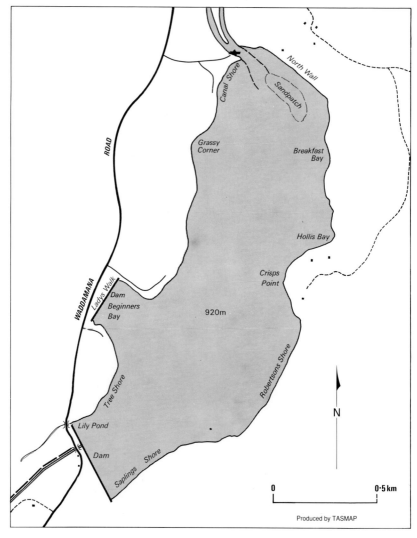

Produced by TASMAP

Boating

As the water is shallow and weedy, small dinghies are most appropriate. A rough access track and launching ramp are located on the western bank of the canal mouth.

Camping

Informal lakeshore camping is popular along the sheltered western shore. The most-used sites include the Canal Shore, Grassy Corner, and the northern shore of Beginners Bay.

Lake Perry

PERCHED LAKE

No trout. See *Fishing in National Parks*, 5.3.

PERRY, LAKE

Tasmap Huon
Drainage Huon system (via the Arve system)
Location Hartz Mountains

A clearwater lake at the foot of a densely-vegetated cirque. There are extensive wadeable shallows near the outflow, and several accessible rocky banks along the rest of the shoreline.

Brown trout of 0.3-0.5 kg are typical, though quite a few attain 1 kg or so.

While spinning is most reliable, there are good dun hatches on warm summer days and the larger fish can sometimes be polaroided.

Access is via a short well-formed foot path. Camping is not encouraged.

See also *Fishing in National Parks*, 5.6.

PET RESERVOIR

Tasmap Hellyer
Drainage Emu system (via the Pet River)

The Pet Reservoir, a domestic supply for Burnie, lies behind a 16 m high earthfill dam. It was formed in 1962 and raised in 1966. Full supply is 268 m above sea level but big drawdowns are to be expected in summer and autumn.

While most shores are gentle and grassy, there are pockets of trees nearby.

The water is usually slightly murky.

Trout stocks

The Pet is primarily a brown trout water. Most fish are the result of natural recruitment from the Pet River, though spawning is often limited because of low flow and stocks are enhanced through liberations of hatchery-reared fish. Most trout taken by anglers weigh 0.6-1 kg and a few exceed 1.3 kg.

Tiger trout (brook x brown hybrids) have been released in recent years but they have failed to make a significant contribution to anglers' bags.

Rainbow trout are not common and are only taken in some years. Most are the result of unrecorded liberations, though some may be escapees from farm dams in the Pet catchment.

Trout liberations (since 1985)

Wild brown trout

YEAR	SIZE	NUMBER
1986	fry	19 000
"	advanced fry	10 000
1987	advanced fry	15 000
"	fry	10 000
1988	fry	7 940
"	advanced fry	15 000
1989	advanced fry	7 940
1990	fry	18 000
"	advanced fry	20 000
1991	fry	16 000

Tiger trout

YEAR	SIZE	NUMBER
1991	advanced fry	700
1992	yearlings	1 100
1993	yearlings	400

The fishing

Trout can sometimes be seen during September/October chasing tadpoles in the shallows. But the most reliable sight fishing occurs on balmy January/February evenings when the mudeyes are on the move.

Though galaxias abound, trout feeding on baitfish are not a major feature.

Spinning and bait casting are very popular among locals.

Special regulations

Boating and camping are prohibited.

PETER, LAKE

Probably contains plenty of slow-growing brown trout. See *Margaret, Lake*.

PETRARCH, LAKE

Tasmap Nive
Drainage Derwent system (via the Cuvier River and Lake St Clair)

A shallow moderately tea-coloured water. The southern end is flanked by heath and woodland, while grass/sedge plains extend from the north-west. There are extensive wadeable shallows along the south-western shore and a large weedy marsh along the north-western shore. Deep water is found along the north-eastern bank and at the outflow.

The water abounds with brown trout. Fish caught in the open shallows are usually 0.3-0.5 kg, those taken in the deep water are usually 0.5-0.7 kg, and some in the marshes exceed 2 kg.

Fly fishers can take big bags by blind-fishing nymphs over the open shallows, but it is best to concentrate on the marsh. Early on calm mornings you are likely to find tailers, and on sunny days polaroiding is worthwhile. Fair hatches and beetle falls occur on hot days in summer and early autumn.

Spinning is best in the deeper water, though small Celtas are effective in the open shallows.

Access is via formed walking tracks from Cynthia Bay (3½-5 hrs each way) and Narcissus (2½-3½ hrs each way). The best campsites are among the trees at the south-eastern end. There are other sites on the exposed north-western plains.

See also *Fishing in National Parks*, 5.4.

Trout from the open shallows in Lake Petrarch. Those in the marsh are bigger and fatter.

PHILLIPS, LAKE

Probably contains plenty of slow-growing brown trout. See *Margaret, Lake*.

PICTON, LAKE

No trout. See *Fishing in National Parks*, 5.2.

PIEMAN, LAKE

Tasmaps Pieman and Sophia
Drainage Pieman River (a major instream impoundment)

Lake Pieman is an uninspiring fishery. Much better sport is found nearby in lakes Rosebery and Mackintosh.

Description

The Reece Dam impounding Lake Pieman is a 122 m high concrete-faced rockfill structure completed by the HEC in 1986. Full supply is 97.5 m above sea level and relatively rapid drawdowns are to be expected.

The tea-coloured water floods a steep densely-forested section of the Pieman River, though much of the vegetation at the dam end was ravaged by wildfire in the early 1980s. While extensive timber-salvage operations were undertaken prior to flooding, some areas were simply too steep to log and there are many stands of drowned trees, especially in the remote corners of the impoundment.

Access and facilities

Sealed roads extend from Tullah and Zeehan to the main boat-launching area at the damsite. Other launching ramps exist at the Wilson River and at the Ring River. The Ring River Road is gated but keys are held by members of the local angling clubs.

Several rugged logging tracks extend to various remote corners of the lake, though most are gated and locked and none are of special significance to anglers.

Access along the shores

Steep banks and impenetrable scrub greatly restrict opportunities for shore-based sport. However, there is limited scope for casting and set-rod fishing at the damsite, the Wilson Bridge and the Ring River boat ramp.

Trout stocks

The Pieman River has long supported plenty of small brown trout and existing stocks were sufficient to provide immediate sport in the new lake.

The impoundment is deep and biologically un-productive and, as expected, there was no great growth boom. Since the first season the average weight has remained at about 0.5 kg. The catch rate is quite good, perhaps 2-4 fish per angler per day, but not good enough to place the fishery in high esteem among anglers.

Rainbow trout (emigrants from lakes Rosebery and Mackintosh) are taken from time to time.

The fishing

Trolling with big Cobras and spoons is most effective, the hot spots being near the mouths of the tributary streams.

Modest rises occur on warm days in summer and autumn.

PIEMAN RIVER

Tasmaps Conical Rocks and Pieman
Drainage Direct to the Southern Ocean

The Pieman supports worthwhile resident browns throughout the year but is only very popular among anglers at sea trout time.

Description

The Pieman River now extends only from the coast to the Reece Dam at Lake Pieman – all of the upper reaches have been inundated by hydro-electric scheme impoundments.

At the heads, there are sedge and bracken flats. Elsewhere the river is flanked by dense wet-forest, though the upper section, from Corinna to the Reece Dam, was ravaged by wildfire in the early 1980s.

The water is tea coloured and is regulated at the foot of the Reece Dam.

The land 500 m each side of the centre-line of the river is a State Reserve and is subject to nor-mal National Park regulations (see introduction to *Fishing in National Parks*, section 5).

Access and facilities

Rough vehicular tracks (4WD only) lead from Granville Harbour and the Reece Dam to the shack area on the southern bank near the heads.

The family car can be taken along the 60 km or so of no-through-road from Waratah to Corinna. In the forest at Corinna there is a good amenities block, informal caravan and tent-sites, and a con-crete launching ramp. Two original buildings from the old gold-mining era, leased from the PWS by local entrepreneurs, are available for rent. While the accommodation is rugged, there are communal gas stoves, generator lighting and hot water. Early booking is essential, especially if you intend to visit at sea trout time. Dinghies are available for hire. A cruise ferry, the *Arcadia II*, operates on a regular basis.

There is no public vehicular access to the base of the Reece Dam, though you can make your way down on foot.

Trout stocks

The trout stocks in the Pieman can probably be traced back as far as the early attempts to estab-lish fish at Lake Lea (see *Lea, Lake*). Resident trout typically weigh 0.3-0.7 kg and can be caught throughout the year.

Sea trout are taken from August to December, the peak time being from mid September to late November. These fish are mostly 0.5-2 kg, though much larger specimens are also reported. A 30 lb fish was mentioned in a Parliamentary report of 1912, and several fish in excess of 9 kg have been taken in recent years.

Relatively small numbers of naturally-spawned rainbow trout were taken in the sections of the river now inundated by lakes Rosebery and Mackintosh. The species is still common in some headwater tributaries (such as the Vale River).

Boat fishing

A strong dinghy or small runabout is essential to enjoy the best of the fishing. The only good launching ramp is at Corinna, though small boats can be taken by 4WD to the heads.

All of the river is suited to trolling and you are best advised to cover as much water as possible until you find a hot spot.

Fly fishers will find good sight fishing only when the trout are chasing whitebait. You need to spend time searching the river for bow-waves, splashes and showering baitfish. Sometimes trout will be found working along the edges among the bands of sparse strap-weed, though the real hot spots are the First Rapid and the Second Rapid some 15-16 km above Corinna (2-3 km below the Reece Dam). While many of the fish taking whitebait will be resident browns, sea trout can account for 50 % or more of the catch.

Shore-based fishing

Fishing from the shore is only attractive when the whitebait are running. There is ample room at the heads, where good bags are taken by spin-ning, bait casting, and blind fishing with wet flies.

At Corinna there is little scope for anything other than set-rod fishing.

Some 100 m below the Reece Dam there is a shallow shingle bank where you often see trout charging around after baitfish, though significant

Sea trout from the Pieman

numbers of trout are likely to be found only in the latter part of the sea trout season (early October to December). This spot is easily accessible from the eastern bank and is ideal for all trouting methods.

The rest of the river is conveniently accessible only if you have a boat.

The Pieman River Power Development

The Pieman River Power Development was approved by the State Government in 1971 and construction began in 1974. Lake Mackintosh was completed in 1981, followed by Lake Murchison in 1982, Lake Rosebery in 1983, and Lake Pieman in 1986. The project was finalised in 1987.

As a result of the development, the Pieman River above the Reece Dam is completely flooded, and flows in the lower reaches are subject to major manipulation. To date this has had little major effect on trout stocks except that baitfish and sea trout now accumulate at the foot of the Reece Dam.

In March 1990 there was a significant fish kill in the Pieman River. Despite early fears of a major spill of toxic waste from nearby mines, the problem was eventually found to be caused by water from the Reece Power Station becoming supersaturated with air. This water caused gas-bubble disease (not unlike divers' bends) among

fish. There was no lasting contamination of the water, nor any major impact on overall trout stocks, and the HEC has taken steps to ensure that the problem does not recur.

PIG RUN CREEK

Tasmaps Forester and St Patricks
Drainage Direct to the North Esk River

A tiny rural creek containing plenty of 0.1-0.2 kg brown trout. Celta fishing and bait casting are most appropriate.

PIGSTY RIVER

See *D'Entrecasteaux River.*

PILLANS LAKE

Tasmap Mersey
Drainage Natural – Derwent system (via James system)
Location Western Lakes

The land surrounding Pillans Lake was devastated by wildfire in 1961. While heath and grass have re-established in some areas, the terrain remains quite barren.

Many shores are rocky and deep, but there are also extensive sand/silt flats. Polaroiding and

A Pillans trout sucks in a nymph

spinning are most reliable, though fair rises occur on warm summer days. Most trout weigh 0.5-1.5 kg. Rainbows are exceedingly scarce.

Numerous tributary streams feed Pillans – and scattered along these are plenty of small stillwaters. The best way to explore these systems is to follow them from mouth to source. Instream lakes generally hold trout up to about 1.5 kg, while dead-end lakes at the heads of tributary runnels are likely to contain trophies.

See also *Fishing in National Parks*, 5.1.

PINE LAKE

Location Southwest National Park

No trout. See *Fishing in National Parks*, 5.2.

PINE LAKE

Tasmap Meander
Drainage Natural – Derwent system (via Great Lake)

Charles Harrison (*Fishing and Tourists*, 1934) wrote:

'In November 1895, it was arranged to make a trip from Deloraine and, in so doing so to stock with trout the Pine Lake, a small sheet some four miles north of Great Lake ... constituting the original stocking ... The trout thrived well in

this lake and reached a size of 8 lb., but once the food supply was overcome they receded in both weight and condition.

In 1944 the SFFC undertook research at the lake and, in an attempt to bolster biological production, laid down manufactured fertilizer. At the same time, the water was restocked with some 8000 brown trout fry. These actions had no appreciable effect on the quality of the fishing.

In 1970-71 some 600 yearling rainbows were turned out, again with no lasting benefit.

Today Pine Lake supports plenty of naturally-spawned brown trout and few fish exceed 0.6 kg.

The water is very exposed and crystal clear. Good rises occur on warm summer evenings.

The upper Liffey River (a small creek) has been diverted into Pine Lake in order to bolster the Great Lake catchment.

As a result of a fungal disease in the nearby native vegetation, the lake was placed under indefinite quarantine in July 1994.

PINE TIER LAGOON

Tasmap Nive
Drainage Derwent system (via the Nive system)

Pine Tier Lagoon contains plenty of small trout and offers even the novice a good chance of bagging fish. It is discussed in detail in the book

277

Trout Guide *(Rob Sloane and Greg French, 1991). A summary only is given here.*

Description

Pine Tier is a narrow elongate storage set in a steep forested valley. It lies behind a 37 m high concrete dam and, as it is used primarily to divert water (via canal) towards Bronte Lagoon, the normal operating range is less than 3 m. Full supply is 670.56 m above sea level.

Water is received from the natural catchments of the Nive and Pine rivers (which drain the Western Lakes) and is characteristically clear. An extensive grassy esplanade, with adjacent weedy shallows, extends along the northern and north-western shores.

History

The Pine Tier Dam was completed in 1953. The drowned streams supported plenty of naturally-spawned browns and rainbows, and there was almost immediate overpopulation. By 1957 some anglers were claiming that only one in five trout were of takeable size.

Trout stocks today

The fishery is maintained entirely by natural recruitment. Brown trout dominate but rainbows account for about 20% of the annual harvest. Typical fish weigh 0.3-0.7 kg.

The fishing

The best wet-fly fishing is found along the marshy margins at the northern end when water is rising after heavy spring rains. At these times it is possible to catch respectable fish of 1 kg or so.

The northern end is also the preferred spot for night-time bait fishing. Worms work well when the water is discoloured after heavy rain, though grubs are favoured at other times.

The eastern shore is ideal for dry fly fishing on warm summer days. Gum beetles are taken eagerly, and it is worthwhile blind searching with a Red Tag if nothing is rising.

All of the deeper shores are suited to lure casting from the banks and drift spinning from boats. The mouths of the Nive and Pine rivers are hot spots. Small Celtas are recommended.

Camping

The most popular camping areas are on the grassy flats at the northern end.

Boating

The only reasonable boat launching area is where the original Gowan Brae Road (now flooded) enters the mouth of the main northern bay.

PINEY CREEK

Tasmap Pieman
Drainage Pieman system (via Lake Pieman)

A small tea-coloured fastwater containing plenty of slow-growing brown trout. It is quite well respected among local bait casters and Celta fishers.

PIONEER DAM

Tasmap Forester
Drainage Ringarooma system
Location Pioneer

The dam at Pioneer was stocked as early as 1906-07 when 350 yearling rainbows were released. Stocking continued until at least the 1940s.

Today the lake is reputed to contain a few browns, but it is not often fished. It is set in flat scrubby woodland, and large beds of dense emergent rushes choke the margins. Access is restricted to a few small sites on the dam wall.

The water is dark with tannin.

PIONEER, LAKE

Tasmap Forester
Drainage Ringarooma system
Location Pioneer

Lake Pioneer is a flooded quarry. The shores incorporate stark-white cliffs, barren quartzite-gravel 'dunes', and pockets of scrub. The surrounding terrain comprises light woodland and dense bush. The water is deep and dark with tannin.

The lake has never been officially stocked but, while it is not a recognised trout fishery, it may well contain a few browns.

PIPERS BROOK

Tasmap St Patricks
Drainage Direct to the Pipers River estuary.

Sea trout are taken from the estuary (see *Pipers River*).

The stream proper is very overgrown but holds plenty of small brown trout.

PIPERS LAGOON

Tasmap Tamar
Drainage Direct to the Meander River

Pipers Lagoon is not a permanent lake but merely a well-defined flood plain. It fishes well when the Meander River is swollen (see *Meander River*).

PIPERS RIVER

Tasmap   St Patricks
Drainage   Direct to Bass Strait

According to early records of the NTAA, brown trout were well established by the turn of the century. A small lot of brook trout yearlings were released in 1904, but without benefit.

Sea trout

The estuary is a clearwater flanked by dunes. The surrounding vegetation progresses from marram grass to heath to light woodland. At low tide the water recedes back to a narrow well-defined channel, exposing extensive white-sand flats.

Small dinghies can be launched at Weymouth and Bellingham and, unless the tide is very high, you can walk upstream along the sand flats.

The sea trout fishing is usually quite good, peaking from late August to late November. During incoming low tides fishing the main channel from the sand is effective. At high tide the hot spots are the head of the estuary (accessible by dinghy) and the lower freshwater reaches.

River residents

Above the tidal reaches, in the vicinity of Weymouth Farm and Back Creek, the river flows across pasture through a narrow band of bush. While access to the water is simple enough, paperbarks and scrub form a canopy, and the long silty broadwaters are too deep to wade. The current is always quite visible, and the water always turbid. While spinning and bait fishing are most practical, the water sometimes floods out into the paddocks providing short-term wet-fly fishing. Brown trout of 0.3-0.7 kg are typical and some grow bigger.

The uppermost reaches, in the rural Bangor, Karoola and Lilydale districts, contain plenty of small brown trout but are largely overgrown. While good bags can be taken from the more accessible stretches on Celtas and baits, I prefer to fish tributaries such as the Second River.

PITT, LAKE

Tasmap   Mersey
Drainage   Mersey system (via the Fisher system)
Location   Chudleigh Lakes

The banks vary from steep rocky drops to grassy flats, and the water is clear.

There is a substantial gutter connection to Lake Explorer and natural recruitment is quite high. Some large fish are reported but most weigh 0.7-1.5 kg.

Polaroiding and spinning are most reliable, though the backwaters provide good wet-fly fishing when levels are very high.

See also *Fishing in National Parks*, 5.1.

PLATYPUS TARN

Possibly no trout. See *Fishing in National Parks*, 5.5.

PLENTY RIVER

Tasmap   Tyenna
Drainage   Direct to the River Derwent at Plenty

The Plenty has a unique place in Australian fishing lore – it was the cradle of brown trout in Australasia.

Description

The Plenty is essentially a fastwater flowing over a shingle bed. The water becomes turbid after heavy rain but clears during dry spells.

The lower 10 km (from the Derwent to Feilton) are flanked by cash crops and marginal pasture, but many banks are fringed with trees and scrub. Due to irrigation demands, summer/autumn flows can be very poor and at times there is little visible flow in some pools. However, many of the deep holes stretch from undercut bank to undercut bank and are well shaded.

The upper reaches flow between steep wooded hills. While most pools are relatively shallow, there is always some flow.

History

The Salmon Ponds, the first trout hatchery in the Southern Hemisphere, was built on the banks of the Plenty in 1862, and the first brown trout and Atlantic salmon were hatched there in 1864 (see *About Our Sportfish*, 2.1 and 2.4). The facility has remained in continuous production and is now maintained as an operational hatchery museum (see *About Tasmania*, section 1).

All salmonid species introduced to the State have been handled at the Salmon Ponds (see *About Our Sportfish*, 2.1-2.6) but, while there have been releases of each to the Plenty (both intentional and otherwise), only brown trout have established.

Trout stocks

A deliberate release of 40 brown trout occurred in April 1865, followed by further stocking from 1866. Early Parliamentary reports show that a 3 lb brown trout was caught in January 1867, and that a 9 ¼ lb fish was taken in June 1868. By 1868 the number of fish seen spawning was 'amazing', and in the 1870s wild river fish of up to 20 lb were handled by hatchery staff. As numbers increased, the average size fell and by the turn of the century the normal size-range was much as it is today.

The river now teems with 0.1-0.5 kg browns but also carries a respectable number of much larger specimens. A limit bag (12 fish) is likely to contain two or more 0.7-1 kg – and anglers who fish regularly expect to take a couple of 2-3 kg fish each season. Some of the large fish are escapees from the Salmon Ponds and some are sea trout, but most are wild river-residents.

Escapees from the Salmon Ponds are common in the lower 4-6 km. You always stand a reasonable chance of catching a rainbow and, depending upon breeding programmes and policy with regard to excess stock, you may also find the occasional brook trout, Atlantic salmon, albino, triploid and/or hybrid.

Traps, weirs and races

In 1885 the Commissioners proposed that a fish trap be constructed on the Plenty River at Redlands so that wild sea trout could be stripped for their ova. By the following winter, the project had been completed. This structure, located a few hundred metres downstream from the Salmon Ponds, has been restored and rebuilt several times. According to the STLAA, major works (including the construction of a penning pond and fish ladder) were undertaken in 1944-45.

The trap has not been used for serious ova collection since the formation of the IFC in 1959, and in recent years it had become quite dilapidated. In 1993 the IFC announced that the Bridgewater branch of the STLAA was again reconstructing the Plenty trap. From a management point of view, the trap is irrelevant (the sea trout maintain themselves by natural recruitment) – but it is certainly of historical significance. Remember that it is illegal to fish within 100 m of any fish trap maintained by the IFC.

Access / Where to fish

The mouth of the Plenty can be reached by walking across open paddocks from the Glenora Road at Plenty. However, most of the stream between Plenty and the Salmon Ponds is very overgrown with willows and difficult to fish.

The best pools (or, at least, the ones with the best fish) are located in the 3 km stretch extending upstream from the Salmon Ponds. A public road leads from the Glenora Road to the Salmon Ponds and, while you are likely to be questioned by IFC staff if you walk through the hatchery grounds armed with a rod, you can (with the landowners' consent) walk across the nearby paddocks.

Feilton, on the upper Plenty River, can be reached via the Plenty Valley Road. Walking upstream from the road bridge is a good strategy if you want to catch good bags of small trout.

The uppermost reaches, some 15 km above Feilton, are also accessible by road. This area offers the least remarkable sport, though there are still plenty of half-pounders.

The nature of the fishing

The Plenty fishes best when levels are moderate to low. While bait casting and Celta fishing are most popular, there is plenty of scope for the fly enthusiast. On hot days you can find a few fish rising to take grasshoppers and beetles and, when the water is clear, polaroiding is worthwhile. But the real action for fly fishers occurs when using large wets and buoyant dries on warm calm evenings. Any fish which moves at dusk is likely to make a savage strike, and you get surprising results even when fishing blind. Evening and night are also the very best times to fool the bigger trout.

PLIMSOLL, LAKE

(shown on many pre-1993 maps as Lake Anthony)

Tasmap　Sophia
Drainage　Pieman system (via the Anthony River)
Location　West Coast Range

Tea coloured Lake Plimsoll was formed in 1993 as a part of the Anthony River Power Development. It lies behind a 47 m high concrete-faced rockfill dam. Full supply is 513.1 m above sea level and the normal operating range is more than 8 m.

The impoundment flooded a vast buttongrass plain and there is little emergent timber. The surrounding peaks are clothed in verdant heath and are nothing less than spectacular.

When the power scheme was approved by Parliament, the upper Anthony catchment was trout-free. Years before the lake formed, the IFC began seeding the streams with brook trout, hoping that sufficient stocks could be established to ensure immediate sport when the lake filled. Natural recruitment in the streams and natural lakes was recorded as early as 1991, and a net survey of the lake in early 1994 showed that overall numbers were exceeding expectations.

Now that the lake has inundated much of the stream network, spawning is largely confined to the remaining 1.5 km of the Anthony River (between Lake Plimsoll and Lake Rolleston). However, there will be some recruitment from two smaller creeks, one midway along the eastern shore and the other a kilometre west of the Anthony. There is little opportunity for spawning in the Henty Canal, and the outflow creek from Lake Selina is accessible to Plimsoll fish only when Lake Plimsoll is approaching full supply.

As good numbers of trout were in the lake at the time of flooding, and ongoing supplementary stocking with hatchery-reared fry and fingerlings is planned, there will be plenty of fish to take advantage of the boom in biological production which typifies new shallow impoundments. Brook trout have already done well in the nearby natural lakes (see *Rolleston, Lake* and *Selina, Lake*) and it seems likely that, over the next few seasons, the average size will rise to 2 kg or more. But militating against the establishment of a true feature-fishery are the planned dramatic drawdowns – drawdowns which will leave much of the lake bed exposed and deny the establishment of dynamic food-rich feeding areas.

Several drowned 2WD spurs leading from the Anthony Road are suitable boat launching areas, though all were gated in 1993-94.

There is ample scope for spinning from the shore.

Fly fishers will probably rely heavily on blind fishing with big wets, though there may be worthwhile mudeye migrations in summer.

Brook trout are difficult to establish but are easily caught. Over-harvesting may become the biggest threat to wild stocks, so a voluntary daily kill of two fish is advocated (release as many as you like).

There are no facilities and, as the surrounding land is wet and uneven, informal camping is largely unappealing.

Brook trout liberations

The stream system

YEAR	SIZE	NUMBER
1986	fingerlings	*
"	adults	+
1987	advanced fry	8 000
1989	advanced fry	1 000
"	small fingerlings	700

* = part-share of 5060
+ = part-share of 250

The lake

YEAR	SIZE	NUMBER
1993	small fingerlings	18 000

See also *West Coast Range*.

A Plimsoll brook trout taken in April 1994 – less than a year after the lake was formed

POA, LAKE

No trout. See *Fishing in National Parks*, 5.1.

POGANA, LAKE

Tasmap   Mersey
Drainage   Derwent system (via the Little River system)
Location   Western Lakes

A clearwater contained by small wooded hills. The shores are rocky and well defined, but most are wadeable. Spinning is usually very worthwhile. Feature fishing for fly fishers occurs in summer and early autumn when there are phenomenal rises to black spinners and terrestrials. Don't forget your polaroids!

Most fish seen weigh 0.6-1 kg, though some attain 1.5 kg.

See also *Fishing in National Parks*, 5.1.

POLYCARP, LAKE

Tasmap   Sophia
Drainage   Henty system (via the Yolande system)
Location   West Coast Range

Records from the Lake Margaret Hatchery show that in October 1930 some 600 yearling trout were liberated into Lake Polycarp – and it is likely that the lake now supports plenty of slow-growing naturally-spawned fish.

The easiest access is cross-country from the north-eastern end of Lake Margaret.

See also *West Coast Range*.

PORT SORELL

Tasmap   Tamar
Drainage   Direct to Bass Strait

At low tide Port Sorell is little more than a network of narrow channels cutting through a wide mud flat. At high tide the water stretches from forested bank to forested bank.

From August to early December the sea trout fishing can be quite remarkable. Incoming tides are best, though it pays to fish over or near the deepwater channels. Hot spots include the beach at the village of Port Sorell, Bakers Point, Squeaking Point, Eagle Point and Finger Point. The waters beneath the bridges on the Frankford Road are also good, though movement along the banks at high tide can be awkward. Boats can be launched at Port Sorell.

All the relevant features, including the channels and place names, are marked on the *Port Sorell* and *Harford* 1:25000 Tasmaps.

The small waters in the Powena Creek system are well worth a look.

POSSUM CREEK

See *Nelson Bay River*

POWENA CREEK

Tasmap Mersey
Drainage Derwent system (via the Pine system)
Location Western Lakes

While the stone/shingle bottomed stream between Lake Antimony and Lake Fanny does not provide good fishing, the myriad lakes between Lake Fanny and the Daisy Lakes are ideal for both spinning and fly fishing. Anglers prepared to put in time exploring the small 'less-likely' tarns are likely to be rewarded with better-than-average brown trout.

See also *Fishing in National Parks*, 5.1.

PRINCESS RIVER

Tasmap Franklin
Drainage King system (via Lake Burbury)

A small tea-coloured fastwater. It was regularly stocked with brown trout fry in the early 1930s and received a part-share of 36 000 rainbow fry in 1934. While the brown trout thrived, the rainbows disappeared (see *King River*).

Today the stream contains lots of 0.2-0.3 kg resident browns, and is also used by lake spawners.

PROMONTORY LAKE

No trout. See *Fishing in National Parks*, 5.2.

PROSSER RIVER

Tasmap Prosser
Drainage Direct to the Mercury Passage

The Prosser system is one of the most noteworthy of the East Coast trout waters.

Description

The water is often very murky but clears appreciably in settled weather.

The lower 10 km winds through a gentle dry-woodland valley. Here the river is a string of long deep broadwaters, most of which are overgrown with native scrub.

From Brockley (near the Tea Tree Rivulet junction) to Buckland, the river is flanked by flat marginal farmland. The water runs through a series of deep pools separated by short marshy

and/or clay-bottomed runnels. Many banks are overgrown with scrub, willows and blackberries.

Above Buckland, between Ardross and Levendale, the setting is mostly native bushland. Normal summer flows are minimal and the river is often reduced to a series of small pools scattered along an exposed shingle/clay bed.

Trout stocks

According to early Parliamentary reports, the Prosser was stocked with brown trout as early as 1878 when 450 fry were released. Wild stocks soon firmly established.

In 1966 there was an experimental release of 150 adult fish. Each year from 1981 to 1983 the river received 75 000 brown trout fry, and in 1986 the dams were stocked with 25 000 brown trout fry. However, stocking has had no observable impact on the quality of fishing.

While the trout population remains relatively small, the size of the fish is good. Most fish taken from the deep pools between the estuary and Buckland weigh 0.3-1 kg and a few attain 2 kg. Above Buckland you encounter a greater percentage of 0.1-0.3 kg fish, though there are still some sizeable specimens in the deep shady lies.

Sea trout and the lower reaches

Sea trout can be taken from August to January, though the runs are never big.

While trout are occasionally caught by native-fish enthusiasts trolling in the estuary, the serious trout fisher is best advised to concentrate on the kilometre of freshwater pools in the wooded gorge between the head of the estuary and the dam. Hot spots are the open rocky banks at the limit of tidal influence, and the big pool at the foot of the dam, though scrub-bashing along the more remote pools can be rewarding indeed.

Even when the sea trout are scarce, you stand a good chance of taking resident browns to 1.3 kg or so.

Domestic rainbows (escapees from sea pens much further south down the coast) were commonly taken during the mid to late 1980s, but none have been reported in recent years (see *About Our Sportfish*, 2.2).

Where to fish for resident trout

The hot spots are: the accessible stretches between the estuary and the Lower Prosser Dam, the pool below the Upper Prosser Dam, and the deep holes between Brockley and Buckland. There are a few good pools in the Zelwood/Ardross area as well, but the quality and quantity of the trout deteriorates as you move further upstream.

The backwater lagoons in the Prosser system often contain good-sized trout. (photo by Frances Latham)

These are several large permanent and semi-permanent backwater lagoons between Brockley and Buckland which become joined to the river during floods and contain a few large brown trout. These waters do not provide feature fishing but are always worth a look if you happen to be passing by.

Spinning

Lure casting is best when levels are high to moderate. As flows subside and the water clears, the trout become increasingly temperamental. Most pools are quite long and deep, so fish-spoon wobblers are appropriate. Celtas are good in the shallows.

Bait fishing

One of the most effective ways to catch trout is by surface fishing with grubs at dusk. Daytime fishing with grasshoppers is effective in summer and autumn.

Fly fishing

Blind casting with wet flies is quite productive when levels are moderately high. Sight fishing is largely confined to balmy evenings when the trout rise to beetles and other terrestrials, though polaroiding is possible when the water is very clear.

The dams

The Lower Prosser Dam is located about 1 km above the estuary. It is an 8 m high concrete structure, built in 1964 to impound water for domestic use at Orford. The dam floods a dry scrubby gorge/valley and access along the banks is awkward. While trout in excess of 1 kg are taken, most serious anglers tend to concentrate on the river below.

The 5 m high Upper Prosser Dam, located about halfway between Orford and Buckland, is also made of concrete. It was formed in 1972 to augment the original water supply. Like the first dam, it is of relatively difficult access and is not held in high regard by local anglers. Nonetheless, it holds plenty of good trout to 1.5 kg – and I have taken big bags near the sluggish inflow late in the season when the trout feed on small tench.

The tributaries

Some of the best angling in the Prosser system is found in Brushy Plains Rivulet and Tea Tree Rivulet. While good fish frequent the Bluff, Sand and Back rivers, these waters are largely overgrown and unappealing. The small headwater tributaries, such as Nelsons Creek, are intermittent and have little to offer for the angler.

PUMP POND

Tasmap Nive
Drainage Derwent system (via the Tarraleah Canals system)

The Pump Pond is a small clearwater lake on the Tarraleah Canal No 2 (completed in 1955). It lies in forest behind a 8 m high earthfill dam. At full supply it is 647.39 m above sea level but drawdowns of more than 4 m are to be expected.

The lake can be fished from the dam wall and adjacent shores, and parts can be waded. There are plenty of 0.3-0.7 kg brown trout and the average catch rate is impressive. Spinning is effective during rough and/or overcast conditions, and there is reliable dry-fly fishing when the weather is fine.

QUAMBY BROOK

Tasmaps Tamar and Meander
Drainage South Esk system (via the Meander River)

Quamby Brook flows through pasture and harbours lots of 0.2-0.4 kg brown trout. According to early NTFA reports, rainbows were released as early as 1917-18, but this species failed to establish.

The lower reaches, from the Meander to Westbury, are choked with willows and are best suited to set-rod fishing. Fly fishing is worthwhile only during floods when the water creeps out beyond the willows into the paddocks.

From Westbury to Golden Valley there is scope for wading and accurate Celta fishing.

QUEECHY POND

Tasmap St Patricks
Drainage North Esk system (via Kings Meadows Rivulet)

Queechy Pond was constructed by the Launceston branch of the NTFA between 1962 and 1969. It is managed for juvenile anglers and is subject to special regulations (check your Fishing Code).

QUEEN RIVER

Tasmap Franklin
Drainage Direct to the King River

A 'dead' stream heavily polluted with metals and sludge (see *King River*). Trout exist in some tributaries, notably the West Queen River and Halls Creek.

QUOIN RIVULET

An intermittent creek with little to offer for the trout fisher.

RAPID RIVER

Tasmap Arthur River
Drainage Direct to the Arthur River

A large tea-coloured fastwater flowing through dense wet-forest. It contains plenty of slow-growing brown trout but, as the only convenient access is via the remote Rapid River (forestry) Road, it is not often fished.

RATTLER RIVER

Tasmap Hellyer
Drainage Direct to the Inglis River at Takone

A small fastwater creek which contains plenty of tiny brown trout. According to early NTFA reports rainbows were released as early as 1911-12 and were still being caught in 1916. None survive today.

RAVENSDALE RIVULET

An intermittent creek with little to offer the trout fisher.

RAYNER, LAKE

Tasmap Tyenna
Drainage Derwent system (via the Tyenna system)
Location Mt Field

In 1961 the STLAA recorded that '*Lake Rayner ... was stocked three years ago, and the rainbow are similar to those in Nichols, but rather better condition*'. It is unlikely that any trout survive today.

See also *Fishing in National Parks*, 5.5.

REBECCA LAGOON

Tasmap Sandy Cape
Drainage Coastal lagoon

Rebecca Lagoon is a small weedy water with a maximum depth of about 1.8 m. There is no scope for natural recruitment of trout.

According to NTFA reports, stocking first occurred in 1951 when 12 000-15 000 brown trout fry were turned out. By 1953 the fish had attained

1 kg or so. Restocking (with advanced brown trout fry) occurred in 1957. In 1959 net-surveys by the SFFC showed that the lake carried trout of 2½-7 lb but that most were infested with worms (see *Curries River Dam*).

In 1961-62 some 10 000 rainbow fingerlings were released, though these '*did not do well*'.

Some 6600 brook trout yearlings were liberated in 1970-71, and by June 1972 there was '*no trace*' of them.

It is unlikely that the lagoon will again be considered for restocking.

REDWATER CREEK

Tasmap Forth
Drainage Direct to the Mersey River near Railton

A small fastwater creek which carries lots of tiny brown trout.

REEDY LAKE

No trout. See *Fishing in National Parks*.

REPULSE, LAKE

Tasmaps Tyenna and Shannon
Drainage Derwent River (a major instream impoundment)

Description

Lake Repulse lies in a forested valley behind a 42 m high concrete-arch dam. It was formed in 1968 as part of the Lower Derwent Power Development. At full supply it is 121.92 m above sea level but drawdowns of more than 5 m are to be expected. The water is often very-slightly turbid and has a faint tinge of tannin.

Access and facilities

There is convenient 2WD access to the damsite, and to the Catagunya Power Station at the head of the lake. Several minor forestry roads extend to the south-western shore from the Dawson Road, all of which are well marked on the *Ouse* 1:25 000 Tasmap.

There are no camping facilities.

A crude boat launching area exists near the southern end of the dam.

Fish stocks

Naturally-spawned brown trout of 0.4-1 kg are quite common. Rainbows are scarce.

Stunted redfin perch abound.

The fishing

There is scope for comfortable shore-based spinning near the southern end of the dam and midway along the eastern shore. Elsewhere you have to contend with scrubby and/or steep banks.

Fly fishing is unremarkable, though good rises occur on warm summer/autumn days when the gum beetles are flying.

REPULSE RIVER

Tasmap Tyenna
Drainage Derwent system (via Lake Repulse)

A small clear fastwater which holds plenty of small resident browns and, late in the season, a few lake spawners.

RESERVOIR LAKES

No trout. See *Fishing in National Parks*, 5.2.

RHONA, LAKE

No trout. See *Fishing in National Parks*, 5.3.

RICHMOND, LAKE

Tasmap Nive
Drainage Direct to the Gordon River

A deep clearwater impounded by steep densely-forested hills. While it contains plenty of very small brown trout, fish to 1 kg or so are common. Lure casting is the most reliable method, though there are fair rises on hot days and fish can be polaroided along the edges whenever there is good light.

The easiest access is a stiff cross-country hike from the Guelph Basin or the Clark Dam (Lake King William). There are limited informal tent sites near the outflow.

Nearby Banana Lake probably contains a much better class of fish, while the lakes to the south (including Warwick and Stuart) probably do not hold trout.

See also *Fishing in National Parks*, 5.3.

RIDGEWAY RESERVOIR

Public fishing is not allowed.

RIENGEENA, LAKE

No trout. See *Fishing in National Parks*, 5.1.

RILEYS CREEK RESERVOIR

Tasmap Huon
Drainage Huon system (via the Kermandie system)

The current 15 m high concrete dam on Rileys Creek was completed in 1962 as a town supply for Geeveston. Forests grow along the western banks, while pasture and orchards extend from the east. There are many rush-lined margins but there is ample scope for shore-based spinning.

The fishery is largely maintained by stocking with hatchery-reared brown trout. Releases of yearlings were made as early as 1959-60, and from 1964-65 there were liberations of wild adults. In recent times stocking with fry has been favoured.

Most trout taken weigh 0.3-1 kg.

Trout liberations (since 1985)

Wild brown trout

YEAR	SIZE	NUMBER
1985	fry	10 000
1986	fry	20 000
1987	fry	20 000
1988	fry	5 000
1989	fry	5 000

RIM LAKE

No trout. See *Fishing in National Parks*, 5.1.

RINGAROOMA RIVER

Tasmaps Cape Portland, Swan Island, and Forester
Drainage Direct to Bass Strait

While the lower half of the river has been severely degraded by tin mining, the upper reaches provide some of the best stream sport in the North-East.

Pollution

Tin was discovered in the Ringarooma catchment in 1875 and by the following year small-scale mining was under way. Substantial operations ensued at Derby, Pioneer and Branxholm. During the boom period (from the 1880s to the 1920s) sluicing had a devastating impact on the river. Since 1948, when the Briseis operation ceased (see *Briseis Hole*), the mineral sludge has been steadily washing downstream. While the estuary and lower freshwater reaches remain choked with silt, the stretch from Moorina to Branxholm is now quite clean.

Trout in the lower reaches today

The estuary area could one-day rehabilitate (the marshes look *so* promising) but currently the silt and sludge render much of the water unsuitable to trout and, while the present status of the trout fishery has not been formally assessed, the area is ignored by anglers.

Reasonable numbers of resident fish frequent the stretch from Moorina to Branxholm, but the best fishing is still where it always has been – above the tin mines.

Trout stocks

According to early Parliamentary reports, the Ringarooma was stocked with brown trout as early as 1881-82. Today the upper reaches carry plenty of 0.2-0.5 kg fish as well as a respectable number to 1.5 kg. When conditions are good you can expect to take big bags.

Rainbows were probably first liberated in the Ringarooma system in 1911-12 (see *Weld River*), though there were subsequent liberations over the next three decades. A significant wild population established in the upper Weld River, and locals claim that the odd fish can still be taken from the Ringarooma itself near the townships of Branxholm and Ringarooma.

Where to fish

The upper Ringarooma is a tea-coloured fast-water flowing through shingly riffles and rocky pools.

From Branxholm to the Dorset junction, the water flows down a densely forested valley. There is ample scope for Celta fishing and clever fly casting, though you must be prepared to wade and/or scrub-bash.

Above the Dorset, the Ringarooma is flanked by flat pasture. While there are patches of scrub, many banks are grassy. When the water is moderately high and murky, upstream worm casting is the preferred method. As levels drop and the water clears, Celta fishing and upstream nymphing become the most reliable methods.

Above the township of Ringarooma there are several stretches where flood waters spill into the paddocks providing modest short-term wet-fly fishing.

Tributary streams

The best tributaries are the Weld (which contains rainbows) and the Dorset, though Ledgerwood Rivulet and the Maurice River are also worth a look.

The very small fastwater creeks in the Ringarooma catchment (such as Federal Creek, Tom

Thumb Creek, and Dunns Creek) contain plenty of tiny brown trout and are well suited to bait casting and Celta fishing.

RINGWOOD CREEK

Intermittent. Not recognised as a trout fishery.

RISDON BROOK RESERVOIR

Probably contains brown trout but public fishing is not permitted.

RIVEAUX, LAKE

No trout. See *Fishing in National Parks*, 5.2.

RIVER O'PLAIN CREEK

Tasmaps St Patricks, Forester, and St Pauls
Drainage Direct to the North Esk River

A tiny overgrown fastwater which carries lots of stunted brown trout. When levels are low, Celta fishing and bait casting result in big bags.

ROBERT TARN

Probably no trout. See *Fishing in National Parks*, 5.5.

ROCKY LAGOON

Tasmap Mersey
Drainage Derwent system (via the Little Pine system)
Location Nineteen Lagoons

Rocky Lagoon is situated in flat moorland, within sight of Lake Botsford on the road to Lake Ada. It is basically a half-sized version of Botsford and similar fishing conditions are encountered.

There is no scope for natural recruitment and the trout fishery is maintained by artificial stocking. The first release occurred in the winter of 1975 when 200 adult browns were turned out. Each year since then it has received a further 50-208 adult browns. While a handful of rainbows (salvaged from Liawenee Canal) were released in 1980, none have been liberated in recent seasons.

Rocky Lagoon is reserved for the use of artificial lures and flies, a restriction which has applied since 1979.

Trout liberations (since 1985)

Wild brown trout

YEAR	SIZE	NUMBER
1985	adults	50
1986	adults	50
1987	adults	200
1988	adults	200
1989	adults	100
1990	adults	100
1991	adults	50
1992	adults	50
1993	adults	50

See also *Fishing in National Parks*, 5.1.

RODWAY, LAKE

No trout. See *Fishing in National Parks*, 5.4.

ROGER RIVER

Tasmaps Circular Head and Arthur River
Drainage Direct to the Duck River

The lower section flows through paddocks but is lined with scrub. It is a series of long deep soft-bottomed pools. Bait and Celta fishers take good bags of brown trout to 0.5 kg, as well as a few specimens to 1 kg or so.

Above the Roger River Road, the river becomes a shallow shingle-bottomed fastwater. The trout are plentiful but stunted, and the fishing is best when levels are low.

Some 170 ha of wet-forest near the Roger River Road has been declared a State Reserve, where normal National Park regulations apply. There are picnic facilities on the riverbank.

ROLLESTON, LAKE

Tasmap Sophia
Drainage Pieman system (via the Anthony system)
Location West Coast Range

Lake Rolleston is one of the new brook trout fisheries in the Henty-Anthony district. Already it has provided good sport – and the future looks great.

Description

The northern half of the lake is surrounded by relatively-flat sedgeland and is easily accessible to anglers. However, the vegetation is thick enough to discourage access along the banks, and there are narrow bands of emergent pin rushes. Bring your waders!

The banks around the southern end are steep, overgrown with dense heath, and largely inaccessible.

The water is tea coloured.

The fishing

The water is ideal for lure casting. If you wade along the shoreline shallows at the northern end and cover as much water as possible (close to the banks and in the depths) you are bound to get strikes.

Fly fishers must be prepared to spend most of their time blind searching with large wets. The tea-coloured water and mottled bottom prohibit effective polaroiding, and the rises are both modest and irregular.

Trout stocks

The lake was first stocked in 1986 (see *Plimsoll, Lake*) and, while stocking with hatchery-reared fish is (at present) ongoing, natural recruitment has taken place. Typical fish weigh 0.5-1.5 kg but some exceed 3.5 kg.

Trout liberations

Brook trout

YEAR	SIZE	NUMBER
1986	fingerlings	*
1987	advanced fry	5 000
1989	advanced fry	10 000
1992	advanced fry	750

*= part-share of 5060

Access and facilities

Access is via the 5 km stretch of very rugged 4WD track which extends from the Anthony Road. The route can be walked in 1-1½ hrs.

A camp, comprising four modest (and decaying) huts exists on the western bank of the Anthony River, less than 1 km north of the lake.

Tent-sites are few and far between – the ground is tussocky, uneven and wet.

See also *West Coast Range.*

ROSEBERY, LAKE

Tasmap Sophia
Drainage Pieman River (a major instream impoundment)

Lake Rosebery is one of the best of the Pieman River Power Development lakes, and is especially attractive to shore-based anglers.

Description

Rosebery, a large tea-coloured storage, began filling in winter 1983. It lies behind a 75 m high

Lake Rolleston – a promising future

concrete dam and is subject to normal drawdowns of up to 8.4 m. Full supply is 159.4 m above sea level.

Much of the country extending from the east and north comprises open sedgeland, while the western and southern shores back up against dense forest. The HEC village of Tullah lies midway along the eastern shore, adjacent to the Murchison Highway

Trout stocks

Stunted brown trout abounded in the natural river system so when the lake formed there was no need for stocking. In the first year locals caught plenty of 0.2-0.9 kg fish and the odd specimen in excess of 2 kg. The average size climbed marginally over the next year and peaked in 1984-85 when fish of 0.5-1.3 kg were common.

Today the water teems with 0.2-0.7 kg trout, and fish in excess of 1.5 kg are rare.

The odd emigrant rainbow trout from Lake Mackintosh was caught in Lake Rosebery in the mid 1980s. In 1991, largely in an attempt to boost

289

the popularity of a flagging fishery, the IFC began stocking with domestic rainbows. Since then rainbows have accounted for up to 20% of the annual harvest, though stocks will crash if liberations of hatchery-reared fish are discontinued.

The official catch rate is poor, about one fish per angler per five days. However, experienced anglers often take big bags, especially on balmy nights when the mudeyes are about.

Trout liberations

Domestic rainbow trout

YEAR	SIZE	NUMBER
1991............fingerlings..............................14 600		
1992............advanced fry............................ 9 000		

Note: in 1993 the IFC promised releases of 15 000 fingerlings during each of the 1993-94 and 1994-95 seasons.

Fly fishing

Sight fishing is reliable only in warm weather when there are rises. As the early months of the angling season are likely to be cold and rough, the best times to visit are in summer and early autumn.

Trout, especially rainbows, can often be found midging in the wind lanes after frosty nights – but you need a boat.

Good mudeye migrations occur throughout summer providing sport for both shore-based and boat anglers. Balmy evenings are best, the hot spots being among the stands of emergent heath.

Falls of beetles happen in late summer and autumn. Trout can then be found mopping-up along the shores, though fishing in the wind lanes further out is usually best.

Lure fishing

Drift spinning and trolling are popular all over the lake. There is also plenty of scope for shore-based sport.

Bait fishing

Surface fishing with grubs is dynamite on calm summer evenings when the mudeyes are about.

Shore-based fishing

There are plenty of open banks suitable for spinning and fly casting – especially along the eastern shore, and the western half of the northern shore. Many locals do much of their fishing at Tullah itself.

Boating

The recommended launching ramps are at the Murchison Bridge and Tullah. The lake is suitable for dinghies (watch the weather!) and runabouts.

Facilities

There are no formal camping areas at Lake Rosebery, though modest sites exist at Lake Mackintosh.

Basic groceries can be bought at Tullah but the open hours are short. Larger stores exist in the village of Rosebery.

Special regulations

Trout spawn late on the West Coast, often in July/August, so the season does not close until the Sunday closest to 31 May. Open day is normal – the Saturday closest to 1 August.

ROSTREVOR RESERVOIR

Tasmap　Little Swanport
Drainage　Direct to Vicarys Rivulet

Description

A 6 m high concrete dam was built on Vicarys Rivulet decades ago. In 1981 the lake was drained and an earth levee formed on the water side of the old dam.

Full supply is less than 20 m above sea level and big drawdowns are to be expected in summer and autumn. The water is surrounded by flat marginal pasture and is always slightly murky. Most shores are shallow, weedy and/or choked with rushes. Deep open water is confined to the levee (at the south-western end).

Fish stocks

There is no scope for natural recruitment of trout. According to the NTFA the *'Rostrevor Estate Dam'* was stocked as early as 1956-57, when 2000 yearling browns were turned out. About 50 adults were released in 1966, but the storage did not feature in the adult-stocking programme. In modern times the fishery has been maintained by regular stocking with brown trout fry. As far as I am aware, there was no stocking of rainbows in 1983 (as recorded by the IFC).

Trout to 1 kg are common and a few attain 3 kg. Tench and eels are also abundant.

Trout liberations (since 1985)

Wild brown trout

YEAR	SIZE	NUMBER
1985............fry...20 000		
1986............fry...10 000		
1988............fry...5 000		
1989............fry...5 000		

The fishing

Spinning from the levee is worthwhile early and late in the angling season.

Set-rod fishing takes trout, though the eels and tench are quite annoying.

Dry-fly fishing is reliable on warm evenings. Tailing fish can sometimes be found in the weedy shallows, especially when the lake is rising, but often you are deceived by tench and eels.

ROTULI, LAKE

Tasmap Mersey
Drainage Derwent system (via the Little River system)
Location Western Lakes

Rotuli teems with 0.2-0.7 kg brown trout. Big bags can be expected when spinning in rough weather and when dry-fly fishing on sunny days. Black spinners and beetles cause intense surface activity in hot weather – and you can polaroid the bigger fish between rises.

The crystal water is contained between steep wooded hills. At low levels you can wade across the narrows at the northern end of the lake, and down the western shore along the edge of the overhanging scrub. At other times you are best advised to fish down the less overgrown eastern banks.

See also *Fishing in National Parks*, 5.1.

ROWALLAN, LAKE

Tasmap Mersey
Drainage Mersey River (a major instream impoundment)

Rowallan is the best of the Mersey Forth Power Development lakes.

Description

Lake Rowallan is impounded in a steep densely-forested valley behind a 43 m high rockfill dam and harbours extensive stands of drowned trees. Full supply is 487.68 m above sea level but draw-downs of up to 21 m are normal, especially in autumn. As levels fall the southern half of the lake recedes dramatically and much of the old river course and adjacent flats become exposed. The dam end is often defined by a steep clay littoral-scar. The water is only faintly tea-coloured.

History of trout stocks

The Rowallan Dam was completed in June 1967 and the lake had reached full supply by the end of the year. The flooded section of the Mersey River had long contained plenty of brown trout, as well as a 'relic' population of rainbows (most probably the progeny of fish released into Lake Meston in 1956-57). By 1968 it had been decided to manage the water as a rainbow trout fishery – a decision which resulted in the closed season

Lake Rotuli

Lake Rowallan – the dam end

being adjusted to protect spawning rainbows, and perhaps some early stocking with hatchery-reared fish. In 1969 it was reported that more rainbows than browns were being caught.

The fish never attained outstanding size and by 1970 typical trout weighed 0.5-1 kg.

Early in 1979 the lake was completely drained to allow for maintenance, but the trout simply retreated to the old river course and the fishery recovered as soon as the lake refilled.

Trout stocks today

The brown trout population is maintained by natural spawning in the Mersey River.

The rainbow population is maintained to some degree by natural spawning of lake fish, and emigrations from the rainbow-only Mersey headwaters. However, the fishery is appreciably enhanced through regular releases of hatchery-reared fry and fingerlings. Rainbows can account for 30-50% of the annual harvest – but when stocking lapses for three of four seasons the catch drops to about 5-10%.

Most trout caught (browns and rainbows) weigh 0.3-1 kg. However, set-rod fishers are more likely to catch small trout, while polaroiders are likely to find fish up to 2 kg.

Trout liberations

Rainbow trout

YEAR	SIZE	NUMBER
1980	fry (W)	10 000
1981	fry (W)	10 000
1985	small fingerlings (W)	10 000
1988	advanced fry (W)	22 500
1992	yearlings (D)	6 000
1993	yearlings (D)	10 000

(W) = wild stock
(D) = domestic stock
Note: in 1993 the IFC promised annual releases of 10 000 rainbow fingerlings.

Fly fishing

Polaroiding from the banks at the dam end of the lake is always worthwhile, though you need a boat to take full advantage of the wind lanes. Good hatches and/or beetle falls occur on warm summer/autumn days, and mudeyes cause surface activity on balmy evenings in late summer.

When the lake is rising and re-flooding the weedy/silty flats at the southern end you can expect to find brown trout foraging in the shallows.

Lure fishing

Spinning from the banks often results in good bags, though it is usually best to drift-spin among the trees.

The best trolling circuits are along the edges of the drowned forests.

Bait fishing

Set-rod fishers must expect to catch small blackfish and small trout (especially rainbows). The best way to take good-sized trout is by cast-and-retrieve fishing at dusk, and by polaroiding in the daytime.

Access and facilities

The only convenient 2WD access is to the eastern shore near the dam. There are two good launching areas, one about 0.2 km south of the dam and another 0.5 km further on.

There is scope for informal caravan and tent camping, though the sites are mostly bare-clay surfaces exposed to wind.

Several 4WD tracks lead from the Mersey Forest Road to the south-eastern shore.

The rugged West Rowallan (4WD) Track, extending along the western bank, runs close to the water at both the northern and southern ends of the impoundment.

Special regulations

The angling season opens on the Saturday closest to 1 October and closes on the Sunday closest to 30 May.

All inflowing waters except the Mersey River are closed to angling at all times.

The Mersey River above Lake Rowallan (above two white posts on opposite banks of the river) is closed to angling from the Sunday closest to 31 March to the Saturday closest to 1 November.

RUBICON RIVER

Tasmap Tamar
Drainage Direct to Port Sorell

A small stream flowing through farmland and pockets of bush. While the lower reaches include some shingly runs, most of the river is deep and sluggish. Many banks are completely overgrown with willows, and the water is usually murky.

Trout stocks

The Rubicon has been a popular brown trout fishery since at least the early 1900s. Rainbows were liberated as early as 1917-18 but failed to establish.

Fish of 1-3 lb were reported in 1918, and in 1949 the NTFA noted that the average weight was nearly 1 lb. Today most resident fish taken by anglers weigh 0.3-0.6 kg, though there are still reasonable numbers in excess of 1 kg.

Fishing for sea trout

Sea trout can be caught in the lower reaches from August to December. The hot spot is below the weir, about 0.5 km above the estuary (1 km above the Frankford Road). There is room for spinning and fly casting.

Fishing for resident trout

In the lower reaches, where the stream flows through bushland, Celta fishing and bait casting are favoured.

The hot spot for fly fishing is in the Avenue Plains where there are long stretches of open grassy bank.

The uppermost reaches, above the Bass Highway, are overgrown and difficult to fish.

RUFUS, LAKE

Tasmap Nive
Drainage Derwent system (via Lake King William)

A deep clearwater impounded by densely-vegetated hills. While access along the banks is arduous, there are narrow shoreline shallows at the outflow end.

The water teems with brown trout to 0.4 kg and specimens in excess of 1 kg are taken from time to time.

Fly fishers can usually polaroid fish cruising over the silt/stone flats and along the overgrown edges, and fair rises occur on warm days in summer and early autumn. Spinning is very productive, especially when the weather is rough.

Access is by foot from the Guelph Basin (Lake King William). It pays to keep close to the northern bank of Rufus Rivulet and to avoid cross-country detours into the dense scrub.

A modest dirt-floored A-frame hut is located on the lakeshore on the northern bank of the outflow. The loft has room to sleep six people. Tent-sites are unattractive and difficult to find.

See also *Fishing in National Parks*, 5.3.

RUSSELL FALLS CREEK

(also known as Falls River)

Tasmap Tyenna
Drainage Derwent system (via the Tyenna system)

The stream between the Tyenna River and Russell Falls teems with small brown trout but is closed to angling at all times. This law helps deter people from trampling on the delicate streamside vegetation adjacent to one of the State's most popular short-walks.

The water above Russell Falls also contains small fish but is very overgrown and seldom fished.

See also *Fishing in National Parks*, 5.5.

RUSSELL RIVER

Tasmap Tyenna
Drainage Direct to the Huon River above Judbury

According to early Parliamentary reports, brown trout were liberated as early as 1877, though by this time fish would already have invaded from the Huon. The NTFA recorded that some 125 000 rainbow fry were liberated in 1917-18, but this species did not establish.

The lower 12 km or so flows through cultivated river-flats, and features deep pools separated by small riffles. Some stretches are overgrown with scrub but there is plenty of room for Celta casting and fly fishing from the banks. Moderate to low flows are best. Trout to 0.5 kg abound.

The upper reaches bounce through dense forest and teem with tiny fish.

SALLY, LAKE

Tasmap Mersey
Drainage Derwent system (via the Pine River)
Location Western Lakes

Lake Sally lies in moorland at the foot of the wooded Great Pine Tier. It is a relatively shallow clearwater with some weedy margins.

While trout can sometimes be found foraging along the drowned edges, polaroiding from the banks is usually most appropriate. The dun hatches can also be very worthwhile, though the trout frequently frustrate by rising beyond casting distance.

Spinning is rewarding at all times of the angling season.

Typical fish weigh 0.5-1.3 kg.

See also *Fishing in National Parks*, 5.1.

SALLY JANE, LAKE

Possibly no trout. See *Fishing in National Parks*, 5.3.

SALOME, LAKE

No trout. See *Fishing in National Parks*, 5.1.

SAMUEL, LAKE

See *London Lakes*.

SAND RIVER

Tasmap Prosser
Drainage Direct to the Prosser River near Brockley

A sluggish creek flowing through marginal farmland. The fishing is similar to that in the Bluff River.

SANDRA, LAKE

No trout. See *West Coast Range*.

SANDSPIT RIVER

Tasmap Prosser
Drainage Direct to Earlham Lagoon

A small creek flowing through forest and pockets of farmland. While summer/autumn flows can be very poor, plenty of brown trout survive in the deep shady clearwater pools. Fish of 0.2-0.5 kg are typical, though some attain 0.8 kg or so. The best results are gained when set-rod fishing in the lower to mid reaches.

SANDY LAKE

Tasmap Mersey
Drainage Derwent system (via the Little Pine system)
Location Nineteen Lagoons

A shallow clearwater best suited to fly fishing. When levels are high tailing trout can be found in the backwaters around the inflow. During normal summer/autumn levels the whole lake can be waded and polaroided. Fish of 0.5-1.5 kg are typical.

See also *Fishing in National Parks*, 5.1.

SANDY BAY RIVULET

Tasmap Derwent
Drainage Direct to the Derwent estuary at Sandy Bay

A tiny turbid creek.

In Sandy Bay the water flows past backyards and is littered with domestic waste.

In the vicinity of Regent Street, the stream is narrow and overgrown with willows and scrub. While most pools are no more than knee deep, they hold a surprising number of brown trout. Fish of takeable size abound and some attain 0.7 kg or so. No doubt the larger trout predate on the abundant galaxias (mostly jollytails). Bait casting is most effective.

In the upper reaches there are several major reservoirs, all of which are closed to public fishing.

SAPPHO, LAKE

No trout. See *Fishing in National Parks*, 5.1.

SATURN, LAKE

No trout. See *Fishing in National Parks*, 5.2.

SAVAGE RIVER

Tasmaps Pieman and Arthur River
Drainage Direct to the Pieman River

A tea-coloured fastwater set in dense rainforest. It contains plenty of slow-growing brown trout but is rarely fished.

SAVAGE RIVER MINE TAILINGS POND

Tasmaps Pieman and Arthur River
Drainage Pieman system (via the Savage system)

Stocked with a total of 128 000 brown trout fry in 1970 and 1971; and restocked with several hundred adults between 1976 and 1977. No formal assessment of the fishery has been made.

SCAMANDER RIVER

Tasmap Georges Bay
Drainage Direct to the Tasman Sea

Sea trout

Fair numbers of sea trout are taken from August to December. While there is room for shore-based sport in the Scamander township and from the grassy banks further up, the tidal reaches can also be fished from a dinghy or small runabout. There is a launching ramp at Scamander.

Spinning, bait fishing and trolling are most popular, though I am told that there are times when wet-fly enthusiasts are able to enjoy good sight fishing.

Resident trout

Between the head of the estuary (at Upper Scamander) and the Avenue River junction, the Scamander River has a rural setting. The water flows fast and clear between scrubby banks. Most of the long shingly pools and riffles are wadeable. The trout grow fast and fish to 0.7 kg or so are quite common. Celta fishing, bait casting and upstream nymphing often result in big bags.

Above the Avenue junction the catchment is forested. There are several attractive long pools in the first 2-3 km, but as you move further up the water dwindles to narrow riffles.

The headwaters contain mostly tiny trout.

According to NTFA reports rainbow trout were released as early as 1906-07, but this species failed to establish.

SEABROOK CREEK

Tasmap Hellyer
Drainage Direct to Bass Strait

A tiny fastwater. Sea trout are taken at the mouth and in the lower freshwater reaches. The stream proper teems with small resident browns.

SEAL, LAKE

Tasmap Tyenna
Drainage Derwent system (via the Broad River)
Location Mt Field

Lake Seal lies between steep thickly-forested slopes with Mt Bridges towering some 300 m above the western shore. While the banks are deep and rocky and access along most shores is extremely arduous, there are extensive wadeable shallows near the outflow.

Anecdotal evidence suggests that the quality of fishing has remained fairly static since at least the 1950s. Brown trout up to 1.5 kg are fairly common, though the angling is often tough. Spinning and polaroiding are usually most appropriate.

The most direct access is by foot track from the Lake Dobson carpark, a walk of about ¾-1 hr (each way).

See also *Fishing in National Parks*, 5.5.

SECOND BAR LAKE

See *Bar Lakes system*.

SECOND LAGOON

Tasmap Meander
Drainage Natural – Derwent system (via the Ouse system)
Location Nineteen Lagoons

A shallow isolated clearwater surrounded by snowgrass flats. While there is no scope for natural recruitment of trout, and there have been no recent liberations, future stocking with hatchery-reared fish and/or wild adults is being considered.

See also *Fishing in National Parks*, 5.1.

SECOND RIVER

Tasmap St Patricks
Drainage Direct to Pipers River

The stream has a rural setting and, while most stretches are heavily overgrown with willows and scrub, there are some grassy banks and wadeable riffles. Celta fishing and bait casting are most appropriate. Brown trout to 0.3 kg abound and some exceed 0.5 kg.

The headwater tributary streams in the Lilydale district abound with tiny fish.

SELINA, LAKE

Tasmap Sophia
Drainage Pieman system (via the Anthony system)
Location West Coast Range

A steep-banked moderately tea-coloured water surrounded by sedge, heath and dense scrub. Access along the banks is arduous but much of the northern shoreline can be waded.

Brook trout were first released in 1986 (see *West Coast Range*) and fish to 3 kg have been taken in recent seasons. Natural spawning has occurred in the outflow stream but, since the inflow is short and silty, continued artificial stocking may be essential for good fishing.

Spinning is most productive early and late in the angling season, though good sport can be had during rough summertime weather. While fly fishers are often forced to fish blind with large wets, good rises can occur on balmy afternoons.

A 2.5 kg Selina brookie

Trout liberations

Brook trout

YEAR	SIZE	NUMBER
1986	small fingerlings	*
1987	advanced fry	6 000
1989	advanced fry	5 000
"	small fingerlings	7 000
1992	small fingerlings	750

* = part-share of 5060

SERPENTINE CREEK

See *Seven Time Creek*.

SERPENTINE IMPOUNDMENT

See *Pedder, Lake*.

SERPENTINE RIVULET

Tasmap Shannon
Drainage Derwent system (via Bronte Canal)

A clearwater stream meandering over a wide

grassy valley-floor. It is a series of long deep-banked pools separated by short riffles. While there are pockets of streamside vegetation, there is plenty of room to fish from the banks.

Brown trout of 0.2-0.6 kg are typical and a few exceed 1 kg. Good bags are taken on Celtas and baits but the real attraction is the summertime polaroiding.

Good trout are also taken from the Serpentine Rivulet Weir.

SEVEN TIME CREEK

(known to locals as Serpentine Creek)

Tasmap St Patricks
Drainage North Esk system (via St Patricks River)

A small fast clearwater containing lots of tiny brown trout.

SHADOW LAKE

Tasmap Nive
Drainage Derwent system (via Lake St Clair)

Shadow Lake contains naturally-spawned browns and rainbows to 3 kg or so. It is a crystal water surrounded by alpine woodland and sedge flats. Large sand/silt flats extend around the northern and western shores – and even the rocky southern banks are wadeable.

When spinning it pays to concentrate on the deep water beyond the shoreline shallows. When conditions are rough you pick up the odd big brown trout, otherwise rainbows of 0.5-1 kg predominate.

Fly fishers are treated to good rises, especially on hot days in summer and autumn when the rainbows take black spinners and beetles. Many risers are less than 0.2 kg but fish of 1-2 kg are common enough. The hot spot is the edge of the drop-off, so wading is essential. Brown trout can sometimes be founding cruising over the shallows – but they are few and far between.

Access involves a 1½-2 hr walk along a well-formed foot track from Cynthia Bay (Lake St Clair).

See also *Fishing in National Parks*, 5.4.

SHANNON LAGOON

Tasmaps Shannon and Meander
Drainage Derwent system (via the Shannon River)

At present Shannon Lagoon cannot be recommended above other waters in the Central

A rainbow from Shadow Lake

Highlands, though some quite basic water management changes could dramatically improve the fishing.

Description

Shannon Lagoon lies in a snowgrass basin at the foot of Great Lake. It is shallow and silty and becomes extremely turbid after wind.

Riparian water, destined for the lower Shannon and Ouse rivers, is released through the lagoon (from Great Lake) only during dry summer months. In wet periods, surplus water is pumped up into Great Lake so that it can be utilized in the Poatina Power Station.

History

In the early years of the Great Lake fishery, the Shannon River discharge was the main spawning area (see *Great Lake*). At this time a small loose rock barrier, designed to keep Great Lake from falling quickly to natural minimum levels, was the only obstruction between the natural Shannon lagoons and Great Lake.

In 1912-13 the first masonry (coffer) dam was built at Miena and by 1915 Great Lake had been raised some 8 feet. Water destined for the Waddamana Power Station was being regulated through the Shannon River by 1916.

In 1922 the small masonry dam was super-seded by the 10 m high Multiple-Arch Dam. At the same time the upper River Ouse was diverted into Great Lake via Liawenee Canal, greatly increasing flows through the upper Shannon. At this time Waddamana was the State's principal power generator so flows remained fairly constant throughout the year.

The new flow conditions suited the snowflake caddis, or 'Shannon moth', and phenomenal hatches soon developed in the Shannon River just below the dam. The 'Shannon Rise' was to become Tasmania's greatest angling attraction. In the early years of the rise, trout averaged more than 5 lb. Fish gorged on the caddis but were rarely easy to catch. Instead, the romance of the unique event was strengthened by the challenging nature of the fishing.

In *The Shannon Rise* (1953) Dick Wigram described it thus:

'At times, a great snowstorm of moth will swirl and eddy above the water. Masses of dead fly, inches thick, lie in all small bays along the bank. Millions of fly crawl on the grass, the bridge, the old fence posts, and then as the sun draws up into the sky, the moth becomes thicker and thicker until it is scarcely possible to recognise a friend on the opposite bank of the river.'

Between 1924 and 1931 the Shannon Power Scheme was constructed, utilising the hydro-

297

electric potential of Great Lake water as it passed between Great Lake and Waddamana. In order to be able to regulate water to the new Shannon Power Station, a 6 m high dam was erected at the outflow of the natural Shannon lagoons. This dam was completed in 1927 but Wigram noted that *'the lagoon was not fully formed until 1930'*.

According to Wigram, from about 1930 the Shannon Rise would usually start at about 4 December and peak about 7 December, though it was normal for good hatches to continue into January and February. At this time the lagoon itself was also a noted fly fishery, tailers and summertime dun feeders being feature attractions. Trout of 6-8 lb were sometimes taken in the early years but, by the 1950s the average size was about 2½ lb.

In 1950 the dam was raised 0.34 m to a full supply of 1017.85 m above sea level.

By 1956 many new power stations had been commissioned in Tasmania and the once steady flow in the Shannon became irregular. As a result, the Shannon began to disappoint, though significant hatches still occurred from time to time and the lagoon continued to provide conventional lake-fishing.

When Great Lake was diverted north in 1964-65 (see *Great Lake*) Shannon Lagoon was denied almost all flow, and earthworks associated with the construction of the new enlarged dam at Miena (completed in 1967) resulted in severe downstream siltation.

While the lagoon was in 1964 raised to 1018.03 m above sea level, the HEC came to fear that the dam could fail if overtopped during unprecedented floods. Accordingly, in 1973 the dam was lowered to 1017.66 m above sea level. This resulted in wave disturbance of the lake bed, compounding the problems of loose silt and turbid water.

Rehabilitation

In the early 1990s engineers reviewed the capacity of the Shannon Dam to cope with flood, and in 1992 the HEC agreed with the IFC to trial a new water-level regime. Water will still be pumped into Great Lake when the lagoon rises above 1017.55 m above sea level, but drawdowns will not exceed 1017.3 m. This should prevent frost damage to the weedbeds (which were often exposed in winter) and help to minimise wave disturbance of the bed. It is hoped that, in the long term, weeds will be able to re-establish over areas of loose silt.

Trout stocks

Shannon Lagoon supports plenty of brown trout

and a few rainbows. Spawning occurs in Burburys Creek, which is crossed by the Lake Highway. Further recruitment is derived from Great Lake (when water is being drawn) and occasional artificial stocking. Fish of 0.7-1.2 kg are typical.

The fishing

Reasonable numbers of tailers can be found along the western shore when levels peak after heavy rain.

Whenever a good flow of clean water is being released from Great Lake (usually for short periods in late summer) the sand/silt bank near the Lake Highway, and the deep channel mouth, are good for polaroiding.

Regulations

Fishing is not permitted in the canals between Shannon Lagoon and Penstock Lagoon.

SHANNON RIVER

Tasmaps Shannon and Meander
Drainage Derwent system (via the Ouse system)

The Shannon embraces a big part of Tasmania's trouting lore. William Senior (*Travel and Trout in the Antipodes,* 1880) noted the Shannon was *'a clear, rapid, handsome river, which, carefully fished, produces sport second to none in Tasmania'*. And after the construction of the Multiple Arch Dam at Miena in 1922, the uppermost section (between Shannon Lagoon and Great lake) became one of the most respected trout fisheries in the world. All this ceased in 1964-65 when Great Lake was diverted north (see *Shannon Lagoon*).

Today, the river below Shannon Lagoon is starved of water and in summer and autumn has little or no flow. There are many pools (even in the highland reaches) which hold significant numbers of 0.2-0.5 kg brown trout, but there is little or no major significance to anglers.

SHARK HOLE

See *Blue Peaks Lakes.*

SHARK LAGOON

See *East Rocky Lagoon.*

SIDON, LAKE

No trout. See *Fishing in National Parks,* 5.1.

SILVER LAKE

Tasmap Mersey
Drainage Derwent system (via the Pine river)
Location Western Lakes

Silver Lake is surrounded by open grassland, though there are wooded areas nearby. There are no extensive wadeable flats and much of the deeper bed is covered with *Isoetes* weed. The main feature is the regular occurrence of exceptional dun hatches. During warm weather from late spring to mid autumn, trout will be found rising freely throughout the day and sometimes all night. Frustratingly, most activity occurs beyond casting distance. However, trout do feed in close to the banks (especially at the narrows) and gulp down well-presented flies.

When there are no rises, or if the duns are hatching too far off shore, it pays to polaroid the edges. This is especially worthwhile when the black spinners are about.

When levels are high the water breaks out into the tussocks and you find the odd tailer.

Lure casters do well in overcast and/or rough weather.

Average fish weigh 0.7 kg and some exceed 1.2 kg.

See also *Fishing in National Parks*, 5.1.

SISTERS CREEK

Tasmaps Table Cape and Hellyer
Drainage Direct to Bass Strait

A moderately tea-coloured fastwater which carries plenty of 0.1-0.3 kg brown trout. In 1921 the NTFA noted that rainbow trout were doing well, and that specimens to 2½ lb were caught in 1920-21. However, this species is no longer present.

The lower reaches, from the coast to a couple of kilometres above Lake Llewellyn, flow through dense bushland and many stretches are covered with a low canopy. There is limited scope for accurate Celta fishing and bait casting.

In the vicinity of the Bass Highway and Myalla the water is flanked by pasture. Many pools are surprisingly deep and fishing from the banks is appropriate. Bait casting with worms and grasshoppers is most popular.

SKINNER, LAKE

Tasmap Tyenna
Drainage Huon system (via the Little Denison system)
Location Snowy Range

A rocky crater-like clearwater surrounded by alpine woodland. It was first stocked in December 1978 when 20 000 rainbow fry were turned out. For several years after this the lake teemed with very small trout, few of which exceeded 0.5 kg. However, natural spawning was modest and, as the original fish died off, the problem of overpopulation eased. When I fished the lake in 1990, there were several year-classes of trout and the biggest fish I caught exceeded 2 kg.

At the instigation of the STLAA, the lake was restocked in April 1991 with 1300 large wild-rainbow yearlings and in February 1994 with 600 large rainbow fingerlings.

While spinning from the banks is most popular, fish are easily polaroided in on-shore wind lanes. Many banks are too deep to wade but in some places it helps to sneak out along the fringes of the overhanging scrub.

Access is via the steep well-defined walking track which leads from the McDougals (logging) Road. The walk takes about 1-1½ hrs each way.

The best tent-sites are near the outflow – but they are small and few.

Strong wind is to be expected and blizzards can occur at any time.

See also *Fishing in National Parks*, 5.2.

SNAKE LAKE

Tasmap Mersey
Drainage Mersey system (via the Fisher system)
Location Chudleigh Lakes

A clearwater impounded by rocky well-defined banks. While mostly too deep to wade, all of the weedy bed is visible from the banks. Spinning and polaroiding are most reliable. Typical brown trout weigh 0.5-1.2 kg.

See also *Fishing in National Parks*, 5.1.

SNUG RIVER

Tasmap D'Entrecasteaux
Drainage Direct to North West Bay

A small creek flowing through dry woodland. In summer and autumn the water dies to a trickle and much of the shingly bed becomes exposed. Small brown trout exist below the falls, but never expect big bags.

SOLITUDE, LAKE

Probably no trout. Good fishing is found nearby at Shadow and Forgotten lakes.

299

SOLOMONS JEWELS

No trout. See *Fishing in National Parks*, 5.1.

SOLVEIG, LAKE

Tasmap Mersey
Drainage Derwent system (via the Pine River)
Location Western Lakes

A clearwater contained between elevated grassy banks. Spinning and bank polaroiding are most reliable, though fair dun hatches occur on warm summer days. Typical fish weigh 0.7-1.2 kg.

See also *Fishing in National Parks*, 5.1.

SONJA, LAKE

Similar to Lake Solveig

SOPHIE, LAKE

No trout. See *Fishing in National Parks*, 5.3.

SORELL CREEK

Tasmap Derwent
Drainage Direct to the Derwent estuary opposite Boyer

A small shingle-bottomed fastwater which carries plenty of 0.1-0.3 kg brown trout. It fishes best when levels are low. Celtas and baits give the best results.

SORELL, LAKE

Tasmap Lake Sorell
Drainage Derwent system (via the Clyde system)

Lake Sorell is the third most popular trout water in Tasmania, behind Great Lake and Arthurs Lake. And the huge annual harvest of trout is bettered only by Arthurs. The water is given extensive coverage in the book Trout Guide *(Rob Sloane and Greg French, 1991). A summary only is given here.*

Description

Sorell is a large natural lake lying in open woodland at 823 m above sea level. It is essentially shallow, with an average depth of 2.4 m and a maximum depth of about 4 m. There are extensive marshes along much of the western shoreline. The open water beyond the marshes can become very murky after strong wind, though general clarity varies from season to season.

Sorell is fed by its natural catchment, and water is conveyed to Lake Crescent via Interlaken Canal. In times of flood, water may also spill into Crescent via Kermodes Drain.

History

Lake Sorell is essentially a natural water, though levels have been manipulated since the 1830s (see *Crescent, Lake*).

In 1871 *Walch's Tasmanian Guide Book* noted that *'Eighty brown trout from the Plenty were put into this lake some time ago'* (evidently some time between 1867 and 1870). In the early 1890s it was reported that there had been small annual stockings of Loch Leven strain brown trout and brook trout.

Lake Sorell featured in several tourist guides of the late 19th century, but there was little advice for anglers. By 1900 the NTFA was claiming that *'no practical results'* of earlier stocking had been seen. Subsequent reports detailed further extensive stocking with brown trout, including sea-run and Loch Leven varieties.

During the 1902-03 season the southern bailiff reportedly netted Sorell and Crescent, taking 40 fish *'up to 12 pounds'*. In the same season some 2000 rainbow trout were released (more ambitious releases of this species followed in ensuing years). Further small liberations of brook trout were reported in the 1904-05 and 1905-06 seasons.

Despite the lack of visitation (or perhaps because of it) the Government built an accommodation house at Interlaken in 1907-08. In this season a few browns and rainbows and the last recorded brook trout were reported to have fallen to *'artificial spinners'*.

The first stripping of brown trout in Mountain Creek (originally known as the Franklin River) took place in the winter of 1907. By 1908-09 the Commissioners had erected a small hatchery at Interlaken *'capable of carrying 160,000 eggs'*. This hatchery was subsequently used for the annual stocking of Sorell and Crescent, though details are sketchy.

By 1919 the STLAA had, with the consent of the Commissioners, erected a new small hatchery at Mountain Creek. During the 1920s many fry were reared at this unit and released into the lake. The hatchery was repaired and rebuilt a number of times and apparently remained functional until the 1940s. It was finally dismantled in 1962.

Despite the fact that angling association reports publicised the Interlaken area and gave details of accommodation, hatchery operations and occasional catch statistics, Sorell and Crescent were largely ignored by anglers until the 1930s. The

NTFA report for 1931-32 suggested that the trout in Lake Sorell *'have until comparatively recent times been almost impossible to capture, no matter what description of bait was offered them. Some believed that this was due to the peculiar colour of the water, others to the possibility of the great abundance of food present. It is, therefore, of interest to note that the trout are now to be caught with the usual lures'*.

By 1935 Sorell had become a popular angling venue. Association records show that the lake continued to be heavily stocked with fish from the Salmon Ponds hatchery throughout the 1940s and 1950s. In 1960, largely as a result of improved scientific advice, the newly created IFC revised stocking policy – and since then there have only been several small-scale experimental releases.

In 1957 a bulldozer was used to improve natural spawning facilities in Mountain Creek, and the stream was further modified in the early 1980s, but in modern times there has been no serious doubt about the ability of the lake to maintain its trout stocks by natural recruitment.

Trout stocks today

Recruitment is principally derived from the intermittent Mountain Creek which supports massive spawning runs each year. Some improvements to the creek have been made to assist spawning and to limit the stranding of trout after flash flooding. Brown trout dominate, though rainbows account for about 10% of the annual harvest. While fish of 0.8-1.5 kg are typical in the open water, many of the brown trout in the marshes weigh 2-3 kg.

Fly fishing

Early-season marsh fishing is a highlight. Memorable sport can be expected if heavy rains from September to November result in rising lake levels. Trout move into the marshes to feed on frogs, tadpoles, aquatic nymphs, snails and galaxias. Ideally you will be able to see trout tailing and bow-waving in the shallows, otherwise it is worthwhile blind-searching pockets of open water with bulky wet flies. In overcast weather trout can be found in the marshes throughout the day. On bright days many fish move into the lake proper or disappear beneath the lush weeds, and dawn and dusk become the best times to fish. The Kermodes and Silver Plains marshes are most easily reached on foot, while the Robinsons, Duck Bay and Dogs Head marshes are more readily available to those with a boat. Brown trout taken from these areas are typically

bigger than those taken in the open waters. Rainbows are normally confined to the lake proper.

It must be recognised that marsh fishing is only at its best for a limited time during spring in some years, essentially being rainfall dependent. Generally blind searching with wet flies from the shore or a boat accounts for the majority of fly-caught fish. The west-facing shores, rocky points and off-shore reefs are the hot spots.

Wet-fly fishing in open water is also productive when trout can be seen slashing and swirling after galaxias. The rocky points and reefs are best in the first two months of the season when the galaxias are spawning. In October and November the trout tend to chase galaxias along the tussock banks and in the marsh drains. In mid to late November tiny transparent galaxia fry school near the surface in open water. In the summer months immature galaxias congregate along the sandy beaches, rocky points and the tussock edges.

Sometimes there are reasonable dun and caddis hatches before the end of October. With the onset of summer, the hatches become more regular. Hot spots include the shallows off Grassy

The marshes generally carry fish bigger than those in the open water. (photo by Rob Sloane)

Point, Blowfly Island, the Hatchery Shore and Murdochs Point.

Trout also respond to black spinners, caddis flies and stone flies which swarm around the tea-tree bushes along the Shepherds Shore, Duck Bay Shore, and the Dago Point to Interlaken shore.

Lure fishing

At the beginning of the season the action is centred on the rocky shorelines and reefs, particularly those adjacent to the major marshes. These seem to be the major spawning areas for the golden galaxias. Casting from the banks or a boat is more efficient than trolling.

While the most spectacular fishing is associated with the galaxia feeders at the beginning of the season, spinning can be very worthwhile at any time along virtually any of the rocky shores. The Dago Point area, the Shepherds Shore, the Hatchery Shore, the Duck Bay shore, St Georges Island and the Dogs Head are all highly regarded.

As the lake is shallow, trolling requires no special depth rigs or sounders. Simply work the open water adjacent to the popular fly fishing and spinning shores. The most productive areas include the Shepherds Shore and across to Grassy Point; between Blowfly Island and Murdochs Point (at high levels); the Hatchery Shore; and from Duck Bay into Kermodes and along Dago Point.

Camping

A major camping and caravan ground has been established by the PWS at Dago Point. This is an attractive site on dry ground, well-sheltered by trees. All facilities except powered sites are available.

Unlike most lakes on the Central Highlands, Sorell is largely surrounded by freehold land and informal lakeshore camping is not encouraged. The Interlaken property owner does permit camping in a traditional area at Silver Plains where basic facilities and formal campsites have recently been established.

Boating

Three boat launching ramps and extensive parking areas are located at Dago Point. The first ramp includes a small jetty, while the middle ramp is sheltered by a rock breakwater.

Small dinghies can also be launched from the roadside at Interlaken and Silver Plains.

There are a number of hidden reefs and extreme care must be exercised when boating – even in open water.

Regulations

Sorell is reserved for the use of artificial lures and flies. All inflowing streams – and radii of 50 m around the mouths of Dogs Head Creek, Silver Plains Creek and Mountain Creek – are closed to angling at all times.

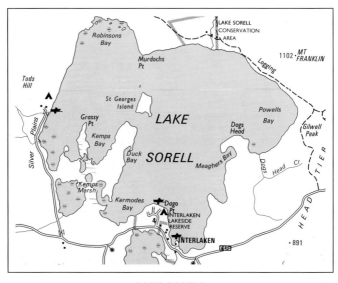

LAKE SORELL

SORELL RIVULET

Tasmap Prosser
Drainage Direct to Pitt Water

According to early Parliamentary reports, brown trout were established by 1869. Rainbow trout were introduced as early as 1917-18 but did not do well.

Today the creek is surrounded by marginal pasture and poor flows are common in summer and autumn. However, the permanent shady pools carry a relatively small number of brown trout to 0.5 kg or so throughout the year.

A few sea trout enter the estuary and lower freshwater reaches during September to January.

SOUTH ELDON RIVER

Similar to the Eldon River

SOUTH LAGOON

Location *Toiberry*

Intermittent. Not recognised as a trout fishery.

SOUTH ESK RIVER

Tasmaps St Patricks, South Esk, St Pauls, and Forester
Drainage Direct to the Tamar estuary

At 201 km the South Esk is the State's longest river – but it flows through dry pasture and carries a relatively small volume of water. The South Esk is the artery of the classic meadow streams, and provides good sport in its own right. The most respected stretch extends from Ormley to Mathinna.

History of fish stocks

Brown trout

It was noted in early Parliamentary reports that in 1866 some 400 ova stripped from the original trout reared at the Salmon Ponds were laid down in hatching boxes at Strathmore (3 km below the Nile junction). A few living trout were produced and these were washed away by flood. The next year, after a fish pond and some new hatching boxes had been constructed, a further 1200 fry were delivered. By 1869 it was claimed that brown trout were established in the system. Large-scale liberations of resident-strain brown trout into the South Esk and its tributaries continued from 1869 to the 1950s – but probably did little to enhance an already-dynamic population.

Sea trout were taken to Launceston as early as 1870, and in 1891-92 a *'small lot'* of Loch Leven fry were liberated into the *'Esk River'*.

Early reports of the NTFA suggest that, allowing for seasonal variation, the average size of the trout in each distinct section of the South Esk has remained fairly static since at least the early 1900s.

Rainbow trout

Early NTAA/NTFA reports show that the first release of rainbow trout occurred in 1898-99, and that a further release of 1000 fry occurred at Pleasant Banks (near Evandale) in 1899-1900. The first rainbow trout was caught at Evandale in 1900-01, and the species was reported to be doing well in 1902. However, despite regular stocking of the South Esk and its tributaries until the 1950s, rainbows failed to establish.

Salmon

Some 3000 Atlantic salmon ova were taken to Launceston in 1884 but most died in transit and only six fry resulted. A further 6000 fry were released in the South Esk in 1885 – and there probably were other liberations – but the species did not establish (see *About Our Sportfish*, 2.4).

Small numbers of sockeye and quinnat salmon were turned out in the early 1900s, but none were ever taken by anglers (see *About Our Sportfish*, 2.5).

Redfin perch

In 1899 the NTAA noted that redfin had been released into the Elizabeth prior to 1893 and had become common in the South Esk. Today the species abounds throughout the lowland reaches.

The Tamar to the Trevallyn Dam

The South Esk between the Tamar estuary and the Trevallyn Dam flows through a steep rocky gorge, over a boulder-strewn bed. Prior to the construction of the dam this stretch was a respected fishery for both resident browns and sea trout. Today the water is diverted at Lake Trevallyn through a tunnel to the River Tamar some 2.5 km below the natural outfall. Unless there is a major flood topping the dam, the flow down the natural bed is now merely a trickle. A fair head of 0.2-0.6 kg resident brown trout frequent the puddles, pools and trickles, and some larger fish are taken from First Basin, but the fishing is relatively poor. I have been told that some sea trout enter the South Esk, but the migrations must be small. Most sea trout now congregate in the River Tamar below the Trevallyn tailrace (see *Tamar, River*).

The area from the Tamar to First Basin is a Launceston City Council reserve laced with sealed flood-lit footpaths. At First Basin there are botanic gardens, a restaurant and a swimming pool.

Some 450 ha between Duck Reach and Lake Trevallyn is a State Recreation Area.

Lake Trevallyn to the Macquarie Junction

This section of the South Esk is wide and deep. Most banks are completely overgrown with willows and are best suited to set-rod fishing. However, away from the major roads there are some open banks and reasonable flood plains. Brown trout of 0.2-1 kg are common and some grow bigger.

Water from Great Lake is diverted via the Poatina Power Station and Brumbys Creek to the Macquarie River. Consequently, the South Esk below the outfall of the Macquarie receives cool water throughout the year, and river levels are prone to sudden fluctuations even in settled weather.

The Macquarie to Clarendon

Above the Macquarie junction the South Esk is a series of wide deep-centred broadwaters and short rock/shingle drops. This stretch is subject to natural flows and can become quite sluggish in times of drought. While the banks are mostly choked with willows, there is some scope for wading.

The water teems with 0.2-0.5 kg brown trout but also carries a few fish in excess of 0.8 kg.

There are fair hatches on calm warm days and, in times of flood, fish forage on the outer edges of the willows. But the fishing is usually much better on the Macquarie or at Brumbys Creek.

Clarendon to the Henrietta Plains

Between Clarendon and the Henrietta Plains there is a vast grassy flood basin. In times of normal flow the river is a series of deep, weedy, moderately-clear broadwaters (many of which have open banks) flanked by a multitude of permanent and semi-permanent backwater lagoons. The backwaters are clearly defined on the *Evandale* and *Nile* 1:25 000 Tasmaps.

Trout in the river proper are mostly 0.2-0.8 kg, while those in the best of the backwaters can attain 2 kg and more.

After heavy rain the river breaks its banks and the trout move out to forage along the flooded banks. The fly fishing can be very good at such times, though it is overshadowed by the backwater fishing on the Macquarie and Meander rivers.

Also, the sport is usually short-lived. The river is likely to swell quickly (within a day) and can become a vast lake. In my experience the fishing is pretty hopeless if you can't get reasonably close to the main river channel.

Good hatches of red spinners occur in late spring and early summer.

Henrietta Plains to Ormley

As early as 1907 the NTFA had commented upon the severe pollution (water discolouration and siltation) of the South Esk below the outfall of the Storeys Creek tin mine. In 1931 a second mine (the Aberfoyle mine at Rossarden) began operation, resulting in even more pollution. For decades the river between Henrietta Plains and Ormley was reduced to a trout fishing wasteland. By the late 1970s, as a result of a winding-back of operations and more strict environmental controls, the mid South Esk had begun to rehabilitate – and in 1982 depleted ore reserves combined with low tin prices forced the closure of the mines. The sediments are now slowly washing away and trout have re-established.

Today the mid South Esk is a string of small weedy broadwaters, shingly riffles and stony-bottomed pools. At times of moderate to low flow the water is clear enough to polaroid.

Ormley to Mathinna

This is the most popular stretch for angling. The water flows between forested hills, cutting through a wide grassy valley-floor. It is relatively cool and fast, featuring a mixture of shingly riffles, wadeable pools, and weedy deepwaters.

Celta fishing is very productive in times of moderate to low flow, and bait casting with grasshoppers is popular in summer and autumn.

The fly fishing is worthwhile, though it is overshadowed by that at the Break O'Day and (further away) Macquarie. In spring and autumn there are fair to good hatches of mayfly spinners (red and black), and in times of flood trout tail in the grassy ditches and depressions adjacent to the banks.

Close to the river are many permanent and semi-permanent backwater lagoons, all well-defined on the *Rossarden* and *St Marys* 1:25 000 Tasmaps. During floods the connecting gutters and grassy edges provide good wet-fly fishing. As levels drop the pools become isolated, weed growth booms, and insects proliferate. In the deepest, most lush lagoons some trout attain 2 kg and more. They rise well and can sometimes be polaroided. The fishing dies away as the pools shrink and become warm.

The headwaters

The South Esk and its tributaries above Mathinna are small shingle-bottomed fastwaters. They hold plenty of small brown trout and are well suited to Celta fishing and bait casting.

The tributary streams

Some anglers seem to have the ability to catch trout on every outing, while others are constantly bemoaning the state of the fishery. Invariably those who do well have thought hard about *where* in the South Esk system to fish. Each stream is at its best only under certain conditions. Tips on deciding where to go are given under *Where to Fish – A Regional Breakdown*, 4.2.

The future

Water in the South Esk system is increasingly under demand for irrigation. Currently the IFC is assessing minimum flow requirements for fish and invertebrates – and it is likely that the RWSC will eventually enforce the maintenance of minimum instream flows.

SOUTH GEORGE RIVER

Tasmap   Georges Bay
Drainage   Direct to the George River

A fastwater stream which carries plenty of 0.1-0.3 kg brown trout.

The lower 4-5 km flow over a shingle bottom through a grassy flat. While many banks are overgrown with willows and scrub, there is plenty of scope for Celta fishing and bait casting.

More than 300 ha of dense wet-forest in the mid reaches is included in the St Columba Falls State Reserve. Here the river flows through shallow pools and riffles, and is well suited to Celta fishing.

The stream above St Columba Falls is flanked by pockets of lush pasture and was once renowned for its rainbow trout. The species was released in the streams at Pyengana as early as 1918-19 and was well established by the 1930s. The IFC reported the continued existence of self-supporting stocks as late as 1966 – but by the late 1970s the rainbows had disappeared. I presume that the rainbows thrived only in the absence of brown trout. Brown trout are now well established, though their origin is unknown.

SPICER, LAKE

No trout. See *West Coast Range*.

SPRING RIVER

No trout. See *Fishing in National Parks*, 5.2.

ST CLAIR LAGOON

Tasmap   Nive
Drainage   Direct to the River Derwent

St Clair Lagoon is a flooded complex of natural lagoons, backwaters, marshes and channels. At normal levels the large main lagoon consists of weedy marshes along the western banks, and open wadeable silt/sand flats over the eastern half. However, when the radial gates at the outflow are closed the water can be raised some 3 m, backing up St Clair Lagoon into Lake St Clair. Water is retained in this manner only when Lake King William is in danger of spilling. In the dry 1980s the water was not manipulated and natural seasonal water cycles took their normal course. The early 1990s have been very wet and artificial high levels have been maintained throughout spring and early summer.

At natural high levels (when flood waters are passing unhindered through the radial gates) fish can be found foraging in the marshes along the western shore. When the water is approaching full supply, there is additional wet-fly fishing among the tea-trees along the eastern shore at the southern end of the Derwent Basin (Lake St Clair).

At natural low levels wade polaroiding along the eastern shore is superb.

In warm weather (at any level) the lagoon also features prolific rises to mayflies, caddis flies, stoneflies and beetles.

Brown trout of 0.3-0.8 kg dominate, especially in the marshes, but rainbows account for up to 15% of the annual harvest.

Artificially-high water at St Clair Lagoon

ST CLAIR, LAKE

Tasmap Nive
Drainage Derwent system (via St Clair Lagoon)

Lake St Clair carries healthy populations of trout and offers good sport.

Description

Crystal clear Lake St Clair is the deepest glacial lake in Australia, depths of up to 174 m having been recorded along the Deep Shore.

The lake is contained between Mt Olympus and the Traveller Range, both of which are long steep and high. On the western banks dense rainforest extends to the water's edge, while on the eastern side there is a mixture of wet-forest and sub-alpine eucalypt forest. Flat woodland extends from the southern and northern shores.

While St Clair is essentially natural, the radial gates at the outfall of St Clair Lagoon can be used to back 3 m of water over both sheets. The Pumping Station can drain Lake St Clair some 6 m below natural minimum levels, though it has not been used since the drought of 1967. The low-profile dam at the outfall of the Derwent Basin (between Lake St Clair and St Clair Lagoon) does not raise Lake St Clair – it serves to prevent St Clair Lagoon from back-washing into the Derwent Basin when Lake St Clair is pumped below the level of its natural outlet.

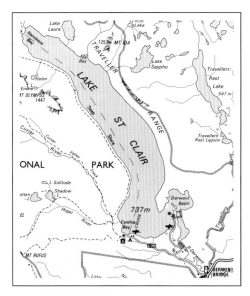

LAKE ST CLAIR

Trout stocks

Trout in Lake St Clair are maintained entirely by natural recruitment, the principal spawning grounds being in the Narcissus and Cuvier rivers. While brown trout dominate, rainbows account for up to 20% of the annual harvest. Typical fish weigh 0.4-0.8 kg, though specimens in excess of 2 kg are taken from time to time.

History

It is likely that brown trout had invaded Lake St Clair from the Derwent before the documented laying down of 2000 ova in streams in the vicinity of the lake in 1877-78. By 1893 the Commissioners had reported that the water was *'teeming with trout'*.

Records from the Plenty hatchery indicate that the first stocking of rainbow trout occurred in 1928 when 100 000 fry were released at Cynthia Bay. In 1934 it was reported that browns to 4 lb and rainbows to 3½ lb were being taken on spinners, and that much larger fish were seen. A further release of 160 000 rainbow fry was undertaken at this time, and heavy stocking with the species continued for several years.

In 1935 some 9000 yearling quinnat salmon were released, but this species failed to establish.

The Tarraleah Power Development was approved by Parliament in 1934 and as a result access to the Lake St Clair was greatly improved. By 1937 the scheme was operational and water was being manipulated at St Clair Lagoon.

During the 1940s heavy stocking continued, especially with rainbow trout. Many of the stock fish were raised at the small hatchery at Lake Margaret on the West Coast. Others were transferred from the hatcheries at Plenty and Miena. The last recorded stocking was the release of 5200 rainbow yearlings in 1948-49. For several years after this time interest turned to the newly formed Lake King William.

Fly fishing

The best early-season wet-fly fishing and summertime rises occur at St Clair Lagoon (see *St Clair Lagoon*). However, the lake proper is still worthwhile.

Wade polaroiding is very good, the best areas being the beaches at Cynthia Bay, the Frankland Beaches and Narcissus Bay.

Wind lane feeders are extremely worthwhile, though you need a boat. There are prolific midge hatches after calm frosty mornings, and reasonable beetle falls occur on warm days in summer and early autumn. The best lanes occur across

St Patricks River

Cynthia Bay, down the main body of the lake, off Fergies Point, and in the Derwent Basin.

Fishing at night with bulky wets or buoyant dries is a reliable fall-back. The best areas are the river mouths at Watersmeet, Narcissus, and Ida Bay. Mild summer/autumn evenings are usually most productive. The activity starts at dusk and often continues throughout the night. Don't be put off by an apparent lack of surface activity – blind searching can be very effective.

Lure fishing

The best areas for shore-based sport are Cynthia Bay, the Frankland Beaches, Ida Bay and Narcissus Bay. Wading is often an advantage.

The traditional trolling area is Derwent Basin. Look for the edges of the reefs and the weedbeds – they are clearly visible in good light. Other good trolling areas are the southern beaches, Cynthia Bay, Echo Point to Narcissus, and Narcissus to Ida Bay.

Access

Vehicular access is limited to the southern end. Access to other shores is restricted to walking (the renowned Overland Track extends along the western bank to Narcissus) or boating. A passenger launch service operates between Cynthia Bay and Narcissus.

Accommodation/Camping

Lake St Clair is part of the Cradle Mountain – Lake St Clair National Park and receives extraordinary visitation from sightseers and bushwalkers. The PWS operates information and management services from the centre of park activity – Cynthia Bay.

The southern end is intensively managed and camping is confined to formal areas at Cynthia Bay. Tent and caravan sites, including a few powered sites, are available. Basic supplies can be bought from the kiosk, which operates year-round.

While camping is not permitted along the southern beaches or at St Clair Lagoon, informal camping is allowed elsewhere. At the far northern end (Narcissus) there is a public bushwalkers' hut capable of sleeping up to 28 people, and many ideal tent-sites. A smaller walkers' hut, capable of sleeping eight people, is located at Echo Point.

All of the National Park is designated 'fuel stove only' and camp fires are totally prohibited.

Public accommodation is available at Cynthia Bay. Hut fees vary according to services provided. Alternatively you will find good accommodation (and meals) nearby at the Derwent Bridge Hotel.

Boating

A concrete ramp is sited at Cynthia Bay. Small motorised dinghies can be hired from the kiosk.

ST JOSEPHS RIVER

Tasmap Hellyer
Drainage Cam system (via St Marys River)

A shallow fastwater flowing over a rock bottom. It is set amid a patchwork of plantation forest, scrub and pasture. There are some grassy esplanades but most banks are heavily overgrown and wading is essential. Big bags of 0.1-0.2 kg brown trout can be taken on Celtas and baits when levels are low.

In 1927 the NTFA noted that rainbow fry were placed in the St Josephs and St Marys rivers *'eleven years ago'* and that even though it had not been restocked until *'recently'* the species had remained plentiful. Soon after brown trout were released above the falls (probably in the 1930s) the rainbows disappeared.

ST MARYS RIVER

Similar to St Josephs River.

ST PATRICKS RIVER

Tasmaps St Patricks and Forester
Drainage Direct to the North Esk River at Watery Plains

Of all the streams in the North Esk system, St Pats is the one most respected by anglers. It is a fast, predominantly hard-bottomed water with long stretches of wadeable riffle. Only some sections of the larger pools are too silty and/or deep to wade. Native scrub, willows and blackberries grow along most banks.

The water becomes very murky after heavy rain but clears appreciably in settled weather.

Brown trout

Early Parliamentary reports indicate that brown trout were established in the North Esk by 1869. William Senior (*Travel and Trout in the Antipodes*, 1880) noted that the stream was of *'favourable repute amongst anglers'* and that there was *'no lack of trout'*. By the turn of the century the water had overpopulated and the overall size and quality of the fish was much the same as it is today. In 1902 the NTFA reported that the average weight of 472 fish caught was little more than ½ lb.

The IFC has been researching the recruitment and survival of trout in the St Patricks system. We know that the fishery is as good today as it was 30 years ago, but we also know that the health of our rivers can no longer be left to chance.

In 1985 the IFC surveyed the river and found that the trout population was much the same as it was at the time of Dr Aubrey Nicholls' survey in 1955 (see *North Esk River*).

Today, when conditions are fair, the proficient angler can expect to take big bags of 0.1-0.4 kg fish. I have taken several brown trout on the fly in excess of 2 kg – usually at night on the edges of log jams and in other likely big-fish lies.

Rainbow trout

The NTFA recorded big liberations of rainbow trout in 1929-30 though, given the already long history of enthusiastic rainbow-stocking by northern anglers, I doubt that these were the first releases. In 1936 anglers were advised that rainbows could be caught in the upper reaches but that, like the brown trout, they were small. Other reports in the 1930s and 1940s continued to mention the apparently stable wild population in the upper reaches. Dr Aubrey Nicholls found rainbows in the Diddleum Plains area in 1955, and the IFC found a slightly larger number there in 1985 (despite zero artificial stocking in the intervening 30 years).

Today rainbows remain confined to the Diddleum Plains area of St Pats and Camden Rivulet, where they account for some 5-10% of the annual trout harvest.

Where to fish

The stretch from the junction with the North Esk to Nunamara flows through a remote forested valley and, while it is ideal Celta water, it is not often fished.

Most angling is done in the water adjacent to the Tasman Highway, and in the Diddleum Plains.

What to fish

In the early months of the season, when the river is swollen and discoloured (but not in flood), casting a worm and spinning result in good bags.

As the weather warms and the water clears, good rises to a variety of aquatics and terrestrials can be expected. Any nondescript dry fly is likely to perform well, though it pays to have caddis, mayfly and beetle imitations. Polaroids are useful, especially for following fish between rises.

When trout are not visible on the surface, traditional upstream nymphing and Celta fishing are good fall-backs.

The tributaries

Most of the tributary streams are tiny shingle-bottomed fastwaters which carry plenty of tiny brown trout. Among the most-fished are Patersonia Rivulet, Coquet Creek, Barrow Creek and Camden Rivulet (which holds rainbows as well). None are as good as the St Pats itself.

See also *Where to Fish – A Regional Breakdown*, 4.2.

ST PAULS RIVER

Tasmaps St Pauls and Break O'Day
Drainage Direct to the South Esk River at Avoca

St Pauls is a series of long, deep rush-lined broadwaters located in flat pasture between forested hills. While some banks are overgrown with tea-tree and scrub, many are quite open. During major floods the river spills into adjacent paddocks. The water is often slightly murky.

St Pauls teems with 0.1-0.4 kg brown trout.

Set-rod fishing with worms is popular when the river floods, and grasshoppers work well in warm weather when fish are rising. Cast-and-retrieve fishing with grubs after dark is a reliable fall-back.

Fly fishing is most productive in November/ December when the trout rise freely to take mayflies (including red spinners) and terrestrials. You often have to cast over rushes and/or scrub – but big bags await the courageous. When the river is lapping the banks, you can usually find fish foraging along the fringes.

There is limited scope for comfortable spinning.

See also *Where to Fish – A Regional Breakdown*, 4.2, 4.10.

STAVERTON CREEK

See *York Creek.*

STOREYS CREEK

Tasmap   St Pauls
Drainage   Direct to the South Esk River below Ormley

Long polluted with tailings from the Storeys Creek and Aberfoyle tin mines (see *South Esk River*). Mining ceased in 1982 and brown trout may have re-established in the lower to mid reaches.

STRAHAN, LAKE

Tasmap   Cape Sorell
Drainage   Isolated coastal lagoon
Location   West of Strahan

A small tea-coloured water surrounded by dense heath which was first stocked in December 1962 with 10 000 rainbow fry. According to NTFA reports, fish had attained takeable size by 1964 and 4 lb by 1967. Restocking with 20 000 rainbow fry occurred in 1982 but, due to poor water quality, no fish survived long enough to be caught by anglers.

STRAHAN LAKES

The Strahan Lakes are a group of isolated coastal lagoons set amid plantation pines in the sand dunes north of Strahan. None are capable of maintaining trout stocks by natural recruitment.

While Lake Bellinger was stocked as early as 1966, there was no major interest in the area until the Forestry Commission began road building in the late 1960s. Lakes Ashwood, Garcia and Bantic were first stocked (with brown trout) in 1970 and liberations continued until 1983. As a result of lobbying from initially enthusiastic local anglers, fishing from motor boats was prohibited in Ashwood, Bellinger and Bantic in 1973.

Lake Ashwood proved to be the most productive and popular water, though Bantic also fished well. Garcia was disappointing.

In recent years local interest has waned and stocking has lapsed.

STUART, LAKE

Probably no trout. See *Fishing in National Parks*, 5.3.

STUMPS LAKE

Tasmap   Mersey
Drainage   Natural – Derwent system (via James system)
Location   Western Lakes

A shallow silt/sand bottomed clearwater surrounded by rocky heathland. When levels are low, wade polaroiding is the best way to fish. After heavy rain the western banks break out into gutters and ditches, creating ideal conditions for wet-fly fishing. Brown trout of 0.5-1.5 kg are typical.

See also *Fishing in National Parks*, 5.1.

STYX RIVER

Tasmaps   Tyenna and Wedge
Drainage   Direct to the River Derwent at Bushy Park

The Styx is a wide, relatively shallow fastwater. The water is tea coloured and, largely because of farming and forestry operations, can become moderately murky after heavy rain. Clarity improves markedly in settled weather.

Description and access

The lowest 10 km pass over a bed of large shingle between hop fields and marginal paddocks. While sections of some pools are quite deep, at normal levels you can wade up the riffles and along the edges of the overhanging scrub.

The Styx River (courtesy Rob Sloane)

The rest of the river is located within dense production forest. Major logging roads, which extend from Karanja to Maydena, cross at several points – but all entry points are gated and vehicular access is possible only by prior arrangement with ANM.

Near the Cataract Rivulet junction, the Styx flows over large shingles and there are numerous shallow rapids and riffles. At moderate to low levels much of the bed is exposed and, by wading and rock-hopping, you can make good progress upstream.

Further up, in the vicinity of the South Styx River, the shingle is more gravel-like and, while there is still plenty of current, there are fewer riffles. Most pools are uniformly shallow and extend from forested bank to forested bank.

Trout stocks

According to early Parliamentary reports brown trout had been conveyed to the Styx by 1869. Today the water teems with naturally-spawned fish in the 0.1-0.3 kg range, but also carries a fair number in excess of 0.5 kg. Trophies of 1.5-3 kg are much more scarce than in the Plenty and Tyenna rivers.

Rainbow trout were liberated as early as 1917 (when 150 000 fry were turned out) but did not establish.

The fishing

The fishing is best when levels are moderate to low. Celta fishing, bait casting and traditional upstream nymphing often result in limit bags. Fair rises occur during hot summer/autumn afternoons.

SULPHUR CREEK

Tasmap   Forth
Drainage   Direct to Bass Strait

A tiny trickle which contains a relatively small population of brown trout. Fish to 0.3 kg are commonly taken, while others exceeding 1 kg are reported from time to time. Bait casting is most practical.

History of trout stocks

Brown trout were released as early as 1901. Rainbows were turned out in 1913 but could not compete with the browns.

SUPPLY RIVER

Tasmap   Tamar
Drainage   Direct to the Tamar estuary

A sluggish, often murky creek draining marginal pasture. While some stretches (including those visible from the Tamar Highway) are overgrown with scrub, there are open banks in the mid reaches. Most pools are too deep and silty to wade.

Brown trout of 0.2-0.3 kg are common and some exceed 1 kg. Bait casting and Celta fishing result in good bags, especially when levels are low. There is also some scope for fly fishing.

SURPRISE, LAKE

No trout. See *Fishing in National Parks*, 5.2.

SURREY LAGOON

Tasmap   Forester
Drainage   Ringarooma system

According to NTFA reports the lagoon was stocked as early as 1934-35 when some 30 000 brown trout fry were turned out. It was restocked several times, the last being when 20 000 rainbow fry were released in 1968. Also, there was probably natural recruitment of brown trout from Davids Creek.

The lake has been dry for many years and is now merely a marshy tussock-flat littered with dead trees and stumps.

SWALLOWS NEST LAKES

No trout. See *Fishing in National Parks*, 5.2.

SWAN RIVER

Tasmaps   Freycinet and Break O'Day
Drainage   Direct to King Bay, Great Swanport

The estuary

The Swan River estuary is a renowned bream fishery and is largely ignored by trout enthusiasts. However, modest to fair runs of sea trout occur each spring, and slobs of 0.5-3 kg are reported from time to time. While most trout are taken by set-rod bream fishers, there appears to be scope for spinning and trolling. Small boats can be launched at Great Swanport, the terminus of the Swan River Road, and the terminus of the Boathouse Road.

Where Great Swanport empties into Great Oyster Bay the water flows over white sand. While this area is rarely fished, it is likely that, during the best runs, sea trout could be seen herding whitebait over the shallows.

The stream

The stream proper flows over loose shingle through dry woodland and marginal pasture. When levels are high the water is murky but at other times it is remarkably clear. As floods subside much of the bed becomes exposed and the current dies to a mere trickle. There are some deep permanent broadwaters, many of which extend from bank to bank, but most pools are small and shallow and provide marginal trout habitat.

The trout are generally slow-growing and relatively scarce. Scrappy fish of 0.2-0.3 kg are typical in the riffles and shallow pools, while specimens in excess of 1 kg can be found in the deeper lies, especially where there is shade and/or undercut banks.

The easiest access is from the Tasman highway at Cranbrook, and from the Old Coach Road at Waters Meeting. Brown trout exist above Hardings Falls, though this is the least respected fishing area.

Celta fishing is reasonably productive when the river is at moderate levels. When the water is still and clear, bait casting is usually more effective, though the numerous galaxias are a nuisance. Polaroiding can be enjoyable but you must be prepared to cover a lot of ground to find just a few worthwhile fish.

While superficially similar to the Swan, tributaries such as the Wye and Cygnet, generally offer better sport. Better sport still is to be found in other drainages, in waters such as the Apsley and St Pauls rivers.

The Swan galaxias

The Swan galaxias *(Galaxias fontanus)* is an endangered species endemic to a few streams in the upper Swan and Macquarie catchments. It is a popular theory that, since *'the species' downstream limit is marked by the upstream limit of brown trout'*, brown trout have forced the fish from a once much-broader range. However, the upstream limit of brown trout is usually a major waterfall – the upstream limit of most native fish. It is likely that the Swan galaxias has evolved in isolation of other galaxiid species and that it has always had a very limited range.

The IFC did not find brown trout above Hardings Falls until 1990, at which time several year-classes were recorded. Some of these fish were old enough to have been present during earlier surveys. However, if the trout *are* recent (illegal) introductions, the Swan galaxias above Hardings Falls may be under threat.

The Swan galaxias has been virtually wiped out by redfin perch in Brodribb Creek (a tributary of the Macquarie) since the creation of Lake Yalleena in the mid 1980s.

In light of the possible recent reduction in the species' range, the IFC has recently translocated the Swan galaxias to selected fish-free headwater tributaries within the Swan catchment.

SYDNEY, LAKE

No trout. See *Fishing in National Parks*, 5.2.

TAILRACE CUT

See *Brumbys Creek*.

TALBOTS LAGOON

Tasmap   Hellyer
Drainage   Arthur system (via the Hellyer system)

With good reason Talbots is the most respected stillwater in the North-West.

Description

The 9 m high rockfill dam on the Wey River was constructed in 1960 by APPM to impound water for its industrial needs. The lake so formed is essentially a clearwater, though some inlets are quite tea-coloured. It is surrounded by production forest.

Trout stocks

Brown trout existed in the Wey prior to flooding and, while some 15 000 fry were liberated in 1981, stocks continue to be maintained almost entirely by natural recruitment. Fish of 1-2 kg are typical and larger specimens are taken from time to time.

In May 1992 some 2000 rainbow yearlings were turned out. These fish quickly attained 1-2 kg and were prominent in anglers' bags. The IFC has since promised annual releases of 500-1000 rainbow fingerlings.

How to fish

While spinners and bait fishers do very well, Talbots is most respected for its fly fishing. In addition to the good polaroiding, fish can be found tailing in the weedy shallows and there are good summer/autumn rises. Mudeyes cause intense activity on muggy evenings in mid to late summer.

Access

Talbots is located in privately owned production forest. All roads are gated and access is possible only by prior arrangement with APPM.

TALINAH LAGOON

Tasmap Mersey
Drainage Derwent system (via the Little Pine system)
Location Western Lakes

Talinah is located 1.5 km west of Ada Lagoon and is best reached by walking along the old vehicular track from the Lake Ada carpark. This route is about 5 km and takes 1-2 hours each way.

Recruitment from the outflow stream is significant and the lake holds plenty of 0.7-2 kg brown trout.

The water is surrounded by snowgrass flats. Most of the bottom is shallow and silty and there are many undercut banks. When levels are high lure casting and wet-fly fishing can be extremely productive. Search the undercuts, flooded gutters, and backwaters. Later in the season wade polaroiding is most reliable, though there is always a chance of finding morning and evening tailers.

See also *Fishing in National Parks*, 5.1.

TALLEH LAGOONS

Tasmap Mersey
Drainage Derwent system (via the Powena and Pine systems)
Location Western Lakes

The most convenient access is via the reasonably well-defined walking track from Lake Ada, a trip of 2½-3½ hrs each way.

The lakes are contained between low sedge-covered hills. They are predominantly shallow with extensive sand/silt flats and some weedbeds.

Mayflies and beetles cause fair rises on warm summer days. Otherwise it pays to wade out and polaroid.

After heavy rain fish can be found foraging along the flooded edges near the inflows and outflows.

Lure casting is good whenever conditions are not too bright and calm.

Brown trout of 0.5-1.2 kg are typical.

See also *Fishing in National Parks*, 5.1.

TAMAR, RIVER

Tasmaps Tamar and St Patricks
Drainage Direct to Bass Strait

The River Tamar, incorporating Port Dalrymple, is the large narrow estuary fed by the North Esk and South Esk rivers. While it is not popular among local fishers (perhaps the superb sport in the meadow streams takes up most of their time) it does boast impressive runs of sea trout.

Description

Most of the estuary has a strong tidal influence. At high water the river backs up into dense pin-rush marshes, while at low water extensive mud flats are exposed.

The surrounding land is a blend of bush, pasture and residential development. Launceston, Tasmania's second largest city, lies at the head.

Trout stocks

Many brown trout are resident in the estuary throughout the year. As with the Derwent, there are more at the head than at the mouth and, while fish of 0.3-1.2 kg are typical, some exceed 4 kg.

Sea trout, the real attraction, are caught from early August to late December, with the peak runs occurring from late September to early December. These fish are mostly 0.5-1.5 kg and some grow much larger.

The history of the trout stocks is discussed under *North Esk River* and *South Esk River*.

The nature of the fishing

The bulk of the estuary is so rarely fished that it is difficult to get a reliable picture of when and how to fish. However, I have had considerable success during my relatively few outings. My advice is to read the notes in this book on fishing in the Derwent, taking special notice of the tendency of trout to utilise the main river channels. Remember, too, that the Tamar does not have the sulphide problem associated with the Derwent's Boyer paper mill.

Where to fish

The real hot spot is the bay below the Trevallyn Power Station. Since 1955 the South Esk has been diverted, via a tunnel at Lake Trevallyn, directly to the western bank of the Tamar, about 2.5 km downstream of the natural mouth (of the South Esk). The Trevallyn station is basically a run-of-the-river operation – Lake Trevallyn has little capacity for storage and the normal river flow passes (more or less) directly through the power house. This means that the discharge is relatively constant, and that the fishing is fairly reliable.

Whitebait, elvers and other migratory fish congregate at the outfall of the power house and the trout (sea run fish and slobs) quickly move in for the kill. As the water is deep and most banks are heavily overgrown with willows, there is only limited scope for shore-based sport. You *can* catch fish from the banks, but you are bound to be frustrated by fish you can see swirling and splashing well out of reach. With a small dinghy you are able to stalk trout as they ambush bait among the willow roots and in open water. Often the water is clear enough to allow you to polaroid your quarry between charges.

The head of the inlet is less than 5 km from the centre of Launceston and is accessible via the West Tamar Highway. There is a launching ramp halfway along the south-eastern bank.

Perhaps the second best spot for angling is the area near the mouth of the North Esk River. I have taken trout from Kings Wharf and along the lowest banks of the North Esk proper. Some locals talk of sea trout entering the South Esk – especially when there is a good flow down Cataract Gorge – but generally this area is a very poor sea trout habitat.

The other places for shore-based fishing are wherever the deepwater channel comes in close to the banks. It can be a battle walking across the rushes and mud flats so I tend to fish steeper rocky banks. My successes have been at Dilston (on the eastern shore), below the Batman Bridge, Mowbray Point (on the eastern shore), Beauty Point (on the western shore), and Bell Bay (on the eastern shore). But if you study the extent and nature of the main deepwater channel and its off-shoots (all well marked on the relevant 1:25 000 Tasmaps) you will find dozens of potential hot spots.

If the Derwent is any gauge, speed boat operators should be able to take good bags throughout the estuary. Despite the lack of enthusiasm from locals, drift spinning and trolling are bound to be deadly. Again a knowledge of the river channels and tides will make all the difference. Launching ramps exist near Launceston, the Trevallyn Power Station, Dilston, Windermere, Mowbray Point, Beauty Point and George Town. All are shown in the *Tasmanian Towns Street Atlas* (see *About Tasmania*, section 1).

Tributaries

The main tributary systems, the North Esk and South Esk, include the best trout streams in the State (see *Where to Fish – A Regional Breakdown*, 4.2).

Many of the small creeks spilling directly into the Tamar are too overgrown and/or intermittent to be of much interest to serious fishers, though most contain small brown trout. The most notable water is the Supply River.

Liberations of rainbow trout into the Tamar creeks (which occurred as early as 1913) proved to be of little benefit.

TARN OF ISLANDS

No trout. See *Fishing in National Parks*, 5.1.

TARRALEAH CANALS

Tasmap Nive
Drainage Derwent system (between Lake King William and Tarraleah)

Though lined with concrete, Tarraleah Canal No 1 and Tarraleah Canal No 2 support plenty of naturally-spawned brown trout (and the odd rainbow) to about 0.7 kg. The forebay, where the two waters meet, is a hot spot. Spinning, dry-fly fishing and bait casting are all recommended.

For history see *King William, Lake*.

TEA TREE RIVULET

Tasmap Prosser
Drainage Direct to the Prosser River at Brockley

The lower 7-8 km flow through marginal pasture and provide quite reasonable trout fishing. While summer/autumn flows are usually poor, many of the pools are long, deep and well shaded. Typical brown trout weigh 0.3-0.7 kg and quite a few attain 1.3 kg.

Gatehouse Marsh (adjacent to the Tasman Highway) is drained by a small channel and looks quite insignificant from the road. However, when the channel is running a banker after heavy rain good trout can be found foraging along the edges.

The best low-water fishing is found in the deep holes above the marsh, about 1 km from the highway. If there is a moderate flow, spinning with light lures works well. When the level is low and water clear, bait casting and fly fishing are most appropriate. Daytime rises are poor, so you rely heavily on polaroiding. In the evenings fish can be found mopping up beetles and other terrestrials.

The forested uppermost reaches are small, largely intermittent and rarely fished.

TEMPLESTOWE LAGOON

Tasmap Break O'Day
Drainage Coastal lagoon

Stocked as early as 1962-63. Restocked with 4000 yearling rainbows in 1965. Did not develop into a viable long-term trout fishery and further liberations are unlikely.

TERRY TARN

Tasmap Mersey
Drainage Derwent system (via the Christys Creek system)
Location Western Lakes

A clearwater impounded by elevated banks. It holds 0.4-1.5 kg brown trout, though often you doubt it. Spinning and bank polaroiding are most appropriate.

See also *Fishing in National Parks*, 5.1.

THE BIG LAGOON

See *Big Lagoon, The.*

THERESA LAGOON

Tasmap Mersey
Drainage Derwent system (via the Powena and Pine systems)
Location Western Lakes

Although spawning appears to be confined to mediocre grounds in the outflow, Theresa contains a relatively large head of 0.4-1.5 kg brown trout. The lake can be effectively fished from the elevated banks, with spinning and polaroiding being most reliable.

See also *Fishing in National Parks*, 5.1.

THIRD LAGOON

Tasmap Meander
Drainage Derwent system (via Double Lagoon and the Little Pine system)
Location Nineteen Lagoons

While natural recruitment is negligible, there have been several poorly-documented liberations of brown trout in recent years.

See also *Fishing in National Parks*, 5.1.

THOMPSONS LAKE

See *Bar Lakes System.*

THOR, LAKE

No trout. See *Fishing in National Parks*, 5.1.

THORNTON RIVER

See *Nelson Bay River.*

THREE ARM LAKE

Tasmap Mersey
Drainage Derwent system (via the Little River system)
Location Western Lakes

The banks are rocky, fringed with dwarf pine and unwadeable. In rough weather lures should be cast parallel to the banks and worked along the overhanging bushes. Fly fishers fare best when polaroiding the banks. The mayfly nymphs crawl out onto the rocks to hatch but the spinner phase can cause intense activity on hot calm days. Brown trout of 0.5-1.2 kg are typical.

The small lakes extending west from Three Arm are mainly shallow and weedy and are best suited to fly fishing. Polaroiding is good in summer and autumn. When levels are very high in spring, trout can sometimes be found foraging in the flooded backwaters adjacent to the inflowing creeks.

See also *Fishing in National Parks*, 5.1.

TIBERIAS, LAKE

Tasmap Lake Sorell
Drainage Derwent system (via the Jordan River)

An intermittent marsh. No doubt brown trout invade from the Jordan during floods. However, water is rarely retained long enough to permit significant trout populations to establish, and prolific weed and rush growth make fishing largely impractical anyway.

TIDDLER, LAKE

Tasmap Mersey
Drainage Derwent system (via the Nive system)

A rocky-shored clearwater set in open woodland. It holds plenty of 0.4-1 kg brown trout and is well suited to spinning and polaroiding.

See also *Fishing in National Parks*, 5.1.

TIN DISH RIVULET

Tasmap Lake Sorell
Drainage South Esk system (via the Blackman River)

A sluggish meadow stream. It drains the relatively fertile saltpan district and the pools feature lush weedbeds. Wet-fly fishing on the flood plains, traditional dry-fly fishing, and polaroiding are most productive. Typical brown trout weigh 0.3-1 kg and a few exceed 1.5 kg.

See also *Macquarie River* and *Where to Fish – A Regional Breakdown*, 4.2.

Lake Tiddler

TIN HUT LAKE

Tasmap Mersey
Drainage Derwent system (via the Little Pine system)
Location Nineteen Lagoons

Tin Hut Lake is a typical dead-end trophy water. Historically most fish taken were naturally-spawned browns from 1.5-4 kg. In December 1986 some 15 000 triploid rainbow fingerlings were liberated. These fish were not prominent in anglers' bags, though several specimens from 2-3 kg were caught in the early 1990s.

While most shorelines are rocky and fairly deep, the northern end features extensive marshes, undercut banks, long snowgrass bars and (during wet periods) productive backwaters.

Early-season spinning is best along the deep undercut banks. As levels drop the trout retreat into the lake body and it then pays to cast well out.

Wet-fly fishing in the flooded marshes and along the undercuts is highly recommended. Even if the fish are not tailing and bow-waving, blind searching will usually produce savage strikes. In summer and autumn polaroiding is most reliable, though trout will sometimes

charge into the shallows after galaxias. Catch-and-release is advocated.

The easiest access is via the disused vehicular track from the western shore of Lake Augusta. The walk (from the Lake Ada road) takes 1-1½ hrs each way.

See also *Fishing in National Parks*, 5.1.

TOOMS LAKE

Tasmap Little Swanport
Drainage South Esk system (via the Macquarie system)

Description

Tooms Lake lies in dry woodland at 464 m above sea level behind a 7 m high concrete dam. Summer/autumn drawdowns are significant but there is no ugly littoral scar. The water is usually moderately turbid.

While many banks are rocky and deep, there are weedy/grassy shallows in Swamp Bay, Wet Bay, Wilsons Bay and the Neck Inlet. There are relatively few pockets of drowned trees.

The big fish at Tin Hut will soon become a thing of the past – unless anglers come to accept catch-and-release.

315

Tooms Lake (photo by Rob Sloane)

History / Trout stocks

The first dam across Tooms River, a crude low-profile structure, was built in 1842 and washed away in 1863. A new dam was built in the mid 1860s and the last major works occurred in 1892.

According to NTFA reports brown trout were well established by 1903-04 when association members took four fish of 6-7 lb. There have been many liberations of brown trout since then, though these probably have done little to enhance stocks derived from natural recruitment.

Rainbow trout were first released sometime between 1904 and 1907. In 1908 the NTFA recorded that 1000 fry were turned out in 1907, but that a total of 1500 fry had been released since 1904. There have been regular (and sometimes large) liberations of rainbow fry and fingerlings ever since. The rainbow population fluctuates markedly with changes in stocking regimes and it is doubtful whether the species could be maintained by natural recruitment alone.

Today most trout taken by anglers weigh 0.5-1 kg. Brown trout to 1.3 kg are reasonably common in the marshes, and experienced locals usually land one or two 2 kg fish each season.

Trout liberations (since 1985)

Wild brown trout

YEAR	SIZE	NUMBER
1987	adults	450
"	fry	45 000
1989	fry	50 000
1990	fry	20 000
1991	fry	30 000
1992	fry	30 000
1993	fry	30 000

Domestic rainbow trout

YEAR	SIZE	NUMBER
1988	large fingerlings	2 000
1989	large fingerlings	3 000
1991	large fingerlings	2 500
1992	large fingerlings	2 500
1993	yearlings	3 000

Note: in 1993 the IFC promised annual liberations of 2000-3000 rainbow fingerlings.

Fly fishing

Feature fishing occurs when levels are high in mid to late spring and the trout move into the marshes to forage on tadpoles and frogs. Generally late evening and early morning are the best times to fish, though under dull conditions you may find a few tails and bow-waves throughout the day. The best places are in the Neck Inlet (thick weed and submerged logs make wading arduous at times), Wet Bay (don't forget to cover the gutters), and Swamp Bay.

Fair rises to red spinners occur on hot summer days. While all shores can be productive, during the predominantly northerly and westerly winds it is best to concentrate on the sheltered water in the Neck Inlet.

Mudeyes stimulate good rises during muggy evenings in mid to late summer. The hot spots are where there are emergent rushes and/or timber.

Autumn is usually more productive than summer. While daytime rises are irregular, evening rises are often superb.

Daytime sight fishing is fickle at any time of the angling season and the truth is that most regular anglers do a lot of blind fishing with traditional wet-flies, the favoured places being the marshes, and over the rocky/grassy reef in Wilsons Bay.

Spinning

The best places for shore-based lure casting are the deeper banks at Axehandle Bay, The White Rocks Shore and near the dam.

Drift spinning along the edges of the marshes in Swamp Bay and the Neck Inlet is very effective when the frogs are about in spring.

Trolling

Trolling is best in spring and autumn, though reasonable catches are made on dull and/or rough days in summer. The White Rocks Shore and the outer edges of the marshes are favoured in spring, while the middle of the lake is preferred in summer and autumn.

Bait fishing

Cast-and-retrieve fishing with cockroaches and grubs is very effective, especially when fish can be seen moving in the marshes. The best times and places are mentioned above in the notes for fly fishers.

TOOMS LAKE

317

Access and facilities

There is 2WD access from the Midlands Highway to the shack area near the dam, and a 4WD track extends to the Neck Inlet. Several boat launching areas exist near the shacks.

Sheltered informal campsites can be found on the grassy banks near the dam end.

TOORAH, LAKE

Tasmap   Mersey
Drainage Derwent system (via the Little River system)
Location Western Lakes

An essentially deep clearwater with well-defined rocky banks. Most of the surrounding vegetation comprises fire-damaged eucalypt woodland, though there are pockets of living rainforest.

Brown trout of 1.3-2 kg are typical. Fly fishing is mostly confined to polaroiding, the shallow south-western shore being the real hot spot. Spinning is productive along all shores.

See also *Fishing in National Parks*, 5.1.

TRAVELLERS REST LAGOON

Tasmap   Nive
Drainage Derwent system (via the Travellers Rest
            River)
Location Western Lakes

A shallow clearwater surrounded by buttongrass flats. When levels are high the water backs up into the moors. As levels moderate all of the lake becomes wadeable.

Spinning is most productive early in the season when the water is high. At other times it is best to concentrate your efforts at Travellers Rest Lake.

Fly fishing is good throughout the year. Tailing fish feature at high levels and polaroiding is productive at other times.

Trout of 1-2 kg are typical and some grow bigger.

See also *Fishing in National Parks*, 5.1.

TRAVELLERS REST LAKE

Tasmap   Nive
Drainage Derwent system (via the Travellers Rest River)
Location Western Lakes

A long, essentially deep clearwater. While most shorelines are steep, rocky, thickly-vegetated and difficult to negotiate, the southern end is surrounded by open moorland and is relatively shallow.

Spinning is worthwhile year-round. Concentrate on the shallows when levels are high, and the deeper water when levels fall.

Wade polaroiding at the southern end is highly recommended. However, those prepared to contend with cramped casting should spend some time wading and scrub-bashing along the wooded shores – some really good fish are spotted cruising along the rocks.

See also *Fishing in National Parks*, 5.1.

Polaroiding at Lake Toorah. The trout takes the dry fly...

... the hook is set...

... and the fight is on!

Cruising in close – Travellers Rest Lagoon

TREVALLYN

Tasmap St Patricks
Drainage South Esk River

The HEC began work on the Trevallyn Power Development in 1950. The lake was formed in 1955 and was destined for mediocrity as a trout fishery.

Description

The turbid waters of Lake Trevallyn lie behind a 33 m high concrete gravity dam. The rising waters drowned a steep lightly-wooded valley, and it is difficult to discern exactly where the South Esk ends and the lake begins. Some gentle grassy slopes flank the north-west – south-east arm at the northern end of the lake.

The dam is primarily used to divert the South Esk to the Trevallyn Power Station on the banks of the Tamar estuary. While drawdowns of more than 8.5 m occur, there is relatively little storage capacity and the normal daily river-flow passes more or less directly through the lake. Spillage down the natural river course occurs only during major floods. Full supply is 126.49 m above sea level.

Trout stocks

The section of river flooded by the Trevallyn Dam was mostly a rock/gravel fastwater, though there were a few deep pools (including the large Third Basin). According to NTFA reports brown trout were plentiful but mainly small and in 'average' condition. It was recognised that there would be sufficient river fish in the new lake to provide immediate sport and the only artificial stocking was a liberation of 500 rainbow yearlings in 1955-56.

In 1956, one year after the formation of the lake, it was noted that the trout population was large and that, while some fish of 2-3 lb were

seen, most were small. By the end of the next season it was conceded that the brown trout *'failed to grow to any size, and the rainbows apparently chose other feeding grounds'*. The average size was said to be 10 inches.

Today the water teems with 0.2-0.5 kg brown trout and fish in excess of 1.2 kg are uncommon. Emigrant rainbows from the Brumbys Creek fish farm are reported every now and then.

Facilities

While most of the land surrounding the lake is privately owned, some 450 ha between the north-eastern shore and Duck Reach (on the lower South Esk) is a State Recreation Area. Public facilities – including toilets, a boat ramp, barbeques and lawns – have been developed at Aquatic Point. However, the Aquatic Point development is open to the public only between 8 am and sunset. Additional facilities, accessible only by boat, are located at Honeymoon Bay.

Boating

Power boats are excluded from a danger zone near the dam and tunnel intake, and from an area set aside for swimming, sailboarding and canoeing. Elsewhere the maximum permissible speed is five knots.

There are launching ramps at Aquatic Point (open from 8 am to sunset) and Hadspen (open all hours).

The fishing

Trevallyn is not a popular trout water – most locals prefer to fish the meadow streams, Brushy Lagoon and/or Curries River Dam (see *Where to Fish – A Regional Breakdown*, 4.2).

Trolling, drift spinning and set-rod fishing account for fair bags, and there are modest rises on warm summer/autumn afternoons.

Comfortable shore-based sport is largely confined to the north-west – south-east arm at the northern end of the lake.

TROUT CREEK

See *Coquet Creek*.

TULLY RIVER

Tasmap Cape Sorell
Drainage Direct to the Henty River

An overgrown tea-coloured fastwater which carries plenty of tiny brown trout. Fishing is best when levels are low. Try Celtas and baits.

TUNGATINAH LAGOON

Tasmap   Nive
Drainage   Derwent system
Location   Central Highlands, north of Tarraleah

Tungatinah gives up more big fish than either Bradys Lake or Lake Binney. While it is not as productive or as popular as Bronte Lagoon, it is certainly worth fishing. Notes on history, water manipulation, trout stocks, and facilities are given under Binney, Lake and Bradys Lake. Detailed information is available in the book Trout Guide *(Rob Sloane and Greg French, 1991).*

How is Tungatinah different from Binney?

Tungatinah is shallower than Binney, and the shores are more open. Much of the northern shoreline is more reminiscent of the grassy banks of Bronte Lagoon than the steep rock/clay slopes bounding most of the Bradys chain.

When and where to fish

The best area for early-season wet-fly fishing and summer polaroiding is along the northern shore, particularly in the flooded marshy corner near the dam wall.

Spinning from the shore or a small boat is usually more effective than trolling.

The canal inflow is popular with set-rod bait fishers.

TWILIGHT TARN

Probably no trout. See *Fishing in National Parks*, 5.5.

TWIN LAKES

No trout. See *Fishing in National Parks*, 5.3.

TWISTED LAKES

No trout. See *Fishing in National Parks*, 5.4.

TWISTED TARN

Tasmap   Tyenna
Drainage   Derwent system (via the Broad system)
Location   Mt Field

Twisted Tarn lies in open alpine woodland just north of the Tarn Shelf. While pencil pines and heath grow along some shores, most of the lake

can be fished from the bank or by wading. The bottom is mostly sand and silt, and the water is crystal clear.

Brown trout of 0.6-1.2 kg are fairly common, and spinning and polaroiding are the most reliable ways to catch them.

Access is by well-formed walking track from Lake Dobson. The round trip incorporating Lake Webster and the Tarn Shelf takes about 5-8 hrs. Pleasant informal campsites can be found near the lakeshore, and there is a public shelter hut nearby at Lake Newdegate.

See also *Fishing in National Parks*, 5.5.

TYENNA RIVER

Tasmap   Tyenna and Wedge
Drainage   Direct to the River Derwent

The Tyenna is a large stream which provides the best fastwater sport in the State.

Description

The water can become quite turbid and slightly tea-coloured after heavy rain, but is usually quite

Upstream nymphing at the Tyenna River (photo courtesy Rob Sloane)

clear. It flows through a series of wide riffles and (mostly small) pools. Most banks are overgrown with trees and scrub – wading is essential.

Trout stocks

Brown trout were taken to *'Russell's Falls'* (an early name for the Tyenna River) in 1870, though by this time fish would already have invaded from the Derwent. The species soon established and continues to be maintained entirely by natural recruitment. While fish of 0.2-0.5 kg are numerous, quite a few attain 1 kg and some exceed 4 kg.

Undoubtedly rainbow trout were periodically released between the turn of the century and the 1950s (see *About Our Sportfish*, 2.2) but wild stocks never established. Late in 1977 the IFC issued a licence for a commercial fish farm on the banks of Russell Falls Creek at National Park, and by 1978 significant numbers of rainbows were being hatched and reared. A second hatchery, on the banks of the Tyenna at Karanja, was approved in 1986. Domestic rainbows from the hatcheries and rearing ponds frequently escape into the Tyenna where they account for up to 30% of the trout taken by anglers. Most of these fish weigh 0.1-0.4 kg, though some exceed 1 kg.

The productivity of the Tyenna is quite extraordinary. The IFC has determined that there are up to 150 trout in every 100 m stretch, including more than 40 of takeable size. This equates to more than 23 kg of fish per 100 m, comparing to just 3-8 kg in similar shingle-bottomed fastwaters elsewhere in Tasmania. The bottom line is that when conditions are fair experienced anglers can expect to take big bags of good-sized fish.

Where to fish

Virtually all of the river from the mouth to Maydena is easily fished and highly recommended. Trout are found above Maydena as well – but much of the water is deep and overgrown. The small fastwater tributaries, such as the Junee River and Marriotts Creek, are full of tiny browns and are not often fished.

When to fish

The best time to fish is when the water is moderate to low – usually in summer and autumn.

Fly fishing

On warm days there are reliable afternoon and evening rises. A variety of terrestrials and aquatics are taken and usually any well-presented nondescript dry-fly will work well.

When there is no obvious surface activity it pays to try traditional upstream nymphing, or even blind fishing with dries.

Bait fishing

Locals often use worms on set-rods in the quieter corners of the deep pools during floods. But the real action occurs as water levels moderate. When there is a fair flow of murky water, upstream casting with worms is dynamite. Later, when the water is clear, grasshoppers are preferred.

Lure fishing

Small (Size 1) Celtas are all you need. Fish can usually be easily caught in bright conditions but, if the going is a little tough, you can always rely on the evening stint to fill the creel. Low levels are best, though you can expect fair results as soon as flood waters begin to ebb.

TYNDALL, LAKE

No trout. See *West Coast Range*.

TYRE, LAKE

No trout. See *Fishing in National Parks*, 5.1.

UNDINE, LAKE

Tasmap   Nive
Drainage   Gordon system (via the Franklin River)

A moderately tea-coloured water surrounded by dense forest. The most convenient access involves a 4 km (1½-2½ hr) cross-country walk from Lake Dixon through buttongrass flats and pockets of thick heath.

While the water teems with 0.2-0.5 kg brown trout, a few fish exceed 1 kg. Spinning is productive in rough weather. Fly fishing is best in warm conditions when the trout can be seen rising and/or cruising the edges.

Better fish are reputed to exist in the small lake 1½ km (¾ hr) west of the north end of Undine. The nearby elevated lakes (including Lake Hermion and perhaps Australia Tarn) have not been invaded by trout.

See also *Fishing in National Parks*, 5.3.

UPPER LAKE JUKES

No trout.

URANUS, LAKE

No trout. See *Fishing in National Parks*, 5.2.

VALE RIVER

Tasmap Sophia
Drainage Pieman system (via the Mackintosh system)

The Vale is one of the most intriguing streams in the State, the two most distinctive features being the wild rainbow trout and the early-season backwater fishing for big browns.

Description

The river between Reynolds Falls and the Speeler Creek junction flows through steep densely-forested gorges and, while it holds plenty of small trout, it is rarely fished.

Feature fishing occurs on the grassy plains in the upper reaches, where the water runs over limestone. From the edge of the plains to the Cradle Mountain link road, the water is a series of shallow broadwaters separated by shingly riffles. While there is plenty of open water, there is also an abundance of lush trailing weeds – both in the pools and in the fast water.

From the link road to the transmission lines the river narrows, in most places being less than 2 or 3 m wide. Most pools are wadeable but there are extensive undercuts and some deep semi-permanent backwater lagoons.

Above the transmission lines the stream fragments, becoming a lacework of narrow channels and honeycombed banks. However, there are many fishable backwaters. Most are grassy flood basins which fill only after heavy rains. Others are permanent and semi-permanent lagoons.

Water colour is variable. At the low end of the plain the stream is often almost transparent, while in the headwater runnels it is distinctly tea coloured. The backwaters also vary, some being dark with tannin and others being crystal clear.

One for tea – Vale River

Fishing the backwater lagoons – Vale River

Access

Access can be made via the link road or via the old vehicular route to Lake Lea. Backpackers will find idyllic informal tent-sites on the plains downstream of the link road, and on the edge of the myrtle forest at the foot of Bonds Range.

Rainbow trout

Rainbow trout were probably first liberated in 1909 or 1910 when the species was taken to Lake Lea. It was believed by many that Lake Lea and the Vale River were connected and it seems that some fish were placed in the stream on the assumption that they would help populate the lake.

Celta fishing and bait casting in the stream proper, downwater of the link road, usually result in good bags of rainbow trout. Traditional upstream nymphing, dry-fly fishing, and night fishing with wet flies are also very effective. Typical rainbows weigh 0.2-1 kg and some grow bigger. I have also taken rainbows, some to 3 kg, from the backwater lagoons, though the species is relatively uncommon in this habitat.

Brown trout

The origin of the brown trout is unclear. Some say that the species has been in the upper reaches for decades. Others insist that they are the result of illegal liberations in the late 1970s or early 1980s.

Brown trout are now found throughout the system, though the best specimens are taken from the headwater runnels and associated backwaters. In this habitat the fish are mostly 0.7-2 kg and quite a few attain 3 kg.

When the river is in flood and spilling into the grassy depressions adjacent to the main channels, fish soon start foraging in the shallows and the wet-fly fishing is superb!

When levels are moderate to low, big fish can be polaroided in the clear permanent and semi-permanent lagoons, and fished up with nymphs from the darker pools.

The future

If the brown trout are recent introductions their average size may already have peaked, and they may eventually displace the rainbows. If the species has been present for a long time, the fishery will already be in balance, and anglers may expect little change in either the average size of fish caught or species composition.

VALLEY LAGOON

(also called Valley Pond)

Tasmap   Forester
Drainage Ringarooma system
Location West of Derby

A deep tea-coloured pond contained between densely-forested banks. From the winter of 1964 to the winter of 1976 it received almost annual consignments of 100-200 adult brown trout. Today stocks are maintained by natural recruitment and the average size is reputed to be small. Set-rod fishing is most popular.

VAUCLUSE RESERVOIR

Tasmap   South Esk
Drainage South Esk system
Location East of Cleveland

A large storage lying behind a high rockfill dam. It is surrounded by marginal pasture and the water is always slightly turbid and tea coloured.

From 1972 to 1976 it was managed as a put-and-take brook trout fishery, receiving a total of 6000 fingerlings and 3000 yearlings. Fish in excess of 1.5 kg were taken by anglers.

Water quality has deteriorated and the lake has not been stocked in recent years.

VENUS, LAKE

No trout. See *Fishing in National Parks*, 5.2.

VERA, LAKE

No trout. See *Fishing in National Parks*, 5.3.

WADLEYS LAKE

Tasmap   Mersey
Drainage Natural – Derwent system (via James system)
Location Western Lakes

Wadleys Lake is surrounded by flat heathland, though there are rocky outcrops and clumps of trees nearby. While some banks are quite deep, there are extensive wadeable shallows. Brown trout to 1.5 kg are common.

Nearby there are several small trophy-brown waters. Unfortunately, between 1989 and 1991 some of these were illegally stocked with domestic rainbows.

See also *Fishing in National Parks*, 5.1.

Take time to explore the small waters near Wadleys

323

WALKER TARN

Tasmap Tyenna
Drainage Derwent system (via the Broad system)
Location Mt Field

Contains the odd better-than-average brown trout. More reliable sport exists nearby at Lake Newdegate and Twisted Tarn.

See also *Fishing in National Parks*, 5.5.

WARATAH, LAKE

Tasmap Hellyer
Drainage Arthur system (via the Waratah River)
Location Waratah

Lake Waratah is actually two small interconnected ponds, formed in 1981 as part of a town beautification project. They are surrounded by lawns and parkland.

As a result of natural overpopulation, the waters teem with 0.2-0.6 kg brown trout. Celta fishing, bait casting and blind fishing with wet flies often result in very big bags. Spectacular daytime and evening rises occur on warm calm days in summer and autumn. While the water is always slightly murky, it is not obviously tea-coloured and fish can sometimes be polaroided along the edges.

WARATAH RESERVOIR

Tasmap Hellyer
Drainage Arthur system (via the Waratah River)
Location Near Waratah

The 6 m high dam was constructed in 1900 as a town supply. Full supply is 608 m above sea level and marked drawdowns can be expected in summer and autumn. While the southern end is bounded by dense forest and scrub, there are grassy flats adjacent to the northern shores. Narrow shoreline marshes are a feature, and the whole storage is littered with emergent tree trunks. Though not obviously tea-coloured, the water is always slightly turbid.

The origin of the trout stocks is obscure (see *Bischoff Reservoir*). Naturally-spawned brown trout of 0.2-0.5 kg are plentiful, and 2 kg fish are reported from time to time. While there is not a recognised wild population of rainbow trout, the IFC in 1993 guaranteed annual releases of 500-1000 rainbow fingerlings at the 'Waratah Lakes'.

When levels are high brown trout sometimes forage in the weedy margins, but feature fly fishing occurs on warm summer/autumn days when there are spectacular rises to mayflies, damselflies and a variety of terrestrials. The big advantages over the Bischoff fishery are that the banks are easily accessible, and fish can be ambushed as

Lake Waratah

Waratah Reservoir

they rise in pockets of open water among the weeds and emergent pin-rushes.

Spinning and bait fishing also work well.

WARWICK, LAKE

No trout. See *Fishing in National Parks*, 5.3.

WATERHOUSE LAKES

See *Big Waterhouse Lake*, *Blackmans Lagoon* and *Little Waterhouse Lake*.

WATERWORKS RESERVOIRS

Public fishing is not allowed.

WAVERLEY, LAKE

Tasmap   St Patricks
Drainage   North Esk system (via Distillery Creek)

An application to flood a marshy *'hazard'* adjacent to the Waverley Primary School was presented to the RWSC in 1977, and in 1980, under

the scrutiny of the Waverley Progress Association, a small dam was constructed. In 1985, with additional funding from the IFC, the current earthfill wall was completed.

The 2.5 ha lake is formally recognised as a Juvenile Angling Pond and can only be fished by people under the age of 17.

The trout fishery is largely dependent upon artificial stocking and the quality of the sport varies accordingly.

Trout liberations

Wild brown trout

YEAR	SIZE	NUMBER
1985	adults	200
1988	fry	?

Note: due to poor documentation this list is likely to be incomplete

Domestic rainbow trout

YEAR	SIZE	NUMBER
1991	yearlings	400
1992	yearlings	300

Note: in 1993 the IFC promised annual liberations of 500 rainbow fingerlings

WAYATINAH LAGOON

Tasmaps   Nive and Shannon
Drainage   River Derwent (a major instream impoundment)

Of the five instream lakes on the lower Derwent, Meadowbank and Wayatinah are by far the best trout fisheries. While Meadowbank is the most popular water, this is really just a function of it being relatively close to Hobart. Wayatinah produces slightly smaller fish but is more productive and more reliable.

Description

Wayatinah is a slightly murky water surrounded by forested hills. It was formed in 1957 following the completion of the 24 m high rockfill dam on the River Derwent. Full supply is 231.03 m above sea level and the normal operating range is less than 2.5 m.

There are two major inflows. The Nive catchment is diverted at Lake Liapootah (some 10 km above Wayatinah) and enters the lagoon not via the old stream bed but from the Liapootah Power Station. A smaller but quite significant contribution comes down the natural course of the River Derwent.

While the lake harbours little emergent timber, there are many drowned logs and submerged tree

325

stumps over the weedy shallows in the northern half.

Trout stocks

The lagoon flooded a section of the Derwent system already well-stocked with brown trout, and continuing natural recruitment from spawning grounds in the River Derwent quickly resulted in overpopulation. Today most fish taken weigh 0.3-0.7 kg and fish in excess of 1.5 kg are uncommon.

Some 5000 rainbow yearlings were liberated in 1957-58 but the species failed to establish. Rainbows are now extremely rare, the few caught being emigrants from the Tarraleah district.

In the mid 1980s a commercial salmon hatchery was established on the banks of the River Derwent immediately above Wayatinah Lagoon (see *About our Sportfish*, 2.4). Many small fish escape, though few are reported by anglers.

Schools of stunted redfin perch abound.

Maintenance in 1981 necessitated the almost complete draining of the lagoon. However, most trout simply retreated to the natural river bed, and the fishery re-established as soon as the impoundment refilled.

Facilities

A formal caravan/camping park, complete with lawns, barbeques and toilets, is located on the western shore north of Wayatinah village.

Boating

Small boats can be launched at the caravan park and at the tunnel outlet (in the south-eastern corner of the lake). As much of the water is shallow and littered with submerged stumps and logs, high-powered speed boats are inappropriate.

Fly fishing

The hot spots for fly fishing are the weedy shallows along the eastern and northern shores.

When levels are rising fish can be found tailing in the weeds and amongst the tea-tree. Late evening and early morning are best, though the action can continue throughout the day when the weather is overcast.

Superb rises to mayflies and beetles happen on warm days in summer and autumn.

Polaroiding is worthwhile when there is plenty of light.

Lure fishing

Lightweight lures are used with good effect by those prepared to wade along the weedy eastern and northern shores. However, just about any accessible bank will deliver fish.

Drift spinning is best adjacent to the weedy shallows.

Trolling is rarely as productive as drift spinning, though fair bags are taken from the deep water over the south-western half of the storage.

WEBSTER, LAKE

Tasmap Tyenna
Drainage Derwent system (via the Broad system)
Location Mt Field

The western shore backs up to a steep forested tier, and the eastern shore is bounded by buttongrass flats. The bottom is rocky and weed-free with extensive wadeable shallows.

An article in *The Mercury* in 1893 reported the stocking of Lake Webster. While there may have been subsequent liberations, there have been no releases in modern times. Today the trout population is large and the average size is disappointing. Most fish weigh about 0.3-0.5 kg and specimens larger than 1 kg are uncommon. Spinning, polaroiding, and night fishing with wet flies commonly result in big bags.

Walking tracks extend from Lake Fenton and Lake Dobson. Both routes take about 1½-2 hrs each way.

See also *Fishing in National Parks*, 5.5.

WELCOME RIVER

Tasmap Welcome
Drainage Direct to Bass Strait

The majority of the Welcome River is located within the vast Woolnorth estate where public access is restricted.

Sea trout are caught in the estuary and lower freshwater reaches.

Numerous brown trout to 0.3 kg are found in the small fastwater creeks near Redpa.

WELD RIVER

Tasmap Forester
Drainage Direct to the Ringarooma River at Moorina

A small wadeable fastwater. The water is tea-coloured and becomes slightly turbid after rain.

Between Moorina and Weldborough the stream flows through a steep densely-forested valley. Above Weldborough it is flanked by pockets of flat pasture, though there is still plenty of bankside vegetation.

While small brown trout exist below Harridge Falls, the upper reaches carry only rainbows.

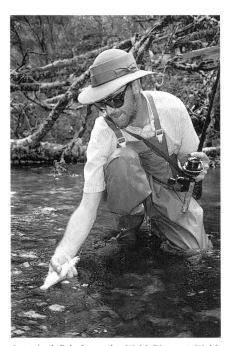

A typical fish from the Weld River at Weld-borough

According to NTFA reports rainbows were liberated as early as 1911 when 2000 fry were distributed in *'Weldborough streams'*. No doubt there were subsequent liberations, but stocks have been maintained entirely by natural recruitment since at least the 1950s. Today the vast majority of fish taken are two-year-olds of about 0.2 kg. However, a few fish survive longer and attain 0.7 kg or so.

While Celta fishing is most popular, there is room in the Weldborough district for comfortable fly casting.

WELD RIVER

Tasmaps Huon, Tyenna, and Wedge
Drainage Direct to the Huon River

The Weld is a productive stream where wild rainbow trout greatly outnumber browns in anglers' bags.

Description

The lower 20 km or so flows through State (production) Forest. While the land adjacent to the river is a blend of forest and sedge flats, all banks are heavily overgrown with trees and scrub. At low levels this stretch is a series of deep rocky pools separated by shallow shingly riffles. You can make good progress upstream by wading, but you must be prepared to scrub-bash around some of the larger pools.

Since 1990 all of the mid to upper catchment has been reserved in an extension of the Southwest National Park.

In the mid reaches, rainforest and dense wet-forest flank the river and the substrate is mostly limestone. There are long riffles, shallow pools, and beds of trailing weeds.

The uppermost reaches are small, shallow and shingly.

During floods the water is heavily tea-coloured but as levels subside the tannin content moderates considerably. Some turbidity associated with forestry operations may be encountered in the lower reaches, especially after heavy rain.

Trout stocks

Brown trout would have invaded the Weld soon after the Huon system was stocked in 1870.

While the origin of the rainbow trout is unclear, the STLAA recorded that the species was well established by the early 1950s.

The upper limit (of distribution) of both species may be in the vicinity of the Weld River Arch – an area of substantial limestone formations, falls and underground channels. I have never seen fish (trout or natives) above the Arch. In fact the upper reaches teem with free-crawling *Anaspides* shrimps – and this species tends to live a cryptic existence when fish are present.

Throughout their range the rainbows tend to outnumber the browns by about ten to one in anglers' bags. While most trout (browns and rainbows) weigh 0.2-0.4 kg, fish to 1 kg are not especially uncommon and I have taken some in excess of 1.5 kg.

Where to fish

The most popular place to fish is the lower section. A forestry road extends from the Denison Road (on the northern side of the Huon River just west of the Little Denison River) to the mouth of the Weld and the Eddy Rapids, though the latter section is of dubious 2WD standard.

There is an alternative 2WD access from Geeveston through the Southern Forests. Some 7 km along the South Weld Road from the Tahune Bridge, a rugged 2WD spur leads to the edge of Glovers Bluff. From here you can scramble down the steep sedge slopes to the riverbank, a descent of about 15-20 minutes. Allow extra time for the uphill return.

The Weld River at the Eddy Rapids

The mid reaches are a rugged wilderness, and the easiest access is via an ill-defined walking route from the north end of the catchment. The 2WD forestry roads leading to the headwaters from Maydena are gated and you need to contact ANM to arrange entry. If you take the Styx Road for 5 km and the Mueller Road for 11 km you will find a short spur track leading to transmission pylon 106. From here there is a blazed route to the Weld River. The first leg, from the carpark to the river some distance above the Arch, takes about ¾-1½ hrs. The track is often littered with fallen horizontal scrub and you must be prepared to spend a good deal of time on your hands and knees. After the first contact with the river you walk downstream for another 1½-2 hrs, this time through classic open-floored closed-canopy rainforest, before meeting the river downstream of the Arch. This area does not offer better fishing than the more accessible lower reaches – but for anglers who like grandeur and solitude it is highly recommended. Remember that this area is a sensitive wilderness zone and that special rules of conduct apply (see introduction to *Fishing in National Parks*, section 5).

How to fish

The angling is always best in summer and autumn when levels are low.

Celta fishing is most popular and can result in big bags even on bright days.

Fly fishers often find fair rises, especially to caddis flies, but otherwise traditional upstream nymphing is bound to get results.

Bait casting with worms and grasshoppers is dynamite in the lower reaches. Remember, though, that bait fishing is not encouraged within the national park.

WENTWORTH DAM

Tasmap Nive
Drainage Derwent system (via the Tarraleah Canal system)

A puddle of clear water lying amid tea-tree behind a low-profile rock dam. See *Hornes Dam*.

WENTWORTH LAKE

(not yet officially named)

No trout. See *Clarence Lagoon*.

WEST COAST RANGE

Tasmaps Sophia and Franklin

Description

Although mostly just 500-700 m above sea level, the West Coast Range is a truly alpine environment. The average annual rainfall is 3.5-4 m and blizzards can occur at any time.

Access

The Anthony Road is a sealed highway running through the heart of the West Coast Range, giving direct access to Lake Plimsoll and passing close to Lake Selina.

There is also a 2WD standard road extending from the Zeehan Highway north of Queenstown to Lake Margaret village, from where you can walk up to Lake Margaret.

Most other roads are of rough 4WD standard only. Of most interest to anglers is the old vehicular track which leads from near Lake Selina to Lake Rolleston. This route can be difficult to negotiate by 4WD but is easily walked.

Trout stocks

Most lakes on the West Coast Range have steep outflows littered with waterfalls and have not been invaded by trout. Some, such as lakes Sandra and

WEST COAST RANGE

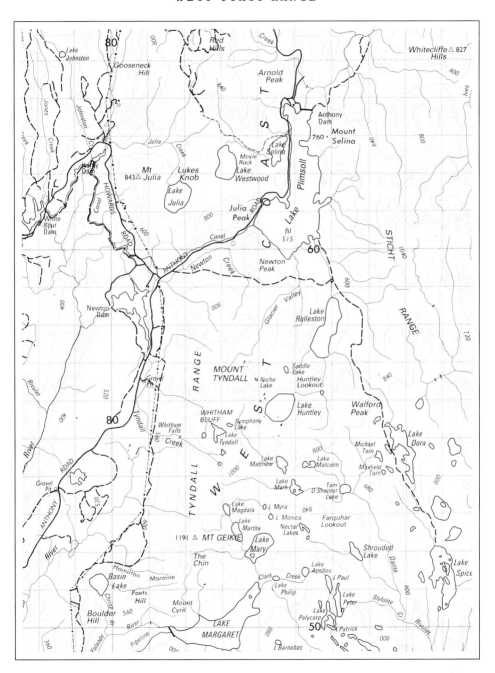

Lake Rolleston

The West Coast Range – brook trout fishing amid spectacular scenery (photo by Carolyn Lee)

Gaye on Mt Murchison, are so isolated that they contain no fish at all – not even the highly invasive (native) climbing galaxia.

The Lake Margaret system was probably stocked early this century (see *Margaret, Lake*) and now supports brown trout. Lake Beatrice was invaded by both brown and rainbow trout from the King River (see *King River*). The only other trout waters are those linked to the Anthony Power Development.

The Anthony Power Development – a new brook trout fishery

The Anthony Power Development was approved by State Parliament in 1983 after the Federal Government prohibited the continuation of the Gordon Below Franklin Dam. Work was completed in 1994.

The scheme involves the diversion of the upper Henty catchment into the Anthony catchment, and a new power station on the Anthony River near Lake Murchison. Impoundments on the upper Henty, White Spur and Newton creeks were completed in 1988, 1989 and 1990 respectively. The main storage, Lake Plimsoll, filled in 1993. Work also began on a dam across the Langdon River – but a re-evaluation of costs and benefits resulted in this project being shelved.

As the power scheme was to be built in an area devoid of trout, it was decided that the impoundments would be stocked with brook trout, the first liberations occurring in the streams in 1986. While the water is acidic and hardly ideal for the species, this stocking programme represents the only realistic hope of establishing a significant wild brook trout fishery in Tasmania (see *About Our Sportfish*, 2.3). Of the impoundments only Lake Plimsoll offers reasonable prospects for anglers. The other waters are small and surrounded by steep densely-vegetated banks – and, since relatively few hatchery-reared brook trout are available, they have not been included in the stocking programme. The Langdon River has received some brook trout, but stocking ceased when it became apparent that the lake would not be formed. There is widespread recognition of the importance of maintaining the integrity of the surrounding natural waters, and so only lakes Selina and Rolleston, which would have been invaded by fish from Lake Plimsoll, are being managed as trout fisheries. Significant natural recruitment has already occurred and the future is promising. However, the species has proven difficult to establish in other waters and catch-and-release is highly desirable at present.

A small water storage, known locally as Langdon Lagoon, was formed behind a crude gravel levee on wet sedgeland adjacent to the Anthony Road (grid ref. 788 540). This was stocked with adults and fingerlings in 1986, with fingerlings in 1987, and with a further 300 fingerlings in 1993. The fish grow well but there is no chance of natural recruitment.

WEST LAGOON

Tasmap South Esk
Drainage South Esk system (via the Liffey system)
Location Toiberry

An intermittent marsh surrounded by flat farmland.

As early as 1914 the NTFA had proposed that the outflow be dammed and a creek diverted into the basin so that a permanent trout fishery could be established. In 1937, amid continued lobbying, it was noted that *'fish up to 11 lb in weight have been taken as now existing'*. Presumably these fish were upstream migrants from the Liffey which had taken advantage of fast-growth conditions in the marsh.

Today the basin is laced with drains and is used for agriculture.

WEST QUEEN RIVER

Tasmap Franklin
Drainage King system (via the Queen River)

A tiny overgrown tea-coloured fastwater. Unlike the nearby East Queen River, it is not heavily polluted and carries plenty of small brown trout.

Of most interest to anglers are the three small reservoirs. Each features steep scrubby banks and provides limited scope for shore-based spinning, fly fishing and bait casting. After being drained for maintenance, lakes 2 and 3 were restocked with brown trout fry in 1987. Natural recruitment results in overpopulation and most fish are very small.

Access is via vehicular spurs from the Lake Margaret Road.

WEST SWAN RIVER

Tasmaps Break O'Day and St Patricks
Drainage Direct to the Swan River at Waters Meeting

The West Swan flows over a bed of loose shingle through dry woodland. At times of moderate to low flow much of the bed is exposed and the water is crystal. Most pools are no more than thigh deep and they become quite warm in summer.

Small brown trout can be taken on Celtas, baits and flies, though you rarely take big bags.

See also *Swan River*.

WESTERN CREEK

Tasmaps Meander and Mersey
Drainage South Esk system (via the Meander River)

The NTFA recorded the liberation of rainbow yearlings in 1906-07 and 1907-08, and noted that large rainbows were caught by anglers in subsequent years. Acknowledging Montana Falls, it is possible that for some years Western Creek was a rainbow-only water.

Today the river teems with small browns.

See also *Meander River*.

WESTERN LAKES

See *Fishing in National Parks*, 5.1.

WESTONS LAKE

Tasmap Mersey
Drainage Mersey system (via the Fisher system)
Location Chudleigh Lakes

Westons Lake is predominantly shallow and weedy.

After heavy rain the lake breaks its banks, filling ditches and gutters and providing exciting wet-fly fishing.

As levels drop, wave action disturbs the bottom and causes discolouration. When polaroiding becomes difficult you are best advised to concentrate on nearby waters such as lakes Lucy Long and Nameless.

Expect brown trout to 2 kg or so.

See also *Fishing in National Parks*, 5.1.

WESTWOOD, LAKE

No trout. See *West Coast Range*.

WEY RIVER

Tasmap Hellyer
Drainage Arthur system (via the Hellyer River)

Essentially a smaller version of the Hellyer River.

Early Parliamentary reports indicate that the 'Way' river was stocked with brown trout as early as 1881, and the NTFA mentioned '*good trout fishing*' in 1904. Today the stream teems with 0.1-0.3 kg brown trout and is best fished by wading upstream when levels are low.

WHITE KANGAROO RIVULET

Tasmaps Derwent and Lake Sorell
Drainage Direct to the Coal River

Typical of south-eastern creeks, the White Kangaroo has limited summer/autumn flows.

The lowest 7-8 km stretch can provide surprisingly good sport for fly fishers and bait casters. It flows through marginal pasture but many banks are overgrown and the large deep pools remain clear and cool throughout the hottest months. The trout (all browns) are mostly 0.2-0.5 kg yet some exceed 1 kg. Fishing is best when levels are moderate to low. Polaroiding is effective and there are modest rises. You can usually pick up one or two fish if you try hard, and the nearby Coal River is a good fall-back on tough days.

The water adjacent to the Brown Mountain Road contains (mostly small) fish throughout the year, but in summer it recedes into small isolated pools and becomes very warm.

Further up, the trout habitat is too marginal to be of interest to anglers.

WHITE SPUR LAKE

Tasmap Sophia
Drainage Natural – Henty system
Location West Coast Range

A small impoundment with steep densely-vege-

tated banks. The 44 m high concrete-faced rock-fill dam was completed in 1989 and serves to divert water via the White Spur and Henty canals into Lake Plimsoll. Full supply is 530 m above sea level and big drawdowns are to be expected.

The impoundment offers little prospect as a trout fishery and has not been stocked, though it may eventually be invaded by brook trout from the Anthony system.

See also *West Coast Range*.

WHITLAM, LAKE

No trout. See *Fishing in National Parks*, 5.3.

WHYTE RIVER

Tasmaps Pieman and Arthur River
Drainage Direct to the Pieman River at Corinna

A tea-coloured fastwater flowing through dense wet-forest. Sea trout are taken from the mouth. Small slow-growing resident browns abound throughout the system.

WIHAREJA LAGOON

Tasmap Shannon
Drainage Derwent system (via the Shannon system)
Location St Patricks Plains

A shallow silt-bottomed natural lagoon located in privately-owned moorland. As the surrounding land is farmed, the water becomes quite murky after heavy rain. However, in settled weather the water clears markedly.

Brown trout stocks are maintained entirely by natural recruitment, and fish of 0.7-1.3 kg are typical.

When the lake breaks out over the grassy verges the trout can be found tailing among the tussocks. As the water recedes polaroiding becomes more effective. Fair rises to mayflies occur in summer.

The shallow water and prolific weed growth can be frustrating for lure casters.

WILKS, LAKE

Tasmap Sophia
Drainage Forth system (via the Dove system)
Location Near Cradle Mountain

Although long reputed to be devoid of trout, in 1990 I noticed several kilo-plus risers. I suspect these fish are the result of recent illegal stocking.

See also *Fishing in National Parks*, 5.4.

WILL, LAKE

No trout. See *Fishing in National Parks*, 5.4.

WILMOT RIVER

Tasmap Forth
Drainage Direct to the River Forth below the Paloona Dam

A slightly tea-coloured fastwater flowing between densely-forested hills.

The lower reaches (accessible from the Wilmot Road at the Alma Bridge, about 1.5 km from the mouth) include some deep broadwaters which hold plenty of small trout as well as a few fish in excess of 1 kg. While access along the banks is arduous, there is plenty of scope for Celta fishing and bait casting.

The mid to upper reaches flow over a shingle bed and comprise shallow pools separated by long riffles. The water teems with 0.2-0.4 kg browns and, when levels are low, Celta fishing, bait casting and traditional upstream nymphing often result in big bags. The easiest access is from Spellmans Bridge on the Wilmot to Upper Castra road.

WILSON RIVER

Tasmap Pieman
Drainage Pieman system (via Lake Pieman)

A tea-coloured fastwater flowing through dense wet-forest. When levels are low it is popular with local Celta fishers. Brown trout to 0.3 kg abound.

WINDERMERE, LAKE

No trout. See *Fishing in National Parks*, 5.4.

WINDY LAKE

No trout. See *Fishing in National Parks*, 5.3.

WINTER BROOK

Tasmaps Forth and Hellyer
Drainage Direct to the River Leven above the Leven Canyon

A small overgrown tea-coloured fastwater which carries plenty of very small brown trout. It is fairly popular among local Celta fishers and bait casters.

WOODS LAKE

Tasmap Shannon
Drainage South Esk system (via the Lake River)

Woods Lake is under-utilised by anglers – but only because of the relatively poor road access. The fishing is discussed in detail in the book Trout Guide *(Rob Sloane and Greg French, 1991). A summary only is given here.*

Description

Woods is a large storage protected by rocky wooded tiers. Full supply is 737.36 m above sea level and the normal operating range is almost 4 m. The water is characteristically milky-green.

Water is received from the natural run-off, occasional releases from Arthurs Lake down the Upper Lake River, and the Ripple Diversion (see *Lagoon of Islands*). The HEC draws water from the lake in summer and autumn to supply its riparian commitment to properties in the Lake River catchment. This became necessary after the formation of Arthurs Lake, which resulted in reduced flows down the Lake River.

Trout stocks

Woods is a wild brown trout fishery maintained entirely by natural recruitment from spawning grounds in the Upper Lake River. The average size and condition of the fish fluctuates with seasonal variations in spawning success and lake levels. Fish of 0.7-1 kg are typical but quite a few attain 2 kg.

History

Brown trout would have invaded Woods from the Lake River and Arthurs Lake by the 1870s. An early Parliamentary report (1893) noted that brook trout had been turned out, but this species did not establish.

In 1904 the NTFA noted the capture of 210 fish (presumably brown trout) averaging about 3 lb, while in 1906 it was reported that Loch Leven strain brown trout provided good sport. The *Handbook of Tasmania* (1908) mentioned that the '*Loch Leven trout*' averaged 3½ lb and that '*Brown trout*' of 8-9 lb were sometimes taken.

Sometime near the turn of the century the lake was enlarged so that water could be stored for use in the Duck Reach Power Station (on the South Esk near Launceston). The HEC puts the year of construction of the first dam at 1905. In 1911 the NTFA noted that the water in the Lake River had become dirty as a result of the '*damming up of Woods Lake*'.

Angling reports of the late 1950s acknowledge the brown trout fishing and mention rainbows to 5 lb. The rainbows may have been emigrants from Arthurs – the species did not establish at Woods.

The present 7 m high rockfill dam at Devils Throat was completed by the HEC in 1962.

Fly fishing

Woods is a good all-round fly water.

Pattersons Flats provide excellent early-season wet-fly fishing. Later, especially in November, tailing fish can be found right around the north-western shores. Early mornings, evenings and overcast days are best.

Good dun hatches occur from November to early autumn, and are dependable providing that the weather is warm and not too rough.

On warm afternoons fish will be found leaping after black spinners and damselflies among trees and bushes along the deeper shores.

Beetles and caddis flies also stimulate surface activity.

Lure fishing

Trolling with Cobras and spoons is popular in the open water across the body of the lake. However, it is usually more productive to drift spin among the gaps around the edges of the weedbeds, and among the logs.

Shore-based spinning is good around the dam and along most other shores. In many areas you need to wade out beyond weed-choked shallows.

Bait fishing

The northern shore provides convenient deep water for set-rod fishing. Night-time cast-and-retrieve fishing is good near the dam and in the marshes.

Access and facilities

Access to the dam is via the Woods Lake Road from the Arthurs Dam at Arthurs Lake. This 15 km route is very rough and is not suited to conventional 2WD cars.

Foot access and 4WD access can be gained to the south-western shore from the Interlaken Road some 3 km east of Lagoon of Islands. However, this route crosses private land and the gates are sometimes locked.

The most popular informal camping sites are on the north-eastern shore near the dam.

Boating

Small boats can be launched near the dam. Car-tops are advisable – the road is not trailer-friendly.

WYE RIVER

Tasmaps Freycinet and Little Swanport
Drainage Direct to the lower Swan River

In many respects the Wye is much like other streams in the Swan system. It flows through vast tracts of marginal pasture and the banks are lined with native trees and scrub. The bed comprises loose shingle and there is practically no weed growth. The water, though surprisingly clear during periods of low flow, is usually very slightly milky. In summer and autumn it is common for there to be no visible flow in the short breaks between the (mostly long) pools. Many of the broadwaters stretch from bank to bank and provide adequate cover for good sized trout. Depths of 2-4 m are common but there is usually at least one wadeable bank.

While most trout weigh 0.2-0.4 kg, each big pool is likely to hold one or more fish in excess of 1.2 kg.

Fishing is best at moderate to low levels. Spinning and bait casting result in fair catches. Polaroiding is good, though you often cover a lot of water without seeing fish. Rises are small and irregular, with most activity occurring in summer at dusk. Blind casting with wet flies at night is a worthwhile fall-back.

Large schools of galaxias exist in most pools, and these fish often snatch baits and flies intended for trout.

YALLEENA, LAKE

Tasmap Little Swanport
Drainage South Esk system (via Brodribb Creek and the Macquarie River)

A privately-owned rainbow fish-out created in the mid 1980s. See *About Our Sportfish*, 2.2.

YEATES LAGOON

Tasmap Mersey
Drainage Mersey system (via the Fisher system)
Location Chudleigh Lakes

A shallow clearwater surrounded by boggy moor-land. The main natural inflow, Yeates Creek, has been diverted upstream of the lagoon resulting in poor summer/autumn levels.

The lake carries plenty of brown trout to 1.5 kg. It received a part-share of 1900 brown trout fry in 1972, though this did little to enhance the already well-established trout population.

See also *Fishing in National Parks*, 5.1.

YOLANDE RIVER

Tasmaps Cape Sorell, Franklin, and Sophia
Drainage Direct to the Henty River

A large steep tea-coloured fastwater flowing through densely-forested gorges. The river proper is of difficult access and, while it carries plenty of slow-growing brown trout, it is rarely fished. The headwaters provide better sport (see *Margaret, Lake*).

YORK CREEK

(termed Staverton Creek in some IFC reports)

Tasmap Forth
Drainage Mersey system (via the Dasher River)

In 1969 and 1972 the IFC noted that the stream carried small rainbow trout and no browns.

YOUD, LAKE

Tasmap Mersey
Drainage Mersey River (an instream lagoon)
Location Western Lakes

Lake Youd is located between Lake Meston and Junction Lake and, like the rest of the upper Mersey system, it is rainbow-only water (see *Meston, Lake*). Since the lagoon is little more than a widening of the river, it carries plenty of 0.2-0.4 kg trout. However, some fish do well in the marshes and attain 1.5 kg or so. Spinning and traditional dry-fly fishing are the most reliable daytime techniques, while wet-fly fishing at dusk is a reliable fall-back. Polaroiding is difficult simply because the bigger fish rarely cruise in shallow water.

Idyllic grassy tent-sites can be found among the trees on the nearby moraines.

See also *Fishing in National Parks*, 5.1.

YOUL, LAKE

Tasmap St Pauls
Drainage North Esk system (via the Nile River)
Location Ben Lomond Plateau

Lake Youl and Youls Tarn are interconnected shallow clearwaters surrounded by moorland. In 1906 the NTFA recorded:
   'Included in this year's stocking was the liberation of 1000 Loch Leven fry in Lake Youl, on the summit of Ben Lomond... carried out by the Fingal Council'.
   It seems that wild stocks did not establish.

A rainbow at Lake Youd

Beyond the Zig Zags

YOULS TARN

See *Youl, Lake.*

ZIG ZAG LAKES

Tasmap Mersey
Drainage Derwent system (via the Little Pine system)
Location Western Lakes (grid ref's 545 660 and 550 665)

The Zig Zags are two clearwaters encircled by relatively-flat heathland. The shores are rocky and mostly well-defined, though there are several small marshy backwaters.

Brown trout of 0.7-1.2 kg are typical. In 1990-91 domestic rainbows were illegally liberated into some of the nearby trophy-brown lakes, but these fish have not featured in anglers' bags.

Spinning and bank polaroiding are most reliable.

See also *Fishing in National Parks*, 5.1.

Acknowledgements

Thanks to:

Rebecca Clay, Ric Dowling, Lester Jones, Frances Latham, Tom Latham, Rob McDonald, Rob Sloane, Pauline Underwood and Karen Ziegler for field assistance.

Rob Sloane and Lester Jones for detailed information on specific waters.

Frances Latham, Rose McDonald, Danny Ray, Rob Sloane and Tony Sloane for manuscript preparation.

Jane Andrew, Ashley Hallam, the IFC, Frances Latham, Carolyn Lee, Steve McArdle, *The Mercury*, Rob Sloane, Viv Spencer, Tasmap and The Wilderness Society for photographs.

The HEC, the IFC (especially Stuart Chilcott, Peter Davies, Wayne Fulton and Andrew Sanger), Rob Sloane, and the RWSC (especially Dave Fuller) for technical information.

Extra thanks to:

Frances Latham and Rob Sloane.
